Modern Trial Advocacy
Analysis and Practice

Modern Trial Advocacy
Analysis and Practice

Steven Lubet
Professor of Law
Northwestern University School of Law
Chicago, Illinois

National Institute for Trial Advocacy

To Linda, my wife

— Summary of Contents —

— Table of Contents —

Table of Contents

Table of Contents

Table of Contents

Table of Contents

Table of Contents

Table of Contents

Table of Contents

Table of Contents

CHAPTER EIGHT — Foundations and Exhibits

Table of Contents

Table of Contents

Table of Contents

Table of Contents

Table of Contents

PREFACE

My goal in writing *Modern Trial Advocacy* has been to stress the importance of theory and analysis in the trial process. A trial is composed of interlocking parts; it is not simply a series of discrete exercises. In isolation, there is no such thing as a good direct examination. A direct examination is good only if it does its job in relation to the other directs, the cross examinations, and the opening statement and final argument.

I have tried to avoid providing rote mechanisms or "recipes" for the various parts of a trial. Instead, I have attempted to emphasize different ways to think about the delivery of argument, the presentation of evidence, and the development of ideas at trial. All lawyers understand that there is no "right way" to try a case. To the extent possible, I have aspired to explain how counsel might identify the multitude of ways to approach a particular problem, and how to go about choosing among them. My working title for this book was *How to Think About Trials.* Although that did not prove catchy enough for publication, it still describes much of the philosophy behind this work.

* * *

We are all, to some extent, captives of our own backgrounds. Lawyers in particular tend to consider the quirks and idiosyncracies of our own locales as universal practices. With the exception of one year, my entire legal career has been spent in Chicago, the only place in the country where lawyers refer to themselves as being "on trial" as opposed to "in trial." I have striven mightily to exorcise all similar Chicagoisms from *Modern Trial Advocacy.* To the extent that some have still slipped in, I apologize.

Chicagoisms or otherwise, none of the examples in this book are intended to illustrate absolute truth. At best, they are to be used as models or samples. Modify them, elaborate on them, enhance them, revise them, and adjust them in whatever manner suits your case.

* * *

Modern Trial Advocacy is organized according to the four principal aspects of planning and conducting trials.

Preface

First, and most important, is the creation of a trial theory, a "story" that accounts for all of the evidence in a way that impels a verdict in your client's favor. The trial theory begins to take shape from the moment you start preparing a case, and continues to be refined throughout every phase of the trial. Part One of this book discusses the development of a trial story, and that concept is refined further in the succeeding chapters.

The remaining three aspects relate to the conduct of the trial. Part Two deals with the examination of witnesses, the persuasive process of developing information on either direct or cross examination. Part Three considers the technical aspects of the trial, making the record through the use of foundations, objections, and responses. Finally, Part Four is devoted to addressing the trier of fact through opening statements, final arguments, and jury selection.

Steven Lubet
Evanston, Illinois
August 1993

ACKNOWLEDGMENTS

I am deeply indebted to Sheila Block who, as senior editor, improved virtually every page of this book. I am also grateful to Robert Burns, Thomas Geraghty, Linda Lipton, Fred Lubet, and James Seckinger for their thoughtful comments and suggestions on content and style. Finally, I must acknowledge the contributions of all of the faculty members who participate in the Trial Advocacy Program at the Northwestern University School of Law. Although there are too many of you to name individually, I want you to know that much of the material in this book is derived from the excellent role modeling that you have provided to our mutual students.

Paulette Van Zant provided splendid secretarial and administrative assistance (as she always does). I am particularly appreciative of Andrew Goldman's hyper-accurate indexing. Jan McGowan contributed outstanding copy editing.

Finally, I am grateful for the support provided to me by the Julius Rosenthal Fund, the William M. Trumbull Fund, the Barnett and Scott Hodes Prize Fund, and the Stanford Clinton Senior Faculty Fund of the Northwestern University School of Law.

Part One
Introduction

— CHAPTER ONE —
Case Analysis, Persuasion, and Storytelling

I. THE IDEA OF A PERSUASIVE STORY
A. Trials as Stories

The function of a trial is to resolve factual disputes. In order to hold a trial it is necessary that the parties be in disagreement concerning historical facts. These disagreements commonly involve the existence or occurrence of events or actions, but they may also turn upon questions of sequence, interpretation, charac-terization, or intent. Thus, trials may be held to answer questions such as these: What happened? What happened first? Why did it happen? Who made it happen? Did it happen on purpose? Was it justified or fair? All of these questions are resolved by accumulating information about past events; if there is no dispute about past events the case should be resolved on summary judgment. [1]

Trials, then, are held in order to allow the parties to persuade the judge or jury by recounting their versions of the historical facts. Another name for this process is storytelling. Each party to a trial has the opportunity to tell a story, albeit through the fairly stilted devices of jury address, direct and cross examination, and introduction of evidence. The framework for the stories — or their grammar — is set by the rules of procedure and evidence. The conclusion of the stories — the end to which they are directed — is controlled by the elements of the applicable substantive law. The content of the stories — their plot and *mise-en-scène* — is governed, of course, by the truth, or at least by so much of the truth as is available to the advocate. Thereafter, the party who succeeds in telling the most persuasive story should win.

But what is persuasive storytelling in the context of a trial? A persuasive story can establish an affirmative case if it has all, or most, of these characteristics: (1) it is told about people who have reasons for the way they act; (2) it accounts for or explains all of the known or undeniable facts; (3) it is told by credible witnesses; (4) it is supported by details; (5) it accords with common sense and contains no implausible elements; and (6) it is organized in a way that makes each succeeding

---

1   *See* Rule 56, Federal Rules of Civil Procedure.

fact increasingly more likely. On the other hand, defense lawyers must often tell "counter-stories" that negate the above aspects of the other side's case.

In addition to persuasiveness, a story presented at trial must consist of admissible evidence, and it must contain all of the elements of a legally cognizable claim or defense.

An advocate's task when preparing for trial is to conceive of and structure a true story, comprising only admissible evidence and containing all of the elements of a claim or defense, that is most likely to be believed or adopted by the trier of fact. This is a creative process, since seldom will the facts be undisputed or susceptible of but a single interpretation. To carry through this process the lawyer must "imagine" a series of alternative scenarios, assessing each for its clarity, simplicity, and believability, as well as for its legal consequences.

B. Planning a Sample Story

Assume, for example, that you represent a plaintiff who was injured in an automobile accident. You know from your law school torts class that in order to recover damages you will have to tell a story proving, at a minimum, that the defendant was negligent. You also know from your evidence class that the story will have to be built on admissible evidence, and you know from your ethics class that the story cannot be based on false or perjured testimony.[2] Your client knows only that when traffic slowed down to allow a fire truck to pass, she was hit from behind by the driver of the other automobile.

How can these basic facts be assembled into a persuasive trial story? First, we know that the story must be about people who act for reasons. Your client slowed down for a fire truck, which explains her actions. But why didn't the defendant slow down as well? Your story will be more persuasive if you can establish his reason.

True, a reason is not absolutely essential. Perhaps the defendant was such a poor driver that he simply drove about banging into other automobiles. On the other hand, consider what the absence of a reason implies. The plaintiff claims that traffic slowed for a fire truck, but the defendant — also part of traffic — did not slow down. Could it be that there was no fire truck? Perhaps there was a fire truck, but it was not sounding its siren or alerting traffic to stop. Is it possible that the plaintiff didn't slow down, but rather slammed on her brakes? In other words, the very absence of a reason for the defendant's actions may make the plaintiff's own testimony less believable.

---

2   *See* Rule 3.3, American Bar Association Model Rules of Professional Conduct (Model Rules); Disciplinary Rules 7-102 and 7-106, American Bar Association Model Code of Professional Responsibility (Model Code).

The skilled advocate will therefore look for a reason or cause for the defendant's actions. Was the defendant drunk? In a hurry? Homicidal? Distracted? You can choose from among these potential reasons by "imagining" each one in the context of your story. Imagine how the story will be told if you claim that the defendant was drunk. Could such a story account for all of the known facts? If the police came to the scene, was the defendant arrested? Did any credible, disinterested witnesses see the defendant drinking or smell liquor on his breath? If not, drunkenness does not provide a persuasive reason for the defendant's actions.

Next, imagine telling your story about a homicidal defendant. Perhaps this wasn't an accident, but a murder attempt. Envision your impassioned plea for punitive damages. But wait, this story is too implausible. How would a murderer know that the plaintiff would be driving on that particular road? How would he know that a fire truck would be attempting to bypass traffic? How could he predict that the plaintiff would slow down enough, or that there would be no other cars in the way? Barring the discovery of additional facts that support such a theory, this story is unpersuasive.

Finally, imagine the story as told about a defendant who was in a hurry. This story accounts for the known facts, since it explains why traffic might slow while the defendant did not. Perhaps the defendant saw the fire truck but was driving just a little too fast to stop in time; or he might have been so preoccupied with the importance of getting somewhere on time that he simply failed to notice the fire truck until it was too late. Moreover, there is nothing implausible or unbelievable about this theory. It is in complete harmony with everyone's everyday observations. Furthermore, details that support the story should not be hard to come by. Was the defendant going to work in the morning? Did he have an important meeting to attend? Was he headed home after a long day? The trial lawyer can find details in virtually any destination that will support the theory of the hurried defendant. Note, however, that while such additional evidence of the defendant's haste will be helpful, the story does not rest upon any external witness's credibility. All of the major elements of the story may be inferred from the defendant's own actions.

How can this last story best be organized? Let us assume that the occurrence of the collision itself is not in issue, and recall that it is important that each fact make every succeeding element increasingly more likely. Which aspect should come first: the presence of the fire truck, or the fact that the defendant was in a hurry? Since the presence of the fire truck does not make it more likely that the defendant was in a hurry, that probably is not the most effective starting point. On the other hand, the defendant's haste does make it more likely that he would fail to notice the fire truck.

Thus, a skeletal version of our story, with some easily obtained details supplied, might go like this: we know there was a collision, but why did it happen? The defendant was driving south on Sheridan Road at 8:35 in the morning. It was the end of rush hour, and he had to be at work downtown. In fact, he had an important meeting that was to begin at 9:00 a.m. sharp. The defendant's parking lot is two blocks from his office. As traffic slowed for a passing fire truck, the defendant didn't notice it. Failing to stop in time, the defendant ran into the plaintiff's car.

Other details might also be available to support this story. Perhaps, immediately following the collision, the defendant ran to a phone booth to call his office. Similarly, there might be "counter-details" for the plaintiff to rebut. The point, however, is to organize your story on the principle of successive supporting detail.

II.   THE ETHICS OF PERSUASIVE STORYTELLING

In the preceding section we discussed the way in which an advocate imagines a persuasive theory or story. We also noted that lawyers are bound to the truth — we are not free to pick stories simply on the basis of their persuasive value. Within this parameter, exactly how much room is there for creative theory choice?

A.   Assuming That You "Know" the Truth

Let us begin with the proposition that in most cases neither the lawyer nor the client will know with certainty what we might call all of the "relevant truth." As in the scenario above, for example, the plaintiff knows her own actions, but has no special knowledge about the defendant. The lawyer, of course, is not free to persuade or coach the plaintiff to alter her own story simply to make it more effective.[3]

This is not to say, however, that legal ethics permit us to do nothing more than put the plaintiff on the witness stand. The lawyer's duty of zealous representation requires further inquiry into the existence of additional details, not to mention the artful use of sequencing and emphasis. For instance, let us assume that the plaintiff has informed her lawyer with certainty that the fire truck was flashing its lights, but not sounding its siren or bell. There is no doubt that an attorney absolutely may not coach the plaintiff to testify that the siren and bell were sounding. Such testimony would be false, perjurious, and unethical.

On the other hand, there is no requirement that the absence of bell and siren be made the centerpiece of the plaintiff's direct examination. Sequencing and emphasis may be used to minimize the adverse impact of this information. Therefore, the direct examination could be developed as follows: "The fire truck was the largest vehicle on the road. It was the standard fire-engine red. All of its lights were flashing brightly — headlights, taillights, and red dome lights. It could be seen easily from all directions. All of the traffic, save the defendant, slowed down

---

3   Rules 3.1, 3.4, and 4.1, Model Rules of Professional Conduct; Disciplinary Rule 7-102(A)(7), Model Code of Professional Responsibility.

for the fire truck. It was not necessary to hear a siren in order to notice the fire truck." Thus, the lawyer has held closely to the truth, while establishing the irrelevance of the damaging information.

B. Assuming That You Don't Know the Truth

A different situation arises when the advocate is not able to identify truth so closely, as in the example above concerning the defendant's reasons for failing to notice the fire truck in time. Recall that we considered a variety of possible reasons, including inattention, drunkenness, and homicide. Some reasons have clear forensic advantages over others. What are ethical limitations on the attorney's ability to choose the best one?

First, it should be clear that we are not bound to accept the defendant's story in the same way that we must give credence to our own client. The duty of zealous representation requires that we resolve doubts in our client's favor.[4] Moreover, we speak to our client within a relationship of confidentiality, which not only protects her communication, but also gives her additional credibility. Without her consent, what our client tells us will go no further, and this knowledge gives her every reason to make a full disclosure.[5] When our client gives us damaging facts (such as the absence of the fire truck's siren), it is even more likely to be true, since she obviously has no reason to inject such information falsely. Conversely, statements that we obtain from the defendant are not necessarily accompanied by comparable indicia of reliability, and we are entitled to mistrust them.

This is not to say that we must always accept information from our clients as revealed wisdom. Clients may mislead us as the result of misperception, forgetfulness, mistake, wishful thinking, reticence, ignorance, and, unfortunately, they occasionally lie. Moreover, opposing parties in litigation usually tell what they perceive as the truth. As a tactical matter, trial lawyers must always examine every statement of every witness for potential error or falsehood. As an ethical matter, however, we should be more ready to assume that our client's words — both helpful and damaging — are likely to be true. It is, after all, the client's case. [6]

Recognizing, then, that we must go beyond the opposite party's version of the facts, we next evaluate the entire universe of possible stories. In our example

---

4   *See* Rule 1.2, Model Rules of Professional Conduct; Disciplinary Rule 7-101, Model Code of Professional Responsibility.

5   *See* Rule 1.6, Model Rules of Professional Conduct; Disciplinary Rule 4-101, Model Code of Professional Responsibility.

6   Note that a lawyer is generally required to accept the client's goals and objectives with regard to litigation. Rule 1.2(a), Model Rules of Professional Conduct. (A lawyer shall abide by a client's decisions concerning the objectives of representation...and shall consult with the client as to the means by which they are to be pursued).

we determined that the "in a hurry" story would be the most persuasive. Simultaneously, we must also determine whether it is an ethical story to tell.

The key to determining the ethical value of any trial theory is whether it is supported by facts that we know, believe, or have a good faith basis to believe, are true. In other words, the story has to be based on facts that are "not false."[7]

Returning to our fire truck case, assume that the defendant has denied that he was in a hurry. He has the right to make this denial, but as plaintiff's lawyers we have no duty to accept it. Assume also that we have not been able to locate a witness who can give direct evidence that the defendant was in a hurry. We do know where and when the collision occurred, and assume that we have also been able to learn numerous facts about the defendant's home, automobile, occupation, and place of employment. The following story emerges, based strictly on facts that we have no reason to doubt.

> The defendant lives sixteen miles from his office. He usually takes the train to work, but on the day of the accident he drove. The accident occurred on a major thoroughfare approximately eleven miles from the defendant's office. The time of the accident was 8:35 a.m., and the defendant had scheduled an important, and potentially lucrative, meeting with a new client for 9:00 a.m. that day. The parking lot nearest to the defendant's office is over two blocks away. The first thing that the defendant did following the accident was telephone his office to say that he would be late.

Our conclusion is that the defendant was in a hurry. Driving on a familiar stretch of road, he was thinking about his appointment, maybe even starting to count the money, and he failed to pay sufficient attention to the traffic. We are entitled to ask the trier of fact to draw this inference, because we reasonably believe its entire basis to be true. The known facts can also support numerous other stories, or no story at all, but that is not an ethical concern. Perhaps the defendant was being particularly careful that morning, knowing how important it was that he arrive on time for his appointment. Perhaps the appointment had nothing to do with the accident. Those arguments can be made, and they may turn out to be more persuasive stories than our own. Our ultimate stories might be ineffective, or even foolish, but they are ethical so long as they are not built on a false foundation.

---

7   *See* Rules 3.1, 3.4(e), and 4.1, Model Rules of Professional Conduct;   Disciplinary Rules 7-102(A)(2) and 7-106(C), Model Code of Professional Responsibility.

C. The Special Case of the Criminal Law

The analysis above, regarding both persuasion and ethics, applies to civil and criminal cases alike. In the criminal law, however, the prosecutor has additional ethical obligations and the defense lawyer has somewhat greater latitude.

A criminal prosecutor is not only an advocate; she is also a public official. It is her duty to punish the guilty, not merely to win on behalf of a client. Therefore, a public prosecutor may not rely upon the "not false" standard for determining the ethical value of a particular theory. Rather, the prosecutor must personally believe in the legal validity of her case, and must refrain from bringing any prosecution that is not supported by probable cause.[8]

Conversely, a criminal defendant is always entitled to plead not guilty, thereby putting the government to its burden of establishing guilt beyond a reasonable doubt.[9] A plea of not guilty need not in any sense be "true," since its function is only to insist upon the constitutional right to trial. Of course, a criminal defendant has no right to introduce perjury or false evidence. However, a criminal defendant need not present any factual defense, and in most jurisdictions a conviction requires that the prosecution "exclude every reasonable hypothesis that is inconsistent with guilt." Thus, so long as she does not rely upon falsity or perjury, a criminal defense lawyer may argue for acquittal — that is, tell a story — based only upon "a reasonable hypothesis" of innocence.

III. PREPARING A PERSUASIVE TRIAL STORY

Assume that you have decided upon the story that you want to tell. It is persuasive. It is about people who have reasons for the way they act. It accounts for all of the known facts. It is told by credible witnesses. It is supported by details. It accords with common sense. It can be organized in a way that makes each succeeding fact more likely.

How do you put your story in the form of a trial?

A. Developing Your Theory and Your Theme

Your case must have both a theory and a theme.

1. Theory

Your theory is the adaptation of your story to the legal issues in the case. A theory of the case should be expressed in a single paragraph that combines an

---

8   *See* Rule 3.8, Model Rules of Professional Conduct; Disciplinary Rule 7-103(A), Model Code of Professional Responsibility.

9   Rule 3.1, Model Rules of Professional Conduct. (A lawyer for the defendant in a criminal proceeding...[may] defend the proceeding as to require that every element of the case be established).

account of the facts and the law in such a way as to lead to the conclusion that your client must win. A successful theory contains these elements:

—*It is logical.* A winning theory has internal logical force. It is based upon a foundation of undisputed or otherwise provable facts, all of which lead in a single direction. The facts upon which your theory is based should reinforce (and never contradict) each other. Indeed, they should lead to each other, each fact or premise implying the next, in an orderly and inevitable fashion.

—*It speaks to the legal elements of your case.* All of your trial persuasion must be in aid of a "legal" conclusion. Your theory must not only establish that your client is good or worthy (or that the other side is bad and unworthy), but also that the law entitles you to relief. Your theory therefore must be directed to prove every legal element that is necessary both to justify a verdict on your behalf and to preserve it on appeal.

—*It is simple.* A good theory makes maximum use of undisputed facts. It relies as little as possible on evidence that may be hotly controverted, implausible, inadmissible, or otherwise difficult to prove.

—*It is easy to believe.* Even "true" theories may be difficult to believe because they contradict everyday experience, or because they require harsh judgments. You must strive to eliminate all implausible elements from your theory. Similarly, you should attempt to avoid arguments that depend upon proof of deception, falsification, ill motive, or personal attack. An airtight theory is able to encompass the entirety of the other side's case, and still result in your victory by sheer logical force.

To develop and express your theory, ask these three questions: What happened? Why did it happen? Why does that mean that my client should win? If your answer is longer than one paragraph, your theory may be logical and true, but it is probably too complicated.

2. Theme

Just as your theory must appeal to logic, your theme must appeal to moral force. A logical theory tells the trier of fact the reason that your verdict must be entered. A moral theme shows why it should be entered. In other words, your theme — best presented in a single sentence — justifies the morality of your theory and appeals to the justice of the case.

A theme is a rhetorical or forensic device. It has no independent legal weight, but rather it gives persuasive force to your legal arguments. The most compelling themes appeal to shared values, civic virtues, or common motivations. They can be succinctly expressed and repeated at virtually every phase of the trial.

In a contracts case, for example, your theory will account for all of the facts surrounding the formation and breach of the contract, as well as the relevant law, say, of specific performance. Your theory will explain why a particular verdict is compelled by the law. Your theme will strengthen your theory by underscoring why entering that verdict is the right thing to do. Perhaps your theme will be, "The defendant would rather try to make money than live up to a promise." Or you might try, "This defendant tried to sell some property, and keep it too." Whatever the theme, you will want to introduce it during your opening statement, reinforce it during direct and cross examinations, and drive it home during your final argument.

B.   Planning Your Final Argument

Good trial preparation begins at the end. It makes great sense to plan your final argument first, because that aspect of the trial is the most similar to storytelling; it is the single element of the trial where it is permissible for you to suggest conclusions, articulate inferences, and otherwise present your theory to the trier of fact as an uninterrupted whole.

In other words, during final argument you are most allowed to say exactly what you want to say, limited only by the requirement that all arguments be supported by evidence contained in the trial record. Thus, by planning your final argument at the beginning of your preparation, you will then be able to plan the balance of your case so as to ensure that the record contains every fact that you will need for summation.

Ask yourself these two questions: What do I want to say at the end of the case? What evidence must I introduce or elicit in order to be able to say it? The answers will give you the broad outline of your entire case.

C.   Planning Your Case in Chief

Your goal during your case in chief is to persuade the trier of fact as to the correctness of your theory, constantly invoking the moral leverage of your theme. To accomplish this, you have four basic tools: (1) jury address, which consists of opening statement and final argument; (2) testimony on direct examination, and to a lesser extent on cross examination; (3) introduction of exhibits, including real and documentary evidence; and (4) absolutely everything else that you do in the courtroom, including the way you look, act, react, speak, move, stand, and sit. The skills involved in each of these aspects of a trial will be discussed at length in later chapters. What follows here is an outline of the general steps to take in planning for trial.

1.   Consider Your Potential Witnesses and Exhibits

Your first step is to list the legal elements of every claim or defense that you hope to establish. If you represent the plaintiff in a personal injury case, then you must offer evidence on all of the elements of negligence: duty, foreseeability, cause-in-fact, proximate cause, and damages. Next, list the evidence that you have available to support each such element. Most likely the bulk of your evidence will be in the form of witness testimony, but some of it will consist of documents, tangible objects, and other real evidence. For each such exhibit, note the witness through whom you will seek its introduction.

You are now ready to make decisions concerning your potential witnesses, by inverting the informational list that you just created.

2. Evaluate Each Witness Individually

Imagine what you would like to say in final argument about each witness you might call to the stand: What does this witness contribute to my theory? What positive facts may I introduce through this witness? Are other witnesses available for the same facts? Is this witness an effective vehicle for my theme? What can I say about this witness that will be logically and morally persuasive?

Once you have assembled all of the "positive" information about each witness, you must go on to consider all possible problems and weaknesses.

a. Factual Weaknesses

Are there likely to be inconsistencies or gaps in the witness's testimony? Does the witness have damaging information that is likely to be elicited on cross examination? If the answer to either question is affirmative, how can you minimize these problems? Can you resolve the inconsistencies by re-evaluating your theory? Can another witness fill the gaps? Can you defuse the potentially damaging facts by bringing them out on direct examination?

b. Evidentiary Problems

Each witness's testimony must be evaluated for possible evidentiary problems. Do not assume that any item of evidence or testimony is automatically admissible. Instead, you must be able to state a positive theory of admissibility for everything that you intend to offer during your case in chief. To prepare for objections ask yourself, "How would I try to keep this information out of evidence?" Then plan your response. If you are not absolutely confident in your ability to counter any objections, you have to go back to the law library.

c. Credibility Problems

How is the witness likely to be attacked? Is the witness subject to challenge for bias or interest? Will perception be in issue? Is there potential for impeachment by prior inconsistent statements? Can you structure your direct examination so as to avoid or minimize these problems?

3. Decide Which Witness to Call

Having evaluated the contributions, strengths, and weaknesses of all of your potential witnesses, you are now in a position to decide which ones you will call to the stand. Your central concern will be to make sure that all of your necessary evidence is admitted. You must call any witness who is the sole source of a crucial piece of information. Except in rare or compelling circumstances, you will also want to call any witness whose credibility or appearance is central to the internal logic or moral weight of your case.

All non-essential witnesses must be evaluated according to their strengths and weaknesses. You will want to consider eliminating witnesses whose testimony will be cumulative or repetitive of each other, since this will increase the likelihood of eliciting a damaging contradiction. You must also be willing to dispense with calling witnesses whose credibility is seriously suspect, or whose testimony has the potential to do you more harm than good.

Once you have arrived at your final list of witnesses, arrange them in the order that will be most helpful to your case. While there are no hard and fast rules for determining witness order, the following three principles should help you decide:

Retention. You want your evidence not only to be heard, but also to be retained. Studies have consistently suggested that judges and juries tend to best remember the evidence that they hear at the beginning and the end of the trial. Following this principle, you will want to call your most important witness first, and your next most important witness last. Start fast and end strong.

Progression. The "first and last" principle must occasionally give way to the need for logical progression. Some witnesses provide the foundation for the testimony of others. Thus, it may be necessary to call "predicate" witnesses early in the trial as a matter of both logical development and legal admissibility. To the extent possible, you may also wish to arrange your witnesses so that accounts of key events are given in chronological order.

Impact. You may also order your witnesses to maximize their dramatic impact. For example, you might wish to begin a wrongful death case by calling one of the grieving parents of the deceased child. Conversely, a necessary witness who is also somewhat unsavory or impeachable should probably be buried in the middle of your case in chief. A variant on the impact principle is the near-universal practice of calling a criminal defendant as the last witness for the defense. This practice has arisen for two reasons. First, it postpones until the last possible moment that time that the lawyer must decide whether to call the defendant to the stand for exposure to cross examination. Second, and far more cynically, calling defendants last allows them to hear all of the other testimony before testifying. (While all occurrence

witnesses are routinely excluded from the courtroom, the defendant has a constitutional right to be present throughout the trial.)

D. Planning Your Cross Examinations

It is inherently more difficult to plan a cross examination than it is to prepare
for direct. It is impossible to safeguard yourself against all surprises, but the
following four steps will help keep them to a minimum.

First, compile a list of every potential adverse witness. Imagine why the
witness is likely to be called. Ask yourself, "How can this witness most hurt my
case?" Always prepare for the worst possible alternative.

Second, consider whether there is a basis for keeping the witness off the stand.
Is the witness competent to testify? Is it possible to invoke a privilege? Then
consider whether any part of the expected testimony might be excludable. For
every statement that the witness might make, imagine all reasonable evidentiary
objections. Do the same thing concerning all exhibits that might be offered through
the witness. For each objection plan your argument, and prepare for the likely
counter-argument. You won't want to make every possible objection, but you will
want to be prepared.

Third, consider the factual weaknesses of each opposing witness. Are there
inconsistencies that can be exploited or enhanced? Is the witness's character
subject to attack? Can the witness be impeached from prior statements? How can
the witness be used to amplify your own theme?

Finally, catalog all of the favorable information that you will be able to obtain
from each opposing witness.

E. Re-evaluating Everything That You've Done

Now that you have planned your case in chief and cross examinations, it is
imperative that you go back and re-evaluate every aspect of your case. Do your
direct examinations fully support and establish your theory? Do they leave any
logical gaps? Are you satisfied that all of your necessary evidence will be admissible?
Will it be credible? Do the potential cross examinations raise issues with which
you cannot cope? Will you be able to articulate your moral theme during most or
all of the direct and cross examinations? If you are unable to answer these questions
satisfactorily, you may need to readjust your theory or theme.

Assuming that you are satisfied with your theory, you should now have an
excellent idea of what the evidence at trial will be. With this in mind, go back again
and rework your final argument. Make sure that it is completely consistent with
the expected evidence, and that it makes maximum use of the uncontroverted
facts. Consider eliminating any parts of the argument that rest too heavily on
evidence that you anticipate will be severely contested. Be sure that you structure

your argument so that you can begin and end with your theme, and invoke it throughout. Finally, outline your opening statement, again beginning and ending with your theme, and raising each of the points to which you will return on final argument.

IV. CONCLUSION

The following chapters discuss all aspects of persuasion at trial, from the opening statement to the final argument. Trial lawyers must master numerous forensic skills, procedural rules, and examination techniques, but your starting point must always be your theory of the case — the story that you want to tell.

Part Two
Examining Witnesses

— CHAPTER TWO —
Direct Examination

I. THE ROLE OF DIRECT EXAMINATION

Cases are won as a consequence of direct examination.

Direct examination is your opportunity to present the substance of your case. It is the time to offer the evidence available to establish the facts that you need to prevail. Having planned your persuasive story, you must now prove the facts upon which it rests by eliciting the testimony of witnesses.

Direct examination, then, is the heart of your case. It is the fulcrum of the trial — the aspect upon which everything else turns. Every other aspect of the trial is derivative of direct examination. Opening statements and final arguments are simply the lawyer's opportunity to comment upon what the witnesses have to say; cross examination exists solely to allow the direct to be challenged or controverted. While we could easily imagine a reasonably fair trial system consisting solely of direct examinations, it is impossible to conceive of anything resembling accurate factfinding in their absence.

Direct examinations should be designed to accomplish one or more of the following basic goals.

A. Introduce Undisputed Facts

In most trials there will be many important facts that are not in dispute. Nonetheless, such facts cannot be considered by the judge or jury, and will not be part of the record on appeal, until and unless they have been placed in evidence through a witness's testimony. Undisputed facts will often be necessary to establish an element of your case. Thus, failing to include them in direct examination could lead to an unfavorable verdict or reversal on appeal.

Assume, for example, that you represent the plaintiff in a case involving damage to the exterior of a building, and that the defense in the case is consent. Even if the question of ownership of the premises is not in dispute, it is still an element of your cause of action. Thus, you must present proof that your client had a possessory or ownership interest in the building, or run the risk of a directed verdict in favor of the defendant.

15

B. Enhance the Likelihood of Disputed Facts

The most important facts in a trial will normally be those in dispute. Direct examination is your opportunity to put forward your client's version of the disputed facts. Furthermore, you must not only introduce evidence on disputed points, you must do so persuasively. The true art of direct examination consists in large part of establishing the certainty of facts that the other side claims are uncertain or untrue.

C. Lay Foundations for the Introduction of Exhibits

Documents, photographs, writings, tangible objects, and other forms of real evidence will often be central to your case. With some exceptions, it is necessary to lay the foundation for the admission of such an exhibit through the direct testimony of a witness. This is the case whether or not the reliability of the exhibit is in dispute.

It is not unusual for a witness to be called only for the purpose of introducing an exhibit. The "records custodian" at a hospital or bank may know absolutely nothing about the contents of a particular report, but nonetheless may be examined solely in order to qualify the document as a business record.

D. Reflect upon the Credibility of Witnesses

The credibility of a witness is always in issue. Thus, every direct examination, whatever its ultimate purpose, must also attend to the credibility of the witness's own testimony. For this reason, most direct examinations begin with some background information about the witness. What does she do for a living? Where did she go to school? How long has she lived in the community? Even if the witness's credibility will not be challenged, this sort of information helps to humanize her, and therefore adds weight to what she has to say.

You can expect the credibility of some witnesses to be attacked on cross examination. In these situations you can blunt the assault by bolstering the witness's believability during direct examination. You can strengthen a witness by eliciting the basis of her knowledge, her ability to observe, or her lack of bias or interest in the outcome of the case.

You may also call a witness to reflect adversely on the credibility of the testimony of another. Direct examination may be used, for example, to introduce negative character or reputation evidence concerning another witness. Alternatively, you may call a witness to provide direct evidence of bias or motive, to lay the foundation for an impeaching document, or simply to contradict other testimony.

E. Hold the Attention of the Trier of Fact

No matter which of the above purposes predominates in any particular direct examination, it must be conducted in a manner that holds the attention of the judge or jury. In addition to being the heart of your case, direct examination also has the highest potential for dissolving into boredom, inattention, and routine. Since it has none of the inherent drama or tension of cross examination, you must take extreme care to prepare your direct examination so as to maximize its impact.

II. THE LAW OF DIRECT EXAMINATION

The rules of evidence govern the content of all direct examinations. Evidence offered on direct must be relevant, authentic, not hearsay, and otherwise admissible. In addition, there is a fairly specific "law of direct examination" that governs the manner and means in which testimony may be presented.

A. Competence of Witnesses

Every witness called to testify on direct examination must be legally "competent" to do so. This is generally taken to mean that the witness possesses personal knowledge of some matter at issue in the case,[1] is able to perceive and relate information, is capable of recognizing the difference between truth and falsity, and understands the seriousness of testifying under oath or on affirmation.[2]

In the absence of evidence or other indications to the contrary, all persons called to the stand are presumed competent to testify.[3] If the competence of a witness is reasonably disputed, it may be necessary to conduct a preliminary examination in order to "qualify" the witness.[4] Such inquiries are usually conducted by the direct examiner, but may also be conducted by the trial judge. In either case, the examination must be directed toward that aspect of competence that has been called into question.

In the case of a very young child, for example, the qualifying examination must establish that the witness is capable of distinguishing reality from fantasy, is able to perceive such relationships as time and distance, and appreciates that it is "wrong to tell a lie." Following the preliminary examination, the adverse party should be allowed an opportunity to conduct a "voir dire," which is a preliminary cross examination limited to a threshold issue such as competence.[5]

---

1   Rule 602, Federal Rules of Evidence.

2   Rule 603, Federal Rules of Evidence.

3   Rule 601, Federal Rules of Evidence.

4   Rule 104(a), Federal Rules of Evidence.

5   *See* Chapter Seven, Section II C (1)(d), *infra* at p. 225.

Note that there are several exceptions to the general rules of competence. Expert witnesses, for example, are excused from the requirement of testifying exclusively from personal knowledge.[6] Judges and jurors are generally disqualified from giving evidence in cases in which they are involved.[7]

B.   Non-leading Questions

The principal rule of direct examination is that the attorney may not "lead" the witness. A leading question is one that contains or suggests its own answer. Since the party calling a witness to the stand is presumed to have conducted an interview and to know what the testimony will be, leading questions are disallowed in order to insure that the testimony will come in the witness's own words.

Whether a certain question is leading is frequently an issue of tone or delivery, as much as one of form. The distinction, moreover, is often finely drawn. For example, there is no doubt that this question is leading:

QUESTION: Of course, you crossed the street, didn't you?

Not only does the question contain its own answer, its format also virtually requires that it be answered in the affirmative.

On the other hand, this question is not leading:

QUESTION: "Did you cross the street?"

Although the question is highly specific and calls for a "yes or no" answer, it does not control the witness's response.

Finally, this question falls in the middle:

QUESTION: "Didn't you cross the street?"

If the examiner's tone of voice and inflection indicate that this is meant as a true query, the question probably will not be considered leading. If the question is stated more as an assertion, however, it will violate the leading question rule.

There are, in any event, numerous exceptions to the rule against leading questions on direct examination. A lawyer is generally permitted to lead a witness on preliminary matters, on issues that are not in dispute, in order to direct the witness's attention to a specific topic, in order to expedite the testimony on non-essential points, and, in some jurisdictions, to refresh a witness's recollection. In addition, it is usually permissible to lead witnesses who are very young, very old, infirm, confused, or frightened. Finally, it is always within the trial judge's discretion to permit leading questions in order to make the examination effective

---

6   Rule 703, Federal Rules of Evidence.

7   Rules 605 and 606, Federal Rules of Evidence.

for the ascertainment of the truth, avoid needless consumption of time, protect the witness from undue embarrassment, or as is otherwise necessary to develop the testimony.

In the absence of extreme provocation or abuse, most lawyers will not object to the occasional use of leading questions on direct. It is most common to object to leading questions that are directed to the central issues of the case, or that are being used to substitute the testimony of counsel for that of the witness.

C. Narratives

Another general rule is that witnesses on direct examination may not testify in "narrative" form. The term narrative has no precise definition, but it is usually taken to mean an answer that goes beyond responding to a single specific question. Questions that invite a lengthy or run-on reply are said to "call for a narrative answer."

An example of a non-narrative question is, "What did you do next?" The objectionable, narrative version would be, "Tell us everything that you did that day."

As with leading questions, the trial judge has wide discretion to permit narrative testimony. Narratives are often allowed, indeed encouraged, when the witness has been qualified as an expert.[8]

D. The Non-opinion Rule

Witnesses are expected to testify as to their sensory observations. What did the witness see, hear, smell, touch, taste, or do? Witnesses other than experts generally are not allowed to offer opinions or to characterize events or testimony. A lay witness, however, is allowed to give opinions that are "rationally based upon the perception of the witness." Thus, witnesses will usually be permitted to draw conclusions on issues such as speed, distance, volume, time, weight, temperature, and weather conditions. Similarly, lay witnesses may characterize the behavior of others as angry, drunken, affectionate, busy, or even insane.

E. Refreshing Recollection

Although witnesses are expected to testify in their own words, they are not expected to have perfect recall. The courtroom can be an unfamiliar and intimidating place for all but the most "professional" witnesses, and witnesses can suffer memory lapses due to stress, fatigue, discomfort, or simple forgetfulness. Under these circumstances, it is permissible for the direct examiner to "refresh" the

---

8   Many lawyers prefer to present expert testimony in narrative form, but this often interferes with effective communication. *See* Chapter Six, Section V C, *infra* at p. 188.

witness's recollection. It is most common to rekindle a witness's memory through the use of a document such as her prior deposition or report. It may also be permissible to use a photograph, an object, or even a leading question.

In order to refresh recollection with a document, you must first establish that the witness's memory is exhausted concerning a specific issue or event. You must then determine that her memory might be refreshed by reference to a certain writing. Next, show the writing to the witness, allow her time to examine it, and inquire as to whether her memory has returned. If the answer is yes, remove the document and request the witness to continue her testimony. Note that in this situation the testimony must ultimately come from the witness's own restored memory; the document may not be offered as a substitute.

III. PLANNING DIRECT EXAMINATIONS

There are three fundamental aspects to every direct examination plan: content, organization, and technique.

Your principal tool in presenting a persuasive direct examination is, of course, the knowledge of the witness. If the underlying content of the examination is not accurate and believable, the lawyer's technique is unlikely to make any noticeable difference. Your primary concern, then, must be content — the existence of the facts that you intend to prove.

The content of a direct examination can be enhanced through the use of organization, language, focus, pacing, and rapport. Effective organization requires sequencing an examination in a manner that provides for logical development, while emphasizing important points and minimizing damaging ones. Questions should be asked in language that directs the progress of the examination without putting words in the witness's mouth. A direct examination uses focus to underscore and expand upon the most crucial issues, rather than allow them to be lost in a welter of meaningless details. Pacing varies the tone, speed, and intensity of the testimony to insure that it does not become boring. Finally, the positive rapport of the direct examiner with the witness is essential to establish the witness's overall trustworthiness and believability.

A. Content

Content — what the witness has to say — must be the driving force of every direct examination. Recall that direct examination provides your best opportunity to prove your case. It is not meant merely as a showcase for the witness's attractiveness or for your own forensic skills. The examination must have a central purpose. It must either establish some aspect of your theory, or it must contribute to the persuasiveness of your theme. Preferably, it will do both.

Begin by asking yourself, "Why am I calling this witness?" Which elements of your claims or defenses will the witness address? How can the witness be used to controvert an element of the other side's case? What exhibits can be introduced through the witness? How can the witness bolster or detract from the credibility of others who will testify? How can the witness add moral strength to the presentation of the case, or appeal to the jury's sense of justice?

Since a witness might be called for any or all of the above reasons, you must exhaustively determine all of the possible useful information. List every conceivable thing that the witness might say to explain or help your case.

Now you must begin to prioritize and discard. This is a ruthless process. In direct examination, length is your enemy. You must work to eliminate all non-essential facts that are questionable, subject to impeachment, cumulative, distasteful, implausible, distracting, or just plain boring.

1. What to Include

First, go through a process of inclusion. List the witness's facts that are necessary to the establishment of your theory. What is the single most important thing that the witness has to say? What are the witness's collateral facts that will make the central information more plausible? What is the next most important part of the potential testimony? What secondary facts make that testimony more believable? Continue this process for every element of your case.

For example, assume that in our fire engine case you have located a witness who saw the defendant driver at an automobile repair shop just a few days before the accident. The witness told you that the defendant was advised that his brakes were in poor repair, but that he left without having them fixed. This is a fact of central importance, and you will no doubt present it in the direct examination. Collateral or supportive facts will include corroborative details such as the time of day, the witness's reason for being in the auto shop, the witness's location during the crucial conversation about the brakes, the reason that the witness can remember the exact language used, and why the witness can identify the defendant. These details, while not strictly relevant to your theory, give weight and believability to the crucial testimony.

You must also be sure to include those "thematic" facts that give your case moral appeal. Returning to the intersection case, perhaps you have an additional witness who will testify that at the time of the collision the defendant was already late for an important meeting. Your theme, then, might be that the defendant was "Too busy to be careful." How can this theme be developed in the testimony of the "auto shop" witness? The answer is to look for supportive details. Was the defendant curt or abrupt with the repairperson? Was he constantly looking at his watch? Was he trying to read "important-looking papers" while discussing the brakes? Did the defendant rush out of the shop? In other words, search for details that support your image of the defendant as busy, preoccupied, and unconcerned with safety.

In addition to central facts and supporting details, your "content checklist" should include consideration of the following sorts of information:

Reasons. Recall that stories are more persuasive when they include reasons for the way people act. A direct examination usually should include the reasons for the witness's own actions. Some witnesses can also provide reasons for the actions of another.

Explanations. When a witness's testimony is not self-explanatory, or where it raises obvious questions, simply ask the witness to explain. In the above "repair shop" scenario it may not be immediately apparent that a casual observer would recall the defendant's actions in such detail. Ask for an explanation:

QUESTION: How is it that you can remember seeing and hearing what the defendant did that morning?

ANSWER: I was at the shop to have my brakes fixed, and it really made an impression on me that he was leaving without taking care of his.

Credibility. The credibility of a witness is always in issue. Some part of every direct examination should be devoted to establishing the credibility of the witness. You can enhance credibility in numerous ways. Show that the witness is neutral and disinterested. Demonstrate that the witness had an adequate opportunity to observe. Allow the witness to deny any expected charges of bias or misconduct. Elicit the witness's personal background of probity and honesty.

2. What to Exclude

Having identified the facts that most support your theory and most strengthen your theme, you may now begin the process of elimination. It should go without saying that you must omit those facts that are "untrue." While you are not required to assure yourself beyond reasonable doubt of the probity of each witness, neither may you knowingly elicit testimony that you believe to be false. By the time you are preparing your direct examinations, you certainly will have abandoned any legal or factual theory that rests upon evidence of this sort.

More realistically, unless you have an extraordinarily compelling reason to include them, you will need to consider discarding facts that fall into the following categories:

Clutter. This may be the single greatest vice in direct examination. Details are essential to the corroboration of important evidence, and they are worse than useless virtually everywhere else. Aimless detail will detract from your true corroboration. In the "auto shop" example, for instance, the witness's proximity to the service counter is an essential detail. The color of the paint in the waiting room is not.

How do you determine whether or not a certain fact is clutter? Ask what it contributes to the persuasiveness of your story. Does it supply a reason for the way that someone acted? Does it make an important fact more or less likely? Does it affect the credibility of a witness? Does it enhance the moral value of your story? If all of the answers are negative, you're looking at clutter.

Unprovables. These are facts that can successfully be disputed. While not "false," they may be subjected to such vigorous and effective dispute as to make them unusable. Is the witness the only person who claims to have observed a certain event, while many other credible witnesses swear to the precise contrary? Is the witness herself less than certain? Is the testimony contradicted by credible documentary evidence? It is usually better to pass up a line of inquiry than to pursue it and ultimately have it rejected. This is not, however, a hard and fast rule. Many true facts will be disputed by the other side, and your case will virtually always turn upon your ability to persuade the trier of fact that your version is correct. Sometimes your case will depend entirely upon the testimony of a single witness who, though certain and truthful, will come under massive attack. Still, you must be willing to evaluate all of the potential testimony against the standards of provability and need. If you can't prove it, don't use it. Especially if you don't need it.

Implausibles. Some facts need not be disputed in order to collapse under their own weight. They might be true, they might be useful, they might be free from possible contradiction, but they still just won't fly. Return to the "auto shop" witness and assume that she informed you that she recognized the defendant because they had once ridden in the same elevator fifteen years previously. You may have no reason to disbelieve the witness, and it is certainly unlikely that anyone could contradict or disprove her testimony. The testimony might even add some support to your theme, say, if the defendant was rushed out of the elevator in an obvious hurry to get to work. Nonetheless, the testimony is simply too far-fetched. If offered, it will give the trier of fact something unnecessary to worry about; it will inject a reason to doubt the other testimony of the witness.

Note, however, that implausibility must be weighed against importance. If the case involved a disputed identification of the defendant, then proof of an earlier encounter might be of sufficient value to risk its introduction.

Impeachables. These are statements open to contradiction by the witness's own prior statements. By the time of trial many witnesses will have given oral and/or written statements in the form of interviews, reports, and depositions. Many also will have signed or authored documents, correspondence, and other writings. With some limitations, the witnesses' previous words may be used to cast doubt upon their credibility; this is called impeachment by a prior inconsistent statement.[9] The demonstration that a witness has previously made statements that contradict her trial testimony is often one of the most dramatic, and damning, aspects of cross examination. Unless you can provide an extremely good explanation of why the witness has changed, or seems to have changed, her story, it is usually best to omit "impeachables" from direct testimony.

Door Openers. Some direct testimony is said to "open the door" for inquiries on cross examination that otherwise would not be allowed. The theory here is that fairness requires that the cross examiner be allowed to explore any topic that was deliberately introduced on direct. For example, in the intersection case the defendant almost certainly would not be allowed to introduce the fact that the plaintiff had been under the care of a psychiatrist. On the other hand, assume that the plaintiff testified on direct that the accident had forced her to miss an important appointment with her doctor, and that the appointment could not be rescheduled for a week due to the nature of the doctor's schedule. In these circumstances the door would be opened, at a minimum, to a cross examination that covered the nature of the appointment and the reason that it could not be rescheduled; in other words, that the plaintiff was on her way to see her psychiatrist.

Another common door opener is the misconceived "defensive" direct examination. It is considered a truism in many quarters that the direct examiner should defuse the cross by preemptively bringing out all of the bad facts. The danger, however, is that you will "defensively" bring out facts that would have been inadmissible on cross examination. Assume, for example, that your client has a prior juvenile conviction for theft. While you might ordinarily want to raise a prior crime yourself in order to explain it or otherwise soften the impact of the evidence, juvenile convictions are almost never admissible. Thus, a defensive direct examination would not only introduce otherwise excludable information, it could very well open the door to further exploitation of those facts on cross. You cannot always avoid door openers, but you must learn to recognize them.

B. Organization and Structure

Organization is the tool through which you translate the witness's memory of events into a coherent and persuasive story. This requires idiom, art, poetry. An artist does not paint everything that she sees. Rather, she organizes shapes, colors, light, and impasto to present her own image of a landscape. In the same manner, a trial lawyer does not simply ask a witness to "tell everything you know," but instead uses the placement and sequence of the information to heighten and clarify its value.

The keys to this process are primacy and recency, apposition, duration, and repetition.

---

9   *See* Chapter Four, Section II, *infra* at p. 119.

Primacy and recency refer to the widely accepted phenomenon that people tend best to remember those things that they hear first and last. Following this principle, the important parts of a direct examination should be brought out at its beginning, and again at its end. Less important information should be "sandwiched" in the middle. In our intersection case the presence of the fire truck may well be the most important part of the plaintiff's testimony. It should therefore be introduced early in her direct examination, and perhaps alluded to again at the end.

Apposition is the placement or juxtaposition of important facts in a manner that emphasizes their relationship. Again looking at the intersection case, a strictly chronological direct examination might have the plaintiff begin by explaining where she was headed on the morning of the accident. Assume now that she was going to an art exhibit that would not open for another hour. The importance and value of this seemingly innocuous fact can be heightened tremendously by "apposing" it to the conduct of the defendant immediately following the accident. Imagine the impact of contrasting the plaintiff's unhurried trip with the following information about the defendant:

QUESTION: Where were you going on the morning of the accident?

ANSWER: I was going to the Art Institute.

QUESTION: Were you in any hurry to get there?

ANSWER: It wasn't going to open for an hour, so I was in no hurry at all.

QUESTION: What did you do immediately after the accident?

ANSWER: I asked the defendant if he was all right.

QUESTION: What did the defendant do immediately following the accident?

ANSWER: He jumped out of his car and ran to a pay telephone. He shouted that he would talk to me later, but first he had to cancel an important appointment.

Duration refers to the relative amount of time that you spend on the various aspects of the direct examination. As a general rule you should dwell on the more important points, using the very length of coverage to emphasize the significance of the topic. Less important matters should consume less of the direct examination. In the fire truck example it should be obvious that the presence and noticeability of the fire engine is central to the plaintiff's case. Although the plaintiff's observation of the truck could be established in a single question and answer, the importance of the subject dictates greater duration for this part of the direct examination:

25

QUESTION: What did you see as you drove south on Sheridan Road?

ANSWER: I saw a fire truck.

QUESTION: Describe it, please.

ANSWER: It was your basic fire truck. It was red, and it had firefighters riding on it. It had lights and a bell.

QUESTION: Were the lights flashing?

ANSWER: Yes, and it was sounding its siren.

QUESTION: How far away were you when you first noticed the fire truck?

ANSWER: I would say almost a block away.

Repetition is a corollary of duration. Important points should be repeated, preferably throughout the direct examination, to increase the likelihood that they will be retained and relied upon by the trier of fact.

Even applying these principles, there is no set pattern for the structure of a direct examination, just as there is no correct way to paint a landscape. The following guidelines, however, will always be useful.

1. Start Strong and End Strong: The Overall Examination

Every direct examination, no matter how else it is organized, should strive to begin and end on strong points. The definition of a strong point will differ from trial to trial. It may be the most gripping and dramatic aspect of the entire examination; it may be the single matter on which the witness expresses the greatest certainty; it may be the case's most hotly disputed issue; or it may be a crucial predicate for other testimony. Whatever the specifics, the strong points of your overall examination should have some or all of these features:

Admissibility. There is little worse than having an objection sustained right at the beginning, or end, of a direct examination. You must be absolutely certain of the admissibility of your opening and closing points.

Theory value. The very definition of a strong point is that it makes a significant contribution to your theory. What does the witness have to say that is most central to the proof of your case?

Thematic value. Ideally, your strongest points will reinforce the moral weight of your case. Try to phrase them in the same language you use to invoke your theme.

Dramatic impact. Dramatic impact at the beginning of an examination will keep the judge or jury listening. Dramatic impact at the end of the examination will help fix the testimony in their memories.

Undeniability. Choose strong points in the hope that they will be vividly remembered. It will do you little good if they are remembered as being questionable or controverted.

In most cases, of course, it will be necessary to use the opening part of the direct examination to introduce the witness and establish some of her background. Thus, the actual "beginning" of the examination should be understood as the beginning of the substantive testimony.

2. Start Strong and End Strong: The Sub-Examinations

Each full direct examination is actually a combination of many smaller sub-examinations. As you move from topic to topic you are constantly concluding and reinitiating the sub-parts of the direct testimony. The "start strong/end strong" rule should not be applied only to the organization of the full direct. It should also be used to structure its individual components.

In our intersection case you might wish to begin and end the substantive part of the plaintiff's examination with evidence about the fire truck. In between, however, you will cover many other issues, including the plaintiff's background, the scene of the collision, and the plaintiff's damages. Each of these component parts of the direct should, if possible, begin and end on a strong point.

In something as simple as setting the scene, consider what elements of the description are most important to your case. Then begin with one and end with another. In the intersection case you might want to lead off with the clarity of the weather conditions in order to establish visibility. Perhaps you would then conclude the scene-setting portion of the examination with this description of the traffic:

QUESTION: Of all of the cars that were present, how many stopped for the fire truck?

ANSWER: All of them, except the defendant.

3. Use Topical Organization

Chronology is almost always the easiest form of organization. What could be more obvious than beginning at the beginning and ending at the end? In trial advocacy, however, easiest is not always best. In many cases it will be preferable to utilize a topical or thematic form of organization. In this way, you can arrange various components of the witness's testimony to reinforce each other, you can isolate weak points, and you can develop your theory in the most persuasive manner. The order in which events occurred is usually fortuitous. Your duty as an advocate is to rearrange the telling so that the story has maximum logical force.

Assume that you are the prosecutor in a burglary case. Your first witness is the police officer who conducted a stake-out and arrested the defendant on the basis of a description that she received from a superior officer. A strict chronology

27

in such a case could be confusing and counterproductive. The witness would have to begin with the morning of the arrest, perhaps explaining the time that she came on duty, the other matters that she worked on that day, and her instructions in conducting the stake-out. She no doubt would have received the description somewhere in the middle of all this activity. Even if relevant, the importance of the surrounding details is not likely to be well understood at the outset of the examination. The officer, sticking to chronological order, would then describe the people she saw at the stake-out location whom she did not arrest. Finally, the witness would come to the defendant's arrival on the scene. Assume, however, that she did not immediately arrest him. Rather, she observed him for some time; perhaps he even left the scene (and returned) once or twice before the eventual arrest.

In plain chronological order, all of this can add up to a rather diffuse story. The officer's reasons for conducting the stake-out are separated from the activity itself; the receipt of the description has no immediate relationship to the apprehension of the suspect. The trier of fact is required to reflect both forward and back on the significance of the data.

A topical organization, however, could provide a framework and that adds clarity and direction to the story. A structure based upon the description of the defendant, rather than chronology, would begin with a description of the arrest itself; then:

QUESTION: Officer, why did you arrest the defendant?

ANSWER: Because he fit a description that I had been given earlier of a wanted burglar.

QUESTION: Did you arrest him as soon as you saw him?

ANSWER: No, I wanted to make sure that he fit the description completely, so I waited until he was standing directly below a street light.

QUESTION: Was there anyone else in the vicinity at that time?

ANSWER: There had been a few people, but nobody who matched the description.

QUESTION: Officer, please go back and tell us how you received the description that led to the arrest of the defendant.

Even in a matter as simple as our automobile collision case, a strictly chronological direct examination of the plaintiff could fail to be either dramatic or persuasive. Imagine beginning the examination with the time that the plaintiff left home that morning. State her destination and her estimated travel time. Describe the weather and traffic conditions. Trace her route from street to street until she arrives at the fateful intersection. Describe the appearance of the fire truck, the plaintiff's reaction, and finally the collision. After slogging through a series of details, some important and some not, the direct examination finally arrives at the most important event — the accident itself.

It would be more dramatic to (1) begin with the collision, (2) explain why the plaintiff had stopped her car, (3) describe the fire truck, (4) describe the response of the surrounding traffic, and (5) contrast that with the actions of the defendant.

4. Don't Interrupt the Action

Every direct examination is likely to involve one, two, or more key events or occurrences. The witness may describe physical activity such as an automobile accident, an arrest, the failure of a piece of equipment, or a surgical procedure. Alternatively, the witness may testify about something less tangible, such as the formation of a contract, the effect of an insult, the making of a threat, the breach of a promise, or the existence of pain following an injury. Whatever the precise subject, it will always be possible to divide the testimony into "action" on the one hand, and supporting details and descriptions on the other.

A cardinal rule for the organization of direct examination is never to interrupt the action. Do not disrupt the dramatic flow of your story, the description of the crucial events, in order to fill in minor details. There can be no more jarring or dissatisfying an experience during trial than when the witness, who has just testified to the sound of a gunshot or the screech of automobile tires, is then calmly asked the location of the nearest street light. The lighting conditions may be important, but they cannot possibly be important enough to justify the discontinuity created by fracturing the natural flow of occurrence testimony.

Many lawyers subscribe to the theory that you should "set the scene" before proceeding to the activity. Following this approach in our automobile case, you would first have the witness describe the intersection, the surrounding traffic, the condition of the streets, and the location of her car, all before proceeding to the events of the collision. This approach is based on the concept that the trier of fact can then place the activities within the framework that you have created.

An alternative approach is first to describe the events themselves, and then to go back and redescribe them while filling in the details of the scene. Assume that the plaintiff in the automobile case has already testified about the events of the accident. You can now go back to set the scene, effectively telling the story a second time: What were the weather conditions when you entered the block where the collision occurred? How much traffic was there when you first saw the fire truck? What direction were you travelling when the defendant's car struck yours?

5. Give Separate Attention to the Details

We have seen that details add strength and veracity to a witness's testimony. Unfortunately, they can also detract from the flow of events. It is therefore usually best to give separate attention to the details, an approach that also allows you to explain their importance.

Assume, for example, that you are presenting the testimony of a robbery victim, and that the central issue in the case is the identification of the defendant. You know that you don't want to detract from the action, so you will present the events of the robbery without interruption. Then you will go back to supply the details that support the witness's ability to identify the defendant:

QUESTION: How far was the defendant from you when you first noticed him?

ANSWER: About 12 or 15 feet.

QUESTION: How much closer did he come?

ANSWER: He came right up to me. His face wasn't more than a foot from mine.

QUESTION: Did you look at his face?

ANSWER: Yes, absolutely. He stared right at me.

QUESTION: For how long?

ANSWER: It was at least a minute.

QUESTION: Was it still light out?

ANSWER: Yes, it was.

QUESTION: Could you see the color of his clothing?

There will be dozens of details available to support the witness's identification. Dispersing them throughout the description of events would both disrupt the testimony and diminish their cumulative importance. The remedy for this problem is to give the details separate attention.

6. Try Not to Scatter Circumstantial Evidence

Circumstantial evidence is usually defined as indirect proof of a proposition, event, or occurrence. The identity of a burglar, for example, could be proven directly through eyewitness testimony. It could also be proven indirectly through the accumulation of circumstantial evidence such as the following: The defendant was seen near the scene of the burglary on the evening of the crime; her scarf was found in the doorway of the burglarized house; she had been heard complaining about her need for a new radio; two days after the crime she was found in possession of a radio that had been taken in the burglary.

None of the above facts taken individually amount to direct proof that the defendant committed the crime. There could be a perfectly innocent explanation for each one. In combination, however, they raise an extremely compelling inference of guilt. In other words, the indirect circumstances accumulate to establish the likelihood of the prosecution's case.

Inferential evidence is at its strongest when a series of circumstances can be combined to lead to the desired conclusion. It is therefore effective to present all of the related circumstantial evidence at a single point in the direct examination, rather than scatter it throughout. This will not always be possible. The logic of a witness's testimony may require that items of circumstantial evidence be elicited at different points in the testimony. Chronological organization will dictate introducing the circumstances in the order that they occurred or were discovered. Even topical organization may require assigning individual circumstances to separate topics. In the burglary case, for example, a topical approach might divide the testimony into areas such as "condition of the premises" and "apprehension of the defendant." The discovery of the scarf and the recovery of the radio would consequently be separated in the testimony.

Nonetheless, it is always a good idea to attempt to cluster your circumstantial evidence. Abandon this technique only when you have settled upon another that you believe will be more effective.

7. Defensive Direct Examination

From time to time it will be necessary to bring out potentially harmful or embarrassing facts on direct in order to blunt their impact on cross examination. The theory of such "defensive" direct examination is that the bad information will have less sting if the witness offers it herself, and conversely that it will be all the more damning if the witness is seen as having tried to hide the bad facts. As we noted above, you should conduct a defensive direct examination only when you are sure that the information is known to the other side and will be admissible on cross examination.

Assuming that you have determined to bring out certain damaging information, be sure not to do it at either the beginning or end of the direct examination. Remember the principles of primacy and recency. By definition, bad facts cannot possibly be the strong points of your case, so you will always want to bury them in the middle of the direct examination.

An extremely useful technique is to allow the trier of fact to "make friends" with your witness before you introduce harmful information. It is a normal human tendency to want to believe the best of people whom you like. Thus, you should give the judge or jury every possible reason to like your witness before offering anything that might have a contrary effect. Recall the last time that you saw a television interview of the neighbors of an arrested crime suspect. They almost inevitably say something like, "He was such a nice man. I can't believe that he would do a thing like that."

If, for example, you have a witness who was previously convicted of a felony, you can reasonably assume that to be fair game for cross examination. You will therefore want to bring out the conviction, in sympathetic terms, during your direct examination. Do not elicit such a fact until you have spent some time "personalizing" the witness. Give the trier of fact a reason to discount the conviction before you ever mention it.

8. Affirmation Before Refutation

Witnesses are often called both to offer affirmative evidence of their own and to refute the testimony of others. In such cases it is usually best to offer the affirmative evidence before proceeding to refutation. In this manner you will accentuate the positive aspects of your case and avoid making the witness appear to be a scold.

As with all principles, this one should not invariably be followed. Some witnesses are called solely for refutation. Others are far more important for what they negate than for their affirmative information. As a general organizing principle, it is useful to think about building your own case before destroying the opposition's.

9. Get to the Point

A direct examination is not a treasure hunt or murder mystery; there is seldom a reason to keep the trier of fact in suspense. The best form of organization is often to explain exactly where the testimony is headed, and then to go directly there.

10. End With a Clincher

Every examination should end with a clincher, a single fact that capsulizes your trial theory or theme. To qualify as a clincher a fact must be (1) absolutely admissible, (2) reasonably dramatic, (3) simple and memorable, and (4) stated with certainty. Depending upon the nature of the evidence and the theory on which you are proceeding, the final question to the plaintiff in our automobile case might be any of the following:

QUESTION: How long was the fire engine visible before the defendant's car struck yours?

ANSWER: It was visible for at least ten seconds, because I had already seen it and stopped for a while when the defendant ran into me.

Or,

> QUESTION: Did the defendant run to the telephone before or after he checked on your injuries?
>
> ANSWER: He ran straight to the telephone without even looking at me.

Or,

> QUESTION: Do you know whether you will ever be able to walk again without pain?
>
> ANSWER: The doctors say that they can't do anything more for me, but I am still praying.

11. Ignore Any Rule When Necessary

By now you will no doubt have noticed that the above principles are not completely consistent with one another. In any given case you will probably be unable to start strong, organize topically, and separate the details, while still getting to the point without interrupting the action. Which rules should you follow? The answer lies in your own good judgment, and can only be arrived at in the context of a specific case. If you need another principle to help interpret the others, it is this: Apply the rules that best advance your theory and theme.

IV. QUESTIONING TECHNIQUE

Since content is the motive force behind every direct examination, you must use questioning technique to focus attention on the witness and the testimony. It is the witness's story that is central to the direct examination; the style and manner of your questioning should underscore and support the credibility and veracity of that story. The following questioning techniques can help you to achieve that goal.

A. Use Short, Open Questions

You want the witness to tell the story. You want the witness to be the center of attention. You want the witness to be appreciated and believed. None of these things can happen if you do all of the talking. Therefore, ask short questions.

Using short questions will help you to refrain from talking, but not every short question will get the witness talking. To do that, you will need open questions.

Don't ask a witness, "Did you go to the bank?" The answer to that short question will probably be an even shorter "Yes." Instead, as much of your direct examination as possible should consist of questions that invite the witness to describe, explain, and illuminate the events of her testimony. Ask questions such as these:

QUESTION: Where did you go that day?

QUESTION: What happened after that?

QUESTION: Tell us who was there.

QUESTION: What else happened?

QUESTION: Describe where you were.

Your witness will almost always be more memorable and believable if you can obtain most of her information in her own words. Short, open questions will advance that goal.

B.   Use Directive and Transitional Questions

You cannot use open questions to begin an examination, or to move from one area of the examination to another. To do so you would have to start with "When were you born," and proceed to ask "What happened next" in almost endless repetition.

A better approach is to use directive and transitional questions. Directive questions, quite simply, direct the witness's attention to the topic that you want to cover. Suppose that you want the witness to address the issue of damages. Ask,

QUESTION: Were you in any pain after the accident?

Having directed the witness's attention, you can now revert to your short, open questions:

QUESTION: Please describe how you felt.

QUESTION: Where else did you hurt?

QUESTION: How has this affected your life?

You may need to use more than one directive question during any particular line of testimony. To fill out the subject of damages, for example, you may need to ask additional questions such as,

QUESTION: Do you currently suffer any physical disabilities?

Or,

QUESTION: Did you ever have such pains before the accident?

Remember that the purpose of a directive question is to direct the witness's attention, not to divert the jury's.

Another problem with short, open questions is that they are not very good at underscoring the relationship between one fact and another. The best way to do this is through "transitional" questions that utilize one fact as the predicate, or introduction, to another. Here are some examples of transitional questions:

QUESTION: After you saw the fire truck, what did you do?

QUESTION: Do you know what the defendant did as the other traffic slowed to a stop?

QUESTION: Once the defendant's car hit yours, did you see him do anything?

Note that directive and transitional questions will tend to be leading. As a technical matter, however, these questions are permissible so long as they are used to orient the witness, expedite the testimony, or introduce a new area of the examination. As a practical matter, objections to directive and transitional questions are not likely to be sustained so long as they are used relatively sparingly and are not asked in a tone that seems to insist upon a certain answer. It is unethical to abuse transitional or directive questions in a way that substitutes your testimony for that of the witness.

C. Reinitiate Primacy

The doctrine of primacy tells us that the trier of fact will pay maximum attention to the witness at the very beginning of the testimony. You can make further use of this principle by continuously "re-beginning" the examination. That is, every time you seem to start anew, you will refocus the attention of the judge or jury. This technique can be called reinitiating primacy, and there are several ways to achieve it:

1. Use General Headlines Questions

Most direct examinations, including even those that are organized chronologically, will consist of a number of individual areas of inquiry. If you treat each such area as a separate examination, you can reinitiate primacy every time you move to a new topic. You can divide the direct into a series of smaller examinations through the use of verbal headlines. Rather than simply move from area to area, insert a headline to alert the judge or jury to the fact that you are shifting gears or changing subjects.

The introduction should be overt. Don't ask,

QUESTION: What happened as you were driving south on Sheridan Road?

35

Instead, announce the new subject by asking,

QUESTION: Were you involved in an accident at the corner of Sheridan and Chase?

Similar headlines might include:

QUESTION: Had you kept your own car in good repair?

Or,

QUESTION: Were you hospitalized?

Or,

QUESTION: Are you still disabled today?

None of these introductory questions would really be necessary to begin the particular segment of testimony. You could simply proceed to the detailed questioning, relying upon the witness to provide the necessary information. You could also write an entire novel without using chapter titles, paragraphs, or even punctuation. The headline question, however, serves the same function as a chapter heading in a book. It divides the "text" and reinitiates primacy.

2. Explain Where You're Going

You can reinitiate primacy even more directly through the use of a few, well-chosen, declaratory statements. Everything that you say during a direct examination does not have to be in the form of a question. You may say to the witness, "Let's talk about the aftermath of the accident." Or, "We need to move on to the subject of your injuries." Such statements are permissible so long as they are truly used to make the transition from one part of the testimony to another, or to orient the witness in some other manner. You cannot, of course, use declaratory statements to instruct the witness how to testify.

3. Use Body Movement

Another way to segment your examination, and thereby reinitiate primacy, is through the use of body movement. Most jurisdictions, although not all, allow lawyers to move rather freely about the courtroom as they conduct their examinations. Unless you are in a court that requires you to remain seated at counsel table or standing at a podium, you can effectively announce the beginning of a new topic by pausing for a moment, and then moving purposefully to a different part of the room. You needn't stride dramatically — a few short steps will usually suffice.

The key to this technique is to stop talking as you move. The silence and movement will reinforce each other, making it clear that one topic has ended and another is about to begin.

D. Use Incremental Questions

Information usually can be obtained in either large or small pieces. Incremental questions break the "whole" into its component pieces, so that the testimony can be delivered in greater, and therefore more persuasive, detail.

A large, non-incremental question might be,

QUESTION: What did the robber look like?

Even a well prepared witness will probably answer this question with a fairly general description. A common response might be,

ANSWER: He was a white male, about 20 or 25 years old, maybe six feet tall.

You might be able to go back to supply any omitted information, but in doing so you will risk giving the unfortunate impression of doing just that — filling in gaps in the witness's testimony. Furthermore, at some point in the backtracking a judge might sustain an objection on the ground that the question — "Describe the robber" — had been asked and answered.

An incremental approach to the issue of identification, on the other hand, would be built upon a set of questions such as these:

QUESTION: Were you able to get a good look at the robber?

ANSWER: Yes, I was able to see him clearly.

QUESTION: How tall was he?

ANSWER: About six feet tall.

QUESTION: How heavy was he?

ANSWER: He was heavy, almost fat, over 200 pounds.

QUESTION: What race was he?

ANSWER: He was white.

QUESTION: And his complexion?

ANSWER: He was very fair, with freckles.

QUESTION: What color was his hair?

ANSWER: He was blond.

QUESTION: How was his hair cut?

ANSWER: It wasn't really cut at all — just sort of long and stringy.

QUESTION: Did he have any facial hair?

ANSWER: A small moustache.

QUESTION: Could you see his eyes?

ANSWER: Yes, he came right up to me.

QUESTION: What color were they?

ANSWER: Blue.

QUESTION: Was he wearing glasses?

ANSWER: Yes, he was.

QUESTION: What sort of frames?

ANSWER: Round wire rims.

QUESTION: Did he have any scars or marks?

ANSWER: Yes, he had a birthmark on his forehead.

QUESTION: Was he wearing a jacket?

ANSWER: He had on a Detroit Pistons jacket.

Depending upon the witness's knowledge, further questions could inquire into other facts. Could the witness see the robber's shirt? What color was it? His trousers? His shoes? Any jewelry? Tatoos?

As you can plainly see, the use of incremental questions, each seeking a single small bit of information, can drive home the accuracy of the identification without seeming to put words in the witness's mouth.

The incremental technique should be used sparingly. It will not work as an overall principle, since the unrestrained use of details will quickly overwhelm the trier of fact. Use it only where the details are available, significant, and convincing.

First and foremost, the details must be available. It will only damage your case for you to ask a series of incremental questions that elicit negative or blank responses.

Second, the details must be significant. You will produce only boredom by providing every conceivable detail regarding every conceivable fact. No one will be interested in the location of the bell on the fire truck or the number of spots on the fire house dalmatian. Rather, you want the fine emphasis on small facts to come as a clear departure from the balance of the examination. What you are implying by the shift should be obvious: "Details weren't crucial before, but they are now. So pay close attention."

Finally, the incremental details have to be convincing; they have to lend verity to the larger point that you are trying to establish. Some details will be meaningless. It is unlikely to help an identification, for example, for the witness to testify that the robber was chewing gum. Other details may not be credible. Even if the witness claims absolute certainty, you probably won't want to offer testimony about the number of fillings in the assailant's teeth.

E. Reflect Time, Distance, Intensity

The very best direct examinations virtually re-create the incidents they describe, drawing verbal images that all but place the trier of fact at the scene of the events. Your pace and manner of questioning are essential to this process.

The timing or duration of an event, for example, is often crucial in a trial; one side claims that things happened quickly and the other asserts that they were drawn out. It is possible to use the pace of questioning to support your particular theory. Assume that you represent the defendant in our fire truck case. His defense is that the fire engine appeared only a moment before the collision, and that he just didn't have enough time to stop his car. The goal of the defendant's direct examination must be to re-create that scene by collapsing the time available to react to the fire truck. Hence, you will ask only a few, fast-paced questions:

QUESTION: When did the fire truck first become visible?

ANSWER: It approached the intersection just as I did.

QUESTION: What was the very first action that you took?

ANSWER: I slammed on my brakes.

QUESTION: How much time did that take?

ANSWER: Less than a second.

Note that this direct examination proceeds quickly, emphasizing both short-ness of time and immediacy of response. This result will be enhanced if you fire off the questions, and if the witness doesn't pause before answering. Strive for the appearance of all but panting for breath.

In contrast, the plaintiff will claim that there was ample time for the defendant to stop. Her direct examination should therefore be drawn out in order to demonstrate exactly how much time there was:

QUESTION: Where was the fire truck when you first saw it?

ANSWER: It was about a quarter of a block away from the intersection.

QUESTION: How far away from you was it?

ANSWER: About 100 yards.

QUESTION: How many other cars were between you and the fire truck?

ANSWER: Three or four.

QUESTION: What did they do in response?

ANSWER: They all stopped.

QUESTION: How long did it take those other cars to stop?

ANSWER: Normal stopping time — a few seconds.

QUESTION: What was the first thing that you did?

ANSWER: I started to pull over to the side.

QUESTION: How long did that take?

ANSWER: Five seconds or so.

QUESTION: What did you do after that?

ANSWER: I brought my car to a stop.

QUESTION: How long did that take?

ANSWER: Well, I applied my brakes right away, and it took a few seconds for the car to stop.

QUESTION: Then what happened?

ANSWER: That's when the other car rear-ended me.

QUESTION: How much time elapsed between the moment when you first saw the fire truck and the time that the defendant's car hit yours?

ANSWER: At least 10 or 15 seconds.

There is every reason not to hurry through this part of the examination. The length, detail, and pace of your questions should be used to demonstrate the validity of your theory: The defendant had plenty of time to stop.

Similar techniques can be used to establish distance and intensity. Draw out your questions to maximize distance; move through them quickly to minimize it. Ask questions at a rapid pace to enhance the intensity of an encounter; slow down to make the situation more relaxed.

A word about ethics is important at this point. Lawyers are often accused of using verbal tricks to turn night into day. That is not what we are discussing here. Rather, the purpose of using "reflective" questioning is just the opposite — to insure that the witness conveys her intended meaning. The techniques and examination styles discussed above are not deceptive, but are useful to illuminate or underscore the content of a witness's testimony. If a witness says that an event took only moments, you can assist in the accurate presentation of that testimony by using a questioning style reflective of suddenness and speed. Use of the wrong style can actually inhibit the witness's communication and positively mislead the trier of fact.

F.   Repeat Important Points

In every direct examination there will be several essential ideas that stand out as far more important than the rest. Do not be satisfied to elicit those points only once. Repeat them. Restate them. Then repeat them again. Then think of ways to restate them again. Since you are not allowed to ask the same question twice (Objection: asked and answered), you will need to employ your lawyer's creativity to fashion numerous slightly different questions, each stressing the same point. Repetition is the parent of retention, and your most important points should arise again and again throughout the testimony, to insure that they are retained by the trier of fact.

The corollary to this principle is that less important points should not be repeated in like manner. Increased attention should be used to make key subjects stand out. If too many points are given this treatment, they will all be made to seem equally unimportant. How do you decide which facts are sufficiently important to bear repetition? The answer is to consider your theory and theme. You will want to repeat those facts that are basic to your logical theory, and those that best evoke your moral theme.

In our automobile accident case, the gist of the plaintiff's theory is that she stopped for a passing fire truck, while the defendant did not. Her single most important fact is definitely the observable presence of the fire truck. Thus, the words "fire truck" should be inserted at every reasonable point during the examination. At the close of her testimony, you want to have created the image that the fire truck dominated the scenery. How many different ways can the witness describe the fire truck? In how many locations can she place it? How many ways can she use it as a reference point for other testimony?

Thematic repetition may be more elusive or subtle. If the plaintiff's theme is that the defendant was "too busy to be careful," you will want to use repetition to emphasize how unbusy the plaintiff was.

Bench and jury trials differ significantly regarding the use of repetition. Juries consist of six or twelve individuals whose attention may sometimes drift. You can never be certain that every juror will have heard and retained every point, so repetition is particularly important. You not only need to drive your key points home, you need to drive them home to everyone. Judges are usually aware of this problem, and they typically will allow a fair amount of latitude for repetition during jury trials.

Bench trials are a different matter. Judges usually expect bench trials to move along swiftly. They don't like to be battered with constant reiteration of the same points. Of course, judges may also be inattentive, but they don't like to be reminded of it. In short, many judges do not like to be treated like jurors, and they will cut off attempts at repetition. Use this technique sparingly in bench trials.

G.   Use Visual Aids

Seeing is believing. In daily life we are accustomed to receive as much as 70% of our information through the sense of sight. Ordinary witness testimony is received primarily through the sense of sound. This makes it harder to follow and harder to retain. You can enhance the effectiveness of almost any witness by illustrating the testimony through the use of charts, photographs, maps, models, drawings, and other visual aids.

Always consider whether the witness's testimony can be illustrated. If the witness is going to testify about a pivotal document, determine whether it can be enlarged or projected on a screen in the courtroom. If the witness is going to testify about an event, create a map or produce an oversize photograph. If the witness will testify about a series of numbers or transactions, use a visual "time line" as your visual aid.

Demonstrations can also serve as visual aids. Ask the witness to re-enact crucial events or to re-create important sounds. "Please show the jury exactly how the defendant raised his hand before he struck you." "Please clap your hands together to show us how loud the sound was." "Please repeat the plaintiff's words in exactly her tone of voice."

Demonstrations must be carefully planned. They have an inevitable tendency to backfire when ill-prepared. Be certain that your expectations are realistic. A witness will not be able to illustrate the loudness of a rifle shot by clapping her hands. Nor will a witness be able to demonstrate the movement of a vehicle by walking about the courtroom. Finally, make sure that your demonstration doesn't look silly. Many lawyers have lost more ground than they gained by asking witnesses to roll around on the floor, climb up on chairs, or dash from one end of the courtroom to the other.

H.   Avoid Negative, Lawyerly, and Complex Questions

For reasons unknown and unknowable, many lawyers think that it makes them sound more professional when they phrase questions in the negative:

QUESTION: Did you not then go to the telephone?

No advocate, judge, juror, witness, English teacher, or speaker of our common language can possibly understand the meaning of that question. Even harder to understand are the two potential answers. What would "yes" mean? "Yes, I did not then go to the telephone?" Or, "Yes, I did." What would "no" mean? "No, I did then go to the telephone?" Or, "No, I didn't."

Furthermore, on direct examination your goal typically is to establish an affirmative case. It is therefore beneficial to phrase your questions so that your witnesses can answer them affirmatively. Do not use negative questions.

You must also avoid "lawyer talk." Many jurors and witnesses will not understand lawyerese, and virtually all will resent it. On the other hand, everyone, including judges, will appreciate plain language. Do not ask,

QUESTION: At what point in time did you alight from your vehicle?

Ask instead,

QUESTION: When did you get out of your car?

Do not ask,

QUESTION: What was your subsequent activity, conduct, or response with regard to the negotiation of an offer and acceptance?

Opt for,

QUESTION: What did you agree to next?

Finally, do not pose questions that call for more than a single item or category of information. Although a witness may be able to sort through a fairly simple compound question — such as "Where did you go and what did you do?" — many will become confused, and more will simply fail to answer the second part. Truly complex questions will almost certainly fail to elicit the answer that you seek.

V.   ADVERSE AND HOSTILE WITNESSES

From time to time it may be necessary to call a witness, such as the opposing party, who will be hostile to your case. Because unfriendly witnesses cannot be expected to cooperate in preparation, most jurisdictions allow the use of leading questions for the direct examination of such witnesses.[10] They fall into two broad categories: adverse and hostile witnesses.

---

10   Rule 611(c), Federal Rules of Evidence.

A. Adverse Witnesses

Adverse witnesses include the opposing party and those identified with the opposing party. Examples of witnesses identified with the opposing party include employees, close relatives, business partners, and others who share a community of interest. It is within the court's discretion to determine whether any particular witness is sufficiently identified with the opposition as to allow leading questions on direct examination.

It is important to alert the court to the fact that you are calling an adverse witness, lest the judge sustain objections to leading questions. In the case of the opposing party, counsel's right to ask leading questions on direct will be obvious. Nonetheless, there is no harm in stating that the witness is being called "as an adverse witness pursuant to Rule 611(c)," or its local analog.

In the case of a non-party adverse witness, it will usually be necessary at the outset to lay a foundation that establishes the witness's identification with the opposition. It may be as simple as in this example:

QUESTION: Please state your name.

ANSWER: My name is Andrew Connor.

QUESTION: Mr. Connor, are you employed by the defendant, South Suburban Country Club?

ANSWER: Yes, I am.

Note that more foundation may be needed, depending upon the nature of the witness's relationship to the adverse party.

In some jurisdictions it may be necessary to request that the court specifically find that the witness is adverse. In others one may lay the foundation and proceed to conduct the examination with leading questions.

B. Hostile Witnesses

A hostile witness is one who, while not technically adverse, displays actual hostility to the direct examiner or her client. The necessary characteristic may be manifested either through expressed antagonism or evident reluctance to testify. Additionally, a witness may be treated as hostile if his testimony legitimately surprises the lawyer who called him to the stand. Whatever the circumstances, it is generally necessary to have the court declare a witness to be hostile before proceeding with leading questions.

C. Strategy

There are limited situations in which it may be profitable to call an adverse witness. The first is where the adverse witness is the only person who can supply an essential element of your case. Thus the witness will have to be called in order to prevent a directed verdict. For the same reason, an adverse witness might also be called to authenticate a necessary document or to lay the foundation for some other exhibit. Finally, and most perilously, an adverse or hostile witness might be called solely for the purpose of making a bad impression on the trier of fact. Needless to say, this tactic has a strong potential to backfire.

In general, adverse (and potentially hostile) witnesses should not be called unless it is absolutely necessary. As noted in the introduction to this section, direct examination provides counsel with an opportunity to build a case. There is therefore great risk involved in calling a witness who will be troublesome, uncooperative, or worse. Moreover, calling an adverse witness allows opposing counsel to conduct, in the midst of your case, a "cross examination" that is very likely to resemble a final argument for the other side. The scope of adverse testimony should therefore be made as narrow as possible.

VI. ETHICS OF DIRECT EXAMINATION

Most of the ethical issues in direct examination involve the extent to which it is permissible to "assist" a witness to prepare or enhance her testimony.

Some issues are relatively easy to resolve. As was discussed earlier in this chapter, for example, it is not unethical to employ "reflective" questioning on direct examination in order to make events seem as though they occurred quickly or slowly.[11] At most, reflective questions will help a witness communicate accurately; they cannot alter the truth. A witness who testifies that an incident happened quickly can be helped, through reflective questioning, to make that point clear. If, on the other hand, the witness states that the events were slow-paced, no amount of reflective direct will effectively change that conclusion.[12]

At the other end of the spectrum, it is absolutely unethical to participate in the creation of false testimony. Lawyers must not ever collude with witnesses in the invention of untrue facts. It is an underpinning of adversary justice that lawyers will act as guardians of the system to prevent the offer of perjured evidence. Without this safeguard, the very justification of adversary litigation is weakened if not destroyed.

The following subsections will discuss variations on this theme.

---

11 *See* Section IV E *supra* at p. 39.

12 This is true of direct examination. On cross examination, of course, the pacing of questions can be used to undermine a witness's conclusory testimony. Regarding the ethics of this sort of examination, see Chapter Three, Section VI D, *infra* at p. 109.

Chapter Two

A. Preparation of Witnesses

A recurring question is the extent to which lawyers may "coach" witnesses in preparation for their testimony. In many countries it is considered unethical for a lawyer even to meet alone with a witness prior to the trial, such is the aversion to the possibility for contamination of the testimony. In the United States, however, we take a far different view. Here it is generally considered incompetent for a lawyer to fail to meet with and prepare a witness in advance of offering her testimony.

The practice of witness preparation is so widespread and entrenched as to be unassailable. It is justified on the theory that witnesses, especially clients, are entitled to the lawyer's help in ensuring that their testimony is presented accurately and persuasively. The justification is compelling. A witness, left to her own devices, might be forgetful, inarticulate, or unaware of the significance of the facts that she relates or omits. People come to lawyers precisely because they want, and are entitled to, assistance in presenting their claims and defenses. It smacks of abandonment to submit a client to examination without first reviewing the potential testimony.

Few would doubt that a lawyer's pretrial counsel should extend to advising a witness to be polite and well-dressed, to answer all of the questions, and to avoid losing her temper. In a sense this advice might be seen as disguising an otherwise ill-mannered, boorish, and evasive client. The more realistic view, however, is that the lawyer is assisting the client to ensure that externalities do not obstruct effective communication. To be sure, there is a point where even recommendations on appearance can verge on fraud. It would, for example, be improper to urge an Islamic or Jewish client to wear a visible cross in order to testify before an all-Christian jury.

More difficult issues arise when counsel attempts to refresh a witness's recollection, to fill in gaps in her story, or to suggest alternative possibilities. Again, this practice is usually justified on the ground that it is necessary to ensure that the truth emerges fully. Witnesses can be forgetful, especially when they are unaware of the legal importance of certain facts.

Thus, a client complaining of a defective product would probably place greatest emphasis on the way that it malfunctioned; he might not think it important that the salesperson helped him select it. A lawyer, however, should know that the seller's participation in selection can result in an implied warranty of fitness for a particular use. It would be wrong to withhold this information from the client, and equally wrong to avoid probing the client's memory for the nature and extent of the seller's representations. Most would agree that the following inquiries are proper:

"Did you speak to a salesperson when selecting the product?"

"What did the salesperson say?"

46

"Did you tell the seller why you needed the product?"

"Did you tell her the use to which you would put it?"

"Did she recommend a particular product to you?"

"Did the salesperson make any promises to you about performance?"

While this line of questioning runs some risk of inducing memories, rather than simply recalling them, it is essential to adequate representation.

Now consider this scenario. The client was asked whether he spoke to the salesperson, and he replied, "Well, I pretty much picked the item out for myself. I really didn't want or need any help." The lawyer continued:

> "I've shopped in those appliance stores and my experience is that the salespeople just won't leave you alone. They're all on commission, and they pretty much stay with you until you buy something. You might not want their help, but sometimes you can't really avoid it. Did anything like that happen to you?"

Is this an aid to the witness's memory, or a not-so-subtle suggestion as to how to improve the story?

There is no good answer to the conundrum, as it essentially rests on the lawyer's intent.[13] It is permissible to invoke common experience in order to help a witness remember details that might have seemed unimportant when they occurred. It is flatly impermissible, even when utilizing an ostensible question, to prompt a witness to add facts that did not really take place.

The key is that counsel must, explicitly and implicitly, prepare the witness to give his or her own testimony, and not the testimony that the lawyer would favor or prefer. Most efforts to assist or empower the witness are ethical. Efforts at substitution or fabrication, no matter how well-cloaked, are not.

B.   Offering Inadmissible Evidence

When evidence is admissible only for a limited purpose, it is unethical to attempt to put it to further use.[14] The obligation of zealous advocacy does not

---

13   Needless to say, blatant efforts to influence the witness's testimony are unethical. The lawyer could not, for example, importune the witness this way: "You cannot win this case unless you testify that the salesperson assured you a specific level of performance. You need to tell me exactly how the seller induced you to buy, and how you were promised that the product would meet your needs."

14   Regarding the misuse of evidence during final argument, see Chapter Ten, Section VI A(3), *infra* at p. 434.

require counsel to ignore or evade the court's rulings with regard to the restricted admissibility of evidence.

By the same token, it is impermissible to prepare a witness to interject clearly inadmissible evidence. Where a motion in limine[15] has been granted, for example, counsel cannot suggest or encourage a witness to use a narrative answer to volunteer the excluded information.

Of course, counsel is not obligated to resolve all evidentiary doubts in favor of the opposition. It is ethical to offer any evidence with regard to which there is a reasonable theory of admissibility. In other words, it is proper to offer evidence so long as counsel can articulate at least one specific and recognizable argument in favor of its admission.[16]

C. Disclosing Perjury

The appropriate response to witness and client perjury has perplexed our profession endlessly. While no ethical lawyer would willingly be a party to perjury, questions arise as how best to prevent it without damaging the principles of confidentiality and zealous advocacy.

There is no doubt that a lawyer may not call a non-client witness who is going to testify falsely,[17] and must "take reasonable remedial measures should non-client perjury occur despite counsel's efforts to avoid it."[18]

The thorny problem is the client. An attorney must certainly take all reasonable steps to dissuade a client from presenting untrue testimony. But what if the client insists on presenting a story that the lawyer firmly believes is false? Or what if the client's perjury on the stand takes the lawyer by surprise, and becomes a *fait accompli* before the lawyer can stop it?

The dilemma is especially acute in criminal cases. Many believe that a criminal defendant has a Constitutional right to take the stand and "tell his story,"

---

15   *See* Chapter Seven, Section II A(2), *infra* at p. 217.

16   This issue is discussed further in Chapter Seven, Section III A, *infra* at p. 247.

17   Rules 3.3(c) and 3.4(b), Model Rules of Professional Conduct.

18   A lawyer shall not "falsify evidence [or] counsel or assist a witness to testify falsely." Rule 3.4(b), Model Rules of Professional Conduct.

   Moreover, "[i]f a lawyer has offered material evidence and comes to know of its falsity, the lawyer shall take reasonable remedial measures." Rule 3.3, Model Rules of Professional Conduct.

   The Commentary to Rule 3.3 provides a three-step approach to "reasonable remedial measures." The lawyer must first remonstrate with the witness to correct the false testimony. If that fails, the lawyer should seek to withdraw "if that will remedy the situation." Since withdrawal will usually be inappropriate in the case of perjury by a non-client, the final step is to make disclosure to the court.

whether the lawyer believes it or not. One commentator has gone so far as to urge that a lawyer's duties of loyalty and confidentiality require actively presenting a criminal defendant's perjured testimony.[19] The great majority of lawyers, judges, and scholars, however, reject this extreme position. The United States Supreme Court has held that there is no constitutional right to testify falsely.[20] The Model Rules of Professional Conduct provide that counsel, in both civil and criminal cases, must take reasonable steps to remedy client perjury, even at the cost of revealing a confidential communication.[21]

The full dimension of the debate over responses to client perjury is beyond the scope of this text. Numerous approaches have been suggested over the years, each supported by its own policies and justifications. It is fair to say, however, that the trend, as outlined in the preceding paragraph, is toward diminished latitude for the client and increased disclosure by counsel.

---

19 Monroe Freedman, *Understanding Lawyers' Ethics,* 109-142 (1990).
20 Nix v. Whiteside, 474 U.S. 157, 106 S.Ct. 988, 89 L.Ed.2d 123 (1966).
21 Rule 3.3(b), Model Rules of Professional Conduct.

— CHAPTER THREE —
Cross Examination

I. THE ROLE OF CROSS EXAMINATION

Cross examination is hard. It is frequently dramatic, often exciting, and in many ways it defines our adversarial system of justice. At bottom, however, cross examination is the ultimate challenge for the trial lawyer. Can you add to your case or detract from the opposition's case by extracting information from the other side's witnesses?

If direct examination is your best opportunity to win your case, cross examination may provide you with a chance to lose it. A poor direct can be aimless and boring, but the witnesses are generally helpful. Your worst fear on direct examination is usually that you have left something out. A poor cross examination, on the other hand, can be truly disastrous. The witnesses can range from uncooperative to hostile, and you constantly run the risk of actually adding weight or sympathy to the other side's case. Moreover, most cross examinations will inevitably be perceived by the trier of fact as a contest between the lawyer and witness. You can seldom afford to appear to lose.

In other words, cross examination is inherently risky. The witness may argue with you. The witness may fill in gaps that were left in the direct testimony. The witness may make you look bad. You may make yourself look bad. And whatever good you accomplish may be subject to immediate cure on redirect examination.

None of these problems can be avoided entirely, but they can be minimized. Although some cross examination is usually expected of every witness, and the temptation is difficult to resist, as a general rule you should cross examine carefully. You must always set realistic goals.

Brevity is an excellent discipline. Many leading trial lawyers suggest that cross examinations be limited to a maximum of three points. While there may often be reasons to depart from such a hard and fast rule, there is no doubt that short cross examinations have much to commend themselves. In terms of your own preparation, setting a mental limit for the length of the cross will help you to concentrate and to organize your thinking. Actually conducting a short examination will minimize risk, add panache, and usually make the result more memorable.

This chapter discusses the general law, content, organization, and basic technique of cross examination. Several more advanced aspects of cross examination — such as impeachment and the use of character evidence — are treated separately in later chapters.

II.   THE LAW OF CROSS EXAMINATION

Cross examination is the hallmark of the Anglo-American system of adversary justice. Protected as a constitutional right in criminal cases, it is also understood as an aspect of due process in civil cases. The law of cross examination varies somewhat from jurisdiction to jurisdiction, but the following rules are nearly universal.

A.   Leading Questions Permitted

The most obvious distinction between direct and cross examination is the permissible use of leading questions. It is assumed that your adversary's witnesses will have little incentive to cooperate with you, and that you may not have been able to interview them in advance. Consequently, virtually all courts allow the cross examiner to ask questions that contain their own answers. Moreover, the right to ask leading questions is usually understood to include the right to insist on a responsive answer.

As we will see below, the ability to use leading questions has enormous implications for the conduct of cross examination.

B.   Limitations on Scope

The general rule in the United States is that cross examination is limited to the scope of the direct. Since the purpose of cross examination is to allow you to inquire of your adversary's witnesses, the scope of the inquiry is restricted to those subjects that were raised during the direct examination.

Note that the definition of scope will vary from jurisdiction to jurisdiction, and even from courtroom to courtroom. A narrow application of this rule can limit the cross examiner to the precise events and occurrences that the witness discussed on direct. A broader approach would allow questioning on related and similar events. For example, assume that the defendant in our collision case testified that his brakes had been inspected just a week before the accident. A strict approach to the "scope of direct" rule might limit the cross examination to questioning on that particular inspection. A broader interpretation would allow inquiries into earlier brake inspections and other aspects of automobile maintenance.

A more generous approach to the scope of cross examination is definitely the modern trend. Undue restriction of cross examination can result in reversal on appeal. Nonetheless, there is no way to predict how an individual judge will apply the scope limitation in any given case; much will depend on the nature of the evidence and the manner in which the lawyers have been conducting themselves.

A few American jurisdictions have adopted the "English rule," which allows wide-open cross examination concerning any issue relevant to the case. In the federal jurisdiction, and some others, the trial judge has discretion to allow inquiry beyond the scope of the direct examination, but the cross examiner is then limited to non-leading questions. Also, in most states a criminal defendant who takes the stand and waives the Fifth Amendment is thereafter subject to cross examination regarding all aspects of the alleged crime.

There are two general exceptions to the "scope of direct" rule. First, the credibility of the witness is always in issue. You may therefore always attempt to establish the bias, motive, interest, untruthfulness or material prior inconsistency of a witness, without regard to the matters that were covered on direct examination. Second, you may cross examine beyond the scope of the direct once the witness herself has "opened the door" to additional matters. In other words, a witness who voluntarily injects a subject into an answer on cross examination may thereafter be questioned as though the subject had been included in the direct.

C. Other Restrictions

A variety of other rules, most of which involve the manner or nature of questioning, also limit cross examinations.

Argumentative questions. You may ask a witness questions. You may suggest answers. You may assert propositions. But you may not argue with the witness. As you may have guessed, the definition of an argumentative question is elusive. Much will depend on your demeanor; perhaps an argumentative question is one that is asked in an argumentative tone. The following is a reasonable working definition: An argumentative question insists that the witness agree with an opinion or characterization, as opposed to a statement of fact.

Intimidating behavior. You are entitled to elicit information on cross examination by asking questions of the witness and insisting upon answers. You are not allowed to loom over the witness, to shout, to make threatening gestures, or otherwise to intimidate, bully, or (yes, here it comes) badger the witness.

Unfair characterizations. Your right to lead the witness does not include a right to mislead the witness. It is objectionable to attempt to mischaracterize a witness's testimony or to ask "trick" questions. If a witness has testified that it was dark outside, it would mischaracterize the testimony to begin a question, "So you admit that it was too dark to see anything . . . ." Trick questions can not be answered accurately. The most famous trick question is known as the "negative pregnant," as in Senator McCarthy's inquisitional, "Have you resigned from the Communist Party?"

Assuming facts. A frequently heard objection is that "Counsel has assumed facts not in evidence." Of course, a cross examiner is frequently allowed to inquire as to facts that are not yet in evidence. This objection should only be sustained when the question uses the non-record fact as a premise rather than as a separate subject of inquiry, thus denying the witness the opportunity to deny its validity. Imagine a witness in the fire truck case who was standing on the sidewalk at the time of the accident. Assume that the witness testified on direct that the defendant never even slowed down before the impact, and said absolutely nothing about having been drinking that morning. At the outset of the cross examination, then, there would be no "facts in evidence" concerning use of alcohol. The cross examiner is certainly entitled to ask questions such as, "Hadn't you been drinking that morning?" The cross examiner should not be allowed, however, to use an assumption about drinking to serve as the predicate for a different question: "Since you had been drinking, you were on foot instead of in your car that morning?" The problem with this sort of bootstrapping is that it doesn't allow the witness a fair opportunity to deny having been drinking in the first place.

Compound and other defective questions. Compound questions contain more than a single inquiry: "Are you related to the plaintiff, and were you wearing your glasses at the time of the accident?" The question is objectionable since any answer will necessarily be ambiguous. Cumulative or "Asked and Answered" questions are objectionable because they cover the same ground twice (or more). Vague questions are objectionable because they tend to elicit vague answers.

III. THE CONTENT OF CROSS EXAMINATION

The first question concerning any cross examination is whether it should be brief or extensive. Although it is standard advice in many quarters that you should refrain from cross examining a witness who hasn't hurt you, in practice almost every witness is subjected to at least a short cross examination. You will seldom wish to leave the testimony of an adverse witness appear to go entirely unchallenged. Moreover, as we will see below, there will often be opportunities to use cross examination to establish positive, constructive evidence. The most frequent decision, then, is not whether to cross examine, but how much. This evaluation must be made at least twice: once in your pretrial preparation and again at the end of the direct examination.

In preparation, you must consider the potential direct examination. What do you expect the witness to say and how, if at all, will you need to challenge or add to the direct? At trial you must make a further determination. Did the actual direct examination proceed as you expected? Was it more or less damaging than you anticipated? You must always reevaluate your cross examination strategy in light of the direct testimony that was eventually produced. This process will often lead you to omit portions of your prepared cross, because they have become unnecessary. It is considerably more dangerous to elaborate on or add to your plan, although this is occasionally unavoidable. In either situation, always remember the risk inherent in cross examination and ask yourself, "Is this cross examination necessary?"

A.   Consider the Purposes of Cross Examination

Though often an invigorating exercise, cross examination should be undertaken only to serve some greater purpose within your theory of the case. A useful cross examination should promise to fulfill at least one of the following objectives:

Repair or minimize damage. Did the direct examination hurt your case? If so, can the harm be rectified or minimized? Can the witness be made to retract or back away from certain testimony? Can additional facts be elicited that will minimize the witness's impact?

Enhance your case. Can the cross examination be used to further one of your claims or defenses? Are there positive facts that can be brought out that will support or contribute to your version of events?

Detract from their case. Conversely, can the cross examination be used to establish facts that are detrimental to your opponent's case? Can it be used to create inconsistencies among the other side's witnesses?

Establish foundation. Is the witness necessary to the proper foundation for the introduction of a document or other exhibit, or for the offer of evidence by another witness?

Discredit direct testimony. Is it possible to discredit the witness's direct testimony through means such as highlighting internal inconsistencies, demonstrating the witness's own lack of certainty or confidence, underscoring lack of opportunity to observe, illustrating the inherent implausibility of the testimony, or showing that it conflicts with the testimony of other, more credible witnesses?

Discredit the witness. Can the witness be shown to be biased or interested in the outcome of the case? Does the witness have a reason to stretch, misrepresent, or fabricate the testimony? Has the witness been untruthful in the past? Can it be shown that the witness is otherwise unworthy of belief?

Reflect on the credibility of another. Can the cross examination be used to reflect, favorably or unfavorably, on the credibility of a different witness?

The length of your cross examination will generally depend upon how many of the above goals you expect to be able to fulfill. It is not necessary, and it may not be possible, to attempt to achieve them all. You will often stand to lose more by over-reaching than you can possibly gain by seeking to cover all of the bases in cross examination. Be selective.

B.   Arrive at the "Usable Universe" of Cross Examination

1. The Entire Universe

In preparing to cross examine any witness you must first determine the broadest possible scope, or universe, for the potential cross examination. From a review of all of the available materials and documents, construct a comprehensive list of the information available from the witness. In keeping with the purposes of cross examination, place each potential fact in one of the following categories:

- Does it make my case more likely?
- Does it make their case less likely?
- Is it a predicate to the admissibility of other evidence?
- Does it make some witness more believable?
- Does it make some witness less believable?

This process will give you the full universe of theoretically desirable information from which you will structure your cross examination.

2. The Usable Universe

You must now evaluate all of the potential facts in order to arrive at your "usable universe." Ask yourself the following questions:

— Is a friendly witness available to present the same facts? There may be no point in attempting to extract answers from an unwilling source if a friendly witness can provide you with the same information. On cross examination you always run the risk that the witness will argue or hedge, or that the information will not be developed as clearly as you would like. Unless you stand to benefit specifically from repetition of the testimony, you may prefer to bypass cross examination that will be merely cumulative of your own evidence.

— Can the information be obtained only on cross examination? You have no choice but to cross examine on important facts that are solely within the knowledge or control of the adverse witness. Such information will range from the foundation for the admission of a document to evidence of the witness's own prior actions.

— Will the facts be uniquely persuasive on cross examination? Some information, though available from a variety of sources, will be particularly valuable when elicited on cross examination. For example, evidence of past wrongdoing may be more credible if it is presented as an admission by the witness herself, rather than as an accusation coming from another. In the automobile accident case, consider the different ways in which evidence of the defendant's driving habits could be admitted. You could produce your own witness to testify that the defendant was a constant speeder. You would have to lay a foundation for this testimony, establishing both the witness's personal knowledge and the consistency of the defendant's "habit."[1] Additionally, your witness would then be subject to cross examination not only on the foundation for the testimony, but also regarding issues such as bias, accuracy, and opportunity to observe. On the other hand, the defendant's own testimony that he loved driving fast cars would be virtually uncontrovertible. It would also bolster the testimony of your own witnesses to the same effect. When possible, it is generally desirable to obtain negative or contested evidence from the mouths of the opposition witnesses.

— How certain is it that the witness will agree with you? Certain information may be completely within the control of a witness for the other side, and it may be uniquely persuasive if elicited during the cross examination of that witness. You must nonetheless consider the contingency that the witness will deny you the answer that you want. You may need to abandon or modify a promising line of cross examination if you do not believe that you will be able to compel the answers that you anticipate. Can the information be confirmed by the witness's own prior statements? Can it be documented through the use of reports, photographs, tests, or other evidence? These and other devices for controlling a witness's testimony on cross examination are discussed in later sections.

The construction of your usable universe depends almost entirely on your mastery of the case as a whole. To prepare for cross examination you must know not only everything that the particular witness is liable to say, but also every other fact that might be obtained from any other witness, document, or exhibit. Your effective choice of cross examination topics will be determined by your ability to choose those areas that will do you the most good, while risking the least harm.

C. Risk Averse Preparation

There are many ways to prepare for cross examination. The following is a "risk averse" method designed to result in a solid, if generally unflashy, cross that minimizes the potential for damage to your case.

Risk averse preparation for cross examination begins with consideration of your anticipated final argument. What do you want to be able to say about this particular witness when you address the jury at the end of the case? How much of that information do you expect to be included in the direct examination? The balance is what you will need to cover on cross.

---

1   *See* Rule 406, Federal Rules of Evidence.

Next, write out the portion of a final argument that you would devote to discussing the facts presented by this particular witness. This will at most serve as a draft for your actual closing,[2] and you should limit this text to the facts contained in the witness's testimony. You need not include the characterizations, inferences, arguments, comments, and thematic references that will also be part of your real final argument. Depending upon the importance of the witness, the length of this argument segment can range from a short paragraph to a full page or more.

It is important that you write your text using short, single-thought, strictly factual sentences. You are not attempting to create literature. Do not worry about continuity, style, or transition. Simply arrange the declarative sentences one after another in the order that you believe will be the most persuasive, referring to the witness in the third person. For example, your argument concerning the defendant in the fire truck case might, assuming that all of these facts were readily available, include the following:

> The defendant awoke on the morning of the accident at 7:00 a.m. He had to be downtown later that morning. He was meeting an important new client. He wanted to get that client's business. He stood to make a lot of money. The meeting was scheduled for 8:30 a.m. The defendant lived 16 miles from his office. He rented a monthly parking spot. That spot was in a garage located two blocks from his office. He left his home at 7:55 a.m. There was a lot of traffic that morning. The accident occurred at an intersection seven miles from downtown. It happened at 8:20 a.m.

An effective paragraph will include the facts that underlie your theory of the case. It should now be a simple matter to convert the text into a cross examination plan. You merely need to take each sentence and rephrase it into a second-person question. In fact, it is often best to leave the sentence in the form of a declaration, technically making it a question through voice inflection or by adding an interrogative phrase at the end. The above paragraph then becomes the following cross examination of the defendant:

QUESTION: You awoke at 7:00 a.m. on the morning of the accident, isn't that right?

QUESTION: You had to be downtown later that morning, correct?

QUESTION: You were meeting an important new client?

QUESTION: You wanted to get that client's business?

---

2   Final argument is treated in Chapter Ten. At this point it is sufficient to note that, while it may be a useful exercise to write out a draft, it is a mistake to read your closing argument from a prepared text.

QUESTION: You stood to make a lot of money?

QUESTION: The meeting was scheduled for 8:30 a.m., correct?

QUESTION: You lived 16 miles from your office?

QUESTION: You rented a monthly parking spot?

QUESTION: That spot was in a garage located two blocks from your office?

QUESTION: You left your home at 7:55 a.m., right?

QUESTION: There was a lot of traffic that morning?

QUESTION: The accident occurred at an intersection seven miles from downtown?

QUESTION: It happened at 8:20 a.m., isn't that right?

Note that the above questions also fit neatly into the "usable universe." Many of the facts are not likely to be available from friendly witnesses. Most others are of the sort that will be most valuable if conceded by the defendant himself. Finally, the facts are nearly all of the sort that can be independently documented, or that the defendant is unlikely to deny.

This technique is useful for developing the content of your cross examination. The organization of the examination and the structure of your individual questions will depend upon additional analysis.

IV. THE ORGANIZATION OF CROSS EXAMINATION

A. Organizing Principles

As with direct examination, the organization of a cross examination can be based on the four principles of primacy and recency, apposition, repetition, and duration. Unlike direct examination, however, on cross examination you will often have to deal with a recalcitrant witness. You may therefore have to temper your plan in recognition of this reality, occasionally sacrificing maximum clarity and persuasion in order to avoid "telegraphing" your strategy to the uncooperative witness. Thus, we must include the additional organizing principles of indirection and misdirection when planning cross examinations.

Three further concepts are basic to the organization, presentation, and technique of virtually every cross examination.

First, cross examination is your opportunity to tell part of your client's story in the middle of the other side's case. Your object is to focus attention away from the witness's direct testimony, and onto matters that you believe are helpful. On cross examination, *you* want to tell the story. To do so, you must always be in control of the testimony and the witness.

Second, cross examination is never the time to attempt to gather new information. Never ask a witness a question simply because you want to find out the answer. Rather, cross examination must be used to establish or enhance the facts that you have already discovered.

Finally, an effective cross examination often succeeds through the use of implication and innuendo. It is not necessary, and it is often harmful, to ask a witness the "ultimate question." Final argument is your opportunity to point out the relationship between facts, make characterizations, and draw conclusions based upon the accumulation of details. Don't expect an opposing witness to do this for you. Lay the groundwork for your eventual argument, then stop. This technique is premised on the assumption that many witnesses will be reluctant to concede facts that will later prove to be damaging or embarrassing. Thus, it may be necessary to avoid informing the witness of the ultimate import of the particular inquiry. This can be accomplished through indirect questioning, which seeks first to establish small and uncontrovertible factual components of a theory, and only later addresses the theory itself. For example, a witness may be loath to admit having read a certain document before signing it; perhaps the written statement contains damaging admissions that the witness would prefer to disclaim. Direct questioning, therefore, would be unlikely to produce the desired result. The witness, if asked, will deny having read the item in question. Indirect questioning, however, may be able to establish the point:

QUESTION: You are a businessman?

QUESTION: Many documents cross your desk each day?

QUESTION: It is your job to read and respond to them?

QUESTION: Your company relies upon you to be accurate?

QUESTION: You often must send written replies?

QUESTION: Large amounts of money can change hands on the basis of the replies that you send?

QUESTION: You have an obligation to your company to be careful about its money?

QUESTION: So you must be careful about what you write?

QUESTION: Of course, that includes your signature?

By this point, you should have obtained through indirection that which the witness would not have conceded directly. The final question should be superfluous.

Misdirection is an arch-relative of indirection, used when the witness is thought to be particularly deceptive or untruthful. Here the cross examiner not only conceals the object of the examination, but actually attempts to take advantage of the witness's own inclination to be uncooperative. Knowing that the witness will tend to fight the examination, the lawyer creates, and then exploits, a "misdirected" image. In our fire truck case, for example, the defendant is extremely unlikely to admit that he should have seen the fire engine; perhaps he would go so far as to deny the obvious. The lawyer may therefore misdirect the defendant's attention, as follows:

QUESTION: Isn't it true that you expected to see a fire truck at that corner?

ANSWER: Certainly not, I never expected a fire truck.

QUESTION: You weren't looking for a fire truck?

ANSWER: No.

QUESTION: You didn't keep your eye out for one?

ANSWER: No.

QUESTION: And you never saw one?

ANSWER: No.

QUESTION: Until, of course, after it was too late?

To be effective in the use of this technique, the cross examination must be organized first to obtain the "misdirected" denial. Note that the above example would not work at all if the questions were asked in the opposite order. In other words, the principle of misdirection works best with an intentionally elusive witness, who needs only to be given sufficient initial rope with which to hoist himself.

B.   Guidelines for Organization

There are a variety of ways in which you can employ the principles discussed above.

1. Do Not Worry About Starting Strong

It would be desirable to be able to begin every cross examination with a strong, memorable point that absolutely drives home your theory and theme. Unfortunately, this will seldom be possible. Most cross examinations will have to begin with a shake-down period, during which you acclimate yourself to the tenor of the witness's responses, and when you also attempt to put the witness in a cooperative frame of mind. Unless you are able to start off with a true bombshell, it will usually be preferable to take the time necessary to establish predicate facts through indirection.

2. Use Topical Organization

Topical organization is essential in cross examination. Your goal on cross examination is not to retell the witness's story, but rather to establish a small number of additional or discrediting points. A topical format will be the most effective in allowing you to move from area to area. Moreover, topical organization also allows you to take maximum advantage of apposition, indirection, and misdirection. You can use it to cluster facts in the same manner that you would on direct examination, or to separate facts in order to avoid showing your hand to the witness.

Assume that you want to use the cross examination of the defendant in the automobile accident to show how busy he was on the day of the collision. You know that he had an important meeting to attend that morning, but he will be unlikely to admit that he might lose the client (and a lot of money) if he arrived late. You can solve this problem by using topical organization to separate your cross examination into two distinct segments: one dealing with the nature of the defendant's business, and the other covering his appointment on the fateful morning.

In the first topical segment you will show that the defendant is an independent management consultant. It is a very competitive business, in which client relations are extremely important. Part of his work involves seeking out potential new clients, whom he is always anxious to please. Since he is a sole proprietor, every client means more money. As a consultant, he must pride himself on professionalism, timeliness and efficiency. He bills his clients by the hour. Time is money. In short, examine the witness on his business background without ever bringing up the subject of the accident. (The defendant's own lawyer almost certainly will have introduced his stable, business-like background; your examination on the same issue would then be within the scope of the direct.)

Later in the examination, after covering several other areas, you will shift topics to the defendant's agenda on the day of the accident. Now it is time to establish the details of his planned meeting and the fact that he was still miles from downtown shortly before it was scheduled to begin. You do not need to obtain an admission that he was running late, or that he was preoccupied. Topical organization has allowed you to develop the predicate facts for that argument before the witness was aware of their implications.

There is another advantage to topical organization on cross examination. Assume, in the example above, that the witness was well-prepared, and that he immediately recognized your reasons for inquiring into his business practices. Because your examination was segmented, however, he could scarcely deny the facts that you suggested. In a portion of the examination limited to the operation of his business it would be implausible for him to deny that his clients value "professionalism, efficiency, and timeliness." If he were to deny your perfectly reasonable propositions, he would make himself look either untrustworthy or defensive. Note that you would not obtain the same result without topical organization. In the middle of the discussion of the morning of the accident, it would be quite plausible for the defendant to testify that this particular new client was not dominating his thoughts.

3. Give the Details First

Details are, if anything, more important on cross examination than they are on direct. On direct examination a witness will always be able to tell the gist of the story; details are used in a secondary manner to add strength and veracity to the basic testimony. On cross examination, however, the witness will frequently disagree with the gist of the story that you want to tell, and use of details therefore becomes the primary method of making your points. You may elicit details to lay the groundwork for future argument, to draw out internal inconsistencies in the witness's testimony, to point out inconsistencies between witnesses, to lead the witness into implausible assertions, or to create implications that the witness will be unable to deny later.

Within each segment of your cross examination, it will usually be preferable to give the details first. No matter what your goal, the witness will be far more likely to agree with a series of small, incremental facts before the thrust of the examination has been made apparent. Once you have challenged, confronted, or closely questioned a witness it will be extremely difficult to go back and fill in the details necessary to make the challenge stick.

Assume that the weather conditions turn out to be of some value to you in the automobile accident case. If you begin your examination of the defendant with questions about the weather you will be likely to obtain cooperative answers. As a preliminary matter you may have no difficulty establishing that it was clear and sunny that day. Perhaps you will have additional details available — the defendant left home without an umbrella, he wasn't wearing overshoes, he didn't turn on his headlights. Conversely, imagine a first question such as, "Isn't it true that you never even tried to stop before the collision?" Now what is the witness likely to say when you ask whether the pavement was dry? Suddenly, the witness may remember all manner of fog and puddles; of course he tried to stop, but the street was just too wet.

There is an additional advantage to beginning a cross examination with details. It allows you to learn about the witness with a minimum of risk. We know that cross examination is not the time to try to gather new information about the case. You should only ask questions to which you know the answer, or where you at least have a good reason to expect a favorable answer. On the other hand, you frequently will not know how a particular witness will react to your questions. Will the witness be cooperative or compliant, or can you expect a struggle every inch of the way? Worse, is the witness slippery and evasive? Even worse, is the witness inclined to mislead and prevaricate? Worst of all, have you misinterpreted the information or made some other blunder in your own preparation? You must learn the answers to these questions before you proceed to the heart of your cross examination. While it may be mildly uncomfortable to receive an unexpectedly evasive answer to a question about a preliminary detail, it can be positively devastating to discover that you are unable to pin down a witness on a central issue. Beginning with details will allow you to take the witness's measure (and to evaluate your own preparation) at a time of minimum impact and risk.

4. Scatter the Circumstantial Evidence

Inferential or circumstantial evidence[3] is most persuasive when a series of facts or events can be combined in such a way as to create a logical path to the desired conclusion. Unfortunately, facts arranged in this manner on cross examination will also be highly transparent to the witness. As you stack inference upon inference your direction will become increasingly clear. A hostile or unfriendly witness will then become increasingly uncooperative, perhaps to the point of thwarting your examination. A far safer approach is to scatter the circumstantial evidence throughout the examination, drawing it together only during final argument.

5. Save a Zinger for the End

The final moment of cross examination may well be the most important. No matter how low-key or friendly your style, almost every cross examination will in some sense be viewed as a contest between you and the witness. Were you able to shake the adverse testimony? Were you able to help your client? In short, did you do what you set out to do? In this regard the final impression that you leave is likely to be the most lasting. Were you able to finish on a high note, or did you simply give up?

It is therefore imperative that you plan carefully the very last point that you intend to make on cross examination. It must be a guaranteed winner, the point on which you are willing to make your exit. Indeed, you should write this point down at the very bottom of your note pad, underlined and in bold letters. It should stand alone, with nothing to obscure it or distract you from it. Then if your entire examination seems to fail, if the witness denies every proposition, if the judge sustains every objection, if the heavens fall and doom impends, you can always skip to the bottom of the page and finish with a flourish. Satisfied that you have made this single, telling, case-sealing point, you may proudly announce, "No further questions of this witness," and sit down.

---

3   Circumstantial evidence is defined and described in Chapter Two, Section III B (6), *supra* at p. 30.

How do you identify your fail-safe zinger? The following guidelines should help:

a. It must be absolutely admissible

There can be no doubt about the admissibility of your intended final point. Nothing smacks more of defeat than ending a cross examination on a sustained objection. If you suspect even for a moment that your zinger might not be allowed, abandon it and choose another. In fact, you should make an entry in the margin of your notes that reminds you of your theory of admissibility. Why is the point relevant? Why isn't it hearsay? How has the foundation been established? Why isn't it speculation?

b. It should be central to your theory

Since your closing point is likely to be the most memorable, you would be best served to make it one of the cornerstones of your theory. If there are eight facts that you must establish in order to prevail, you would like to end each cross examination on one of them. This may not always be possible. Not every opposing witness will testify about an essential matter, and it is important to insure admissibility by keeping your zinger well within the scope of the direct. Or it may be possible to undermine the witness's credibility by ending on a point that is collateral to your basic theory.

c. It should evoke your theme

The very purpose of a trial theme is to create a memorable phrase or invocation that captures the moral basis of your case. The closing moments of cross examination, therefore, constitute the perfect time to evoke your theme. Attention will never be more focused and memorability will never be higher. Imagine that the plaintiff in the fire truck case was taken directly to a hospital, but that the unhurt defendant went on to his office after filling out a police report. If your theme is "Too busy to be careful," you can close your cross examination with these two questions: You made it to your office later that morning, didn't you? Taking care of business, I suppose? You know that the answer to the first question will be "Yes." You don't care about the answer to the second one.

d. It must be undeniable

It should be obvious by now that your final question must be undeniable. The end of your cross is not the time to argue or quibble with the witness. There are two good ways to insure undeniability.[4]

First, choose a fact that you can document. Look for something that can be proven from a prior statement of the witness or some other tangible exhibit or

---

4   The subject of controlling the witness and insuring favorable answers is discussed at greater length in Section V, *infra* at p. 68.

writing. If evidence of that sort is unavailable, select a point that has already been made in the testimony of other opposition witnesses, thereby making a denial either implausible or inconsistent with the balance of the other side's case.

Second, phrase your question in terms of bedrock fact, making sure that it contains nothing that approaches a characterization. The more "factual" your question, the less possible it is for the witness to deny you a simple answer. In the automobile accident case, for example, a purely factual closing question would be, "You arrived at your office later that morning?" The same point, but made with a characterization, would be, "You were so busy that you went straight to your office?" The witness can argue with you about the interpretation of the word "busy," but arrival at his office is a fact.

Remember that cross examination may be followed immediately by redirect examination. Your closing question on cross may provide the opening subject for redirect. Thus, another aspect of undeniability is that the point must not be capable of immediate explanation. For example, the fire truck defendant may have gone straight to his office, but only to retrieve medicine for his heart condition. After that he might not have worked for the next three days. You can omit those facts on cross examination, but you can be sure that they will be developed on redirect. Since that point can be explained, it is not sufficiently "undeniable" for use as a closing question.

e. It must be stated with conviction

No matter what your closing question, you must be able to deliver it with an attitude of satisfied completion. If the subject makes you nervous, worried, or embarrassed, then you must choose another. It is neither necessary nor desirable to smirk, but you must exhibit confidence that your parting inquiry has done its work.

C. A Classic Format for Cross Examination

Because almost all cross examinations will be topical, there can be no standard or prescribed form of organization. The following "classic format" is designed to maximize witness cooperation. Of course, you may have a goal in mind for your cross examination other than witness cooperation; in that case, feel free to ignore or alter this approach. As a rule of thumb, however, you can best employ principles such as indirection and "detail scattering" by seeking information in this order.

1. Friendly Information

Be friendly first. Begin by asking all questions that the witness will regard as non-threatening. These will often be background questions. For example, medical malpractice cases are often based upon errors of omission, and you may intend to argue in closing that the defendant physician, by virtue of her extraordinary training, should have known about certain available tests. You can start your cross examination, then, by asking friendly questions about the defendant's medical education, residency, fellowships, and awards. Most people, even defendants on trial, like to talk about their achievements. There is little doubt that a witness will be the most forthcoming when asked about aggrandizing information at the very outset of the cross examination.

2. Affirmative Information

After exhausting the friendly information, ask questions that build up the value of your case, rather than tear down the opposition's. Much of this information will fill in gaps in the direct testimony. In fact, a good way to plan this portion of the cross is to list the information that you reasonably hope will be included in the direct. Whatever is omitted from the witness's actual testimony will form the core of your affirmative information section. Although adverse witnesses may not be enthusiastic about supplying you with helpful information, they will be unlikely to fight you over answers that might logically have been included in their own direct.

3. Uncontrovertible Information

You can now proceed to inquire about facts that damage the opposition's case or detract from the witness's testimony, so long as they are well-settled or documentable. On these questions a witness may be inclined to hedge or quibble, but you can minimize this possibility by sticking to the sort of information that ultimately must be conceded.

4. Challenging Information

It is unlikely that a witness will cooperate with you once you begin challenging her memory, perception, accuracy, conduct, or other aspects of her testimony. Therefore it is usually desirable to proceed through friendly, affirmative, and uncontroverted information before you begin to take sharper issue with the witness. At some point, of course, you will have to ask most witnesses questions that they will recognize as challenges: "Mr. Defendant, the fact is that the first thing you did after the collision was to telephone your office?" Such questions are necessary. When used in their proper place they will not prevent you from first exploiting the other, more cooperative testimony from the witness.

5. Hostile Information

Hostile information involves directly confronting the witness. You may be able to extract the necessary answers to hostile questions, but certainly you can eliminate all hope of cooperation both then and thereafter. Hostile questions involve assaults on the witness's honesty, probity, peacefulness, character, or background. "Didn't you spend time in prison?" "You never intended to live up to the contract?" "That was a lie, wasn't it?"

6. Zinger

Always end with a zinger. You know why.

V. QUESTIONING TECHNIQUE

You know what you want to cover on cross examination, and you know the order in which you want to cover it. How do you ask questions that will insure your success?

The essential goal of cross examination technique is witness control. As we noted above, your object on cross examination is to tell your client's story. This requires that you set the agenda for the examination, that you determine the flow of information, and that you require answers to your questions. In short, you must always be in control of the witness and the testimony. This does not, by the way, mean that you must appear to be in control, and it certainly does not mean that you must be domineering, rude, or overbearing toward the witness. In this context, control means only that the examination follow the course that you have selected, and that the information produced be only that which you have determined helpful.

Control, therefore, can be either non-assertive or assertive. With a cooperative or tractable witness, control may mean nothing more than asking the right questions and getting the right answers. A hostile, evasive, or argumentative witness may require that you employ more assertive means.

There are numerous questioning techniques, to be discussed below, that you can employ to ensure witness control. At a minimum, however, every question on cross examination should have all of the following bedrock characteristics:

— *Short.* Questions on cross examination must be short in both execution and concept. If a question is more than ten words long, it is not short in execution. Try to shorten it. If a question contains more than a single fact or implication, it is not short in concept. Divide it.

— *Leading.* Every question on cross examination should be leading. Include the answers in the questions. Tell the witness exactly what to say. Cross examination is no time to seek the witness's interpretation of the facts. It is the time for you to tell a story by obtaining the witness's assent. A non-leading question invites the witness to wander away from your story.[5]

---

5   There are a few situations in which you may want to ask a non-leading question on cross examination. This chiefly occurs when you are absolutely certain that the witness must answer in a certain way, and you believe that the dramatic value of the answer will be enhanced by having it produced in the witness's own words. If, for example, you are cross examining a witness with a prior felony conviction, you might ask the non-leading question, "How many years did you spend in prison after you were convicted of perjury?" Even in low-risk situations such as this, however, the technique has been known to backfire. Use it sparingly, if at all.

— *Propositional.* The best questions on cross examination are not questions at all. Rather, they are propositions of fact that you put to the witness in interrogative form. You already know the answer — you simply need to produce it from the witness's mouth. Every question on cross examination should contain a proposition that falls into one of these three categories: (1) you already know the answer; (2) you can otherwise document or prove the answer; or (3) any answer will be helpful. An example of the latter sort of question would be the classic inquiry to a witness who must admit having previously given a false statement: "Were you lying then, or are you lying now?"

A. Planning for Control

Control of a witness on cross examination begins with your plan and is achieved, in large measure, on your notepad. In other words, a cross examination is only as good as your outline.

1. Avoid Written Questions

Many beginning lawyers like to write out all of the questions that they intend to ask on cross examination. This can be an excellent drill, since it will concentrate your thinking and sharpen your specific questions. As we will see below, much of the art of cross examination involves asking short, incremental, closely sequenced questions. Since this is an unnatural style for many lawyers, it can be useful indeed to write out the questions first in order to make sure that they conform to this ideal.

When it comes to the actual examination, however, it is usually a mistake to read from a prepared list of questions. The great majority of lawyers use notes, of course, but not in the form of written questions. Reading your questions will deprive your examination of the appearance of spontaneity. For all but the most accomplished thespians, reading from a script will sound just like reading from a script, or worse, a laundry list. It will be almost impossible to develop any rhythm with the witness.

Reading from a set of questions will also deprive you of the control that comes from eye contact with the witness. The witness will be less likely to follow your lead, and you will be less able to observe the witness's demeanor of telltale signs of nervousness or retraction. Witnesses often betray themselves or open doors during cross examination, and you must constantly be ready to exploit such an unplanned opportunity. Needless to say, that will not happen if you are tied to a set of written questions.

There are even drawbacks simply to keeping your notes in the form of a set of written questions. First, this format encourages bobbing your head up and down from pad to witness. Even if you do not read the questions, you will spend an inordinate amount of time looking away from the witness. A more serious difficulty is the increased likelihood of losing your place. This is not a small problem. Notes based on written questions will be much longer than an outline, and the questions will all tend to look alike. The possibility of losing your place on a page, or being unable to find the page that you need, is extreme. Almost nothing is more embarrassing or damaging than being unable to continue a cross examination because your notes have become disorganized.

Written questions are best used as a pre-examination device. Write them out, study them, hone them, rearrange them, and then discard them in favor of a topical outline.

2. Using an Outline

The purpose of your outline should be to remind you of the points that you intend to make on cross examination, and to ensure that you do not inadvertently omit anything. Do not regard your notes as a script, but rather as a set of cues or prompts, each of which introduces an area of questioning. Beneath each of the main prompts you will list the key details that you intend to elicit from the witness.

Your outline can follow the same format that you have used since high school. Principal topics are represented by Roman numerals, subtopics are denoted by capital letters, and smaller points or component details are represented by Arabic numerals. Although the form for academic outlines goes on to involve lower case letters, small Roman numerals, and other levels *ad infinitum*, the outline for a cross examination will become too complex if it extends beyond the third level.

The main topics for the cross examination of the defendant in the fire truck case would probably include the defendant's background, the events of the accident, and his post-accident conduct. In abbreviated form, an outline for that cross examination might look like this:

I. **Background**
    A. **Business consultant**
        1. Sole proprietor
        2. Clients are important
        3. Timeliness and efficiency
    B. **Locations and distances**
        1. His home
        2. His office
        3. Parking lot

II. **Accident**
   A. **Plans for day**
      1. Left home at 7:55 a.m.
      2. Meeting at 8:30 a.m.
   B. **Weather**
   C. **Fire truck**
      1. Didn't see
      2. Didn't hear
      3. Didn't stop

III. **Post-accident**
   A. **Ran to phone office/client**
   B. **Didn't call ambulance for plaintiff**

Note that the use of subparts will vary according to the importance of, and your need to remember, discrete details. Depending upon your level of confidence, for example, you might want to fill in additional details for the weather conditions. On the other hand, you can usually expect to remember what was important to your case about the weather.

More importantly, note that the indented headings make it very easy to follow an outline in this form. It is not organized merely to tell the story, it also has a visual pattern that allows you to keep your place. Even when you lose your place, the sparsity of words makes recovery that much simpler. Moreover, the use of single-word or short-phrase headings should allow you to keep your outline short. It may be possible to limit your notes to a single sheet of paper, and it should almost never be necessary to use more than a few pages.

Finally, your zinger has to be the very last Roman numeral at the bottom of the final page of your outline. Even if you do not fill the last page, put the zinger at the bottom so that it will have maximum visual impact. You will want it to stand out when you need it.

3. "Referencing" Your Outline

Once you have drafted the outline for your cross examination, you should proceed to "reference" it. Referencing allows you to refresh the recollection of forgetful witnesses, and to impeach or contradict witnesses who give you evasive, unexpected, or false answers.

Across from every important subtopic and crucial detail, make a note that records the source for the point that you intend to make. You need not reference the major topic headings, but other than that it will often prove useful to reference your notes line by line. At a minimum, you must reference every point that you consider essential to your case, as well as those that you expect to be controverted or challenging to the witness. For example, assume that you know about the defendant's meeting plans because he testified to them at his deposition. At the point in your outline where you reach the defendant's intended destination on the morning of the accident, make a note of the page and line in his deposition where he testified that he had an 8:30 a.m. meeting with an important client.

In addition to deposition transcripts, reference sources can come from letters, reports, memoranda, notes, and even photographs. The best sources, of course, are the witness's own prior words. Adequate secondary sources may include documents that the witness reviewed, acted upon, or affirmed by silence. In most circumstances, the testimony of a different person, though perhaps useful, will not be a reliable source for referencing a cross examination.

Many lawyers prepare their outlines by first drawing a vertical line slightly to the right of the center of the page. They then write the outline for the examination on the left side of the line, while references are noted on the right side. The right column may also be used for note-taking during the witness's direct examination. The first part of such a note pad would look like this:

Cross Examination of Defendant

I. Background	
A. Business consultant	Dep., p.6, line 11
1. Sole proprietor	Dep., p.7, line 2
2. Clients important	Dep., p.26, line 23
3. Timeliness	Dep., p.19, line 4
B. Locations and distance	
1. His home	Dep., p.2, line 16
2. His office	Lease
3. Parking lot	Rental contract

It is also useful to devote the top of your first page to a sort of mini-reference chart, where you list all of the important times, dates, and addresses in the case. Although by the time of trial you may think that you know these details as well as your own name, no lawyer is forever safe from "drawing a blank" on crucial details at crucial moments. The last thing you want to do is cross examine a witness as to her whereabouts for the wrong date. Cautious lawyers have even been known to write the names of the key witnesses — including their own clients — at the top of the first page.

B. Questions That Achieve Control

Having organized and outlined the cross examination, we are now ready to consider the precise techniques that provide maximum control over a witness's testimony. Many of the following rules will seem familiar, since most are based upon the principles of apposition, duration, indirection, and misdirection. As with all of trial advocacy, it will seldom be possible to apply every rule in any given examination (although some lawyers have managed somehow to break every rule during a single examination). Rather, you must use your own good judgment to determine which principles will be most effective in your particular situation.

1. Use Incremental Questions

Cross examination should proceed in a series of small, steady steps. No matter how certain you are that a witness must grant you an answer, there is always a risk that she will disagree. Disagreement almost always hurts. While it is true that you may often bring a witness back under control,[6] at a minimum that effort will generally waste time and distract attention from your more important goals.

The larger the scope of your question, the more likely you are to give the witness room to disagree. It is therefore preferable to divide areas of questioning into their smallest component parts. For example, assume that you are about to cross examine the defendant in the fire truck case. You want to establish the distance from his parking garage to his office, in order to show that he was in a hurry to get to his meeting that morning. You could ask one question: "Your parking garage is located three blocks from your office, isn't it?" If the witness says "yes" you will have achieved your purpose, but what will you do if the witness says "no"? Make no mistake about it: no matter how carefully you have planned your cross examination, some witnesses will find a way to say "no." In the above scenario, for example, the defendant may decide that the distance is not quite three blocks, since his office building is not exactly on the corner. Or he may quibble with you over whether you can call the parking lot "his" garage. In fact, you may even have made a mistake about the facts. In any event, you can head off such potential problems by asking incremental questions, such as these:

---

6   Techniques for reasserting control are discussed in Section V D, *infra* at p. 89.

QUESTION: You have a monthly parking contract at the Garrick garage?

QUESTION: The Garrick is located at the northwest corner of Randolph and Dearborn?

QUESTION: Your office is located at 48 South Dearborn?

QUESTION: The shortest distance from the Garrick to your office is to go south on Dearborn?

QUESTION: First you must cross Randolph? Then you must cross Washington? Then you must cross Madison?

QUESTION: And your office is further south on that block, isn't it?

This technique allows you to do two things. First, it blocks the escape route for a witness who is inclined to argue or prevaricate. The incremental questions provide small targets for a witness's inventiveness. More importantly, it lets you know early in the sequence whether the witness is likely to disagree with you. The use of incremental questions allows you to test the witness for cooperation, and to determine whether your own factual assumptions are correct, before you reach an embarrassing point of no return.

2.   Use Sequenced Questions for Impact

Sequencing may be used on cross examination for a variety of purposes. First, as on direct, you may use sequencing (or apposition) to clarify your story or enhance its impact upon the trier of fact. Eliciting two facts in close proximity can underscore relationships, contrasts, inconsistencies, connections, or motives. In the fire truck case, you may sequence your cross examination so that the defendant testifies within a very short time about the important meeting that he had to attend on the morning of the accident and his earlier decision to leave the auto repair shop without servicing his brakes. The apposition of these otherwise disparate facts can help develop your theme, "Too busy to be careful."

The defendant, of course, will not want to draw the connection for you that his busy professional life leads him to neglect safety. You may be able to control the witness, however, by sequencing your examination in a way that multiplies the impact of two otherwise unconnected facts.

3.   Use Sequenced Questions for Indirection

Unfortunately, what is clear to the jury will also be clear to the witness. Alerted that you have decided to exploit his busy schedule, the defendant may decide not to concede so readily the key details of his visit to the mechanic. In such situations you may use sequencing not for clarity and impact, but for indirection. You may therefore decide simply to abandon apposition, and instead to "scatter" the information about the defendant's busy schedule.

Alternatively, however, you may still use sequencing to make your point. The key lies in the order of the examination. Assume that you still want to elicit in close proximity the information about the repair shop and the client meeting. Neither event is a necessary predicate to the other; which one should you establish first?

Although it may seem counter-intuitive, the answer is to save the "surest" topic for last. In the above example, you can probably be the most "sure" that the defendant will admit going directly to his office following the accident. The issue is purely factual, and there are, no doubt, other witnesses who will place him at the office that morning. You can also be fairly sure that the witness will admit having been at the repair shop, since again there will be witnesses to place him there. On the other hand, you must be decidedly less sure that he will concede that he opted not to have his brakes fixed because he was busy that day. The defendant's motivations are his own, and they can seldom be established from a collateral source.[7]

Thus, motivation is your touchiest subject. It should therefore come at the beginning of your sequence, for two reasons. First, recall that the witness will be most cooperative before he understands where the examination is headed. Since proof of motivation depends most on the witness's own cooperation, you will want to address that issue at the beginning of that part of the examination. Second, you know that you want to conclude every area of the examination successfully. You will therefore save your more "provable" points for last.

How will this particular exercise in sequencing work? Assume that the brake shop incident occurred on Monday, and that the accident was on Friday. Begin by asking the witness about his business schedule on that Monday. Do not bring up automobile repairs until you have completely established all of his appointments and time commitments for that day. Then ask him about his visit to the mechanic, concluding with the fact that he did not leave his car there. You may now go on to the day of the accident, establishing that the defendant went on to his office following the collision. Through careful sequencing you should be able to maintain sufficient control of the witness and keep both events in close apposition.

4. Use Sequenced Questions for Commitment

Using sequenced questions in combination with incremental questions may occasionally allow you to compel an unwilling witness to make important concessions. Facts can often be arranged in a manner that gives their progression a logic of its own. When the initial facts in a sequence are sufficiently small and innocuous, a witness may be led to embark upon a course of concessions that will be impossible to stop.

---

7   This discussion assumes that you do not have available a prior statement from the defendant that admits the facts that you are seeking to establish.

Suppose that you represent the defendant in the fire truck case, and you want to prove that the plaintiff was not as seriously injured as she claims. There is, of course, absolutely no possibility that the witness will admit to having exaggerated her injuries. On the other hand, she may initially admit the accuracy of a series of smaller, more innocuous assertions. Note that the sequencing of the following questions commits the witness to a premise that will later be expanded in a way that she will not be able to deny:

QUESTION: You have testified that the accident has interfered with your enjoyment of life?

QUESTION: For example, you have given up playing tennis?

QUESTION: Tennis, of course, requires considerable physical exertion?

QUESTION: Because of that, you have dropped your membership in the North Shore Tennis Club?

QUESTION: One of your other interests is the fine arts, isn't that right?

QUESTION: In particular, you admire the French impressionists, correct?

QUESTION: Of course, the accident has not diminished your appreciation for the French impressionists?

QUESTION: In fact, you are a fairly serious student of 19th century art?

QUESTION: You share that interest with your friends and children, don't you?

QUESTION: You have maintained your membership in the Art Institute, haven't you?

QUESTION: You attended the special Monet exhibition, didn't you? And your membership allowed you to bring along some friends as guests, correct?

QUESTION: And in fact, you have continued to serve as a guide for schoolchildren?

QUESTION: Being a guide, of course, involves accompanying the children throughout the museum?

Sequencing was used in this example to commit the witness to several premises that were later expanded in a way that she would be unable to deny. Tennis is strenuous. She continues to enjoy the French impressionists. She was able to keep up with her friends at a crowded museum exhibit. And eventually, she is still capable of chasing children around the Art Institute.

5. Create a "Conceptual Corral"

As we have seen, the purpose of cross examination is often to "box in" a witness so that crucial facts cannot be averted or denied. It is often useful to think of this process as building a "conceptual corral" around the witness. After building the first three sides of the corral, you may then close the gate with your final proposition.

Each side of the conceptual corral is formed by a different sort of question. One side consists of the witness's own previous admissions or actions, another is formed by undeniable facts, and the third is based upon everyday plausibility. The length of any particular side, or the extent to which you will rely on any of the three sorts of information, will differ from case to case. With almost every witness, however, the three sides of the corral can be constructed to form an enclosure from which the witness cannot escape.

Suppose that you want to prove that the defendant in the accident case ignored the fire truck. That proposition will be the gate of your corral; you won't make it obvious until all three sides have been put into place.

The first side is formed by the witness's own admissions, gathered from his deposition, documents in the case, or his earlier testimony on direct: He was driving south on Sheridan Road, he was late for an appointment, he had over 10 miles yet to go, he had to park three blocks from his office, he didn't hit his brakes before the collision.

Side two consists of undeniable facts that have already been established or that can readily be proved by other witnesses: The fire truck was the largest vehicle on the road. It was red. The other traffic stopped. The weather was clear.

The last side is based upon plausibility. A fire truck can be seen at a distance of over 100 yards. Fire trucks have red lights to increase their visibility. Traveling at 30 miles per hour, it only takes about 90 feet to stop an automobile.

The three sides having been constructed, the gate will simply fall into place: The defendant could only have missed the fire truck by ignoring the roadway.

Note that the fourth side of the corral often will not require any questions at all. Admissions, facts, and plausibility will frequently be all that you need to establish your ultimate point. And, as we will discuss below, it is usually preferable not to confront the witness with your ultimate proposition.

6. Avoid Ultimate Questions

It will often be tempting to confront an adverse witness with one last conclusory question: "So you just ignored the fire truck, didn't you?" Resist this temptation. If you have already established all of the incremental facts that lead to your conclusion, then you will have little to gain by making the question explicit.

At best you will repeat what has become obvious, and at worst you will give the witness an opportunity to recant or amend the foundational testimony.

Even worse, you may not have established the incremental facts as fully as you thought. Under these circumstances, you can expect the witness not only to disagree with your ultimate proposition, but to be prepared to explain exactly why you are wrong.

The classic approach to cross examination calls for the lawyer to elicit all of the facts that lead to the ultimate conclusion, and to then stop. The final proposition is saved for final argument. By saving the ultimate point for final argument, you ensure that the witness will not be able to change or add to the testimony. To a certain extent, you also avoid informing opposing counsel of your argument, and you diminish the likelihood of having your position refuted either on redirect or through another witness.

While some writers state flatly that you should always save your ultimate point for argument, a more flexible rule is also more realistic. Perhaps it could best be stated as "Save the ultimate point for argument, unless you are certain that it will be inescapable." For example, the witness may already have admitted your ultimate point during her deposition. Or your proposition might have been so firmly established by the evidence as to be undeniable. In rare cases you might want the witness to disagree with your conclusion, so that you may exploit the sheer implausibility of the denial. Short of these circumstances, however, the safest route is generally to be satisfied with establishing a chain of incremental facts, and to reserve the capstone for argument.

7. Listen to the Witness and Insist on an Answer

There is more to controlling a witness on cross examination than asking the right questions. You must also make sure that you have gotten the correct answers. This requires that you listen to the witness. Even the most painstakingly prepared question can elicit the wrong answer. The witness may not have understood you, or she may have detected an ambiguity in your inquiry. Some witnesses will argue with you for the sake of argument, some will try to deflect your examination, and some will simply answer a question different from the one that you asked. In any event, you must always recall that it is the witness's answer that constitutes evidence, and you must listen carefully to ensure that the evidence is what you expected.

You can often correct an incorrect answer by restating your question. Consider the following scenario from the fire truck case:

QUESTION: Isn't it true that all of the other traffic stopped for the fire truck?

ANSWER: How would they know to stop? There was no siren.

QUESTION: You didn't answer my question. All of the other cars did stop?

ANSWER: Yes.

In the above example, the defendant apparently decided that he did not want to respond to the cross examiner's question, so he deflected it by answering a different question. An inattentive lawyer might have interpreted that answer as a denial, or otherwise let it go by. The advocate listened more carefully, however, and was able to obtain the precise information sought.

Note as well that the cross examiner in this situation would be equally satisfied with either an affirmative or negative answer. If the defendant admitted that all of the other traffic stopped, then the point is made. If the defendant insisted that the traffic hadn't stopped, he would be subject to contradiction by numerous other witnesses. Either way, the cross examination would be successful. The greatest problem, then, is the non-answer. There are many techniques for requiring difficult or evasive witnesses to answer your questions,[8] but the first step is always to listen to the witness and to insist upon an answer.

C. Questions That Lose Control

The pitfalls of cross examination are well known: refusals to answer, unexpected answers, argumentative witnesses, evasive and slippery witnesses. Significantly, virtually all of these problems derive from the same basic error on the part of the cross examiner — failure to control the testimony.

Control of testimony on cross examination means ensuring (1) that all of your questions are answered with the information that you want, and (2) that no information is produced other than what you have requested. In other words, the witness must answer your questions, and only your questions. An examination goes slightly out of control when a witness hedges or withholds answers. It goes seriously out of control when a witness begins to spout entirely new information.

While some witnesses are intractable by nature, it is more usual that lawyers bring these problems upon themselves. Certain questions, and styles of questioning, constitute virtual invitations to a witness to set up an independent shop. The most common of these are detailed below. From time to time there may be a reason to use one of the following sorts of questions, but as a general proposition they are all to be avoided.

1. Non-leading Questions

The cardinal rule on cross examination is to use leading questions. The cardinal sin is to abandon that tool. We have discussed at length the advantages of stating your questions in the form of leading propositions. For some reason,

---

8   *See* Section V D, *infra* at p. 89.

however, many lawyers seem impelled to drift into non-leading questions once an examination has begun. You can control a witness this way:

QUESTION: You were 30 feet away from plaintiff's car when you first applied your brakes, correct?

But you lose the witness when you ask,

QUESTION: How far from the plaintiff's car were you when you applied your brakes?

Why would a lawyer make such an elementary mistake? The principal reason no doubt lies in lack of confidence. It is awkward to put words in another person's mouth. We do not generally conduct conversations by telling others exactly what to say. It is even more uncomfortable when you are uncertain about the content yourself. How odd it feels to tell the driver of an automobile exactly where and when he applied his brakes. An easy response mechanism to this unease is to revert to a more natural style of discourse. Just ask what happened. And so we all occasionally fall into the trap of turning control of the examination over to the witness.

The solution to this problem is preparation. If you are unsure of where the witness applied his brakes, of course you will not tell him that it was thirty feet. So be sure. Read his deposition, scour the police report, measure the skid marks, talk to other witnesses, calculate his speed and stopping distance. Then, once you are certain that there is no plausible denial, tell him exactly what he did. Because your leading question is based upon verifiable facts, the great likelihood is that the witness will agree with you. If the witness disagrees, all is still well and good. After all, you have the facts to use in further cross examination or to introduce through another witness.

There are two legitimate reasons to suspend temporarily the use of leading questions. Neither is without its risks, and both should be used with care. First, you will occasionally need to learn a bit of information from a witness in order to continue a cross examination. For example, there might have been two routes available to the fire truck defendant to reach his office from the scene of the accident. Having prepared thoroughly, you know that you will be able to show that he was already so late that neither route would have gotten him to his appointment on time. Thus, even if you don't know the answer to the question, you can safely ask a non-leading question: "What road did you intend to take downtown?" You need that information to structure the balance of your examination, and you can handle whichever answer you are given. Never employ this approach because you are curious or because you hope that the answer will be helpful. The potential for backfiring is great. You must truly be certain that you need to ask an informational question, and that you have prepared alternate examinations depending on which answer you are given.

Second, and even less frequently, you may believe that an answer will have more impact if it comes in the witness's words instead of yours. Sometimes this works, but often it does not. Suppose that you are cross examining the fire truck plaintiff on the extent of her injuries. You know that she is still able to work at her job, and that she recently went on a three-day camping trip. It would indeed heighten the drama of the moment if you could obtain the damning testimony in her own words:

QUESTION: Ma'am, please tell us all of the things that you were able to do on your recent camping trip.

ANSWER: Oh, I was able to hike, fish, swim, pitch the tent, carry my backpack, and sleep on the ground.

Perhaps the witness testified to all of that during her deposition. By the time of trial, however, the more likely scenario will be:

QUESTION: Ma'am, please tell us all of the things that you were able to do on your recent camping trip.

ANSWER: I was hardly able to do anything. Everything I tried caused me pain, even sleeping.

Non-leading questions might have a terrific potential impact, but leading questions have the incalculable advantage of greater safety. Consider:

QUESTION: Ma'am, you went on a three-day camping trip?

ANSWER: Yes.

QUESTION: You went hiking?

ANSWER: Yes, but it caused me pain.

QUESTION: You went fishing and swimming?

ANSWER: Yes.

QUESTION: You pitched the tent?

ANSWER: Yes, but that hurt, too.

QUESTION: You stayed out in the woods for three days?

ANSWER: Yes.

Note that the witness may be able to argue with you notwithstanding your use of leading questions. The difference, however, is that short, leading questions limit her ability to do so, while increasing your ability to bring her back under control. Furthermore, the "yes, but" nature of her embellishments necessarily make them less persuasive.

Still, there may be times when it is truly advantageous to extract cross examination testimony in a witness's own words. This technique is most likely to work when the information you are after is well-documented, factual, and short. In the above example, assuming that you have adequate deposition testimony, you might be able to use non-leading questions to the following extent:

QUESTION: Where did you spend last Labor Day weekend?

ANSWER: At Eagle River Falls.

QUESTION: What is Eagle River Falls?

ANSWER: It is a campground.

That is enough; do not push your luck. Since the last thing you want to do is lose control of the testimony, now is the time to go back to leading questions.

2.   "Why" or Explanation Questions

There is virtually never a need to ask a witness to explain something on cross examination. If you already know the explanation, then use leading questions to tell it to the witness. If you do not already know the explanation, then cross examination surely is not the time to learn it. No matter how assiduously you have prepared, no matter how well you think you understand the witness's motives and reasons, a witness can always surprise you by explaining the unexplainable.

The greatest temptation to ask for an explanation arises when a witness offers a completely unexpected answer. The dissonance between the expectation and the actual response cries out for resolution. The natural reaction is to resolve the inconsistency by asking the witness, "Please explain what you mean by that." Unfortunately, the witness will be more than happy to explain, almost always to the detriment of the cross examiner. The following scenario is not unrealistic:

QUESTION: Your parking garage was located three blocks from your office, correct?

ANSWER: Yes.

QUESTION: And the sidewalks are always very crowded between 8:00 and 8:30 in the morning?

ANSWER: That's right.

QUESTION: You usually have to wait for one or more traffic lights between the garage and your office, don't you?

ANSWER: I do.

QUESTION: So you have to plan on at least ten minutes to get from your garage to your office, right?

ANSWER: No, that is not right. I usually make it in three to five minutes.

QUESTION: Please explain how you can travel that distance, under those circumstances, in only three to five minutes.

ANSWER: It's simple. There is an express bus that travels that route in a bus lane. I get on in front of the garage and its next stop is right in front of the office. Even in heavy traffic it never takes more than five minutes, since the bus lane is always clear and the traffic lights are coordinated.

There are numerous common questions that invite such long, unwelcome answers. They should all be excised from your cross examination vocabulary. Do not ask a witness to explain. Do not ask a "why" question. Do not ask a question that begins with "How do you know," or "Tell us the reason." If you receive an unexpected answer, the fault probably lies with the original question. The best solution is usually to move on or rephrase your inquiry.[9] It cannot help you to allow the witness to dig the hole a little deeper.

Asking a witness to explain is the equivalent of saying, "I've grown tired of controlling this cross examination. Why don't you take over for a while?"

3. "Fishing" Questions

Fishing questions are the ones that you ask in the hope that you might catch something. It has been said before and it is worth repeating here: Do not ask questions to which you do not know the answers. For every reason that you have to think that the answer will be favorable, there are a dozen reasons you haven't thought of, all of which suggest disaster.

Very few lawyers actually intend to go fishing during cross examination; most lawyers plan only to elicit information that they have developed during preparation for trial. Nonetheless, temptation has been known to strike. A witness, during either direct or cross, may expose an enticing, but incomplete, morsel of information. It is difficult to resist exploring such an opening, just to see if anything is really there. That is how the fishing starts.

In our intersection case, for example, suppose that during discovery the plaintiff produced medical reports indicating that she would need to participate in

---

9   Reasserting control in such situations is discussed in greater detail below. *See* Section V D *infra* at p. 89.

extensive physical therapy for the next several years. During her direct testimony at trial, however, she has unexpectedly stated that, "My doctor said that I did not need to go to physical therapy any longer, and I ended it several months ago." The suggestion seems obvious; her injuries are not as severe as was previously thought, and she is now well on the way to resuming her normal life. Defense counsel immediately sees a vision of reduced damages. The temptation to go fishing on cross is now nearly irresistible; the defendant's lawyer wants to make sure that the record is clear as to the plaintiff's recovery.

Unfortunately, defendant's counsel is likely to "catch" information sharply different from that which was sought:

QUESTION: You have told us that your doctor terminated your physical therapy.

ANSWER: That is correct.

QUESTION: Isn't that because your recovery has been quicker than was expected and you don't need the therapy any longer?

ANSWER: No. It is because the therapy was too painful and I wasn't making any progress.

The defendant's lawyer in the above scenario had a good reason to hope that the "therapy" questions would produce helpful information. The most important part of the answer, however, was unknown. Counsel simply had no way of predicting what the witness would say as to why the physical therapy ended. Reasonably hoping to turn up a good answer, counsel instead made the plaintiff's case stronger. That is what can happen when you go fishing.

4. Long Questions

Long questions have an almost limitless capacity to deprive a cross examiner of witness control. Recall that short, single-fact, propositional questions give a witness the least room to take issue with your point. By contrast, long questions, by their very nature, multiply a witness's opportunity to find something with which to disagree. The more words that you use, the more chance there is that a witness will refuse to adopt them all.

A second problem with long questions is that they are easily forgotten or misunderstood. Even a witness with every reasonable intention can be misled or baffled by a lengthy question. Thereafter, the witness may insist on answering the question that she thought you asked, rather than the one that you meant to ask.

Finally, long questions diminish your ability to enlist the judge in your efforts to control a witness. It is a little-known, and even less acknowledged, characteristic of trial judges that they do not all tend to pay close attention to attorneys' questions, particularly in jury trials. It is, after all, the answer that constitutes evidence. Given the principle of primacy, long questions have the greatest potential to lose a judge's attention. In ordinary circumstances this is not of great moment, since the judge's impression, or even understanding, of the question may not be essential. Once a witness has avoided answering, however, the judge's perception of the question can become crucial.

Counsel will often want to request the judge to direct a witness to answer a question "yes or no." Understandably, a judge will only be likely to do this if she has heard and comprehended the entire question. Even if your question is completely susceptible of a "yes or no" answer, a judge who has tuned out the last two-thirds of your inquiry is extremely unlikely to restrict the witness's answer.

There is no fixed point at which a question becomes "long." Some inquiries, depending upon the nature of the concept and the cooperativeness of the witness, may call for more words than others. A useful rule of thumb is that any question of ten words or fewer may be considered "short." You may wish to exceed this length, but only for a reason.

5. "Gap" Questions

"Gap" questions constitute an especially enticing subset of explanation questions. Interestingly, they are often most irresistible to lawyers who are particularly well-prepared or attentive.

Imagine that you are the prosecutor in a hit and run case. You know the date on which the crime occurred, but because there were no eyewitnesses, you have been able to narrow the time of the crime only to a six-hour window. The defendant has raised the defense of alibi. You have thoroughly researched the law and meticulously prepared the facts of your case, which is based entirely on circumstantial evidence. The defendant has taken the stand and testified in his own defense. Listening carefully, you were surprised to notice that he left several half-hour gaps in his alibi.

The defendant is now available for cross examination. The temptation may be overwhelming to alert the jury to the gaps in the defendant's alibi: "Mr. Defendant, you told us where you were at 2:00 p.m., but you didn't say anything about 2:30 p.m., did you?" Do not ask that question; you will lose control. It is an unspoken invitation to the witness to fill in the gap. Even if the witness does not take the opportunity to complete his alibi, you can be certain that opposing counsel will do it for him on redirect. The far better tactic is to allow the omission to remain unexplained, and then to point it out during final argument.

Gaps are found in direct testimony more often than one might expect. A witness may neglect to testify about one of a series of important events, or may omit testimony concerning a crucial document. Alternatively, a witness might leave out important evidence on damages, or may fail entirely to testify as to an element, such as proximate cause, of the opposition's case.

How can you avoid the temptation to ask "gap" questions? The key is to remember that it is the opposition's burden to prove their case. Everything that they leave out of their case works in your favor. In most circumstances the absence of proof can be interpreted as negative proof.[10]

Of course, your opposition may also create gaps in their testimony by design, purposely leaving out facts that damage their case but are helpful to yours. Needless to say, you will want to address these omissions during your cross examination. The fatal "gap" questions are the ones that are directed at omissions in the other side's case. A useful way to keep this distinction in mind is the following: Do not cross examine on omissions in testimony. Do cross examine on the absence of facts.

Thus, when your opposition has failed to prove something, simply allow the gap to remain. Comment on it during final argument, not cross examination.

6. "You testified" Questions

Another common method of surrendering control to a witness is through the use of questions that seem to challenge the witness to recall the content of her earlier direct testimony. These can be referred to as "you testified" questions, because they inevitably contain some variant on those words. Each of the following is a "you testified" question:

QUESTION: You testified that the assailant had brown hair?

QUESTION: Wasn't it your testimony that you left your house at 8:00 a.m.?

QUESTION: On direct examination you testified that the last possible delivery date was May 17, didn't you?

What is wrong with these questions? In each case they seem to call for relevant information. They are all leading. They are all short. They are all propositional.

---

10   The most obvious exception to this rule is a criminal defendant's decision not to testify at all, from which no negative inference may be drawn.

The problem with "you testified" questions is that they invite the witness to quibble over the precise wording used on direct examination. The exact language of the witness's earlier answer is seldom essential,[11] but the "you testified" format inflates its apparent importance, often almost to the point of seeming to pick a fight. Imagine these answers to the above questions, with the witness's unspoken thoughts given in parentheses:

QUESTION: You testified that the assailant had brown hair?"

ANSWER: No. (I testified that he had sort of sandy brown hair.)

QUESTION: Wasn't it your testimony that you left your house at 8:00 a.m.?

ANSWER: That was not my testimony. (I said that I believed that I left my house at approximately 8:00 a.m.)

QUESTION: On direct examination you testified that the last possible delivery date was May 17, didn't you?

ANSWER: I do not believe that is correct. (I think I said that we could not accept delivery any later than May 17.)

Even if you have correctly remembered the witness's precise testimony down to the last word, there is no guarantee that the witness will remember it equally well. At best, you may end up with a response on the order of, "I cannot remember whether those were my exact words." At that point you have lost control, since the examination has now shifted away from your agenda and onto the issue of the superiority of your memory. The court reporter can be called upon to resolve the dispute, but that exercise, at a minimum, will be disruptive to your pace. Besides, you might turn out to be embarrassingly wrong.

It is far less risky, and generally much more effective, to cross examine witnesses on facts and events, rather than on prior testimony: "You left your home at 8:00 a.m.?" "You expected delivery no later than May 17?" In situations where you want to make it clear that you challenge the witness's version of events, use a formulation such as this one: "You now claim that the assailant had brown hair?"

---

11 The precise wording of a witness's previous answer can be essential when you intend to impeach the witness through the use of a prior inconsistent statement. In that situation it is usually necessary, and indeed some courts require, that you "recommit" the witness to the testimony that you intend to impeach. Thus, the classic foundation for impeachment by a prior inconsistent statement includes a preliminary "you testified" question. Note, however, that the subject of the impeachment is the witness's earlier testimony, and not the actual underlying events. For further information on the specifics of impeachment, *see* Chapter Four, Section II *infra* at p.119.

It may be helpful to think of possible cross examination questions using the following hierarchy. As a general rule, you should prefer questions that are higher on the list:

Best, direct your questions to what happened.

Next, direct your questions to what the witness claims happened.

Last, direct your questions to what the witness said happened.

The closer you can stay to "real life," the less likely you are to lose witness control.

7. Characterizations and Conclusions

Another way to risk losing control on cross examination is to request that a witness agree with a characterization or conclusion. Assume that you are cross examining the complaining witness in a robbery case. The witness testified on direct that the crime occurred at midnight on a seldom-traveled country road. Your defense is misidentification. Wishing to take advantage of the time and place of the events, you ask this question:

"It was too dark to see very well, wasn't it?"

You have just asked the witness to agree with your characterization of the lighting conditions. The witness, being nobody's fool, answers:

"I could see just fine."

Instead, you should have asked the witness about the facts that led you to the characterization: the sun had gone down, there was no moon that night, there were no street lamps, there were no house lights, there were no illuminated signs. The characterization could then be saved for final argument.

Some outstanding trial lawyers, through force of personality, splendid preparation, or stunningly good luck, have been quite successful in obtaining a witness's agreement to their characterizations. In the above example, it would be of inestimable value to have the witness concede that it was too dark to see very well. For most lawyers, however, the risk to these questions usually outweighs the gain.

Bear in mind that it may be difficult to draw the line between characterization and fact. It will depend on the specifics of the case, the inclinations of the witness, the context of the question, and numerous other factors. On the one hand, a question such as, "It was midnight?" is clearly one of fact. On the other hand, a question such as, "Your identification was mistaken?" is no doubt a characterization. There are numerous possibilities in between. Even the question, "It was too dark to see?" might be regarded as either characterization or fact, depending upon the witness's background. While most people would regard that statement as conclusory — who is to say when it becomes too dark to see? — a photo-physicist, or perhaps a forensic ophthalmologist, might regard the inquiry as calling for an absolute fact.

Recognizing the impossibility of stating an absolute rule, the wisest course is to examine your questions for their potential to be taken as characterizations. Then make sure that you phrase them as facts.

D. Reasserting Control

Notwithstanding your best efforts and preparation, some witnesses will inevitably wander beyond your control. Your perfectly reasonable question may result in an absolute torrent of unwelcome, and uncalled for, information. While your first reaction to such testimony may range from anger to panic, the better response is to ask yourself, "Why is this witness out of control?" Once you have answered that question, you can proceed to apply the techniques for reasserting witness control.

A witness typically falls out of control in one of three ways: (1) she has refused to agree with you; (2) she has been invited to explain an answer; or (3) she is being impermissibly uncooperative.[12] In the first two instances the problem is your fault, and you can usually cure it with further questions. In the third case the witness is at fault, and you may need help from the judge.

1. Refusal to Agree

a. Determine why the witness has refused to agree

What happens when you ask a short, propositional, leading question and the witness simply disagrees with you? You are well prepared, you have done your homework, your question is in good form, you know what the answer should be — but the witness will not give you the right answer. The witness is clearly beyond your control, but why?

Imagine that you have asked a purely factual leading question, but that the witness will not give you the answer that you expect. Perhaps things have gone along the line of one of the following scenarios:

QUESTION: You are the plaintiff's next door neighbor, aren't you?

ANSWER: No, I am not.

---

12 A fourth circumstance, where the witness has changed her testimony, will be covered in the discussion of impeachment. *See* Chapter Four.

Or,

> QUESTION: When you entered the operating room the chief surgeon was already there, wasn't she?
>
> ANSWER: That is not correct.

Or,

> QUESTION: Wasn't the gun sitting on the desk?
>
> ANSWER: No.

In each of these situations you expected an affirmative answer, but you received a resounding negative. Why did it happen? As Shakespeare's Cassius remarked, "The fault, dear Brutus, is not in our stars, but in ourselves."[13] Unless the witness is lying,[14] intentionally uncooperative,[15] or sincerely mistaken,[16] you received the wrong answer because of the nature of your question. This usually happens for one of three reasons: (1) you were wrong about your facts; (2) you included a "compound detail"; or (3) your question contained an "imbedded" characterization.

In the first example above it is possible that you were simply wrong on the facts. This happens to everyone. Perhaps the witness lives across the street or down the block from the plaintiff. Perhaps your investigator gave you erroneous information. Perhaps the police report that you relied upon was incorrect. Perhaps you simply got two witnesses confused. These are all common occurrences.

In the second example it is likely that the cross examiner included what we will call a compound detail. Recall the question: "When you entered the operating room, the chief surgeon was already there?" The chief surgeon's presence in the operating room exactly at the time of the witness's entry is an extra detail. It may be superfluous, but it gives the witness the opportunity to seize upon that nuance as a reason for answering "No" to the entire question. The witness is not disagreeing about the chief surgeon's presence, but only about the timing of her arrival. Note, by the way, that the question is not technically compound in form; it asks only for a single fact. Still, the inclusion of an unnecessary detail has the effect of "compounding" the question and releasing the witness from control.

---

13 *Julius Caesar,* Act I, Scene 2, line 134.

14 If the witness is lying or otherwise changing her testimony you will, of course, impeach her through the use of her own prior statement. We know that you have access to a prior statement or other impeaching material, because otherwise you would not have asked the question in the first place. Regarding the mechanics of impeachment, *see* Chapter Four.

15 Methods for dealing with impermissibly uncooperative witnesses are discussed in Section V D(3), *infra* at p. 100.

16 If the witness is mistaken, you will refresh her recollection.

Finally, the question in the third example, while appearing factual on its face, may have been interpreted by the witness as including a characterization. This sort of "imbedded characterization" is frequently the reason for an unexpected negative answer. How could a question so purely factual be taken as an imbedded characterization? The witness, after all, was asked whether the gun was on the desk. That question calls only for a simple observation; there is no room for interpretation. If all of the facts point to the gun's location on the desk, how can this witness respond otherwise? The answer is that one person's fact may indeed be another's characterization. Although you may be quite confident that the piece of furniture in question is a desk, the witness may regard it as a vanity or computer table. Moreover, the distinction may be important to the witness, if, for example, there had been several similar pieces of furniture in the room.

b. Retreat to constituent facts

Once you have determined why a witness has refused to agree with you, you can generally bring the witness back under control simply by asking further questions. Of course, you will never ask a witness for an explanation or elaboration. Rather, your following questions should "retreat to constituent facts." This method can work regardless of the reason the witness has chosen to disagree. It involves breaking your original question into a series of ever-smaller "constituent facts," until the basis of the witness's disagreement can be eliminated.

The retreat to constituent facts is a retreat only in the tactical sense. By using this method you are not giving up or abandoning your line of questioning. You are "retreating" from an insistence that the witness adopt your exact language. By changing your wording, while maintaining the substance of your question, you can effectively reassert control over the witness. In other words, you can accomplish your advocacy objective without the need for direct confrontation.

i. Mistaken facts

In employing the retreat to constituent facts, you must first consider that you may have been mistaken in the first place. If your facts were wrong, then the witness obviously will not agree. Reconsider your question. Are you certain of its premise? Are you depending upon a reliable source? Is the answer you want truly beyond controversy? If you conclude that the witness may have disagreed with you because of misinformation, then rephrase your question to include only those facts of which you are the most certain.

In the next-door-neighbor example above, for instance, your retreat might take the following form:

QUESTION: You are the defendant's next door neighbor, aren't you?

ANSWER: No, I am not.

QUESTION: It is true that you know the defendant?

ANSWER: Yes, that is true.

QUESTION: And you do live near the defendant?

ANSWER: Yes, I do.

At this point, having established the constituent facts of which you are the most certain, you will stop. Of course, if the witness denies knowing or living near the defendant, then it is obvious that something else is wrong with your cross examination. Under those circumstances your best recourse is to move on to another line of questioning, and to reexamine your notes and files during a break in the testimony.

ii. Compound details

Compound details are those which are unnecessary to the question, but which have the effect of compounding the inquiry and making possible a denial or disagreement. You can usually reassert control over the witness simply by rephrasing your question without the superfluous detail. Note, however, that not all details are "compound"; some may be quite necessary, even crucial, to your case. Consider the two following examples:

QUESTION: You saw a red car run the stop light, didn't you?

QUESTION: The next car that you saw was red, correct?

In the first question the car's color may well be irrelevant. So long as the witness saw a car run the stop light, it may not matter what color it was. If your case does not depend on the color of the automobile, you may rephrase the question by omitting the detail and retreating to a constituent fact: "You did see a car run the stop light?"

In the second question, on the other hand, it seems apparent that the color of the car does matter, since the cross examiner has taken pains to point out that the very next automobile was red. Thus, the detail is probably not compound. You can proceed to ask another question to establish that the witness did indeed see a car, but at some point the color will have to be established as well.

Identifying compound details, then, calls for the exercise of judgment. Only the lawyer who prepared the case will know whether a particular detail is essential or unnecessary. In either event, however, you can begin to reassert control over the witness by disaggregating the details and continuing your examination on the basis of constituent facts. Consider the operating room example from the previous section:

QUESTION: When you entered the operating room the chief surgeon was already there, wasn't she?

ANSWER: That is not correct.

QUESTION: Well, you did enter the operating room?

ANSWER: I did.

QUESTION: You and the chief surgeon were present in the operating room at the same time?

ANSWER: We were.

QUESTION: You observed the operation?

ANSWER: Yes.

QUESTION: The chief surgeon was there when the procedure began?

ANSWER: She was.

Note that the cross examiner was able to elicit all of the important facts, while omitting the compound detail. Of course, if the exact time of the surgeon's entry was relevant to the case, another approach would have to be taken. Such an approach, as utilized with "imbedded characterizations," is discussed in the next section.

iii. Imbedded characterizations

"Imbedded characterizations" are statements that appear to be factual but which, upon examination, turn out to contain unspoken characterizations or assumptions. In the example in the introductory section above we saw that even a simple noun like "desk" can contain an imbedded characterization, since the term expresses an assumption as to the intended use for the piece of furniture.

Our language, as imprecise as it is, is filled with opportunities for the use of imbedded characterizations. They may arise through the use of technical language, professional or occupational jargon, slang, or as we saw above, simply as the result of a differentiated understanding of an otherwise simple noun or verb.

Imagine, for example, that a murder was committed on a Hollywood sound stage, just as a studio tour was passing through. A member of the cast was charged with the crime, and has raised the SODDI[17] defense. One of the tourists has testified on direct and is now being cross examined:

QUESTION: You were on the set when you heard a shot?

ANSWER: I was.

QUESTION: You looked over and saw a gun on the floor?

---

17   Some Other Dude Did It.

ANSWER: I did.

QUESTION: It was at the feet of the best boy?

ANSWER: No, I don't think so.

As it happens, "best boy" is the professional term for the first assistant electrician on a film crew. The lawyer, apparently a Los Angeles native, thought nothing about using this term. The tourist-witness, however, gave the term its ordinary meaning, and therefore gave the cross examiner the wrong answer.

Of course, the "best boy" story is a fanciful example, since only the most star-struck lawyer would fail to recognize it immediately as containing an ambiguity. Even still, the characterization can be unpacked via retreat to constituent facts:

QUESTION: You were on the set when you heard a shot?

ANSWER: I was.

QUESTION: You looked over and saw a gun on the floor?

ANSWER: I did.

QUESTION: It was at the feet of the best boy?

ANSWER: No, I don't think so.

QUESTION: Well, it was at the feet of a member of the film crew?

ANSWER: Yes, that's right.

QUESTION: And that person was holding a tool box?

ANSWER: Yes, I believe he was.

QUESTION: He was wearing an apron?

ANSWER: Yes.

QUESTION: And he was off to the side, away from the actors?

ANSWER: Correct.

At this point the constituent facts have been established: The weapon was seen near a member of the crew, not in the vicinity of the defendant-actor. It is not necessary to insist that the witness adopt the lawyer's language, or even to define the term "best boy." Facts are important, not words, and it is almost always possible to rephrase a question so as to employ more basic facts.

How would one retreat to constituent facts concerning a more realistic question? Assume that you are cross examining an eye witness to a crime that occurred at 8:30 p.m. on May 21. You want to establish that it was too dark for anyone to see clearly, but the witness will not agree with your imbedded characterization. Therefore, you retreat to constituent facts:

QUESTION: It was already dark at the time of the crime, wasn't it?

ANSWER: No, I wouldn't say so.

QUESTION: Well, it was 8:30 p.m., wasn't it?

ANSWER: Yes.

QUESTION: And it was still May?

ANSWER: Of course.

QUESTION: The sun had set?

ANSWER: Yes.

QUESTION: The street lights had gone on?

ANSWER: I think that is right.

QUESTION: The cars had their headlights on?

ANSWER: I believe so.

QUESTION: Certainly it was no longer daylight, correct?

ANSWER: Correct.

At this point you will stop. You have elicited the constituent facts that establish "darkness." It is not necessary to drag a concession out of the witness that it was too dark to see; the facts, and your final argument, will speak for themselves. Note also that most of the constituent facts can be proven through other means. The time of the sunset can be shown from Weather Bureau publications, and the time of street light illumination should be available from municipal records. Thus, a witness who disagrees with your constituent facts can be shown as untrustworthy during your case in chief.

Imbedded characterizations lurk everywhere. They are particularly tricky precisely because they generally involve a witness's unforeseen interpretation of a term or idea. It is important, therefore, not to become obsessed with avoiding imbedded characterizations. To do so would turn your cross examination into an interminable series of overwhelming details. You should never ask, "Was the gun on a piece of furniture with a flat horizontal surface and four vertical legs?" Go ahead and ask whether it was on the desk. By the same token, go ahead and ask the witness whether it was dark. Maybe she will agree with you, in which case there will be no need to retreat to constituent facts.

It is only when the witness unexpectedly disagrees that you must break your reasonable question into its smallest factual components. This places a premium on quick reaction. Since you cannot plan a response to a witness's unexpected answer, how can you know which constituent facts to use? It is impossible to list constituent facts for every noun and verb in your cross examination, just in case you might need them.

The answer lies in your theory of the case. You may not anticipate a witness's answer to your question, but you should always know why you asked the question. Why was the question necessary? How will it contribute to your final argument? What did you want to prove? The answers to these questions should almost always supply you with more than sufficient constituent facts.

2. Invited Explanation

a. Determine why the witness has explained

Most witnesses launch into unsolicited explanations because they think that they have been requested, or at least allowed, to do so. Whenever a witness begins to answer you at length, you must ask yourself what it was about the question that the witness took as a cue. Certainly you did not directly ask the witness to explain something, but perhaps the question was long, compound, fishing, or a "gap" question.

In addition to those enumerated in the previous section,[18] many questions contain implicit invitations to explain. Questions that use words such as "yet" and "still" are often regarded by witnesses as challenges that call for explanations. Consider this example, in which the last question uses both of the challenging words:

QUESTION: Immediately before the accident you were waiting for a bus?

ANSWER: That's right.

QUESTION: The bus was coming from the north, wasn't it?

ANSWER: Correct.

QUESTION: You had to look north for your bus?

ANSWER: I did.

QUESTION: The accident took place to the south of the intersection?

---

18   *See* "Questions that Lose Control," Section V C, *supra* at p. 79.

ANSWER: I guess it did.

QUESTION: Yet you still say that you could see the accident clearly?

ANSWER: Well, I turned my head when I heard the brakes screech.

Note that the "yet, still" question added virtually nothing to the examination, other than to alert the witness to the need for an explanation.

Other questions that frequently evoke explanations include those that are argumentative or unfair. Every time you take issue with or confront a witness, and especially when you mischaracterize testimony, you are inviting the witness to offer an explanation. This is not to say that you should never confront a witness during cross examination; indeed, it frequently is essential that you do so. Rather, you must be aware that confrontation will not always result in meek acquiescence on the witness's part. On the other hand, you should not knowingly mischaracterize a witness's testimony, for reasons both tactical and ethical.

In any event, the first step toward reasserting control of an explaining witness is to understand why the witness has begun to explain. This knowledge is crucial, so that you may avoid perpetuating your mistake in your subsequent questions.

b.   Reasserting control, part one

How do you reassert control over a witness whom you have, even if unintentionally, invited to explain an answer? For many lawyers, the initial reaction to the beginning of an explanation is somewhere between panic and fury. It is not hard to imagine the mental response when the unwanted explanation begins to emerge: The witness is not supposed to be doing this! The witness is just supposed to be giving the answer that I want! The witness is being unfair!

In these circumstances it is not surprising that the first tendency is to try to get the witness to shut up. Most lawyers try to achieve this in one of two ways: the impolite and the not-so-polite.

The rude way to terminate a witness's explanation is simply by interrupting with an instruction to the witness on the order of "Please just answer the question." Slightly more polite is the common interjection that begins, "Thank you, you have answered my question." Both interruptions ignore the fact that the witness was invited to explain. While the lawyer may not have recognized the invitation as it was issued, there is no guarantee that the judge or jury will take the attorney's side of the dispute. In fact, there is every reason to think that the judge and jury will take the witness's side. Nobody likes to see a witness interrupted.

As a rule of thumb, it is best to avoid interrupting a witness. Not only will you appear rude, but the tactic is likely to be ineffective. The witness may persist in explaining or the judge may insist that you allow the explanation to go forward. More to the point, even when your interruption is successful, the explanation is almost certain to be elicited on redirect examination. You will have lost "rudeness" points for no reason.

There are really only two situations that call for interrupting a witness. The first is when you believe that the witness is about to blurt out some devastating fact that is otherwise absolutely inadmissible. Under these circumstances redirect examination is not a concern, and you do indeed need to shut up the witness. The second situation in which you may want to interrupt a witness is when the witness deserves it, and you, consequently, have earned the right to interrupt. This occurs when the witness, despite your valiant efforts to be reasonable and precise, insists on continuing to volunteer collateral information. This witness is actually being impermissibly uncooperative, and the techniques for resolving this problem are discussed below.[19] Suffice it to say here that you should hesitate to interrupt even when you are dealing with a flagrantly uncooperative witness.

Well, if you are not going to interrupt the witness, what can you do? As a first line of defense, there are a fair number of non-verbal techniques that can be used to get a witness to stop talking. A stern look can be surprisingly effective, especially when the witness knows that she has gone beyond the legitimate bounds of your original question. Guilt, even for those on the witness stand, plays its part in human motivation. A second approach is to raise your hand in the universal "stop" symbol. This works particularly well if you do it at a natural pause in the witness's testimony, or when the witness displays some hesitancy about continuing.

A pause or hesitation by the witness is an excellent opportunity to recover the initiative by putting an entirely new question to the witness. Artfully done, this will not seem like an interruption, but rather as though you simply moved on after allowing the witness to finish the reply. This technique works best when it can be accomplished unobtrusively. Try to "slide" your question into the space where the witness is catching her breath or visibly deciding whether to continue. You do not need to change the subject entirely, but your question should be new. Be certain that it does not resuggest the subject of the explanation that you are attempting to abort.

These first three techniques — glare, upraised hand, and fill-in-the-blank — will sometimes work. Sometimes they will not. Their effectiveness depends in large part upon the level of control that you established in the balance of your examination of the witness. A witness who has become accustomed to answering short, leading, propositional questions will be more likely to stop explaining. In contrast, a witness who repeatedly has been given latitude to explain will be inclined to continue doing so. Additionally, your own level of confidence, not to mention the

---

19   See Section V D(3) *infra* at p. 100, regarding the reassertion of control over an impermissibly uncooperative witness.

witness's natural degree of loquaciousness, will play a large part in your ability to reassert control through these means.

c. Reasserting control, part two

Assuming that you cannot stare or "slide" the witness back under control, what are your remaining alternatives? While this may seem counter-intuitive or insufficiently activist, the best approach for coping with invited explanations may well be to do nothing. Allow the witness to finish the answer and then proceed to another question that does not invite explanation.

Recall that we are dealing here with a witness who has been allowed or invited to explain. It is therefore unnecessary, and may be counterproductive, to attempt to prove that the witness took unfair license. Many lawyers attempt to discipline the witness or otherwise make a point by saying something such as:

QUESTION:　You haven't answered my question. Can you please answer yes or no?

Or,

QUESTION:　Are you finished? Would you like to answer my question now?

Or,

QUESTION:　Please listen carefully. I am going to ask you a very simple question.

While these questions, and others like them, may be satisfying to the ego, they accomplish little and may actually result in making the witness more combative. It is very unlikely that the witness will retract the previous answer. "Was I explaining? I'm sorry. The answer should have been that I could not really see." That simply will not happen. Once an invited explanation has been given it is almost certain to stand. Do not argue about it or attempt to undo it; your time will be better spent making sure that it does not happen again. There is no reason to announce that you are going to ask a simple question. Just ask one.

The best way to bring an "invited" witness back under control is to terminate the invitation. Make sure that the next question is short, propositional, and leading. Ask yourself what it was about the previous question that was taken as an invitation, and then cure the problem with your next question. Recall the witness to the intersection accident who was invited to explain with a "yet, still" question. Instead of arguing with her, bring her back under control by reverting to controlling questions:

QUESTION: Immediately before the accident you were waiting for a bus?

ANSWER: That's right.

QUESTION: The bus was coming from the north, wasn't it?

ANSWER: Correct.

QUESTION: You had to look north for your bus?

ANSWER: I did.

QUESTION: The accident took place to the south of the intersection.

ANSWER: I guess it did.

QUESTION: Yet you still say that you could see the accident clearly?

ANSWER: Well, I turned my head when I heard the brakes screech.

QUESTION: So before you turned your head you were looking to the north.

ANSWER: Yes.

QUESTION: And the accident occurred to the south of where you were standing.

ANSWER: That is right.

A witness who is inclined to play fairly will generally be brought back under control if you ignore the explanation and proceed with leading questions. Some witnesses will continue to interject information and to explain every answer, whether invited to or not. These witnesses are impermissibly uncooperative, and the techniques for dealing with them are discussed in the next section.

3. Impermissible Lack of Cooperation

Not all witnesses are inclined to play fairly. Some witnesses are overtly partisan, some are subtly uncooperative, and some are just plain ornery. While there is no requirement that a witness facilitate or enhance the goals of your cross examination, there is a requirement that the witness, within her ability, provide fair answers to fair questions. Unfair answers take a number of forms, including speechmaking, deflection, and obstinance.

Speechmaking occurs when a witness insists on responding to a question with an uninvited explanation. In contrast to the invited explanation, where some aspect of the question encouraged the witness to explain the answer, a speechmaking witness is actually attempting to take control of the cross examination by inserting an explanation where none has been called for:

QUESTION: Didn't the accident occur at 8:20 a.m.?

ANSWER: Yes it did.

QUESTION: You had a business meeting scheduled for 8:30 that same morning, didn't you?

ANSWER: It really wasn't a very important meeting. We were just going to exchange a few papers. One of my partners could easily have taken care of it, and, in fact, I had pretty much decided to skip it by the time I left home.

The witness in this example believes that he has figured out where the cross examination is headed, and he has determined to cut off the line of questioning by offering an explanation in advance. There was nothing about the question that prompted or suggested the need for an immediate explanation, but the witness's own agenda nonetheless impelled one.

Deflection occurs when the witness decides to answer a question other than the one that was asked:

QUESTION: You know that traffic must stop for fire trucks, don't you?

ANSWER: There was no bell and no siren; I had no reason to stop.

Here the witness ignored the question, interjecting instead the information that he believes will be most helpful to his case.

Finally, a witness is obstinate when he simply refuses to answer the question, either by hedging the answer or by arguing with the cross examiner:

QUESTION: You left home at 8:10 that morning?

ANSWER: I guess so.

QUESTION: It is an eight-mile drive to your office?

ANSWER: You could say that.

QUESTION: You had a business meeting that morning?

ANSWER: It depends on what you mean by business.

QUESTION: It was important that you be on time?

ANSWER: Don't you try to be on time for your meetings?

This witness, in essence, has refused to participate in the cross examination. He does not want to answer any questions, so he responds with a series of non-answers.

In each of the above examples the witness was impermissibly uncooperative. The questions were simple, straightforward, and easily capable of "yes or no" answers. The witnesses, however, intentionally sought to thwart the cross examination. How can such witnesses be brought back under control?

There are two basic methods for reasserting control over intentionally uncooperative witnesses. The first is to do it yourself; the second is to ask the judge for help.

a. Obtaining help from the judge

As a cross examiner you are entitled to reasonably responsive answers from a witness. It is the judge's obligation to ensure not only that the witness respond to your questions, but also to "strike" any answers that are unresponsive. Thus, the ultimate solution to the problem of the impermissibly uncooperative witness is to seek the judge's intervention:

QUESTION: Your Honor, could you please instruct the witness to answer my question?

QUESTION: Your Honor, could you please direct the witness to answer that question yes or no?

QUESTION: I move to strike that answer as non-responsive to my question, and I request that the Court instruct the jury to disregard it.

There are a number of reasons, however, to be wary of seeking the judge's help in controlling your witness on cross examination.

First, early recourse to the judge may seem petty or picky. Just as lawyers do not object to every conceivably objectionable question, there is no reason to go running to the judge every time a witness fails to answer in precisely the manner that you expected. It looks bad, maybe even childish, to go looking for outside help when circumstances do not really call for it.

Moreover, many judges dislike interceding in cross examinations. They expect the lawyers to handle their own questioning, and they do not want to appear to take sides between a lawyer and a witness. Some judges, regrettably, have a nasty habit of not paying attention during jury trials, and they will be unable to tell whether your request is reasonable. For these reasons, a request for help from the judge is often met with something like "Proceed, counsel" or "Just ask another question."

Finally, never underestimate the possibility that the judge might disagree with you. You may think that the question can be answered "yes or no," and you might think that the witness was clearly non-responsive, but the judge might have an entirely different view of things. Imagine the difficulty of returning to a cross examination following this scenario:

LAWYER: Your Honor, will you please direct the witness to give me a "yes or no" answer?

COURT: I don't think that your question can be answered "yes or no." The witness is entitled to explain.

Or,

LAWYER: I move to strike the last answer as unresponsive to my question.

COURT: I think that the answer was perfectly responsive, given the nature of your question. Proceed, counsel.

How, then, can you be certain of obtaining the court's help when you ask for it? And in the process, how can you avoid appearing petty or ineffectual when you finally resort to the judge? The answer is to earn the right to seek outside assistance with the witness, by first attempting to reassert control by yourself. This method will not only validate your later attempt to invoke judicial authority, it will also have the added benefit of demonstrating to the witness the futility of any subsequent efforts to evade your questions.

If your own attempts to control the witness do not succeed, there will still be an opportunity to turn to the judge. By that time, of course, you will have demonstrated that you are not being petty and, with luck, you also will have ensured that you have the judge's full attention.

b. Reasserting control by yourself

The one thing that you can always do in cross examination is to ask more questions.

i. Pointed repetition

You can frequently reassert control over even a recalcitrant witness simply by repeating your original question, while using your voice or demeanor to emphasize the need for a direct answer:

QUESTION: You had a business meeting scheduled for 8:30 that same morning, didn't you?

ANSWER: It really wasn't a very important meeting. We were just going to exchange a few papers. One of my partners could easily have taken care of it, and, in fact, I had pretty much decided to skip it by the time I left home.

QUESTION: You DID have a business meeting scheduled for 8:30 that morning, didn't you?

Many witnesses will provide you with an answer at this point. Some will continue to resist. In these circumstances, an explanation from you may help:

QUESTION: You DID have a business meeting scheduled for 8:30 that morning, didn't you?

ANSWER: Like I said, it wasn't very important.

QUESTION: We will discuss importance in a little while. Right now I am asking you whether you had a meeting scheduled for 8:30 that morning.

If the witness refuses to answer at this point, he has obviously decided never to answer. There is little point to squabbling with the witness, although there are a few additional rhetorical flourishes that work from time to time:

QUESTION: Mr. Witness, surely you do not deny that you had a business meeting scheduled for 8:30 that morning?

In any event, assuming that the information is important to your case, you have by this time earned the right to go to the judge.

ii. Discipline

A witness who deflected your question can frequently be brought back under control if you restate the question firmly. If this doesn't work, there are a variety of ways to "discipline" the witness by pointing out the flaw in the deflection:

QUESTION: You know that traffic must stop for fire trucks, don't you?

ANSWER: There was no bell and no siren; I had no reason to stop.

QUESTION: But my question was this: You know that traffic must stop for fire trucks?

ANSWER: What I am trying to tell you is that there was no siren, so why should I stop?

QUESTION: Mr. Witness, you are 35 years old, aren't you?

ANSWER: Yes, I am.

QUESTION: You have been driving an automobile for over 15 years?

ANSWER: That seems right.

QUESTION: You took driver's education in high school?

ANSWER: I did.

QUESTION: You passed the written test to get your license?

ANSWER: Of course.

QUESTION: And you passed subsequent written tests for periodic renewals.

ANSWER: I did.

QUESTION: So can't you agree with me that the rules of the road require you to stop for fire trucks?

ANSWER: I guess so.

QUESTION: And you have known that for years, haven't you?

Note that the cross examiner in the above example earned the right to discipline the witness. The original question was short and factual; it did not invite an explanation. The witness was then given a second chance to answer. Only after the repeated deflection did the cross examiner set out to bring the witness to heel. The identical technique would have been considerably less useful under other circumstances. If the witness had not persisted in the refusal to answer, or if the question had been less precise, the lawyer's "disciplinary" line of questions might have appeared to be nasty or bullying.

There are a number of ways to "discipline" a witness. One of the surest is to confront the witness with his own previous words or actions. While impeachment through the use of prior statements is covered in a later chapter,[20] the following is a short example of using the witness's own prior actions to reassert control:

QUESTION: You know that traffic must stop for fire trucks, don't you?

ANSWER: There was no bell and no siren; I had no reason to stop.

QUESTION: Well, you did eventually hit your brakes, didn't you?

ANSWER: Yes.

QUESTION: As soon as you saw the fire truck?

ANSWER: Yes.

QUESTION: And that was because you knew that traffic had to stop for fire trucks, isn't that right?

This technique involves the use of short, factual questions that combine to demonstrate the utter reasonableness of the original question. By painstakingly eliciting the logical basis for the inquiry you, in a sense, shame the witness into providing you with a direct answer.

---

20   *See* Chapter Four *infra* at p. 111.

More aggressive means are also available. A final method of reasserting control, short of seeking the court's assistance, is through the judicious use of what we might call semi-sarcasm. Sarcasm is always risky in the courtroom, especially for beginning lawyers, and it should be used only when the witness clearly deserves it. Save this approach for the truly evasive, partisan, or oily witness — the witness who has resisted your every well-moderated effort to extract a plain answer:

QUESTION: You left home at 8:10 that morning?

ANSWER: I guess so.

QUESTION: Well you know that you left home, don't you?

ANSWER: Yes.

QUESTION: And you testified earlier that you left at about 8:10 a.m., right?

ANSWER: Yes.

QUESTION: So it isn't a guess at all when I say that you left home at 8:10 on the morning of the accident?

Similarly,

QUESTION: It is an eight-mile drive to your office?

ANSWER: You could say that.

QUESTION: Is there a reason that you don't want to say that?

ANSWER: No.

QUESTION: So it is eight miles to your office?

Or,

QUESTION: You had a business meeting that morning?

ANSWER: It depends on what you mean by business.

QUESTION: You were wearing your jacket and tie, weren't you?

ANSWER: Yes.

QUESTION: You weren't going golfing at 8:30 that morning?

ANSWER: No.

QUESTION: You were headed toward your office?

ANSWER: Yes.

QUESTION: Toward your place of business, right?

And finally,

QUESTION: It was important that you be on time?

ANSWER: Don't you try to be on time for your meetings?

QUESTION: Unfortunately, the rules of evidence do not allow me to answer your questions, but I would like you to answer mine. You don't have a problem with that, do you?

ANSWER: No.

QUESTION: Good. You do try to be on time for your business meetings, don't you?

Semi-sarcasm, as illustrated above, is a questioning technique that is aimed at exposing the groundless obstinacy of the witness's answers. It is called "semi-sarcasm" precisely because its goal is not to demonstrate the lawyer's superior wit and intelligence, but rather to underline the witness's unreasonable lack of cooperation. Such sarcasm comes more easily to some lawyers than to others. Some judges and juries receive it well, others do not. The decision to use semi-sarcasm is a personal one, with one near-universal requirement. You can only use this technique on a witness who truly deserves it.

VI. ETHICS OF CROSS EXAMINATION

While lawyers generally consider cross examination to be an "engine" of truth-seeking, we are often criticized for using cross as a device for distortion and obfuscation. And in truth, like all powerful rhetorical tools, cross examination can be used to mislead and deceive. Accordingly, certain ethical principles have developed that circumscribe a lawyer's use of cross examination.

A. Basis for Questioning

1. Factual Basis

Many cross examinations contain inherent assertions of fact. Indeed, many of the best cross examination questions are strictly "propositional." Consider these examples from the fire engine case:

QUESTION: You did not have your brakes fixed, did you?

QUESTION: You slept on the ground while on your camping trip, correct?

QUESTION: You were on your way to an important business meeting, right?

QUESTION: You have continued to work as a guide at the Art Institute, haven't you?

Each question contains a single fact that counsel is urging to be true. The danger arises that counsel might also propose baseless or knowingly false points. The witness, of course, can deny any untrue assertions, but the denials are likely to ring hollow in the face of an attorney's presumably superior persuasive skills. Enormous damage can be done by false or groundless accusations. Imagine the impact of this examination:

QUESTION: Isn't it true that you had been drinking on the morning of the accident?

ANSWER: No, not at all.

QUESTION: Didn't you arrive at Mayer's Bar at 7:00 a.m.?

ANSWER: Certainly not.

QUESTION: Well, the truth is that you ran up an $8.00 tab that morning, didn't you?

ANSWER: No.

QUESTION: $8.00 would cover at least four drinks, right?

ANSWER: I'm telling you that I wasn't drinking.

The precision of the details in the questions appears to add verity to the cross examination, while the denials can be made to appear superficial. The cross examiner's ability to control the interchange puts the witness at an extreme disadvantage. This cross examination raises no problems if the witness was indeed drinking at Mayer's Bar, but it is intolerable if the charge is untrue.

To protect against the unscrupulous use of cross examination, it is required that every question have a "good faith" basis in fact.[21] Counsel is not free to make up assertions, or even to fish for possibly incriminating material. Rather, as a predicate to any "propositional" question, counsel must be aware of specific facts that support the allegation.

2. Legal Basis

The "good faith basis" for a cross examination question cannot be comprised solely of inadmissible evidence. Counsel cannot allude to any matter "that will not

---

21 A lawyer shall not "in trial, allude to any matter that the lawyer does not reasonably believe is relevant or that will not be supported by admissible evidence." Rule 3.4(e), Model Rules of Professional Conduct.

be supported by admissible evidence."[22] Thus, a good faith basis cannot be provided by rumors, uncorroborated hearsay, or pure speculation.

Allegations lacking a basis in admissible evidence may lead to a sustained objection, an admonition by the court, or even a mistrial. Moreover, many jurisdictions require counsel to offer admissible extrinsic evidence to "prove up" certain assertions made on cross examination, such as past conviction of a felony.

B.   Assertions of Personal Knowledge

It is unethical to "assert personal knowledge of facts in issue . . . or state a personal opinion as to the justness of a cause, the credibility of a witness, the culpability of a civil litigant or the guilt or innocence of an accused."[23] While this problem most frequently occurs during final argument,[24] it also arises during cross examination.

Cross examination questions often take a "Do you know?" or "Didn't you tell me?" format. Both types of question are improper, because they put the lawyer's own credibility in issue. "Do you know?" questions suggest that the lawyer is aware of true facts which, while not appearing on the record, contradict the witness's testimony. "Didn't you tell me?" questions argue that the witness and the lawyer had a conversation, and that the lawyer's version is more believable. In either case, the questions amount to an assertion of personal knowledge.[25]

C.   Derogatory Questions

It is unethical to ask questions that are intended solely to harass, degrade, or humiliate a witness, or to discourage him from testifying.

D.   Discrediting a Truthful Witness

To what extent may cross examination be used to discredit the testimony of a witness whom counsel knows to be telling the truth?

The answer to this question is reasonably straightforward in criminal cases. Defense counsel is entitled to insist that the government prove its case through evidence that is persuasive beyond a reasonable doubt. Thus, witnesses must not

---

22   *Id.*

23   Rule 3.4(e), Model Rules of Professional Conduct.

24   *See* Chapter Ten, Section VI A(1), *infra* at p. 432.

25   "Do you know?" questions may be permissible in limited circumstances. A witness claiming compendious knowledge, for example, could legitimately be questioned as to her lack of certain information. Similarly, a character witness could be questioned concerning unknown facts about a witness's reputation. In each situation, however, the question must have a good faith basis.

only be truthful, they must also be convincing to the required degree of certainty. A discrediting cross is simply an additional safeguard.

Conversely, a criminal prosecutor has a public duty to avoid conviction of the innocent. A truthful witness, therefore, should not be discredited simply for the sake of the exercise.

The rule is less certain in civil cases. It is clear, however, that a witness cannot be degraded or debased simply to cast doubt on otherwise unchallenged testimony. On the other hand, true factual information may be used to undermine the credibility of a witness whose testimony is legitimately controverted.

E.   Misusing Evidence

The same rules apply on cross as on direct with regard to misusing evidence that has been admitted for a limited purpose.[26]

---

26   *See* Chapter Two, Section VI B, *supra* at p. 47.

Part Three
Making the Record

—CHAPTER FOUR—
Impeachment

I. INTRODUCTION
A. Categories of Impeachment

While much cross examination[1] consists of demonstrating inaccuracies or rebutting a witness's testimony, impeachment is intended actually to discredit the witness as a reliable source of information. Successful impeachment renders the witness less worthy of belief, as opposed to merely unobservant, mistaken, or otherwise subject to contradiction. There are three basic categories of witness impeachment, each of which provides a reason to place less credence in a witness's testimony.

Perhaps the most common method of impeachment is the use of a prior inconsistent statement, action, or omission. The elicitation of a prior inconsistency demonstrates that the witness's current testimony is at odds with her own previous statements or actions. In essence, this examination says, "Do not believe this witness because her story has changed."

A second method of impeachment is the use of character, or "characteristic" evidence. This form of impeachment is aimed at demonstrating that the witness possesses some inherent trait or characteristic, unrelated to the case at hand, that renders the testimony less credible. Perhaps the witness is a convicted felon or suffers a memory defect. This examination says, "This witness is not trustworthy on any matter, because of who he is."

---

1   It was once considered improper for a lawyer to "impeach one's own witness" on the theory that a lawyer who called a witness to the stand for direct examination had "vouched" for the witness's credibility. The techniques of impeachment, therefore, arose in the context of cross examination. The rule against impeaching your own witness has been abolished. *See* Rule 607, Federal Rules of Evidence. As a technical matter, impeachment may now occur during either direct or cross examination. As a practical matter, however, impeachment during direct examination is unusual. This chapter, therefore, will treat impeachment as a device to be used on cross examination.

Finally, "case data" impeachment involves the establishment of facts that make the witness less reliable, although only within the context of the case at trial. The witness might have a financial interest in the outcome of the case, or might be prejudiced against one of the parties. In other words, "Give less weight to the witness because of her relationship to the case."

B. Perfection of Impeachment

Impeachment generally begins and ends during cross examination. When a witness concedes the existence of the impeaching information, nothing further needs be done and the cross examiner may go on to other matters. If, however, the witness denies the truth of the impeaching matter, the cross examiner may be required to perfect or complete the impeachment by offering extrinsic evidence,[2] or evidence that is adduced through the testimony of someone other than the subject of the impeachment. This can occur whether the original impeachment was based upon prior inconsistency, character, or case data. For example:

QUESTION: Didn't you tell the investigating police officer that the traffic light was green for the southbound traffic?

ANSWER: No, I did not.

Or,

QUESTION: Isn't it true that you were once convicted of forgery?

ANSWER: That is not true.

Or,

QUESTION: You are a substantial investor in the company that is the defendant in this case, correct?

ANSWER: I'm sorry, you are incorrect.

In each of these circumstances the impeachment can be perfected only by calling an additional witness or offering other affirmative evidence that proves the existence of the impeaching fact. In the above examples, the extrinsic evidence might take the form of testimony from the investigating police officer, a certified

---

2   In a majority of jurisdictions the cross examiner is required to be able to complete impeachment in at least some situations, most notably the assertion that the witness has been convicted of a felony. In some jurisdictions it is not necessary to perfect an impeachment, even where the witness has denied the truth of the cross examiner's questions, so long as there was a "good faith basis" for the original inquiry. Even where not required, the cross examiner is usually allowed to perfect the impeachment.

copy of the forgery conviction, or the introduction of business records from the defendant corporation.

Thus, impeachment generally should not be attempted unless a witness or other evidence is reasonably available to complete the impeachment. Moreover, the perfecting evidence must be independently admissible; there are no special rules of evidence for the completion of impeachment. You cannot perfect impeachment through the use of evidence that is hearsay, improperly authenticated, speculative, lacking in foundation or otherwise inadmissible.

The consequence of failing to complete an attempted impeachment can be severe. Depending upon the nature of the alleged impeaching fact, the result can range from a stern admonition and instruction from the judge, to an order striking some or all of the cross examination, and perhaps all the way to a mistrial or reversal on appeal. Even in circumstances that do not require impeachment to be perfected, failing to do so can be damaging to your case. The witness's denial of your allegation will go unrebutted, and opposing counsel will no doubt underscore that fact during final argument.

C. Tactical Considerations

Impeachment is a powerful tool. Unlike "standard" cross examination, which may rely on unspoken premises and subtle misdirection, there can be no mistaking or hiding the intended impact of impeachment. All three kinds of impeachment are inherently confrontational. They challenge the witness's believability, perhaps even her veracity. For this reason, it is best to use the techniques of impeachment sparingly, both to preserve the potency of the method and to avoid crying wolf over unimportant details.

1. Impeach the Witness Only on Significant Matters

It is important to avoid impeaching witnesses on irrelevant, trivial, or petty inconsistencies. The process of impeachment, particularly through the use of prior inconsistency, is generally so confrontational that there is a great risk of creating an annoying dissonance between expectation and reward. If the "punch line" fails to justify the build-up, the result can be embarrassing or damaging to your case. Imagine this scenario, for example, in the trial of the fire truck case that we have been using throughout; the plaintiff is being cross examined:

QUESTION: You testified on direct examination that you heard the siren, saw the flashing lights, and then slowed down, correct?

ANSWER: Correct.

QUESTION: You have given an earlier statement?

ANSWER: Why, yes I did.

QUESTION: You spoke to the investigating police officer?

ANSWER: That is right.

QUESTION: You knew that you had to be truthful with the police officer?

ANSWER: Of course.

QUESTION: Didn't your earlier statement say, "I saw the flashing lights, then I heard the siren, which caused me to slow down at once?"

ANSWER: Yes, I believe that is what I said.

Although the plaintiff has, in some technical sense, been impeached, the inconsistency involved is so slight as to be inconsequential. What difference does it make whether the witness first heard the siren or saw the lights? The essential point — that the fire truck was using its warning signals and that traffic slowed down — remains completely intact. The cross examiner, however, has squandered valuable capital by confronting the witness, wasting time, and emerging with nothing to show for those efforts. A jury's near-certain response would be, "Is that all you can do?" A judge's response would be even less charitable.

This principle of "significance" does not apply only to prior inconsistencies. Other forms of impeachment also should only be used on important matters. Charges of prejudice or bias, for instance, should only be made when they are truly likely to make a difference to the way in which the witness will be perceived.

2. Impeach the Witness Only on True Inconsistencies

The purpose of impeachment through the use of a prior inconsistency is to show that the witness has made contradictory statements. The technique works only when the two statements cannot both be true. If the two statements can be harmonized, explained, or rationalized, the impeachment will fail. For example:

QUESTION: You testified on direct that the bank robbers drove away in a blue car, correct?

ANSWER: Yes.

QUESTION: You gave a statement to the police right after the robbery, didn't you?

ANSWER: Yes, I did.

QUESTION: You told the police that the robbers drove off in a turquoise car, didn't you?

Although different words were used, the two statements are not inconsistent. It does not detract from the witness's credibility that she once referred to the car as turquoise, and that she later called it blue.

3. Impeach a Witness Only When Success Is Likely

Failed impeachment can be disastrous. A lawyer who begins an assault that cannot be completed will look ineffective at best and foolishly overbearing at worst.

Impeachment can succeed only when the source of the impeachment is readily available. For that reason the outline of your cross examination must be indexed to the sources of your information, including all of the witness's prior statements. Do not begin your impeachment until you have the prior statement firmly in hand, and have located the precise page and line that you intend to use to contradict the current testimony.

Do not rely on your memory. Even your clear recollection that the witness's deposition was diametrically contrary to her new testimony will have a way of betraying you when you turn to the transcript and read her exact words. It makes much more sense to pause and review your notes before attempting to impeach a witness than it does to have to stop in the middle when you cannot find the right material.

4. Do Not Impeach Favorable Information

Impeachment is not like mountain climbing. It should not be undertaken simply because it is there. The purpose of impeachment is to cast doubt on the credibility of some or all of a witness's testimony. There is nothing to be gained by casting doubt on testimony that was helpful to your own case. Thus, even if an opposing witness has given a prior inconsistent statement, it should not be used to impeach favorable trial testimony.

Assume that the defendant in the fire engine case testified at trial that immediately after the accident he ran to a telephone booth to call his office. In contrast, at deposition he testified that his first action was to check the damage to his BMW, and that he went to the telephone booth only after making sure that the plaintiff was not seriously injured.

The two statements are clearly inconsistent, and the witness is technically open to impeachment. The trial testimony, however, is actually more helpful to the cross examiner's case. Recall the possible plaintiff's theme that the defendant was "too busy to be careful." The defendant's admission that his first thought was to telephone his office fits beautifully into that theme. While his hard-heartedness in checking on his BMW before looking into the plaintiff's injuries might also be useful to the cross examiner's case, this information does not go directly to any theory of liability or damages. The cross examiner therefore will not want to undercut the trial testimony (about the immediate phone call) by impeaching it with the deposition transcript (about checking on his BMW).

5. Consider the "Rule of Completeness"

The "Rule of Completeness" provides that once a witness has been impeached from a prior inconsistent statement, opposing counsel may request the immediate reading of additional, explanatory portions of the same statement. Under the Federal Rules of Evidence, for example, the adverse party may introduce any other part of the statement "which ought in fairness to be considered contemporaneously with it."[3]

Thus, even a true gem of an impeaching statement may be immediately undercut if some other part of the impeaching document explains or negates the apparent contradiction. Assume that the following impeachment of the plaintiff has taken place in our fire truck case:[4]

QUESTION: You testified on direct examination that as a result of the accident you are no longer able to ride your bicycle, correct?

ANSWER: Correct.

QUESTION: On deposition, however, didn't you testify as follows: "Just last week I rode my bicycle over four miles to the Botanic Garden."?

ANSWER: Yes, I did say that.

The above impeachment obviously hurts the plaintiff's claim for damages.

The effectiveness of the impeachment is undercut, if not entirely destroyed, however, if the following statement from the same deposition is immediately admitted into evidence: "I try to do everything I can to minimize the limitations of my injury. Sometimes I try too hard. That bike trip to the Botanic Garden put me back in the hospital for two days; I'll never try that again."

There is little to gain and much to lose by impeaching a witness only to see the impeachment come completely undone within a matter of minutes. Always scour the impeaching document for other information "which ought in fairness to be considered contemporaneously" with the impeachment.

---

3   *See* Rule 106, Federal Rules of Evidence.

4   The form of the impeachment has been truncated so as to emphasize the point about the Rule of Completeness.

6. Consider Refreshing the Witness's Recollection

Not every gap or variation in a witness's testimony is the result of an intentional change. Witnesses often become confused or forgetful. A witness may have testified inconsistently with her prior statements quite innocently or inadvertently. In these circumstances it will often be possible to use the prior statement to refresh the witness's recollection, rather than to impeach her credibility. The technique for refreshing recollection is the same on cross examination as it is on direct.[5] In many courts, however, a cross examiner will be allowed to refresh a witness's recollection without first being required to establish that the witness's memory has been exhausted. For example:

QUESTION: You testified on direct examination that you went directly from the scene of the accident to the hospital.

ANSWER: That is right.

QUESTION: You also testified to these matters when your deposition was taken, didn't you?

ANSWER: I am sure that I did.

QUESTION: Please look at page 166 of your deposition, which I am now handing to you, and tell me when you have finished reading it.

ANSWER: I am done.

QUESTION: Does that refresh your recollection as to whether you did anything before going to the hospital?

ANSWER: Yes it does.

QUESTION: In fact, you went to the telephone and called your office first, didn't you?

ANSWER: Yes I did.

The strict requirements for refreshing recollection are usually somewhat relaxed on cross examination because the cross examiner cannot expect much cooperation from the witness. It is one thing on direct examination to refresh the recollection of a witness who admits to a memory lapse, but it is quite another on cross examination to refresh the memory of a witness who has omitted some fact

---

5   See Chapter Two, Section II E, *supra* at p. 19.

without realizing it. Judges therefore tend to leniency, and opposing counsel often abstain from objecting, if only to avoid the unpleasant necessity of impeachment.

D. Evidentiary Considerations

Prior inconsistent statements that were given under oath are admissible as substantive evidence; they can be used to prove the truth of the original statement.[6] Prior inconsistent statements that were not given under oath are generally admissible for the limited purpose of impeachment; they can be used only to reflect on the credibility of the witness.[7]

Under traditional theories of evidence, prior out-of-court statements of witnesses are hearsay, and therefore not admissible as substantive evidence. They are admissible, however, as impeachment under the theory that the offer is intended only to reflect on the witness's credibility, and not actually as proof of the facts contained in the statement. Consider the following example:

QUESTION: You testified on direct examination that the southbound traffic had the green light?

ANSWER: Yes.

QUESTION: In your statement to the police officer, didn't you say that the southbound traffic had a red light?

ANSWER: I did.

The witness's earlier statement to the police officer was obviously made out of court. It therefore would be hearsay if offered to prove that the light actually was red, since that would go to the "truth of the matter asserted."[8] The statement is not hearsay, however, if it is only offered to show that the witness has changed her testimony. Under those circumstances, the statement is not offered to prove that the light was red, but only that the witness is an unreliable source for the color of the light.

---

6   Rule 801(d)(1)(A), Federal Rules of Evidence.

7   Prior inconsistent statements that were not given under oath may occasionally be used as substantive evidence if they qualify for some exception to the hearsay rule. For example, the prior statement of a party is admissible as a party admission whether or not it was made under oath. *See* Rule 801(d)(2), Federal Rules of Evidence. The same would be true of declarations against interest, excited utterances, or present sense impressions. Rule 803, Federal Rules of Evidence.

8   *See* Rule 801(c), Federal Rules of Evidence.

The traditional rule has been altered somewhat by modern practice. Under the Federal Rules of Evidence a prior inconsistent statement is not considered hearsay if it was originally made under oath at a trial, hearing, other proceeding, or in a deposition.[9] Thus, if the witness in the example above had made the earlier statement at her deposition, rather than to a police officer, it would then be admissible as substantive proof that the light was indeed red.

What is the importance of this distinction? Isn't the difference between substantive evidence and impeaching evidence simply too fine for most juries to comprehend? It is true that judges' limiting instructions are frequently ignored or misunderstood. In some situations, however, it may make a difference if the judge instructs the jury to "consider the witness's prior statement only as impeachment, and not as substantive evidence."

More frequently, the difference between impeaching and substantive evidence will be relevant to the determination of issues of law. For example, only substantive evidence should be considered in deciding whether the plaintiff has made out a prima facie case. Similarly, a reviewing court should not consider strictly impeaching evidence in deciding whether a verdict was supported by sufficient evidence. Finally, a court may restrict a lawyer's final argument if evidence that was admitted for a limited purpose is sought to be used as substantive proof.

In consequence, it is usually preferable to impeach a witness through the use of a sworn statement if one is available, since that approach allows the greatest latitude for later use of the evidence.

II.   PRIOR INCONSISTENT STATEMENTS

One of the most dramatic aspects of any trial is the confrontation of a witness with his own prior inconsistent statement. This is the moment that cross examiners live for—the opportunity to show that the witness's current testimony is contradicted by her own earlier words. Properly conducted, this form of impeachment is not only effective on cross examination, it also can provide extremely fruitful final argument:

> "Ladies and Gentlemen, Mr. Kaye is simply unworthy of belief. He couldn't even keep his story straight himself. Right after the accident, he told Officer Berkeley that the light was red. By the time of trial it had mysteriously changed to green. The best you can say about Mr. Kaye is that he doesn't know what color the light was."

---

9   Rule 801(d)(1)(A), Federal Rules of Evidence.

Prior inconsistent statements damage a witness's credibility because they demonstrate that the witness has changed his story. Depending upon the nature and seriousness of the change, the witness may be shown to be evasive, opportunistic, error-prone, or even lying. To accomplish any of these goals, of course, it is necessary that the prior statement be clearly inconsistent with the current testimony, and that it be directed to a subject of true significance to the case. Semi-inconsistencies concerning tangential matters will have little or no impact.[10]

There are three steps necessary to impeach a witness with a prior inconsistent statement: (1) recommit; (2) validate; and (3) confront. Each of the three steps will be treated in detail below. Before proceeding to consider the separate elements of impeachment, the following illustration, though somewhat truncated, will place the entire process in perspective.

Recommit:

QUESTION: Mr. Kaye, you testified during your direct examination that the traffic light was green for the southbound traffic.

ANSWER: That is right.

Validate:

QUESTION: Immediately after the accident you spoke to Officer Berkeley?

ANSWER: I did.

QUESTION: You understood that it was important to tell Officer Berkeley exactly what you saw?

ANSWER: Yes.

QUESTION: You spoke to the police officer on the very day of the accident?

ANSWER: Correct.

QUESTION: So obviously the events were fresh in your mind?

ANSWER: Yes.

QUESTION: Since then over a year has gone by?

ANSWER: Yes.

---

10   For discussion of tactical considerations in impeachment, see Section I C, *supra* at p. 113.

QUESTION: After you spoke to Officer Berkeley, she asked you to sign a statement, didn't she?

ANSWER: Yes, she did.

QUESTION: You read and signed the statement, didn't you?

ANSWER: Yes.

Confront:

QUESTION: Please look at Exhibit Number 39 for identification, and tell me if you recognize your signature at the bottom of the page.

ANSWER: I do.

QUESTION: Isn't this the statement that you signed for Officer Berkeley?

ANSWER: It is.

QUESTION: Please read it through and tell me when you have finished.

ANSWER: I am finished.

QUESTION: Doesn't your statement say the following: "At the time of the accident, the traffic light was red for the southbound traffic."

ANSWER: Yes, that is what the statement says.

QUESTION: That is the statement that you signed for Officer Berkeley?

ANSWER: Yes.

This illustration contains all of the elements of impeachment with a prior inconsistent statement. We will discuss each of those elements in considerably more detail below.

A. The Process of Impeachment

1. Recommit the Witness

The first step in impeaching a witness with a prior inconsistent statement is to recommit the witness to his current testimony:

QUESTION: Mr. Kaye, you testified on direct examination that the light was green for the southbound traffic, correct?

The purpose of recommitting the witness is to underscore the gulf between the current testimony and the prior statement. There is no evidentiary requirement that the witness be allowed to repeat the direct testimony. On the other hand, it is difficult to imagine how the two statements could be effectively contrasted without restating the testimony that is about to be impeached.

There are two ways to recommit a witness to the about-to-be-impeached testimony. One is traditional and one is elegant.

a. The traditional way

The traditional method of recommittal is to restate the witness's direct testimony, and to ask the witness to reaffirm it. Thus, the witness's current statement is made absolutely clear, so that there can be no doubt about its content when it is eventually impeached. In order to use this method you must restate the direct testimony as accurately as possible. Paraphrases or summaries may result in a series of arguments or quibbles with the witness that can detract from the impeachment.

It is equally important, however, for the cross examiner to avoid giving the witness an unbridled opportunity simply to repeat the direct testimony. It is therefore crucial to use short, leading questions during this phase of recommittal. Do not, as in the example that follows, ask a witness to repeat his direct testimony:

QUESTION: Mr. Kaye, what color did you say that the light was for the southbound traffic?

Instead, tell the witness what his previous testimony was:

QUESTION: Mr. Kaye, you testified on direct examination that the light was green for the southbound traffic.

The difference between these two approaches is that the leading question retains control over the witness and prevents the witness from embellishing upon or improving his answer. Moreover, the second approach allows you to use vocal inflection and facial expression to inject a note of doubt as to the accuracy of the testimony that you are repeating. When you ask a witness to repeat his testimony, there is an inevitable suggestion that the testimony is important. On the other hand, when the cross examiner repeats the testimony, it is possible to inject a note of skepticism that will convey just the right measure of doubt.

Depending upon the severity of the impending impeachment, it may be possible to ask the question in a form that is doubtful indeed:

QUESTION: Mr. Kaye, on direct examination you told defendant's counsel that the light was green for the southbound traffic?

Or in extreme cases,

QUESTION: Mr. Kaye, the story that you told on direct examination was, and I quote, that "the light was green for the southbound traffic."

The traditional approach has the benefit of predictability and recognizability. By quoting the direct examination you are almost assured that the witness will agree with you, and thereby allow you to proceed with the impeachment. Furthermore, since impeachment has been accomplished in this manner for generations, virtually all judges will recognize what you are doing, and this alone may obviate any lurking evidentiary problems.

The inescapable drawback to the traditional approach is that, by definition, it restates the witness's direct testimony. Furthermore, the repeated testimony will almost always be damaging, since you wouldn't bother impeaching it if it had not damaged your case. Sometimes the repetition can seem endless:

QUESTION: Mr. Kaye, you testified on direct examination that the light was green for the southbound traffic.

ANSWER: The light was definitely green for the southbound traffic.

QUESTION: And that was your testimony on direct examination?

ANSWER: Yes. The light was green for the southbound traffic.

Now the testimony has been repeated three times, although the cross examiner will only be allowed to impeach it once.

b. The elegant way

An elegant alternative to the traditional approach avoids this difficulty by rephrasing the direct examination in language that is beneficial to the cross examiner's own case. As we noted above, there is no strict rule of evidence that requires a cross examiner to repeat verbatim the witness's about-to-be-impeached testimony. The purpose of recommitment is only to focus attention on the inconsistency between the courtroom testimony and the prior statement. It is therefore possible to recommit the witness to the content of the current testimony without repeating it word for word. The content, in turn, can be phrased in a virtually unlimited number of ways.

Consider the simple traffic light example that was used in the previous section. The witness testified on direct examination that the light was green for the southbound traffic, but his statement to the police was just the opposite. It is your theory that the light was red for the southbound traffic. Rather than repeat the direct testimony, the cross examiner can recommit the witness as follows:

QUESTION: Mr. Kaye, the light was red for the southbound traffic, correct?

ANSWER: No, that is not true.

QUESTION: Mr. Kaye, I would like to show you the statement that you gave to Officer Berkeley.

You can now proceed to impeach the witness with his own prior statement.

This format for recommittal avoids repetition of the direct testimony. It also allows you to describe your own case in affirmative language: "Wasn't the light red for the southbound traffic?" Since your case rests on the proposition that the light was red for the southbound traffic, you profit from stating that affirmative fact as often as possible.

The impeachment that follows will not be directed at the witness's direct testimony that the light was green, but rather at his denial during cross examination that the light was red. The effect, of course, will be the same.

There is a further benefit to the elegant method of recommitment. It creates an outside opportunity that the witness will agree with you. Should lightning strike and the witness agree that the light was indeed red, impeachment will be unnecessary. What's more, the witness's revised testimony as to the color of the light will be admissible as substantive evidence, not merely as impeachment.[11]

Even in the far more likely situation, where the witness does not agree to change his testimony, the elegant approach to recommitment can make it appear as though you expected the witness to agree. This, in turn, will give greater credence to your own case. There is little risk to this approach, since you will have the impeaching document firmly in hand.

There are two difficulties with the elegant approach. First, precise phrasing becomes extremely important, since you cannot rely simply on repeating the witness's own testimony. Counsel must find a way of restating the witness's earlier testimony that not only puts the cross examiner's case in an affirmative light but is also faithful to the direct examination. Finally, the witness's denial must be subject to immediate contradiction by the impeaching document. This is a far more daunting task, particularly when it arises unexpectedly in the heat of trial, than simply confronting a witness with his own earlier direct examination.

The second difficulty is one that always confronts an elegant technique. Judges may not recognize it. Lawyers and judges have been taught that repetition of the direct testimony is a necessary prelude to impeachment via prior inconsistent statement. We have seen that recommitment is really nothing more than a rhetorical technique that is intended to focus attention on the disparity between

---

11   *See* Section I D *supra* at p. 118.

the two statements. Many older practitioners, however, may tend to view traditional recommitment as a mandatory litany, or even as an evidentiary foundation.
With some judges this problem may be acute, since they will tend to allow the
familiar and to disallow what they do not recognize.

c. Deciding

The decision as to which form of recommitment to use will depend upon a
number of factors.

How complex is the impeachment? If the concept being impeached is subtle,
detailed, or complex, it may well be better to use the traditional method of
recommitment. Under these circumstances you will not want to risk an argument
with the witness, or forfeiting the understanding of the judge, so it may be best to
rely upon the witness's own words to set up the impeachment. Conversely, if the
concept being impeached is simple, and particularly if it can be easily restated
through the use of an antonym, there is little risk to employing the elegant method.

How impeachable were the witness's own words? A witness will occasionally
say something that is contrary to a prior statement, but without using words that
are directly contradictory. Perhaps the witness testified on deposition that the
defendant was her best friend, and then testified at trial that she "really didn't see
the defendant all that often." While the two statements are inconsistent, they are
not clearly contradictory. The deposition testimony is not really impeaching of the
trial testimony. Even though the two statements differ significantly in spirit,
repetition of the witness's direct examination cannot be used to set up an effective
impeachment. The elegant method of recommitment, however, addresses this
problem by rephrasing the direct testimony in affirmative, and therefore more easily
impeachable, form. The cross examiner can put the question directly to the witness:
"Isn't it true that you are the defendant's best friend?" If the witness admits the
relationship, then there will be no need for impeachment. If the witness denies the
relationship, she may then be impeached with the deposition transcript.

How often do you intend to impeach the witness? If the witness's testimony
was riddled with inconsistencies, and if you intend to impeach her concerning
more than one or two of them, the traditional method of recommitment has definite
advantages. By continually referring to the discordance between direct examination and prior statements, the repeated impeachment will have the effect of
undercutting the witness's entire direct examination. If the witness is only to be
impeached once or twice, then the elegant method may make the individual points
more effectively.

Will you attempt to refresh the witness's recollection? Occasionally it is
effective to use a prior inconsistent statement to refresh a witness's recollection,

rather than as impeachment.[12] Since this technique relies upon the premise of the witness's own forgetfulness, it is more likely to succeed when the traditional method of recommitment is employed. It will be far easier for a witness to agree that she forgot something during direct examination than it will be for her to admit that the denial contained in her immediately previous answer was a memory lapse.

2. Validate the Prior Statement

Once the witness has been recommitted, the next step in the impeachment is to validate the prior statement. The initial purpose of validation is to establish that the witness actually made the impeaching statement. Depending upon the circumstances of the case, further validation may be employed to accredit or demonstrate the accuracy of the earlier statement, as opposed to the witness's direct testimony.

a. Basic validation of written statements

The basic format for validating a witness's prior written statement is simply to establish when and how the earlier statement was made:

QUESTION:　Did you give a statement to Officer Berkeley immediately after the accident?

Or,

QUESTION:　Your deposition was taken at my office in March of last year, correct?

Although the basic process of validation is straightforward, care must still be taken to avoid ambiguity. For example, while lawyers understand what is meant by "giving" a statement, to some witnesses that may suggest a level of formality was not actually present. Remedy this problem by eliciting constituent facts:

QUESTION:　You spoke to Officer Berkeley immediately after the accident?

QUESTION:　Officer Berkeley was taking notes during your conversation?

QUESTION:　At the end of the conversation Officer Berkeley gave you a handwritten statement to read?

QUESTION:　That statement contained a description of what you had seen that day?

QUESTION:　You read the statement?

12　*See* Section I C(6), *supra* at p. 117.

QUESTION: After reading it, you signed it?

In the same fashion, the witness's deposition can be validated without the use of compound questions, and also in a manner that explains the deposition process to a jury:

QUESTION: You came to my office in March of last year?

QUESTION: There was a court reporter present?

QUESTION: Your attorney was also there?

QUESTION: You were placed under oath?

QUESTION: I asked questions and you gave answers, correct?

QUESTION: While you were being questioned, the court reporter was taking down your testimony?

QUESTION: Several weeks later you were given a copy of the transcript?

QUESTION: You read and signed the transcript?

The final step in basic validation is to show the written statement to the witness in order to have her confirm that it is indeed her own. As with all exhibits, the statement must be marked and shown to opposing counsel.[13] The validation may then proceed as follows:

QUESTION: Let me show you Exhibit 9; please tell me when you are done examining it.

QUESTION: Isn't this the statement that you signed after speaking to Officer Berkeley?

This method can be used to validate business documents, memoranda, signed depositions and interrogatories, letters, and other writings that carry the witness's signature. In the case of an unsigned deposition transcript,[14] other means of final validation will have to be used, such as:

---

13 Regarding the handling of exhibits, see Chapter Eight.

14 Depositions may be recorded by audio or videotape, in which case, even if later transcribed, they may not result in a signed transcript. Rule 30(b)(4), Federal Rules of Civil Procedure. In any event, the signing of a transcript can be, and frequently is, waived by the witness and the parties. Rule 30(e), Federal Rules of Civil Procedure. Finally, a witness may have failed, neglected, or refused to sign the transcript. In these circumstances the transcript generally can still be used as though it had been signed. *Id.*

QUESTION: At the end of the deposition you were asked if you wanted to read and sign it, correct?

QUESTION: And you stated that you would waive your right to read and sign the deposition transcript?

As we will see below, the witness will later be given an opportunity to admit or deny having given the specific deposition testimony being used for impeachment.

b. Accreditation of prior statements

The fact that a witness has made a prior inconsistent statement is impeaching, but it does not necessarily demonstrate that the witness's current testimony is false or inaccurate. After all, the earlier statement may have been erroneous and the direct testimony correct. It is therefore frequently advantageous to show that the first statement was made under circumstances that make it the more accurate of the two. Since the two statements are by definition mutually exclusive, there is a natural syllogism: if the earlier statement is true, then the current testimony must be wrong. Thus, the "accreditation" of the prior inconsistent statement can further detract from the witness's credibility.

Of course, no witness is likely to admit that her out-of-court statement was more accurate than her sworn testimony. It is therefore usually necessary to accredit the prior statement through the use of circumstantial evidence. Many indicia of accuracy can be attributed to the witness's earlier statement, including importance, duty, and proximity in time.

i.   Accreditation through importance

A witness's earlier statement can be accredited by showing that the witness had an important reason to be accurate when giving it. Assume that the victim of a robbery testified on direct examination that the robber was wearing a Chicago Bulls sweatshirt:

QUESTION: Immediately after the robbery you called the police?

QUESTION: Officer Elliott came to your home?

QUESTION: At that time, the robber was still at large?

QUESTION: Of course, you wanted to help Officer Elliott catch the criminal?

QUESTION: So it was very important that you give Officer Elliott a full and complete description?

QUESTION: A careless or incomplete description would make Officer Elliott's job harder, wouldn't it?

QUESTION: You certainly didn't want anyone else to be robbed?

QUESTION: So you gave Officer Elliott the best information that you could?

QUESTION: Didn't you tell Officer Elliott that the robber was wearing a Detroit Pistons shirt?

This form of validation establishes the witness's reason to be as accurate and truthful as possible at the time that the original description was given. The inconsistent later description will therefore be less credible.

Circumstantial importance can be shown in a wide variety of situations. Assume that the plaintiff in a contract case has testified on direct examination that he had agreed orally with the defendant that a large shipment of vegetables would be delivered no later than May 17:

QUESTION: Your company receives deliveries on its loading dock?

QUESTION: The loading dock is run by the dock supervisor?

QUESTION: The receipt of deliveries is very important to your company?

QUESTION: So the dock supervisor must have accurate information about which deliveries are expected?

QUESTION: Refrigeration space must be available for perishables?

QUESTION: Dock hands have to be there to unload the merchandise?

QUESTION: It is very important that you not take possession of the wrong goods, because that could result in liability?

QUESTION: That is why you always communicate with the dock supervisor in writing?

QUESTION: On May 11, you sent a memorandum to the dock supervisor, correct?

QUESTION: Doesn't that memorandum state, "Our next shipment of vegetables will arrive on May 19. Please be sure that sufficient refrigeration space is available"?

By establishing the importance of the written communication with the dock supervisor, the cross examiner has also established the greater likelihood that the goods really were expected on May 19, as opposed to May 17, as the witness claimed during direct examination.

The importance of some prior statements can only be demonstrated indirectly. Assume that the owner of a nearby gas station witnessed the accident in our fire truck case. The witness later signed a statement prepared by an insurance investigator[15] which stated that the fire engine was not sounding its siren. On direct examination, however, the witness testified that he heard a siren. Because the statement to the insurance investigator was of no special importance to the witness, the cross examiner will accredit it indirectly:

QUESTION: The gasoline business operates on a very small margin?

QUESTION: As owner, you are responsible for the bottom line?

QUESTION: Small mistakes can be costly?

QUESTION: You wouldn't want to write a check for the wrong amount?

QUESTION: You wouldn't want to sign an invoice that charged you too much?

QUESTION: You wouldn't want to accept a bill of lading for the wrong supplies?

QUESTION: So you have to be careful about what you sign?

Since the witness cannot realistically deny taking care with his signature, the signed statement to the investigator has been circumstantially accredited. The contrary testimony has therefore been discredited.

ii. Accreditation through duty

A prior statement can also be accredited by showing that the witness was under either a legal or business duty to be accurate. The most common example of a statement given under a legal duty is prior testimony, either at trial or deposition. Here is an example of accrediting deposition testimony:

QUESTION: You came to my office in March of last year?

QUESTION: There was a court reporter present?

QUESTION: Your attorney was also there?

---

15 The cross examiner will refer to the statement as having been taken only by an "investigator," taking pains to ensure that the testimony omits the word "insurance." A jury's knowledge of the existence of liability insurance is usually regarded as so devastating to the defendant's case that it is generally inadmissible. *See* Rule 411, Federal Rules of Evidence. In circumstances such as the instant example, most courts would grant a motion in limine excluding evidence that the investigator worked for an insurance company. Before the witness took the stand he would be instructed to omit the word "insurance" from his testimony. Regarding motions in limine, See Chapter Seven, Section II A(2), *infra* at p. 217.

QUESTION: You were sworn to tell the truth?

QUESTION: That was the same oath that you took here today?

QUESTION: You did tell the truth at your deposition?

QUESTION: You promised to give accurate answers?

QUESTION: You promised to tell me if there were any questions that you did not understand?

QUESTION: I asked questions and you gave answers, correct?

QUESTION: All of your answers at the deposition were under oath?

An even greater duty can often be shown if the prior testimony occurred in court:

QUESTION: You testified in an earlier hearing in this case?

QUESTION: That testimony took place right here in this courtroom?

QUESTION: Judge Fairchild was presiding, just as she is here today?

QUESTION: You were sworn to tell the truth?

QUESTION: You knew that Judge Fairchild wanted you to tell the truth?

Business duties may also be used to accredit a prior statement. Assume that a high school student has been charged with a crime, and that one of her teachers has testified that the student was present in his class at the time of the offense. The attendance report, however, has the student marked absent.

QUESTION: One of your jobs as a high school teacher is to take attendance?

QUESTION: You fill out an attendance form and send it down to the school office?

QUESTION: Your attendance figures are entered onto a master roll?

QUESTION: And that roll is eventually sent on to the superintendent's office?

QUESTION: Attendance figures are used to determine state funding for your school?

QUESTION: They are also used to determine allocation of resources?

QUESTION: The filing of attendance reports is considered in your own annual review?

QUESTION: The filing of attendance reports is part of your job description?

QUESTION: The filing of attendance reports is included in your union contract?

QUESTION: A teacher could be suspended for serious errors in his attendance reports, isn't that right?

This accreditation creates a circumstantial basis for preferring the information in the attendance report to the witness's later inconsistent testimony.

iii.   Accreditation through proximity in time

Because human memory inevitably fades, an earlier statement can be accredited because it was given closer in time to the events being described. This source of accreditation can be employed whether the impeaching material is a written statement, a deposition transcript, or a business document. Recall the robbery victim from the earlier example:

QUESTION: Immediately after the robbery you called the police?

QUESTION: Officer Elliott came to your home?

QUESTION: You spoke to Officer Elliott about the events of the robbery?

QUESTION: This was less than an hour after the robbery occurred?

QUESTION: The events of the robbery were obviously very fresh in your mind when you spoke to Officer Elliott?

QUESTION: And now over a year has gone by, correct?

The value of proximity in time can be emphasized by pointing out intervening events that may have caused the witness's memory to dim. In the same robbery case, assume that Officer Elliott testified on direct testimony that she arrested the defendant, who was wearing a Chicago Bulls sweatshirt. Her police report, however, states that the defendant was wearing a Detroit Pistons shirt:

QUESTION: Officer Elliott, immediately after you arrested the defendant you filled out a police report, correct?

QUESTION: You completed your report within an hour of making the arrest?

QUESTION: At the time that you wrote your report, the defendant was still in a holding cell?

QUESTION: The defendant was still available to you, if you had wanted to confirm any of the details of your report?

QUESTION: In any event, when you wrote the report, the events of the arrest were still fresh in your mind?

QUESTION: And now over a year has gone by, correct?

QUESTION: During the intervening year you have made at least 50 additional arrests?

QUESTION: You have had to write reports concerning each of those 50 arrests?

QUESTION: And you always try to write arrest reports as soon as you can, while the events are fresh in your mind, correct?

Proximity in time will only accredit a statement that was given significantly earlier than the trial testimony. You can scarcely use this method to accredit a deposition that was taken two weeks before trial.

iv. Evidentiary and ethical considerations

Recall that a prior inconsistent statement, unless given under oath, generally is not admissible as substantive evidence.[16] Thus, no matter how strongly accredited, an unsworn prior statement may only be used to detract from the credibility of the witness's current testimony.

Why, then, would a lawyer want to go to such lengths to accredit a statement by showing importance, duty, or proximity in time? Isn't the witness sufficiently impeached once it is established that a prior inconsistent statement was made?

The answer is that the accreditation of the first statement reflects negatively on the accuracy of the witness's testimony. If the statement to the investigator is accurate and the filling station owner did not hear a siren, then the witness's later testimony that there was a siren must necessarily be incorrect. On the other hand, if the circumstances surrounding the statement to the investigator are suggestive of unreliability, then the trial testimony may be credible after all. The strength of the original statement contributes directly to the weight of the impeachment.

On the other hand, the contents of the unsworn prior statement cannot be used to establish an affirmative fact. The prior statement may be used to discount the testimony of the gas station owner, but not to prove the actual absence of the

---

16 A prior inconsistent statement may be admissible as a party admission, or perhaps as a present sense impression or an excited utterance. If there is such an independent basis for the statement's admissibility, then it can be used as substantive evidence whether or not it was also offered as impeachment.

siren. Furthermore, the prior statement cannot be considered in ruling upon the sufficiency of the evidence for the purposes of a motion for a directed verdict.

Thus, on the basis of the impeachment counsel can argue:

The service station owner has testified that the fire engine was sounding its siren, but that testimony is not worthy of your belief. Just days after the accident, when the events were fresh in his mind, the witness gave a reliable statement that he heard no siren at all. The station owner is a careful man who reads what he signs. There is no reason on earth for him to have given such a statement if there actually had been a siren.

Counsel cannot argue:

We know that the fire engine was not sounding its siren. We know that because the service station owner said so in the statement that he gave just days after the accident. Let me read you the statement: "I saw the fire truck's lights, and I was surprised that there was no siren." This proves that the siren was not sounding.

A judge will often allow the use of a prior inconsistent statement subject to a limiting instruction that it can be considered only for the purpose of reflecting upon the witness's credibility. Even when such an instruction has not been given, the evidentiary limitation on the use of prior statements is often implicit in the circumstances of their admission into evidence.

Attorneys will often seek to avoid the impact of the "substantive evidence" rule by cleverly structuring their arguments to the jury in such a way as to intimate that an impeaching statement should be accepted as substantive proof. Nonetheless, if an out-of-court statement has been admitted for a limited purpose, it is improper to attempt to convert it into substantive proof through the "back door." Indeed, if the judge has actually instructed the jury not to consider a statement as substantive evidence, it is unethical to attempt to evade the judge's ruling in the hope that the court and opposing counsel will not notice.

3. Confront the Witness with the Prior Statement

The final stage of impeachment is to confront the witness with the prior statement. The purpose of this confrontation is to extract from the witness an admission that the earlier statement was indeed made; recall that it is the fact of the prior inconsistency that is admissible as impeachment. This confrontation need not be "confrontational." It is frequently sufficient merely to require the witness to admit making the impeaching statement, since most impeachment is based upon a witness's forgetfulness, confusion, or embellishment. Hostility or accusation should be reserved for those rare situations when the witness can be proven to be lying or acting out of some other ill motive.

To be effective, the confrontation must be accomplished in a clear and concise manner that leaves the witness no room for evasion or argument. The classic approach is simply to read the witness's own words. In confronting the gas station owner from the fire truck case, the cross examiner will end the impeachment by reading from the witness's statement:

QUESTION: Now just after the accident, didn't you tell the investigator, "I saw the fire truck's lights, and I was surprised that there was no siren?"

ANSWER: Yes, I did.

The confrontation can be enhanced, and counsel can be more assured of agreement from the witness, by directing the witness to read along from the impeaching statement. Give a copy to the witness and proceed:

QUESTION: Please take a look at Exhibit 14; isn't that the statement that you signed?

ANSWER: Yes, it is.

QUESTION: Now please look at the first sentence of the last paragraph, and read along with me. Doesn't your statement say, "I saw the fire truck's lights, and I was surprised that there was no siren?"

There are two cardinal rules to be followed in confronting a witness with a prior inconsistent statement: (1) Do not ask the witness to read the statement aloud, and (2) do not ask the witness to explain the inconsistency. Both of these rules are applications of basic principles of cross examination.

Asking a witness to read aloud from an impeaching document is the same as asking a wide-open, non-leading question; it surrenders control of the examination to the witness. The cross examiner has no way of knowing how clearly, loudly, or accurately the witness will read the statement. It is not unknown for a witness, either mistakenly or intentionally, to read from an entirely different portion of the document. It is nearly certain that the witness will not read with inflection that emphasizes the inconsistency.

Impeachment will be more effective when the cross examiner reads the impeaching matter in a loud, clear, contrasting tone of voice. While some attorneys believe that they can make a dramatic point by eliciting the words from the witness's own mouth, for most lawyers the risk of this approach will far outweigh the possible gain.

An even riskier way to lose control of the examination is to ask the witness to explain the inconsistency between a prior statement and the trial testimony. There is almost never a reason to ask a witness to explain something on cross examination, and the middle of impeachment is no time to experiment with exceptions to this rule. At best the witness will take the opportunity to muddle the clarity of the impeachment; at worst the witness will launch into a facile explanation that undercuts the entire line of examination. A variety of questions might function as invitations to explain. Do not ask a witness to agree that the two statements are inconsistent or different. Except in unusual circumstances, do not ask a witness to concede that she has "changed her story." Questions of this sort are likely only to produce argument, and argument is likely to engender explanation.

Properly conducted, each line of impeachment will conclude on a lawyer's highlight. You will read the impeaching statement in a manner that underscores the inconsistency between the witness's own previous words and the testimony just given in court. There will be no mistaking the implication, and the witness will necessarily concede that the prior statement indeed was given.

4. Special Cases

a. The denying witness

Some witnesses may deny some or all of the predicates to impeachment. They may refuse to reconfirm their own direct testimony, they may resist validating the circumstances of the impeaching statement, or they may deny ever having made the prior statement. Most of these difficulties can be dealt with through the use of basic cross examination principles.

The simplest problem is the witness who refuses to reaffirm the direct testimony. The easy remedy is to have the court reporter read back the original testimony, and then to re-put the question to the witness. In any but the shortest trial, however, it may take the court reporter some time to find the precise place in the transcript where the testimony can be found. Indeed, if the testimony to be impeached occurred on an earlier day of the trial, the court reporter may have changed. Unfortunately, not every trial judge will have the patience to wait while the exact testimony is located.[17]

There are a number of solutions to this problem. The first solution is to avoid the problem entirely by making sure that your notes contain a word-for-word rendition of the testimony that you intend to impeach. That will make it more difficult for the witness to deny your accuracy, and it will also make the judge and

---

17 This problem is obviated if counsel has been able to afford the purchase of "daily copy" of the transcript. Testimony likely to be impeached can be marked by the court reporter. In that case, you need only turn to the appropriate page and read the testimony to the witness. The court reporter's certification at the end of the transcript is sufficient proof of authenticity.

jury more inclined to view a denying witness as a quibbler. Second, as with any cross examination that runs into a compound detail or imbedded characterization,[18] you can break the question into its constituent parts. Imagine that the filling station owner in the fire truck case refused to reaffirm his direct testimony. Rather than take the time to search through the court reporter's notes, counsel could proceed as follows:

QUESTION: You testified on direct testimony that you clearly heard the siren of the fire engine, correct?

ANSWER: I do not believe that I said that.

QUESTION: You did testify about the fire engine?

ANSWER: Yes, I did.

QUESTION: Are you telling me that you did not hear the siren?

ANSWER: No.

QUESTION: All right, so your current testimony is that you did hear the siren?

ANSWER: That is right.

Note that use of the "elegant" method of recommitment would prevent this problem. If the cross examiner asked, "You did not hear a fire truck siren, did you?" the witness would either have to agree or disagree with the assertion. If the witness agrees, then there is no need to proceed with impeachment. If the witness denies the assertion, then that denial can be impeached without regard to his exact words on direct examination.

A witness who will not validate the circumstances of a prior statement can be handled in the same manner. Break the cross examination into small, constituent facts that the witness cannot deny. It is also effective to confront the witness with the negative implications of the denial. In the robbery scenario, for example, imagine that the witness will not agree to the importance of the description given to Officer Elliott:

QUESTION: Immediately after the robbery Officer Elliott came to your home?

ANSWER: Yes.

---

18   *See* Chapter Three, Section V D, *supra* at p. 89.

QUESTION: At that time, the robber was still at large?

ANSWER: I guess so.

QUESTION: Of course, you wanted to help Officer Elliott catch the criminal?

ANSWER: I just wanted to get my things back.

QUESTION: Well, the robber had your things, didn't he?

ANSWER: Yes.

QUESTION: So it was very important that you give Officer Elliott a full and complete description?

ANSWER: I just did the best I could under the circumstances.

QUESTION: You did the best you could to give a good description, right?

ANSWER: Yes.

QUESTION: You certainly wouldn't have intentionally misled Officer Elliott?

ANSWER: No, of course not.

QUESTION: And you wouldn't have left anything out?

ANSWER: Not on purpose.

QUESTION: You certainly didn't want anyone else to be robbed?

ANSWER: Of course not.

QUESTION: And you were the only one that Officer Elliott could talk to about a description?

ANSWER: Yes.

QUESTION: So you gave Officer Elliott the best information that you could, didn't you?

ANSWER: I did.

Since the true circumstances of the statement contribute to its validity, the witness cannot avoid supplying the cross examiner with the accrediting information.

Finally, some witnesses will disclaim ever having made the impeaching statement:

QUESTION: Didn't you tell Officer Elliott that the robber was wearing a Detroit Pistons shirt?

ANSWER: No, I never said that.

If the prior statement was in writing, the witness can then be confronted with the impeaching document. Further denial will lead to the admission of the impeaching document into evidence.[19]

A stickier problem arises when the prior statement was oral rather than written. Assume that the robbery victim spoke to Officer Elliott but did not sign a written statement. Even if Officer Elliott included verbatim notes in the police report, that document cannot be used to complete the impeachment because it is not a prior statement of the witness. Thus Officer Elliott would have to be called to the stand and examined about the description that the witness gave orally during the investigation:

QUESTION: Didn't you interview the victim immediately after the robbery?

ANSWER: Yes.

QUESTION: And he told you that the robber was wearing a Detroit Pistons shirt?

ANSWER: Yes, he did.

Should Officer Elliott also deny the cross examiner's assertion, then the police report can be utilized either for impeachment or to refresh recollection.

b. The lying witness

Prior inconsistent statements are generally used to cast doubt on witnesses' credibility, but not to accuse them of outright falsehood. It is usually enough to argue that a witness has forgotten the facts or has exaggerated her testimony, without attempting to paint her as a liar. Viewed purely as a matter of persuasion, it is easier to get a jury to accept that a witness is in error than it is to establish that the witness is guilty of deliberate falsehood. The witness may have a tolerable explanation for the inconsistency, or she may have other redeeming personal qualities that can create juror sympathy if she is attacked too harshly.

Nonetheless, some witnesses are liars. Some of the liars can be exposed through the use of their own prior inconsistent statements. Some witnesses even admit having contradicted their testimony by lying in the past.

---

19   For a discussion of perfecting impeachment, see Section I B, *supra* at p. 112.

Lying witnesses can be confronted directly, since almost nothing will be more damaging to a witness's credibility than proof of past prevarication. Perhaps the most frequently encountered admitted liar is the criminal defendant who has become the government's witness against a codefendant:

QUESTION: You testified on direct that you participated in the crime with Mr. Snyder?

ANSWER: I did.

QUESTION: You were arrested for that crime on December 19?

ANSWER: Yes, I was.

QUESTION: Right after your arrest you were questioned by Officer Bowman?

ANSWER: That is right.

QUESTION: You told Officer Bowman that you didn't know anything about the crime?

ANSWER: Yes, but that was not true.

QUESTION: You claim now that you were lying to Officer Bowman?

ANSWER: That is right.

QUESTION: You claim that you lied to Officer Bowman in order to keep yourself out of trouble?

ANSWER: Yes.

QUESTION: So you admit to being a liar?

ANSWER: I guess so.

Note that the cross examiner has taken care not to validate the witness's claim that the original denial was a lie. Defense counsel wants the original denial of involvement to be true, and the current testimony, which implicates the defendant, to be false. Thus, the cross examiner uses the prior inconsistent statement only to establish the witness's willingness to lie.

5. The Timing of Impeachment

To be used effectively, impeachment should fit into the overall strategy of your cross examination. If you intend to impeach a statement that was made during the witness's direct examination, you can place it anywhere in your own cross examination. Assuming that you have multiple points to make, at what stage of the cross examination should you make use of the prior inconsistent statement?

140

Impeachment

The basic principles for the organization of cross examination also apply to impeachment. It is usually advisable to maximize cooperation by beginning with inquiries that do not challenge or threaten the witness. For the same reason, initial questions are usually employed to build up your own case, as opposed to controverting the opposition's. These are not hard and fast rules, but they do form a sound framework within which to begin thinking about organization.

Since impeachment is often threatening or confrontational, it is usually advisable to save it until you have exhausted the favorable information that you intend to obtain from the witness. Only once the witness's cooperation is no longer important to your success should you move on to the past inconsistency.

There is such a thing as gentle impeachment, where a witness is reminded nicely that she made a contrary statement in the past. A close cousin to refreshing recollection, this form of impeachment can be used safely at almost any point in the cross examination.

A third approach to timing is to "discipline" the witness by conducting a good, strong impeachment at the very beginning of the cross examination. This technique should be used when you anticipate some difficulty in controlling the witness. By teaching the witness right from the start of the examination that you have the tools to compel the answers that you are entitled to, the witness's tendency to wander or argue may be minimized. You will sacrifice cooperation, but this is a witness from whom you had not expected cooperation in the first place.

It is crucial to consider impeachment within the context of the entire cross examination. If you are using topical organization, then you will probably want to impeach the witness on any relevant matter at some point during that aspect of the examination. In the fire truck case, for example, assume that the defense attorney is cross examining the filling station owner on his ability to see and hear the fire engine. Even though there is a fair amount of favorable information to be gathered on this issue, it also makes sense during this portion of the examination to impeach the witness with his earlier statement that he did not hear a siren. The clarity and continuity of the examination is more important than preserving the witness's good will. Of course, there is nothing to prevent you from saving the impeachment until the very end of your examination on the sound and appearance of the fire truck.

The technique of apposition is also relevant to impeachment. Recall from our discussion of the trial as a persuasive story that good stories are told about people who act for reasons. Impeachment, then, is most effective when the examination also provides a motive for the witness's inconsistency. Perhaps intervening facts led to a convenient memory lapse? Or perhaps the witness had an opportunity to confer with other interested parties? In suitable cases, the use of apposition can make it clear that the witness's inconsistency is due to something other than coincidence or mistake. The classic example of apposing impeachment to an intervening event is the cross examination of a criminal defendant who has agreed to testify for the government:

QUESTION: You testified on direct that you participated in the crime with Mr. Snyder?

ANSWER: Yes, I did.

QUESTION: You were arrested for that crime on December 19?

ANSWER: Yes, I was.

QUESTION: Right after your arrest you were questioned by Officer Bowman.

ANSWER: That is right.

QUESTION: You were then charged with the crime and you pleaded "not guilty."

ANSWER: Yes.

QUESTION: About three weeks later you had a conversation with the prosecutor, right?

ANSWER: Right.

QUESTION: The prosecutor offered you a plea bargain?

ANSWER: She did.

QUESTION: You agreed to plead guilty, and to testify against Mr. Snyder?

ANSWER: Yes.

QUESTION: And in exchange you would receive a sentence of probation?

ANSWER: Yes.

QUESTION: That was your deal?

ANSWER: I guess so.

QUESTION: But you spoke to Officer Bowman before you ever made any deals, right?

ANSWER: Yes.

QUESTION: And before you made any deals, you told Officer Bowman that you didn't know anything at all about the crime.

ANSWER: Yes.

QUESTION: It was only after your deal that you came into court to testify that you participated in the crime along with someone else.

ANSWER: That is right.

The cross examiner has not only shown that the witness told inconsistent stories, but has also established the witness's motive for making the change.

Although lacking the drama of a plea bargain, other examples of intervening events that might be tied into impeachment can include contact with an attorney or investigator, becoming a party to the lawsuit, changes of employment, discussions with family members, exposure to media accounts of the underlying events, or anything else that might, overtly or subtly, influence a witness to change his story.

Thus far, we have been discussing the impeachment of a witness's direct testimony. This situation allows counsel the maximum opportunity to plan and organize for the later impeachment. The need to impeach a witness, however, will frequently arise for the first time during cross examination. The cross examiner asks a reasonable question and, surprise, the witness provides a wholly unexpected answer. At that point there is no reason to wait or experiment with the niceties of fine organization. If you have the ammunition, impeach the witness on the spot.

B.   Ethical Concerns

Two primary ethical issues arise in the context of impeaching a witness through the use of a prior inconsistent statement. The first issue, attempting to use the statement for a purpose other than that for which it was admitted, was discussed at some length earlier.[20] It bears repeating.

It is unethical for a lawyer to "allude to any matter which the lawyer does not reasonably believe is . . . supported by admissible evidence."[21] Once a judge has ruled that certain evidence is admissible only for a limited purpose, it is inadmissible on those issues for which it has been excluded. In light of a limiting instruction, no lawyer can reasonably believe otherwise. Thus, it is unethical to "allude" to a purely impeaching statement as though it had been admitted as substantive evidence.[22]

---

20   *See* Section II A(2)(b)(iv) *supra* at p. 133.

21   Rule 3.4(e), Model Rules of Professional Conduct.

22   As has been noted previously, many prior statements may be admitted both for impeachment and as substantive evidence.

The second ethical issue in impeachment involves the admonition not to allow a witness to explain the inconsistency. Assuming that there may be a perfectly reasonable explanation for the discrepancy between two statements, is it ethical to prevent the witness from explaining?

The answer lies in the fact that it is not truly possible for a cross examiner to prevent a witness from providing an explanation. It will always be possible for opposing counsel to ask the witness to elaborate during redirect examination. No admissible evidence can ultimately be excluded as the result of cross examination tactics. Thus, the most that the cross examiner can accomplish will be to prevent the witness from explaining an inconsistency during cross examination. As an advocate, it is the cross examiner's task to present the evidence that is favorable to her client; the very purpose of redirect is to allow the other side to fill in gaps, remedy errors, and correct misperceptions. Thus, leaving potential explanations to redirect is perfectly permissible under the adversary system.

An explanation would carry more weight if it could be given in the midst of cross examination. It will necessarily seem somewhat hollow and apologetic occurring after the fact during redirect. That again is a consequence of advocacy. Recall that the witness had an opportunity during direct examination to offer the earlier statement and explain its seeming inconsistency with current testimony. Having passed up the chance to offer that testimony during direct examination, a witness can hardly complain that it is unethical for the cross examiner not to allow it during cross.

III. OTHER PRIOR INCONSISTENCIES

In addition to prior inconsistent statements, witnesses may also be impeached through the use of prior omissions or silence, as well as on the basis of prior inconsistent actions.

A. Impeachment by Omission or Silence

Impeachment by omission generally follows the same theory as impeachment with a prior inconsistent statement. The witness's current testimony is rendered less credible because when she told the same story earlier it did not contain facts that she now claims are true. In essence, the impeachment is saying, "Do not believe this witness, because she is adding facts to her story." In other words, "If those things are true, why didn't you say them before?"

To be impeaching, the witness's prior omission must be inconsistent with the current testimony. A prior omission is not impeaching, or even admissible, if it occurred in circumstances that do not render it incompatible with the witness's testimony from the stand. The following example, as should be obvious, does not constitute impeachment by omission:

QUESTION: You have testified today that the fire engine was sounding its siren, correct?

ANSWER: Yes.

QUESTION: You took a final examination in your Property class last week, didn't you?

ANSWER: Yes, I did.

QUESTION: Nowhere on your final exam did you write that you heard a fire engine's siren, did you?

The cross examination is wide of the mark because the omission is entirely consistent with the witness's testimony about the siren. There was no reason for the witness to include the facts of the accident on a final examination.

Impeachment by omission, then, rests upon the establishment of circumstances that create a dissonance between the witness's previous silence and the story that is now being told. The stronger the dissonance, the more effective the impeachment.

What circumstances create the necessary discontinuity between omission and testimony? We can begin by looking at opportunity, duty, and natural inclination.

1. Opportunity

The first requirement is opportunity. A witness cannot be impeached by virtue of previous silence if she was not given the opportunity to speak. Moreover, this must include the opportunity to provide the information that is now being challenged at trial. Thus, a witness cannot be impeached on the basis of omission at a deposition unless a question was asked that reasonably called for that information. The following example illustrates the minimum necessary for impeachment:[23]

QUESTION: You have testified that you heard the fire truck siren?

ANSWER: Yes.

QUESTION: During your deposition I asked you this question: "After you first saw the fire truck, what else did you see or hear?"

ANSWER: That is right.

---

23 For the sake of brevity, most of the build-up for the use of the deposition has been omitted.

QUESTION: And you answered, "I heard the screech of brakes and I saw the BMW slam into the back of the other car."

ANSWER: I believe that was my testimony.

The witness was impeached, if not devastated, by the omission of the sound of the siren in response to a question that reasonably called for it. In contrast, the following example is not impeaching:

QUESTION: During your entire deposition you never once mentioned hearing the fire truck's siren, did you?

ANSWER: I do not believe that anyone asked me about what I heard.

Proof of opportunity, however, is not always sufficient to allow impeachment by omission. A witness who neglects the opportunity to provide information may have misunderstood the question, or may have been temporarily forgetful or confused. The cross examiner must usually go further to show that the absent statement would have been made if it had been true. This can be shown by virtue of either duty or natural inclination.

2. Duty

A witness who was under a duty to provide or record information cannot easily be forgiven its absence. Under these circumstances, the natural conclusion to be drawn from the omission of a fact is that the fact did not occur. Impeachment by omission can be tremendously enhanced by building up the obligation involved in the witness's prior statement. In the context of a deposition, the accreditation might proceed as follows:

QUESTION: You recall having your deposition taken?

QUESTION: You came to my office along with your own attorney?

QUESTION: There was a court reporter present who placed you under oath?

QUESTION: That was the same oath that you took here in court today?

QUESTION: I asked you to tell me if you did not understand any of my questions?

QUESTION: I asked you to tell me if you were unable to give full and complete answers?

QUESTION: And you agreed to answer all of my questions to the best of your ability?

QUESTION: After the deposition was concluded, you had the opportunity to read it over?

QUESTION: You were able to make any corrections or additions that you wanted?

QUESTION: You signed the transcript without making any additions?

QUESTION: Didn't I ask you the following question, "After you noticed the fire truck, what else did you see or hear?"

ANSWER: That is right.

QUESTION: You did not ask me to rephrase that question?

ANSWER: I guess not.

QUESTION: Nothing prevented you from giving a full answer?

ANSWER: No.

QUESTION: And your only answer was, "I heard the screech of brakes and I saw the BMW slam into the back of the other car."

ANSWER: I believe that was my testimony.

QUESTION: Nowhere else in your deposition did you say or add anything about hearing a siren?

ANSWER: I do not believe that I did.

Duty is easily established when the witness previously testified under oath. Duty can also be shown in a wide variety of other circumstances. A prime example is the police report. Assume that the officer in the scenario below arrested the defendant on a charge of narcotics possession; on direct examination the officer testified that the defendant also vigorously resisted arrest:

QUESTION: Officer, immediately after the arrest, you filled out a police report, correct?

QUESTION: It is one of your official duties to fill out such a report?

QUESTION: In fact, police reports are required by both municipal statute and state law, isn't that right?

QUESTION: There are also departmental regulations on the manner in which the reports are to be filled out?

QUESTION: Doesn't one of those regulations state, quote, "Every felony arrest report must contain all information relevant to the apprehension and prosecution of the offender?"

QUESTION: So it is your duty to include in your report "all information relevant to the apprehension and prosecution of the offender," right?

QUESTION: On the day that you arrested the defendant, you certainly wanted to do your duty?

QUESTION: Now, you testified here today that the defendant resisted your arrest, and even took a swing at you?

ANSWER: Yes, that is right.

QUESTION: Resisting a police officer is a crime, isn't it?

ANSWER: Yes, it is.

QUESTION: And trying to hit a police officer can surely lead to "prosecution of the offender," can't it?

ANSWER: It can.

QUESTION: Please look at your police report, which has been marked as Exhibit 6. Read it through carefully, and tell me when you are finished.

ANSWER: I am done reading.

QUESTION: Isn't this the report that you were under a duty to complete?

ANSWER: Yes.

QUESTION: A duty imposed both by law and departmental regulations?

ANSWER: Yes.

QUESTION: There is not a single word in your report about the defendant resisting arrest?

ANSWER: No.

QUESTION: And there is not a single word in your official report about the defendant taking a swing at you, is there?

ANSWER: No, there is not.

Note that it is impossible to use the "elegant" method of recommitment when impeaching by omission. The witness's exact testimony must be used in order to illustrate the importance of the omission.

Business duty can also be used as a predicate to impeachment by omission. It can be shown that a witness did not include facts in a docket entry, a sales record, a service report, a transmittal letter, a bill of lading, an invoice, or any of numerous other documents that are expected to contain complete records of transactions. In the intersection case that we have frequently used as an example, assume that an automobile mechanic testified that she had examined the defendant's brakes and recommended that they be repaired, but that he declined to have any work done:

QUESTION: Ms. Duxler, you testified that you examined the defendant's brakes and recommended that they be repaired?

ANSWER: Yes, I did.

QUESTION: When the defendant brought his car in for repairs, you filled out a work sheet, didn't you?

ANSWER: Yes.

QUESTION: The work sheet is the record that your shop keeps of all the work that is done on any car, correct?

ANSWER: Yes.

QUESTION: It is also the form that you use to calculate charges for labor and parts?

ANSWER: It is.

QUESTION: You do charge for the labor involved in making inspections, don't you?

ANSWER: Yes, we do.

QUESTION: So it is an important part of your job to record all of the work that you do?

ANSWER: That is right.

QUESTION: Let me show you Defendant's Exhibit 4. Please tell me when you have finished reading it.

ANSWER: I am done.

QUESTION: That is your work sheet for the defendant's car on the day he brought it in to you, correct?

ANSWER: It is.

QUESTION: The work sheet includes an entry for "replace windshield wiper blades," correct?

ANSWER: It does.

QUESTION: And that is because you did replace the wiper blades, right?

ANSWER: We did.

QUESTION: It contains an entry for "change oil and filters," right?

ANSWER: Right.

QUESTION: Because you did change the oil?

ANSWER: We changed it.

QUESTION: There is no entry whatsoever on that work sheet that says anything about inspecting brakes, is there?

ANSWER: It isn't on here.

The witness's business duty to include an entry on brake inspection, if an inspection was indeed performed, is established by the question regarding labor charges for inspections. The other entries on the form are used to underscore the glaring absence of anything concerning the purported brake inspection. This is the syllogism of impeachment by omission: The witness appears to have written down everything she did; she wrote nothing down about a brake inspection; therefore, she did not perform a brake inspection.

3. Natural Inclination

Even if no duty can be established, impeachment by omission can still be accomplished. Previous silence can be inconsistent with a current statement if the earlier omission occurred in circumstances where the witness should have been naturally inclined to speak. Imagine that a witness testified at trial that he had seen several children break into a neighbor's garage and steal a bicycle. It would impeach the witness to point out that he had never mentioned this occurrence to either the neighbor or to the children's parents, since a natural inclination is to report such matters to the persons affected. In other words, "If you really saw the kids steal a bicycle, why didn't you say anything at the time?" While it is true that the witness was under no legal or business duty to alert his neighbor to the theft, it is nonetheless a reasonable inference that he would have told his neighbor if the theft had really happened. It is a natural inclination to help your friends and neighbors.

Natural inclination can be found in a wide variety of circumstances and relationships. A crime victim should be naturally inclined to give the police a complete description of the criminal. Parents should be naturally inclined to give safety warnings to their children. Employees should be naturally inclined to complain about adverse working conditions to their employers. The key to this form of impeachment by omission is accreditation of the circumstances that give rise to the inclination to speak. Consider the case of a crime victim:

QUESTION: You testified on direct that you were able to identify the defendant because of the scar on his forehead?

ANSWER: Yes.

QUESTION: Immediately after the crime you were interviewed by a police officer?

ANSWER: Yes, I was.

QUESTION: You knew that the officer wanted your help in catching the criminal?

ANSWER: I did.

QUESTION: And you knew that you were the only one who could give a description of the criminal?

ANSWER: Yes, I was the only one who was robbed.

QUESTION: Of course, you didn't want anyone else to be robbed?

ANSWER: Certainly.

QUESTION: So you gave the officer all the help that you could?

ANSWER: Yes, I did.

QUESTION: But you never once told the officer that the criminal had a scar on his forehead?

ANSWER: No, I guess I didn't.

Can the witness in this example deflect the impeachment by replying that the officer never asked whether the robber had a scar? Obviously not, since a crime victim should be naturally inclined to volunteer that sort of information, whether directly asked about it or not.

Another example can be found in "missing complaint" situations. Assume that the tenant in a commercial lease case seeks to break a tenancy on the ground that the building did not provide adequate security. The plaintiff's testimony concerning poor security could be impeached if there had been no previous complaints about conditions:

QUESTION: You testified on direct that the security situation in the building makes it impossible for you to do business there?

ANSWER: That is absolutely correct.

QUESTION: That is because security is very important to you and your customers, right?

ANSWER: Yes, it obviously is.

QUESTION: You have never written a letter to building management complaining about security, have you?

ANSWER: No.

QUESTION: You never requested a meeting to discuss security, did you?

ANSWER: Well, no.

QUESTION: You paid your rent by check each month?

ANSWER: Yes.

QUESTION: But you never sent a note complaining about security along with the rent check, did you?

ANSWER: No, we didn't.

The absence of complaints is impeaching because a business owner would naturally be inclined to complain about something so important to business. Since there were no complaints, the logic of the impeachment is that conditions could not have been so bad as the plaintiff is now claiming.

B. Prior Inconsistent Actions

Finally, a witness may be impeached on the basis of prior inconsistent actions. The witness's current testimony is rendered less credible by pointing out that she did not act in conformity with her own story on some previous occasion: "If what you are saying now is true, why did you act inconsistently in the past?"

Unlike impeachment through prior inconsistent statements or omissions, no elaborate set-up is necessary for the use of prior inconsistent actions. It is sufficient simply to put the questions to the witness. Return to the commercial lease case from the preceding section, and assume that the business owner testified about the poor security in the building. With no further elaboration, the cross examiner may proceed as follows:

QUESTION: Your business hours are 9:00 a.m. to 10:00 p.m.?

QUESTION: You have not shortened your hours?

QUESTION: You have not installed closed circuit television cameras?

QUESTION: You have not put in additional lighting?

QUESTION: You have allowed your own teen-aged children to work the evening shift?

Each of these instances of the witness's own conduct, if admitted or otherwise proven, detracts from the credibility of the plaintiff's testimony that security conditions were intolerable.

The impeachment might be enhanced further still through the use of a set-up that takes advantage of the principle of apposition:

QUESTION: You testified on direct examination that security conditions are intolerable?

ANSWER: That is right.

QUESTION: You claim to be in fear for your customers' safety?

ANSWER: Absolutely.

QUESTION: You keep your store open until 10:00 p.m.?

ANSWER: Yes.

QUESTION: And security conditions are so bad that you have had your own teen-aged children work the evening shift?

The witness's claim of danger is flatly inconsistent with his actions in allowing his children to work in the store at night. Note, however, that the use of sarcasm is often risky. Many lawyers would prefer simply to make this point during final argument.

IV. CHARACTER AND "CHARACTERISTIC" IMPEACHMENT

Character impeachment refers to the use of some inherent trait or particular characteristic of the witness, essentially unrelated to the case at hand, to render the testimony less credible. The thrust of the impeachment is to show that the witness, for some demonstrable reason, is simply not trustworthy.

The most common forms of characteristic impeachment include conviction of a crime, defect in memory or perception, and past untruthfulness.

A. Conviction of a Crime

A witness may be impeached on the basis of his or her past conviction of certain crimes. While the specifics vary from state to state, under the Federal Rules of Evidence a conviction is admissible for impeachment only if the crime

(1) was punishable by death or imprisonment in excess of one year under the law under which [the witness] was convicted, and the court determines that the probative value of admitting this evidence outweighs its prejudicial effect to the defendant, or (2) involved dishonesty or false statement, regardless of the punishment.[24]

In addition, the Federal Rules provide that convictions generally may not be used if they are more than ten years old,[25] and that juvenile adjudications are inadmissible under most circumstances.[26]

The theory behind impeachment on the basis of conviction of a crime is that criminals are just less trustworthy than other witnesses. Thus, the characteristic of having been convicted of a qualifying crime may be admissible to discredit a witness, without regard to the issues in the particular case. This makes great sense with regard to crimes such as perjury, forgery, and theft by deception, but it is somewhat less compelling concerning crimes such as assault or criminal damage to property. Why would a six-year-old conviction for, say, vandalism have any bearing on a witness's credibility in a current contract dispute? It is for this reason that Federal Rule 609(a)(1) provides that before allowing the impeachment to proceed the court must determine whether the probative value of admitting the evidence outweighs its prejudicial effect. Note, however, that no such balancing test is required if the impeaching crime involved dishonesty or false statement.

Once it has been determined that a conviction can be used for impeachment, relatively little technique is involved in the cross examination:

QUESTION: Isn't it true, Ms. Minkler, that you were once convicted of the crime of aggravated battery?

ANSWER: Yes.

QUESTION: You were convicted on October 12, 1988, correct?

ANSWER: Yes.

QUESTION: That was a felony?

---

24 Rule 609(A), Federal Rules of Evidence.

25 Specifically, evidence of a conviction under this rule is not admissible if a period of more than ten years has elapsed since the date of the conviction or of the release of the witness, whichever is the later date, unless the court determines, in the interests of justice, that the probative value of the conviction substantially outweighs its prejudicial effect. Rule 609(b), Federal Rules of Evidence.

26 See Rule 609(d), Federal Rules of Evidence.

ANSWER: It was.

QUESTION: And you were sentenced to two years of probation?

ANSWER: I was.

QUESTION: That conviction took place in this very courthouse?

ANSWER: It did.

As a rule, the impeachment is limited to the details of the conviction; the facts and circumstances of the crime are generally inadmissible.[27] Because of this, the importance of the impeachment can easily be lost if the cross examiner collapses it all into one or two questions. It is far more effective to draw out the impeaching information, as in the above example, into a series of short questions, each of which deals with a single fact. Repetition of terms such as "crime," "conviction," and even "convicted criminal" will add weight to the impeachment.

If the witness denies having been convicted, the cross examiner must be able to complete the impeachment by introducing a certified copy of the judgment or order of conviction.

B.   Past Untruthfulness and Other Bad Acts

We have discussed the rules governing impeachment on the basis of a criminal conviction. What of a witness's bad acts that were not the subject of a conviction? A witness who has lied in the past, whether or not prosecuted and whether or not under oath, may well be likely to lie during current testimony. On the other hand, past misconduct of some sort is a near-universal human condition, and trials could easily become bogged down if lawyers are allowed free rein to cross examine witnesses on any and all of their old misdeeds.

The Federal Rules of Evidence strike a balance by allowing the impeachment of witnesses on the basis of specific instances of past misconduct, apart from criminal convictions, only if they are probative of untruthfulness. Thus, a witness can be impeached with evidence that he has lied on a specific previous occasion, but not on the basis of previous violence. Moreover, the trial judge has discretion to exclude evidence even of past untruthfulness. Finally, incidents of prior untruthfulness may not be proven by extrinsic evidence.[28] The cross examiner is stuck with the witness's answer.

---

27   The facts and details of the crime may become admissible, however, if the witness or opposing counsel "opens the door."

28   Rule 608(b), Federal Rules of Evidence.

Impeachment on the basis of past untruthfulness is therefore a very tricky matter. You must be certain that the witness will "own up" to the charge, since you will be unable to prove it otherwise.

C. Impaired Perception or Recollection

A witness can also be impeached on the basis of inability to perceive or recall events.

Perception can be adversely affected by a wide variety of circumstances. The witness may have been distracted at the time of the events, or his vision may have been obscured. The witness may have been sleepy, frightened, or intoxicated. The witness may have poor eyesight, or may suffer from some other sensory deficit. Any of these, or similar, facts can be used to impeach the credibility of a witness's testimony.

As with so much else in cross examination, this form of impeachment is usually most effective when counsel refrains from asking the ultimate question. Assume, for example, that a witness in a burglary case identified the defendant during direct examination. The cross examiner is primed for impeachment, knowing that the witness had just awakened from a nap when he observed the burglar. The focus of the impeachment will be on the witness's diminished ability to perceive:

QUESTION: The burglary occurred in the middle of the afternoon?

ANSWER: Yes.

QUESTION: You had been taking a nap on the couch?

ANSWER: Yes.

QUESTION: It was light outside?

ANSWER: It was.

QUESTION: But you were still able to sleep, correct?

ANSWER: Yes.

QUESTION: Then you heard a sound?

ANSWER: I did.

QUESTION: It must have taken a moment to awaken you?

ANSWER: I suppose so.

QUESTION: You couldn't have known right away where the sound was coming from?

ANSWER:	No, I guess not.
QUESTION:	So you had to orient yourself?
ANSWER:	Yes.
QUESTION:	Then you sat up?
ANSWER:	I did.
QUESTION:	Then you looked around?
ANSWER:	That's right.
QUESTION:	You saw someone by the window?
ANSWER:	Right.
QUESTION:	That must have come as quite a shock?
ANSWER:	It certainly did.
QUESTION:	The man had his back to the window?
ANSWER:	Yes.
QUESTION:	And the light was coming through the window?
ANSWER:	Yes, it must have been.

At this point, the cross examiner will stop. The constituent facts of the impeachment have been established; the witness's perception was obviously impeded. Any further questioning is likely to be taken by the witness as an invitation to explain, thus threatening counsel's control of the examination. The argument is certainly clear: The witness was groggy, surprised, and a little frightened; the burglar's face was in a shadow; the identification is therefore suspect. The point is to save these conclusions for final argument, rather than to attempt to extract them directly from the witness.

The concept of impaired perception relates to the witness's ability to perceive at the time of the original events. In contrast, the concept of impaired recollection involves the occurrence of intervening events damaging to the witness's recall. Such events can be as mundane as the mere passage of time, or as dramatic as a head injury.

V.   "CASE DATA" IMPEACHMENT

Some facts are impeaching only within the circumstances of a particular case. They would be innocuous, or perhaps even helpful, in any other context. The most

157

common forms of case data impeachment are based on the witness's personal interest, motive, and bias or prejudice.

A. Personal Interest

A witness who is personally interested in the outcome of a case may be inclined to testify with less than absolute candor. Whether consciously or subconsciously, it is a well-recognized human tendency to shape one's recollection in the direction of the desired outcome.

Impeachment on the basis of personal interest is therefore geared to take advantage of this phenomenon, by pointing out just how the witness stands to gain or lose as a consequence of the resolution of the case. The technique is common in both civil and criminal cases, and it may be applied to both party and non-party witnesses.

Perhaps the clearest example of impeachment on the basis of personal interest arises when the witness is the defendant in a serious criminal case:

QUESTION: You are the defendant in this case?

ANSWER: Yes.

QUESTION: You understand that if you are found guilty you can be sentenced to many years in the penitentiary?

ANSWER: I guess so.

QUESTION: The penitentiary is a terrible place?

ANSWER: That is what I hear.

QUESTION: No one would ever willingly spend years in jail?

ANSWER: Certainly not.

QUESTION: Of course, if you have an alibi, then you might not have to go to prison?

ANSWER: I guess not.

QUESTION: But only if the jury believes you?

ANSWER: That is right.

QUESTION: As it turns out, you do have an alibi, don't you?

ANSWER: I was not there when the crime was committed.

Impeachment

QUESTION: And your testimony will keep you out of prison if the jury
believes it?

Indeed, the defendant's interest in his own testimony is so obvious that the
point is often best left for final argument.

In civil matters, the parties often stand to receive (or lose) great amounts of
money depending upon the verdict in the case. As with the criminal defendant,
the interest of both civil plaintiffs and defendants is generally apparent. Moreover,
since there is always a plaintiff and defendant in each case, this form of interest
will often cancel itself out. The financial interest of non-party witnesses, however,
may not be quite so obvious, and will therefore frequently be the target of
impeachment.

In the following example, assume that the witness has been called to the
stand on behalf of the plaintiff in a will contest. The witness testified on direct that
the testator did not appear to be "of sound mind" at the time that the challenged
will was executed:

QUESTION: You are not a party to this case, are you?

ANSWER: I am not.

QUESTION: But you are the plaintiff's business partner?

ANSWER: Yes, I am.

QUESTION: You will receive no funds directly if the will is thrown out?

ANSWER: Right. I am not involved at all.

QUESTION: But your business partner is involved.

ANSWER: Yes, I suppose so.

QUESTION: He will become the sole beneficiary if the will is found invalid.

ANSWER: I believe that is true.

QUESTION: Your business showed a large loss last year, didn't it?

ANSWER: Yes, we did.

QUESTION: You lost over $1,000,000, didn't you?

ANSWER: Something like that.

QUESTION: You have loaned over $400,000 to the business yourself,
haven't you?

ANSWER: I have.

QUESTION: You could lose that money if the business enters bankruptcy?

ANSWER: Yes.

QUESTION: Your business needs an infusion of capital?

ANSWER: We do.

QUESTION: And if that doesn't come from someone else, it might have to come from you?

ANSWER: I suppose that is right.

QUESTION: If this will is upheld, your business partner will not receive a penny?

ANSWER: I guess that is right.

QUESTION: And you have testified that the testator was not of sound mind when she left her estate to someone other than your business partner?

Two things about this example are noteworthy. First, the value of the impeaching fact is strictly dependent upon the circumstances of this case. This impeachment would be impossible, even laughable, if it were attempted in a case that did not involve this unique confluence of events: challenged will, business partner, failing company, and personal loan. Unlike "characteristic" impeachment, which can be used in virtually any matter, "case data" impeachment is limited to its particular circumstances.

This observation leads to the second point. Case data impeachment is most valuable when the cross examiner takes full advantage of the technique of apposition. The impeaching facts have the most weight when they are developed in conjunction with the other "case data" that explain their significance. The above witness's status as the plaintiff's business partner might be viewed as mildly impeaching standing alone. The witness's credibility is eroded far more significantly, however, when the additional facts — failing business, cash shortage, and outstanding personal loan — are elicited in close succession.

The most effective use of case data impeachment requires the advocate to search the record, and often to search beyond the record, for specific bits of information that can be accumulated to challenge some witness's credibility. This is true, as we have just seen, for impeachment on the basis of interest. It is also true, as we shall see below, for impeachment on the basis of motive, bias or prejudice.

B. Motive

A witness's testimony may be affected by a motive other than financial interest. The witness may have a professional stake in the issues being litigated, or may have some other reason to prefer one outcome to another. In the will contest from the previous section, imagine that the lawyer who drew the will was called to the stand to testify with regard to its validity:

QUESTION: You are the lawyer who drew the will?

ANSWER: Yes.

QUESTION: You also arranged for it to be executed?

ANSWER: I did.

QUESTION: You were there at the signing?

ANSWER: I was.

QUESTION: You called your secretary and receptionist into your office to act as witnesses?

ANSWER: That is correct.

QUESTION: You could not have done those things if the testator had been incompetent?

ANSWER: Of course not.

QUESTION: You could not arrange for an incompetent person to execute a will?

ANSWER: No, I couldn't.

QUESTION: It would be unprofessional for you not to notice a person's obvious lack of mental faculties?

ANSWER: It would be a mistake.

QUESTION: So the challenge to this will is also a challenge to your own professional observations?

ANSWER: I suppose you could put it that way.

QUESTION: And, of course, your testimony today is that the testator was perfectly lucid at all times?

This witness may be inclined to testify in such a way as to vindicate her earlier judgment. While she has no direct interest in the distribution of the estate, she is still impeachable on the basis of motive. Other commonly encountered motives include emotional attachment, revenge, chauvinism, pre-existing belief, or adherence to a school of thought.[29] In all cases, apposition is the key.

C. Bias or Prejudice

Bias and prejudice generally refer to a witness's relationship to one of the parties. A witness may be well-disposed, or ill-inclined, toward either the plaintiff or the defendant. Sadly, some witnesses harbor prejudices against entire groups of people.

Bias in favor of a party is often the consequence of friendship or affinity:

QUESTION: You are the defendant's younger brother?

QUESTION: You grew up together?

QUESTION: You have helped each other out throughout your lives?

QUESTION: Now your brother is charged with a crime?

QUESTION: He is in trouble?

QUESTION: He needs help?

QUESTION: And you are here to testify?

Nothing is more case-specific than this sort of impeachment. It has forensic value if and only if the witness's brother is the defendant in the case. Nothing can be presumed about case data; research and exploration are always required. When it comes to bias and prejudice, even close familial relationships have the potential to cut both ways:

QUESTION: You are the defendant's younger brother?

QUESTION: You grew up together?

QUESTION: He was always beating you up?

QUESTION: He seemed to have all of life's advantages?

QUESTION: It was hard to follow in his successful footsteps?

QUESTION: Everyone was always comparing you to him?

QUESTION: He teased you and called you names?

---

29   This motive is most frequently used to impeach expert witnesses.

Impeachment

QUESTION: You were always resentful of him?

QUESTION: You swore that you would get even?

QUESTION: Now your older brother is charged with a crime?

QUESTION: After all these years, his success seems to have run out?

QUESTION: And you have come to court today to testify against him?

As with all case data impeachment, the establishment of bias or prejudice requires careful development through the use of small, individual facts. This sort of impeachment is made doubly difficult by the fact that it is hard to avoid "telegraphing" your strategy. Once the witness realizes that you intend to impugn his objectivity, he will very naturally attempt to avoid admitting the component facts of your impeachment. In the fraternal scenario above, for example, the typical witness would do everything possible to deny the existence of lifelong resentment of his older brother. Thus, the cross examiner would not risk this line of examination unless the witness's grudge could be sufficiently documented through letters, prior statements, or the testimony of other witnesses.

Witnesses are similarly loath to admit to racial, ethnic, or other group prejudices. Effective impeachment on this basis therefore depends upon the initial elicitation of incontrovertible facts such as prior statements, organizational memberships, or other provable past actions.

— CHAPTER FIVE —
Redirect Examination and Rehabilitation

I.   PURPOSE OF REDIRECT

Redirect allows counsel an opportunity to respond to the cross examination. Redirect may be used for a number of purposes. The witness may be asked to explain points that were explored during the cross, to untangle seeming inconsistencies, to correct errors or misstatements, or to rebut new charges or inferences. In other words, the purpose of redirect is to minimize or undo the damage, if any, that was effected during the cross examination.

Cross examiners are universally cautioned not to ask "one question too many." In a nutshell, redirect is the time to ask exactly those additional questions that the cross examiner purposefully left out.

II.   LAW AND PROCEDURE
A.   Scope

Because redirect is allowed for counteracting or responding to the cross examination, the material that can be covered on redirect is technically limited to the scope of the cross. The interpretation of this rule varies from court to court; some are quite strict and others are fairly lenient. Almost all courts, however, insist that counsel is not free to introduce a wholly new matter on redirect. The redirect must always have some reasonable relationship to the cross examination.

The scope rule adds considerable hazard to the tactic of "sandbagging," or withholding crucial evidence from the direct examination in order to raise it following the cross. Counsel who reserves an important item of testimony from direct runs the risk that the issue will not be covered on cross, and that it will therefore be excluded from redirect as well. Accordingly, there is little to be gained, and much to lose, by sandbagging, especially since redirect examination is usually followed by recross. Even when successful in deferring certain testimony to redirect, counsel cannot succeed in insulating the witness from recross examination.

There is, however, one situation in which reserving evidence until redirect may be helpful. A witness may have an effective response to a potential line of cross examination. Counsel, however, may have no way of knowing whether the cross examiner will pursue those particular issues. Thus, it can be prudent to withhold the explanation until redirect, rather than to insert it defensively during the main direct.[1]

B. Rules of Evidence

All of the rules of direct examination apply equally to redirect examination. Leading questions are prohibited, witnesses may not testify in narrative form, testimony must come from personal knowledge, lay opinions are limited to sensory perceptions, and the proper foundation must be laid to refresh recollection.

Many courts, however, allow a certain amount of latitude during redirect, especially with regard to leading questions. Even without indulgence, leading questions are always permissible to direct the witness's attention or to introduce an area of questioning. A certain amount of leading may be necessary on redirect, in order to focus the examination on the segment of the cross examination that you wish to explain or rebut.

C. Recross Examination and Additional Redirect

Redirect examination may be followed by recross which may be followed by additional redirect, and so on into the night. Each additional examination is limited to the scope of the one that immediately preceded it. Thus, recross is restricted to the scope of the redirect and a second redirect would be confined to the scope of the recross. There is no right to continue an infinite regression of successive "re-examinations." Rather, it is within the court's discretion to allow or deny a request for, say, re-recross. Most judges routinely allow at least one redirect and one recross.

D. Reopening Direct Examination

Reopening direct examination is an alternative to redirect. It can be employed where counsel needs to pursue a line of questioning that is beyond the scope of the cross examination. It is strictly within the court's discretion to allow counsel to reopen a direct examination.

III. PLANNED REDIRECT

Most redirect examinations cannot be thoroughly planned, since each must be closely responsive to the preceding cross examination. Nonetheless, it is possible to anticipate that certain areas will have to be covered on redirect, and to plan accordingly.

---

1 Situations that may call for this approach are addressed below in Section III, *infra* at p. 166.

It is not always possible to know which lines of cross examination will actually be pursued. Counsel would not want to use the direct examination to explain away a cross that might never materialize. Thus, an explanation may be best reserved for redirect, in the event that the cross examination ultimately probes that particular area. It is both possible and necessary to plan for such contingencies.

For example, a witness may have given a prior statement that is arguably impeaching. While there may be a perfectly reasonable response to any apparent inconsistency, it would undermine the witness to bring up the earlier statement during the direct. An explanation would only make sense once the cross examiner actually effected the impeachment. Consequently, the best plan in this situation is probably to defer the explanation until the redirect.

A similar situation arises where there is credible objection to the anticipated cross examination. A witness's past criminal act, for example, might be excludable.[2] The direct examiner certainly would not want to bring up a prior crime or other bad act, even to justify the circumstances, without first determining whether an objection to the cross examination will be sustained. Again, the wisest approach may be to hold the explanation for redirect.

In both of these situations, and others like them, it is possible to plan a segment of the redirect — including preparation of the witness — just as one would plan a direct examination. Note, however, that both examples involve only rejoinders to potential cross examination. The technique of withholding testimony until redirect is not recommended for affirmative evidence or elements of your case.

IV. FOREGOING REDIRECT

Redirect examination is not always necessary. As with all witness examinations, redirect should only be pursued if it will contribute to your theory of the case.

There is no need to ask additional questions if the witness was not appreciably hurt by the cross examination. Additionally, some damage cannot be repaired; it is a mistake to engage in redirect examination if the situation cannot be improved. The worst miscalculation, however, is to surprise the witness with a redirect question. Do not ask for an explanation unless you are certain that the witness has one.

As a further hazard, redirect exposes the witness to recross. If redirect is waived there can be no additional cross examination. Even a single question on redirect, however, can subject the witness to significant further cross examination, so long as it stays within the applicable scope.

---

2   Rule 404(b), Federal Rules of Evidence.

Finally, an unnecessary redirect risks repeating, and therefore re-emphasizing, the cross examination. It can also trivialize the effect of the direct by rehashing minor points.

V. CONDUCTING REDIRECT

Content is the most important aspect of redirect examination. The redirect should concentrate on a few significant points that definitely can be developed. As noted above, these can typically include explanations, clarifications, or responses.

A. Explanations

Explanations are best obtained by asking for them. Focus the witness's attention on the pertinent area of the cross examination and then simply ask her to proceed:

QUESTION: Defense counsel pointed out that you did not visit your doctor immediately following your camping trip at Eagle River Falls. Why didn't you go to the doctor right away?

This approach can also be used to bring out clarifying facts, made relevant by the cross examination:

QUESTION: How soon after the camping trip did you visit the doctor?

A witness may have been frustrated by the control exerted by the cross examiner. If the level of control seemed unfair or unjustified, this can be pointed out during the redirect. Consider:

QUESTION: Defense counsel seemed very concerned that you did not go to the doctor immediately after your camping trip, but she didn't ask you for an explanation. Would you like to explain?

Or,

QUESTION: I noticed that defense counsel cut you off when you tried to continue your answer about the camping trip. What was it that you wanted to say?

Or,

QUESTION: There was a lot of cross examination about your camping trip, but counsel didn't ask you anything about what your doctor eventually prescribed for you. What treatment did you get?

While the introductions in the above examples are arguably leading, they are probably permissible efforts to direct the witness's attention. Nonetheless, preambles of this sort should not be overused. They are likely to be effective only where the cross examination truly was overbearing or oppressive.

B. Rehabilitation

Redirect can be used specifically for rehabilitation of a witness who has been impeached with a prior inconsistent statement.

1. Technique

The technique for rehabilitation is similar to that used for any other explanation. Direct the witness's attention to the supposed impeachment and request a clarification. It may be that the alleged inconsistency can be easily resolved, or that the earlier statement was the product of a misunderstanding or misinterpretation. Whatever the explanation, it is important to conclude the rehabilitation with an affirmative statement of the witness's current testimony.

In the following example the plaintiff in the fire truck case testified on direct examination that the fire engine had been sounding its siren and flashing its lights. On cross examination she was impeached with her deposition, in which she stated that the fire truck "had not been using all of its warning devices." She might be rehabilitated on redirect, as follows:

QUESTION: In your deposition you said that the fire truck was not using all of its warning signals. Can you explain how that fits in with your testimony today about the lights and the siren?

ANSWER: When I answered the deposition question I was thinking about the horn as an additional warning signal, and as far as I can recall the fire truck was not sounding its horn.

QUESTION: Which warning devices was the fire truck using?

ANSWER: It was definitely sounding its siren and flashing all of its red lights.

2. Prior Consistent Statements

A witness can also be rehabilitated through the introduction of a prior consistent statement. Although a witness's own previous out-of-court account would ordinarily be hearsay, a prior consistent statement is admissible to "rebut an express or implied charge . . . of recent fabrication or improper influence or motive."[3]

Accordingly, once the cross examiner suggests that the witness has changed her story, the direct examiner may show that the witness's testimony is consistent

---

3   Rule 801(d)(1)(C), Federal Rules of Evidence.

with an earlier report or other statement. Note that in some jurisdictions a prior consistent statement is admissible only if it predates the inconsistent statement used for impeachment.

— CHAPTER SIX —
Expert Testimony

I. INTRODUCTION

Most witnesses are called to the stand because they have seen, heard, or done something relevant to the issues in the case. Such persons are often referred to as ordinary witnesses, lay witnesses, or percipient witnesses. Whatever the term used, the testimony of such witnesses is generally limited to those things they have directly observed or experienced, as well as reasonable conclusions that can be drawn on the basis of their sensory perceptions. In short, lay witnesses must testify from personal knowledge,[1] and they may not offer opinions.

Expert witnesses comprise an entirely different category. An expert witness is not limited to personal knowledge, and may base her testimony on information that was gathered solely for the purpose of testifying in the litigation. Moreover, under the proper circumstances an expert witness may offer an opinion that goes well beyond her direct sensory impressions. An expert may opine on the cause or consequences of occurrences, interpret the actions of other persons, draw conclusions on the basis of circumstances, comment on the likelihood of events, and may even state her beliefs regarding such seemingly non-factual issues as fault, damage, negligence, avoidability, and the like.

Expert witnesses may be helpful in a wide variety of cases. Experts can be used in commercial cases to interpret complex financial data, in tort cases to explain the nature of injuries, or in criminal cases to translate underworld slang into everyday language. Properly qualified, an expert can be asked to peer into the past (as when an accident reconstructionist re-creates the scene of an automobile collision), or predict the future (as when an economist projects the expected life earnings of the deceased in a wrongful death case). In some cases expert testimony is required as a matter of law. In legal or medical malpractice cases, for example, it is usually necessary to call an expert witness in order to establish the relevant

---

1   *See* Chapter Eight, Section II A, *infra* at p. 268 concerning the requirement of personal knowledge.

171

standard of care; in narcotics cases the prosecution usually must call a chemist or other expert to prove that the substance in question is actually an illegal drug.

Given the extraordinarily broad scope of expert testimony, and its extreme potential for influencing the judgment of the trier of fact, certain rules have developed regarding the permissible use, extent, and nature of expert testimony.

II. STANDARDS FOR EXPERT TESTIMONY

A. Areas of Expertise

Rule 702 of the Federal Rules of Evidence provides that expert opinions are admissible where the expert's "scientific, technical, or other specialized knowledge will assist the trier of fact to understand the evidence or to determine a fact in issue." Thus, there are two threshold questions. Does the witness possess sufficient scientific, technical, or other specialized knowledge? And will that knowledge be helpful to the trier of fact?

An early and widely accepted test for both knowledge and helpfulness was taken from *Frye v. United States.*[2] Under the *Frye* rule, scientific testimony was admissible only if the tests or procedures used by the expert had gained "general acceptance" within the scientific community. Accordingly, novel or innovative processes could not be used as the basis for expert testimony until they had been adopted, or at least recognized, by the scientific community at large. It was up to the court, on the basis of either testimony or judicial notice, to pass on the general acceptance of the expert's approach before allowing the information to be given to the jury.

In recent years, many states have moved to a more relaxed standard that allows an expert to vouch for the validity of her own methods, with the jury making a factual determination as to whether they are credible. While this approach has the advantage of allowing "cutting edge" technologies into the courtroom, it runs the risk of allowing a jury to be persuaded by idiosyncratic theories that are superficially appealing but scientifically questionable. There has lately been a reaction against the use of so-called "junk science" in the courtroom, with the issue yet to be definitively decided. Needless to say, it is essential to determine which test for admissibility will be used prior to offering scientific evidence.[3]

---

2   293 F. 1013 (D.C. Cir. 1923).

3   As this edition was in press the United States Supreme Court decided *Daubert v. Merril Dow Pharmeceuticals,* ___ U.S.___, holding that the *Frye* test had been superseded by the Federal Rules of Evidence. Under *Daubert,* "general acceptance" is not a necessary precondition to the admissibility of scientific evidence in federal courts. Rather, the trial judge must make a

It is important to recognize that scientific evidence is only one branch of expert testimony. Other forms of expertise may range from an anthropologist's knowledge of cultural norms and customs, to a carpenter's understanding of how wooden slats can be joined. Since testimony of this nature will not depend upon the use of tests, procedures, or comparisons, the question of "general acceptance" will not usually arise.

B. Scope of Opinion

It was once considered improper for an expert to offer an opinion on the "ultimate issue" in the case, as this was regarded as "invading the province of the jury." This restrictive convention often led to extremely elliptical testimony, with the expert testifying to a series of inferences and opinions but not drawing the most obvious factual conclusions. This process was further complicated by the difficulty of determining exactly what were the ultimate issues in a case.

The Federal Rules of Evidence now provide that expert testimony, if otherwise admissible, "is not objectionable because it embraces an ultimate issue to be decided by the trier of fact." The only exception is that an expert in a criminal case may not state an opinion as to whether the defendant "did or did not have the mental state or condition constituting an element of the crime charged or a defense thereto."[4]

Judges vary on their interpretations of the "ultimate issue" rule. Some courts will allow experts to opine on virtually any issue, including such case-breakers as whether the plaintiff in a personal injury case was contributorily negligent or whether the defendant in a tax evasion case had unreported income. Other judges draw the line at what they consider to be legal conclusions. So, for example, a medical expert in a malpractice case would no doubt be allowed to state that certain tests were indicated and that the defendant had not performed them. Many judges would also allow the expert to testify that the failure to order the tests fell below the standard of care generally exercised by practitioners in the relevant community, although this might be considered an "ultimate issue in the case." Most judges, though not all, would balk at permitting the expert to testify that the defendant's conduct constituted malpractice, on the theory that malpractice is a legal conclusion that is not within the specialized knowledge of a medical expert.

---

preliminary assessment of the scientific validity of the reasoning and methodology that underlies the profferred testimony.

Note that *Daubert* was decided as a matter of federal evidentiary law, and that the states may not adopt its holding.

4   Rule 704(b), Federal Rules of Evidence.

C. Bases for Opinion

Under the Federal Rules of Evidence an expert can testify to her opinion with or without explaining the facts or data on which the opinion is based.[5] In theory, then, an expert, once qualified, could simply state her opinion on direct examination, leaving the cross examiner to search for its basis.[6] In practice, of course, this approach is rarely followed, since the expert's opinion could hardly be persuasive until its foundation is explained. The practical effect of the rule is to allow the witness to state her opinion at the beginning of the examination, followed by explication, rather than having to set forth all of the data at the outset.

A related issue is the nature of the information that an expert may rely upon in arriving at an opinion. At common law, experts could give opinions only on the basis of facts that were already in evidence. One way for an expert to comply with this requirement was to observe the actual testimony by sitting through the trial. The only alternative to this expensive and cumbersome routine was for the attorney offering the expert testimony to precede it with an elaborate "hypothetical question" that recited all of the facts — either admitted or eventually to be admitted — needed by the expert as the basis for an opinion.

The hypothetical question was usually the preferred option, if only because it was less costly, but it had numerous drawbacks. Because they had to include every relevant fact, the hypotheticals were often long, boring, and impossible to follow. Worse, the omission of a single fact could conceivably invalidate the entire hypothetical, as could the inclusion of a fact that was not eventually admitted into evidence. Trial lawyers spent countless hours, and appellate courts devoted untold pages, to discussion of the technical adequacy of expert hypotheticals.

The Federal Rules of Evidence have abolished the need for this highly stylized ritual. An expert witness may now testify on the basis of "facts made known to him at or before the hearing."[7] Moreover, those facts or data need not be admissible in evidence, so long as they are "of a type reasonably relied upon by experts in the particular field."[8]

While it is certain that an expert may *rely* upon inadmissible data, it is less clear whether the expert may *recite* that data as support for her testimony. For

---

5   Rule 705, Federal Rules of Evidence.

6   "The expert may in any event be required to disclose the underlying facts or data on cross-examination." Rule 705, Federal Rules of Evidence.

7   Rule 703, Federal Rules of Evidence.

8   *Id.*

example, forensic pathologists regularly rely upon toxicology reports in determining the cause of death. A pathologist could presumably reach an opinion based upon such a written report, even if it would be hearsay if offered at trial.[9] The question, however, is whether the expert, having accepted the report, may also testify as to its contents.

The majority view is that an expert may explain the bases of her opinion, even if this involves relating otherwise inadmissible evidence. Thus, the pathologist in the above hypothetical could testify to the contents of the toxicology report. This view is supported by the eminently logical argument that it is meaningless to allow a witness to rely on information, and then preclude her from supporting her opinion. The minority position is that Rule 703 was not intended to be either a principle of admissibility or an independent exception to the hearsay rule, as evidenced by the fact that it is neither found nor referenced in the section of the Federal Rules that defines hearsay and its exceptions. Under this approach our pathologist could state how and why she relied upon the toxicology report, but she could not state the toxicologist's findings.[10]

III. THE EXPERT'S OVERVIEW

Just as a lawyer cannot succeed without developing a comprehensive theory of the case, neither will an expert be effective without a viable, articulated theory. An expert's theory is an overview or summary of the expert's entire position. The theory must not only state a conclusion, but must also explain, in common-sense terms, why the expert is correct. Why did she settle upon a certain methodology? Why did she review particular data? Why is her approach reliable? Why is the opposing expert wrong? In other words, the expert witness must tell a coherent story that provides the trier of fact with reasons for accepting, and, it is hoped, internalizing, the expert's point of view.

The need for a theory is especially true in cases involving "dueling experts." It is common for each of the opposing parties in litigation to retain their own expert

---

9 While the toxicologist could definitely testify to her own conclusions, a written report containing those same conclusions would be hearsay because it is an out-of-court statement offered to prove the truth of its own contents. It is possible that the report might be admissible as a business record, but that would require the testimony of either the toxicologist or some other qualified person to lay the foundation for the exception. Thus, in the absence of supporting testimony, the report could not be admitted.

10 The difference between the two positions is most acute when the source of the expert's opinion is not only unadmitted but also inadmissible, as could be the case if there were some flaw in the toxicology report that prevented its acceptance as a business record.

witnesses. The trier of fact is then faced with the task of sorting through the opinion testimony and choosing which witness to believe. It is likely that both experts will be amply qualified, and it is unlikely that either will make a glaring error in her analysis or commit an unpardonable *faux pas* in her testimony. The trier of fact will therefore be inclined to credit the expert whose theory is most believable.

Consider the following case. The plaintiff operated a state-wide chain of drive-in restaurants, but was put out of business by the defendant's allegedly unfair competition. Assume that summary judgment was granted in favor of the plaintiff on the issue of liability, and that the court set the case for trial on damages. Each side retained an expert witness who generated a damage model.

Not surprisingly, the plaintiff's expert opined that the restaurants, had they not been driven out of business, would have earned millions of dollars over the following five years. The defendant's witness, however, held the view that the stores would have been marginally profitable, with total profits amounting to no more than a few hundred thousand dollars. Each witness backed up her opinion with computer print-outs, charts, and graphs. Both used reliable data and all of their figures were rigorously accurate.

The rival experts reached different conclusions because they followed different routes. The plaintiff's expert calculated lost profits as a function of population growth and driving habits, opining that the revenues at drive-in restaurants would rise in proportion to expected increases in population and miles driven. The defendant's witness, on the other hand, estimated damages on a "profit-per-store" basis, taking the plaintiff's average profit for the existing restaurants and multiplying them by the number of outlets that the plaintiff planned to build.

Faced with this discrepancy, the task for counsel is to present the expert testimony in its most persuasive form. Whichever side you represent, it should be obvious that a simple recitation of your expert's methods will be unlikely to carry the day. After all, we have assumed that both experts were meticulously careful within the confines of their respective approaches. For the same reason, the trier of fact will probably be unimpressed by an expert who reviews in detail all of her calculations. Numbers are boring in any event, and both experts are sure to have been accurate in their arithmetic.

Instead, the key to this case is to persuade the trier of fact that your expert chose the correct approach. The plaintiff's expert must be asked to explain *why* lost profits can be determined on the basis of population growth; the defendant's expert has to support her reliance on profits-per-store. The prevailing expert will not be the one with the greatest mastery of the details, but rather the one who most successfully conveys the preferability of her theory. The most painstakingly prepared projection of population growth cannot succeed in persuading a jury if they ultimately decide that only profits-per-store can give them an accurate assessment of damages.

The importance of theory extends to all types of expert testimony. It is necessary, but not sufficient, for your expert to be thorough, exacting, highly regarded, incisive, honorable, and well prepared. Her testimony will suffer if she cannot support her opinion with common-sense reasons.

IV. OFFERING EXPERT TESTIMONY

There is a certain logic to the direct examination of most experts. While the particulars and details will vary, there are a limited number of possible patterns for organizing the testimony. It is absolutely necessary, for example, to qualify the expert before proceeding to her opinion. The following is a broad outline that can accommodate the specifics of most expert testimony.

A. Introduction and Foreshadowing

The first step is to introduce the expert and explain her involvement in the case. Since expert testimony is qualitatively different from lay testimony, it is a good idea to clarify its purposes for the jury so that they will understand what they are about to hear.[11] Ask the witness how she came to be retained and why she is present in court.

Moreover, the technical requirements of presenting expert testimony often result in a considerable time gap between the introduction of the witness and the substantive high points of her testimony. Thus, it is generally desirable to foreshadow the expert's opinion at the very outset of the examination.

The plaintiff's damages expert in the example from the preceding section might be introduced as follows:

QUESTION: Please state your name.

ANSWER: Dr. Andrea Longhini.

QUESTION: Dr. Longhini, have you been retained to reach an expert opinion in this case?

---

11 It is obviously unnecessary to explain the purpose of expert testimony in bench trials.

ANSWER: Yes.

QUESTION: Did you reach an opinion concerning the plaintiff's lost profits?

ANSWER: Yes, I have calculated the amount of money that the plaintiff would have earned.

QUESTION: We'll talk about your opinion in detail in a few minutes, but right now we have to talk about your qualifications to testify as an expert in this case.

B.   Qualification

To testify as an expert, a witness must be qualified by reason of knowledge, skill, experience, training or education.[12] This is a threshold question for the judge, who must determine whether the witness is qualified before permitting her to give opinion testimony. The qualification of the witness, then, is a necessary predicate for all of the testimony to follow. Care must be taken to qualify the expert in a manner that is both technically adequate and persuasive.

1. Technical Requirements

The technical requirements for qualifying an expert witness are straightforward. It is usually adequate to show that the witness possesses some specialized skill or knowledge, acquired through appropriate experience or education, and that the witness is able to apply that skill or knowledge in a manner relevant to the issues in the case.

Thus, the minimal qualifications for the financial expert in the restaurant case could be established as follows:

QUESTION: Dr. Longhini, could you please tell us something about your education?

ANSWER: Certainly. I have an undergraduate degree in business from Notre Dame and a Ph.D. in Economics from the University of California.

QUESTION: What work have you done since receiving your doctorate?

---

12   Rule 702, Federal Rules of Evidence.

ANSWER: I was a professor in the Economics Department at Temple University for six years. Then I left to start my own consulting firm, which is called Longhini & Associates.

QUESTION: Do you have a specialty within the field of economics?

ANSWER: Yes, my specialty is business valuation.

QUESTION: Has business valuation been your specialty both at Temple University and at Longhini & Associates?

ANSWER: Yes.

QUESTION: What is the field of business valuation?

ANSWER: It is the study of all of the components that contribute to the fair value of a business, including anticipated future profits, assets, receivables, good will, and investment potential.

The above examination confirms the expert's qualifications by reason of both education and experience. Dr. Longhini should now be able to give an opinion as to the projected profits for the restaurant chain.

There are, of course, many other areas of basic qualification beyond education and business experience. Examples include specialized training, continuing education courses, teaching and lecturing positions, licenses and certifications, publications, consulting experience, professional memberships, awards, and other professional honors.

The establishment of basic qualifications, however, should not be counsel's entire objective. It is equally, if not more, important to go on to qualify the witness as persuasively as possible.

2. Persuasive Qualification

The technical qualification of an expert merely allows the witness to testify in the form of an opinion. Counsel's ultimate goal is to ensure that the opinion is accepted by the trier of fact. Persuasive qualification is particularly important in cases involving competing experts, since their relative qualifications may be one basis on which the judge or jury will decide which expert to believe.

It is a mistake, however, to think that more qualifications are necessarily more persuasive. An endless repetition of degrees, publications, awards, and appointments may easily overload any judge or juror's ability, not to mention desire, to pay careful attention to the witness. It is often better to introduce the witness's detailed resumé or curriculum vitae,[13] and to use the qualification portion of the actual examination to focus in on several salient points.[14]

It is usually more persuasive to concentrate on a witness's specific expertise, as opposed to her more generic or remote qualifications. Every economist, for example, is likely to hold a doctorate, so there is comparatively little advantage to be gained by spending valuable time expounding your expert's academic degrees. Similarly, there is usually scant reason to go into matters such as the subject of the witness's doctoral thesis, unless it bears directly on some issue in the case.

On the other hand, an expert's credibility can be greatly enhanced by singling out qualifications that relate specifically to the particular case. Thus, it would be important to point out that the witness has published several articles directly relevant to the issues in the case. It would be less useful to take the witness through a long list of extraneous articles, even if they appeared in prestigious journals. Other case-specific qualifications may include direct experience, consulting work, or teaching that is connected to an issue in the case.

Experience is often more impressive than academic background. So, for example, a medical expert may be more impressive if she has actually practiced in the applicable specialty, as opposed to possessing knowledge that is strictly theoretical. When presenting such a witness, then, counsel should typically dwell on her experience, pointing out details such as the number of procedures she has performed, the hospitals where she is on staff, and the numbers of other physicians who have consulted her.

Finally, it is frequently effective to emphasize areas of qualification where you know the opposing expert to be lacking. If your expert has a superior academic background, use the direct examination to point out why academic training is important. If your expert holds a certification that the opposing expert lacks, have her explain how difficult it is to become certified.

3. Tender of the Witness

In some jurisdictions it is necessary, once qualifications have been concluded, to tender the witness to the court as an expert in a specified field. The purpose of

---

13 An expert's resumé might technically be considered hearsay. Expert qualifications, however, are notoriously boring, and most judges will jump at the chance to move things along by allowing the introduction of a resumé. For the same reason, it is common for counsel to stipulate to the introduction of resumés for all expert witnesses. Alternatively, a resumé might be admissible as a business record.

14 The expert's resumé should rarely be used as a complete substitute for examination on qualifications, since this would deprive counsel of the opportunity to emphasize the witness's most compelling virtues.

the tender is to inform the court that qualification has been completed, and to give opposing counsel an opportunity either to conduct a voir dire of the witness or to object to the tender.[15] In the restaurant example above, the financial expert would be tendered as follows:

COUNSEL: Your Honor, we tender Dr. Andrea Longhini as an expert witness in the field of business valuation and the projection of profits.

It may be an effective tactic to tender an expert witness to the court even in jurisdictions where a formal tender is not required. First, tendering the witness signals that the qualification segment has been completed and requires opposing counsel either to object or accede to the witness's qualifications. By forcing the issue early in the examination, the direct examiner can avoid being interrupted by an objection to the witness's qualifications at some more delicate point in the testimony. Additionally, assuming that the judge rules favorably on the tender, counsel in effect has obtained the court's declaration that the witness is, indeed, an expert. This will give additional weight to the opinions that follow.

C. Opinion and Theory

Following qualification, the next step in the direct examination of an expert witness is to elicit firm statements of opinion and theory.

1. Statement of Opinion

The Federal Rules of Evidence provide that an expert "may testify in terms of opinion or inference and give his reasons therefor without prior disclosure of the underlying facts or data, unless the court requires otherwise."[16] Consequently, once the witness has been qualified (and accepted as an expert in jurisdictions requiring a formal tender and ruling), she may proceed to express her opinion without additional foundation. In other words, she may state her conclusions without first detailing the nature or extent of her background work or investigation.

Many attorneys believe strongly in taking advantage of the "opinion first" provision. Expert testimony tends to be long, arcane, and boring. The intricate

---

15 Opposing counsel may utilize voir dire examination to attempt to develop deficiencies in the witness's qualifications. This is done in the midst of the direct examination for two reasons. First, if it can be shown that the witness truly is not qualified, there will be no reason to continue the direct examination. Second, objections raised as a consequence of voir dire can often be cured through additional direct examination. Note that voir dire on qualifications, as with all voir dire examination, should be limited to the eventual admissibility of the expert testimony and should not be used as a substitute for cross examination regarding weight or credibility.

16 Rule 705, Federal Rules of Evidence.

details of an expert's preparation are unlikely to be interesting, or even particularly understandable. They will be even less captivating if they are offered in a void, without any advance notice of where the details are leading or why they are being explained. On the other hand, a clear statement of the expert's conclusion can provide the context for the balance of the explanatory testimony. Compare the two following vignettes, each taken from the "fast food" example above:

QUESTION: Dr. Longhini, what did you do to arrive at your opinion in this matter?

ANSWER: My first step was to gather all of the available data regarding vehicle registrations and anticipated population growth in the state.

QUESTION: Then what did you do?

ANSWER: I correlated population growth with expected vehicle miles to arrive at a reasonable estimate of "miles per person" over each of the next five years.

QUESTION: How was that calculation performed?

Even the most diligent and attentive juror would be baffled by this examination. What is the relevance of vehicle miles and population growth to fast food profits? The nature of the witness's computation is meaningless in the absence of some connection to his opinion in the case. Indeed, the more thoroughly the witness explains her calculations, the more incomprehensible they will become. In contrast, consider the following:

QUESTION: Dr. Longhini, do you have an opinion as to the profits that the plaintiff's restaurant chain would have made, if they hadn't been forced out of business?

ANSWER: Yes, I do.

QUESTION: What is your opinion?

ANSWER: I believe that the restaurant chain would have earned at least $3.2 million over the next five years, if they had been able to stay in business.

QUESTION: How did you reach that opinion?

ANSWER: I based my calculations on the state's projected population growth, combined with the probable demand for fast-food, drive-in restaurants.

This examination is far more understandable. By providing her opinion at the outset, the expert allows the trier of fact to comprehend the significance of the following details. The jury will be much more able to understand the relationship between lost profits and the data on vehicle registration and population growth.

2. Statement of Theory

Once the expert's opinion has been stated, immediately provide the underlying theory. The theory should furnish the nexus between the expert's conclusion and the data used to support the conclusion. In other words, the examination should follow this pattern: (1) here is my opinion; (2) here are the principles that support my opinion; (3) here is what I did to reach my final conclusion.

In the fast food example, the expert's theory should explain *why* population growth and vehicle miles are reliable indicators of projected profits:

QUESTION: Dr. Longhini, why did you base your calculations on the state's projected population growth?

ANSWER: The demand for fast food will rise as population grows. This is particularly true because teenagers and parents of young children are the largest purchasers of fast food, and they are also two of the groups that increase most rapidly as population goes up.

QUESTION: Why did you also consider growth in vehicle miles?

ANSWER: Drive-in restaurants are especially sensitive to vehicle miles. As people drive more they are exposed to more drive-in restaurants, and they therefore buy more meals.

QUESTION: What did you conclude from these relationships?

ANSWER: I concluded that the profitability of a drive-in restaurant chain will rise in proportion to a combination of general population growth and increases in miles driven.

QUESTION: Did you consider only population growth and vehicle miles?

ANSWER: Of course not. I began by determining the chain's profits under current conditions, and I used those figures as a base. Then I projected them forward for five years, using the government's statistics for population and driving.

QUESTION: Please tell us now exactly how you did that.

Note how this examination provides the context for the explanation to follow.

D. Explanation and Support

Having stated and supported her theory choice, the expert can now go on to detail the nature of her investigation and calculations. The trier of fact cannot be expected to take the expert at her word, so the validity and accuracy of her data and assumptions must be established.

1. Data

The expert should be asked how she chose and obtained her data. She should also explain why her information is reliable. In the scenario above, for example, the expert could point out that government statistics on population and vehicle miles are used to make many crucial decisions such as the configuration of traffic lights, the expansion of highways, and even the construction of schools.

The expert should also be asked to describe any tests or computations that she performed.

The treatment of underlying data is one of the trickiest aspects of expert testimony. Many experts will be in love with their data, and they will be anxious to lay them out in excruciating detail. Unfortunately, most judges and jurors will have little tolerance for lengthy descriptions of enigmatic scientific or technical processes. Counsel must therefore strike a balance, eliciting a sufficiently detailed treatment of the data to persuade the jury of its reliability but stopping well short of the point where their attention span is exhausted.

It is not sufficient for the expert simply to relate the nature of the data. Rather, the expert should go on to explain how and why the data support her conclusions.

2. Assumptions

Most experts rely upon assumptions. The financial expert in the fast food case, for example, would no doubt assume that the relationship between sales and population growth would continue at historical rates. The expert would also probably assume a certain "discount rate" for reducing his projection to present value. There is obviously nothing wrong with using appropriate presumptions, but their validity should be explained:

QUESTION: Dr. Longhini, did you make any assumptions in reaching your opinion that the plaintiff's restaurant chain would have earned $3.2 million in profits?

ANSWER: Yes, I assumed that fast food sales would continue to increase in proportion to population, at the same rate as they had in the past.

QUESTION: Why did you make that assumption?

ANSWER: The restaurant chain was put out of business, so there were no actual sales to look at. I therefore had to project their most likely sales, and for that I had to assume a base figure to project forward.

QUESTION: What did you use as your base figure?

ANSWER: I used the average growth for the entire industry.

QUESTION: Why did you use the industry average?

ANSWER: I used the industry average precisely because it is an average of all of the companies in that particular business. That way I could be sure that I wasn't using a figure that was abnormally high or abnormally low.

It is not necessary to explain or outline every hypothesis used by your expert, but the more important assumptions should be noted and supported.

E. Theory Differentiation

In cases involving dueling experts there will also be competing theories. Properly prepared and presented, each expert will attempt to persuade the trier of fact that her theory ought to be accepted. It can be particularly effective, therefore, to ask your expert to comment on the opposing expert's work. This technique can be called theory differentiation, because it is most convincing when your expert discusses the shortcomings of the opposition theory.

In the previous sections we have seen illustrations taken from the testimony of the plaintiff's financial expert in a case involving lost profits. Now consider this example of theory differentiation, offered by the expert witness for the defendant:[17]

QUESTION: Please state your name.

ANSWER: Benjamin Haruo.

QUESTION: Dr. Haruo, have you had an opportunity to review the work done in this case by Dr. Andrea Longhini?

ANSWER: Yes, I have.

QUESTION: Do you agree with Dr. Longhini's damage projections?

ANSWER: No, I do not.

---

17   For the purpose of this example, assume that the witness has been identified and qualified.

QUESTION: Why not?

ANSWER: Dr. Longhini based her estimate on a combination of population growth and milage assumptions, and this approach cannot yield a reliable result.

QUESTION: Why is that?

ANSWER: Because it assumes too much. Dr. Longhini's theory is that restaurant revenues will inevitably rise along with population and automobile miles. While this might possibly be true for the entire restaurant industry, there is no reason to think that it would be true for any particular chain of restaurants. To reach a dependable result for an individual chain you would have to consider many other factors.

QUESTION: What factors are those?

ANSWER: At a minimum you would have to consider location, market niche, product recognition, potential competition, specific demographics, and general economic climate.

QUESTION: Did Dr. Longhini consider any of those factors?

ANSWER: No, she did not.

QUESTION: Could you please give us an example of how location could affect the profit projections?

ANSWER: Certainly. Population always grows unevenly. Even if the overall population rises in a state or a city, it might stay constant or fall in certain areas. Therefore, a restaurant chain might not be able to take advantage of population increases if all of their outlets were placed in stagnant or declining locations.

The defense expert has deftly exposed the flaws in the plaintiff's theory. There are two advantages to such theory differentiation. First, it enables the expert to concentrate on major issues, as opposed to picking out petty mistakes. Second, it allows the expert to avoid personal attacks. In essence, the above example has Dr. Haruo saying: "I have no personal quarrel with Dr. Longhini; she simply chose an inadequate theory." This "high road" approach will contribute to the dignity and persuasiveness of the witness.

The timing of theory differentiation can be important. Plaintiff's counsel generally will want to establish her own theory first, before proceeding to criticize the defense expert. Depending upon the circumstances of the case, plaintiff's counsel might even want to forego theory differentiation entirely during her case in chief, and to recall her expert for that purpose on rebuttal.

The defense, on the other hand, should address the plaintiff's expert's theory at some point during the direct examination of the defendant's own expert. This can be done early in the examination (in order to rebut the plaintiff's expert immediately and forcefully), or it can be done toward the end of the testimony (in order to allow the defense expert to build up the positive aspects of her own theory before turning her attention to the opposition).

F. Conclusion

An expert's direct examination should conclude with a powerful restatement of her most important conclusions.

V. PERSUASIVE TECHNIQUES FOR DIRECT EXAMINATION

Most of the direct examination methods discussed in Chapter Two can be used effectively with expert witnesses. In addition, the following techniques are specifically applicable to expert testimony.

A. Humanize the Witness

Many experts from scientific, technical, or financial backgrounds may appear aloof, intimidating, or even arrogant to jurors who do not share their special expertise. It is therefore important to humanize these witnesses as much as possible in the course of the direct examination. If permitted in your jurisdiction, this can be done by bringing out personal and family background information, and by allowing the witness to talk about more than strictly professional matters.

B. Use Plain Language

Virtually every field of expertise creates its own technical and shorthand terms, and expert witnesses will be inclined to use arcane and jargon-laden speech without even thinking about it. It is counsel's job to guide the witness away from the use of jargon and into the realm of everyday speech. There are three basic means to accomplish this task.

First, thoroughly prepare the witness to avoid complex, professional terms. Spend sufficient time with the witness before trial so that she will understand the importance of plain, simple language.

Second, ask for an explanation when your witness lapses into her native tongue, whether it is finance-talk, engineeringese, or accounting-speak. This should be done gently and without reprimand or condescension, as in this example:

QUESTION: Dr. Schenkier, do you have an opinion as to why the pressure plate failed?

ANSWER: Yes. My tests indicate that the fastening bolts were over-torqued.

QUESTION: What do you mean when you say over-torqued?

ANSWER: I mean that the bolts were turned too far when they were tightened.

Finally, and possibly most important, counsel must avoid the temptation to adopt the expert's word choices. Too many lawyers, perhaps out of a desire to appear erudite or knowledgeable, tend to examine expert witnesses using the expert's own jargon. Such examinations can take on the characteristics of a private, and completely inaccessible, conversation between the lawyer and the witness. It is bad enough when lawyers use legalese; it is worse when they embrace the private speech of another profession. Consider the following:

QUESTION: Dr. Breskin, what injuries did you observe?

ANSWER: I observed multiple contusions on the anterior upper extremities.

QUESTION: Was there anything remarkable about the contusions?

ANSWER: Yes. They varied in color, which indicated that they had been inflicted at different times.

QUESTION: Did the location of the contusions indicate anything further to you?

ANSWER: Yes. Their anterior location suggested that they had been inflicted from a superior position.

The lawyer and doctor are talking about bruises. The witness chose to use the term "contusions" because it is medically precise, and the lawyer's adoption of the term encouraged the doctor to continue using it. While the lawyer may have succeeded in demonstrating his medical sophistication, he may have done so at the cost of the jury's comprehension.

C.   Avoid Narratives

Most judges will allow expert witnesses considerable freedom to testify in narrative fashion. Many lawyers believe that they should take advantage of this leeway, and they therefore encourage their experts to present their testimony in long, uninterrupted segments. This is a mistake. Long narratives are hard to follow and hard to digest.

Expert Testimony

Anyone who ever sat through a long lecture or speech should understand how difficult it is to pay attention to a speaker for an extended period of time. This is particularly true of expert testimony, which often concentrates on complex or intricate details. Allowing an expert to testify in a long, unbroken stretch invites juror inattention.

Recall the discussion of the importance of primacy in basic direct examination: the judge and jury remember best what they hear first. This concept applies to individual answers as well as to complete examinations. A new answer begins every time counsel asks a question. In other words, every question to the expert reinitiates primacy and refocuses the listeners' attention. Unless the expert is an extraordinarily skilled speaker, a narrative answer will have no comparable points of reinitiation. The opportunity to continuously highlight the testimony will be lost.

Counsel can avoid narrative answers and reinitiate primacy by punctuating the expert's testimony at logical breaking points:

QUESTION: Dr. Haruo, what is the significance of location in projecting profits for a chain of drive-in restaurants?

ANSWER: Location is probably the single most important factor when it comes to profitability in any retail business. Even if the overall trend in an industry is upward, a poorly located business is unlikely to benefit. This is especially true of the restaurant business.

QUESTION: Please explain.

ANSWER: The restaurant business is intensely local in nature. There are very few restaurants that attract people from great distances. Most people eat near their homes, their places of work, or their shopping destinations. So a restaurant in an undesirable neighborhood or in a declining business district simply will not draw customers.

QUESTION: Why is that?

ANSWER: Many restaurants depend heavily on luncheon trade. People on their lunch break usually do not have more than an hour, so a restaurant will not be able to draw this business unless it is located near a fairly large number of employers. No matter how well the economy is doing, a restaurant will not do well at lunch time if it is located in an area that happens to have experienced a downturn.

Note that the lawyer in this example did not cut off the witness and did not limit the expert to unnaturally short answers. The lawyer did, however, use strategically interjected questions to break up the narrative, thereby continually re-emphasizing the expert's testimony.

D. Use Examples and Analogies

Many complex ideas can be made understandable with examples, analogies, or metaphors. Expert witnesses should be encouraged to clarify their testimony through the use of such imagery. Consider the following use of an example to flesh out a relatively abstract concept:

QUESTION: Dr. Haruo, please give us an example of how a restaurant chain might do poorly, even in a state with an expanding population and increasing vehicle miles?

ANSWER: Certainly. Many urban areas have experienced population growth that is basically limited to the suburbs. A restaurant chain that was concentrated in the central city would show almost no increased profitability as a result of that growth. In fact, its profits might well decline because of the population shift. That is why location is such an important factor.

An analogy could serve the same purpose:

QUESTION: Dr. Haruo, could you please explain the importance of location a little further?

ANSWER: Well, maybe it would help to think about it this way. Imagine a baseball league with eight teams. If the top two or three pennant contenders are all located in big cities they will obviously draw a lot of fans. On the other hand, a cellar-dwelling team in a small city would probably play to an empty stadium. So even if the league's overall attendance went up, that wouldn't help to fill the seats for the last place team. A poor location is a lot like being stuck in last place.

Counsel should not take the witness by surprise with a request for an example or metaphor. The time to consider using these explanatory tools is during preparation, not on the spur of the moment in the midst of direct examination.

E. Use Visual Aids

The direct examination of almost every expert can be enhanced through the use of visual displays. Since expert testimony may be hard to follow, it can be particularly effective to portray the expert's concepts with charts, graphs, drawings, or models.

A physician's testimony, for example, can be brought to life with an anatomical model or a series of colored overlays. Financial experts should illustrate their testimony with graphs or tables. An architectural or engineering expert should use diagrams or scale models. The possibilities for visual aids are practically infinite, limited only by counsel's (and the expert's) imagination.

F.   Use Internal Summaries

Because of the potential length and complexity of expert testimony, it is important to highlight significant points through the use of internal summaries. Ask the expert to point out the relevance of the most critical steps in her analysis. Request that she summarize the implications of her findings.

Think of the expert's testimony as containing a series of steps or elements. At the conclusion of each step the expert should explain how she got there, why it is important, and where she is going next, as in the following example from the testimony of the defendant's expert in the drive-in case:

QUESTION: Dr. Haruo, please summarize your objections to Dr. Longhini's methodology?

ANSWER: The problem with Dr. Longhini's approach is that she failed to consider several of the most important factors in determining profitability. Her reliance on population and vehicle miles led her to dramatically overestimate the restaurant chain's likely profitability. Her study was especially deficient because it did not account for either location or potential competition.

QUESTION: Were you able to conduct a more comprehensive study?

ANSWER: Yes. I conducted a study that included the six most important factors, all of which were omitted by Dr. Longhini.

G.   Use the Concept of Consensus

Almost every field of expertise contains several contending schools of thought. Opposing experts often arrive at different opinions because they approach the issues from distinct perspectives. For example, a strict Freudian psychologist is likely to evaluate a patient's mental state quite differently from a Gestalt therapist.

Your expert's testimony can be made more persuasive if you can show that she has presented the mainstream view, as opposed to a novel or untested theory. This can be done by stressing such credentials as university affiliation, professional certification, or other indicia of widespread acceptance. The question of consensus can also be approached directly:

QUESTION: Dr. Haruo, what is the consensus view on the projection of retail business profits?

ANSWER: The strong consensus is that multiple factors have to be considered, and that location is the single most import variable.

QUESTION: Is Dr. Longhini's method within that consensus?

ANSWER: No. Dr. Longhini basically tries to take a short cut. She substitutes population growth for all other factors. I do not believe there is a single business school in the United States that teaches students to project profits that way.

H. Use Leading Questions When Called For

Two recurrent problems in expert testimony are boredom and pomposity. Many experts are inclined to drone on at length over unimportant details. Others present themselves with an air of overweening self-importance, especially in the course of presenting their credentials. Both of these difficulties can be resolved through the judicious use of leading questions.

Counsel can often cut through a welter of details by using a leading question to direct the witness to the heart of the matter. Consider the examination of a chemist, called to testify as to the composition of substance. The process used by the witness may have been comprised of many steps. A judge or jury, however, would quickly become bored with a blow-by-blow recitation of the entire procedure. Counsel can shorten the questioning by using a few leading questions:

QUESTION: Did you perform a chemical analysis?

ANSWER: Yes.

QUESTION: Did that analysis consist of a six-step process?

ANSWER: Yes, it did.

QUESTION: Did you perform all six steps in accordance with accepted procedures?

ANSWER: Yes.

QUESTION: What were your results?

Leading questions were permissible in the above example because they were preliminary. If the adequacy or scrupulousness of the chemist's tests were in issue, however, leading questions would neither be allowed nor advisable. While it is a useful technique to use leading questions to skip over minor details, they should never be used as a substitute for the witness's own testimony concerning important issues.

Leading questions can also be used to make the witness seem less haughty or pretentious. Even an inherently modest witness may have some difficulty testifying to a list of glowing qualifications without appearing arrogant. Other witnesses do not even try to tone down the self-laudation. Imagine a series of answers along this line: "I am the author of *Principles of Business Valuation,* which is widely regarded as the leading treatise in the field. My book won three national awards, and it is regularly assigned at over 40 business schools." While the witness is no doubt justly proud of this achievement, the recitation may sound too self-important.

In contrast, counsel can elicit the same information through leading questions:

QUESTION: Are you the author of *Principles of Business Valuation?*

ANSWER: Yes, I am.

QUESTION: I understand that your book is widely regarded as the leading treatise in the field.

ANSWER: Well, I think others would have to make that judgment.

QUESTION: Let me put it this way. Your book won three national awards, didn't it?

ANSWER: Yes, it did.

QUESTION: And isn't it regularly assigned at over 40 business schools?

ANSWER: I believe that it is.

Again, the leading questions in this example may be considered preliminary because they are directed solely at the witness's qualifications.

I. Encourage Powerful Language

There is a tradition in many technical fields of hedging or qualifying the language in which conclusions are expressed. This makes great sense when discussing research, since one's results are always subject to further inquiry. Thus, it is not uncommon for professionals to use terms such as "to the best of my knowledge," or "according to current indications," or "as far as we can tell." While this language is meant to convey open-mindedness as opposed to uncertainty, it can be fatal to a witness's testimony in a courtroom.

To prevent inadvertent miscommunication, expert witnesses should be prepared to testify in straightforward, unequivocal terms. Experts should be

193

cautioned to avoid language that unintentionally qualifies or hedges their results, using instead wording that emphasizes accuracy and certainty.

Here is an example of weak language:

ANSWER: My best estimate at this time is that the restaurant chain would have earned approximately $3.2 million.

In fact, the witness has conducted an exhaustive study and is completely certain, within the bounds of professional competence, that $3.2 million is the correct figure. That certainty can be better expressed through more powerful language:

ANSWER: I have calculated lost profits at $3.2 million.

Or,

ANSWER: My projections show that the restaurant chain would have earned $3.2 million.

Or,

ANSWER: The result of my study is a determination of lost profits in the amount of $3.2 million.

The substitution of authoritative terminology for weak language may require a process of education for the witness. Of course, if the expert's conclusions really are tentative or provisional, counsel should not attempt to persuade the witness to testify otherwise.

J.   Use Enumeration

Audiences most often pay closer attention to information presented in numbered lists. Expert witnesses should therefore be encouraged to introduce concepts in terms of factors or considerations, rather than launching into extended explanations. The following is a good example of enumeration:

QUESTION: Dr. Haruo, what is your opinion of Dr. Longhini's study?

ANSWER: There are three basic problems with Dr. Longhini's study.

QUESTION: What are those problems?

ANSWER: First, she projected profits on the basis of only two factors. Second, she failed to consider location, which should have been the most important element. Third, she doesn't seem to recognize that population growth can be extremely uneven.

Counsel can now ask the witness to explain each of the three points. Note that the introduction of each point will reinitiate primacy, and therefore heighten the jury's attention.

K.   Consider Inoculation

Expert witnesses may be open to several distinct lines of cross examination.[18] Counsel should therefore consider conducting a certain amount of explanatory or defensive direct examination to "inoculate" the witness against cross examination on such matters as the payment of fees, the use of presumptions, reliance on secondary sources, and the like.

L.   Do Not Stretch the Witness's Expertise

It may be tempting to try to stretch a witness's expertise, either as a cost-saving measure or in an effort to enlarge the scope of her testimony. Both of these undertakings are misguided. It is risky, bordering upon unethical, to seek to have an expert testify outside of her legitimate field.

In the restaurant scenario we have seen examples of testimony from financial experts on the question of lost profits. Although the plaintiff's expert was called and qualified solely with regard to the issue of damages, some attorneys might venture to have the witness offer an opinion on liability as well. Perhaps the witness might do double duty by testifying that the defendant's pricing practices were predatory.

There are two immediate problems with this approach. First, it is unlikely that a single economist would really possess expertise with regard both to damage modeling and pricing practices. Second, even assuming sufficient expertise, once the witness takes a position on liability she will be compromised as an impartial arbiter of damages. A witness who advances too many favorable opinions may quickly come to be seen as a shill or hired gun.

More troubling is the possibility that some lawyers might try to inveigle the expert to offer opinions that are truly beyond the scope of their expertise. Such testimony, if given, puts the witness out on a limb that may well be sawed off during cross examination. Tactics aside, experts are intended to be both qualified and independent. It is therefore unethical to attempt to persuade a witness to exaggerate her qualifications, or to tamper with the independence of her views. Honorable experts will not allow attorneys to influence their opinions, and counsel must always respect this position. If an expert's ultimate conclusions are not sufficiently favorable, one need not call her as a witness.

---

18   Cross examination of expert witnesses is discussed in Section VI, *infra*, at p. 196.

VI. CROSS EXAMINATION OF EXPERT WITNESSES

Most of the basic approaches to cross examination discussed in Chapter Three can also be adapted to expert testimony. In addition, there are certain tools that can be used primarily or most effectively with expert witnesses.

Research, as much as technique, lies at the heart of expert witness cross examination. Counsel cannot conduct an adequate cross examination without first thoroughly investigating all of the technical aspects of the expected testimony. It is often said that you cannot cross examine an expert without first becoming an expert yourself.

Moreover, your research should extend beyond the expert's subject matter area and into the witness's own professional background. Counsel should read everything the witness has ever published, and should also attempt to obtain transcripts of prior trial and/or deposition testimony. There is nothing so effective as impeaching an expert with her own prior assertions. Other fruitful areas of investigation may include the expert's professional affiliations, past clients, governmental positions, and the like. Such research should not be viewed as an effort to dig up dirt (although once in a lifetime you might stumble across something juicy), but rather as an attempt to obtain a rounded picture of the expert's professional status. Many experts have become closely associated with certain positions over the course of their careers, and this knowledge can be of considerable assistance in shaping a cross examination.

The research necessary to cross examine an expert witness will necessarily vary considerably from case to case. The balance of this section is therefore limited to techniques that can be applied to expert witnesses in general.

A. Challenge the Witness's Credentials

An expert witness's credentials are subject to challenge either on voir dire or during cross examination. Voir dire may be used to object to the legal sufficiency of the expert's qualifications, while cross examination is the time to attack their weight.

1. Voir Dire on Credentials

Once the proponent of an expert has concluded the qualification segment of the direct examination, opposing counsel is entitled to conduct a voir dire of the witness. A voir dire examination temporarily suspends the direct so that the opponent of the proffered evidence can inquire as to its evidentiary sufficiency. With regard to the qualification of experts, this means that opposing counsel can interrupt the direct examination in order to conduct a mini-cross limited to the issue of the witness's credentials.

In jurisdictions that require the tender of expert witnesses, voir dire typically proceeds once the witness is proffered to the court:

PROPONENT: Your Honor, we tender Dr. Benjamin Haruo as an expert on the subject of lost profits.

COURT: Any objection, counsel?

OPPONENT: Your Honor, we would like the opportunity to conduct a voir dire examination.

COURT: You may examine the witness on the subject of his qualifications to testify.

In jurisdictions where tender is not utilized, it is necessary for opposing counsel to interpose an objection at the point where the witness begins to offer an opinion. Do not wait to be invited by the court:

PROPONENT: Dr. Haruo, do you have an opinion as to the profits that the plaintiff would have earned if the restaurant chain had not been driven out of business?

OPPONENT: Objection. Your Honor, we would like an opportunity for voir dire of this witness before he is allowed to give opinion testimony.

COURT: You may examine the witness on the subject of his qualifications to testify.

Note that voir dire is limited generally to the question of the admissibility of evidence. Thus, voir dire regarding an expert's credentials is restricted to the foundation for the witness's ability to opine on the issues in the case. In other words, is the witness "qualified as an expert by knowledge, skill, experience, training, or education?"[19] The witness may proceed with her testimony so long as he meets this minimum requirement. Voir dire is not the time to launch into a wide-ranging attack on the expert's integrity, methods, data, or bias.

It is frequently an uphill battle to persuade a judge that a proffered witness should not be allowed to testify as an expert. Judges often respond to such objections by ruling that they go only to the weight, and not the admissibility, of the expert testimony.

Nonetheless, it is possible to disqualify an expert through the use of voir dire. Purported experts can be disqualified by establishing the remoteness of their

---

19 Rule 702, Federal Rules of Evidence.

credentials, the inapplicability of their specialties, the lack of general acceptance of their purported expertise, or the unreliability of their data.

One caution. Counsel must decide whether to request that voir dire be conducted outside the presence of the jury. On one hand, it never hurts for the jury to hear negative information about a witness. On the other hand, a witness's credibility may be strengthened if an aggressive voir dire is unsuccessful and the court rules that the witness is, indeed, an expert.

2. Cross Examination on Credentials

The court's ruling that a witness may testify as an expert means only that the witness possesses sufficient credentials to pass the evidentiary threshold. It still may be possible to diminish the weight of the witness's qualifications during cross examination. There are three basic methods for discrediting the value of a witness's credentials.

a. Limit the Scope of the Witness's Expertise

Although a witness may be well-qualified in a certain area or sub-specialty, it may be possible to recast the issues of the case in such a way as to place them beyond the witness's competence. Assume, for example, that the plaintiff's expert in the restaurant scenario was tendered and accepted as an expert on lost profits:

QUESTION: Dr. Longhini, your primary consulting work involves business valuation, correct?

ANSWER: That is my profession.

QUESTION: Issues of valuation usually involve an existing business, right?

ANSWER: That is the usual case.

QUESTION: People come to you when they want to buy or sell a business, or when they have to value it for estate tax purposes, or perhaps when there is a divorce?

ANSWER: Yes, those are all typical situations for business valuation.

QUESTION: You wouldn't call yourself a management consultant, would you?

ANSWER: No, I do not get involved in operations.

QUESTION: Because your work is basically evaluative?

ANSWER: Exactly.

QUESTION: So someone who wanted assistance in expanding a business would need to go to a different consultant, wouldn't they?

ANSWER: Correct.

QUESTION: For example, there are consultants who specialize in site evaluation, correct?

ANSWER: Yes, there are.

QUESTION: But you do not do that yourself?

ANSWER: No, I do not.

QUESTION: So if I wanted to evaluate the best possible locations for my business outlets, you would recommend that I consult someone else, isn't that right?

ANSWER: Yes, I suppose that I would refer you.

Counsel may now argue that the crucial issue of location is beyond Dr. Longhini's expertise, and that her opinion regarding lost profits should therefore be discounted.

b. Stress Missing Credentials

An expert witness may be minimally qualified to testify, but still lack certain important certifications, degrees or licenses. Assume for example that the plaintiff in a personal injury case has called his psychotherapist to testify on the issue of damages. The witness was tendered and accepted as an expert, and has completed his direct testimony. This cross examination followed:

QUESTION: Mr. Halperin, your degree is in social work, correct?

ANSWER: Yes, I have an MSW and I am a licensed psychotherapist.

QUESTION: You do not have a doctorate in clinical psychology, do you?

ANSWER: No, I do not.

QUESTION: And of course you are not a psychiatrist?

ANSWER: That is correct.

QUESTION: I notice that your stationery lists your name as Donald Halperin, MSW.

ANSWER: Yes, that is right.

QUESTION: I have seen other social workers with the letters ACSW after their names. What does ACSW stand for?

ANSWER: It stands for Accredited Clinical Social Worker.

QUESTION: That is an additional certification that some social workers earn, correct?

ANSWER: Yes, that is correct.

QUESTION: But you have not achieved that certification, have you?

c. Contrast Your Expert's Credentials

It is most effective to point out an adverse witness's missing credentials when their absence can be contrasted with your own expert's superior qualifications. In the following example, assume that the plaintiff called a practicing attorney as an expert witness in a legal malpractice case. This scenario is taken from the defendant's cross examination:

QUESTION: Ms. Grant, I understand that you are a member of the American Bar Association Section of Litigation, correct?

ANSWER: Yes, I am.

QUESTION: The American Bar Association Section of Litigation is open to any lawyer who is willing to pay the dues, correct?

ANSWER: That is right.

QUESTION: So you were not elected or chosen by your peers for membership in that section, were you?

ANSWER: Nobody is.

QUESTION: I assume that you are familiar with the American College of Trial Lawyers?

ANSWER: I am.

QUESTION: That organization consists of lawyers who specialize in litigation and the trial of cases, correct?

ANSWER: I believe so.

QUESTION: Membership in the American College is limited to two percent of the lawyers in any given state, isn't that right?

ANSWER: I think that is right.

QUESTION: And individuals have to be proposed and elected to membership in the American College of Trial Lawyers?

ANSWER: I understand that to be the process.

QUESTION: You are not a member of the American College, are you?

ANSWER: No, I am not.

QUESTION: Are you aware that Ms. Bowman, the defendant's expert witness, is a member of the American College of Trial Lawyers?

ANSWER: I understand that she is.

Experts' credentials can be contrasted on bases other than certification. It is fair game to point out your own witness's greater or more specific experience, your witness's teaching or publication record, or any other disparity that will enhance your expert and diminish the opposition.

Note, however, that all of the rules of basic cross examination apply here as well. You must be satisfied to elicit the fact of the contrasting qualifications. It will do you little good to argue with the opposing witness, or to try to extract a concession that her credentials are inadequate.

B. Obtain Favorable Information

It will often be possible to obtain favorable concessions from the opposing party's expert witness. As with all cross examination, it is usually wisest to attempt to extract such information near the beginning of the examination. Needless to say, one must be positive of the answers before launching into this sort of cross examination.

In general, the helpful material available from opposing experts will fall into the following categories.

1. Affirm Your Own Expert

Even experts who ultimately disagree may have many shared understandings. You may therefore contribute to the accreditation of your own expert by asking the opposing expert to acknowledge the reliability of your expert's data, the validity of her assumptions, or the caliber or her credentials.

2. Elicit Areas of Agreement

In addition, it may be possible to elicit concessions from the opposing expert that go to the merits of the case. The adverse expert may, for example, be willing to agree with several of your major premises, even while disagreeing with your ultimate conclusion. Consider this cross examination of the defense expert in the drive-in restaurant case:

QUESTION: Dr. Longhini, you are dissatisfied with the nature of Dr. Haruo's study of lost profits, correct?

ANSWER: Yes, I have trouble with Dr. Haruo's methodology.

QUESTION: But you do agree, don't you, that the chain had been operating as a going concern?

ANSWER: Yes, I do.

QUESTION: In fact, the restaurant chain had made a profit every year they were in business?

ANSWER: I believe that is correct.

QUESTION: And every one of their outlets was profitable, correct?

ANSWER: I think that is right.

QUESTION: So someone must have been able to select profitable locations, right?

ANSWER: I suppose so.

QUESTION: Dr. Haruo assumed that the chain would continue to choose good locations, isn't that right?

ANSWER: That is implicit in his model.

QUESTION: And you did not conduct an independent study of favorable or unfavorable restaurant locations, did you?

ANSWER: No, I did not.

QUESTION: So you have not data that you can point to that would contradict Dr. Haruo's assumption?

ANSWER: I do not.

3. Criticize the Opposing Party's Conduct

Finally, it may be possible to draw from an opposing expert significant criticism of her own party's conduct. Though the expert reached a final conclusion favorable to the party, she may be unwilling to approve of all of their underlying actions. For example:

QUESTION: Dr. Haruo, in order for you to reach your opinion on damages it was necessary for you to review all of the plaintiff's financial records, correct?

ANSWER: Yes, that is correct.

QUESTION: Isn't it true that the plaintiff company did not keep accurate store-by-store records?

ANSWER: Yes, they aggregated their financial information, rather than breaking it down store-by-store.

QUESTION: The absence of store-by-store information must have made your job more difficult.

ANSWER: I found that I was able to achieve accurate results on the basis of state-wide projections.

QUESTION: I understand your position. Still, you could have projected profits for each individual restaurant if the available financial data had been more precise, isn't that true?

ANSWER: Yes, that is true.

QUESTION: But because of the plaintiff's aggregate record keeping, you were not able to do that?

ANSWER: No one could have made such projections on the basis of that data.

C. Use of Learned Treatises

One form of cross examination unique to expert witnesses is impeachment through the use of a learned treatise. Under the Federal Rules of Evidence an expert witness may be confronted with statements contained in "published treatises, periodicals, or pamphlets on a subject of history, medicine, or other science or art," so long as they are established as reliable authority.[20]

Contrary to the belief of many lawyers and judges, it is not necessary to establish that the witness has relied on the particular treatise, or even that the witness acknowledge it as authoritative. Under the Federal Rules the reliability of a learned treatise may be established either by admission of the witness, or by other expert testimony, or by judicial notice.[21] Impeachment, then, could conceivably take this form:

---

20   Rule 803(18), Federal Rules of Evidence.
21   Rule 803(18), Federal Rules of Evidence.

QUESTION: Are you familiar with Lubet's *Modern Trial Advocacy?*

ANSWER: Certainly.

QUESTION: Do you regard it as authoritative in the field?

ANSWER: Absolutely not.

QUESTION: I want to read you a passage from Lubet's *Modern Trial Advocacy.*

OPPONENT: Objection, Your Honor. The witness testified that Lubet is not regarded as an authority.

QUESTION: Your Honor, we will produce other expert testimony that Lubet's *Modern Trial Advocacy* is regarded as an authoritative text.

COURT: You may proceed.

Of course, it is far more persuasive when the witness agrees that the treatise is indeed recognized as a leading authority. You can insure such a favorable response by restricting your impeachment to widely recognized sources. Alternatively, you can utilize the expert's deposition to determine exactly what treatises she will accept as reliable.

In either case, once the reliability of the treatise is confirmed, the impeachment may proceed one of two ways. You may read a passage from the treatise into evidence without asking the expert any questions about it; the Federal Rules require only that the passage be called to the witness's attention. The more traditional approach is to ask the witness whether she agrees with the particular quotation. At that point the witness must either accede or disagree. If she accepts the statement, your job is done. If she disagrees, you may argue later that she is out of step with recognized authority.

Finally, note that this rule allows an excerpt from a learned treatise to be read into evidence, but that the treatise itself may not be received as an exhibit.

D. Challenge the Witness's Impartiality

Expert witnesses are supposed to be independent analysts, not advocates. The worst thing you can say about an expert witness is that she has altered her opinion to fit a party's needs. Accordingly, it can be very effective to cross examine an expert on the issue of bias, if the material is there to be exploited. Cross examination on bias falls into three basic categories.

1. Fees

Most experts in litigation are retained and paid significant fees. While the acceptance of money in exchange for testimony would initially seem to be a fruitful area for cross examination, the reality is somewhat less promising.

First, the trier of fact is likely to understand that no witness could afford to perform extensive tests or analyses without being compensated. Second, all experts in the case are probably being paid, so there is little ground to be gained by making a point of it on cross examination when your own expert is equally vulnerable. Finally, most experienced experts will be adept at turning such challenges aside.

It is generally productive to cross examine an expert concerning her fee only in fairly limited circumstances. For example, it may demonstrate bias if the fee is extraordinarily large. Similarly, it may be evidence of something less than objectivity if the witness has a large unpaid fee outstanding at the time that she testifies.

Certain fee arrangements are unethical; these will be discussed in the section on ethics and expert testimony.[22]

2. Relationship with Party or Counsel

An expert's relationship with a party or with counsel may also indicate a lack of impartiality. Some witnesses seem to work hand in glove with certain law firms, testifying to similar conclusions in case after case. While such an ongoing relationship is not proof of bias, it does suggest that the association may have been sustained for a reason.

The extent of the repeated retention is important. It will usually be of little significance that an expert worked on two or three cases for one law firm over a fairly lengthy period. After all, the firm might prize the witness precisely for her independence. On the other hand, it can become questionable when a firm has engaged the same expert on a dozen or more occasions. While there may be a perfectly innocent explanation for this constancy, it is certainly reasonable to bring it out on cross examination.

The same analysis obtains to witnesses who have testified repeatedly for the same party, although retained by different law firms.

Finally, some cases may involve testimony by in-house experts, perhaps a company's own accountant or engineer. In most cases, such experts are susceptible to no more suggestion of bias than would be any other employee. In some situations, however, the in-house expert's own judgment will be at issue in the

---

22 *See* Section VII, *infra* at p. 211.

case. An accountant, for example, may have failed to see that a debt was under-collateralized; an engineer may not have not have foreseen the need for more exacting tolerances. In these circumstances the cross examination must bring out the witness's personal stake in the outcome of the litigation.

3. Positional Bias

With or without regard to past retention, some experts seem wedded to certain professional, scientific, or intellectual positions. Experts frequently come to testify only for plaintiffs or only for defendants. Others reach only one of a range of conclusions. Some psychiatrists, for example, have been known never to find a single criminal defendant to be sane or competent. Where they exist, these rigidly held positional biases can be exploited effectively on cross examination.

4. Preparation for Cross Examination on Bias

Diligent preparation is required before cross examining an expert witness on bias. Partiality is a serious accusation to make against an expert witness, and it should not be levelled without a good faith basis for the claim. Cross examination is not the time to make random inquiries, much less baseless charges, as to lack of objectivity or independence.

It is essential that counsel use discovery and investigation to explore thoroughly all of an expert's potential biases. Cross examination can then be limited to those assertions that can be supported in fact.

E. Point Out Omissions

An expert may be vulnerable on cross examination if she has failed to conduct essential tests or procedures, or if she has neglected to consider all significant factors. The question of neglected tests or experiments will depend upon the unique factors of each case. You must pursue thorough discovery to determine whether processes were short-cut or slighted, preferably after first consulting your own expert.

Other sorts of omissions are more commonplace. Witnesses are frequently asked to give evaluations concerning the validity or accuracy of other experts' work. A consulting pathologist, for example, might be asked to re-evaluate the protocol of an autopsy conducted by the local medical examiner. No matter how prominent, a "second-opinion" witness can almost always be undermined by the fact that she did not conduct the primary investigation:

QUESTION: Dr. Fine, you reach a conclusion quite different from the conclusions reached by Dr. Barry, correct?

ANSWER: Yes.

QUESTION: Of course, you did not perform an autopsy yourself, did you?

ANSWER: No, I did not.

QUESTION: In fact, your information comes exclusively from Dr. Barry's autopsy protocol?

ANSWER: That is right.

QUESTION: So you have relied on Dr. Barry for all of your factual information, isn't that right?

ANSWER: Yes, I have.

QUESTION: You know nothing of the actual circumstances of the autopsy, other than what you have learned from Dr. Barry's report?

ANSWER: Correct.

QUESTION: So at least with regard to gathering information, you have trusted Dr. Barry's work.

This technique is not limited to "re-evaluating" experts. It can be employed, in different form, with regard to any witness who relies exclusively on information provided by others:

QUESTION: Dr. Fine, you base your opinion solely on an examination of hospital records, correct?

ANSWER: Correct.

QUESTION: You did not examine the decedent yourself, did you?

ANSWER: No, I did not.

QUESTION: So your opinion can only be as good as the information you received, right?

ANSWER: I suppose so.

QUESTION: If any of that information were faulty, that could affect the basis for your opinion, correct?

ANSWER: Yes, depending upon the circumstances.

QUESTION: The same would be true of missing information, right?

ANSWER: Right.

QUESTION: You'll agree with me, won't you, that firsthand observation is preferred for the purpose of diagnosis?

ANSWER: Yes, it is preferred.

Finally, many experts will testify on the basis of statistics or studies compiled from other sources. Frequently, such experts will not have investigated the reliability of the underlying data, and this can leave them vulnerable to cross examination.

F. Substitute Information

1. Change Assumptions

As we have seen, almost all experts must use assumptions of one sort or another in the course of formulating their opinions. An expert's assumptions, however, might be unrealistic, unreliable, or unreasonably favorable to the retaining party. It can be extremely effective, therefore, to ask the witness to alter an assumption, substituting one that you believe to be more in keeping with the evidence in the case. Consider this scenario from the drive-in restaurant case:

QUESTION: Dr. Longhini, your lost-profits calculation includes an assumption that vehicle miles will continue to grow at the rate of 4%, correct?

ANSWER: Yes, that is the figure I used.

QUESTION: Will you agree that numerous factors can influence the growth of vehicle miles?

ANSWER: Yes, I think that is obvious.

QUESTION: For example, vehicle miles actually fell during the oil embargo?

ANSWER: I believe that is true.

QUESTION: And if vehicle miles were to rise at a rate of less than 4%, your estimate of lost profits would have to be reduced, correct?

ANSWER: Yes, that is right.

QUESTION: In fact, if we used an assumption of 2%, your estimate of lost profits would have to be reduced by over $600,000?

ANSWER: I haven't done the calculation, but it should be something in that range.

When the substituted assumption calls for recalculation, it is generally most effective to do the math in advance, rather than asking the witness to do it on the spot. A request that the witness perform the computation is an invitation to quibble.

2. Vary the Facts

A related technique is to vary the facts upon which the expert has relied, or to suggest additional facts, as in this example from the restaurant case:

QUESTION: Dr. Longhini, you are aware that the plaintiff's most profitable outlet was in the Lincoln Walk Mall, correct?

ANSWER: Yes.

QUESTION: And the continued existence of that outlet was a fact that you relied on in calculating your result, right?

ANSWER: That is right.

QUESTION: But if the entire Lincoln Walk Mall were to close due to bankruptcy, then you would have to change your conclusion, isn't that right?

ANSWER: I suppose that is correct.

QUESTION: Well, you couldn't have a profitable restaurant in a closed mall, could you?

ANSWER: Of course not.

As with all cross examination questions, counsel must have a good faith basis for asserting new or varied facts to an expert witness.

3. Degree of Certainty

It is also possible to challenge an expert's degree of certainty by suggesting alternative scenarios or explanations:

QUESTION: Dr. Haruo, you believe that the plaintiff's history of profitability is largely attributable to location, correct?

ANSWER: Yes, I think that location is, and has been, the most important factor.

QUESTION: But there are other factors that contribute to profitability, correct?

ANSWER: Certainly.

QUESTION: Some of those factors would be product quality, value, or market demand, correct?

ANSWER: Yes.

209

QUESTION: You are surely familiar with the term "destination shopping," aren't you?

ANSWER: Of course.

QUESTION: That means that people will travel to seek out value or quality or amenities, regardless of the location, correct?

ANSWER: That does happen.

QUESTION: Well, you didn't interview the plaintiff's customers, did you?

ANSWER: Of course not.

QUESTION: So you cannot be sure that location was of primary importance to them, can you?

ANSWER: I can't look into their minds.

QUESTION: Isn't it possible that the plaintiff's customers sought out their restaurants because of value or quality?

ANSWER: It is possible.

QUESTION: So it is also possible that location was not the primary factor in plaintiff's profitability?

4. Dependence on Other Testimony

The opinion of an expert witness often depends upon facts to be established by other witnesses. Thus, the expert's testimony may be undermined, not by anything you ask the expert directly, but rather by challenging its factual underpinnings during the cross examination of the fact witnesses. It is necessary only to obtain the expert's concession that the other witness's facts are essential to her opinion:

QUESTION: Dr. Longhini, part of your opinion is based on Ms. Van Zant's statement that she was certain that the restaurant chain would have been able to obtain funding for continued expansion, correct?

ANSWER: Correct.

Counsel need examine the expert no further, so long as Ms. Van Zant's certainty of funding can later be shaken or refuted. The connection — that the expert's opinion is weakened — may be drawn during final argument. Alternatively, counsel could ask the expert to concede that the opinion would have to be changed if the expansion money were not available.

G. Challenge Technique or Theory

The most difficult, though frequently the most tempting, form of expert cross examination is to challenge the witness's method, theory, or logic. It is possible, but extremely unlikely, that an expert will agree that she made a mistake or that her reasoning is faulty. In most cases you have little to gain by confronting an expert with any but the most glaring flaws, since that will only afford her an opportunity to explain. It is usually far more effective to use your own expert to point out the opposition's errors, and then to draw your own conclusions during final argument.

VII. ETHICS OF EXPERT EXAMINATION

A. Fees

Unlike other witnesses who can be reimbursed only for expenses, an expert may be paid a fee for preparing and testifying in court.[23] There is authority that an expert's fee must be "reasonable," but that limit has never been well-defined.[24] In any event, an unreasonably large fee would render the witness extremely vulnerable on cross examination.

A more salient restriction is the rule against paying contingent fees to expert witnesses, which is found in virtually every jurisdiction.[25] Contingent fees are prohibited because they provide the expert with an unacceptable incentive to tailor her opinion to the interests of the party retaining her.

Expert testimony should be objective, and the expert's compensation therefore should not be dependent on the outcome of the case or the content of her opinion. Thus, it is also unethical to raise or lower an expert's hourly rate on the basis of the result of the initial research or evaluation.[26]

---

23 Rule 3.4(b) comment 3, Model Rules of Professional Conduct. *See also* DR 7-109(C), Model Code of Professional Responsibility.

24 DR 7-109(C)(3), Model Code of Professional Responsibility. This provision has been superseded in most states by Rule 3.4 of the Model Rules of Professional Conduct, the text of which does not carry over the reasonableness requirement. The Comment to Rule 3.4 defers to state law on the subject of fees, again making no reference to reasonableness.

25 The rule is explicit in the Model Code of Professional Responsibility: "A lawyer shall not pay, offer to pay, or acquiesce in the payment of compensation to a witness contingent upon the content of his testimony or the outcome of the case." DR 7-109(C), Model Code of Professional Responsibility. The Comments to the Model Rules of Professional Conduct point out that "the common rule in most jurisdictions is that it is . . . improper to pay an expert witness a contingent fee." Rule 3.4, comment 3, Model Rules of Professional Conduct.

26 Most experts bill at a constant hourly rate. An expert whose evaluation leads to a favorable opinion may presumably be retained for further hours to be spent on preparation, deposition, and trial testimony. While this additional work will obviously lead to greater total compensation, it is not considered a contingent fee.

B. Influencing Testimony

Lawyers typically retain experts for one reason only: in order to help win the case. Given the expense involved, there may be a temptation to view the expert as simply another member of the team who can be enlisted to provide whatever advocacy is necessary. Thus, it is not unknown for attorneys to attempt to persuade experts to alter the content of their opinions. This is wrong. It is no more acceptable to attempt to persuade an expert to change her opinion than it would be to try to convince a percipient witness to change his account of the facts. The entire system of expert testimony rests upon the assumption that experts are independent of the retaining attorneys. Counsel must take care not to attempt or appear to use the fee relationship to corrupt the expert's autonomy.[27] It is similarly unethical to attempt to color an expert's testimony by withholding damaging facts or by providing false information or data.

As with other witnesses, it is not unethical to assist an expert to prepare for trial. Counsel may inform the witness of the questions to be asked on direct examination, and may alert the witness to potential cross examination. An expert may be advised to use powerful language, to avoid jargon, to use analogies, to refrain from long narratives, or to use other means that will help her convey her opinion accurately.

C. Disclosure and Discovery

The Federal Rules of Civil Procedure, and the corresponding rules in most states, contain limitations on discovery and disclosure with respect to expert witnesses.[28] In brief, experts are divided into two categories: those who are expected to testify and those who are retained only as consultants. Although there are exceptions, only testifying experts are generally subject to discovery.[29] Purely consulting experts, other than in extreme circumstances, are exempt from discovery.[30]

---

27 Rule 3.4(b) of the Model Rules of Professional Conduct provides that a lawyer shall not "counsel or assist a witness to testify falsely." An expert's opinion can be false if it is induced by a desire to please counsel or obtain compensation, as opposed to an objective investigation of the facts and circumstances of the case. *See also* DR 7-102(A)(6), Model Code of Professional Responsibility.

28 Rule 26(b)(4), Federal Rules of Civil Procedure.

29 The Federal Rules seem to place limitations on the discovery that can be had from testifying experts, but in practice these limitations are usually waived by stipulation of the parties or canceled upon motion or by order of the court. Rule 26(B)(4)(A), Federal Rules of Civil Procedure.

30 Rule 26(B)(4)(B), Federal Rules of Civil Procedure.

The question that arises is whether it is ethical to attempt to interview an opposing party's consulting witness, from whom formal discovery is not available. The courts are divided on this issue. Some jurisdictions hold that Rule 26, or its equivalent, is intended to shield non-testifying experts from all disclosure, formal or informal. Other courts have held that the discovery rules apply only to discovery, and that extramural interviews are permissible. There is also a third approach that allows supervised interviews, but only with leave of court. Needless to say, counsel must take care to determine the relevant jurisdiction's law on this issue before attempting to interview the opposition's non-testifying expert.[31]

---

31   This issue is treated at length in Underwood and Fortune, *Trial Ethics,* 185-194 (1988).

— CHAPTER SEVEN —
Objections

I. MAKING THE RECORD

There is a technical, as well as an artistic, side to trial advocacy. The laws of evidence and procedure govern the manner in which a trial proceeds. It is not sufficient for information to be persuasive and elegant, or even true; it must also be admissible under the law of evidence and presented properly under the rules of trial procedure. The process of bringing and contesting information before the court and jury is called making the record.

Making the record involves a series of steps. Attorneys offer evidence in the form of testimony and exhibits. Some of this evidence may become the subject of objections, in which case the trial judge is called upon to make rulings on admissibility. The admissible evidence is presented before the fact-finder. If properly preserved, both the evidence and the objections may eventually be reviewed by an appellate court.

In order to make a record, it is necessary to operationalize the rules of evidence and procedure. It is not enough to understand the theory of the hearsay rule, one must also be able to recognize hearsay on an almost instinctual level, and to articulate a persuasive objection at virtually any given moment. It is not enough to comprehend the foundation for the admission of a past recollection, it is also necessary to be able to elicit the foundation in a manner that will be persuasive to the trier of fact. In other words, making the record calls for knowledge, judgment, decisiveness, adaptability, and reflexes.

This chapter will discuss the use of objections. The next chapter will cover two related aspects of making a trial record: exhibits and foundations.

Objections are the means by which evidentiary disputes are raised and resolved. Objections may be made to an attorney's questions, to a witness's testimony, to the introduction or use of exhibits, to a lawyer's demeanor or behavior, and even to the conduct of the judge.

Most of a trial advocate's energy is understandably devoted to the content of her case. What do the witnesses have to say? What facts are available to prove the case? How can the opposition be undermined? Which events are central to the proof? Is it possible for several different stories to be harmonized? A persuasive story rests upon the manner in which facts can be developed, arranged, and presented to the trier of fact. It is equally, and sometimes more important, however, that the advocate also be well-versed in the technical side of trial advocacy. A well-conceived and tightly constructed story cannot persuade a jury if its crucial elements are not admitted into the record, or if the opposition has had the benefit of using substantial amounts of inadmissible evidence.

II. OBJECTIONS

A. Purpose and Function

1. Use of Objections at Trial

An objection is a request that the court rule on the admissibility of certain testimony or evidence. The purpose of objecting is to prevent the introduction or consideration of inadmissible information. Although the process of objecting has become associated in the popular mind with contentiousness and even hostility, that need not be the case. Our adversary system relies upon opposing attorneys to present evidence, and the judge to decide upon its admissibility. An objection, then, is nothing more than a signal to the judge that there is a disagreement between counsel concerning the rules of evidence or procedure. When there are no objections, which is the overwhelming majority of the time, the judge can allow evidence to come into the record without the need for a specific ruling. If we had no process of objecting, the trial judge would have to rule upon every separate answer and item of evidence. Unless the process is abused or misused, trials are actually expedited by the judge's ability to rely upon counsel to object to questionable evidence.

Objections can be made to questions, answers, exhibits, and virtually anything else that occurs during a trial.

An attorney's question may be objectionable because of its form, or because it calls for inadmissible evidence. A question is objectionable as to form when it seeks to obtain information in an impermissible way. For example, a leading question on direct examination is improper because it tells the witness what answer is expected.[1] Even if the answer itself would be admissible, the question is disallowed because of its suggestiveness. Compound questions, vague questions, and argumentative questions, to name a few, are also objectionable as to form.

Conversely, a question phrased in proper form may nonetheless call for inadmissible evidence. The information sought may be irrelevant, privileged, or hearsay. An objection may be made when it is apparent from the question itself that the answer should not be admitted. The question, "What is your religious

---

[1] Leading questions are discussed in greater detail in Section IV A(1), *infra* at p. 250.

belief?" is in proper form. Any answer, however, would be inadmissible under most circumstances by virtue of the Federal Rules of Evidence.[2] The question is therefore objectionable.

Even in the absence of an objectionable question, a witness may respond with an inadmissible answer. The answer might volunteer irrelevant information, it might contain unanticipated hearsay, or it might consist entirely of speculation. For example, a direct examiner could ask the perfectly allowable question, "How do you know that the traffic light was red?" only to receive the hearsay reply, "Because someone told me just last week." Opposing counsel would no doubt object to the answer and move that it be stricken from the record.

Finally, objections may be made to anything else that might have an impermissible impact on the trier of fact. A lawyer can object if opposing counsel raises her voice to a witness or approaches the witness in an intimidating manner. Objections can be made to the manner in which exhibits are displayed, or to the position of chairs and tables in the courtroom. Even the judge's words and actions are not immune to objection, although it is admittedly awkward to ask the court to rule on the permissibility of its own conduct.

2. Use of Objections before Trial

It is not always necessary to wait until trial to move for the exclusion of evidence. Motions in limine are available to obtain pretrial rulings on evidence that is potentially so harmful that even mention of it may prejudice the jury. A motion in limine asks the judge to rule that the offending evidence be found inadmissible, and that it not be offered or introduced at trial.[3]

A motion in limine can be based on any of the substantive rules of evidence. Note, however, that the motion usually will not be granted merely because the subject evidence is objectionable. An additional showing is usually required that the evidence is so damaging that once it is mentioned a sustained objection at trial will not be sufficient to undo its prejudicial impact.

a. Effect of Granting the Motion

Once granted, a motion in limine excludes all references to the subject evidence. Not only is the evidence itself disallowed, but counsel may not offer it or refer to it in a question. Evidence excluded in this manner also may not be

---

2   Evidence of the beliefs or opinions of a witness on matters of religion is not admissible for the purpose of showing that by reason of their nature his credibility is impaired or enhanced. Rule 610, Federal Rules of Evidence.

3   A motion in limine may also be used to obtain an advance ruling that evidence is admissible. With such a ruling in hand counsel can better frame her trial theory, and can also plan witness examinations so as to avoid the possibility of reversible error. Nonetheless, this "reverse" use of the motion in limine is fairly unusual.

mentioned during jury selection, opening statements, or closing arguments. In the appropriate situation witnesses may be instructed not to volunteer testimony concerning the excluded evidence.

For example, assume that the plaintiff in a contract action had been convicted of disorderly conduct while participating in a peace demonstration during the 1960s. The conviction is clearly not admissible under the Federal Rules of Evidence[4]. An order granting plaintiff's motion in limine would prevent defense counsel from inquiring about the conviction during the cross examination of the plaintiff. It would also bar mention of the conviction during jury selection, opening statement, and closing argument. Finally, the defense attorney could be required to instruct all of her witnesses to refrain from mentioning the plaintiff's past conviction.

Alternatively, the court might grant only some portion of a motion in limine. The court may exclude some, although not all, of the subject evidence, or could enter an order limiting its use. In the above example, it is conceivable that the judge might rule that the conviction is admissible for impeachment, but only if the plaintiff first offers evidence of his own good character.[5] In that case, the conviction could still not be mentioned during jury selection or opening statement, but it might become admissible once the plaintiff took the stand.

b. Effect of Reserving Ruling on the Motion

Judges may reserve ruling on motions in limine, as it is often difficult or impossible to determine whether evidence should be excluded until the trial is under way. The admissibility of some evidence may depend upon the foundational testimony that precedes it. In such circumstances the judge might want to delay ruling until the trial evidence is more fully developed.

To prevent prejudice to the moving party, many judges will instruct counsel to refrain from mentioning the subject evidence until the reserved motion can be ruled upon. This will generally require the offering attorney to wait until she believes the foundation has been established, and then to approach the bench for a decision on the motion in limine.

c. Effect of Denying the Motion

The denial of a motion in limine does not necessarily mean that the subject evidence is absolutely admissible. It may mean only that there are insufficient grounds to take the step of excluding it before the trial begins. Thus, even where a pretrial motion has been denied, an objection to the same evidence at trial might be sustained.

---

4   Rule 609, Federal Rules of Evidence.

5   *See* Rule 404(a)(1), Federal Rules of Evidence.

If possible, the court should be asked to clarify the meaning of an order denying a motion in limine. Has the evidence been found admissible, or is it simply too soon to decide?

3. Preservation of the Record on Appeal

Appellate courts typically will not consider issues that were not originally raised in the trial court. The admission of evidence generally cannot be reviewed unless it was the subject of a motion in limine, or a timely objection was made at trial.[6] Thus, objections serve not only to alert the trial judge to the need for a ruling, they also define the scope of the evidentiary issues that can be considered on appeal.

B. The Decision to Object

1. The Process of Decision-making

In the heat of trial the decision on whether to object to some item of evidence must usually be made literally on a split-second basis. A question on either direct or cross examination typically lasts less than ten seconds, and a long question will go on for no more than twenty seconds, yet within that time counsel must recognize, formulate, and evaluate all possible objections. The concentration required is enormous and there is no opportunity for letup; counsel must pay exquisite attention to every question and every answer, lest some devastating bit of inadmissible evidence sneak its way into the record. There is no room for even the slightest lapse.

The decision-making process consists of three distinct phases. Counsel must first recognize the objectionability of the particular question, answer, or exhibit. This is often the easiest step, since many questions simply "sound wrong." In addition, it is often possible to rely upon certain key words and phrases to jog the objection reflex. Questions that use words such as "could" or "might" or "possible" commonly call for speculation. Questions that ask about out-of-court statements or conversations must clear the hearsay hurdle.

Following recognition, the next task is to formulate a valid objection. Does the question truly call for speculation, or is it an acceptable lay opinion? Is the out-of-court statement inadmissible hearsay, or does it fall within one of the many exceptions? Even if there is a potentially applicable exception, is it possible to present a counter-argument in favor of excluding the evidence? This is the sort of analysis that can fill pages in an appellate opinion or an evidence casebook, but

---

6   *See* Rule 103(a)(1), Federal Rules of Evidence. The only exception is in the case of "plain error," in which case the appellate court can take notice of egregious errors affecting substantive rights, even if they were not brought to the attention of the trial judge. *See* Rule 103(d), Federal Rules of Evidence.

trial counsel must undertake it within the five or ten seconds during which a viable objection can be made.

Finally, counsel must evaluate the tactical situation in order to determine whether the objection is worth making. It is well worth noting that not every valid objection needs to be made. There is little point to objecting if opposing counsel will be able to rectify the problem simply by rephrasing the question, or if the information is not ultimately harmful to your case. Moreover, there are often good reasons to refrain from objecting.

2. Reasons Not to Object

a. Jurors' Reactions

Objections are tiresome. They interrupt the flow of the evidence, they distract attention from the real issues at hand, and they have an awful tendency to degenerate into posturing and/or whining. It is always possible that the objecting lawyer will lose points with the judge or jury by constantly interrupting the opposition.

It was once widely held that jurors hate objections, and that this alone was reason enough to avoid objecting in all but the most pressing circumstances. More recent thinking on the subject is that jurors understand the need for lawyers to object and see it as part of counsel's job, so long as it is not overdone. Juror reaction, then, becomes a reason to utilize objections wisely and sparingly, but not to stand in fear of making them at all.

b. Judge's Reaction

Fear of losing, however, remains a substantial reason to refrain from objecting. No lawyer can predict with certainty that a judge will agree with his or her objections. A judge may overrule an objection because she misunderstood it, because her knowledge of the law of evidence is inadequate, or because she just wants to move the trial along without interruption. A judge might also overrule an objection because it was meritless, foolish, or contemptuous. Whatever the reason, it hardly enhances counsel's stock to be overruled regularly when making objections. It is therefore necessary to evaluate the risk of losing when deciding whether to object.

Bear in mind, however, that an unmade objection cannot preserve the record for appeal. Only an objection that is presented and overruled can later be considered by the appellate court. Reticence in objecting can therefore result in the waiver of important issues. Fear of losing should never be the sole determining factor in deciding whether to object. It can even be tactically advantageous to make and lose an objection, since this may lay the groundwork for a successful appeal.

c. Opponent's Reaction

What goes around comes around. Counsel who objects at every turn will eventually find her own examinations punctuated by the intercessions of the opposing lawyer. This sort of interchange serves no good end, and can only detract from the dignity and value of the adversary system.

In a well-prepared trial involving experienced counsel it would not be surprising for hours, even days, to go by without a single objection. When objections are made, they are directed at important items of evidence whose admissibility is seriously in doubt. While this standard cannot be achieved in every case, it is one to which we all might aspire.

3. Deciding to Object

The decision to object must be made in reference to your theory of the case. Concerning every potential objection, always ask: Will the exclusion of the evidence contribute to my theory of the case? Unless the exclusion of the evidence actually advances your theory, there is generally no need to raise an objection.

The principal contribution that an objection can make to your theory of the case is to prevent the admission of truly damaging evidence. Thus the maxim, "Do not object to anything that doesn't hurt you." You can refine the decision even further by asking these two additional questions: Even if the information is harmful, can it be accommodated by other means? Even if the objection is sustained, will the information eventually be admitted after another question or through another witness?

a. Accommodating Harmful Evidence

Harmful information can often be accommodated through explanation or argument. Indeed, the function of the theory of the case is precisely to anticipate the use of harmful information and to develop a story that both accounts for and devalues it. Consider the case of a plaintiff in a personal injury case being cross examined on the issue of damages. She testified on direct that the injuries to her hand prevented her from engaging in many activities that she previously had enjoyed, including oil painting. The cross examiner, armed with information gained in discovery, has determined to show that plaintiff's inability to paint is of no great value:

QUESTION: You used to engage in oil painting, and now you can't? Correct?

QUESTION: You even considered becoming a professional artist?

QUESTION: You tried to sell your paintings in a local gallery?

QUESTION: But not a single person ever bought one, right?

QUESTION: You even gave up painting several times out of frustration, didn't you?

QUESTION: In fact, just before the accident the gallery owner told you that your paintings could not even be displayed there any longer, isn't that right?

QUESTION: The fact is, you were never any good at all at painting, were you?

Should the plaintiff's counsel have objected to these questions? Her inability to sell her paintings seems irrelevant to her current injuries, since she did not claim loss of income. The gallery owner's statement appears to be hearsay. The parting shot was surely argumentative. And the purpose of the examination was to damage the plaintiff.

On the other hand, the information can be accommodated. Imagine the plaintiff's explanation, either during cross examination or on redirect:

ANSWER: I never painted for money. It was just my way of relaxing and enjoying myself.

ANSWER: Being in the gallery was nice, but the real joy came from holding the brush and creating the images.

ANSWER: I suppose I wasn't that good in some people's eyes, but just standing at the easel and creating was enough for me. Now I can never do that again.

Or imagine the final argument of plaintiff's lawyer:

Maybe my client wasn't the best painter in the world, but it was a hobby that brought her inner peace. It was a way for her to lose the troubles of the day. Even if the paintings were bad, that harmed no one. She seeks damages not from the loss of a profession or job, but from the loss of her enjoyment of life. So what if she was a poor painter? Does that give the defendant the right to crush her hand so that she can no longer even hold a brush? And who knows, perhaps she would have improved? Perhaps she would have been discovered? Now she will never know.

In other words, the plaintiff's theory of damages can accommodate, perhaps even benefit from, the nasty cross examination. Counsel therefore must choose. Is it better to object in the hope of terminating the line of questioning, or is there more to be gained by weaving the cross examination into the plaintiff's own case? There is no definite answer to this question, other than to note that reflexive objection is not always the optimum solution.

b. Eventual Admissibility

A further consideration is the eventual admissibility of the information. When a question is improper solely as a matter of form, it can generally be cured simply with rephrasing. An objection, therefore, is quite unlikely to result in the actual exclusion of any evidence. This is particularly true of leading questions on direct examination:

QUESTION: Isn't it true that you had the green light as you approached the intersection?

OBJECTION: Counsel is leading his own witness.

THE COURT: The objection is sustained.

QUESTION: What color was the traffic light as you approached the intersection?

ANSWER: It was green.

In this example the objection to the leading question accomplished nothing in the way of excluding evidence, and may actually have emphasized the witness's testimony that the light was green. Counsel would have been just as well off not making it. Of course, the persistent use of leading questions to feed answers to a witness is quite another matter. In those circumstances an objection should almost always be made. The use of an occasional leading question, however, is so easily cured that experienced counsel seldom object.

A variation on this theme occurs when information is objectionable coming from one witness but conceivably admissible if elicited from another. Hearsay provides a good example, as in this direct examination of the defendant driver in an intersection case:

QUESTION: Did you speak to anyone following the accident?

ANSWER: Yes, I spoke to a crossing guard who was standing on the corner.

QUESTION: Did the crossing guard tell you what he saw?

ANSWER: Yes.

QUESTION: What did the crossing guard tell you that he saw?

OBJECTION: Hearsay.[7]

THE COURT: Sustained.

Here, the objecting lawyer has succeeded in keeping the crossing guard's observations out of evidence, but only for the time being. What will happen when the crossing guard testifies?

QUESTION: What is your occupation?

ANSWER: I am a crossing guard.

QUESTION: Did you see the accident?

ANSWER: Yes I did.

QUESTION: What did you see?

No objection is possible, since the crossing guard will be testifying as to his own direct observations.

Most situations are hardly so clear-cut. The crossing guard may not be available to testify, or he might give testimony that is much less favorable to the defendant. The guard might be subject to impeachment or might suffer a memory lapse. There is no hard and fast rule that counsel should refrain from objecting simply because another witness is available to give unobjectionable testimony. On the other hand, the ultimate admissibility of the information is definitely a factor to be considered in deciding whether to object.

If the harmful information cannot be accommodated and if it is unlikely to be admitted later, then objecting is a no-risk proposition. All other situations call for the exercise of judgment.

4. Planning

We have just catalogued a long list of factors to be considered in deciding whether or not to raise any particular objection. Even in the computer age it is difficult to imagine anyone actually running through all of these factors in the five or so seconds available between question and response. How, then, can full consideration be given to the objection decision?

The answer, as in so much of trial advocacy, lies in planning. Given the scope of modern pretrial discovery, there is no reason to postpone the objection decision until the very moment when the answer is falling from the witness's lips. The

---

7   Note that no objection was made to the earlier question, "Did the crossing guard tell you what he saw?" An objection at that point would have been premature, since only the content of the statement will be hearsay. Regarding the timing of objections, see Section II C(1)(c), *infra* at p. 225.

general content, if not the precise words, of most important testimony is known to all counsel before the witness ever takes the stand. Most documents and tangible exhibits must be tendered to opposing counsel in advance of trial.

Objection strategy should therefore be planned in the same manner as is direct or cross examination. For each opposition witness, counsel's preparation should include consideration of all possible objections to every reasonably anticipated area of testimony. The potential objections should be weighed against the standards discussed in the above sections, and counsel should come to at least a tentative conclusion as to whether an objection is worth making. The same process should be applied to every expected exhibit and document. It is also necessary to consider the likely content of the opposition's cross examination of your own witnesses, and to determine the value of any possible objections.

The best of planning, of course, will not free counsel from the need to make split-second decisions. The evidence will rarely come in exactly as was expected, and the context of the trial may require last-minute adjustments to strategy and approach. Nonetheless, a good deal of the evidentiary background work can and should be done prior to trial.

C. Making and Meeting Objections

The format for making and meeting objections differs somewhat from state to state and even from courtroom to courtroom, so you will need to tailor your approach to objections to local practice. If in doubt about the requirements in a particular jurisdiction, one should always inquire. What follows here is a generalized description of the majority approach.

1. Making an Objection

The standard method of raising an objection is to stand and state the grounds for the objection:

"Objection, Your Honor, relevance."

"Objection, counsel is leading the witness."

"Your Honor, we object on the ground of hearsay."

"Objection, no foundation."

In a jury trial it may also be advisable to add a descriptive tag line, so that the jury will understand the basis of the objection:

"Objection, hearsay, Your Honor. The witness cannot testify to what somebody else said."

"We object to the leading questions; counsel is testifying instead of the witness."

225

In any event, it is necessary to give the precise basis for the objection in order to preserve the issue for appeal. In most jurisdictions, simply stating "objection" is understood only to raise the ground of relevance. If such a "general objection" is made and overruled, all other possible grounds are waived for appeal.[8] It is also necessary actually to state that you are making an objection. For some reason many attorneys are inclined only to comment on the inadequacy of the evidence, most commonly something like, "Your Honor, I fail to see the relevance of counsel's last question." A rebuke from the judge often follows. "It doesn't matter whether or not you see it. Just make an objection if you have one, counsel."

a. Speaking Objections

A speaking objection goes beyond the simple objection/grounds formula described above. Some attorneys find it necessary or fulfilling to launch into an extended discourse on the bases for their objections before allowing the judge to rule or opposing counsel to speak:

> "Objection, Your Honor, that question calls for hearsay. The witness's personal notes constitute an out-of-court statement, even though the witness is present on the stand. They do not qualify either as business records or as past recollection recorded, and in any event there has been no foundation."

While there is no absolute rule against speaking objections, most judges do not like them. Since the judge is often ready to rule as soon as the initial objection is made, speaking objections are seen as time-wasting and laborious. Judges generally consider it their prerogative to request argument, and may resent it when counsel fails to wait for the invitation.

b. Repeated Objections

It is often necessary to raise the same objection to a number of questions in a row. Perhaps your initial objection was sustained, but your opponent is persistent in attempting to introduce the inadmissible evidence through other means. Perhaps your initial objection was overruled, and you feel bound to protect your record for appeal as opposing counsel asks a series of questions in elaboration. In any event, an awkward feeling inevitably arises when it is necessary to object repeatedly, on the same ground, to question after question.

The least obtrusive way to raise a repeated objection is to say "same objection" at the end of each of opposing counsel's questions. The judge can then repeat her ruling and the trial can proceed in a relatively uninterrupted fashion. If your objections are being sustained, the judge will no doubt tire of reiterating her ruling

---

8   Note, however, that a "general objection" that is sustained may be affirmed on appeal if there is any valid basis for the objection.

and will eventually instruct opposing counsel to move on to another line of questioning.

If your "same objections" are being consistently overruled, the judge is likely to tire of them even sooner. At some point she will probably inform you that "I have ruled on that issue, counsel. There is no need for you to continue to object." Now you will risk the judge's ire if you continue to object, but you also risk waiving an issue on appeal if some future question expands on the theme in a way that was not quite covered by your earlier objections.

The solution to this conundrum, which will often be suggested by the trial judge, is the "standing objection." The theory of the standing objection is that a single objection will be considered to "stand" or apply to an entire line of questioning, without the need for repeated interruptions. The problem with standing objections is that it may be difficult in the future to determine exactly which questions and answers were covered. Although the meaning of the standing objection may be apparent to everyone present in the courtroom, the cold transcript presented to the appellate court may seem to tell an entirely different story. It is for this reason that standing objections are to be avoided if possible.

Should a judge insist that you proceed by way of standing objection, it is imperative that the objection be articulated as clearly as possible. Avoid the following scenario at all cost:

THE COURT: Counsel, you may have a standing objection to that line of questioning.

COUNSEL: Thank you, Your Honor.

THE COURT: Ask the next question.

Imagine the dilemma of an appellate court charged with reviewing this record for error. What is the evidentiary basis of this standing objection? How long will it obtain? How should it be interpreted if some of the following questions contain new issues or subtle variations? The appellate court will be confused and unhappy; this is not a record of which counsel can be proud.

The alternative, once the trial judge has informed you that a standing objection looms in your future, is to take matters into your own hands:

THE COURT: Counsel, you may have a standing objection to that line of questioning.

COUNSEL: Thank you, Your Honor. For the record, we object to all further testimony concerning any conversations between the defendant and Ms. London, including Ms. London's alleged references to the investigative report. Ms. London's statements are hearsay and the comments on the content of the report are double hearsay. Additionally, the secondary evidence concerning the report violates the best evidence rule.

THE COURT: Very well. Ask the next question.

Although not perfect, this record is far better than the one preceding it. No recitation of a standing objection is ambiguity-proof. Counsel must remain alert for nuances in the testimony that require the raising of a new objection.

c. Timing

Having determined what to say when initiating an objection, one must consider when to say it. The general rule is that an objection must be made as soon as it is apparent that it is called for. On the other hand, an objection may be premature if it interrupts an incomplete question or if it anticipates testimony that may or may not be given. To be timely, an objection must come neither too early nor too late.

Most objections to questions should be held until the examiner has had the opportunity to complete the question. Not only is it rude to interrupt, but the final version may turn out not to be objectionable. On a more pragmatic level, many judges will refuse to rule on an objection until the question has been completed. An interrupting objection, then, merely insures that the question will be stated twice, thereby emphasizing its objectionable information or implications.

There are times, however, when it is necessary to interrupt the questioner. Some questions are objectionable not because of what they will elicit, but because of what they assert. A question may contain a damaging suggestion or proposition which, once heard by the jury, cannot be wholly remedied by objection. Such questions must be interrupted in order to cut off the interrogator's inadmissible statement. For example, a cross examiner may be about to question a witness about an inadmissible criminal conviction. Imagine this scenario:

QUESTION: Isn't it true that you were convicted of the crime of selling heroin?

OBJECTION: Objection, Your Honor, that was a juvenile offense. It is inadmissible under Rule 609(d).

THE COURT: Sustained.

Although the objection was sustained,[9] the jury has already heard the inadmissible, though nonetheless damning, truth about the witness. It would obviously have been far more effective to cut off the question earlier:

---

9   In reality, it is most likely that this information would have been the subject of a pretrial motion in limine. For the purposes of this illustration, assume that for some reason no pretrial motions were made.

QUESTION: Isn't it true that you were con—

OBJECTION: Objection, Your Honor. Counsel is seeking information that is prohibited under Rule 609(d).

THE COURT: Sustained.[10]

Even if it does not interrupt a question, an objection may be premature if the examination has not yet reached the point where the inadmissibility of the answer has become certain. An objection must be made immediately before the inadmissible answer, not in anticipation of it. It is not uncommon for a diligent and eager lawyer to object one question too soon, as in the following example:

QUESTION: Did you have a conversation with Ms. London?

OBJECTION: Objection, Your Honor, hearsay.

THE COURT: Overruled. At this point the only question is whether a conversation occurred. The witness may answer.

ANSWER: Yes, I had a conversation with Ms. London.

QUESTION: Did Ms. London tell you anything about the investigation report?

OBJECTION: Hearsay, Your Honor.

THE COURT: Still too soon, counsel. Proceed.

ANSWER: Yes, she did.

QUESTION: What did Ms. London tell you about the investigation report?

OBJECTION: Objection on the ground of hearsay.

THE COURT: Sustained.

The first two objections were overruled because under the hearsay rule only the content of the out-of-court statement is inadmissible. The fact of the conversation is admissible evidence.

Timing the objections to questions is relatively easy. Often, however, a witness will respond to a seemingly proper question with a wholly inadmissible response. The timing in these situations is trickier since, by definition, the answer was not foreshadowed by the question. The general rule is that an objection must be made as soon as the inadmissible nature of the answer becomes apparent. This necessarily means interrupting the witness. For example:

---

10   If the judge does anything other than immediately sustain the objection, the objecting lawyer will want to approach the bench for argument.

QUESTION: When did you begin your investigation of the defendant's financial situation?

ANSWER: I began the investigation as soon as I received an anonymous letter charging that —

OBJECTION: We object on the grounds of hearsay and foundation.

THE COURT: Sustained.

It will not do to allow the witness to finish the answer, because by then the jury would have heard the testimony and the harm would be done.

Unfortunately, it is not always possible to recognize and respond to inadmissible testimony before it happens. Counsel may be momentarily distracted or may suffer from rusty reflexes. And some witnesses, either innocently or by design, just have a way of slipping improper testimony into the record. When this happens counsel's only recourse is the motion to strike:

QUESTION: Are you the comptroller of the defendant corporation?

ANSWER: The only thing I knew about skimming funds came through the rumor mill.

OBJECTION: Objection, hearsay. We move to strike that answer.

THE COURT: Sustained. The answer will be stricken from the record.[11]

In a jury trial it is also important that the judge instruct the jury to disregard the inadmissible answer:

QUESTION: Will Your Honor please instruct the jury to disregard that last answer?

THE COURT: Yes, certainly. Ladies and gentlemen, you are to disregard the answer that the witness just gave. Proceed.

While this sort of curative instruction is hardly a satisfying remedy, it is the best that can be done under the circumstances. In many jurisdictions the request for a curative instruction is a necessary predicate to raising the issue on appeal.

d. Witness Voir Dire

The basis for an objection may not always be apparent from the question or even the answer. Counsel may have access to information that is not yet in the

---

11 Note that the "stricken" testimony will not actually be deleted from the transcript. For the purpose of review on appeal it is necessary that all of the witness's testimony, as well as all of the rulings of the court and the arguments of counsel, appear on the transcript. Thus, the testimony is stricken only in the legal sense, not literally.

record, but which negates the admissibility of some part of a witness's testimony. This information can be brought to the judge's attention through witness voir dire. The term voir dire is derived from "law French" which was once in use in English courts; it means "speak the truth."

In the context of witness examination, voir dire refers to a limited cross examination for the purpose of determining the admissibility of evidence. The voir dire examination interrupts the direct and gives the opposing lawyer a chance to bring out additional facts that bear directly on the admissibility of some part of the balance of the testimony. Counsel who wishes to conduct voir dire must ask permission of the judge:

QUESTION: Whose signature is on that document?

ANSWER: It appears to be the defendant's.

OBJECTION: Your Honor, we object to that testimony, and ask leave to conduct a limited voir dire of the witness.

THE COURT: You may proceed with voir dire of the witness.

OBJECTION: You did not see the document being signed, did you?

ANSWER: No.

OBJECTION: You have never seen the defendant sign his name, have you?

ANSWER: No.

OBJECTION: You have never received any signed correspondence from the defendant, have you?

ANSWER: No.

OBJECTION: Your Honor, it is obvious that the witness cannot identify the signature from her own personal knowledge. We renew our objection to the testimony and move to strike the previous answer.

Voir dire examination is most commonly utilized with regard to the qualifications of an expert witness or the foundation for a document or exhibit, but it can be used in other situations as well. Note that following voir dire the offering attorney is entitled to conduct additional examination aimed at re-establishing the admissibility of the evidence.

2. Responding to Objections

Many judges like to rule on objections as soon as they hear them, without even a response from opposing counsel. Believing that they know the law and have been attentive to the proceedings, judges often consider it a waste of time to entertain argument. In truth, a majority of evidentiary objections present no great problems in jurisprudence. A judge can sustain or overrule a good many objections without recourse to counsel's views.

It is common, therefore, for opposing counsel to make no response to an objection unless invited to do so by the judge:

QUESTION: What did the police officer say to you?

OBJECTION: Objection, hearsay.

THE COURT: What about it, counsel?

QUESTION: It is not hearsay because . . .

The judge might also signal the desire for a response non-verbally, perhaps by looking at counsel or by nodding in counsel's direction. It is important to be on the alert for such gestures, since failure to respond might be interpreted by the judge as waiver.

a. Requesting Argument

Many objections will not be readily susceptible of summary disposition because they raise subtle or complex legal issues. Aspects of an objection may escape the judge, or may require consideration of additional information that is not apparent from the record. In these circumstances counsel cannot rely on an invitation to argue from the judge, and will need to inform the court, as politely as possible, that argument is necessary. It is preferable to do this before the judge has ruled, if that can be accomplished without interrupting. An effective signal is to stand while the objection is being made, in order to alert the judge that argument is desired.

Despite counsel's best efforts, the judge may rule on a disputed objection without input from the opposing side. If the point is important, counsel cannot be shy about letting the judge know that there is another side to the objection:

QUESTION: What did the police officer say to you?

OBJECTION: Objection, hearsay.

THE COURT: Sustained.

QUESTION: Your Honor, we would like to be heard on that.

THE COURT: Very well, what do you have to say?

QUESTION: The statement falls under the "present sense impression" exception.

THE COURT: I see. Overruled. The witness may answer.

b. Specific Responses

The key to responding to any objection is specificity. A judge who has agreed to listen to argument on an objection has indicated that she is persuadable. A good argument will result in the admission of the evidence only if it provides the judge with a good reason to overrule the objection. Tell the judge exactly why the proffered evidence is admissible. Some lawyers, for reasons known only to themselves, respond to objections by repeating the evidence and exhorting the judge to admit it. The following scenario is not at all unusual:

QUESTION: What did the defendant do immediately after the accident?

ANSWER: He began yelling at his eight-year-old son.

OBJECTION: Objection. The defendant's relationship with his son is irrelevant.

THE COURT: It does seem irrelevant. What do you have to say, counsel?

QUESTION: It is very relevant, Your Honor. It shows that he was yelling at his child.

This response communicates very little to the judge. What is the probative value of the defendant's conduct? Note how much more effective it is when counsel explains why the evidence is being offered to the court:

QUESTION: What did the defendant do immediately after the accident?

ANSWER: He began yelling at his eight-year-old son.

OBJECTION: Objection. The defendant's relationship with his son is irrelevant.

THE COURT: It does seem irrelevant. What do you have to say, counsel?

ANSWER: The defendant's anger at his son tends to show that he was distracted by the child just before the accident. It goes directly to negligence, Your Honor.

The judge may or may not agree with your assessment of the case, but at least she will have the benefit of your analysis.

c. Limited Admissibility

Evidence may be inadmissible for some purposes, yet admissible for others. When responding to objections it is extremely important to advise the judge of the precise purpose for which the evidence is offered.

For example, evidence that a dangerous condition has been repaired is generally inadmissible to prove negligence.[12] Counsel cannot argue to the jury, "Of course the owner of the car took inadequate care of the automobile; he had his brakes repaired just two days after the accident." On the other hand, evidence of the repair is admissible to prove ownership of the automobile. Counsel can argue, "The defendant denies that he was responsible for the upkeep of the car, but he was the one who ordered and paid for the repair of the brakes just two days after the accident."

With this dichotomy in mind, consider the possible objections and responses in the cross examination of the defendant:

QUESTION: Didn't you have your brakes repaired just two days after the accident?

OBJECTION: Objection, Your Honor, this testimony violates Rule 407.

THE COURT: What do you have to say, counsel?

QUESTION: We are offering it only to prove ownership and control, Your Honor.

THE COURT: The evidence will be received, but only for that limited purpose. Ladies and gentlemen of the jury, you are to consider this evidence only for the purpose of showing ownership and control of the automobile. You must not consider it as proof of any negligence on the part of the defendant.

If the court does not immediately give a limiting instruction, one should be requested by the attorney whose objection was overruled.

d. Conditional Offers

The admissibility of certain testimony, particularly with regard to relevance, may not always be immediately clear. This is a frequent occurrence on cross examination, since counsel may be utilizing the technique of indirection[13] or otherwise attempting to avoid being too obvious about the direction of the cross. Nor is such subtlety unknown on direct examination. In either case, the ultimate

---

12   *See* Rule 407, Federal Rules of Evidence.

13   *See* Chapter Three, Section V B(3), *supra* at p. 74.

admissibility of the evidence might depend upon other testimony to be developed through later witnesses.

In these circumstances counsel may respond to an objection by making a "conditional offer." This is done either by promising to "tie it up later," or, preferably, by explaining to the court the nature of the evidence that is expected to follow. For example:

QUESTION: Isn't it true that you had an important meeting scheduled for the morning of the accident?

OBJECTION: Objection. The witness's business schedule is not relevant.

THE COURT: What is the relevance of that inquiry, counsel?

PROPONENT:We intend to introduce evidence that the defendant had a meeting scheduled with a prospective client, that he was already late for the meeting at the time of the accident, and that he stood to lose a great deal of money if he didn't arrive on time. The question is therefore directly relevant to show that he was speeding and inattentive.[14]

THE COURT: Based on that representation I will allow the testimony, subject to a motion to strike if you don't tie it up.

A conditional offer is always subject to the actual production of the later evidence. The testimony can, and should, be stricken if counsel's representations are not fulfilled.[15]

e. Planning for Objections

Being specific is a challenge. When you are interrupted in mid-examination by a maddening objection, the precise, and hopefully devastating, reply may not spring spontaneously to your lips. It is therefore essential to plan for likely objections as part of the overall preparation for trial.

Planning for relevance objections should be nearly automatic, since it is really part and parcel of developing your theory of the case. Recall that every question that you ask, indeed every item of evidence that you put forward, should be calculated to advance your theory of the case. By definition, then, you will have considered the probative value of each question before the trial ever starts. To respond to a relevance objection, you will really need to do nothing more than explain to the judge why you offered the evidence in the first place. In other words,

---

14 Depending upon the sensitivity of the information, it would be appropriate to request that the argument on such an objection be conducted outside the presence of the witness.

15 *See* FRE 104(b).

"The testimony is relevant, Your Honor, because it contributes 'X' to my theory of the case."

Other objections may not be as easy to anticipate. At a minimum, however, trial preparation should include an evaluation of the admissibility of every tangible object, document, or other exhibit that you intend to offer into evidence or use for demonstrative purposes. It is similarly necessary to do an "admissibility check" on all testimony involving conversations, telephone calls, meetings, and other out-of-court statements. Finally, potential objections should be considered for all opinions, conclusions, calculations, and characterizations that you expect to elicit. Why is the evidence relevant? What is the necessary foundation for its authenticity? Does the witness have sufficient personal knowledge? Is there a hearsay problem? Might it be privileged?

f. Judicious Non-responses

It is not necessary to fight to the death over every objection. Counsel can frequently avoid an objection by rephrasing the offending question, either before or after the judge rules.

Since the precise language of a question is seldom of vital importance, it should be possible to circumnavigate virtually any objection as to form. Leading questions, compound questions, and vague questions can all be cured. Even if your original question was perfectly fine, you may be able to move the trial along, and earn the gratitude of judge and jury, by posing the same inquiry in different words.

Other objections that can be undercut through rephrasing include personal knowledge, foundation, and even relevance. For example:

QUESTION: Did the plaintiff follow his doctor's advice?

OBJECTION: Objection. Lack of personal knowledge.

QUESTION: Let me put it this way. Did the plaintiff say anything to you about his doctor's advice?

ANSWER: Yes.

QUESTION: What did he say?

ANSWER: He said that he would rather risk the consequences than stay in bed all day.

Note that in this scenario the examination was made stronger by rephrasing the question in response to the objection.

Making and meeting objections involves a certain amount of gamesmanship. No lawyer likes to be seen as an evidentiary naif or pushover. From time to time it may be tactically important to stand behind a question, if only to establish your mastery of the rules. Another alternative is to rephrase a question without saying so. In the above example the attorney neither withdrew the question nor overtly rephrased it, but rather said, "Let me put it this way." Problem solved.

D. Arguing Objections

1. Where

As an initial matter, lawyers usually argue objections from wherever they happen to be standing or sitting when the issue first arises. Even in a jury trial, most objections are resolved without anyone moving from their location. The language of objecting is arcane, and in most circumstances it does no harm to have the discussion in the presence of the jury.

Occasionally, however, it is important that the jury not hear the content of the argument. It may be necessary to recite the expected testimony so the judge can rule on the objection, or to refer to other evidence that has not yet been admitted. In these circumstances, either side may request that the argument take place out of the presence of the jury.

The most common way of insulating the jury from the attorneys' argument is for counsel to approach the bench and hold, in whispered tones, a sidebar conference. Alternatively, the jury can be excused from the courtroom while counsel argue. This latter approach is used fairly infrequently, and only in the case of extended arguments, since it is cumbersome and time-consuming to shuffle the jury in and out of the courtroom.

A sidebar can be called by the court or requested by either the party making or the party responding to the objection. Typically, the lawyer whose case is most likely to be harmed by disclosures in the course of the argument requests the sidebar. Ethical counsel, however, will volunteer the need for a sidebar whenever she realizes that her own argument may prejudice the other side. The opposition's failure to ask for argument outside of the jury's presence should not be taken as license to make statements containing potentially inadmissible evidence. Unfortunately, this practice is all too common. It has no place in a trial between professionals.

2. How

Arguments on objections should be conducted as a conversation between counsel and the court. The general scenario is for objecting counsel to argue first, followed by the attorney who offered the evidence, and concluding with a reply from the objector. In practice, however, the format is often much less formal, with the judge asking questions and counsel responding.

If there is one signal rule in arguing objections, it is that counsel should not argue with, or even address, each other. It is the judge who will make the ruling and the judge who must be convinced. It is ineffective, distracting, and even insulting to the court when counsel turn to each other to argue their objections:

PLAINTIFF'S COUNSEL: Your Honor, our objection to the testimony is lack of foundation.

DEFENDANT'S COUNSEL: What more foundation could you want, counselor?

PLAINTIFF'S COUNSEL: Well, you could start with a basis for personal knowledge.

DEFENDANT'S COUNSEL: He already testified that he is the comptroller. Isn't that enough for you?

No matter how foolish, trite, or easily disposed of the other side's position seems, avoid speaking directly to opposing counsel. All of your arguments should be made to the court. If, in the course of an argument, you are ever tempted to turn to opposing counsel, remember that she is being paid to disagree with you. There should be nothing in the world that you can say to make her alter her position. Her job is to take the other side of the issue. The judge, by contrast, is employed to keep an open mind. The judge can be persuaded, but only if you take the trouble to address the court directly.

Your evidentiary arguments will be most convincing if they are delivered with a tone of firm conviction. When you argue an objection you are asking the judge to do something — either to admit or exclude evidence. The wrong decision can lead to reversal, a matter of at least passing professional concern to the judge. Your argument, then, should give the judge a reason for ruling in your favor. Emotive histrionics, of course, will be counterproductive. The sort of diffidence or lassitude often displayed by attorneys when arguing to the bench is also unlikely to succeed. A judge, despite the robe, is human. If you do not believe in your argument, why should she?

Finally, counsel must be certain actually to obtain a ruling on every objection. Judges may often prefer to avoid ruling on objections, either because they didn't hear them, don't understand them, or simply because they want to reduce the possibility of being reversed on appeal. In some courtrooms this practice has been raised to the level of a fine art:

OBJECTION: Objection, Your Honor, relevance.

THE COURT: Rephrase the question, counselor.

Or,

OBJECTION: Objection, counsel is leading the witness.

THE COURT: The question is leading. Proceed.

Or,

> OBJECTION: We object on the ground of hearsay.

> THE COURT: The witness cannot testify to what someone else said. Ask another question.

In none of the above examples did the judge actually rule on the objection. If evidence is received or withheld on the basis of these non-rulings, counsel will have a difficult time making an argument for reversal on appeal. The court never actually ordered anyone to do anything; it was all left in the hands of counsel.

The remedy to this sort of decision by default is simply to insist politely on a ruling:

"Before we proceed, Your Honor, I have an objection pending."

"Has the court ruled on counsel's objection?"

"May we please have a ruling, Your Honor?"

Here and there a judge may be chagrined, but few will ever be offended by an attorney's request that evidence either be admitted or not. A clear record is in everyone's best interest.

E.   Once the Judge Has Ruled

The judge's ruling on an objection is not necessarily the end of that particular discourse. Counsel must remain alert to protect and develop the record. Both the proponent of the evidence (offering lawyer) and the opponent (objecting lawyer) may have more yet to do.

1.   Objection Overruled

a.   Proponent's Job

The proponent's job when an objection is overruled is to ensure that the evidence actually makes its way into the record. In other words, the proponent must make sure that the witness answers the question that the judge has just ruled to be permissible. The following is an all-too-frequent scenario:

> QUESTION: After the accident, what did the crossing guard say to you?

> OBJECTION: Objection, Your Honor, the question calls for hearsay.

> QUESTION: Your Honor, it has already been established that the crossing guard observed the accident immediately before making the declaration, so it qualifies as either an excited utterance or a present sense impression.

THE COURT: Yes, I think there is a hearsay exception there. Overruled.

QUESTION: What is the next thing that you did?

ANSWER: I went to a telephone and dialed 911.

Despite the court's ruling, the witness was never given an opportunity to answer the original question. The proponent, apparently flushed with victory, just went on to another subject.

A variation on this theme occurs when the witness's answer has been interrupted or when the arguments on the objection overlap the testimony. Moreover, even when the witness was able to get an answer out, the import of the testimony may have been drowned out by the subsequent wrangling over the objection.

Some lawyers utilize the dubious tactic of having the court reporter read back the prior question and answer (if there was one) following an overruled objection. While this approach is technically correct, it has very little forensic merit. Presumably, the lawyer has prepared an examination that is designed for maximum impact. Counsel knows which words to emphasize and knows how the witness is likely to respond. Why would an attorney choose to forego the persuasive force of her own examination in favor of turning it over to the inevitably monotonous reading of a court reporter? It is the lawyer, not the stenographer, who has been retained to represent the client.

Following an overruled objection, the proponent's safest course is to repeat the question, and to be sure to get a clear answer from the witness.

b. Opponent's Job

The opponent's job following an overruled objection is to stay alert to the possibility of excluding all or some of the offending evidence.

In the first instance, the opponent of the evidence should not withdraw an objection. Many lawyers, perhaps out of embarrassment or obsequiousness, seem to think that they can gain points with the trial judge by withdrawing an objection once it has been overruled. In fact, the opposite is true. Having already taken the court's time by making and arguing an objection, one can only convey indecision or lack of seriousness by withdrawing it immediately thereafter. Even more to the point, withdrawing an objection has the effect of waiving the issue for appeal.

In any event, once an objection has been overruled, the objecting lawyer must continue to scrutinize the subsequent testimony. Perhaps the witness will not testify in the manner that was promised by the proponent of the evidence in her argument to the court. For example:

QUESTION: After the accident, what did the crossing guard say to you?

OBJECTION: Objection, Your Honor, the question calls for hearsay.

QUESTION: Your Honor, it qualifies as either an excited utterance or a present sense impression.

THE COURT: Yes, I think there is a hearsay exception there. Overruled.

ANSWER: She said that she didn't really see what happened, but that it looked as though . . .

OBJECTION: Your Honor, I renew my objection. If the witness didn't really see the accident then she can't have a present sense impression.

THE COURT: Yes. The objection will be sustained on those grounds.

Alternatively, other grounds for objection may become clear in the course of the testimony, or perhaps the witness will begin volunteering evidence that is inadmissible for some additional reason. In the above scenario counsel could also have objected on the ground that the declarant's statement ("it looked as though . . .") was speculative.

2. Objection Sustained

a. Proponent's Job

A sustained objection means that the proponent of the evidence has been denied the opportunity to place the testimony or exhibit into the record. This ruling leaves the proponent with two tasks.

i.   Offer of proof

The proponent's first task is to protect the record by making an offer of proof. When a witness is not allowed to testify, the record is silent as to the content of the evidence. An appellate court reviewing the record, however, must know the content of the omitted material in order to determine whether the judge's ruling was reversible error. The offer of proof is the means by which counsel can place into the record a description of the excluded testimony,[16] so that the right to an effective appeal may be preserved.[17] An offer of proof also gives the trial court an opportunity to reconsider its ruling on the basis of a more complete description of the excluded evidence.

---

16 When a proffered exhibit, as opposed to testimony, is not admitted, it usually remains part of the record as an exhibit "for identification" as opposed to an exhibit "in evidence." Thus, exhibits can generally be reviewed by an appellate court without the need for an offer of proof.

17 Rule 103(a)(2), Federal Rules of Evidence.

There are three generally accepted ways to present an offer of proof. The first method is to excuse the jury and proceed with the examination of the witness. This approach has the obvious benefit of accuracy, since the witness's actual testimony will be preserved. It is also time-consuming and somewhat awkward, and for those reasons it is only employed in exceptional circumstances.

The most frequently utilized method of presenting an offer of proof is for counsel to summarize the excluded testimony. For example:

QUESTION: What did the crossing guard say to you immediately after the accident?

OBJECTION: Hearsay, Your Honor.

THE COURT: Sustained.

QUESTION: May I make an offer of proof?

THE COURT: Certainly. Proceed.

QUESTION: If the witness were allowed to testify, he would state that the crossing guard made the following statement to him: "I saw the fire truck and heard the siren. All of the traffic stopped except for the red car in the left lane, which just ran right into the back of the blue car without even slowing down."

THE COURT: Very well. The ruling stands. Ask another question.

Although certainly time-efficient, the summarization method has its drawbacks. One problem is that it is very easy to leave out crucial information. In the above scenario, for example, the offer of proof contains nothing to show that the crossing guard's statement would qualify under an exception to the hearsay rule.[18] A further problem is that enterprising and less than scrupulous lawyers have been known to pad their summaries with "testimony" far more favorable than the witness ever would have produced.

The third approach to offers of proof is the submission to the court of witness statements, reports, or deposition transcripts. This method can have the benefit of both thoroughness and brevity, as follows:

"Your Honor, we submit as an offer of proof pages 12-21 of the witness's deposition, which we have marked for identification as Plaintiff's Exhibit 8."

---

18 *See* Rules 803(1) and (2), Federal Rules of Evidence.

Or,

"Your Honor, this witness gave a written statement to Officer Lucas, which has been marked as Defendant's Exhibit 11. If we were allowed to proceed the witness would testify to the facts contained in that statement, which we present as an offer of proof."

This method is used relatively infrequently, however, due at least in part to the difficulty of assembling the right written materials at exactly the right time.

ii. Keep trying

The proponent's second task in the face of a sustained objection is to keep trying to have the evidence admitted. When a judge sustains an objection, the ruling usually applies only to the specific question (or answer) and grounds that were then before the court. Unless the judge says so explicitly, the ruling does not extend to the ultimate admissibility of the underlying evidence. In other words, a sustained objection says only that "the evidence cannot be admitted based on the testimony and arguments heard so far." It does not say that "the evidence cannot ever be admitted no matter what you do." Counsel generally has the option to offer the evidence through other means.

These "other means" may consist of nothing more than rephrasing a question. Any objection as to form — leading, compound, vague, argumentative — can be cured by altering the language of the inquiry. Leading questions on direct examination can easily be restated:

QUESTION: You had the green light when the defendant's car hit yours, didn't you?

OBJECTION: Objection, leading.

THE COURT: Sustained.

QUESTION: What color was your light when the defendant's car hit yours?

ANSWER: It was green.

Objections are frequently sustained not because of the form of the question, but because of some missing predicate in the testimony. Objections to foundation can be cured by eliciting additional foundation. Objections to a witness's lack of personal knowledge can be remedied with further questions showing the basis of the witness's information. Relevance objections can be overcome through continued questioning aimed at demonstrating the probative value of the original question. In the following cross examination the witness is the defendant in an intersection accident case:

QUESTION: Immediately after the accident you started yelling at your twelve-year-old son, didn't you?

OBJECTION: Objection, relevance.

THE COURT: Sustained.

QUESTION: Well, your twelve-year-old son was in the car at the time of the accident, wasn't he?

ANSWER: Yes.

QUESTION: He was sitting in the front seat?

ANSWER: Yes, he was.

QUESTION: He had a "boom box" with him, didn't he?

ANSWER: He did.

QUESTION: And there was a "heavy metal" tape in the boom box?

ANSWER: I guess that is what you call it.

QUESTION: That music can be awfully loud, can't it?

ANSWER: I suppose so.

QUESTION: Most adults find it extremely annoying, don't they?

ANSWER: I couldn't really say.

QUESTION: Are you aware that the police report says that the boom box was still playing in your front seat when they arrived at the scene?

ANSWER: I remember something like that.

QUESTION: And immediately after the accident you yelled at your son, did't you?

OBJECTION: Same objection.

QUESTION: Your Honor, I believe we have established the likelihood that the defendant was distracted by his son's music. Yelling at the child is probative on that issue.

THE COURT: Yes, I see your point. Overruled.

The same approach can work for hearsay objections. Additional facts can often be established that will qualify a statement for an exception to the hearsay rule. Moreover, out-of-court statements may sometimes be recast in the form of conduct or observations. In the following example a police officer has just testified on direct examination that she received a radio dispatch that a crime had been committed:

QUESTION: What was the content of the radio bulletin from the dispatcher?

OBJECTION: Objection, hearsay.

THE COURT: Sustained.

QUESTION: What did you do immediately after receiving the alert?

ANSWER: I drove to the corner of Grand Avenue and State Street.

QUESTION: What did you do there?

ANSWER: I began looking for a suspect wearing glasses and a white lab jacket.

The effect of the sustained hearsay objection was avoided by continuing the examination on the admissible subject of the witness's actions, as opposed to the inadmissible subject of the dispatcher's out-of-court statement.

It is not always possible to overcome a sustained objection. Some testimony will be flatly inadmissible, no matter how many approaches counsel attempts. On the other hand, there are often numerous routes to admissibility, and a sustained objection usually closes off only one. Keep trying.

b. Opponent's job

When an objection is sustained the opponent of the evidence has been successful. This should bring satisfaction to the objector, and in some cases even rejoicing, but it is never a reason to rest on your laurels. The very next question may ask for the identical evidence, in which case an additional objection must be made. A sustained objection will be a temporary victory indeed if the proponent of the evidence succeeds in having it admitted later in the witness's testimony. This is not uncommon. Successful objections can come undone as soon as the objector relaxes vigilance:

QUESTION: Who told you to begin your financial investigation?

ANSWER: I received an anonymous note charging that —

OBJECTION: Objection, hearsay.

THE COURT: Sustained.

QUESTION: What caused you to begin investigating?

245

ANSWER: There was a charge that money had been skimmed from one of the trust accounts.

QUESTION: How did you learn of the charge?

ANSWER: I received a note.

The opponent of the evidence in this case let down her guard. When the first hearsay objection was successful, she allowed her attention to lapse. She therefore failed to notice that the identical testimony was being introduced as the "cause" of the investigation. The information, of course, is no less hearsay (and no less anonymous) the second time around. A second objection should have been made.

The cardinal rule when your objection is sustained is don't fall asleep.

3. Evidence Admitted for a Limited Purpose

If the evidence is admitted for a limited purpose, the opponent's job is to ask for a limiting instruction that explains the nature of the court's ruling. Most judges give such an instruction as a matter of course. Counsel may occasionally want to forego the limiting instruction, on the theory that it will only call attention to the harmful evidence.

4. Theory Re-evaluation

Rulings on objections govern the flow of evidence at trial. The availability of evidence forms the underpinning of every attorney's theory of the case. Theory planning, in turn, involves calculated predictions as to the admissibility of evidence. It may be, therefore, that the court's ruling on a particularly important objection will require counsel to re-evaluate her theory of the case.

Evidentiary rulings must be understood in the context of the entire case. They are not merely passing successes or failures; they can be crucial turning points in the progress of the case. If an essential item of evidence is excluded, or if some controversial proof is admitted, counsel may have to switch theories, or abandon a claim or defense, even if this occurs in mid-trial.

In some instances the effect of an evidentiary ruling may be only to strengthen or weaken your case. If the court excludes some testimony of one of your witnesses, you might be able to proceed as planned, but with a lesser volume of evidence. Recall the fire engine/intersection case that we have been using as an example. The plaintiff's theory was that the defendant caused the accident because he was hurrying to a business meeting for which he was already late. Assume that the court, for whatever reason, sustained an objection to testimony that the defendant was seen rushing from his home that morning with his tie undone and a coffee cup in his hand. This ruling diminishes the proof available to the plaintiff, but so long as other evidence is available, the "hurrying to work" theory can remain intact.

Other missing testimony might vitiate entirely one of your claims. Return to the fire engine case and assume now that an objection was sustained to evidence that the defendant had declined to have his brakes repaired despite a mechanic's advice to the contrary. Following this ruling, the entire claim of negligent maintenance will probably have to be scrapped. Plaintiff's counsel will be in trouble indeed if she does not have a back-up theory available.

Theory alterations cannot be well made on the spur of the moment. As a consequence, trial preparation must always take into consideration the possible effects of evidentiary rulings. It is not enough to plan to make objections. Counsel must go further to determine the impact on her theory if the objection is overruled and the evidence is admitted. By the same token, it is not sufficient to anticipate one's response to the opposition's objections. It is also necessary to plan conceivable theory adaptations in the event that those objections are sustained.

III. ETHICS AND OBJECTIONS

Ethical issues frequently arise in the context of making and meeting objections. Because the objecting process is one of the most confrontational aspects of the trial, it often tests counsel's reserves of good will, civility, restraint, and sense of fair play. The three most common problems are discussed below.

A. Asking Objectionable Questions

As we have discussed above, assessing the likely admissibility of evidence is an essential component of trial preparation. There is no question that counsel may offer any evidence that she believes is either clearly or probably admissible. What about evidence that is probably inadmissible? Is it ethical to offer such testimony in the hope that either opposing counsel will fail to object or that the judge will make an erroneous ruling?

It is ethical to offer any evidence over which there is a reasonable evidentiary dispute. Our adversary system calls upon each attorney to make out the best case possible, and relies upon the judge to rule on disputed issues of law. Valuable evidence should not be preemptively excluded on the basis of counsel's assessment, so long as there is a reasonable basis in the law for its admission.

As we have seen, an attorney is usually wise to refrain from objecting to every objectionable question or answer. This raises the possibility that opposing counsel may choose not to object to testimony, even if its admissibility is open to debate. That decision is the opposition's to make, and there is no need for an attorney to save them from having to make it.

By the same token, the judge is the arbiter of the law. If her evaluation of admissibility is different from counsel's, then the judge is correct, at least until the matter reaches an appellate court.[19] This is not a novel concept. Boswell reported that Dr. Johnson took the same position with regard to arguing a case which he knew to be weak:

> Sir, you do not know it to be good or bad till the Judge determines it.
> * * * An argument which does not convince yourself, may convince the Judge to whom you urge it: And if it does convince him, why, then, Sir, you are wrong and he is right.[20]

This principle does not, however, relieve counsel of all responsibility to cull inadmissible evidence from her case. A corollary to counsel's right to offer evidence for which there is a reasonable evidence is the obligation to refrain from offering evidence for which there is no reasonable basis. As stated in the Model Rules of Professional Conduct, a lawyer shall not

> [I]n trial, allude to any matter that the lawyer does not reasonably believe is relevant or that will not be supported by admissible evidence . . . [21]

In other words, it is unethical to offer evidence knowing that there is no reasonable basis for its admission. Even though opposing counsel might neglect to object, and even though the court might err in its ruling, the adversary system does not extend so far as to allow the intentional use of improper evidence. Indeed, one of the justifications for the adversary system is precisely that counsel can be relied upon to perform this minimum level of self-policing.

When does counsel have a reasonable belief as to the admissibility of evidence? This determination lies within the thought processes of the individual lawyer. For this reason it is unlikely that any single proffer would ever result in discipline, although repeated efforts to offer clearly inadmissible evidence could lead to sanctions in an extreme case.

The test of ethical conduct, however, cannot be found in the likelihood of punishment. An appropriate rule, therefore, is to consider it improper to offer evidence that cannot be supported by an articulatable theory of admissibility. Counsel should be able to complete, with specific and recognizable legal arguments, the sentence that begins, "This evidence is admissible because . . . ." If the only conclusion for the sentence is "Because it helps my case," then there is not a reasonable basis for the offer.

---

19 There may be purely tactical reasons to abstain from offering proof of questionable admissibility. If the trial judge admits the evidence over objection, and counsel relies on it in winning her case, that same evidence may later become the basis for reversal on appeal.

20 2 Boswell, *The Life of Johnson* 47 (Hill Ed. 1887).

21 Rule 3.4(e), Model Rules of Professional Conduct.

Finally, it is unethical to attempt to use the information contained in questions as a substitute for testimony that cannot be obtained. Some lawyers apparently believe that the idea of zealous advocacy allows them to slip information before a jury by asserting it in a question, knowing full well that the witness will not be allowed to answer. The usual scenario is something as follows:

LAWYER: Isn't it true that you were once fired from a job for being drunk?

OBJECTION: Objection, relevance.

LAWYER: I withdraw the question. (*Sotto voce*: Who cares about the ruling? I never expected to get it in, but now the jury knows that the witness is a drunk.)

This conduct, even if the information is true, is absolutely unethical. Testimony is to come from witnesses, with admissibility ruled upon by the court. It subverts the very purpose of an adversary trial when lawyers abuse their right to question witnesses in order to slip inadmissible evidence before the jury.

B.   Making Questionable Objections

The same general analysis applies to the use of objections as it does to the offer of evidence. Counsel need not be positive that an objection will be sustained, but must only believe that there is a reasonable basis for making it. Again, under the adversary system it is up to the judge to decide whether to admit the evidence.

The license to make questionable objections is available only if counsel is truly interested in excluding the subject evidence. That is, an attorney may make any reasonable or plausible objection, but only so long as the purpose of the objection is to obtain a ruling on the evidence. As we will see in the following section, objections may also be employed for a variety of ulterior purposes, most of which are unethical.

C.   Making "Tactical" Objections

Many lawyers, and more than a few trial advocacy texts, tout the use of so-called "tactical" objections. Since an objection is the only means by which one lawyer can interrupt the examination of another, it is suggested that objections should occasionally be made to "break up" the flow of a successful examination. An objection can throw the opposing lawyer off stride, or give the witness a rest, or distract the jury from the content of the testimony. This advice is usually tempered with the admonition that there must always be some evidentiary basis for the objection, but the real message is that an objection may be used for any purpose whatsoever, so long as you can make it with a straight face.

This view is unfortunate. It amounts to nothing more than the sneaky use of objections for a wholly improper purpose. No judge would allow a lawyer to object on the ground that the opposition's examination is going too well. The fact that disruption can be accomplished *sub silentio* does not justify it. The same is true of other "tactical" uses of objections. It is unethical to use a speaking objection to communicate with the jury or to suggest testimony to a witness.

The tactical use of objections is widespread and seldom punished. The use of "colorable" objections to accomplish impermissible goals can insulate a lawyer from discipline, but it does not make the practice right.[22] The "true exclusion" standard being urged here may well be unenforceable by judges; it is virtually impossible to evaluate a lawyer's thought process to determine the underlying reason for any particular objection. The standard is, however, attainable by any lawyer who is committed to practice in good faith.

IV. A SHORT LIST OF COMMON OBJECTIONS

A complete discussion of evidentiary objections is beyond the scope of this book. The following list of some frequently made objections (and responses) is intended only as a reference or guide, not as a substitute for a thorough knowledge of evidence and procedure.

This section provides a brief description of the grounds for each objection, followed by an equally brief statement of some possible responses. Where appropriate, citations are made to the Federal Rules of Evidence (FRE).

A. Objections to the Form of the Question (or Answer)

1. Leading Question

A leading question suggests or contains its own answer. Leading questions are objectionable on direct examination. They are permitted on cross examination. *See* FRE 611.

Responses. The question is preliminary, foundational, directing the witness's attention, or refreshing the witness's recollection. The witness is very old, very young, infirm, adverse, or hostile. Leading questions can most often be rephrased in non-leading form.

---

22 Racial or religious discrimination can also be accomplished, at least on a small scale, through undetectable means. One can often find an arguable excuse for bad actions. In this context it is easily recognizable that hiding one's motivation does not justify the result.

2. Compound Question

A compound question contains two separate inquiries that are not necessarily susceptible of a single answer. For example, "Wasn't the fire engine driving in the left lane and flashing its lights?"

Responses. Dual inquiries are permissible if the question seeks to establish a relationship between two facts or events. For example, "Didn't he move forward and then reach into his pocket?" Other than to establish a relationship, compound questions are objectionable and should be rephrased.

3. Vague Question

A question is vague if it is incomprehensible, or incomplete, or if any answer will necessarily be ambiguous. For example, the question, "When do you leave your house in the morning?" is vague, since it does not specify the day of the week to which it refers.

Responses. A question is not vague if the judge understands it. Many judges will ask the witness whether he or she understands the question. Unless the precise wording is important, it is often easiest to rephrase a "vague" question.

4. Argumentative Question

An argumentative question asks the witness to accept the examiner's summary, inference or conclusion, rather than to agree with the existence (or non-existence) of a fact. Questions can be made more or less argumentative depending upon the tone of voice of the examiner.

Responses. Treat the objection as a relevance issue, and explain its probative value to the court: "Your Honor, it goes to prove . . . ." (It will not be persuasive to say, "Your Honor, I am not arguing." It might be persuasive to explain the non-argumentative point that you are trying to make). Alternatively, make no response, but wait to see if the judge thinks that the question is argumentative. If so, rephrase the question.

5. Narratives

Witnesses are required to testify in the form of question and answer. This requirement insures that opposing counsel will have the opportunity to frame objections to questions before the answer is given. A narrative answer is one which proceeds at some length in the absence of questions. An answer that is more than a few sentences long can usually be classified as a narrative. A narrative question is one that calls for a narrative answer, such as, "Tell us everything that you did on July 14." Objections can be made both to narrative questions and narrative answers.

Responses. The best response is usually to ask another question that will break up the narrative. Note that expert witnesses are often allowed to testify in narrative fashion, since technical explanations cannot be given easily in question-and-answer format. Even then, however, it is usually more persuasive to interject questions to break up big answers.

6. Asked and Answered

An attorney is not entitled to repeat questions and answers. Once an inquiry has been "asked and answered," further repetition is objectionable. Variations on a theme, however, are permissible, so long as the identical information is not endlessly repeated. The asked and answered rule does not preclude inquiring on cross examination into subjects that were covered fully on direct. Nor does it prevent asking identical questions of different witnesses. (Judges do, however, have the inherent power to exclude cumulative testimony. *See* FRE 611(a).)

Responses. If the question has not been asked and answered, counsel can point out to the judge the manner in which it differs from the earlier testimony. Otherwise, it is best to rephrase the question so as to vary the exact information sought.

7. Assuming Facts Not in Evidence

A question, usually on cross examination, is objectionable if it includes as a predicate a statement of fact that has not been proven. The reason for this objection is that the question is unfair; it cannot be answered without conceding the unproven assumption. Consider, for example, the following question: "You left your home so late that you only had fifteen minutes to get to your office." If the time of the witness's departure was not previously established, this question assumes a fact not in evidence. The witness cannot answer yes to the main question (15 minutes to get to the office) without implicitly conceding the unproven predicate.

Responses. A question assumes facts not in evidence only when it utilizes an introductory predicate as the basis for another inquiry. Simple, one-part cross examination questions do not need to be based upon facts that are already in evidence. For example, it would be proper to ask a witness, "Didn't you leave home late that morning?," whether or not there had already been evidence as to the time of the witness's departure. As a consequence of misunderstanding this distinction, "facts not in evidence" objections are often erroneously made to perfectly good cross examination questions. If the objection is well taken, most questions can easily be divided in two.

8. Non-responsive Answers

It was once hornbook law that only the attorney who asked the question could object to a non-responsive answer. The theory for this limitation was that opposing counsel had no valid objection so long as the content of the answer complied with the rules of evidence. The more modern view is that opposing counsel can object if all, or some part, of an answer is unresponsive to the question, since counsel is entitled to insist that the examination proceed in question-and-answer format. Jurisdictions that adhere to the traditional view may still recognize an objection that the witness is "volunteering" or that there is "no question pending."

Responses. Ask another question.

B. Substantive Objections

1. Hearsay

The Federal Rules of Evidence define hearsay as "[A] statement, other than one made by the declarant while testifying at the trial or hearing, offered in evidence to prove the truth of the matter asserted." FRE 801(c). Thus, any out-of-court statement, including the witness's own previous statement, is potentially hearsay. Whenever a witness testifies, or is asked to testify, about what she or someone else said in the past, the statement should be subjected to hearsay analysis. Statements are not hearsay if they are offered for a purpose other than to "prove the truth of the matter asserted." For example, consider the statement, "I warned him that his brakes needed work." This statement would be hearsay if offered to prove that the brakes were indeed defective. On the other hand, it would not be hearsay if offered to prove that the driver had notice of the condition of the brakes, and was therefore negligent in not having them repaired. There are also numerous exceptions to the hearsay rule.

Responses. Out-of-court statements are admissible if they are not hearsay, or if they fall within one of the exceptions to the hearsay rule.

In addition to statements that are not offered for their truth, the Federal Rules of Evidence define two other types of statements as non-hearsay. The witness's own previous statement is not hearsay if (A) it was given under oath and it is inconsistent with the current testimony;[23] or (B) it is consistent with the current testimony and it is offered to rebut a charge of recent fabrication;[24] or (C) it is a statement of past identification. *See* FRE 801(d)(1). In addition, an admission of a

---

23 Regarding the use of prior inconsistent statements for impeachment, see Chapter Four, Section II, *supra* at p. 119.

24 Regarding the use of prior consistent statements for rehabilitation, see Chapter Five, Section V B(2), *supra* at p. 169.

party opponent is defined as non-hearsay, if offered against that party. FRE 801(D)(2).

Some of the more frequently encountered exceptions to the hearsay rule are as follows:

Present Sense Impression. A statement describing an event made while the declarant is observing it. For example, "Look, there goes the President." FRE 803(1).

Excited Utterance. A statement relating to a startling event made while under the stress of excitement caused by the event. For example, "A piece of plaster fell from the roof, and it just missed me." FRE 803(2).

State of Mind. A statement of the declarant's mental state or condition. For example, "He said that he was so mad he couldn't see straight." FRE 803(3).

Past Recollection Recorded. A memorandum or record of a matter about which the witness once had knowledge, but which she has since forgotten. The record must have been made by the witness when the events were fresh in the witness's mind, and must be shown to have been accurate when made. FRE 803(5).

Business Records. The business records exception applies to the records of any regularly conducted activity. To qualify as an exception to the hearsay rule, the record must have been made at or near the time of the transaction, by a person with knowledge or transmitted from a person with knowledge. It must have been made and kept in the ordinary course of business. The foundation for a business record must be laid by the custodian of the record, or by some other qualified witness. FRE 803(6).

Reputation as to Character. Evidence of a person's reputation for truth and veracity is an exception to the hearsay rule. Note that there are restrictions other than hearsay on the admissibility of character evidence. FRE 803(21). *See also* FRE 404; 405.

Prior Testimony. Testimony given at a different proceeding, or in deposition, qualifies for this exception if (1) the testimony was given under oath; (2) the adverse party had an opportunity to cross examine; and (3) the witness is currently unavailable. FRE 804(b)(1).

Dying Declaration. A statement by a dying person as to the cause or circumstances of what he or she believed to be impending death. Admissible only in homicide prosecutions or civil cases. FRE 804(b)(2).

Statement Against Interest. A statement so contrary to the declarant's pecuniary, proprietary, or penal interest, that no reasonable person would have made it unless it were true. The declarant must be unavailable, and certain other limitations apply in criminal cases. FRE 804(b)(3).

Catch All Exception. Other hearsay statements may be admitted if they contain sufficient circumstantial guarantees of trustworthiness. The declarant must be unavailable, and advance notice must be given to the adverse party. FRE 804(b)(5).

2. Irrelevant

Evidence is irrelevant if it does not make any fact of consequence to the case more or less probable. Evidence can be irrelevant if it proves nothing, or if it tends to prove something that does not matter. FRE 401, 402.

Response. Explain the relevance of the testimony.

3. Unfair Prejudice

Relevant evidence may be excluded if its probative value is substantially outweighed by the danger of unfair prejudice. Note that evidence cannot be excluded merely because it is prejudicial; by definition, all relevant evidence must be prejudicial to some party. Rather, the objection only obtains if the testimony has little probative value and it is unfairly prejudicial. The classic example is a lurid and explicit photograph of an injured crime victim, offered to prove some fact of slight relevance, such as the clothing that the victim was wearing. The availability of other means to establish the same facts will also be considered by the court. FRE 403.

Responses. Most judges are hesitant to exclude evidence on this basis. A measured explanation of the probative value of the testimony is the best response.

4. Improper Character Evidence, Generally

Character evidence is generally not admissible to prove that a person acted in conformity with his or her character. For example, a defendant's past burglaries cannot be offered as proof of a current charge of burglary. A driver's past accidents cannot be offered as proof of current negligence. FRE 404(a).

Responses. A criminal defendant may offer proof of good character, which the prosecution may then rebut. FRE 404 (a)(1).

Past crimes and bad acts may be offered to prove motive, opportunity, intent, preparation, plan, knowledge, identity, or absence of mistake. FRE 404(b).

5. Improper Character Evidence, Conviction of Crime

As noted above, the commission, and even the conviction, of past crimes is not admissible to prove current guilt.

The credibility of a witness who takes the stand and testifies, however, may be impeached on the basis of a prior criminal conviction, but only if the following requirements are satisfied: The crime must have been either (1) a felony, or (2) one which involved dishonesty or false statement, regardless of punishment. With certain exceptions, the evidence is not admissible unless it occurred within the last ten years. Juvenile adjudications are generally not admissible. FRE 609.

Note that the impeachment is generally limited to the fact of conviction, the name of the crime, and the sentence received. The details and events that comprised the crime are generally inadmissible.

Responses. If the crime was not a felony, the conviction may still be admissible if it involved dishonesty. If the conviction is more than ten years old, it may still be admissible if the court determines that its probative value, supported by specific facts and circumstances, substantially outweighs its prejudicial effect. FRE 609.

6. Improper Character Evidence, Untruthfulness

As noted above, the past bad acts of a person may not be offered as proof that he or she committed similar acts. Specific instances of conduct are admissible for the limited purpose of attacking or supporting credibility. A witness may therefore be cross examined concerning past bad acts only if they reflect upon truthfulness or untruthfulness. Note, however, that such bad acts (other than conviction of a crime) may not be proved by extrinsic evidence. The cross examiner is stuck with the witness's answer. FRE 608(b).

Responses. Explain the manner in which the witness's past bad acts are probative of untruthfulness.

7. Improper Character Evidence, Reputation

Reputation evidence is admissible only with regard to an individual's character for truthfulness or untruthfulness. Moreover, evidence of a truthful character is admissible only after the character of the witness has been attacked. FRE 608(a).

Responses. Explain the manner in which the reputation evidence is probative of truthfulness or untruthfulness.

8. Lack of Personal Knowledge

Witnesses (other than experts) must testify from personal knowledge, which is generally defined as sensory perception. A witness's lack of personal knowledge may be obvious from the questioning, may be inherent in the testimony, or may be developed by questioning on voir dire. FRE 602.

Responses. Ask further questions that establish the witness's personal knowledge.

9. Improper Lay Opinion

Lay witnesses (non-experts) are generally precluded from testifying as to opinions, conclusions, or inferences. FRE 701.

Responses. Lay witnesses may testify to opinions or inferences if they are rationally based upon the perception of the witness. Common lay opinions include estimates of speed, distance, value, height, time, duration, and temperature. Lay witnesses are also commonly allowed to testify as to the mood, sanity, demeanor, sobriety, or tone of voice of another person.

10. Speculation or Conjecture

Witnesses may not be asked to speculate or guess. Such questions are often phrased as hypotheticals in a form such as, "What would have happened if . . .."

Responses. Witnesses are permitted to make reasonable estimates rationally based upon perception.

11. Authenticity

Exhibits must be authenticated before they may be admitted. Authenticity refers to adequate proof that the exhibit actually is what it seems or purports to be. Virtually all documents and tangible objects must be authenticated. Since exhibits are authenticated by laying a foundation, objections may be raised on the ground of either authenticity or foundation. This subject is discussed in greater detail in Chapter Eight.

Responses. Ask additional questions that establish authenticity.

12. Lack of Foundation

Nearly all evidence, other than a witness's direct observation of events, requires some sort of predicate foundation for admissibility. An objection to lack of foundation requires the judge to make a preliminary ruling as to the admissibility of the evidence. FRE 104. The evidentiary foundations vary widely. For example, the foundation for the business records exception to the hearsay rule includes evidence that the records were made and kept in the ordinary course of business. The foundation for the introduction of certain scientific evidence requires the establishment of a chain of custody. The following list includes some, though by no means all, of the sorts of evidence that require special foundations for admissibility: voice identifications, telephone conversations, writings, business records, the existence of a privilege, dying declarations, photographs, scientific tests, expert and lay opinions, and many more. This subject is discussed in greater detail in Chapter Eight.

Responses. Ask additional questions that lay the necessary foundation.

13. Best Evidence

The "best evidence" or "original document" rule refers to the common law requirement that copies or secondary evidence of writings could not be admitted into evidence unless the absence of the original could be explained. Under modern practice, most jurisdictions have significantly expanded upon the circumstances in which duplicates and other secondary evidence may be admitted.

Under the Federal Rules of Evidence, "duplicates" are usually admissible to the same extent as originals. Duplicates include carbons, photocopies, photographs, duplicate print-outs, or any other copies that are made by "techniques which accurately reproduce the original." FRE 1001-1003.

Other secondary evidence, such as oral testimony as to the contents of a document, is admissible only if the original has been lost or destroyed, is unavailable through judicial process, or if it is in the exclusive possession of the opposing party. FRE 1004.

Responses. Ask additional questions demonstrating either that the item offered is a duplicate, or that the original is unavailable.

14. Privilege

Numerous privileges may operate to exclude otherwise admissible evidence. Among the most common are attorney-client, physician-patient, marital, clergy, psychotherapist-patient, and a number of others that exist either by statute or at common law. Each privilege has its own foundation and its own set of exceptions. FRE 501 did not change the common law privileges, but note that state statutory privileges may not obtain in federal actions.

Responses. Virtually all privileges are subject to some exceptions, which vary from jurisdiction to jurisdiction.

15. Liability Insurance

Evidence that a person carried liability insurance is not admissible on the issue of negligence. FRE 411. This exclusion is necessary because it is generally assumed that juries will be promiscuous in awarding judgments that they know will ultimately be paid by insurance companies. The improper mention of liability insurance may be considered so prejudicial as to warrant a mistrial.

Responses. Evidence of liability insurance may be admissible on some issue other than negligence, such as proof of agency, ownership, control, or bias or prejudice of a witness. FRE 411.

16. Subsequent Remedial Measures

Evidence of subsequent repair or other remedial measures is not admissible to prove negligence or other culpable conduct. FRE 405. The primary rationale for this rule is that parties should not be discouraged from remedying dangerous conditions, and should not have to choose between undertaking repairs and creating proof of their own liability.

Responses. Subsequent remedial measures may be offered to prove ownership, control, or feasibility of precautionary measures, if controverted. FRE 407. Evidence of subsequent repair may also be admissible in strict liability cases, as opposed to negligence cases.

17. Settlement Offers

Offers of compromise or settlement are not admissible to prove or disprove liability. Statements made during settlement negotiations are also inadmissible. FRE 408.

Responses. Statements made during settlement discussions may be admissible to prove bias or prejudice of a witness, or to negate a contention of undue delay. FRE 408.

— CHAPTER EIGHT —
Foundations and Exhibits

I. EVIDENTIARY FOUNDATIONS

A. The Requirement of Foundation

Before any evidence can be considered at trial, there must be some basis for believing it to be relevant and admissible. This basis is called the foundation for the evidence. Depending upon the nature of the evidence, the foundation may be painfully complex or strikingly simple. The law of evidence determines exactly which facts form the predicate for the admission of all testimony and exhibits. In any event, the question of foundation is directed to the judge, who must make a preliminary determination as to whether the particular evidence will be received.[1]

Regarding much testimony, foundation is so obvious that it is almost overlooked as a formal aspect of the trial. For example, the basic foundation for eyewitness, or percipient, testimony is that the witness observed relevant events and is able to recall them. This foundation is typically established as a means of introducing the witness, virtually as a matter of course. For example:

QUESTION: Where were you on the afternoon of March 17?

ANSWER: I was at the corner of Main and Ridge.

QUESTION: What did you see?

ANSWER: I saw an automobile collision.

It has now been shown that the witness has personal knowledge of relevant facts. On the basis of this foundation, and in the absence of some objection that is not apparent from the example, the witness should be allowed to describe the collision. Of course, not all foundations are so straightforward. Many require the proof of substantial predicate facts, as will be discussed below.

---

1   *See* Rule 104, Federal Rules of Evidence.

Foundations are required in the interest of both efficiency and fairness. In order to conserve the court's time, evidence will not be heard unless there is first a threshold showing of relevance and admissibility. In the above example, for instance, there would be no reason for a court to hear a narrative about the accident from a witness who was not qualified to describe it.

Similarly, fairness dictates that an adversary be given notice of the basis for offering evidence before it is actually received. Imagine this scenario at the very beginning of a direct examination:

QUESTION: What is your name?

ANSWER: Ryan Black.

QUESTION: Please describe the automobile accident that occurred at the corner of Main and Ridge last March 17.

In the absence of some basis for the witness's testimony, opposing counsel has no way of knowing whether the proffered evidence will be competent or inadmissible. The witness may be about to testify on the basis of speculation or hearsay. Foundation is therefore required in order to prevent unfair prejudice.

B. Components of Foundation

There are three universal aspects to virtually all evidentiary foundations. To be received, evidence must be shown to be (1) relevant, (2) authentic, and (3) admissible under the applicable laws of evidence. While the discrete elements of foundation will differ according to the nature of the evidence and the purpose for which it is offered, these three considerations must always apply.

1. Relevance

Relevance defines the relationship between the proffered evidence and some fact that is at issue in the case. Evidence will not be admitted simply because it is interesting or imaginative. Rather, it must be shown to be probative in the sense that it makes some disputed fact either more or less likely. The relevance of most evidence is generally made apparent from the context of the case, but occasionally it must be demonstrated by the establishment of foundational facts.

In the intersection example above, the relevance of the testimony is made clear by the recitation of the date and place of the witness's observation. The witness is about to testify concerning the collision at issue, not just any accident. Note, however, that this basic foundation might not always be adequate. Had there been more than one accident on March 17 at the corner of Main and Ridge, the witness would have to provide additional identifying facts before testifying to the events. What time was the witness there? What colors were the automobiles involved?

2. Authenticity

The concept of authenticity refers to the requirement of proof that the evidence actually is what the proponent claims it to be.[2] In other words, evidence is not to be admitted until there has been a threshold showing that it is "the real thing." The judge decides whether an item of evidence has been sufficiently authenticated, and the criteria vary according to the nature of the evidence involved. In many jurisdictions the strict rules of evidence do not apply to the court's preliminary determination of admissibility.[3]

We generally think of authentication as it applies to tangible evidence such as documents, physical objects, or photographs. Is that really the contract that the parties executed? Is this actually the machine part that caused the injury? Does the photograph fairly and accurately depict the scene of the accident? Before any exhibit can be received a foundation must be established that adequately supports the proponent's claim of authenticity. Note that the court's initial ruling on authenticity is preliminary. It bears only on admissibility and is not binding as a factual determination. Opposing counsel may continue to controvert the genuineness of the exhibit, and the trier of fact (either judge or jury) remains free ultimately to reject the exhibit.

The requirement of authenticity is not, however, limited to tangible objects. It also applies to certain testimonial evidence. For example, a witness generally may not testify to a telephone conversation without first establishing her basis for recognizing the voice of the person on the other end of the line.[4] That is, the identity of the other speaker must be authenticated.

3. Specific Admissibility

While evidence will generally be received if it is relevant and authentic, the law of evidence contains a host of specific provisions that govern the admissibility of various sorts of proof. In many cases evidence can be admitted only following the establishment of foundational facts. Most exceptions to the hearsay rule, for

---

2   See Rule 901(a), Federal Rules of Evidence, which provides: "The requirement of authentication or identification as a condition precedent to admissibility is satisfied by evidence sufficient to support a finding that the matter in question is what its proponent claims."

3   *See e.g.* Rule 104(a), Federal Rules of Evidence: "Preliminary questions concerning the . . . admissibility of evidence shall be determined by the court . . . . In making its determination it is not bound by the rules of evidence except those with respect to privilege."

4   Alternative means for authenticating telephone conversations are discussed in Section II B(2), *infra* at p. 271.

example, require such a preliminary showing. Similarly, a foundation must be laid for the admission of evidence of habit or routine practice,[5] or for the admission of evidence of subsequent remedial measures.[6] It is impossible to generalize about such prerequisites, except to say that the advocate must be aware of the rule of evidence under which each item of evidence is proffered. As is discussed in detail below, a foundation can then be tailored to meet the rule's requirements.

C. Establishing Foundations

1. Using a Single Witness

The most common approach to the establishment of a foundation is simply to call a witness who can provide the necessary facts, and then to offer the evidence after that testimony has been elicited. Consider this example from the direct examination of the plaintiff in our fire engine case:[7]

QUESTION: Do you recognize the object that I am showing you, which has been marked as plaintiff's exhibit 12?

ANSWER: Yes, it is the neck brace that I got from my doctor.

QUESTION: When did you get it from your doctor?

ANSWER: When I was discharged from the hospital following the accident.

QUESTION: What is it made of?

ANSWER: Stiff plastic.

QUESTION: Do you still wear it?

ANSWER: Yes, I have to wear it at least eight hours a day.

Counsel may now offer the neck brace into evidence. Its relevance to the issue of damages is apparent from the context of the case, its authenticity as the actual neck brace has been established by the witness, and there are no special evidentiary considerations that govern the admission of this real evidence.

---

5   *See* Rule 406, Federal Rules of Evidence.

6   *See* Rule 407, Federal Rules of Evidence.

7   This example is slightly truncated. A fuller discussion of the steps for offering real evidence is found in Section III B(1), *infra* at p. 288.

2. Using Multiple Witnesses

Some foundations cannot be laid by a single witness. In such cases counsel must establish separate parts of the foundation from each of several witnesses before offering the evidence. In a purse-snatching case, for example, it may be necessary to call two witnesses in order to lay the foundation for the admission of the stolen purse. First, the arresting officer:

QUESTION: Officer, do you recognize prosecution exhibit 1?

ANSWER: Yes. It is a lady's purse that was in the possession of the defendant when I arrested him.

The officer has laid some of the foundation, but not all of it. The defendant's possession of a purse is not relevant until it is shown to have been stolen. It is therefore necessary to call the crime victim:

QUESTION: Ma'am, do you recognize prosecution exhibit 1?

ANSWER: Yes. It is my pocketbook.

QUESTION: Before today, when was the last time that you saw it?

ANSWER: The last time I saw it was when it was ripped off of my shoulder by a purse snatcher.

Now the purse is admissible. The victim provided the missing aspect of relevance, and she also authenticated the purse as the object that was stolen.

Note that it is possible to combine both direct and cross examinations to lay a single foundation. Thus, defense counsel can begin to lay a foundation during the cross examination of a plaintiff's witness and can conclude the foundation during the defendant's case in chief. Assume, for example, that the defendant wants to introduce a letter from the plaintiff. To be admissible, it must be shown both that the plaintiff wrote the letter and that the defendant received it. Defense counsel can begin the foundation during the plaintiff's case by having the plaintiff authenticate his own signature on cross examination. The foundation can later be completed by having the defendant testify during her own case that the letter was actually received.

3. Conditional Admissibility

It is not always possible to complete a foundation during the testimony of a single witness. However, a witness who is responsible for part of the foundation will in many cases have other important information concerning the exhibit. In the absence of a special rule, this witness could not testify about the exhibit until a second witness had been called to complete the foundation. Only then could the first witness return to the stand to complete his testimony about the exhibit.

Fortunately, such an awkward and inefficient procedure is generally not necessary. The courts have developed the doctrine of conditional admissibility, which allows the temporary or conditional admission of the evidence based upon counsel's representation that the foundation will be completed through the testimony of a subsequent witness.[8]

In the above purse-snatching case the prosecution might want to elicit further testimony about the purse from the arresting officer:

QUESTION: Officer, do you recognize prosecution exhibit 1?

ANSWER: Yes. It is a lady's purse that the defendant was concealing under his jacket when I arrested him.

QUESTION: Officer, please show us how the defendant was concealing the purse when you arrested him.

DEFENSE COUNSEL: Objection. There is no foundation for this demonstration.

PROSECUTOR: Your Honor, we will complete the foundation when we call the victim, who will testify that exhibit 1 is the same purse that was stolen from her.

COURT: On the basis of counsel's representation, the objection is overruled.

The further testimony of the officer has been conditionally allowed, subject to the perfection of the foundation. In the event that the victim does not identify the purse, all of the conditionally accepted testimony will be subject to a motion to strike.

4. Using Adverse Witnesses

Potentially complex foundations can often be simplified through the use of adverse examination. In a case where executed contracts have been exchanged through the mail, for example, it may be extremely difficult for one party to authenticate the other party's signature. This problem can be completely alleviated, however, simply by calling the opposing party as an adverse witness:

---

8   Rule 104(b) of the Federal Rules of Evidence provides: "When the relevancy of evidence depends upon the fulfillment of a condition of fact, the court shall admit it . . . subject to . . . the introduction of evidence sufficient to support a finding of the fulfillment of the condition."

QUESTION: Are you the defendant in this case?

ANSWER: I am.

QUESTION: Is this your signature at the bottom of plaintiff's exhibit 1?

ANSWER: Yes, it is.

The signature has now been authenticated.

5. Cross Examination

Foundation requirements apply equally during cross and direct examinations. Testimonial foundations must be laid on cross examination for personal knowledge, voice identification, hearsay exceptions, and in every other circumstance where a foundation would be necessary on direct examination. In addition, there are special foundations for certain cross examination techniques such as impeachment by past omission or prior inconsistent statement.

It is also often necessary to use cross examination to lay the foundation for the admission of exhibits. Defense counsel in particular can avoid the need to call adverse witnesses by attempting to establish foundations for her own exhibits while cross examining a plaintiff's witness.

In some jurisdictions, however, exhibits cannot actually be offered other than in counsel's case in chief. In such jurisdictions you may proceed to elicit the appropriate foundational testimony during cross examination, but you must delay actually offering the exhibits until the other side has rested. Following this rule, a plaintiff's attorney who develops the foundation for exhibits while cross examining defense witnesses must wait until the defense has rested, and may then offer the exhibits on rebuttal.

The "case-in-chief" rule is very difficult to justify analytically. Counsel can develop affirmative testimonial evidence on cross examination, and there is no good reason to treat real or documentary evidence any differently. Moreover, delaying the offer of an exhibit until after cross examination also delays any objections to the exhibit. This may prove awkward in situations where an objection is sustained for some technical reason, and the witness is no longer on the stand to cure the defect.

It is far preferable to be able to offer exhibits on cross examination. Nonetheless, the case-in-chief rule must be followed where it exists.

II. FOUNDATIONS FOR TESTIMONIAL EVIDENCE

A. Personal Knowledge

Witnesses are expected to testify from personal knowledge.[9] The most common sort of personal knowledge is direct sensory perception: information gained through sight, hearing, touch, taste, and smell. Witnesses may also have personal knowledge of more subjective information, such as their own intentions or emotions, or the reputation of another person.

Whatever the content of the witness's testimony, it is necessary to lay a foundation showing that the witness is testifying either from personal knowledge or on the basis of an acceptable substitute, as in the case of expert testimony.[10]

In the case of sensory perception, the basic foundation is simply that the witness was in a position to observe or otherwise experience the relevant facts:

QUESTION: Where were you on the afternoon of March 17?

ANSWER: I was at the corner of State and Madison.

QUESTION: What were you doing?

ANSWER: I was watching the St. Patrick's Day Parade.

QUESTION: Please tell us what you saw.

Or,

QUESTION: What was your last meal before you went to the hospital?

ANSWER: I had a tuna sandwich at a restaurant called Kate's Corner.

QUESTION: How did it taste?

ANSWER: It was warm, and it tasted sort of sour.

QUESTION: Did you finish it?

ANSWER: No, because of the way it tasted.

9　*See* Rule 602, Federal Rules of Evidence: "A witness may not testify to a matter unless evidence is introduced sufficient to support a finding that he has personal knowledge of the matter. Evidence to prove personal knowledge may, but need not, consist of the testimony of the witness himself."

10　Expert witnesses are not required to testify from personal knowledge. *See* Rule 703, Federal Rules of Evidence. The foundation for expert testimony is discussed in Chapter Six, Section II, *supra* at p. 172.

In ordinary circumstances, it is not necessary to establish more than the witness's general basis for testifying. Witnesses are assumed to have all of their senses in order, so, for example, counsel is not required to show that the witness's eyesight is unimpaired or that the witness was familiar with right-tasting tuna sandwiches.

In some situations, however, additional foundation may be called for to establish fully the basis of the witness's testimony:

QUESTION: Where were you on the afternoon of March 17?

ANSWER: I was in my office on the 28th floor of the National Bank Building.

QUESTION: What were you doing?

ANSWER: I was watching the St. Patrick's Day Parade.

QUESTION: Were you able to see the people on the floats?

ANSWER: Yes.

QUESTION: How is that?

ANSWER: I was using binoculars.

Or,

QUESTION: What happened when you were standing in the workshop?

ANSWER: I heard a high-pitched, mechanical, whining sound in the next room.

QUESTION: Could you tell what it was?

ANSWER: Yes.

QUESTION: How could you tell?

ANSWER: I have worked in the workshop before, and I heard that sound when I saw the machines operating.

QUESTION: What was the sound?

The foundations in the above scenarios are actually slightly overdone. In simple cases such as these, most witnesses will be allowed to provide the basis of the perception either before or after testifying to the facts. Thus, in the machine shop example most judges would allow the witness first to identify the noise and then to explain why she could recognize it.

Apart from the personal knowledge rule, special foundations are required for certain sorts of testimony. Special foundations may also be necessary to bring testimony within an exception to the hearsay rule. These foundations are discussed in the following sections.

B. Special Foundations for Certain Testimonial Evidence

While most testimony requires a showing of personal knowledge, certain testimony calls for the establishment of additional foundational facts.

1. Conversations

Witnesses are often called upon to testify to conversations between two or more parties. In order to authenticate the conversation, and thereby allow opposing counsel to conduct a meaningful cross examination, testimony concerning a conversation generally must be supported by a foundation establishing the date, time, and place of the conversation, as well as the persons present at the time. For example:

QUESTION: Did you complain to anyone about the quality of the printing job?

ANSWER: Yes, I spoke to the store manager, Elaine McIntyre.

QUESTION: When did you speak to the manager?

ANSWER: On the same day that I refused to accept the product: April 18.

QUESTION: About what time was that?

ANSWER: I believe that it was just before noon, but it may have been somewhat later.

QUESTION: Where were you when you spoke?

ANSWER: We were at the service counter.

QUESTION: Was anybody else present?

ANSWER: There was a clerk nearby, but she wasn't involved in the conversation.

QUESTION: Please tell us what was said during that conversation.

This foundation demonstrates the authenticity of the conversation. The witness's ability to relate the time, date, place, and participants provides sufficient evidence that the conversation happened as she says it did. It is not necessary to lay the foundation with minute precision. In the above scenario the witness would not be required to provide the clerk's name, or the exact time of the conversation. The foundation is sufficient so long as it fulfills its purpose of providing opposing counsel with reasonably sufficient information with which to challenge or contest the witness's testimony.

Note, however, that the authentication of the conversation does not resolve any hearsay or other evidentiary problems that may be raised by its content. Those issues must be addressed separately, often necessitating the development of additional foundation.

2. Telephone Conversations and Voice Identification

The foundation for a telephone conversation includes the additional element of voice identification, or of a reasonable circumstantial substitute.

a. Voice Identification

Voice identification can be based on personal familiarity that either precedes or post-dates the telephone conversation in question.[11] For example:

QUESTION: Did you complain to anyone about the quality of the printing job?

ANSWER: Yes, I telephoned the store manager, Elaine McIntyre, as soon as I opened the first package.

QUESTION: How do you know that you were speaking to Ms. McIntyre?

ANSWER: I recognized her voice. I have been going to that print shop for years, and I have spoken to her many times in person.

The witness could also base voice identification on a subsequent contact with the store manager:

QUESTION: Did you complain to anyone about the quality of the printing job?

ANSWER: Yes, I telephoned the store manager, Elaine McIntyre, as soon as I opened the first package.

---

11 *See* Rule 901(b)(5), Federal Rules of Evidence.

QUESTION: Had you ever met Ms. McIntyre?

ANSWER: Not at that time.

QUESTION: How do you know that you were speaking to Ms. McIntyre on the phone?

ANSWER: I spoke to her in person the next day, and I recognized her voice as the same person from the phone call.

There is no strict time limit for voice identification based on subsequent contact, although a lengthy time lapse will obviously detract from the weight to be given to a contested identification.

b. Circumstantial Evidence; Listed Numbers

In the absence of a basis for voice identification, circumstantial evidence can be used as the foundation for a telephone conversation. A telephone call placed by the witness can be authenticated by showing that the call was made to a listed number.[12] Again:

QUESTION: Did you complain to anyone about the quality of the printing job?

ANSWER: Yes, I telephoned the store as soon as I opened the first package.

QUESTION: How did you obtain the number?

ANSWER: I looked it up in the telephone book.

QUESTION: Did you dial the number that was listed in the book?

ANSWER: Yes.

QUESTION: What did you say when the telephone was answered?

ANSWER: I said that I wanted to complain about the quality of the printing job that I had just picked up.

Under the Federal Rules of Evidence, the above foundation is sufficient in the case of a business, so long as the conversation related to "business reasonably

---

12 *See* Rule 901(b)(6), Federal Rules of Evidence, which uses the phrase "the number assigned at the time by the telephone company to a particular person or business."

transacted over the telephone."[13] There is a presumption that the person who answers a business telephone is authorized to speak for the business.

In the case of an individual, however, the foundation must also include "circumstances, including self-identification, [that] show the person answering to be the one called."[14]

c. Other Circumstantial Evidence

Numerous other circumstances can be used to authenticate telephone conversations. Subsequent verifying events can form the foundation for telephone calls either placed or received by the witness. In the following example, the witness both placed and received a telephone call:

QUESTION: Did you ever speak to Mr. Zenner after the incident?

ANSWER: Yes, I looked his number up in the telephone book and I called his home.

QUESTION: Did you speak to Mr. Zenner?

ANSWER: No, a woman answered the telephone.

QUESTION: What did you do?

ANSWER: I left my name and number, and I asked for Mr. Zenner to call me back.

QUESTION: Did you ever receive a return call?

ANSWER: Yes, I received a call the next day.

QUESTION: What did the party say?

ANSWER: He said, "This is Mr. Zenner. I am returning your call from yesterday."

Note that the placement of a call to an individual's listed number is not alone sufficient to lay the foundation for a conversation. Additional verifying facts must be established. In this example, both the first and second conversations are verified by the following circumstances of the return call: (1) Zenner's self-identification; (2) the stated response to the initial message; and (3) the listing of Zenner's number in the telephone directory.

---

13   *Id.* at 901(b)(6)(B).

14   *Id.*

Circumstantial evidence authenticating telephone calls *received* by a witness must include specific information that tends to identify the caller. Calls *placed* by the witness are commonly authenticated circumstantially on the basis of the number dialed. Such evidence can include reference to listings other than in the telephone directory, perhaps on company stationery or advertising material.

3. Prior Identification

Under the Federal Rules of Evidence a witness may testify to his or her previous, out-of-court identification of an individual.[15] While such evidence is most commonly offered in criminal cases to bolster the in-court identification made at trial,[16] it also has its uses in civil matters. The foundation for this testimony is that the out-of-court identification was made by the witness after perceiving the person identified:

QUESTION: Were you able to see the person who stole your car?

ANSWER: Yes. He was driving away in it just as I got home from work. I saw him from the shoulders up.

QUESTION: How far away were you when you first saw him?

ANSWER: I was about 30 feet away.

QUESTION: Did you ever see him again?

ANSWER: Yes, I picked him out of a lineup.

QUESTION: Where and when was that?

ANSWER: About four days later at the police station.

QUESTION: Please describe the circumstances of the lineup.

ANSWER: There were five men standing in a row. They were all about the same height and they were all wearing blue jeans and

---

15 Rule 801(d)(1)(C), Federal Rules of Evidence. Note that statements of prior identification are excluded from the definition of hearsay, and therefore are admissible to "prove the truth of the matter asserted."

16 In-court identifications may be less than compelling, since the physical arrangement of the courtroom will often serve to point the witness in the direction of the party to be identified. In criminal cases, for example, the defendant will usually be seated at counsel table next to the defense lawyer. Out-of-court identifications, on the other hand, are more likely to test the witness's initial observation. Proof that the witness picked the defendant out of a lineup, for example, will significantly bolster the subsequent in-court identification.

flannel shirts. I identified the man who was second from the left.

QUESTION: Was that the same man whom you identified here in court today?

ANSWER: Yes.

4. Habit and Routine

Testimonial evidence of habit or routine practice may be admitted as circumstantial evidence that a person or organization acted in a similar fashion on a particular occasion.[17] The subject matter of such testimony can range from an individual's clothing preferences to a business's routine for mailing letters. In each case, the evidence of a regular custom or practice is offered to prove that the individual or business acted in the same way at a time relevant to the issues at trial.

To lay the foundation for evidence of habit or routine practice, it is necessary to call a witness with personal knowledge of the regular conduct of the person or organization involved. Furthermore, counsel must establish that the asserted conduct was, in fact, of a consistently repeated nature. This can be accomplished through proof of either extended observation or of the existence of a formal policy or procedure.

a. Individual Habit

The most common foundation for an individual's habit is through evidence of a pattern of conduct repeated over a substantial period of time. The alleged habit must be clearly differentiated from independent or distinct activities.

In the following example, assume that the defendant is charged with stabbing a man to death. Pleading self-defense, the defendant claims that it was the victim who attacked him with a knife, which he took away and used to defend himself. Habit evidence will be offered by the prosecution to show that the defendant always carried a knife:

QUESTION: How long have you known the defendant?

ANSWER: About five years.

QUESTION: In what context do you know him?

ANSWER: We are neighbors. He lives next door to me.

---

17   Rule 406, Federal Rules of Evidence.

QUESTION: During the last five years, how often have you seen the defendant?

ANSWER: On average, I would say that I have seen him at least twice a week.

QUESTION: On those occasions, did you ever see the defendant carry a knife?

ANSWER: Yes. He always carried a hunting knife strapped to his belt.

QUESTION: How often did you see the defendant with a hunting knife?

ANSWER: Whenever he went out of the house, he always had that knife on his belt.

QUESTION: Did you ever see him go out of the house without a knife on his belt?

ANSWER: Only once.

QUESTION: What was that occasion?

ANSWER: He was going to a wedding in a tuxedo.

The evidence of the defendant's constant habit over an extended period of time is admissible to prove that he was carrying a knife on the date in question.

b. Business Practice

The routine practice of a business or organization may be established either through direct observation or through evidence of an existing policy or practice. In the following example, assume that a dispute exists over whether an employee's references were checked before she was hired by a large corporation. Although the employee's file was marked "OK," no one can specifically remember making the reference checks. The company must therefore rely on proof of their business practice. First, through direct experience:

QUESTION: What is your position at the Judson Corporation?

ANSWER: I work in personnel. I am in charge of checking references.

QUESTION: How long have you held that position?

ANSWER: Six years.

QUESTION: How do you go about checking references?

ANSWER: Once a potential employee has been approved by the department head, the next step is to check references. The file comes to me and I personally telephone every listed reference.

QUESTION: What happens after you telephone the references?

ANSWER: If all of the references are positive I mark the file "OK" and send it on to the personnel manager. If they are negative I mark it "failed" before I send it on.

QUESTION: Have you ever marked a file "OK" when you haven't telephoned the references?

ANSWER: No. Not in my entire six years at the Judson Company.

QUESTION: Was that the practice that you followed during April of last year?

ANSWER: Absolutely.

QUESTION: Did anyone else handle reference checks during that period?

ANSWER: No. I was the only one.

The witness's testimony of her own business routine is proof that she adhered to that custom during the time period in question.

Now assume that there were a number of employees who did reference checks during the relevant time period and that several of them have left the company. Furthermore, the "OK" notation on the file was made by a rubber stamp:

QUESTION: What is your position at the Judson Corporation?

ANSWER: I work in personnel. I am in charge of checking references.

QUESTION: How long have you held that position?

ANSWER: Six years.

QUESTION: Do other employees also check references?

ANSWER: Yes. Over the years there have been four or five of us who have made the actual telephone calls.

QUESTION: Does the Judson Company have a written policy regarding reference checks?

ANSWER: Yes. Once a potential employee has been approved by the department head, the next step is to check references. The file comes to our department and someone personally telephones every listed reference. If all of the references are positive the file is stamped "OK" and sent on to the personnel manager. If they are negative it is stamped "failed" before it is sent on.

QUESTION: Was that policy provided in writing to every employee in your department?

ANSWER: Yes.

QUESTION: Does the written policy of the Judson Company permit a file to be stamped "OK" if the references have not been telephoned?

ANSWER: Definitely not.

QUESTION: Was that policy in effect during April of last year?

ANSWER: Yes it was.

Even without personal observation, the witness's knowledge of the company's business policy[18] provides a sufficient foundation for the introduction of the routine practice.

5. Character and Reputation

Evidence of a person's character generally is not admissible to prove that "he acted in conformity therewith on a particular occasion."[19] For example, counsel may not offer proof of a person's dislike of children as evidence that he committed a kidnapping. There are, however, a number of exceptions that allow the admission of character evidence for a variety of purposes.[20] Each exception requires the establishment of its own foundation.

a. Other Crimes or Past Misconduct

Following the general rule, evidence of past crimes or other wrongful conduct is not admissible to prove the occurrence of a specific event. Three previous burglaries cannot be offered to show that a defendant is a burglar, nor can three previous automobile accidents be used to prove that a tort plaintiff was guilty of

---

18 Since the witness testified to the content of a written policy, further foundation might be necessary to comply with the "best evidence" or "original writing" rule. *See* Section V B, *infra* at p. 314.

19 Rule 404(a), Federal Rules of Evidence.

20 The uses of character evidence for impeachment are discussed in Chapter Four, Section IV, *supra* at p. 153.

contributory negligence. Past misconduct, including uncharged crimes, may, however, be admitted for other purposes "such as proof of motive, opportunity, intent, preparation, plan, knowledge, identity, or absence of mistake or accident."[21]

The foundation for such evidence must include the specifics of the past act as well as the circumstances that make it usable for a permissible purpose in the case at trial. Assume that the defendant in the following example is an employer who is being prosecuted for intentionally failing to pay last year's employee withholding taxes to the government. The defendant admits the conduct, but claims that it was an unintentional oversight. The prosecution has called a tax examiner to the stand:

QUESTION: What is your occupation?

ANSWER: I am an auditor for the Internal Revenue Service.

QUESTION: Have you audited the records of the defendant's business?

ANSWER: Yes, I audited the records for the last seven years.

QUESTION: Exactly what records did you review?

ANSWER: I looked at all of the payroll records, including the time sheets and check stubs for every employee.

QUESTION: Were you able to determine anything with regard to withholding taxes?

ANSWER: Yes. In each of the last seven years the amount of money withheld from employees' paychecks was more than the amount paid over to the government.

QUESTION: What was the difference last year?

ANSWER: Last year the defendant withheld $55,000 more from employees than was paid to the government for their withholding taxes.

QUESTION: And in the preceding six years?

ANSWER: The amounts for the previous six years were $40,000; $32,000; $51,000; $39,000; $46,000; and $42,000.

---

21 Rule 404(b), Federal Rules of Evidence.

QUESTION: Did the defendant submit withholding tax returns in each of the last seven years?

ANSWER: Yes. They were submitted and signed by the defendant in each of the last seven years, but they never accurately reflected the amount of money deducted from employees' paychecks.

The defendant has not been charged with failing to pay withholding taxes other than in the most recent year. The government may not offer the other tax records to show that the defendant was an habitual tax cheat. Nonetheless, evidence of the past misconduct is admissible to show either intent or absence of mistake in filing last year's return.

Note that the foundation included the basis of the witness's knowledge, the precise records that were reviewed, the relationship of the records to the withholding return, the years in which underpayments were made, and the defendant's personal involvement in signing the returns.

b. Reputation for Untruthfulness

Once a witness has testified, it is permissible for the opposing party to offer evidence of the witness's reputation in the community for untruthfulness. This is typically done by calling another witness to the stand who has knowledge of the first witness's reputation in the community. This evidence can be offered only to reflect on the credibility of the first witness's testimony.

The foundation for such reputation evidence includes identification of the relevant community, the basis of the witness's knowledge, and the nature of the first witness's reputation during a relevant time period. Note that the "community" involved may be residential, professional, social, or the like. Assume that the plaintiff has already testified in our fire engine case. The defendant has now called a witness to testify regarding the plaintiff's reputation for untruthfulness:

QUESTION: Do you know the plaintiff?

ANSWER: Yes, I have known her for four years.

QUESTION: In what context do you know her?

ANSWER: We belong to the same hiking club. It's called the Campside Walkers.

QUESTION: Are you familiar with the plaintiff's reputation for truth and veracity among the Campside Walkers?

ANSWER: Yes. Her reputation is very bad. She is regarded within the club as an untruthful person.

QUESTION: Was that her reputation as of last Tuesday when she testified?

ANSWER: Yes it was.

In many jurisdictions a witness may also testify as to her opinion of a previous witness's untruthfulness.[22] The foundation is similar to that for reputation testimony:

QUESTION: Do you know the plaintiff?

ANSWER: Yes, I have known her for four years.

QUESTION: In what context do you know her?

ANSWER: We belong to the same hiking club, the Campside Walkers.

QUESTION: How often have you spoken to the plaintiff during those four years?

ANSWER: Well, the club meets once a month and both of us usually attend the meetings. In addition, we have gone on many long hikes together and on at least three occasions we went on weekend camping trips.

QUESTION: Based on your contacts with the plaintiff, do you have an opinion concerning her truthfulness?

ANSWER: Yes, I do. My opinion is that she is not a truthful person.

Once a witness has given reputation or opinion evidence concerning another's untruthfulness, the cross examiner may then inquire as to "relevant specific instances of conduct."[23] Additionally, once the character of a witness has been attacked, the proponent of the witness may proceed to offer evidence of the witness's good reputation for *truthfulness.*

c. Character Traits of Criminal Defendant or Crime Victim

Notwithstanding the general rule, a criminal defendant may always offer evidence of a pertinent character trait such as honesty, truthfulness, or peacefulness. This evidence may come in the form of reputation, opinion, or specific incidents of conduct. The foundation for favorable character trait evidence is the same as is other reputation, opinion, or specific conduct situations. Once the accused has offered evidence of good character, the prosecution may offer the same

---

22 Rule 405(a), Federal Rules of Evidence.

23 *Id.*

sorts of evidence in rebuttal.[24] It is up to the defendant to initiate the admissibility of character evidence; the prosecution may not launch a pre-emptive attack.

In the same vein, a criminal defendant may offer evidence of a relevant character trait of the crime victim, which may then be rebutted in similar fashion by the prosecution.[25] Finally, even in the absence of initial evidence from the defense, the prosecution may use reputation, opinion, or specific conduct evidence of the "peaceful" character traits of a homicide victim in order to prove that the victim was not the "first aggressor."[26]

C. Foundations for Hearsay Statements

The rule against hearsay excludes evidence of out-of-court statements if offered to prove the truth of the matter asserted.[27] Numerous exceptions to the hearsay rule allow for the admissibility of out-of-court statements, provided that the necessary foundation is established. The foundations for those exceptions that apply primarily to testimonial evidence are discussed below. Foundations for hearsay exceptions that typically apply to documentary evidence are discussed in a later section.[28] The following sections are intended only as an outline of the foundations for the various hearsay exceptions, not as a complete treatment of the complexities or rationale for the hearsay rule itself.

1. Party Admissions

Out-of-court statements made by the opposing party are generally admissible to prove the truth of the matter asserted. Party admissions constituted a hearsay exception at common law, and are excluded from the definition of hearsay under the Federal Rules of Evidence.[29] Notwithstanding the approach of the Federal Rules,

---

24 Rule 404(a)(1), Federal Rules of Evidence.

25 Note that Rule 412, Federal Rules of Evidence, places severe restrictions on the admissibility of evidence concerning the past conduct or reputation of victims of rape or sexual assault. Specifically, "reputation or opinion evidence of the past sexual behavior of an alleged victim of such rape or assault is not admissible." *Id.* at Rule 412(a). A similar provision applies to direct evidence of the victim's past conduct. Virtually every state has adopted some version of this important and beneficial rule.

26 Rule 404(a)(2), Federal Rules of Evidence.

27 *See* Rule 801, Federal Rules of Evidence.

28 *See* Section V C, *infra* at p. 316.

29 Rule 801(d)(2), Federal Rules of Evidence.

most lawyers continue to find it convenient to refer to the "exception" for admissions by a party-opponent.

In brief, the previous statements of the opposing party are admissible if: (1) the witness can authenticate the statement, (2) the statement was made by the party against whom it is offered, and (3) the statement is adverse to the opposing party's claim or defense.[30] In the following example the witness is a police officer who investigated an automobile accident. The direct examination is being conducted by plaintiff's counsel:

QUESTION: Officer, did you speak to anyone after you arrived at the scene of the accident?

ANSWER: I spoke to both drivers, Mr. Weiss and Ms. Gable.

QUESTION: Was that the same Mr. Weiss who is the defendant in this case?

ANSWER: Yes.

QUESTION: Who was present when you spoke with Mr. Weiss?

ANSWER: Only the two of us.

QUESTION: When did that conversation take place?

ANSWER: At approximately 10:00 a.m. on March 17.

QUESTION: Where did it take place?

ANSWER: At the intersection of Ridge and Main.

QUESTION: Did Mr. Weiss say anything about the cause of the accident?

ANSWER: Yes. He said that he never saw the other automobile until just before the impact.

---

30 Party admissions may be received in written as well as testimonial form. The foundation for a written party admission— such as a letter, memorandum, or report—is the same as that for an oral one. Where the admission is contained in a document, however, all of the other general requisites for the admissibility of an exhibit must be present.

The defendant's out-of-court statement is admissible. The witness heard the statement and can identify it as having been made by the party against whom it is being offered. The content of the statement itself demonstrates its adverse nature. The party admission doctrine applies only to statements offered *against* the party-declarant. The plaintiff in the above example could not elicit her own favorable statements to the investigating police officer.[31]

The party admission exception also applies to statements made by the agent or employee of a party.[32] In these situations there are two additional elements to the foundation: (1) the declarant was an agent or employee of the opposing party at the time that the statement was made, and (2) the statement concerned a matter that was within the scope of the agency or employment. In the following example, assume that the plaintiff is the Quickset Printing Company, which has sued the defendant for nonpayment on a large duplicating order. The defendant is testifying on direct examination:

QUESTION: Did you speak to anyone at Quickset after you received the order?

ANSWER: Yes. I went back to the shop and I spoke to the manager.

QUESTION: How do you know that you were speaking to the manager?

ANSWER: I have been doing business with Quickset for years, and I have spoken to the manager many times.

QUESTION: What did you say to the manager?

ANSWER: I said that the order was defective and that I would not pay for it.

QUESTION: Did the manager respond?

ANSWER: Yes. She said that she didn't expect anyone to pay for defective work, and that she would speak to the owner of the company.

Agency and scope having been established, the manager's out-of-court statement is admissible. Note that the testimony also contained a reference to the defendant's own out-of-court statement concerning the defective nature of the

---

31 The plaintiff's statements to the officer might, however, be admissible on some other theory such as "excited utterance" or "state of mind." *See* Sections II B(3) and (4), *infra* at p. 274-5.

32 Rule 801(d)(2)(D), Federal Rules of Evidence.

order. While the defendant could not offer her own statement as a party admission, it is admissible to provide the context for the manager's response.

2. Present Sense Impression

The present sense impression exception allows the admission of out-of-court statements "describing or explaining an event or condition made while the declarant was perceiving the event or condition, or immediately thereafter."[33] The foundation for the exception, then, is that: (1) the declarant perceived an event; (2) the declarant described the event; and (3) the description was given while the event occurred or immediately afterwards. A witness may testify to her own previous statement of a present sense impression, as in this example taken from the fire engine case:

QUESTION: Where were you at about 8:30 a.m. last March 17?

ANSWER: I was at the corner of Sheridan and Touhy, walking west on Touhy.

QUESTION: Were you with anyone?

ANSWER: Yes, I was with my two children, who are four and six years old. My neighbor was also with us.

QUESTION: Was your attention drawn to a vehicle at that time?

ANSWER: I saw a fire engine headed west on Touhy Avenue.

QUESTION: Was the fire engine using its warning signals?

ANSWER: It was flashing its lights and sounding its siren.

QUESTION: Did you say anything about the fire engine to anyone?

ANSWER: Yes. I told my children to listen to the siren and to look for the fire truck. I think that my exact words were something like, "Listen kids, whenever you hear a siren like that it means that you have to look out for a fire engine."

QUESTION: When did you say that to your children?

ANSWER: Right as the fire truck was passing.

A witness also can often testify to a present sense impression statement made by another. It is generally necessary for the statement to have been made in the

---

33   Rule 803(1), Federal Rules of Evidence.

witness's presence, in order to satisfy the foundational requirement of personal knowledge.[34]

3. Excited Utterance

The excited utterance exception is quite similar to the present sense impression rule, allowing for the admission of hearsay when the statement relates "to a startling event or condition made while the declarant was under the stress of excitement caused by the event or condition."[35]

The foundation for an excited utterance is that (1) the declarant perceived a startling event or experienced a stressful condition; (2) the declarant made astatement concerning the event or condition; and (3) the statement was made while the declarant was under the stress of the event or condition.

As with present sense impressions, a witness may testify to her own excited utterance or to that of another.

4. State of Mind

"State of mind" provides one of the broadest exceptions to the hearsay rule, as it allows the admission of statements concerning the declarant's "then existing state of mind emotion, sensation, or physical condition (such as intent, plan, motive, design, mental feeling, pain, and bodily health)."[36]

---

34 It is possible, however, to "stack" hearsay exceptions so as to allow testimony concerning secondhand statements. Imagine, for instance, the following chain of events in the fire truck case: A passenger in the defendant's car heard the siren and described it to the defendant, saying,"listen, I think I hear a fire truck siren." The defendant later mentioned the passenger's remark to the investigating police officer. The officer would be allowed to testify as follows:

QUESTION: Did the defendant say anything to you about a siren?

ANSWER: Yes. The defendant said that his passenger told him something like, "Listen, I think I hear a fire truck siren."

The passenger's statement is a present sense impression, and the defendant's recounting of it is a party admission. Each out-of-court statement falls under an independent exception to the hearsay rule. Assuming that the proper foundations are laid, the police officer's testimony is therefore admissible. *See* Rule 805, Federal Rules of Evidence.

The further intricacies of the treatment of "hearsay within hearsay" are beyond the scope of this chapter and will not be discussed in any greater detail.

35 Rule 803(2), Federal Rules of Evidence.

36 Rule 803(3), Federal Rules of Evidence.

The foundation for this exception is that the statement actually be probative of the declarant's mental, emotional, or physical condition. This can best be demonstrated by the content of the statement itself. Apart from the content of the statement, there is no special foundation for the state of mind exception. However, the witness still must establish the authenticity of the statement by testifying as to (1) when the statement was made, (2) where it was made, (3) who was present, and (4) what was said. Note also that the statement must have been made during the existence of the mental, emotional, or physical condition that it describes.

5. Statement Made for Medical Treatment

The foundation for this exception is that the declarant made a statement for the purpose of obtaining medical care or diagnosis. The statement may be made to a physician, medical worker, or other person, so long as its purpose was to obtain or facilitate treatment. The statement may include medical history or past symptoms, but it must relate to a present bodily condition.[37]

6. Dying Declaration

The hearsay exception for dying declarations requires the following foundation: (1) The declarant made a statement while believing that his or her death was imminent, (2) concerning what he or she believed to be the cause of death.[38] At common law it was also required that the declarant actually had died, but under the Federal Rules it is sufficient that the declarant be unavailable as a witness.[39]

The declarant's belief that death was imminent can be established by surrounding circumstances, such as the nature of an illness or injury, or by the declarant's own words. The content of the statement will generally be sufficient to show that it related to the declarant's belief as to the cause of death.

Under the Federal Rules, dying declarations are admissible only in civil cases or homicide prosecutions. The exception is not available in criminal cases other than homicides.

III. EXHIBITS

A. The Role of Exhibits

Exhibits are the tangible objects, documents, photographs, video and audio tapes, and other items that are offered for the jury's consideration. Exhibits are the only form, apart from the testimony of witnesses, in which evidence can be

---

37   Rule 803(4), Federal Rules of Evidence.
38   Rule 804(b)(2), Federal Rules of Evidence.
39   Rule 804(b), Federal Rules of Evidence.

received. Spoken testimony typically presents the jury with a recitation of the witness's memories and perceptions. As effective as testimony might be, it remains a second-hand account that is, at best, once removed from the jury's own experiences. Exhibits, on the other hand, allow the jurors to utilize their own senses and perceptions. It is one thing to hear somebody describe, for example, the texture of a piece of cloth; it is quite another actually to run your hand over the material itself. Your direct experience will be infinitely more informative than listening to another person's description. Having touched the cloth you will remember it better, you will appreciate more of its nuances or details, and you will be far less likely to change your mind about it in the future.

Life is full of experiences that cannot truly be described, and exhibits bring reality into the courtroom in a way that spoken testimony will never approach. Imagine the melody of the last popular song that you heard on the radio. No matter how simple the tune, even the most gifted critic cannot recapture it in words. The use of an audiotape, however, can re-create the experience almost exactly. The same is true of visual exhibits. Think of a scene as commonplace as the street immediately outside the room in which you are sitting. It would take hours to describe everything that you could see there, and even then you would be unable to capture all of the colors, distances, spatial relationships, angles and other particulars. A photograph can depict these details, and numerous others, all at once.

At trial, exhibits enhance or supplement the testimony of the witnesses. Exhibits can make information clearer, more concrete, more understandable, and more reliable. The sections immediately following will discuss the general procedures for the introduction of exhibits.

B. Types of Exhibits

While the categories tend to overlap and the lines cannot be drawn with precision, it is often helpful to think of exhibits as falling into these three categories: (1) real evidence, (2) demonstrative evidence, and (3) documentary evidence.

1. Real Evidence

The term "real evidence" generally refers to tangible objects that played an actual role in the events at issue in the trial.

The proceeds or instrumentalities of the crime are often introduced in criminal cases. Typical examples might include the "marked money" recovered in a suspect's possession, the bullet casing found at the scene of the crime, an item of clothing that the defendant was wearing when arrested, or a quantity of narcotics seized by the police.

Real evidence is also used in all categories of civil cases. In personal injury cases it is common for plaintiff's counsel to introduce objects that allegedly caused or contributed to the injury. Such real evidence might include a frayed wire that led to a steering failure or a rusty canister that failed to contain a corrosive liquid. Similarly, defense counsel in a tort case would be expected to introduce the actual safety devices that were available to, but ignored by, the plaintiff. Real evidence in a commercial dispute might include samples of allegedly non-conforming goods.

Photographs, while obviously different from tangible objects, are so close to reality that they are also often treated as real evidence.

Documents such as contracts, memoranda, letters, and other primary writings can also be considered real evidence, although the special rules that apply to out-of-court writings generally make it more convenient to treat "documentary evidence" as a separate category.

2. Demonstrative Evidence

The term "demonstrative evidence" refers to exhibits that did not play an actual role in the events underlying the case, but that are used to illustrate or clarify a witness's testimony. Demonstrative evidence can take the form of models, graphs, diagrams, charts, drawings, or any other objects that can explain or illustrate issues in the case.

A familiar form of demonstrative evidence is the simple intersection diagram on which a witness can indicate the locations of the automobiles involved in an accident. The intersection itself, not the diagram, would constitute real evidence of the configuration of the streets. The diagram, however, may be used to demonstrate the relative positions of the cars, traffic signals, and witnesses. It is easy to see why demonstrative evidence can be superior to real evidence — the intersection cannot be transported into the courtroom. And even if the jury were to be taken to the scene of the accident, it would still be extremely difficult for the lawyers to push real automobiles around at the instruction of the witnesses.

Another common type of demonstrative evidence is the "comparison" object. In many cases it is not possible to produce the original objects involved — they may have been destroyed, lost, or concealed. It is therefore permissible to use a similar object for the purpose of illustration. Imagine an automobile accident in which a young child was injured. If the child's safety seat was destroyed in the crash, either party could use an identical seat to demonstrate, for example, how the child fit into it and how it was fastened.

More complex displays may range from an anatomical model to an elaborate "day in the life" videotape depicting the daily routine of a disabled accident victim. An anatomical model of a human shoulder can be used to show the effects of surgery on an individual's ability to move or work. "Day in the life" videotapes have been used with great impact to demonstrate the limitations and obstacles faced by accident victims, and the extraordinary effort and expense that is necessary to cope with severe injuries.

The distinguishing feature of demonstrative evidence is that it is lawyer-generated. Real evidence exists by virtue of the activities of the parties and witnesses in the case. Counsel can search for it, discover it, preserve it, and utilize it, but a lawyer can never create real evidence. Demonstrative evidence is not intrinsic to the case. It is never handed to counsel, but must be developed by the attorneys as an aspect of the presentation of the case.

The production of demonstrative evidence is a creative task. It allows counsel, in effect, to dream about ways of presenting a case, and then to fashion those dreams into a persuasive reality. The attorney must constantly ask, "How can I make this testimony more concrete?" Or, "How can I help the jury visualize this point?" Or, "Is there a way to accentuate the relationship between these two ideas?" The answer will often be found in the development of demonstrative exhibits.

3. Documentary Evidence

"Documentary evidence" is the term used to refer to virtually all writings, including letters, contracts, leases, memoranda, reports, and business records. Written documents, almost by definition, contain out-of-court statements, and they are typically offered because their contents are relevant to the case. Thus, most documents face hearsay hurdles in a way that real and demonstrative exhibits do not. Tangible objects are admitted into evidence because of what they *are*; documentary exhibits are admitted because of what they *say*.

The value of documentary evidence cannot be overstated. Intrinsic writings can provide proof of past events in a way that mere testimony cannot. Imagine a criminal case in which the defendant has raised an alibi defense, claiming that on the day of the crime he was visiting relatives in a distant city. The testimony of the defendant and his family is relevant and admissible to establish the alibi, but it will be subject to vigorous attack on cross examination. A signed hotel receipt for the date in question stands to be far more persuasive than any witness as to the defendant's whereabouts.

Documentary evidence has the power to *document* past events. Barring fraud or forgery, contemporaneous writings often provide the best proof possible. For that reason, counsel must always take pains to ensure that all potentially relevant documents are discovered. Thorough searches must be made not only of the client's files, but also of every conceivable third-party source. Many businesses, institutions, and even individuals keep copious records and notes. It is the lawyer's job to inquire into and investigate every conceivable source of favorable documentary evidence.

Perhaps more than any other form of evidence, however, documents have the potential to overwhelm the trier of fact. Only the most determined judge or juror will have the patience to wade through a foot-tall stack of reports in order to extract some evidentiary gem. Thus, while your search for documents should be exhaustive, your presentation of documents must be judicious. Truly important exhibits can be emphasized effectively only if trivial or repetitive ones are omitted. The final section of this chapter deals in greater depth with the persuasive use of documentary evidence and other exhibits.

C. Pretrial Procedures for the Admission of Exhibits

The foundations for various exhibits can be lengthy and cumbersome, even though the eventual admissibility of the exhibit is not really in doubt. At trial, foundation testimony can be boring and repetitive; worse, it can distract attention from the truly contested issues in the case. For this reason, the courts have developed a number of streamlined procedures that allow pretrial rulings on the admissibility of exhibits, including real, demonstrative, and documentary evidence.

1. Pretrial Conferences and Orders

Many jurisdictions now require pretrial conferences, especially in large or complex cases. Under the Federal Rules of Civil Procedure, for example, parties may be required to attend one or more pretrial conferences at which there may be "advance rulings from the court on the admissibility of evidence."[40]

Many federal judges have adopted a routine practice of requiring the parties to submit written pretrial orders identifying every exhibit that they anticipate offering at trial. Counsel must also indicate whether or not they object to each other's proposed exhibits, giving the basis for the objection. Where there is no objection, the exhibit will automatically be received. Rulings on contested exhibits may be made at a pretrial conference, or may be reserved until trial.

In jurisdictions utilizing extensive pretrial practice, every exhibit may be ruled upon in advance of the trial. Lawyers will therefore know exactly which exhibits have been admitted and which have been refused, thereby freeing counsel of the necessity of expending valuable trial time on unnecessary foundations.

2. Motions in Limine

Even in the absence of a formalized pretrial process, it is possible to secure advance decisions on the admissibility of exhibits through the use of the motion in limine.[41] Contrary to some popular opinion, the motion in limine is not merely the civil analog to the motion to suppress evidence in criminal cases. Although the motion in limine is most commonly used to obtain the exclusion of evidence, there

---

40 Rule 16(c)(4), Federal Rules of Civil Procedure.

41 *See* Chapter Seven, Section II(A)(2), *supra* at p. 217.

is no reason that it cannot also be used affirmatively to seek a ruling that certain evidence is admissible. "In limine" means "at the threshold," and there is nothing about the motion that restricts its use to excluding evidence.

The reason to object to evidence before trial is obvious. An order barring the use of an exhibit will prevent opposing counsel from referring to it during the opening statement or from displaying it to the jury while ostensibly laying a foundation.

It can be equally useful to obtain a pretrial ruling allowing an exhibit into evidence. Advance knowledge of the admissibility of an exhibit will allow counsel to prepare an opening statement that takes full advantage of the exhibit, but which does not risk a reprimand from the court or reversible error. By the same token, knowing that an exhibit has been admitted will permit the attorney to work it more easily into direct and cross examinations. It may even be worthwhile to lose an affirmative motion in limine, since the early exclusion of an exhibit will enable counsel to adapt her approach to the witnesses, or even to change her trial theory.

3. Stipulations

In situations where judicial involvement is unavailable, impractical, or unnecessary, pretrial admissibility of an exhibit may still be obtained by stipulation. A stipulation is an agreement between counsel as to some aspect of the case. Lawyers may stipulate, for example, to the filing of an amended pleading, or to the existence of a certain set of facts. While judges are technically free to reject stipulations, this is seldom done other than in the case of over-reaching or abuse.[42]

Stipulations to the admissibility of exhibits are almost uniformly honored by the courts, since they really amount to nothing more than a pretrial agreement not to object to certain evidence. Since the stipulating attorney would be equally free to refrain from objecting at trial, the end result of the stipulation is to save time for all concerned.

There is no formal procedure for obtaining a stipulation.[43] Any lawyer may request a stipulation from opposing counsel, who may either refuse or accede. This

---

42 It was once common practice for attorneys to cooperate with one another by stipulating to numerous continuances or extensions of time. Most courts now attempt to curtail this abusive practice.

43 Note that a judge may require proposed stipulations to be presented as part of a pretrial order or at a pretrial conference. Rule 14(c), Federal Rules of Civil Procedure. This does not, however, prevent the parties from arriving at stipulations on their own.

can be done by letter, telephone conversation, at a meeting, or in court. Informal stipulations, however, and especially oral ones, have a maddening way of dissolving or becoming ambiguous at trial. It is therefore desirable to reduce stipulations to writing, preferably in the form of a signed document. Even when oral stipulations between counsel have been stenographically recorded, either in court or at a deposition, it is wise to review a transcript before relying too heavily on the stipulation during trial preparation.

Finally, it is important for all parties that stipulations be as precise as possible. If the stipulation is to the admissibility of an exhibit, the object or writing must be specifically identified, and the stipulation should also include any understood limitations on the exhibit's use.

4. Requests to Admit

Modern discovery practice allows counsel to obviate the need to lay many foundations at trial. Under the Federal Rules of Civil Procedure,[44] and comparable provisions in most states, any party may serve "Requests for Admission" on any other party. The opposing party must then either admit or deny the request, and may suffer sanctions for making false denials.

The federal rules specifically provide for a request to admit "the genuineness of documents."[45] Once opposing counsel has admitted the genuineness of a document, no objection on that ground can be made to its admissibility at trial.

Additionally, counsel may serve requests to admit the "truth" of virtually any fact relevant to the case. Such facts definitely include all of the elements of the foundations for exhibits. A carefully drafted request to admit can result in the admissibility of even an otherwise contested exhibit.

Opposing counsel is free to deny any of the facts presented in a request for admission. Significant sanctions, however, may attend false or dilatory denials, or other evasive replies.[46] Moreover, failure to respond to such a request is, under the federal rules, treated as an admission.

D.   Offering Exhibits at Trial

Whether they consist of real, demonstrative, or documentary evidence, there is one basic protocol for offering exhibits at trial. Although the details vary

---

44   Rule 36(a), Federal Rules of Civil Procedure.

45   *Id.*

46   Rule 37(c), Federal Rules of Civil Procedure.

somewhat from jurisdiction to jurisdiction, the following steps form a nearly universal procedure.[47]

1. Mark the Exhibit for Identification

Every exhibit should be marked for identification *before* it is offered into evidence, or even referred to in the course of a trial. Marking the exhibit identifies it for the record so that it will be uniquely recognizable to anyone who later reads a transcript of the proceedings. References to "this letter" or "the first broken fastener" may be understood in the courtroom, but they will be meaningless to an appellate court. "Defendant's exhibit three," on the other hand, can mean only one thing, assuming that the exhibit was appropriately marked and identified.

Exhibits are generally marked sequentially, and further identified according to the designation of the party who has first offered them. Thus, the exhibits in a two-party trial will be called plaintiff's exhibit one, plaintiff's exhibit two, defendant's exhibit one, defendant's exhibit two, and so forth. In multiple-party trials it is necessary to identify an exhibit by the name, and not merely the designation, of the party who offers it. Accordingly, you will see references to plaintiff Bennett exhibit one, or Weber exhibit two. In some jurisdictions plaintiffs are expected to use sequential numbers for their exhibits, while defendants are requested to use letters. Hence, plaintiff's exhibit one and defendant's exhibit A. The details of the particular marking system are unimportant, so long as it produces a clear and understandable indication of which exhibit is which.

The "mark" itself usually takes the form of a sticker placed directly on the object or document. Stickers are available in a variety of forms. Many attorneys use color-coded sets that already contain the words plaintiff or defendant, with a space left blank for the number assigned to each exhibit.

It was once the prevailing practice to have the court reporter or clerk mark each exhibit in open court. Often counsel was required to ask the judge's permission to have an exhibit marked. This time-consuming procedure has been widely replaced by the premarking of exhibits, either at a pretrial conference or in the attorney's office.

The term "marked for identification" means that the exhibit has been marked, and can be referred to in court, but has not yet been admitted into evidence.

---

47 Subsequent sections of this chapter will discuss the foundations for various sorts of exhibits. Most sections will include examples of these foundations. For the sake of brevity, these examples will be limited to the evidentiary foundations and will not include the technical protocol for offering the exhibits. Readers should assume that in each example the sponsoring attorney would go on to follow the general procedure for offering exhibits as is outlined below.

Exhibits that have been marked for identification may be shown to witnesses and may be the subject of limited examinations for the purpose of establishing a foundation, but they usually may not be shown to the jury.

The distinction between exhibits that have and have not been admitted is crucial. Many jurisdictions, however, have abolished the "for identification" notation as redundant. All exhibits need to be marked, and the record will show which have been allowed into evidence even in the absence of a special inscription.[48]

2. Identify the Exhibit for Opposing Counsel

Exhibits should be identified for opposing counsel before they are shown to the witness. This may be done by referring to the exhibit number or by indicating its designation in the pretrial order if one has been prepared. In some jurisdictions you may be expected actually to hand or display the exhibit to opposing counsel before proceeding.

In any event, these common courtesies allow opposing counsel to confirm that the exhibit is the same one that was produced during discovery or that was discussed and marked at the pretrial conference. Opposing counsel is also afforded an opportunity to make an early objection to the use of the exhibit.

3. Examine the Witness on the Foundation for the Exhibit

Having identified the exhibit, you may now proceed to lay the foundation for its admission.

a. Show the Exhibit to the Witness

The first step is to show the exhibit to the witness. This is typically done by handing it to the witness.[49] If the exhibit is something as large as a life-sized model or an enlarged photograph, you may point to it and direct the witness's attention. In either case you should announce for the record what you are doing, using a shorthand description of the exhibit, as well as its identification number:

COUNSEL: Ms. Bowman, I am handing you defendant's exhibit eleven, which is a letter dated July 26.

---

48 Moreover, the presence or absence of the "for identification" notation can be misleading. The judge's decision on admissibility is determinative, as shown by the trial record. Examining an exhibit to see if the clerk has stricken the words "for identification" can lead to disastrous results if the clerk misunderstood or failed to hear the court's ruling.

49 In some jurisdictions it is necessary to obtain the court's permission before you approach the witness. In other courtrooms you may simply walk up to the witness, so long as you do it politely.

The description ensures clarity. The term "defendant's exhibit eleven" will mean nothing to the jury and even less to someone reading the transcript. Many lawyers prefer to have the witness give the initial description of the exhibit, but this approach unnecessarily cedes control of the examination. The witness, especially on cross examination, might give a misleading or inadmissible description. In any event, the witness will have plenty of opportunity to describe the exhibit during the identification phase of the testimony.

Your initial description of the exhibit must be scrupulously neutral. While you are allowed to ask a leading question on preliminary matters, you are not allowed to begin arguing your case under the pretext of laying a foundation. Thus, you cannot say:

COUNSEL: Ms. Bowman, I am handing you defendant's exhibit eleven, which is the letter in which the plaintiff agreed to provide repair service at no additional cost.

The date of the letter, and perhaps the name of its author, would be sufficient. If the very description of the exhibit is in issue, you may briefly describe what it "purports" to be.

b. Identify the Exhibit

The next step is to have the witness identify the exhibit. The witness should state the basis for her familiarity with the exhibit, and then describe it in some detail:

QUESTION: Have you ever seen plaintiff's exhibit seven before?

ANSWER: Yes, I have seen it many times.

QUESTION: What is plaintiff's exhibit seven?

ANSWER: It is a piece of the stationery that I received when my order was delivered from Quickset Printing.

QUESTION: How is it that you recognize it?

ANSWER: I remember how it looked when I took it out of the box.

Numerous variations are possible once the witness has examined the exhibit: Are you familiar with the exhibit? Do you recognize the exhibit? Are you able to identify the exhibit? While it is technically necessary to establish initially that the witness has a basis for giving a description, it is often possible to elicit the description first: "What is it? How do you know?"

c. Complete the Foundation for the Exhibit

In some situations, particularly those involving real evidence, the identification of the exhibit will provide a sufficient foundation for admission. In other circumstances the foundation will be much more elaborate, perhaps calling for chain of custody or the establishment of a hearsay exception. These and other foundations for the introduction of real, demonstrative, and documentary evidence are discussed at length in subsequent sections of this chapter.

4. Offer the Exhibit into Evidence

Once the foundation has been completed, the exhibit can be offered into evidence. Jurisdictions vary as to the formality with which this must be done. In the simplest version:

COUNSEL: Your Honor, we offer plaintiff's exhibit three.

Some courts, however, expect a more highly mannered presentation:

COUNSEL: Your Honor, we move that the identifying mark be stricken and that plaintiff's exhibit three be received as plaintiff's exhibit three in evidence.

In any case, the exhibit must be shown to the judge, who will then ask opposing counsel if there are any objections to its admission. [50] At this point it is sufficient to recall that objecting counsel is entitled to request a limited cross examination of the witness (voir dire), which will be restricted to the subject of the admissibility of the exhibit.

5. Publish and Use the Exhibit

Once an exhibit has been received it can be "published" to the jury and also used as a basis for further testimony.

a. Publication

The term "publication" refers to the communication of the exhibit to the jury. Exhibits may be published in a variety of ways. Large objects and oversize graphics are usually turned toward the jury. Smaller objects typically are handed to the jurors and passed among them. Documents can be enlarged and displayed, passed among the jurors, or read aloud. The choice of publication method is customarily left to

---

50 The process for arguing objections is discussed in Chapter Seven.

counsel, although the court may deny leave to use overly dramatic, prejudicial, or dangerous means.[51]

While the right of publication follows inherently from the admission of the document, the court still exercises discretion over the timing and manner of publication. Consequently, it is necessary to obtain the judge's permission to communicate an exhibit to the jury:

COUNSEL: Your Honor, may I show defendant's exhibit six to the jury?

Or,

COUNSEL: May I have leave to publish plaintiff's exhibit three by passing it among the jurors?

Or,

COUNSEL: Your Honor, may the witness read prosecution exhibit nine to the jury?

There is no requirement that the entire exhibit be published. In the case of a lengthy document or voluminous record, it is appropriate to ask a witness to read only the portions that you deem most important. The entire exhibit, however, must be made available to the jury for inspection, as well as to opposing counsel for use on cross examination.

b. Using the Exhibit

Once an exhibit has been admitted into evidence, it can be used to illustrate or amplify a witness's testimony. In addition to publishing it to the jury, a witness can give further testimony that interprets or otherwise explains the significance of the exhibit.

Tangible objects can be used in demonstrations. A witness can show how a gun was aimed or how a tool was used. Maps, diagrams, and photographs can be used to illustrate the movement of persons and vehicles, the locations of incidents, or the relationship and distances between stationary objects. It is permissible to have witnesses mark directly on the exhibit, or to use velcro "stick-ons" to elaborate on her testimony. These techniques will be discussed further in the section below on demonstrative evidence.

Additionally, once an exhibit is in evidence, a witness can testify about its contents:

---

51 Section VI, *infra* at p. 324, discusses the persuasive use of exhibits, including effective methods of publication to the jury.

QUESTION: Do the words in defendant's exhibit nine have a particular meaning in your profession?

QUESTION: Why was the color of the stationery, plaintiff's exhibit one, so important to you?

QUESTION: What did you do once you received plaintiff's exhibit twelve?

QUESTION: What was your reaction when you saw Mr. Marshall holding defendant's exhibit four?

The right to testify about an exhibit is constrained by the applicable rules of evidence. Contrary to a frequently heard objection, however, an exhibit is not required to "speak for itself."

Finally, be aware that once an exhibit has been admitted it may be used, subject to the rules of evidence, in the examination of any witness, not only the witness who introduced it.

IV. FOUNDATIONS FOR REAL AND DEMONSTRATIVE EVIDENCE

A. Real Evidence/Tangible Objects

Real evidence must be shown to be relevant and authentic. Did the object actually play a role in the facts of the case? Does it tend to prove (or disprove) some issue in contention? Is the object in court *really* the one that we are talking about? If these conditions are met, the evidence will usually be admitted.[52]

The relevance of real evidence is typically established by the context of the case, and often requires no additional attention when it comes to laying the foundation. Authenticity, on the other hand, must always be carefully established, as it is the fact of authenticity that qualifies the exhibit as *real* evidence.

In many cases the authenticity of real evidence can be shown by a witness's recognition of the exhibit. Other cases require a more detailed and complex foundation, usually referred to as chain of custody.

---

52 Rule 403, Federal Rules of Evidence provides an exception: "Although relevant, evidence may be excluded if its probative value is substantially outweighed by the danger of unfair prejudice, confusion of the issues, or misleading the jury, or by considerations of undue delay, waste of time, or needless presentation of cumulative evidence."

This provision is often applied to real evidence.

1. Recognition of the Exhibit

The authenticity of real evidence can be established through the testimony of a witness who is able to recognize the item in question. Many objects can be identified by virtue of their unique features. Others may have been given some identifying mark in anticipation of litigation. In either case, the witness must testify (1) that she was familiar with the object at the time of the underlying events, and (2) that she is able to recognize the exhibit in court as that very same object.

In the following example, the plaintiff in a property damage case will be asked to lay the foundation for an item of personal property:

QUESTION: Do you recognize plaintiff's exhibit one?

ANSWER: Yes, it is an oil painting that was left to me by my grand-mother.

QUESTION: How is it that you can recognize it?

ANSWER: Until the fire, it hung over our mantle and I used to look at it almost every day.

QUESTION: Was it in your house at the time of the fire?

ANSWER: Yes it was. It was one of the first things that I tried to salvage after we were allowed back into the house.

QUESTION: Is plaintiff's exhibit one the same oil painting that you re-moved from your house after the fire?

ANSWER: Yes.

QUESTION: Is plaintiff's exhibit one in the same condition as it was when you removed it from your house after the fire?

ANSWER: Yes, it is.

While an oil painting is likely to be unique and easily recognizable, other exhibits are more fungible. Police officers, and others who are familiar with litigation, often solve this problem by placing identifying marks on tangible objects. In the following example, a police officer will lay the foundation for a child's safety seat that was found at the scene of an automobile accident:

QUESTION: Officer, did you recover any personal property at the scene of the accident?

ANSWER: Yes, I removed a child's safety seat from the back seat of the plaintiff's automobile.

QUESTION: What did you do with the car seat after you removed it?

ANSWER: I wrote my initials on the back of the seat, along with the date of the accident.

QUESTION: Showing you defendant's exhibit six, is this the same child's safety seat that you removed from the back of the plaintiff's automobile on the date of the accident?

ANSWER: Yes, it is.

QUESTION: How do you know?

ANSWER: Because it has my initials and the date written on the back, in my own handwriting.

QUESTION: Is defendant's exhibit six in the same condition as it was when you retrieved it from the plaintiff's automobile?

ANSWER: Yes, it is.

The above foundation is sufficient for the admission of the car seat, so long as the exhibit is only being offered only to prove the presence of the child seat in the plaintiff's automobile. The question on condition is technically superfluous, unless the condition of the car seat is in issue. Nonetheless, judges are accustomed to hearing the "same condition" question, so it is usually a good idea to include in the foundation for any tangible object.

An exhibit may still be admissible even if its physical condition has changed between the incident and the time of the trial. Under those circumstances, the foundation must include an explanation of any changes:

QUESTION: Have there been any changes to the car seat since the time that you retrieved it from the plaintiff's automobile?

ANSWER: Yes. It is now much dirtier, and some of the plastic has been chipped or scratched.

QUESTION: Other than those changes, is defendant's exhibit six in the same condition as it was when you removed if from the plaintiff's car?

ANSWER: Yes.

In both the oil painting and the car seat examples, it was unnecessary for the witness to account for the whereabouts of the exhibit between the incident and the trial. This is because the witnesses were able to supply all of the information necessary to authenticate the exhibits. In other circumstances, however, a foundation will need to include a chain of custody.

2. Chain of Custody

A chain of custody establishes the location, handling, and care of an object between the time of its recovery and the time of trial. A chain of custody must be shown whenever (1) the exhibit is not uniquely recognizable and has not been marked, or (2) when the exhibit's physical properties are in issue.

a. The Need for a Chain of Custody

Many objects are not inherently identifiable. A case might involve a defective piece of industrial machinery, a damaged automobile part, a contaminated food product, or a mis-applied hospital dressing. In none of these situations is a witness likely to recognize the relevant object with any certainty. While it is possible that some of these items might have been marked for later use in litigation, most people (other than police officers and trial lawyers) do not go around scratching their initials on objects to ensure their admissibility. Furthermore, some exhibits cannot be marked at all. Vegetation samples, tissue samples, liquids, and narcotics all have physical properties that defy marking.

A chain of custody is also necessary whenever the exhibit has been subjected to testing or analysis, or when other aspects of its condition or composition are at issue in the case. An object that has been tested is likely to have passed through many hands on its way to the courtroom. Because the test results can be invalidated by mishandling, tampering, or alteration of the exhibit, it is necessary to account for its possession and care at least between the time that it was recovered and the time that it was analyzed. The same holds true for an item that is used to display some physical property in the courtroom; a chain must be established to show possession of the exhibit from the time of the underlying incident until its production in court.

b. Establishing a Chain of Custody

A chain of custody must, at a minimum, be sufficient to show that the object in the courtroom is the same one that was involved in the events being considered at trial. This can usually be accomplished by tracing the possession of the item as it passed from hand to hand. In some situations it is also necessary to show that the object was stored during the intervening period in a manner that was secure from tampering or inadvertent change. In either case, it may be necessary to call more than one witness in order to complete the chain.

In the following example, an automobile mechanic was injured when a tire exploded as it was being mounted. The tire manufacturer has been sued, and the defective tire will be offered solely to show that it was manufactured by the defendant. The first witness is the garage manager:

QUESTION: Where were you when the plaintiff was injured?

ANSWER: I was standing about 30 feet away when I heard the noise of a loud explosion.

QUESTION: What did you do?

ANSWER: I ran over to where the plaintiff was lying on the ground. He was covered with blood, and there was a ragged tire lying right next to him.

QUESTION: Were there any other tires nearby?

ANSWER: No, that was the only one.

QUESTION: Did you do anything with the tire?

ANSWER: Yes. I picked it up and put it in my office.

QUESTION: Were there any other tires in your office at the time?

ANSWER: No.

QUESTION: Did you ever do anything else with the tire that you found next to the plaintiff?

ANSWER: Yes. About a week later a company superintendent came to investigate the injury. He asked to take the tire, and I gave it to him.

QUESTION: Had the tire been in your office the entire time between the injury to the plaintiff and the time that you gave it to the company superintendent?

ANSWER: Yes.

QUESTION: Were there any other tires in your office during that time?

ANSWER: No.

The garage manager has completed the first part of the chain. Note that the tire has not yet been produced in court. The next witness is the company superintendent:

QUESTION: Did you obtain a tire in the course of your investigation of this injury?

ANSWER: Yes. I went to speak to the garage manager about two weeks after the incident, and he gave me a tire that he had kept in his office.

QUESTION: What did you do with that tire?

ANSWER: I brought it back to company headquarters and placed it in my office.

QUESTION: From that day until today, were there any other tires in your office?

ANSWER: No.

QUESTION: Did the tire that you got from the garage manager ever leave your office?

ANSWER: Yes, I brought it with me to court today.

QUESTION: Showing you plaintiff's exhibit one, is this the tire that you obtained from the garage manager and that you brought with you to court today?

ANSWER: Yes, it is.

The chain of custody is now sufficient to establish the identity of the tire. Even though the company superintendent did not witness the accident or initially recover the tire, there is enough evidence to show the continuity of possession. Since in this example the tire is being offered only to prove who manufactured it, physical properties are not in issue. It is therefore unnecessary to show that the tire was kept under lock and key during the intervening period. While it is remotely conceivable that someone could have sneaked into either office and affixed a fraudulent logo to the tire, it is usually unnecessary for a chain of custody to exclude all such unlikely possibilities.[53]

If the tire had been given to an engineering consultant for stress analysis, a more elaborate foundation would be required. It would be necessary to show that measures were taken to safeguard the condition of the tire from the time it was recovered at least until it reached the laboratory for testing. With most exhibits this is accomplished by placing the item in a sealed container, usually marked with a date and a person's initials or some other distinctive notation. If the exhibit is removed for testing, the container is typically resealed and re-marked once the test has been completed. Organizations that frequently collect evidence, such as police departments and hospitals, generally have developed routine chain-of-custody procedures for isolating and preserving potential exhibits.

---

53   If there were evidence of such tampering, however, a more elaborate chain would be required.

B. Photography and Other Recording Devices

Photographs and other recordings bridge the gap between real and demonstrative evidence. While a visual or audio recording of any sort is, strictly speaking, an illustration of a past event, its capacity to portray a scene with accuracy is so great that many courts treat photographs and other recordings as tantamount to real evidence.

1. Still Photographs

The basic foundation for the admission of a still photograph is that it "fairly and accurately" portrays the scene shown. In all but a few situations it is not necessary to call the photographer to the stand. It is generally possible to introduce a photograph through the testimony of any witness who is familiar with the scene as it appeared at a relevant time. In the following example the witness is the owner of a home that was destroyed by fire. A photograph of the house will be offered as evidence of damages.

QUESTION: Were you the owner of the house located at 208 Oak Street?

ANSWER: Yes.

QUESTION: How long did you live there?

ANSWER: About eight years, until the fire.

QUESTION: So, of course, you are familiar with the appearance of your home before the fire.

ANSWER: Yes, certainly.

QUESTION: Does plaintiff's exhibit eleven fairly and accurately show your home at 208 Oak Street, as it appeared on the day before the fire?

ANSWER: Yes, it does.

Because the witness is familiar with the appearance of the house, it is not necessary to call the photographer or to inquire into the circumstances in which the photo was taken. Nor is it necessary to show that the photo was taken on the day before the fire, so long as the picture "fairly and accurately" depicts the house as it appeared on the relevant day.

If there had been any alterations in the appearance of the house, the photo could still be admitted once the changes had been explained. The admissibility of the photo will depend upon the significance of the changes.

QUESTION: Were there any changes in the appearance of your house between the time of exhibit eleven and the time of the fire?

ANSWER: Yes. The house had been painted, so the color was blue instead of white.

Because the value of the destroyed property will not be affected by the color of the paint, this foundation is sufficient. It is certainly possible, however, for the admission of a photograph to be refused because of discrepancies between the scene at the time it was taken as opposed to the scene at the time of the relevant events.

In some circumstances it may be necessary to call the photographer to the stand, as in cases where the photograph was taken using special or unusual techniques. Additionally, while most photographs are offered to show how some-thing *looked* at a particular time, some photographs are offered to prove that something *occurred* at a certain time. It is usually necessary to produce the testimony of the photographer if the date or occasion of the occurrence in the photograph are in issue.

One last word about magic words. It has become a virtual reflex for lawyers to introduce photographs by asking whether they "fairly and accurately" depict the scene portrayed. Many judges have come to believe that the phrase "fairly and accurately depict" is a required part of the foundation for a photograph. It is not. Any language should be acceptable, so long as it authenticates the photograph as a reliable representation of a relevant scene. Nonetheless, it may be advisable to use the magic words. Judges often expect them and opposing counsel will be less likely to object.

2. Motion Pictures and Videotapes

As with photographs, a motion picture or videotape may be authenticated by any witness who is familiar with the scene or scenes portrayed. It is necessary to call the operator of the camera only if special features were employed, or if the date of the filming is in issue.

A more difficult problem arises in the case of remote taping, when no person actually observed the events as they were recorded. In these circumstances the foundation must include additional information on operating procedures as well as the condition of the equipment.

3. Audiotapes

The foundation for an audiotape recording depends upon the purpose for which it is offered. A tape recording that is submitted merely as a voice exemplar, for example, may be authenticated by any witness who is able to recognize the voices of the various speakers. The same holds true for recorded music, as might be offered in a copyright dispute. The foundation can be laid by any witness who is familiar with the material recorded.

Audiotapes are perhaps most commonly offered to prove the content of a conversation. Such tapes have often been made surreptitiously, as in the case of police wiretaps. As might be expected, the foundation for these tapes may be quite involved. The simplest case is presented when the tape was made by a participant to the conversation,[54] or where the conversation was overheard by a person who may be called as a witness:

QUESTION: Did you have a conversation with Richard Martine on September 21?

ANSWER: Yes, I did.

QUESTION: Was that conversation recorded?

ANSWER: Yes. I recorded it myself.

QUESTION: Is prosecution exhibit eight the recording that you made of that conversation?

ANSWER: Yes.

QUESTION: How do you know?

ANSWER: Because I have listened to it several times.

QUESTION: Does prosecution exhibit eight contain an accurate recording of the conversation that you had with Richard Martine on September 21?

ANSWER: Yes, it does.

While this foundation is generally adequate,[55] many lawyers prefer to elicit more extensive testimony concerning the reliability of the equipment used in the recording and the safekeeping (chain of custody) of the tape between the time of the recording and the time of trial. Such a foundation may be necessary if the

---

54 Please note that state laws vary regarding warrantless audiotape recordings. In many states it is a criminal offense to tape record a conversation without the consent of every person involved. Other states allow tape recording so long as at least one participant in the conversation consents. Every jurisdiction, of course, allows law enforcement personnel to make surreptitious tape recordings upon obtaining a warrant. The admissibility of a tape recording is obviously affected by its legality.

55 Note that the authentication of a tape recording does not obviate the need for the recorded conversation to be brought within an exception to the hearsay rule.

authenticity of the tape is in issue, or if no witness is available to testify to the content of the conversation as it occurred.

4. X Rays and Similar Images

X rays, and other images produced by means such as computerized axial tomography (CAT scans) and magnetic resonance imaging (MRIs), are essentially photographs of the body's internal composition. While it is a scientifically reliable fact that x rays generally produce a "fair and accurate" representation of the bone structure, there is no person who can provide eyewitness testimony comparing an x ray and a live patient's actual skeleton. Fortunately, courts have long been willing to take judicial notice of the validity of x rays, and the same now holds true for CAT scans and MRI films.

Consequently, the foundation for the admission of x rays and similar technologies has been streamlined since the time when it was considered necessary to prove both the scientific basis for the process, the competency of the technician, and the good working condition of the particular machine.

It is now generally considered sufficient for a physician or other qualified person to testify that an x ray, CAT scan, or MRI is a fair representation of the internal structure of a given patient's body. The identifying marks on the film (which allow the physician to recognize which x ray belongs to which patient) are usually considered to be business records of the hospital or clinic.[56]

C. Demonstrative Evidence

Demonstrative evidence is used to illustrate, clarify, or explain other testimony or real evidence. When such an exhibit is sufficiently accurate or probative, it may be admitted into evidence and even given to the jury when they retire to deliberate. A closely related type of exhibit is the "illustrative aid," which may be used to assist a witness in explaining testimony, but cannot be given to the jury as evidence.

The line between "evidence" and "aid" cannot be clearly drawn, but it is possible to imagine a continuum based on accuracy. Scale exhibits, such as models, maps, and diagrams, are extremely accurate and are usually considered demonstrative evidence; rough free-hand drawings may be useful devices, but their lack of precision makes them more likely to be limited to use as visual aids.

---

56 Regarding the foundation for the business records exception to the hearsay rule, see Section V C(1), *infra* at p. 316.

1. Admissible Demonstrative Evidence

a. Maps, Charts, and Diagrams

The foundation for a map, chart, blueprint, or other diagram is essentially the same as that for a photograph. The witness must be familiar with the scene, location, or structure as it appeared at a relevant time, and must testify that the exhibit constitutes a fair representation.

Additional foundation is necessary if the exhibit is drawn to scale. If the witness prepared the exhibit herself, she may testify to the manner in which she prepared it and the steps that she took to insure its accuracy. Following this approach it may be necessary to call two witnesses: one who prepared the exhibit and another who can testify regarding the facts or events in issue. Note that in many cases witness testimony will not be necessary to establish scale, since the notation on official maps, plats, and surveys may be self-authenticating,[57] and the court may take judicial notice of the accuracy of commercially produced maps and charts.[58]

b. Models and Reproductions

The foundation for a model or reproduction is similar to that for a photograph. The witness must be familiar with the real location or object, and must testify to the model's accuracy. Issues regarding scale are identical to those concerning maps and diagrams.

Litigation often calls for the use of generic, as opposed to specific, models. A medical expert in a personal injury case might want to use an anatomical model to illustrate her testimony. A scale representation of a human shoulder joint will not be an exact model of the plaintiff's own shoulder joint. Nonetheless, it should be possible sufficiently to authenticate such a model. To do so, the witness must testify that the model will be useful in explaining her testimony:

QUESTION: Doctor, what is plaintiff's exhibit twelve?

ANSWER: It is a scale model of a human shoulder joint.

QUESTION: Would the use of plaintiff's exhibit twelve assist you in explaining the injury to the plaintiff's shoulder?

ANSWER: Yes. All human shoulder joints are basically the same.

---

57   *See* Rule 902(5), Federal Rules of Evidence.
58   *See* Rule 201(b), Federal Rules of Evidence.

A final type of model is the "similar" object. If the actual object is unavailable, a similar object may be used to illustrate a witness's testimony. A defective product, for example, might be destroyed in the same accident that causes an injury. A defect could be "modeled," however, by using an identical product produced by the same company.

2. Illustrative Aids

Exhibits that are insufficiently accurate to be allowed into evidence may often still be used for illustrative purposes. The foundation includes a witness's testimony that the exhibit will assist in explaining her testimony, as well as a general explanation or description of the inaccuracy. In the following example the witness has produced a free-hand drawing of an intersection:

QUESTION: What is defendant's exhibit five?

ANSWER: It is a drawing of the intersection of Forest and Main.

QUESTION: Did you make that drawing yourself?

ANSWER: Yes, I did.

QUESTION: Does defendant's exhibit five generally show the configuration of the streets at Forest and Main as they appeared on the date of the accident?

ANSWER: Yes, it shows the location of the streets and the locations of the traffic signs.

QUESTION: Is defendant's exhibit five drawn to scale?

ANSWER: It is the best I could do, but it is not drawn to scale.

QUESTION: Would defendant's exhibit five still help you to explain your testimony about the accident?

ANSWER: Yes, it would.

The above foundation is sufficient to allow the witness to use the diagram in the course of her testimony. The eventual admissibility of the diagram, however, will depend upon the court's assessment of its accuracy. Free-hand drawings are often inadmissible because they tend to distort distances, spatial relationships, angles, sight lines, and similar information. For that reason, as well as the notorious unreliability of witness-produced drawings, it is generally preferable to use commercially prepared diagrams.

V. FOUNDATIONS FOR DOCUMENTS

In addition to the usual issues of relevance and authenticity, the foundation for a document usually includes two other elements. Because documents invariably contain out-of-court statements, they must be brought within an exception or exclusion to the hearsay rule. Additionally, the proffer must comply with the "best evidence" or "original writing" rule.

A. Authentication

The authentication of documents typically requires proof of authorship or origin, and may also call for proof of transmission or receipt. The existence of a lease, for example, may not be probative unless it can be shown to bear the signatures of the contending parties. Similarly, the existence of a product recall letter is meaningless unless it was transmitted to the affected consumers. Thus, unlike tangible objects, the foundation for documentary evidence may include more than simple recognition.

On the other hand, it is unusual for the physical condition or safe keeping of a document to be in issue. Chain of custody, therefore, is seldom a component of the foundation for documentary evidence, although it may be required if the paper has been subjected to testing or if the writing appears to have been altered or amended.

1. Handwriting and Signature

The signature or other handwriting on a document can be authenticated through a variety of means. A witness may recognize a signature based on past observation or may authenticate it on the basis of circumstantial evidence. Other possibilities include expert testimony and in-court comparison by the trier of fact.

A witness may always authenticate her own handwriting or signature. A witness may also authenticate the handwriting of another if sufficient familiarity can be shown:

QUESTION: Please examine defendant's exhibit two and tell me if you recognize the signature at the bottom of the page.

ANSWER: Yes, I do recognize the signature.

QUESTION: Whose signature is it?

ANSWER: It is Ruth Arroyo's.

QUESTION: How are you able to recognize it?

ANSWER: I have seen Ruth sign her name many times, and I recognize the handwriting as hers.

It is not necessary, however, for the witness actually to have seen the person sign her name. Circumstantial evidence can also support the required degree of familiarity:

QUESTION: How is it that you are able to recognize Ruth Arroyo's signature?

ANSWER: We have corresponded over the years, and it is the same signature that I have seen on her letters.

QUESTION: How do you know that those letters came from Ms. Arroyo?

ANSWER: Because she would usually answer questions that I had written to her in my letters.

Note that extended correspondence is not a requisite. A non-expert witness can identify a signature on the basis of a single past event or sample, so long as familiarity was not acquired for the purpose of litigation.[59]

An expert witness can authenticate a signature on the basis of comparison to a single identified specimen,[60] and the trier of fact, either court or jury, can make its own comparison on the basis of an authenticated exemplar.[61] In the case of comparison to be made by an expert or the trier of fact, the known specimen must still be authenticated. This can be accomplished through the testimony of a witness, as above, by stipulation, or by having the alleged signator write out an exemplar in open court.

2. Circumstantial Evidence of Authorship or Origin

Many documents are printed or typewritten, and do not contain signatures or other handwriting. Unless such a document is somehow uniquely marked, it will need to be authenticated via circumstantial evidence. Such evidence can be in the form of a letterhead, seal, or stamp, or it can be provided by the context of the case:

QUESTION: Do you recognize defendant's exhibit six?

ANSWER: Yes, it is a price list that I received from Quickset Printing.

---

59 Rule 901(b)(2), Federal Rules of Evidence.

60 Regarding the qualification of an expert witness, see Chapter Six.

61 Rule 901(b)(3), Federal Rules of Evidence.

QUESTION: How do you know that defendant's exhibit six came from Quickset Printing?

ANSWER: Well, it is on stationery that says Quickset Printing at the top of the page.

QUESTION: Is there any other reason that you know that defendant's exhibit six came from Quickset Printing?

ANSWER: Yes. I called the telephone number listed for Quickset in the directory and I asked the person who answered the phone to send me a price list. This price list arrived in the mail two days later.

The above foundation is more than sufficient to authenticate the document. Note that, notwithstanding the admission of the document, the opposing party remains free to controvert its origin or authorship. Authentication is a threshold question, and it is not dispositive of the ultimate issue.

3. Mailing or Transmission

The admissibility of a document will often depend upon its receipt by, or at least transmission to, another party. This is an authenticity issue, since the document is made admissible only by its status as one that was actually or constructively *received*. In other words, proof of mailing authenticates the document as truly having been sent to the other party.

Mailing can be proven either directly or through evidence of a routine business practice.[62] Direct proof of mailing can be given in a single sentence: "I placed the document in an envelope, with the correct address, and I deposited it in the United States mail with sufficient postage." The following is an example[63] of the "business practice" approach to proof of mailing:

QUESTION: Does your organization have a routine practice for the handling of outgoing mail?

---

62 *See* Section II B(4), *supra* at p. 275, for a discussion of the foundation for habit and routine practice evidence.

63 In a real trial the witness would probably be permitted to explain the entire mailing procedure in a single, narrative answer. This example uses multiple questions and answers in order to underscore the individual elements of the foundation, as well as to avoid giving the impression that narratives are generally allowed.

ANSWER: Yes, we do.

QUESTION: Please tell us, step by step, what that practice is.

ANSWER: The secretary prepares an envelope as soon as a letter is typed, taking the address from the address block on the letter itself.

QUESTION: What is the next step?

ANSWER: Then the letter and the envelope are given back to the person who wrote it. That person proofreads the letter, and signs it if there are no corrections.

QUESTION: What happens next?

ANSWER: The letter is given back to the secretary, who makes any necessary corrections. If there are no corrections, or once any corrections have been made and approved, the secretary seals the letter in the envelope and places it in the out box.

QUESTION: What is the next step?

ANSWER: The letters in the out box are picked up twice each day by someone from the mail room. The letters are taken to the mail room where they are weighed and run through the postage meter. The metered mail is taken to the local post office twice each day, once at about noon and once at 5:00 p.m.

QUESTION: Was that procedure in place on December 19?

ANSWER: Yes, it was.

Other than personal delivery, the postal service was once the only common form of transferring documents. Today there are numerous other means, including electronic mail, overnight express services, and telefax machines. The basic foundation for proof of transmission is the same, no matter which mode of communication is utilized. A witness may provide direct proof of transmission ("I put it in the fax machine and I dialed the listed number"), or may testify as to the organization's practice for handling outgoing documents.

B.   The Original Writing ("Best Evidence") Rule

The so-called "best evidence" rule was once a formidable obstacle to the admission of documentary evidence. In its harshest form, the rule excluded all but the original copy of any writing, unless certain conditions could be met. Today, the rule has been softened considerably, and now allows for the easy admissibility of most copies.[64] The rule constitutes an authenticity requirement, but its terms are sufficiently unique so as to call for separate treatment.[65]

The essence of the "original writing" rule is that the content of a document can be proved only by producing the original, or an acceptable duplicate, unless the original is lost, destroyed, or unavailable. Because under most circumstances a duplicate is admissible on the same terms as the original, the rule now operates primarily to exclude testimonial summaries or paraphrases of a document. Note also that the original writing rule applies only to proof of a document's content, not its signing, acknowledgment, or delivery.

As noted above, a duplicate may be substituted for the original in most situations. The Federal Rules of Evidence define the term "duplicate" quite broadly, so as to include essentially all accurate reproductions, including carbons, photocopies, telefaxes, and computer-printed duplicates.[66]

Duplicates are not admissible, however, where "a genuine question is raised as to the authenticity of the original."[67] Thus, for example, a photocopy of a contract cannot be offered if one of the parties can support a claim that her signature was forged on the original.

In any event, there are exceptions to the original writing rule. The original is not required if it (1) has been lost or destroyed, (2) is unobtainable, or (3) is in the possession of an opponent who has refused to produce it.[68] Invocation of an exception requires the establishment of a foundation.

---

64 Rule 1002, Federal Rules of Evidence states the basic original writing requirement: "To prove the content of a writing, recording, or photograph, the original writing, recording, or photograph is required, except as otherwise provided in these rules or by Act of Congress."

    Rule 1003, however, goes on to allow the admissibility of most duplicates: "A duplicate is admissible to the same extent as an original unless (1) a genuine question is raised as to the authenticity of the original or (2) in the circumstances it would be unfair to admit the duplicate in lieu of the original."

65 As everyone knows, the "best evidence" rule has nothing to do with whether or not a document is the best evidence of any particular proposition, which is why most commentators now choose to refer to it as the "original writing" or "original document" rule. Judges and lawyers, perhaps because they thrive on confusion, have persisted in using the "best evidence" terminology.

66 *See* Rule 1001(4), Federal Rules of Evidence, which provides as follows: "A "duplicate" is a counterpart produced by the same impression as the original, or from the same matrix, or by means of photography, including enlargements and miniatures, or by mechanical or electronic rerecording, or by chemical reproduction, or by other equivalent techniques which accurately reproduce the original."

67 Rule 1003(1), Federal Rules of Evidence.

68 Rule 1004, Federal Rules of Evidence.

In the following example the witness claims to have received a threatening letter from the defendant:

QUESTION: Did you receive a letter from the defendant?

ANSWER: Yes, I did.

QUESTION: How do you know that it was from the defendant?

ANSWER: I recognized his handwriting, which I have seen many times.

QUESTION: Do you still have the letter?

ANSWER: No, I do not.

QUESTION: What happened to it?

ANSWER: I lost it when I moved to a new apartment.

QUESTION: What did the letter say?

The witness, having explained the loss of the original, may now testify as to the letter's content.[69] Similar foundations are necessary for the other exceptions to the rule.[70]

C.   Foundations for Hearsay Exceptions

The offer of a document inevitably sets the hearsay bell ringing in opposing counsel's mind. While writings may be admissible for non-hearsay purposes, such as proof of notice or acceptance, they are frequently submitted precisely to prove that their contents are true. Various exceptions are available to allow the use of such documents, each requiring its own foundation. The more common exceptions are discussed in the following sections.

1. Business Records

Business records can include ledgers, accounts, calendar entries, memoranda, notices, reports, statements, and similar writings. All of these documents constitute

---

69   Note that compliance with the original writing rule goes only to authenticity. A document may still be excluded if it is otherwise hearsay. In this example, however, the letter, having been written by the defendant, qualifies as a party admission.

70   The most involved foundation is necessary when the original is asserted to be in the possession of a party opponent. The Federal Rule allows secondary evidence if "[a]t a time when an original was under the control of the party against whom offered, he was put on notice, by the pleadings or otherwise, that the contents would be a subject of proof at the hearing, and he does not produce the original at the hearing . . . ." Rule 1004(3), Federal Rules of Evidence.

hearsay if they are offered to prove that their contents are true. Thus, the entries in a loan company's account book would be hearsay if submitted as proof that a certain loan was not repaid in time.

Fortunately for the world of commerce, the "business records" exception to the hearsay rule allows for the admission of most such records, so long as they can be shown to meet certain requirements. Under the Federal Rules, the records of any regularly conducted activity are admissible if they (1) were made at or near the time of a transaction or event; (2) were made by, or based on information transmitted from, a person with knowledge; (3) were kept in the course of a regularly conducted business activity; and (4) were made as a part of the regular practice of that business activity.[71]

It is not uncommon to use the approximate words of the rule in order to lay a foundation for the exception:

QUESTION: Are you employed by the Quickset Printing Company?

ANSWER: Yes, I am the accountant and bookkeeper.

QUESTION: Do you recognize plaintiff's exhibit three?

ANSWER: Yes I do. It is our ledger book.

QUESTION: What is the function of your ledger book?

ANSWER: We use it to record all of our credit sales, and all of the payments that we receive.

QUESTION: Are the entries in plaintiff's exhibit three made at or near the time of the sales or payments?

ANSWER: Yes.

QUESTION: Are the entries made by or transmitted from a person with knowledge of the sales and payments?

ANSWER: Yes.

QUESTION: Are those entries made as a part of the regular business practice of Quickset Printing?

ANSWER: Yes.

---

71 Rule 803(6), Federal Rules of Evidence.

QUESTION: Is the ledger book, plaintiff's exhibit three, kept in the regular course of business?

ANSWER: Yes, it is.

The foundation for the exception is now complete. Note that the witness does not need to be the keeper or custodian of the records, but may be any "person with knowledge."[72] The term "business" is defined broadly to include any "business, institution, association, profession, occupation, and calling of every kind, whether or not conducted for profit."[73] Furthermore, the absence of an entry is also admissible on the basis of the same foundation, so long as it is the type of matter of which a record was regularly kept.[74]

The basic foundation for the business records exception can be expanded upon as circumstances dictate. In dealing with records that are more complex, intricate, questionable, or exotic than ledger books, it is often desirable to have the witness spend more time explaining their use and reliability. It is worth keeping in mind, however, that judges are accustomed to hearing the foundation's magic words, and that objections are less likely to be made or sustained when you use them, too.

2. Computer Print-outs

Computer-generated print-outs have become a common form of business record. In the early days of computing it was considered necessary to prove that computer data entry and retrieval systems were reliable means for storing information, but this is no longer the case.

The Federal Rules specifically recognize "data compilations" as an acceptable form of business record. Thus, the foundation for a computer print-out is basically the same as that for any other business record:

QUESTION: Are you employed by the Quickset Printing Company?

ANSWER: Yes, I am the accountant and data manager.

QUESTION: Do you recognize plaintiff's exhibit three?

ANSWER: Yes, I do. It is a print-out of our accounts receivable.

QUESTION: How was plaintiff's exhibit three generated?

---

72 Rule 803(6), Federal Rules of Evidence.
73 *Id.*
74 Rule 803(7), Federal Rules of Evidence.

ANSWER: We use a computer program to record all of our credit sales and all of the payments that we receive. We can then print out the information whenever we need it.

QUESTION: Are the entries made on your computer system at or near the time of the sales or payments?

ANSWER: Yes.

QUESTION: Are the computer entries made by or transmitted from a person with knowledge of the sales and payments?

ANSWER: Yes.

QUESTION: Are those entries made as a part of the regular business practice of Quickset Printing?

ANSWER: Yes.

QUESTION: Are your computer records kept in the regular course of business?

ANSWER: Yes, they are.

Note that only the computer entries, and not the print-out, need to have been made "at or near the time of the transactions."

3. Summaries

Many business records or other sets of data are so lengthy and ponderous that they cannot be conveniently produced in court. Even if they could be produced, they may be so extensive and technical as to be impenetrable. In these circumstances it is permissible to substitute a "chart, summary, or calculation" that fairly presents the relevant information in a usable or understandable form.[75]

The foundation for such a summary includes these elements: (1) the original documents are so voluminous that they cannot be conveniently examined in court; (2) the witness has examined the original data; (3) the witness is qualified to produce a summary of the information; and (4) the exhibit is a fair and accurate summary of the underlying information. The witness in the following example is an economist who has been called to testify regarding a company's net worth:

---

75   Rule 1006, Federal Rules of Evidence.

QUESTION: What is your occupation?

ANSWER: I am an economist.

QUESTION: Have you examined certain records of the Quickset Printing Company?

ANSWER: Yes.

QUESTION: Please describe all of the documents that you examined.

ANSWER: I looked at all of the books and records of the company, including their pay records, tax records, fringe benefit records, insurance records, accounts payable, accounts receivable, inventories, mortgages, and appraisals of their real property.

QUESTION: Why did you examine those records?

ANSWER: It was necessary to look at all of that information in order to arrive at a figure for their net worth.

QUESTION: Can you describe the volume of the materials that you examined?

ANSWER: All in all, I would say that they would fill three or four large binders.

QUESTION: Do you recognize plaintiff's exhibit nineteen?

ANSWER: Yes, it is a summary that I prepared of the Quickset records.

QUESTION: What does plaintiff's exhibit nineteen contain?

ANSWER: It shows their outstanding assets and liabilities, which then gives us their net worth.

QUESTION: Is plaintiff's exhibit nineteen a fair and accurate summary of the corporate records of Quickset Printing?

ANSWER: Yes.

It is also necessary for the original records to be made available for examination by the other parties. This aspect of the foundation can be established through testimony or by stipulation.

4. Recorded Recollection

A witness's written notes, or other recorded recollection, may be admitted into evidence only if the witness, at the time of trial, "has insufficient recollection to enable him to testify fully and accurately."[76] The foundation for this exception to the hearsay rule comprises these elements: (1) the witness once had personal knowledge of the relevant facts or events; (2) the witness cannot currently recall the events fully and accurately; (3) the witness previously made an accurate memorandum or record of the facts; (4) at a time when the events were fresh in his or her memory.

The witness in the following example has sued an insurance company for failure to pay a property damage claim:

QUESTION: Is it possible for you to name all of the items that were destroyed in the fire at your home?

ANSWER: No, we lost everything. I am sure that I would not be able to name every item, or even most of them.

QUESTION: Before the fire, had you ever made a list of your belongings?

ANSWER: Yes, I inventoried all of the more valuable or significant items, and I put the list in my safe deposit box.

QUESTION: How did you make that list?

ANSWER: It was easy. I went from room to room and wrote down each thing as I saw it.

QUESTION: Was the list accurate when you made it?

ANSWER: Yes, it was.

QUESTION: Showing you plaintiff's exhibit one, is this the list of belongings that you made?

ANSWER: It is.

QUESTION: After reviewing the list, would it be possible for you to remember all of the items on it?

ANSWER: No, there are too many.

The foundation for the witness's recorded recollection is not complete. Note that the witness testified that she could not recall all of the items even after reviewing the list. This testimony fulfills the requirement that the witness be unable to testify "fully and accurately." If the witness *could* recall all of the items, then her recollection would be "refreshed," and this particular hearsay exception would

---

76   Rule 803(5), Federal Rules of Evidence.

not be available. The witness would, of course, be able to testify as to her renewed recollection.[77]

Under the Federal Rules, a document containing a recorded recollection may only be read into evidence; the record itself cannot be received as an exhibit unless offered by the adverse party.[78] Some state jurisdictions simply allow the admission of the document.

5. Public Records

There are a number of hearsay exceptions that allow for the admissibility of public records, statistics, and reports. Such records are generally admissible if they were made by a public office or agency and they set forth (1) the activities of the office or agency; or (2) matters observed pursuant to a duty imposed by law; or (3) in limited circumstances, certain investigative findings; or (4) officially required records of vital statistics.[79]

Because most government records are "self-authenticating," it is not usually necessary to call a witness to testify to their authenticity.[80] While it is technically necessary to call a witness to establish the "governmental duty" elements of the foundation, most courts will take judicial notice of the fact that agencies are required by law to record their activities and observations, particularly where the obligation is imposed by a statute or regulation.

Note that the Federal Rule places two limits on the use of this hearsay exception in criminal cases. First, "matters observed by police officers and other law enforcement personnel" do not qualify for the exception, even if contained in a report made pursuant to a duty imposed by law. Second, investigative findings are admissible in criminal cases only if offered *against* the government.

6. Absence of Public Record or Entry

Public records may also be used to show the non-occurrence of events. The foundation for this evidence is (1) that such events, occurrences or matters were regularly recorded in some form; (2) by a public office or agency; and (3) that a diligent search has failed to disclose a record of a particular fact or event. This evidence may be offered by certification from the appropriate official, in which case no witness needs to be called. The evidence may also be offered via testimony:

---

77   The techniques for refreshing recollection are discussed in Chapter Two, Section II E, *supra* at p. 19.

78   Rule 803(5), Federal Rules of Evidence.

79   *See* Rules 803(8) and 803(9), Federal Rules of Evidence.

80   Rule 902, Federal Rules of Evidence.

QUESTION: Do you hold a public position in this state?

ANSWER: Yes, I am the chief clerk at the Liquor Control Commission.

QUESTION: Does your agency keep records of the liquor licenses issued in this state?

ANSWER: Yes, we keep a record of every license as it is issued, as well as the payment of each annual licensing fee.

QUESTION: Are those records regularly made and preserved as part of the public business of your agency?

ANSWER: They are.

QUESTION: Have you conducted a diligent search to determine whether this state has ever issued a liquor license to an organization called the Park City Club?

ANSWER: Yes, I have.

QUESTION: What was the result of that search?

ANSWER: No such license has ever been issued.

7. Previous Testimony

The transcript of a person's previous testimony may be admitted into evidence if (1) the declarant is currently "unavailable" to testify; (2) the testimony was given under oath in court or at a deposition; (3) the party *against* whom the testimony is being offered had a fair opportunity to examine the witness when the testimony was originally given.[81] Note that this exception allows the admission of the earlier statement as a substitute for current testimony. Unlike the use of prior testimony for impeachment, there is no requirement that the previous testimony be inconsistent with the declarant's current position.

Under the Federal Rule, a witness can be deemed "unavailable" for a variety of reasons, including: (1) the valid assertion of a privilege; (2) persistent refusal to testify; (3) inability to attend the hearing due to illness; (4) death; (5) failure of memory; or (6) absence from the hearing notwithstanding the efforts of the proponent of the testimony to procure attendance.

The elements of the foundation for this exception will frequently be established through judicial notice. The court, for example, will usually take notice of

---

81   Rule 804(b)(1), Federal Rules of Evidence.

the fact that a party had an opportunity to cross examine the declarant at the earlier hearing or deposition. It may occasionally be necessary to produce proof of unavailability, as in the case of a witness who failed to respond to a subpoena.

8. Party Admissions

The party admission exception applies to documents as well as to oral statements. A party admission can be contained in a letter, report, memorandum, journal, progress chart, or virtually any other form of writing. Once the exhibit has been authenticated, the only remaining foundation is that it was made or adopted by a party against whom it is being offered, or by an agent, servant, or employee of such a party.

VI. PERSUASIVE USE OF EXHIBITS

The previous sections dealt with the technical aspects of offering exhibits. The admission of an exhibit, however, is only part of counsel's task. It is equally important to ensure that exhibits are presented and used as persuasively as possible.

A. Persuasive Foundations

Because foundations are technical matters that are principally directed to the court, it is easy to lose sight of their impact on the jury. There are two approaches that can be used to keep jurors from being confused, bored, or annoyed by foundations.

1. Minimalism

Whenever possible, use stipulations and pretrial rulings to avoid the need for developing foundations in court. If foundational testimony must be presented, keep it as short as possible. Leading questions, permissible on preliminary matters, can be used to move the testimony along.

Several elements of a foundation can frequently be combined in a single sentence. The business records foundation, for example, can be summed up in only two questions:

QUESTION: Were the entries made at or near the time of the transaction by a person with knowledge, or transmitted by a person with knowledge, of the transaction?

QUESTION: Were the records made and kept in the ordinary course of business?

These questions are technically compound, but few lawyers or judges will be concerned with that nicety at the expense of expediting such a boring aspect of the trial. The above language will be unfathomable to most jurors, but it will be over with in a hurry. It is not usually important for the jury to understand a technical foundation, and it may well be better to have them baffled and happy than well-educated and resentful.

2. Maximalism

Foundations are not always rote technicalities. Particularly where the authenticity of the exhibit is in issue, the thoroughness of the foundation can play an important role in jury persuasion. In such circumstances it is important to develop the foundation fully, taking care to use language that the jurors will understand.

Using another business records situation, assume that the defendant company in the following example is being sued for non-payment of a bill for supplies. The defendant's records show that payment was made in cash, and the plaintiff contests the accuracy of the entry. The witness is the defendant's bookkeeper:

QUESTION: What are your duties as bookkeeper at the Mills Company?

ANSWER: I am in charge of all purchase, payment, and receipt records.

QUESTION: Does your job require you to keep a record of payments?

ANSWER: Yes, every time we make a payment I make an entry in the disbursement column of our ledger.

QUESTION: Showing you defendant's exhibit one, is this the ledger that you referred to?

ANSWER: Yes it is.

QUESTION: What do the entries in defendant's exhibit one, the ledger, show?

ANSWER: They show the amount, the form of payment, the person or company we paid, and the name of the person who made the payment.

QUESTION: How soon after each payment do you make the entries?

ANSWER: Within 24 hours.

QUESTION: How do you get the information?

ANSWER: Each person who makes a payment reports it directly to me, and I enter it in the book.

QUESTION: Were the entries in defendant's exhibit one made in any particular order?

ANSWER: They are entered in the order of the date on which each payment was made.

325

QUESTION: Is it a regular part of your job to make the entries in exhibit one?

ANSWER: Yes.

QUESTION: Is it a regular part of your job to keep defendant's exhibit one up to date?

ANSWER: Yes it is.

QUESTION: Does defendant's exhibit one contain an entry for a payment to Quickset Printing last January 4?

ANSWER: Yes it does.

QUESTION: At the time of that entry, were you aware of any dispute between your employer and Quickset?

ANSWER: No, it was just another regular entry.

The above foundation was long, but it was necessary to show the reliability of the entry. As with any direct examination, details add credibility.

A detailed foundation can make an exhibit more persuasive even when its authenticity is not in dispute. The following example is a battery prosecution in which the defendant is alleged to have struck the victim with a length of pipe. The original pipe was not recovered, and the prosecution is seeking to introduce a similar pipe as demonstrative evidence. A sufficient foundation could be laid by the victim's testimony that the exhibit is "identical" to the one with which he was hit. A longer foundation, however, could be much more effective:

QUESTION: Please take prosecution exhibit five in your hand, and tell me when you have finished examining it.

ANSWER: I have finished.

QUESTION: Is exhibit five similar to the pipe that the defendant hit you with?

ANSWER: Yes, it is.

QUESTION: Is it the same weight as the defendant's weapon?

ANSWER: Yes, it is the same weight.

QUESTION: Is it the same length as the defendant's pipe?

ANSWER: Yes.

QUESTION: Is it as big around as the pipe that the defendant used?

ANSWER: Yes.

QUESTION: Are there any differences at all between prosecution exhibit five and the pipe that the defendant used to beat you?

ANSWER: They are exactly alike.

Following this foundation, the jury should have a full appreciation of the exhibit not merely as a model, but as a dangerous weapon. Further demonstrations with the pipe, once it is admitted into evidence, will drive the point home even more.

3. Magic Words

Whether utilizing the minimalist or maximalist approach to foundations, counsel must always reckon with the potency of magic words. Many foundations—including those for photographs, business records, and the authenticity of conversations—have become routine to the point that convenient phrases are now frequently confused with legal requirements. No matter what some judges may think, though, it is not necessary to introduce every photograph by asking whether it "fairly and accurately depicts" the scene involved. As far as the law of evidence is concerned, it would be just as acceptable to ask whether the photograph "shows everything in the scene just as it appeared on the date in question." Hundreds of other variations would serve just as well.

Nonetheless, there is precious little to be gained by arguing with judges or opposing lawyers who are determined to hear the magic words. In the end, it is just easier to say "fairly and accurately depict" than it is to convince the court that your more thoughtful version of the foundation is legally sufficient.

Magic words get results, and must therefore be part of every attorney's repertoire. For the benefit of a jury you will often want to lay a foundation in more readily understandable language, but this should not prevent you from falling back on the expected jargon, either in response to an objection or as an extra "fail-safe" line of questions at the end of your preferred foundation.

B.   Creative Exhibits

The most valuable exhibits in any case seldom step forward and present themselves. Rather, they must be sought after, searched out, and discovered. Often they must be developed and created. Even those exhibits that are simply handed to counsel by the client can be presented in an enhanced form. The following sections discuss creative means of finding, developing, and presenting exhibits.

1. Looking for Exhibits

It is essential to ensure your complete access to all real and documentary exhibits. While you will rarely want to introduce everything that you find, you cannot adequately represent your client until you have examined every potential item of evidence. No competent attorney would go to trial without having learned the identity of every witness, and exhibits are essentially silent witnesses. You must find them all.

a. Documentary exhibits

The most obvious initial source for documentary exhibits is your own client. Whether the case involves a commercial transaction, a tort, or a crime, it is likely that your client will bring you some paper that has bearing on the case. It is an error to assume that your client has shown you everything. This is true both of sophisticated business clients and naive individuals. An extremely important aspect of trial preparation consists of reviewing with your client (and your client's personnel) all possible sources for documentary evidence.

Modern discovery rules allow counsel wide access to documents in the possession of the opposing party. Attorneys commonly phrase documents requests in scattergun terms, requesting something on the order of "all writings, papers, and documents relevant to, purporting to be relevant to, discussing, touching upon, or otherwise generated or maintained with reference to" one or more of the issues involved in the particular case. Most lawyers respond to such broad requests in good faith, but a greater degree of specificity will go a long way toward ensuring that crucial documents are not inadvertently omitted and that the request can be enforced if necessary.

Finally, counsel should never ignore the possibility that important documents may be in the hands of non-parties. While non-parties are not subject to ordinary discovery, they will often be cooperative to the point of turning over significant evidence on request. When cooperation is not forthcoming, subpoenas are usually available.

Whether documents are being sought from your client, the opposition, or from non-parties, you must know what you are looking for in order to be reasonably confident that you have found everything that you might be able to use. But how can you know what you are looking for, when what you are looking for is unknown? The answer to this seeming paradox lies with the lawyer's skills of analysis. You are looking for the things that must — or should, or might — exist.

Recall that the word "document" is both a noun and a verb. Documents exist in order to document events and occurrences. Thus, for every act, event, occurrence, or detail in your case, you must ask, "How might this fact be documented?" The answer to that question will inform your search for documentary evidence, and help you decide whether to seek the evidence in the hands of your client, the opposition, or some non-party.

Consider, for example, a robbery prosecution in which the defendant claims an alibi. Robberies, unless occurring in front of a surveillance camera, are seldom documented. An alibi, however, has potential. If the defendant claims to have been shopping at or near the time of the crime, for instance, look for purchase receipts or credit card slips. A defendant who claims to have been out of town might be able to produce, or lead you to, hotel registrations. Bear in mind that credit card companies keep records of card usage, and that some computerized systems now even record the time of the transaction. It can therefore be possible to pinpoint an individual's presence at a retail store, a parking lot, a gasoline station, or a restaurant.

The point of this is not simply the value of obtaining credit card receipts, but rather the importance of *imagining* where documentation exists and then seeking it out. Were the relevant transactions the subject of a report? Of correspondence? Of a memorandum? Did anyone at the meeting take written notes? Did anyone dictate notes? Was there a sign-in sheet? Were any photographs taken? Is there a calendar entry? Were work orders filled out?

b. Real Evidence

Real evidence must be tracked down with the same determination as documentary evidence. What objects should exist that will support (or controvert) your theory of the case? Such objects can be as large and obvious as traffic signs, or as small and insubstantial as fiber samples or skin scrapings. Forensic science has made enormous strides in recent years. While some investigatory techniques are more reliable than others, and many are not as reliable as their proponents claim, you will not be able to use any of them unless you first determine what to look for.

2. Developing Exhibits

All exhibits fall essentially into two categories: those that predate the litigation and those created by the attorneys. The pre-litigation, or integral, exhibits must be taken as they are found, but counsel has wide latitude in shaping and developing other exhibits for use at trial. Some of the more common sorts of lawyer-generated exhibits are discussed below. The creation of these, and similar, exhibits should be considered in virtually every case.

a. Deposition Transcripts

Although not commonly thought of as exhibits, deposition transcripts are indeed physical objects that did not exist before the litigation. They come into being only as a consequence of arrangement and questioning by counsel. The words on the printed page can under some circumstances be shown to, as well as read to, the jury. An enlargement of a key section of an adverse witness's testimony can make an extremely effective exhibit when used on cross examination.

b. Photographs and Videotapes

As we noted in the foundation section, it is extremely easy to have photographs admitted into evidence. They only need to portray accurately a relevant scene in order to be received. With this in mind, you will almost always want to photograph important objects or locations that bear on your theory of the case.

Although it is not necessary to call the photographer in order to authenticate a photograph, it is often a good idea to employ a professional photographer to take any desired photographs. Amateurs, even working with good equipment, can make errors in focus, lighting, or composition. A professional will understand how to capture the desired scene, while avoiding extraneous or misleading information.

It is now possible to use videotapes in much the same way that still photography has been used for years. Instead of photographing the scene of an accident, for example, counsel should consider videotaping not only the scene, but also the viewpoints of the parties as they approached the scene. A still photograph can capture only a limited amount of information about a physical space, while a videotape can more accurately convey information concerning perspective, spatial relationships, and even speed.

c. Models

Models can be simple or elaborate, but they are almost always useful in explaining a series of events. Depending upon the size of the case and the available litigation budget, models can range from to-scale duplicates of entire buildings, to commercially available reproductions of human organs or joints.

d. Diagrams and Maps

Diagrams are perhaps the simplest and most ubiquitous form of lawyer-generated exhibit. Virtually no automobile accident case would be complete without an intersection drawing, and many other cases use street grids, floor plans, or other diagrams on which to place the occurrence of physical events. One of the advantages of a diagram is that it can be marked to indicate the locations of signs, objects, or witnesses, as well as the movement of persons and things.

e. Explanatory Graphs and Charts

Photographs, models, and diagrams all represent physical objects and occurrences. Graphs and charts, on the other hand, help explain concepts and ideas. A simple "time line," for example, can clarify the sequence in which crucial events occurred. Similarly, a pie chart can help a witness explain loss of income or allocation of damages. It is entirely permissible for a witness to illustrate her testimony in addition to describing it in words. Counsel can help the witness communicate by assisting in the development of graphs and charts.

3. Presenting Exhibits

The presentation of an exhibit can be as important as its composition or foundation. No matter how well thought out, no matter how solidly admissible, an exhibit will not accomplish its purpose if it is not understood and accepted by the trier of fact. As with any aspect of witness examination, there are certain principles that can generally be applied to the presentation of exhibits at trial:

a. Advance Preparation

The best exhibits are usually those prepared in advance of trial. This principle applies to both selection and design.

While some cases involve only two or three exhibits, many cases will see the production of dozens, if not hundreds, of documents. A careful trial plan will determine precisely which of these exhibits are the most significant, and will treat them in such a way as to emphasize their importance. As with direct examination, clutter is the enemy of coherent document presentation. Even if thirty or forty documents are necessary to establish every element of your case, the advocate's duty is to cull out the three or four (or perhaps even five or six) that have the most impact. This must be done in advance of trial. It will not do to wait for the witnesses' testimony before you decide which exhibits to highlight. First, your decision about the value of the exhibits should drive the preparation of your witness examinations, not the other way around. Second, the documents that you intend to rely upon most should be enlarged or otherwise prepared for an impressive presentation.

In addition to selecting key integral documents for enhanced presentation, effective trial preparation also involves the design of lawyer-generated exhibits. Particularly when it comes to diagrams and graphs, an ounce of professional preparation is usually worth several pounds of courtroom drawing. The lawyer must decide whether a witness's testimony can be improved through the use of a chart, graph, or diagram. If so, the desired exhibit should be developed in advance of trial.

While it is permissible for witnesses to draw on blackboards or posterboards while testifying, this approach usually should be avoided. Free-hand drawing is unreliable under the best circumstances, and witnesses are notoriously prone to make embarrassing mistakes when called upon to draw in a courtroom. Use of a blackboard, in particular, seldom leads to a satisfying result. Whether the blackboard drawing is made by the witness or the attorney, it will often be either too small to be seen or so large as to run out of space. The time spent drawing will be wasted at best and distracting at worst. Lighting conditions may make even the boldest lines difficult to see, and the chalk will inevitably squeak at the most dramatic moment of the testimony.

Essential features of an exhibit such as scale, perspective, and proportion can only be assured when entrusted to a professional illustrator. If professional assistance is not an alternative, then counsel must take care to create the best diagram possible.

b. Size

Exhibits must be seen to be appreciated. When creating an exhibit, create a big one. When using integral exhibits, such as pre-existing documents, make enlargements.

There is no reason for a lawyer-produced exhibit to be visually inaccessible. Charts, graphs, and diagrams should be made on oversize pieces of stiff poster board. Thin tagboard is unacceptable, since even a masterpiece will be useless if it cannot be made to stand up. It is also necessary to ensure that a display easel will be available in the courtroom.

Ordinary documents can be enlarged. While it is neither necessary nor desirable to enlarge every document, the crucial few should be enlarged to poster size and mounted for display. The most important exhibits to enlarge are those that support your theory of the case. In a case involving extended correspondence over the terms of a contract, for example, counsel may want to enlarge only the two letters showing the final offer and acceptance. Alternatively, trial strategy might dictate enlarging letters that contain certain terms or conditions. In any event, the enhanced presentation of a limited number of exhibits can underscore their importance and drive home your trial theory.

An overhead projector can also be used to display documents. Unfortunately, the visual quality of overhead projection is often poor. The exhibit may be distorted or the image may be faint. Although overhead transparencies are inexpensive and easy to obtain, photographic enlargements are to be preferred if possible.

Photographs, whether pre-existing or taken at counsel's direction, should also be enlarged. Even an 8 x 10 photograph cannot easily be seen from the usual distance between the jury box and the witness stand. If the film quality permits, crucial photographs should be further enlarged to poster size, or reproduced as 35mm slides.

c. Copies

Counsel should enter the courtroom with enough copies of every exhibit. At a minimum, this should include an original, additional copies for the witness and the judge, and copies for each opposing attorney, if they have not already been produced. Distributing copies at the appropriate time in the examination will prevent delays and can forestall objections. There is little more awkward and distracting than a lawyer leaning over a witness's shoulder while they attempt to share an exhibit.

When enlargements are impractical or unavailable, counsel should also make enough copies of the exhibits, whether documents or photographs, to distribute to

332

the jurors. With the court's permission, the copies can be given to the jurors as the witness testifies to the foundation. Alternatively, counsel might wish to delay passing out the copies until the exhibit has been admitted, or even until the end of the examination, so as to avoid having the jurors' attention distracted during the witness's testimony.

It is increasingly common for documents to be admitted at the pretrial conference. When this occurs it is possible to assemble all of the documents into a bound or loose-leaf "exhibit book," copies of which can be provided to court, to each juror, and to witnesses as necessary.

Part Four
Addressing the Fact Finder

— CHAPTER NINE —
Opening Statements

I. INTRODUCTION: THE ROLE OF THE OPENING STATEMENT
A. The Opening Moment

Opening statement, the advocate's first opportunity to speak directly to the jury about the merits of the case, marks the beginning of the competition for the jury's imagination. This moment is crucial, since the mental image that the jurors hold while hearing the evidence will directly influence the way that they interpret it. The attorney who is successful in seizing the opening moment will have an advantage throughout the trial, because the jury will tend to filter all of the evidence through a lens that she has created.

The importance of access to the jury's imagination cannot be underestimated. We are accustomed to receiving most of our information through the sense of sight, but at trial the jurors will obtain most of their information through the oral testimony of witnesses. They will hear descriptions and recountings of past events, but in almost all cases they will not actually see an enactment of the crucial occurrences. They will, however, envision the events as they believe them to have occurred. Each juror will summon her own mental images of the facts, objects, locations, and transactions that are described from the witness stand. The details and context of these images will, in turn, influence the juror's decision.

Consider, for example, the image that is brought to mind by the words "billiard parlor." Each person who hears that term is likely to think of a specific location that she once visited (or saw on television or in a movie), and to use it as a reference in calling up a mental picture of a similar locale. Billiard parlors, in most people's experience, are probably formal, reserved, well-lighted, reasonably open, and fairly respectable. Thus, events occurring in a billiard parlor will have a certain cast to them. Jurors with this scene in mind will tend to fit the events into that image, that is, to view them in a "billiard parlor" sort of way.

On the other hand, consider the image evoked by the words "pool room." Now many people would probably envision a place that is smoky, dark, perhaps slightly threatening, and probably a little seedy. Things happen differently in pool rooms than they do in billiard parlors. Visibility is better in a billiard parlor; things happen more furtively in a pool room. A stranger might be questioned in a billiard parlor, but a confrontation is more likely in a pool room. In other words, the initial mental image dictates, or at least suggests, a variety of assumptions about the nature, context, and likelihood of events.

These assumptions, of course, are not graven in stone. They can be altered, dispelled, or contradicted by the evidence. Still, the creation of an initial image can be a powerful tool. Recall how Professor Henry Hill in *The Music Man* convinced the citizens of River City to purchase the instruments for a boys' band. He described their "trouble with a capital T and that rhymes with P and that stands for pool." The townsfolk listening to Professor Hill envisioned their children sinking en masse into depravity and delinquency, because of the mental picture evoked by "Pool." He would not have been a quarter so persuasive if he had preached that they had "trouble with a capital T and that rhymes with B and that stands for billiards." The image just isn't that compelling.

Your task in an opening statement is to engage the jury's imagination — to help them begin to imagine the case your way. As we shall see below, this forensic task is complicated by the legal function that the opening statement plays in the conduct of the trial.

B. Legal Function

Opening statements exist in order to assist the jury in understanding the evidence to be presented at trial. Of course, we hope that the evidence will be self-explanatory, but in even the best-organized cases, evidence is often presented in a disjointed, if not utterly discontinuous manner.

As witnesses are called to the stand, each testifies only as to what he or she knows about the case. Thus, even the simplest narrative may be divided among many witnesses. Moreover, a single witness may have information concerning the beginning and the end of a chain of events, but may know nothing about intervening occurrences. That testimony will have to be filled in by an entirely different witness. It may not be possible to call witnesses in the most desirable or logical order, due to logistical problems or unavailability. Exhibits present their own unique set of challenges, since the witness necessary to lay the foundation for a document may not be the one who can adequately explain its content.

The very structure of the trial compounds the problem: the flow of direct testimony is inevitably, indeed intentionally, interrupted by cross examination. The defendant's evidence, no matter where it might reasonably fit into the overall narrative, is always delayed until after the plaintiff's entire case has been presented. The potential for confusion is great and unavoidable.

To reduce the possibility of jury confusion as a result of the manner in which evidence is introduced, the courts have developed the concept of the opening statement. At the very beginning of the trial jurors are presented with an overview of the case, so that they will be better equipped to make sense of the evidence as it is actually presented. The institutional purpose of the opening statement, then, is to ease the jury's burden by making the trial more understandable; it is not intended to give the lawyers another crack at pleading the case. For this reason, many courts have held that the presentation of an opening statement is a privilege, not a protected right, and that the privilege may be withheld in situations where opening statements will not be helpful to the jury.

Thus, we have the basis of the "non-argument" rule. The courts and commentators are virtually unanimous that opening statements may only be used to inform the jury of "what the evidence will show." Counsel may not argue the case during opening, but is restricted to offering a preview of the anticipated testimony, exhibits, and other evidence. This limitation results in a highly stylized set of rules for the presentation of opening statements, and it informs almost everything else that there is to be said on the subject.

C. Advocacy

As an advocate, your governing principle in presenting an opening statement should be to use it as an opportunity to advance your theory of the case. This is not as easy, or as obvious, as it sounds.

Given the strictures placed upon the content of opening statements, it may be all too easy for a lawyer to slip into complacency. Since the legal function of the opening is limited to a preview of the evidence, many lawyers take the approach of simply listing the witnesses or describing the general tenor of the expected testimony and exhibits. In other words, they discuss only what the "evidence will be." This is a serious mistake, as it squanders the potential benefits of the opening moment.

A far more useful, and equally permissible, approach is to discuss what the "evidence will show," rather than merely what it will be. The distinction is not semantic. Telling the jury "what the evidence will be" is a neutral formulation, geared toward providing a simple synopsis of the trial to come. Explaining "what the evidence will show," on the other hand, requires you to consider the relationship between the expected evidence and the conclusions and outcomes that you want the jury to reach. In our intersection case, for example, the projected evidence might be that a fire truck approached the intersection, and that the defendant did not stop his car. From the plaintiff's perspective, however, the evidence hopefully will show that the defendant had ample opportunity to observe the fire truck, which was flashing its lights and sounding its siren, but that he was so distracted that he did not notice it.

Counsel need not feel limited to an antiseptic listing of the evidence to come. Rather, explain to the jury what propositions will be proven and exactly how they will be proven. So long as you avoid lapsing into argumentative form, you may explicate your theory of the case. While you may not urge the jury to reach certain conclusions, you may arrange your discussion of the facts so that the conclusions are inevitable. Many tools are available to accomplish this goal. In brief, a well-developed opening statement will take advantage of some or all of the following concepts:

Choice of facts. In every opening statement you must decide which facts to include and which to leave out. While you will obviously want to emphasize the facts that you find helpful, there is also considerable risk to telling an incomplete or illogical story.

Sequencing. The order of facts may be as important as the nature of the facts. Recall the question that resulted in the downfall of the Nixon administration: "What did the President know and when did he know it?"

Clarity of description. It is one thing to mention a fact, but it is better to describe it with sufficient detail and clarity as to engage the jury in your own mental portrait.

Common sense. Common sense is used both to judge and predict outcomes. An opening statement cannot be successful if its story doesn't jibe with everyday experience. On the other hand, a jury's reflexive resort to common sense can be used to lead them to a desired conclusion. Consider an opening statement that begins this way: "The defendant woke up late; he had an important meeting to go to; the meeting was to be held far from his home; the defendant drove to the meeting." Without saying more, common sense suggests that the defendant was in a hurry.

Moral attraction. An opening statement can be made more attractive when it tells a story that people want to accept. The evidence can be described in a context of shared values or civic virtues, so as to add moral force to your client's position. In the intersection case, for example, the plaintiff's evidence will be that she stopped for the fire truck. On the other hand, the evidence will *show* that the plaintiff knew that it was important not to get in the way of a fire engine, and so she stopped to let it pass.

In the final analysis, the most successful opening statements are those that explain exactly how you intend to win your case.

II. THE LAW OF OPENING STATEMENTS

A. The Rule Against Argument

As we noted above, the rule against argument is inherent in the very concept of the opening statement. Our system of law, based as it is on the production of testimony and exhibits, has no place for argument that precedes the introduction of evidence. Indeed, jurors are cautioned against discussing the case even among themselves before all of the evidence has been presented. Jurors are not supposed to begin making up their minds until they have heard all of the evidence. Therefore, the limited function of the opening statement is to create a context for the jury's understanding. Thus, argument is improper during opening statements.

1. Defining the Rule

The rule against argument is easier to state than to define. Moreover, application of the rule will vary from jurisdiction to jurisdiction, and even from courtroom to courtroom. No matter how the rule is articulated, it is almost never hard and fast. Most judges recognize that "argument" is a relative concept, and allow lawyers a reasonable amount of latitude.

As a general rule, opening statement ends and argument begins when counsel attempts to tell the jury how they should reach their decision. So long as the opening is comprised only of a description of the evidence there obviously is no problem. Difficulties arise only when the advocate engages in interpretation or exhortation. You may not urge the jury to draw inferences from facts or to reach certain conclusions. You may not explain the importance of certain items of evidence, or suggest how evidence should be weighed. It is improper to comment directly on the credibility of witnesses. Finally, an opening statement may not be used to appeal overtly to the jury's sense of mercy or justice.

For example, it would be proper to tell the following story to a jury during the opening statement in a personal injury case:

Just before the accident the plaintiff was sitting in a tavern. In less than an hour and a half he consumed at least four shots of whiskey. He bought a round for the house and then he left. He left in his car. The accident occurred within the next twenty minutes.

It would be improper argument, however, to continue in this vein:

The plaintiff was obviously drunk. No person could drink four whiskeys in that amount of time without feeling it. Only an alcoholic or a liar would even claim to have been sober under those circumstances.

The second paragraph violates the argument rule not only because it draws the conclusion that the plaintiff was drunk, but also because it tells the jury how to evaluate the plaintiff's anticipated testimony: "Only an alcoholic or a liar would claim to have been sober."

2. Guidelines

A number of guidelines or rules of thumb have been developed for determining when an opening statement has drifted into argument.

The witness test. One possible test is to question whether a witness will actually testify to the "facts" contained in the opening statement. If so, the opening is proper. If not, it has become argument. In the tavern example above, for instance, witnesses will be able to testify to the plaintiff's presence in the bar and his consumption of liquor; therefore the initial paragraph is appropriate. No such witness, however, would be allowed to testify to the conclusion that the plaintiff is a liar or an alcoholic. Accordingly, the second paragraph is impermissible.

The verification test. An alternative measure is to determine whether the content of the opening statement can be verified, the theory being that facts are verifiable while argumentative conclusions are not. Note that this analysis can be more flexible than the witness test, since the comment that the plaintiff was drunk is subject to verification. On the other hand, the "alcoholic or liar" comment continues to fail under this test as well.

The "link" test. A final approach is to consider whether the opening statement contains facts with independent evidentiary value, or whether the attorney has had to provide a rhetorical link in the probative chain. Again we see that the first paragraph above is just fine; it consists entirely of classic evidence. The second paragraph, however, is pure rhetoric. It becomes probative only when counsel supplies the explanation, or link, that "no person could drink that amount of whiskey without showing it."

Each of these tests is more holistic than legalistic. There are no case holdings or rules of court that detail how a particular jurisdiction will apply the rule against argument. Even a seasoned trial judge may not be able to explain exactly why an objection was sustained to some portion of an opening statement. As a practical matter, it may be best to keep in mind the principle that "argument" occurs when counsel seeks to tell the jury *how* they should go about reaching their decision.

3. Other Considerations

In addition to the words spoken and the evidence marshalled by counsel, a variety of other considerations may lead a judge to conclude that an opening statement has crossed the line into argument. Some of these are detailed below:

Tone of voice. Words that appear neutral on the printed page may become argumentative by virtue of the tone in which they are delivered. Sneering, sarcasm, volume, or vocal caricature can all transform an acceptable opening into an impermissible one.

Rhetorical questions. The use of rhetorical questions is inherently argumentative. Such questions can be used to suggest disbelief, as in, "What could she possibly have been thinking of?" Alternatively, they can be used as a statement of incontrovertible certainty, such as, "What other answer could there be?" In either case, they strongly signal argument when used in an opening statement.

Repetition. Although an excellent persuasive device when used elsewhere in a trial, repetition can lead an opening statement into forbidden territory. In the tavern scenario above, for example, imagine that the first paragraph of the plaintiff's opening statement was embellished this way:

> Just before the accident the plaintiff was sitting in a tavern. In less than an hour and a half he consumed at least four shots of whiskey. Not two or three, but four. He bought a round for the house and then he left. He left in his car. That's right, he drove away from the tavern. He opened the car door, got behind the wheel, put the key in the ignition, started the engine, shifted into first gear, and proceeded to drive down the road. There will be two witnesses who will testify to plaintiff's consumption of alcohol. And three different witnesses will testify that they saw the plaintiff drive away from the bar in his own car.

Although each of the facts in this extended paragraph could stand as non-argumentative, some judges would no doubt consider the extreme repetition as going too far.

B.   Comments on the Law

Closely related to the rule against argument is the general proscription against discussing law during opening statements. The rationale is the same. Opening statements are allowed for the purpose of organizing and previewing the evidence for the jury. Not until the end of the case will the court instruct the jurors on the law. The instructions presumably will be comprehensive, and therefore will not require a preview. Indeed, it is usually impossible to predict all of the jury instructions until all of the evidence has been admitted. In any event, to the extent that the jury requires advance information about the law, this can come from the judge in the form of a preliminary instruction.

Nonetheless, it is virtually impossible for counsel to avoid some discussion of the law during any but the simplest opening statement. It is the law, after all, that determines the relevance and importance of the facts being previewed. Without some explanation of the legal issues, a jury will have no way to tell whether certain facts are significant, or merely window dressing.

In a drunk driving prosecution, for example, it would obviously be permissible for the prosecutor to inform the jury that the defendant's blood alcohol level was .12 per cent. Whatever test might be applied, this is clearly a provable fact that is subject to verification. It is also a fairly meaningless fact unless the jury is also informed of the jurisdiction's legal test for intoxication, which in most states is .10 per cent or less.

Perhaps more to the point, assume that the following opening statement, consistent with the facts, was given by the plaintiff's attorney in a personal injury case:

> Ladies and gentlemen, shortly after the accident, the defendant was taken to a local hospital. A blood sample was drawn and it was analyzed for the presence of alcohol. The result was that her blood contained .08 per cent alcohol. We will present the expert testimony of Dr. Irene Coleman, who will testify that a blood alcohol level of .08 per cent will result in the impairment of reflexes, response time, and judgment. Dr. Coleman will testify that, in her opinion, that blood alcohol level would significantly interfere with the safe operation of an automobile.

Note that the entire opening statement is devoted to the description of provable evidence. The material is well organized, and it will surely assist the jury in understanding the evidence of intoxication, which will probably be presented through the testimony of two or three different witnesses. There has been no mention of the law.

Defense counsel, however, might wish to give the following opening statement:

> Ladies and gentlemen, the legal limit for intoxication in this state is .10 per cent blood alcohol. The defendant's blood was sampled in the emergency room within 30 minutes of the accident. The test showed that her blood alcohol level was only .08 per cent, which is .02 per cent below the level for legally operating an automobile in this state. Dr. Alex Benjamin will testify in this case that the defendant's blood alcohol level could not have significantly changed in the 30 minutes between the accident and the blood test. Her blood alcohol level was within the legal limit at the time of the accident.

The defendant's opening statement, to make any sense at all, must be allowed to include some information about the law. The jury cannot possibly assess the value of the other evidence without the reference to the state statute. Thus, most judges would consider this defendant's limited discussion of the law to be an acceptable part of the opening statement.

It would not be acceptable, however, for either of the parties to argue for an interpretation or construction of the law. Plaintiff's counsel could not, for example, use the opening statement to urge the jury to ignore the legal limit and concentrate on the defendant's impaired reflexes. By the same token, defense counsel could not posit that statutory intoxication is all that matters, and that the jury should ignore any other evidence of inebriation.

These positions might be suitable for final argument. Neither, however, would be permissible during opening statements. In both cases the attorney is attempting to provide the jury with a method for reaching their decision, rather than with a guide to understanding information as it is presented.

Most judges attempt to steer a middle course when it comes to discussion of the law during opening statements. It is almost always permissible to frame the legal issues for the jury. A sentence or two devoted to an explanation of the legal significance of the evidence will also usually be allowed. Once the discussion of the law becomes intricate, lengthy, or controversial, however, an objection will usually be sustained.[1]

C. Persuasion

While argument is prohibited during opening statements, persuasion is not. Indeed, persuasion is unavoidable. The test of relevance provides that evidence is not admissible unless it tends to prove or disprove some matter at issue in the case. Accordingly, few of the facts outlined in an opening statement will be "neutral." Most facts will be favorable to one side or the other. So long as counsel refrains from suggesting conclusions to be drawn from the facts, it is permissible to arrange them in an order that maximizes their favorable impact. Furthermore, persuasive ordering of the facts by both counsel will typically assist the jury in understanding the case, since they will then be able to see just how the parties' stories diverge.

The persuasive ordering of facts can be accomplished either through incremental development or through contrast. Incremental development involves the successive ordering of a series of discrete facts, each building upon the last, until the desired conclusion becomes obvious. Although the facts will be related, they need not be presented in chronological order. The following example demonstrates how the plaintiff might use incremental development in our fire engine case:

> The defendant awoke at 7:20 a.m. He had an important meeting scheduled with a potential new client for 8:30 that morning. The client had not yet decided whether to hire the defendant, but the account would have been worth a lot of money. The meeting was to be held downtown, which was 12 miles from the defendant's home. The defendant showered, shaved, dressed, and ate a quick breakfast. He went to his car, which was parked about a block away. All of this took approximately 50 minutes. By the time the defendant got to his car it was 8:10 a.m. He had 20 minutes left before the new client was scheduled to arrive at his office.

---

1 It should go without saying that an incorrect statement of the law is objectionable, even if made only in passing or for the purpose of framing the issues for the jury.

Note that the example begins when the defendant woke up, skips ahead to the information about the scheduled meeting, and then goes back to describe the rest of the defendant's morning routine. Other facts, of course, could be added to show how seriously late the defendant was, and therefore how likely he was to drive carelessly or too fast. The point is that the individual events build upon each other to explain, without saying so, why the defendant would have been driving negligently.

Contrast is the juxtaposition of contradictory facts, most often used in an opening statement to demonstrate the implausibility of some aspect of the opposing case. The defendant in the fire engine case might use contrast this way:

> The plaintiff in this case is seeking damages for pain and suffering and lost income. She claims a permanent disability. You will see medical bills offered into evidence that start with the date of the accident and which continue right through to last December 10. You will also see a receipt for the purchase of a new backpack and camp stove, purchased by the plaintiff last May 17. She went to the doctor on May 15, she bought her backpack on May 17, and she went camping at Eagle River Falls on May 20. She returned to town on May 27. Her next visit to the doctor was not until July 19.

Without resort to argument, the simple contrast between the medical bills and the camping trip casts doubt on the plaintiff's allegation of permanent injury.

The line between persuasive ordering and argument is crossed when counsel attempts to inject judgments, conclusions, or other means of reaching a decision into the opening statement. It is fair game to present facts showing, say, that the plaintiff requires a large judgment to be fully compensated:

> Each morning when the plaintiff wakes up he needs assistance in getting out of bed. He cannot walk to the bathroom himself. He cannot bathe or clean himself. He cannot fix his own breakfast. If he wants to read a newspaper or a book, someone must get it for him. Each day, for 24 hours, he must pay a nurse or housekeeper to do all of the things that other people are able to do for themselves.

It is not fair game, however, to continue in this vein: "The plaintiff could just as easily be your own neighbor or relative; he deserves your generosity."

III. STRUCTURE AND ELEMENTS

If a trial is a persuasive story, the opening statement is the attorney's first opportunity to tell the whole story without distraction or interruption. Not until final argument will counsel again be able to speak directly to the jury. All other communication will be filtered through the awkward, and often opaque, process of witness examination. If your theory is to be presented in its entirety, opening statement is the time to do it. Because of the conventions that control the content and form of the opening statement, it is particularly important to pay careful attention to its structure and elements.

A. Communicate Your Theory

The single most important rule concerning opening statements is to present a coherent theory of the case. You will, of course, have developed such a theory in your pretrial preparation, since no case can be won without one. The challenge now is to communicate it clearly, succinctly, and persuasively.

Recall that a trial theory is the adaptation of a factual story to the legal issues in the case. Your theory must contain a simple, logical, provable account of facts which, when viewed in light of the controlling law, will lead to the conclusion that your client should win. In short, you will want to use the opening statement to explain to the jury why the verdict should be in your favor.

A successful theory will be built around a persuasive story. Ideally, such a story will be told about people who have reasons for the way they act; it will explain all of the known or undeniable facts; it will be told by credible witnesses; it will be supported by details; and it will accord with common sense. Thus, your opening statement should, at some point and in some manner, address all of these elements:

What happened? The crucial events in your story will be the ones that speak to the legal elements of your claim or defense. If you represent the plaintiff in a tort case, your opening statement should contain sufficient facts from which a conclusion can be drawn that the defendant was negligent. The defendant's opening, on the other hand, should emphasize facts pointing toward his own caution or the plaintiff's fault.

Why did it happen? It is not sufficient to list the facts. A story is most persuasive when it explains why events occurred as they did. It is particularly important to explain why individuals acted as they did, since a compelling reason for an action will tend to rule out or negate alternative possibilities. For example, you may explain that the defendant in a collision case was driving slowly and carefully just before the accident. This story will be more persuasive if it can be supported with a reason. Perhaps she was returning from an antique auction, carrying an expensive and fragile chandelier in her back seat. Obviously, then, she would be inclined to be more than normally cautious. Her reason for driving slowly not only supports her version of events, but it also makes less likely a claim by the plaintiff that she careened around a corner at high speed.

Which witnesses should be believed? Trials almost always revolve around conflicting testimony,[2] with one set of witnesses supporting the plaintiff's theory and another supporting the defendant's. It is improper to argue the credibility of witnesses in your opening statement, but you may, and should, provide the jury with facts that bolster your own witnesses and detract from the opposition's. While too much background can easily clutter your opening statement and distract the jury, positive information — such as education, community ties, and family responsibility — should be provided to humanize your key witnesses. Bias, motive, prejudice, and interest in the outcome of the case are always relevant to a witness's believability. Explain the facts that demonstrate your own witnesses' lack of bias; include as well the facts that demonstrate the motive or interest of the opposition. For example:

> Two experts will testify as to the cause of the fire. The plaintiff will call Fire Chief Olson, who will testify that he investigated the fire as part of his normal professional duties. Chief Olson concluded that the fire was accidental. He was not paid by either of the parties. He was simply doing his job. The defendant's expert is Dr. Jane Larson. She does not work for the city or the state; she is a private investigator. All of her income is derived from private clients. She was hired by the defendant to reach an opinion about the cause of the fire in this case, and she was paid $110 an hour to do so. She will testify that the fire was caused by arson.

How can we be sure? As should be apparent from the examples above, the persuasiveness of an opening statement, indeed the persuasiveness of virtually any aspect of a trial, is often established through the use of details. Broad assertions can stake out territory and raise issues, but it is most often the details upon which the truth will be determined. An essential element of an opening statement, then, is the judicious use of details in support of the accuracy, dependability, or believability of your facts.

Does it all make sense? Finally, the theory you present in opening, or at any other point in the trial, must make sense when it is measured against the everyday experiences of the jurors. The provision of reasons, biases, or details, no matter how compelling they are to your way of thinking, will accomplish nothing if the jurors cannot place them into a context that they understand and accept. It is meaningless to suggest that a witness should be believed because she received an

---

2   It is sometimes the case that none of the testimony is in conflict, and that the jury is required only to determine the legal consequences of undisputed facts. These situations are relatively rare. Even when they do occur, the jury may be called upon to determine the relative weight to be given to certain witnesses' testimony. For example, personal injury cases in which liability is clear are often submitted to the jury solely on the issue of damages. In these cases there will often be no testimony contradicting the plaintiff's injury, but the jury will still have to decide how much weight, which is to say credibility, to give to the plaintiff's rendition of damages.

"A" on her contracts exam in law school. Although that detail may make her praiseworthy in some eyes, it is not a common sense indicator of honesty.

B. Communicate Your Theme

Your trial theme, as distinct from your theory, should be expressed in a single sentence that captures the moral force of your case. A theme communicates to the jury the reason that your client deserves to win. Thus, introducing a theme in opening is particularly effective as a persuasive matter, since it can focus the jury's attention on a cognitive image that you will return to throughout the trial.

Nonetheless, using a theme in your opening statement presents some difficulty. Unlike a trial theory, a theme is intended to reflect upon or interpret the evidence, rather than simply to describe or outline it. Overuse or constant repetition of your theme may bring you perilously close to argument. Most judges, however, will allow the statement of a theme at both the beginning and end of an opening statement, especially when it is phrased in terms of fact, as opposed to opinion or characterization.

One possible theme for the plaintiff in the fire engine case is that the defendant was "too busy to be careful." This theme can be used at the beginning of the opening as a reference point for the information about the defendant's course of conduct on the morning of the accident:

Ladies and Gentlemen, this is a case about a driver who was too busy to be careful. On the morning of the accident he woke up late. He had to be at an important meeting downtown that morning, and he had less than an hour left in which to get there.

Although there is a sense in which "too busy to be careful" is a conclusion, it is used here solely as an introduction to the facts that follow. Moreover, it is a conclusion of the sort that the rules of evidence generally allow lay persons to draw. Busyness and carefulness are ordinary incidents of life that are easily recognized without questionable inferences. Therefore, the theme "too busy to be careful" can almost certainly be invoked at the outset of the plaintiff's opening statement.

On the other hand, it is possible to conceive of a theme that is too tendentious for use in opening. Perhaps the plaintiff wants to use the theme that "the defendant had no business being on the road." This phrase is entirely judgmental. It will not clarify or elucidate whatever facts may follow, as it is aimed strictly at invoking moral condemnation. While we all probably share a common understanding of what it means to be busy, no similar uniform meaning can be attributed to "no business being on the road." In closing argument it will be perfectly appropriate to argue that the defendant had no business being on the road, but the phrase goes too far for use in an opening statement.

C. Utilize Primacy

The principle of primacy posits that in all aspects of a trial a jury will remember best those things that they hear first. The opening statement therefore provides a double opportunity to utilize primacy. The first few minutes of your opening statement constitute the "beginning of the beginning," and therefore have the potential to be among the most memorable moments of the trial. Put them to good use.

It is essential not to waste your opening moments on trivia or platitudes. Get right to the point. State your theme. Explain the most important part of your theory. Lay the groundwork for a crucial direct or cross examination. Foreshadow your closing argument. Above all, do not spend your most precious minutes meandering through a civics-class exposition on the virtues of the American jury system.

In the fire engine case, the plaintiff might want to open something like this:

This is a case about a defendant who was too busy to be careful. Because he failed to stop for a fire truck, he smashed his car right into the back of the plaintiff's automobile. The fire truck was flashing its lights and sounding its siren. All of the other drivers noticed the fire truck and stopped. Except the defendant. He had his mind on an important meeting, so he kept on driving until it was too late. Now the plaintiff will never take another step without feeling pain. Let me tell you exactly what happened.

The above opening is direct and to the point. It states theory and theme right at the outset, and launches immediately into the facts that support the plaintiff's case. The three central points that the plaintiff will make are all mentioned: The fire truck was clearly visible, all of the other traffic stopped, but the defendant was preoccupied and caused the accident.

Contrast the following example on behalf of the defendant:

I am the attorney for the defendant, who is seated with me here at counsel table. On the defendant's left is my co-counsel. It is now our opportunity to present our opening statement. Because the evidence at trial may be introduced in a disjointed fashion, an opening statement can serve as a road map to help you understand the evidence. Imagine, if you will, the picture on the cover of a jigsaw puzzle: it helps you put together the pieces inside. And that is what I would like to do now.

The plaintiff's opening moment is obviously more persuasive. While the defendant has done a reasonably good job of explaining the philosophy behind allowing openings, the plaintiff has begun establishing her case.

There might be some argument for the defendant's approach if there were truly some possibility that the jury would not understand an opening statement without the explanatory metaphors. In fact, the opposite is true. The picture on the cover of a jigsaw puzzle is self-explanatory; everyone knows why it is there. You will never see a paragraph on the cover of the box explaining why the puzzlemaker provided you with a picture. In fact, you might worry about the puzzle if there was such an explanation.

Not all platitudes need to be excluded from the opening statement. There is a place in every lawyer's repertoire for a little schmaltz about the virtues of the jury system. You may wish to introduce your client and co-counsel, if the judge hasn't already done so. You might even want to say a few words about the relationship between the opening statement and the rest of the trial. It is not at all wrong to do any of these things. Just don't do them first.

Two principles can guide your selection of material for the beginning of the opening statement: impact and relationship.

Impact. Your opening statement should begin with the information that you hope will have the greatest impact on the jury. What facts most support a verdict in your favor? What issues will be most hotly contested? Which witness will you rely upon the most? Choose the point that you most hope the jury will take with them when they retire to deliberate.

Relationship. There will be many important evidentiary facts in most trials. Since you will want the jury to remember them all, it may be difficult to decide just which ones to begin with. This decision can be made easier if, in addition to impact, you consider the relationship of the information to some other aspect of the trial. Will the testimony of your key witness be attacked? Will you need to undermine or impeach the testimony of an opposition witness? Will your closing argument rely upon certain inferences or conclusions? You can use the first moments of your opening statement to begin developing the points to which you intend to return.

D. Utilize Issues

Your case can be only as persuasive as the theory behind it, and your theory can only be persuasive if it ties the evidence to the legal issues. Your opening statement, then, must address the legal issues in your case. Ultimately, the jury will not be asked to conclude whether a particular witness is a good person or whether events occurred in a certain order. Such decisions may be reached along the way, but they are only important to the extent that they affect the actual verdict in the case. Defense counsel may do a stunning job of convincing the jury that the plaintiff is foolish or forgetful, but she will lose her case unless she also persuades them that the defendant was not negligent.

It is imperative, therefore, that your opening statement explain to the jury why your facts are important to their decision. Although a statement of importance may seem to approach argument, recall that the opening statement's purpose is to assist the jury in understanding the evidence. A serial presentation of facts, no matter how beautifully organized or well delivered, cannot be understood clearly without some mention of the purpose for which the evidence will be offered. Accordingly, it would be unusual for a judge to disallow a reasonable explanation of the issues toward which the evidence is directed.

Assuming that the fire engine case is being tried in a comparative negligence jurisdiction, the defense may want to show that the plaintiff was partially at fault for the accident. The opening statement could simply list a set of facts that comprise the plaintiff's contribution to the accident, and hope that the jury draws the right conclusion: the plaintiff didn't pull over; the plaintiff's brake lights were not working; and, although she claims otherwise, the plaintiff may not have been wearing her glasses. It will be more persuasive, however, and truly more helpful to the jury, if the opening first explains the import of the evidence:

> One issue in this case is whether the plaintiff herself contributed to the accident. You see, even if the defendant was negligent in some way, the law still asks whether the plaintiff was partially at fault as well. And if she was at fault, then any damages would have to be reduced. The evidence will definitely show that the plaintiff was at fault. When she saw the fire truck she slammed on her brakes, right in the middle of the road. She didn't pull over to the side. She didn't leave a clear lane for the car that was immediately behind her. That made it impossible for the following driver, my client, to avoid the accident. Furthermore, her brake lights weren't working on the day of the accident. She knew that they weren't working, but she hadn't gotten around to getting them fixed. So when she slammed on her brakes, my client had no way of knowing that she was going to make a sudden stop, instead of pulling over into the parking lane.

The statement of the law is an acceptable part of this opening statement because it is correct, neutral, and closely related to the facts that follow. It is helpful because it focuses attention on the import of the facts concerning the plaintiff's driving. The evidence is going to be offered not to show that the plaintiff was generally a poor driver, but rather to show exactly how she contributed to the accident in this case.

Note, by the way, that the excerpt above does not include the disputed fact that the plaintiff wasn't wearing her glasses. Once the legal issue is used as a preface for the evidence, it becomes obvious that the plaintiff's absent glasses are not essential to the defendant's theory of the case. The defendant's theory is that the plaintiff stopped too quickly, not that she failed to see the fire truck or react in time. Therefore, the claim of missing glasses, a fact that surely would be included in any rote rendition of the negative evidence, becomes expendable. Counsel can omit the disputed, and perhaps unprovable, fact from her opening statement.

Cognitive theory suggests that a jury will seldom deliberate to a conclusion on each discreet fact presented at trial. Rather, the jurors typically will attend to a series of "turning points" or crucial issues. Opening statements stand to be most effective when they anticipate these turning points and therefore comprise issue-oriented discussion of the facts.

E. Utilize the Evidence, Don't Just Display It

There is a world of difference between utilizing evidence and merely displaying it. Displaying evidence is a vice most common to unprepared or disorganized lawyers, and it is frequently the result of insufficient attention to theory and analysis. While no diligent attorney would intentionally use the opening statement to list a series of facts in a purely random order, many lawyers are attracted to the allure of some seemingly natural organization. Such reference to an external guideline, chronology being the most common, is not utilization of the evidence, since the organizing principle is something independent of the client's position. Utilization of the evidence, however, involves the purposeful ordering of the facts, as we have discussed above, in the manner most supportive of counsel's theory of the case.

1. The Problem with Natural Organization

"Natural" organization can be seductive. It is easy to organize an opening statement on a "witness-by-witness" basis. It is comfortable to organize an opening statement according to chronology. Ultimately, however, both of these methods may result in nothing more than a display of the evidence, rather than a structure that is most persuasive under the circumstances. There is no law of nature that says that obvious principles are the most convincing, or even the most understandable. An advocate defaults in her duty if she allows the accident of witness observation or the serendipitous occurrence of events to replace dynamic organization and analysis.

a. Avoid witness summaries

The "witness-by-witness" approach, in particular, is to be avoided. It is a mystery why many lawyers think that they can help the jury understand the case by naming all of the witnesses and outlining the expected testimony of each. Recall that the very purpose of the opening statement, indeed its underlying justification, is to overcome the disjointed fashion in which the witnesses will produce evidence at trial. Witness-by-witness rendition of the facts is unlikely to produce a coherent story when the witnesses take the stand and testify for themselves. This method of organization becomes no more helpful simply because a lawyer has substituted a summary of the testimony for the actual direct and cross examinations.

Imagine that plaintiff's counsel in the fire engine case opted for the "witness" approach in her opening statement:[3]

> Ladies and gentlemen, you will hear a number of witnesses testify in this case. Let me tell you about some of them.
>
> The plaintiff will testify that on the morning of the accident she was driving south on Sheridan Road. As she approached the intersection of Sheridan and Touhy, she saw a fire truck approaching from the west. It was flashing its lights and sounding its siren, so she applied her brakes and stopped her car immediately. Suddenly, another car, driven by the defendant, crashed into her from behind.
>
> Bonnie Middleton was a firefighter on Engine Number 7 on the day of the accident. She will tell you that the weather was clear and dry that day. She will also describe the call that her engine company received and the fact that they followed their standard procedure when they left the firehouse — flashing their lights and sounding their siren. The fire engine headed east on Touhy, in the direction of Sheridan Road.
>
> You will also hear from Nate Lipton. Nate is an auto mechanic. He will testify that just a week before the accident the defendant came into Nate's garage for some repair work. Nate advised the defendant to have his brakes relined, but the defendant was too busy. He left without having the brake job done.

The drawback of this method should be readily apparent. Even though the information attributed to each of the above witnesses was intentionally abbreviated, the opening statement quickly became boring and hard to follow. In a real opening statement it would be necessary to flesh out the anticipated testimony in greater detail, resulting in an even more protracted, and less compelling, narrative. Moreover, as the number of witnesses increases, the disjointed nature of the opening would increase as well. As hard as it is to continue to pay attention to short descriptions of three witnesses, it would be that much harder to pay attention to longer renditions of six, ten, or more.

A still greater problem with the witness approach, however, is that it obstructs counsel's ability to develop a theory of the case. Your theory will seldom depend upon which witness provides a particular piece of information,[4] but it will always

---

3   The vignette that follows is intentionally truncated in the interest of readability. A real opening statement would obviously contain longer versions of each witness's anticipated testimony. This version, however, contains sufficient information to make the necessary point about use of the witness-by-witness approach.

4   There will be circumstances in which it *is* important which witness testifies to a particular fact. This situation is considered in Section IV B(6), *infra* at p. 366.

depend upon how the various facts fit together. In the scenario above, the witness-oriented fragmentation of the story makes it impossible for the attorney to explain, or even intimate, the relationship between the presence of the fire truck and the poor condition of the defendant's brakes. While clever jurors will no doubt be able to intuit a connection, the job of the advocate is not to leave such constructions to chance. Consider the following alternative:[5]

> The weather was clear and dry on the morning of the accident. Fire Engine Company Number 9 received a call to respond to a fire, and the crew boarded their truck and left the firehouse, headed east on Touhy toward Sheridan Road. In keeping with standard procedure, they sounded their siren and flashed their lights from the moment that they left the station. At that same time, the plaintiff was driving south on Sheridan. As she approached the intersection with Touhy, she saw and heard the fire truck, so she immediately applied her brakes. She had plenty of time to stop. The defendant, whose car was directly behind hers, didn't stop. At one point he slammed on his brakes, but it was too late. As hard as he hit his brakes, it did not keep him from crashing right into the plaintiff's car. You should know that the defendant's brakes were not in good repair. Only a week before he had taken his car in for some work. The mechanic told him that his brakes needed relining, but he declined to have the work done. It was less than seven days later when those same brakes proved not to be good enough to stop his car and prevent what has turned out to be a lifetime of pain for my client.

This story is far more cohesive than the witness-based account. It brings all of the vehicles together at the fateful intersection, without the necessity of the jurors having to keep a running account of their whereabouts. It connects the fire engine's use of lights and siren directly to the cause of the accident. Finally, it shows that the defendant might have been able to stop his car, but for the poor maintenance of his brakes. In other words, this approach to the opening statement takes what would otherwise be a nasty, but isolated, fact about the defendant, and transforms it into a key supporting element of the plaintiff's theory of the case.

b. Be wary of chronology

Chronology is an obvious, natural, and often useful organizing technique for opening statements. All events in the real world, after all, occur in chronological order. Moreover, we are all used to thinking of life in chronological terms. It is for this very reason, in fact, that opening statements have become part of the trial: to allow lawyers to take individual witness accounts and meld them into a single chronological narrative.

---

5   This vignette is also abbreviated. An actual opening statement would contain more facts, but all of the essentials are contained in this scenario.

Still, it is all too easy, and sometimes counterproductive, automatically to allow chronology to establish the organization of an opening statement. Simply because events occurred in a certain order is not a sufficient reason to present them that way to a jury. This is especially the case when your story involves simultaneous, or nearly simultaneous, events that took place in different locations.

i. The drawbacks of chronology

In the fire truck case, for instance, a strict chronology might begin with the time that the plaintiff left her home. The defendant probably left his home shortly thereafter, and the fire engine left the station last of all. None of this ordering should matter to either party's story, however, since the only important fact is their concurrent arrival at the fateful intersection. While it may not undermine either opening statement to detail the order in which the vehicles departed, it will certainly clutter the stories with useless, and perhaps confusing, details.

Chronology can also interfere with the logical exposition of your theory. The plaintiff's theory in the fire truck case is that she stopped for the fire engine, as required by law, but the defendant did not. The defendant was at fault because he was preoccupied and failed to keep a proper lookout. Perhaps he was speeding, and perhaps his brakes performed inadequately due to poor maintenance. The various elements of this theory both precede and follow the accident itself. For example, the defendant woke up late before the collision, but he ran to the phone to cancel his meeting after the collision. Both of these facts directly support the theory that the defendant was in a hurry that morning. Even though they occurred at different times, they can have more impact if they are presented together.

Similarly, consider the importance of the defendant's failure to have his brakes repaired. If the opening statement were presented in strict chronology, that fact would be introduced to the jury before they had any way to measure its importance. Of course, no matter when the jury hears it, it sounds bad for the defendant to have ignored a warning about his brakes. But a chronological recitation will separate this fact from the moment of the accident, thus requiring the jury to reach back in their memories in order to recall its importance.

The brake story is most persuasive when it is added to the events of the accident, not when it precedes them. Presented first, the brakes story, at best, will evoke curiosity: "I wonder why that will turn out to be important?" Presented after the account of the accident the brake story should result in understanding: "Oh, so that is why he didn't stop in time." As an advocate, you should almost always prefer to have the jury understand your theory, rather than wonder about it.

ii. The uses of chronology

Despite the drawbacks mentioned above, the judicious use of chronology is an essential part of every opening statement.

Chronological development should always be used to explain independent events. Every trial can be understood as a series of sub-events, which fit together to comprise the entire story. The order of these sub-events is always open to manipulation by counsel. The sub-events themselves, however, have their own internal logic, which generally can be understood only when explained chronologically.

The fire engine case provides an excellent illustration of this principle. The plaintiff's case consists of at least the following four sub-events: (1) the collision itself; (2) the defendant's hurried morning; (3) the defendant's failure to repair his brakes; and (4) the fire department's policy of always sounding the siren on a vehicle that is responding to a call. These four elements, and of course there may be others, can be arranged in a variety of ways to make the case more persuasive. Once the overall structure has been determined, however, it will make most sense, as you reach each individual component, to detail it chronologically. Suppose that plaintiff's counsel has decided to organize her opening statement in the same order that the sub-events are given above. After going through the facts of the accident in the same sequence in which they occurred, she would proceed to develop the secondary components by relying upon the chronology of each one:

> Why didn't the defendant stop, when all of the other traffic did? We know that he woke up late that morning, and that he had an important meeting to attend downtown, which was scheduled to begin only slightly over an hour later. By the time he washed and shaved, and went to the garage where his car was parked, he only had twenty minutes left to get to his meeting. It was eleven miles from his home to his office. As he headed south on Sheridan Road, every delay made him that much later for his meeting.

> By the time he got to the corner of Sheridan and Touhy he only had 12 minutes or so before his meeting was to start, yet he still had eight miles to go. We know that the fire truck was already at that corner, flashing its lights and sounding its siren. There is no evidence that the defendant intentionally ignored the fire truck, but he obviously didn't respond to it in time. Although at some point he hit his breaks, he still went crashing into the back of my client's car.

> Was there something wrong with the defendant's brakes? Could he have stopped in time if they had been working better? We know that just a week before the accident he had his car in for servicing. The mechanic advised him to have his brakes relined, but the defendant

decided not to take the time to have the repair work done. He left the garage without having his brakes fixed.

We also know that the fire truck gave the defendant plenty of warning. It was flashing its lights and sounding its siren. We know this because it has always been strict fire department policy to use these warning signals whenever an engine is responding to a call. And so it was that day. Engine Number 9 was responding to a call, so, as one of the firefighters will tell you herself, the lights and siren were being used with full force.

Note, by the way, the reference to the testimony of the firefighter in the paragraph about the fire truck's lights and siren. Even though the story is not being presented in a witness-by-witness fashion, it will often be helpful to refer to the source of certain evidence, particularly when you know that it will be disputed. This technique will be developed at greater length below.[6]

Although the sub-events as units are presented out of chronology, internally each one is detailed basically as it occurred. The result of this approach is that the jury will be able to understand the context of the entire story, as well as the precise nature of the individual occurrences that comprise the story.

2. Using Details Persuasively

As we have seen, the utilization of evidence in an opening statement depends upon the persuasive arrangement of major propositions and supporting details. While the application of this approach will vary tremendously from case to case, the following few generalizations should prove helpful:

a. Big ideas, then details

As a general rule, an opening statement should be organized as a series of big ideas, each of which is immediately supported by persuasive details.

As we have discussed above, jurors will tend to resolve a case on the basis of certain turning points or crucial issues. Details can be marshaled to make your version of these turning points more persuasive. For example, one major issue in the fire truck case will be whether or not the engine was sounding its siren just before the accident. If the jury decides that there was a siren, it will be more likely to bring back a plaintiff's verdict; if there was no siren, then the defendant has a better chance. Thus, the use of the siren is a turning point in the trial. The plaintiff's position on this issue can be made more likely through the addition of details: the fire truck was responding to a call; there is a departmental policy to use the siren

---

6   *See* Section III E(2), *infra* at p. 356.

whenever responding to a call; the driver of the truck was an experienced firefighter, well aware of the policy; other motorists stopped their cars.[7]

The details, however, have little meaning when offered on their own. They become important only in light of the turning point on which they are offered. The fact that the fire truck was responding to a call doesn't tell us anything about the way that the accident happened, but it does tell us that the truck was almost certainly using its siren. In the same vein, the jury will have no reason to care about the experience level of the fire truck driver, until it is first informed that the use of the siren is an issue in the case. It is for this reason that details are best used to follow up or support the initial explication of a bigger idea.

b. Weave in the witnesses

While the witness-by-witness approach is unlikely to result in an effective opening statement, this does not mean that individual witnesses should not be mentioned in the course of your opening. To the contrary, it is often quite important to inform the jury of the source of a specific fact or the precise nature of some anticipated testimony. The key is to weave the information about the witnesses into the narrative, so that the witness references arise in the context of your theory of the case.

As we have been discussing, the use of the siren is likely to be a turning point in our fire truck case. The plaintiff says that there was a siren, and the defendant says that there was not. The plaintiff's opening statement can bolster her position by weaving in witness information when her narrative reaches the siren issue:

> Just as she reached the intersection, the plaintiff saw and heard an approaching fire truck. It was sounding its siren and flashing its lights. We know that the siren was operating because Lieutenant Bonnie Middleton, the driver of the fire truck, will testify that she always sounds the siren when she is answering a call. That is fire department policy, and Lieutenant Middleton is a decorated firefighter who has been with the department for over ten years. Perhaps, for whatever reason, the defendant didn't hear the siren, but Lieutenant Middleton will testify that she is certain that she was doing her official duty — that is, using her audio and visual alarms — on the day when the accident occurred.

Used in this manner, the information about Lieutenant Middleton corroborates and strengthens the plaintiff's theory of the case. It neither stands alone, as an isolated description of the witness, nor does it interfere with the flow of the

---

7 In the absence of details, the "siren question" would simply be a matter of the plaintiff's word against the defendant's. Note, then, that one value of the details is that they add persuasive force to the plaintiff's theory without relying upon her own credibility. This, in turn, makes the plaintiff all the more credible, since her version of events is supported by objective facts.

narrative. Rather, it adds unapologetic support to the plaintiff's theory at the precise moment when support is likely to be most readily understood.

c. Raise credibility when it counts

Once the witnesses have been woven into the narrative, a question still remains as to when and how to deal with their credibility. Although the non-argument rule prevents counsel from commenting directly on the believability of a witness, this point can still be made quite handily through the use of attributive details. It would be an error, however, to attend to the reliability of every witness whom you mention in your opening statement.

In reality, the veracity of most witnesses is unlikely to be challenged. Building up a witness whom no one is likely to tear down will only add verbiage to your opening statement, and therefore violates the "anti-clutter" principle. Worse, by engaging in unnecessary damage control you run the risk of actually damaging the credibility of the witness whom you are attempting to endorse.

Conversely, it is also problematic to use your opening statement to attack the credibility of a witness who has not yet testified. It is a natural instinct to want to give someone the benefit of the doubt, and in the absence of the person whose integrity you are trying to impugn you may give the impression of being disingenuous or unfair.

This is not to say that the credibility of witnesses should never be addressed in opening statements, but rather that the issue generally should be raised overtly only in fairly narrow circumstances. Passing comments on credibility typically present no problem when they are positive in nature. Plaintiff's remark that the fire truck driver was an experienced firefighter, for example, was short enough not to constitute clutter and reasonable enough not to undercut the witness. Note, however, that throwaway lines that are negative in character may still seem catty, or worse. If you are going to say something bad about someone, it is usually best to say it directly.

In any event, extended treatment of credibility is usually best left to situations where a witness is likely to be challenged, or where some item of evidence is seriously in dispute.

A plaintiff who expects one of her witnesses to be attacked should consider doing some advance work to establish the witness's credibility. Once the jury has been given a reason to trust a witness, it will be more difficult for the other side to damage him. There is some risk to this, of course, since the anticipated assault may never actually materialize. Moreover, this is a tricky subject to introduce without damning the witness through faint praise. It won't help your opening statement, much less your case, to announce that "some people consider this witness to be a liar, but we will prove that he is as honest as the day is long."

Advance accreditation of a witness, then, should be accomplished in as positive a manner as possible. Humanize the witness. Give the jury a chance to come to like the witness. Explain the witness's many fine qualities. Likable people are more apt to be accepted as truthful, even after negative information has been offered by the other side. Thus, the best defense to an anticipated attack, and certainly the first method to consider, is to build up the witness without any reference to the way you expect him to be maligned. Let it come as an unpleasant surprise when opposing counsel starts taking the low road against the perfectly reasonable witness you have described.[8]

On the other hand, defense counsel should almost always rise to the defense of a witness who has been disparaged during the plaintiff's opening. Particularly where you intend to rely on the witness's testimony to establish an element of your case, it is important not to allow an attack to go unanswered. If you do not defend your witness, the jury may very well infer that he is indefensible. You will have lost important ground before the testimony has even begun.

The defense of a witness's credibility need not consist of a point-by-point refutation of any charges made by the other side, although false charges certainly should be rebutted or denied. It may, however, be more effective simply to use your opening to paint a contrary picture of the witness. Consider this response in a situation where plaintiff's attorney has accused a key defense witness of shading his testimony to help out a friend:

> Plaintiff's counsel said some really nasty things about Mr. Alexander. I don't want to dignify them by repeating them, and I am not going to name-call any of the plaintiff's own witnesses. The actual evidence in this case, though, is going to show that Mr. Alexander is responsible, dependable, and honest. He was born and raised right here in town. He graduated from State University with a degree in education, and he has been a teacher ever since. Mr. Alexander works ten hours a day in an inner city school, trying to help kids get a better chance in life. At 3:30 when the other teachers go home, Kenny Alexander stays late supervising the drama program. On weekends he tutors kids who need some extra help. He has been named teacher of the year four different times. Kenny Alexander didn't ask to be involved in this case, he just happened to be a witness. Sure, he's a friend of the defendant's, but Kenny will tell you, that couldn't possibly affect his testimony. You'll see and hear Ken Alexander, and you can judge plaintiff's charges for yourselves.

---

8   The issue of whether your opening statement should address negative facts about your own witnesses is discussed in Section IV D, *infra* at p. 372.

The charge of biased testimony is difficult to refute. No contrary facts can be presented, and the claim only stands to be strengthened by descent into an "is so/is not" sort of confrontation. The best approach, therefore, is often to explain why the witness couldn't possibly testify to anything but the truth.

Finally, where the trial involves seriously conflicting issues of fact, it is important to use the opening statement to stress the superior credibility of your own witnesses. In the fire truck case, for instance, the use of the siren might be a significant factual dispute. The plaintiff could deal with the question this way:

> The plaintiff heard the fire truck's siren and immediately stopped her car. The defendant has claimed that there was no siren. But you don't need to rely on the plaintiff alone in order to resolve this dispute. Lieutenant Bonnie Middleton will testify that she was using her siren as she always did. Lieutenant Middleton has been with the fire department for over a decade. She has no interest in this case one way or another, but she has received numerous commendations for her excellent work as a firefighter. She teaches courses at the departmental academy, and she was the first woman in the entire state to be promoted to the rank of lieutenant.

If there were no question about the siren it would not be necessary to go into Lieutenant Middleton's background. The factual dispute, however, gives added importance to enhancing her credibility.

IV. CONTENT

The range of triable subjects being virtually limitless, is it possible to define what goes into a good opening statement? Of course, every good opening statement, no matter what the case, contains enough information to help you win the trial, but not so much as to distract the jury or risk exploitation by the other side. The following considerations should be helpful in most trials.

A. True and Provable

Every fact that you include in your opening statement must be true and provable. We have already seen that the law limits opening statements to a preview of the evidence that will be presented once the trial begins. It is not enough, however, that some witness may be willing to make a certain statement. The ethics of our profession require that we never knowingly be involved in presenting false evidence. This stricture applies not only to offering testimony, but also to outlining the case during the opening statement.

As we discussed earlier, the concept of truth takes a very specific form in the context of the adversary system. Since the jury, or judge, is assigned the role of deciding the truth of facts, counsel is generally obligated only to present one competing version of events. An attorney does not need to subject potential witnesses to a polygraph examination, or be convinced of a witness's truthfulness beyond a reasonable doubt. The attorney may not, however, present evidence known to be fraudulent. Stated conversely, while you needn't be persuaded to a moral certainty, you must have some reasonable basis for believing a fact to be true before you can offer it from the witness stand or use it during your opening statement. It does not matter how good it makes the story, it does not matter how well it fits your theory of the case, it does not matter how incontrovertible your position might be: no fact may be used in an opening statement unless it meets the "not knowingly false" test of validity.

Conversely, even assuredly true facts should not be used in an opening statement until they have been subjected to the test of provability. While there may occasionally be reasons to depart from this principle, you should, as a general rule, omit from your opening statement any fact that you are not certain you will be able to prove at trial.

An opening statement is in many ways a promise to the jury. By making a definitive statement about the future evidence, you have committed yourself to produce that evidence. If your witnesses turn out to be less conclusive than your opening statement, you may seem at best to have overstated your case. At worst, you may seem deliberately to have misled the jury. The same thing can happen when promised evidence fails to materialize, either because the court declines to admit it or because it turns out to be unavailable. Even if the jury doesn't immediately realize that there has been a gap between your opening and your proof, you can be certain that opposing counsel will point it out during final argument.

1. Your Central Evidence

Your strongest evidence should generally occupy pride of place in your opening statement. The central evidence will be a combination of: (1) the facts most essential to your case, and (2) the facts least likely to be disputed.

In the fire truck case it is central to the plaintiff's position to prove that she did indeed stop for a fire engine. The opening statement, if it does nothing else, must firmly establish in the jury's mind the presence of the truck and its use of its warning signals. Even if these facts will be disputed, they must be developed in the opening statement because the plaintiff cannot win without them.

Additionally, the plaintiff's opening statement should make liberal use of undisputed evidence, even if it is not absolutely necessary to the case. The plaintiff can win the fire truck case without proving that the defendant was in a hurry. On the other hand, many of the specifics of the defendant's rushed morning cannot be controverted, which obviously makes them all the more persuasive. Thus, the plaintiff should be sure to include facts such as the time and importance of the defendant's business meeting that morning, the distance from his home to his office, the route that he had to drive, his parking arrangements, and his dash to the phone booth immediately after the collision.

2. Questionable Evidence

How strong or central must evidence be in order to gain a place in your opening statement? What should you do with evidence of dubious admissibility?

For the purpose of inclusion in your opening statement, or for later use at trial for that matter, you can regard all of your evidence as having two predominant attributes: necessity and provability. Each of these qualities, in turn, can be imagined as a continuum. The necessity level of any item of evidence can range from absolute to basically dispensable. Provability will vary to the same extent. The higher a necessity value that you assign to any fact, the less provability is required for including it in your opening statement. By the same token, evidence that is more provable can be less essential.

Note, however, that every opening statement is limited in time; you can't, and shouldn't, use everything. Thus, for both aspects of evidence there is a point of diminishing return. Remotely provable facts should generally be omitted no matter how important they might turn out to be. Facts only tangentially related to your theory of the case should also be left out, no matter how unquestionable they are.

Many lawyers believe that counsel should always err on the side of excluding information from the opening statement, particularly when the issue is admissibility. Why risk promising something that you will not be able to deliver? Even if you present your opening without the questionable evidence, you will still be able to offer it at trial. If it turns out to be admitted you can make full use of it during the closing argument. This approach quite clearly minimizes the risk that your opening statement will backfire.

Some attorneys, however, are of the view that such risk aversion leads to unnecessary self-censorship. By purging your opening statement of everything that is subject to objection, you may lose the opportunity to tell the most coherent and complete story possible. Furthermore, notwithstanding your own doubts, opposing counsel may decide not to object to the evidence in question. Then you will have excluded it from your opening statement for no reason at all. Attorneys who take this position therefore place primary emphasis on the importance of the evidence, and correspondingly less value on the likelihood of its eventual admission.

At this point in the discussion, two caveats are absolutely necessary. First, it is unethical to use an opening statement to discuss evidence for which there is no reasonable basis to offer. There is a line to be drawn between evidence that may be subject to objection and that which is obviously inadmissible. While one need not defer in advance to the possibility of an arguable objection, counsel cannot ethically sneak information before a jury where there is no chance of having it properly admitted. It is acceptable to run the risk of inadmissibility, but it is entirely cynical, unacceptable, and wrong to expound clearly inadmissible evidence during an opening statement.

Second, in situations where a motion in limine has been allowed, it is unethical (and perhaps contumacious) to use the opening statement to refer to evidence that has been excluded by the court. The grant of a motion in limine rules out all mention of the evidence, not simply its offer through the testimony of a witness. Many judges also make it a practice to reserve ruling on motions in limine while instructing counsel not to allude to the subject evidence during opening statements.

B. The Operative Facts

The most important part of any opening statement is its treatment of the operative facts. Facts win lawsuits. Everything else — organization, presentation, theme development — must be seen as an aid to communication of the facts of the case.

It goes without saying that there can be no recipe for presenting the facts of a case. Each trial is unique. Some call for delicate innuendo; others may benefit from a frontal assault. Some cases rest heavily on the credibility of witnesses, while others depend on the timing of events. Often, however, the operative facts of a case will include some or all of the following:

1. Action and Key Events

Many cases revolve around one or more actions or key events. Most cases involving personal injury, crimes, medical malpractice, or property damage, to name only a few, require the description of a series of physical occurrences. An earlier section discussed the importance of using chronology to detail a single discrete event, as well as its frequent misuse as a device to outline an entire case.[9] This section addresses other aspects of presenting an account of the key events.

Whether representing the plaintiff or the defendant, it is important to use the opening statement to begin to paint a picture of the events in a way that helps the jury visualize the case from your client's point of view. To do this effectively, you must first have created your own mental image which will, of course, be consistent with the testimony to be given later by your own witnesses. The importance of preparation cannot be overemphasized. You must know precisely how, and in what terms, your witnesses will relate each incident. You must be familiar with all of the physical evidence, and you must, if possible, have visited the site of the events.

---

9   *See* Section III E(1), *supra* at p. 351.

Competent counsel should never risk the possibility of dissonance between the events portrayed in the opening statement and those that emerge from the witnesses' testimony.

In depicting events, nouns and verbs are often more helpful than adjectives and adverbs. This may seem counterintuitive, since we commonly think of modifiers as adding descriptive depth. Consider, however, which of the following accounts is more evocative of the crime. First, a short paragraph that makes maximum use of adverbs and adjectives:

> It was a heinous, horrible crime. The defendant's actions were inhuman and awful. He brutally grabbed at the victim's gold chain, fiercely yanking it away. He left an ugly, ugly bruise on the victim's neck. Unsatisfied with the proceeds of the armed robbery, the defendant then coldly and wantonly stabbed the victim twice, leaving his jacket lying in a bloody heap. It was indeed a cowardly act, taken against a defenseless victim.

Now consider a paragraph with virtually no modifiers at all:

> The defendant placed his knife against the victim's body. Without waiting, he grabbed the gold chain from the victim's neck and wrenched it until it snapped, leaving bruises on the victim's neck that didn't heal for over a week. Although he had already taken what he wanted, he twisted the knife into the victim's shoulder, turning it as he pushed, and watched as the blood welled to the surface. Then he stabbed the victim again, until the blood soaked the jacket all the way through.

The second paragraph is more vivid, not only because of its slightly greater length,[10] but primarily because it describes the deeds as they occurred. In contrast, the first paragraph actually short-circuits the action by substituting value-laden modifiers for an account of the events themselves.

Of course, it would be foolish, if not impossible, to attempt to deliver an opening statement free of modifiers. Adjectives and adverbs are useful precisely because they convey compact meanings. Often they are indispensable. It is impossible to describe a red rubber ball without using the word "red."

Counsel must bear in mind, however, that modifiers frequently stand for judgments rather than for descriptions. Words like heinous, brutal, and awful, or lovely, wonderful, and grand may convey the lawyer's opinion about something, but they do not depict a vision of the events themselves.

---

10 It inevitably takes more words to write without adjectives and adverbs, since one of the functions of a modifier is to compress concepts into a single word.

2. The Physical Scene

The meaning and legal significance of events is often dependent upon their location. Actions that are lawful or innocuous in one locale may become the basis of liability if they occur somewhere else. It is negligent to drive an automobile on the wrong side of the road. It may be an unfair labor practice for management to approach potential union members in their homes. It may violate a zoning ordinance to operate a law practice from one's home. Similarly, the physical details of a particular setting may affect issues such as probability, credibility, or visibility.

It is of great importance, therefore, to use your opening statement to set the scene for major events. While virtually all commentators agree that the scene should be set apart from a description of the action itself, there is divided opinion as to the sequence in which a scene should be described. Many lawyers suggest putting all of the details in place before going on to portray the action. In this way, the jury will already be aware of the physical details as the events unfold. Alternatively, you may describe the action first, and then go back to fill in the specifics of the setting. The theory behind this approach is that the importance of the events should be obvious, but the importance of the details will require some context to become apparent. There is no reason to care about the location of a stop sign until we know that there was a collision in the middle of the intersection.

Setting a scene involves describing a potentially unlimited number of details. It is essential that your opening statement dwell on those details that are significant to your case, while avoiding those that are merely clutter. In the fire truck case, for example, it is important for the plaintiff to note that the pavement was dry, since that would affect the defendant's stopping distance. The height of the curb, however, would be extraneous under virtually any theory of the case.

3. Transactions and Agreements

Most business cases involve written and oral communications far more than they do physical occurrences. In many ways these non-physical events may be more difficult to describe during an opening statement, since there is little or no activity to depict. Nonetheless, when a case turns on the interpretation of a document or the meaning of a series of telephone calls, counsel must search for a way to bring the transaction to life.

The surest way not to bring a business transaction to life is to parse it out in minute chronological detail. It is generally far better to begin at the end. Explain the gist of the agreement, and then go back to fill in only those details that are necessary to support your interpretation. There is no need, for example, to recount every telephone conversation that went into the negotiation of a purchase order. It will usually be sufficient to delineate the terms of the order itself, supported by an account of one or two crucial conversations.

It is not enough, however, simply to recite the terms of an agreement, and then to point out that it was either kept or broken. While such an approach may, in the driest sense, convey your theory, it will not add moral weight to your case. Recall that your trial theme is intended to provide the jury with a reason for wanting to rule in your favor. This can only be done if you are able to explain the "rightness" of your interpretation of the contract. Why were the particular terms so important? Why was your client's reliance on the other party justified? Why will the other party's interpretation lead to chaos and disaster for the entire republic?

4. Business Context

Business context can be crucial to an appreciation of many agreements and transactions. Words may have specialized meanings, or unspoken expectations may be understood by all of the parties. Detailing the business context of a contract or other transaction may be the equivalent of setting the scene for an automobile accident.

Business context can include information on industry practice, course of dealings, production standards, insurability, cost of credit, lines of authority, agency, normal business hours, grievance procedures, and a host of other factors that may form the backdrop for even the simplest transaction.

5. Relationship of the Parties

As much as any physical detail, the past relationship of the parties can speak volumes about the merits of a case. It will add a whole new dimension to a contracts case if it is revealed that there had been a history of misunderstanding between the buyer and the seller. Past animus can be used to show motive or malice. A tradition of reliability, on the other hand, can be used to establish the reasonableness of a party's actions.

6. Motives and Motivations

As we have consistently seen, stories are more persuasive when they are told about people who have reasons for the way they act. An opening statement, therefore, should always attempt to stress the motivations for the parties' actions. The activity that you describe will be far more plausible if, at the same time, you are also able to explain why the people involved acted as they did.

It must be stressed, however, that the opening statement is not the time to speculate about a person's secret motives. The opening statement must develop motive in the same way that it treats everything else — through the preview of evidentiary facts. The rule against argument applies with full force, and probably then some, to the discussion of motive.

Thus, motivation must be carefully established through the use of discrete, incremental facts. You cannot say that the plaintiff is greedy. You can point out five previous occasions on which the plaintiff sued for breach of contract, each one based upon an imperceptible flaw in the goods delivered.

7. Amount of Damages

There are two schools of thought regarding the treatment of damages during the plaintiff's opening statement. One approach is to make the discussion of damages a significant part of the opening, explaining the nature of the injury and the amount that is being sought. The theory here is to acclimate the jury to the fact that the plaintiff will be requesting substantial monetary compensation. Where the amount sought is extremely large, many lawyers believe that it will take some time for the jury to become used to thinking about such big numbers. Thus, they like the process to begin as soon as possible.

Other lawyers believe that damage amounts will have little meaning until the jury actually has heard the evidence. It will be difficult for them to think in terms of awards until they have at least begun to make up their minds about liability. This is thought to be particularly true about big numbers, as it may make the lawyer and client seem greedy to begin talking about large verdicts before any evidence has been introduced. Lawyers who hold this view generally discuss the facts that support damages, but do not mention a specific figure. Note, however, that there is little reason not to state a precise figure for damages in, for example, a commercial case where the amount is liquidated.

Finally, a large majority of defense counsel refrain from discussing damages during the opening statement. Even where the plaintiff's damage figure is inflated or unrealistic, many defense lawyers fear that they will appear to concede liability if they seem to quibble about the amount of damages right at the outset of the case. Some lawyers choose to make only a passing reference to the plaintiff's request, stating something to the effect that, "Even if the defendant was at fault, the evidence will show that the plaintiff's number is far more than would be necessary for fair compensation." Others do not even go this far. Of course, where the defendant has admitted or stipulated to liability, the case will be tried only on the question of damages. Since the amount of compensation is the only issue, the defendant obviously must address it during the opening statement.

C. The Opposition Case

It is always difficult to decide how much attention to give to the opposition case. Plaintiff's counsel must determine whether to anticipate and respond to the expected defenses. Defendant's counsel has to consider whether and how much to react to the plaintiff's opening.

1. Plaintiff's Opening

Unlike final arguments, there is no rebuttal in opening statements. The plaintiff gets to address the jury only once, and without the advantage of knowing what the defendant's opening will be. No matter what defense counsel says, plaintiff's attorney will not be able to respond directly until the end of the trial. This can be especially troublesome in cases where the defendant presents an affirmative defense. Since an affirmative defense, by definition, raises issues that go beyond the plaintiff's own case, the plaintiff faces a delicate problem in dealing with them during the opening statement. Should the plaintiff ignore the affirmative defense, thereby foregoing the opportunity to reply to it at the outset of the trial? Or should the plaintiff respond to the defense in advance, in essence forecasting the defendant's case?

A solution to this problem is to construct the discussion of the plaintiff's own case in such a way as to blunt any rejoinders that the defendant might raise. In a simple automobile accident case, for example, plaintiff's counsel can build up the plaintiff's level of care and skill while driving, without ever mentioning the defense of contributory negligence.

Unfortunately, not all defenses are equally amenable to this approach. Assume, for instance, that you represent the plaintiff in a sales transaction. Your client contracted to sell industrial machinery to the defendant. Your client contends that the goods were shipped, but no payment was received. There are at least three possible defenses: (1) the goods were never received, due to some fault of the plaintiff; (2) they were received, but they were defective; or (3) payment was made.

To negate fully any of these claims, the plaintiff, at a minimum, must refer to the defense itself. Consider the defense of defective products. To be sure, a general statement that the goods conformed to the contract will be sufficient to stake out the plaintiff's position. But a truly persuasive story will require the plaintiff to confront and refute each of the shortcomings asserted by the defense. In the absence of this discussion in the plaintiff's opening, the jury will hear only about what was wrong with the shipment. It is conceivable that plaintiff's counsel might run through every single specification, explaining that the goods conformed across the board, but this itemization could go on forever without informing the jury of the precise issue in dispute. It would make far more sense for the plaintiff to focus her opening statement on exactly the defects claimed by the defendant.

In some cases, then, the plaintiff has little choice but to anticipate the defendant's opening statement. Here are some guidelines:

Your case first. Give primary attention to the strongest aspects of your own case. The opening statement is your opportunity to begin to capture the jury's imagination. Don't get them started imagining the things that might be wrong with your case. Accentuate the positive. To the extent possible, defenses should be treated as technicalities or annoyances.

Be certain. The process of discovery should allow you to know with some certainty exactly which defenses will be raised. There is no reason to survey all of the holes that the defendant might try to punch in your case. Concentrate on the principal defenses.

No apologies, no sneers. When it comes time to discuss the opposition's case, your tone should be firm, unapologetic, and straightforward. If you seem overly concerned or worried about a defense, it will suggest that there are indeed problems with your case. By the same token, you shouldn't sneer or be entirely dismissive; after all, you are the one who is introducing the issue. Moreover, you can't expect the jury to share your disdain for the defendant's position when they haven't even had a chance to hear it yet.

Minimize witness references. There is an inherent difficulty in predicting what the other side's witnesses are going to say. Opening statements are allowed, after all, to allow you to assist the jury by previewing your own evidence. Not having prepared or organized the other side's case, you would be hard put to explain how you can help the jury by guessing at what it might be.

In this vein, it has even been suggested that it is improper for counsel to preview testimony from opposition witnesses. The theory behind this position is that you may only use your opening statement to explain what you expect the evidence to show, and that you cannot be certain what the opposition evidence will be. Given the reality of deposition practice and pretrial orders, however, it is obvious that in most cases you will have a good idea of just how the opposing witnesses will testify. Even if a witness ends up not being called, in most jurisdictions you will have the opportunity to call the witness yourself.

Nonetheless, it is a good idea to refer to the other side's case in summary only, and to avoid direct quotations from their witnesses. There is something discordant about a lawyer predicting how opposing witnesses will testify. Additionally, there is a tremendous chance that, following such an opening, the other side's witnesses will testify differently, if only to spite you. Finally, recall that the purpose of anticipating the defendant's opening statement is to allow you to build up your own case, not to expound on the details of theirs.

There are situations where explicit quotations may be helpful. It can be devastating to read from a document that the defendant produced or to quote directly from the defendant's own deposition. The key to this approach is to be sure (1) that the quotations are accurate, (2) that they are meaningful standing alone and do not require extensive context, and (3) that you have an independent evidentiary basis for introducing them yourself.

Finally, it must be noted that the Fifth Amendment prohibits prosecutors from so much as suggesting that the defendant will testify. The Fifth Amendment does not, however, prevent the prosecutor from reading from a confession or prior statement of the defendant, so long as the statement itself has not been ruled inadmissible.

2. Defendant's Opening

Many lawyers believe that thorough preparation includes planning every word of the opening statement in advance. This is true only to a point. While plaintiffs and prosecutors have the luxury of knowing exactly how they will open their cases, defense lawyers must be more flexible. It is a tremendous advantage to deliver the second opening statement, and defense counsel can only take advantage of this opportunity by being ready to respond to at least some aspects of the plaintiff's opening. No matter how well you have prepared your case, it is a mistake to be tied to a scripted opening statement. Responses or rejoinders to the plaintiff's opening can be fruitful in the following situations:

Denials. The civil plaintiff's opening statement, and even more so the criminal prosecutor's, is essentially an accusation. Its entire thrust is to tell a story that accuses the defendant of negligence, breach of contract, criminal acts, or some other negative conduct. After hearing such an extended charge against the defendant, the jury's first inclination will be to ask the question, "Well, is it true?" The defendant, then, absolutely must respond with a denial. Anything short of a denial is likely to be regarded as evasion, equivocation, or worse, an admission of fault.

While defense counsel can plan to deny the plaintiff's allegations, it can be a mistake to plan exactly *how* to deny them. Generic denials tend to sound exactly like generic denials; they lack force because they do not meet the opposing party head-on. It can be much more effective and persuasive to pick up on the plaintiff's opening and to deny their claims using some of the same language in which they were made.

Care must be taken not to echo the insinuations of the plaintiff's charge. There is no reason to repeat all of the nasty evidence that the plaintiff claims to be able to produce. On the other hand, it is necessary to recognize that the plaintiff has made specific charges, and to explain specifically how they will be rebutted.

This is a poor example of a denial in a defendant's opening statement, because it is too general to carry any weight:

The defendant denies any and all negligence on his part. He denies that he was anything less than a careful driver, and he denies that he caused the plaintiff any harm.

370

This is a worse example because it gives too much credence to the plaintiff's case:

> The plaintiff has claimed that my client was preoccupied with an important business meeting on the morning of the accident. It is their position that he was thinking about how to attract a lucrative new client, instead of paying attention to the road. This is all untrue. We will prove that the accident was the plaintiff's own fault.

This is a better example; it responds directly to the plaintiff's central claim, but it does so by building up the defendant's own case, not by reiterating the plaintiff's:

> Contrary to the plaintiff's claim, my client was anything but "too busy to be careful." We will prove that he was driving well within the legal speed limit and that he was keeping a proper and careful lookout. He had plenty of time to get to his office that morning, but the plaintiff herself stopped her car in the middle of the street, rather than pulling over to the right as the traffic laws require.

Controverted evidence. It is also important to respond directly to the plaintiff's version of significant controverted evidence. Simply telling your own independent story is not sufficient, since that will not allow you to explain why the facts in support of your version are superior. It is also risky to expect the jury to keep the plaintiff's opening in mind, and then to appreciate the implications of the contrary facts as you reveal them. Instead, you should make it apparent that you are contradicting the plaintiff's factual claims:

> Plaintiff's counsel claimed that my client neglected to have his brakes repaired. The facts are that he took his car in for a tune-up and the mechanic said only that he should have his brakes "looked at" within the next 10,000 miles. The evidence will show that the defendant took care of all scheduled maintenance completely according to the manufacturer's timetable, and that he had no reason to think that his brakes were not functioning properly.

Should defense counsel simply begin talking about brakes, the jury might take it as a concession that defendant's brakes were a problem. The defense case is therefore made much stronger by pointing out how the defendant's facts contradict the plaintiff's claim.

Omissions. The absence of evidence can be as telling as the evidence itself. Defense counsel should therefore be ready to respond not only to what was said in plaintiff's opening, but also to what was not said. While it would be argumentative to accuse opposing counsel of concealing information, it is perfectly proper to point out evidentiary gaps in the plaintiff's opening statement. Assume, for example, that liability has been stipulated in the fire engine case, and that it is being tried solely on the issue of damages:

Plaintiff's counsel spoke at some length about the plaintiff's injuries. She did not, however, give you all of the facts about the plaintiff's current physical condition. The evidence will show, for example, that the plaintiff spent a week last summer camping at Eagle River Falls. She carried a backpack, she slept on the ground, and she hiked every day. Plaintiff's counsel did not tell you that the trip was planned for a week and she stayed the full week. It was not necessary for her to leave early. After the week of roughing it, she simply went home. She didn't go to a hospital, or even to her family doctor. On the other hand, there will be absolutely no evidence in this case that the plaintiff lost any income as a result of her injuries.

Credibility. Finally, it is imperative that defense counsel reply to comments concerning the credibility of witnesses. If plaintiff's counsel trumpeted the superior credibility of her witnesses regarding a central issue or disputed fact, then you must react either by building up your own witnesses or by pointing out why and how the plaintiff's witnesses have feet of clay. Even if you did not originally intend to address credibility, you should not allow the plaintiff's position to stand unrebutted. This is even more important when the integrity of one of your own witnesses has been attacked. In these circumstances silence may be seen as a tacit admission; use your opening statement to go to bat for your witness.

D. Bad Facts and Disclaimers

Should your opening statement ever mention negative information that is likely to come out about one of your own witnesses? There is divided opinion on this issue. The traditional view is that you will appear to be hiding any bad facts that you do not mention, and that you can defuse the impact of such facts by bringing them out yourself. Thus, most lawyers favor making at least a casual reference to such matters as felony convictions, admissible "bad acts," and other provable misconduct.

More recently, however, it has been suggested that jurors do not expect lawyers to say anything negative about their own witnesses, and that by doing so you actually call greater attention to the damaging information. There will be time enough to respond to charges after they have actually been made; there is no need to lead the bandwagon yourself.

To date, there have been no objective studies that validate either position. Whether to introduce damaging information about your own witnesses remains a matter of judgment, and no doubt the answer will differ with the context of the case. A prudent middle ground, however, is always to keep bad information, or even the suggestion of bad information, to an absolute minimum. You will want to exhibit the highest possible level of confidence and belief in your own witnesses. Thus, negative information should never be mentioned until you have laid out all of the positive facts about the witness. If you believe that you must defuse a ticking bomb, do it quickly and without fanfare.

Defense counsel, of course, does not need to wonder if any of her witnesses will be attacked during the plaintiff's opening statement. She has the advantage of going second. Thus, for defense counsel there will seldom, if ever, be a situation where it is necessary to raise damaging facts in order to head off the opposition. If the jury didn't get the bad news when the plaintiff opened, there should be scant reason to deliver it during the defendant's opening statement.[11]

E. Legal Issues

As was noted above, it is frequently important to use the opening statement to introduce the legal issues to the jury.[12] A statement of legal issues will put the significance of the facts into clear perspective. Explanations of the law should be brief and to the point. It is far better to weave them into the context of the story, as opposed to "string-citing" all of the legal issues at once.

F. Introductions

At some point in the opening statement it will be necessary to introduce yourself, your client, and any co-counsel. Even if the judge has already introduced all of you, it is a common courtesy to do it again yourself. While there is a natural inclination to begin with introductions, they are not really important enough to warrant the use of your opening moment. It is usually better to start with a strong statement of your theory and theme, and then proceed to the introductions at a natural breaking point.

G. Request for Verdict

Your opening statement should almost always conclude with a request for, or explanation of, the verdict that you will seek at the end of the trial. This request should be made in general terms: "At the end of the case we will ask you to return a verdict that the defendant was not guilty of negligence." The opening statement is not the time for a lengthy discussion of verdict forms or special interrogatories.

---

11 It is possible, of course, that the plaintiff will introduce negative information into evidence, notwithstanding the fact that it was not mentioned during the opening statement. Defense counsel should nonetheless be wary of advance disclosure during her opening. First, the plaintiff may decide not to offer the damaging evidence, or if offered it may not be admitted. Second, much unpleasant information can be developed only on cross examination, in which case there will be time enough to defuse it (if that is your choice) during the witness's direct. Finally, the bad facts might be introduced during plaintiff's case in chief, in which case cross examination will be immediately available to the defendant, and it is unlikely to appear that the defendant was trying to conceal the material.

12 *See* Section II B, *supra* at p. 341.

H. Bromides and Platitudes

There are numerous opening statement bromides and platitudes that have become venerated traditions among some members of the bar. While certain of these clichés have fallen from general use in recent years, others have taken on a life of their own, being repeated by generation after generation even though they have little, if any, intrinsic meaning. A few of the conventions have their limited uses. Here follows a short list of topics, phrases and slogans that are usually best omitted from your opening statements.

The civics lesson. Some lawyers begin their opening statements with a paean to the American jury system. This invocation is unlikely to help your case, since it has absolutely no persuasive value one way or the other. It may convince the jury that you are a patriotic lawyer, but it is just as likely to convince them that you have very little to say on the merits. There is a time to thank the jury for their service and to indicate your respect for the job that they are doing, but it is not at the beginning of your opening statement. The civics lesson, by the way, should be distinguished from a discussion in criminal cases of the concept of proof beyond a reasonable doubt. Reasonable doubt, unlike a generalized discourse on the jury system, is virtually always an essential element of the defendant's case that must be addressed during opening statements.

The neutral simile. It is not uncommon for a lawyer to begin an opening statement with an extended simile that is intended to explain the function of the opening. An opening statement, the jury might be told, is like the picture on the cover of a jigsaw puzzle box. Or it might be like a road map, or like the directions for assembly of a compact disk player. None of these similes are really worthwhile. They communicate absolutely nothing about your case, but they are damaging in the sense that they waste your opening moment. If your opening statement is good, the simile will be unnecessary. If your opening statement is disorganized or vague, no simile or metaphor will save it.

"Not evidence." Perhaps the hoariest opening line in the history of opening statements is the caution to the jury that "What I am about to say to you is not evidence; the evidence will be presented in the form of witness testimony, documents, and exhibits." Although this introduction is now heard less and less, it was once considered *de rigueur* for opening statements. Because it still survives in some quarters, the reasons for abandoning this line bear repeating. Telling the jury that your opening statement is not evidence is the rough equivalent of telling them to ignore what you are about to say. No one has ever claimed that opening statements are evidence, so there is no reason to disclaim the idea. You want the

jury to pay attention to your opening; you should therefore say nothing that will tend to diminish its importance.[13]

"The evidence will show." Opening statements are limited to a description of "what the evidence will show." This rule has led some lawyers to conclude that every fact mentioned in the opening statement must be preceded with an introductory phrase such as, "We expect the evidence to show that the fire engine was flashing its lights," or "we intend to prove that the defendant had not repaired his brakes," or "there will be evidence that the defendant was already late for an important business meeting at the time of the collision." There is no harm at all in occasionally reminding the judge and jury that you are indeed forecasting evidence that is yet to come. It is hopelessly distracting, however, to use such a phrase as a preface to every item of evidence. It is entirely possible to deliver a complete opening statement without ever once saying "the evidence will show . . . ." At most, the line should be used at wide intervals, simply as an acknowledgment that the opening is a preview.

V. DELIVERY AND TECHNIQUE

It would be very easy to overemphasize the significance of presentational skills in delivering an opening statement. While the popular misconception may be that dramatic style can win trials, the truth is that well-developed facts almost always triumph over dramatics. Only once you have generated your theory of the case and organized your opening statement to present it most effectively should you turn your attention to delivery techniques. This does not mean that delivery is irrelevant, but only that the substance of the case must come first.

Recognizing the secondary importance of technique, here are some useful guidelines.

A. Do Not Read

Do not read your opening statement from a prepared text. Only the most skilled professional actors can deliver a scripted speech and still appear to be spontaneous and sincere. Everyone else will seem to be stilted or labored. Your goal during the opening should be to communicate directly to the jury, not to lecture to them from a manuscript. You will want to make eye contact, you will

---

13 There is one situation in which there may be some value to reminding a jury that an opening statement is not evidence. In criminal cases the prosecution often presents a very comprehensive and compelling opening statement. Since the defense may not wish to commit themselves to putting on a case, they are often left with very little to say in response. Moreover, the defense will frequently rely most heavily on cross examination, as opposed to the development of an affirmative case. In these circumstances it can be helpful to use the opening statement to explain that the prosecution opening, no matter how powerful it seemed, simply was not evidence. Note that in these circumstances the "not evidence" disclaimer is raised about the opposition opening, not your own.

want to pick up on the jury's reactions, and you will want to respond to objections and rulings by the court. Defense counsel, moreover, will want to reply to challenges, weaknesses, and omissions in the plaintiff's opening statement. A written opening statement will prevent you from doing any of these things effectively.

Much the same can be said of attempting to memorize your opening statement. While exceptional memorization is better than reading, you will still run the risk of forgetting a line (or more), of losing your place, or of being thrown off track by an objection. Very experienced lawyers may be able to deliver opening statements from memory. Novices should be wary of trying.

The best approach is often to deliver the opening statement from an outline. It should be possible to list all of your major points, as well as the most important supporting details, on one or two sheets of paper. An outline will allow you organize the material as well as ensure that you don't leave anything out, while avoiding all of the perils of reading or memorization. Although some lawyers believe that any use of notes is distracting to the jury, it is far more likely that jurors understand the need to use some notes whenever you are speaking at length. The key, of course, is for your notes to be unobtrusive. Hence, the outline as opposed to the text.

B. Use Simple Language and Straightforward Presentation

The opening statement should be reasonably straightforward and direct. It is a time to allow your facts to speak for themselves, and not a time for emotional pleas or impassioned argument. In any event, the court will not allow you to make elaborate use of metaphors, literary allusions, biblical quotations, or any of the other rhetorical devices that can be so helpful during final argument.

While you should never talk down to a jury, simple language is generally the best. There is no word so eloquent that it is worth risking the understanding of a single juror. Your opening statement can be perfectly sophisticated without relying upon language that you won't hear on the evening news. There is no reason to say that the defendant in the fire truck case "procrastinated" in having his brakes repaired; say instead that he "put off having his brakes fixed."[14] Most of all, do not use legalese. It isn't impressive even to lawyers, and it will tend to confuse, bore, and even aggravate the jury.

---

14 Readers have no doubt observed that this book does not shy away from big words. Nor should it; our language is rich and it is made richer by the use of interesting and precise words. But writing is one thing, and trying cases is another.

C. Use Movement for Emphasis and Transition

To the extent that it is allowed by the judge,[15] you can add considerable force to your opening statement simply by moving about in the courtroom. Movement can be used most effectively to make the transition from one topic to another, or to emphasize a particular point.

Movement for transition. Every time you change subjects during your opening statement, take a step or two to one side or the other. If you are standing at the lectern, your movement could be as slight as a shift to its side. By using your body in this manner you signal to the jury that one subject has ended and another is about to begin. This motion, in turn, will have the effect of reinitiating primacy. The jury's attention will refocus, and you will then have a new "opening moment" in which to take advantage of the jury's heightened concentration and retention.

Movement for emphasis. Deliberate body movement always concentrates the jury's attention. Movement toward the jury will concentrate it even more. Whenever you reach a particularly important point in your opening statement, you can emphasize it by taking a step or two in the jury's direction. As your movement becomes faster and more purposeful, you will emphasize the point even more. Two caveats regarding the use of this technique should be fairly obvious: don't run and don't hover over the jury. The invasion of their space can be seen as overbearing or even threatening. Note also that your important point should not be made while you are walking, since the jury might be paying more attention to your motion than to your words. Instead, use a transition sentence while you are moving toward the jury, then stop, pause a moment, and deliver your crucial point while standing perfectly still. The contrast will emphasize the issue even more.

Pacing. Pacing is bad. It distracts the jury. Far worse, it also deprives you of the ability to use movement for emphasis. If you are constantly walking back and forth in the courtroom, you cannot use a few well-chosen steps to underscore the significance of a critical detail. This can be especially crippling in an opening statement, since the rule against argument otherwise severely limits your ability to accent issues for the jury.

Lectern. Most, although not all, courtrooms come equipped with a lectern. Many experienced attorneys move the lectern aside during opening statements so that nothing will stand between themselves and the jury. They either speak without using notes, or they use a few small index cards. This is an excellent approach if you are able to use it. Most lawyers, however, need more notes and are more

---

15 In some jurisdictions counsel is required always to remain at the lectern. In a few jurisdictions the attorneys must conduct the entire trial while seated at counsel table. Most judges, however, allow lawyers to move rather freely about the courtroom, especially during opening statements and closing arguments. If you are not familiar with a particular judge's practice, make a point of finding out before the trial begins.

comfortable using a lectern as home base. There is nothing wrong with speaking from a lectern, and you will not lose your case if you take a note pad with you when you deliver your opening statement. The key is to use the lectern without being chained to it. Feel free to move out to the side of the lectern, or even across the courtroom, returning to your staging ground when you have finished emphasizing a point or when you need to refer to your notes.

D. Visuals and Exhibits

Your openings statement need not be confined to your words alone. The use of visual aids and exhibits can enormously enhance the value of your presentation.

Exhibits. Since the purpose of the opening statement is to explain what the evidence will show, you are entitled to read from or display documents and other exhibits that you expect to be admitted into evidence. If the case involves a contract, quote from the central clause. If you plan to offer a key letter into evidence, have it enlarged and show it to the jury during your opening statement. Use a pointer so that the jury can read along with you as you recite the opposing party's damning admission. During your opening statement you may be able to show the jury photographs, models, maps, and charts, as well as other tangible exhibits such as weapons, machinery, or even prosthetics. There is some risk, of course, in displaying an exhibit that may not ultimately be admitted.[16] Under modern practice, however, this problem can usually be alleviated by obtaining a pretrial ruling on admissibility.

Visual aids. In addition to displaying actual exhibits, you may also use visual aids during your opening statement. The general rule is that any visual aid must be likely to help the jury to understand the eventual trial evidence. Thus, lawyers have been allowed to show "time lines" to the jury, or to draw free-hand diagrams that will not later be offered. There are limitations, of course. The visual aids must fairly summarize the evidence, they cannot be misleading, and they cannot be argumentative. You could not, for example, produce a chart captioned "Three Reasons Not To Believe The Plaintiff." Visual aids should be shown to opposing counsel before your opening statement begins. It is advisable also to show visuals to the court and to obtain advance permission for their use.

Other evidence. Not all exhibits are visual. It is permissible to play tape recordings during opening statements — such as legally tapped telephone conversations or 911 emergency calls — if they will later be offered into evidence. It is conceivable that creative counsel might even make use of olfactory or tactile evidence, although this possibility seems remote.

---

16 Regarding references to "questionable evidence" during opening statements, *see* Section IV A(2), *supra* at p. 362.

VI. ADDITIONAL CONSIDERATIONS

A. Motions and Objections

Objections are fairly unusual during opening statements. It may seem rude to interrupt when the other lawyer is speaking directly to the jury, and a general convention has developed that most attorneys will try to avoid objecting during opposing counsel's opening. There are times, however, when objections are called for and should be made.

1. Common Objections

The most common objection during an opening statement is to improper argument. Most judges will sustain this objection only when the argument is extended or outrageous. An argumentative sentence or two will be unlikely to draw an objection, and even more unlikely to see one sustained. Drawn out argument, however, should be objected to. There is no convention that allows opposing counsel to transform the opening statement into a final argument. Be particularly alert to extended argument on the credibility of witnesses.

It is also objectionable to discuss or explain the law during opening statements. Again, some brief mention of the applicable law is permissible, and in fact, unavoidable. Lengthy discourse on the law, and especially misstatement of the law, should draw an objection.

It is both objectionable and unethical for counsel to express a personal opinion during the opening statement, or to assert personal knowledge of the facts of the case.[17] The purpose of this rule is to prevent attorneys from offering "facts" that will not be in evidence, and also to prevent the trial from becoming a referendum on the believability of the lawyers. This rule is intended to prevent lawyers from saying things like, "Believe me, I know what happened and I wouldn't lie to you." It is not intended to preclude the occasional use of phrases such as "I think" or "I'm sure." An objection on this ground is most likely to be sustained when opposing counsel discusses her own investigation of the case, or makes reference to her own credibility.

While opening statements are required to preview only the evidence that will ultimately come before the jury, objections usually will not be sustained on the ground that counsel is discussing inadmissible evidence. A lawyer is entitled to take a chance that her evidence will be admitted, and most judges will not rule on evidentiary objections during the opening statements. If you truly believe that evidence should be excluded, then your proper course of action is to make a motion in limine before the trial, not to raise an objection during opposing counsel's

---

17 In fact, it is unethical for counsel to express a personal opinion or assert personal knowledge of the facts at any point during the trial. *See* Rule 3.4(e), Model Rules of Professional Conduct 3.4(e); DR 7-106(C)(3) & (4), Model Code of Professional Responsibility.

opening statement. On the other hand, it is possible that the opposition might take you completely by surprise by trying to slip some outrageously inadmissible and prejudicial tidbit into their opening statement. If that is the case, by all means object. It is unethical for an attorney to "allude to any matter that the lawyer does not reasonably believe is relevant or that will not be supported by admissible evidence."[18]

It is entirely objectionable to refer to evidence that has been excluded via motion in limine or other pretrial ruling.

Finally, it is worth noting that there is no such objection as, "That is not what the evidence will be." Opposing counsel presents her case and you present yours. You will naturally disagree as to what the evidence will show. If counsel ultimately fails to live up to the commitments given during her opening statement, then you can pound that point home during your final argument. For the same reason, there is also no such objection as "Mischaracterizing the evidence." If a characterization amounts to argument, object to it. Otherwise, opposing counsel is free to put whatever spin she can on the evidence.

2. Responding to Objections

An objection during your opening statement can be distracting. Lengthy argument, however, can be even more disruptive. Any time that you spend speaking to the court is time that you are not speaking to the jury. In all but exceptional circumstances, then, it is usually best to wait for the judge to rule on an objection, and then to proceed.

If the objection is overruled, you may thank the court and pick up where you left off. If the objection is sustained, you must adapt your opening to the court's ruling. For example, if your theme has been declared argumentative you must figure out a way to recast or truncate it so that you can continue to use it without objection.

Consider the "Too busy to be careful" theme that we have posited for the fire truck case. Although it is unlikely, imagine that the court has sustained an objection to the use of that phrase during your opening statement. Don't ask for reconsideration or try to explain why you weren't being argumentative. A small adjustment to your opening should be sufficient:

> The evidence will show that the defendant was extremely busy on the morning of the accident. The evidence will also show that the defendant was not careful. He was busy because he had an important meeting scheduled with a new client. He was running late for the meeting, and

---

18 Rule 3.4(e), Model Rules of Professional Conduct; DR 7-106(C)(1), Model Code of Professional Responsibility.

he wanted to get there on time. We know that he wasn't careful, because he kept on driving when all of the other traffic stopped for a fire truck. The truck was flashing its lights and sounding its siren, but the defendant didn't notice it until it was too late.

Finally, many judges are adept at avoiding rulings on objections during opening statements. The following scenario is not uncommon:

ATTORNEY: Objection, Your Honor. Counsel is engaging in improper argument.

COURT: Argument is not permitted during opening statements. Proceed.

The judge has neither sustained nor overruled the objection. What should you do? The best approach is usually to modify your opening statement slightly, as an indication to the court that you understand the need to avoid argument. The judge, in effect, has cautioned you, and you should not take that as license to binge on argumentation.

3. Motions and Curative Instructions

Once an objection is sustained the opening statement is allowed to continue. Occasionally the offending portion of the opening statement is so damaging that the objecting lawyer must request a curative instruction from the court. This should be done primarily when opposing counsel has engaged in lengthy argument, or has referred to evidence that has already been excluded.

Curative instructions are obtained by asking the court to "instruct the jury to disregard counsel's comments." Some judges then instruct the jury in rather perfunctory terms, while others actually make some effort to ensure that the jury will not consider the improper comments. In either case, the decision to request a curative instruction is a touchy one, since the instruction itself might serve to emphasize exactly the point that you want the jury to disregard.

Nonetheless, in many jurisdictions you cannot appeal on the ground of improper comments during opening unless you first objected and then requested a curative instruction. Paradoxically, it is not uncommon for appellate courts then to hold that the instruction rectified any harm.

In extreme cases, a motion for a mistrial can be made on the basis of improper comments during the opening statement. To warrant a mistrial, opposing counsel's improper statement must have been so prejudicial and damaging as to have destroyed irrevocably the possibility of a fair trial.

B.   Bench Trials

A judge, unlike a jury, is obviously familiar with the manner in which evidence is produced at trial. Does a judge ever require help in understanding the evidence? Is there a place for opening statements in bench trials?

In all but extremely complex cases, most judges prefer to eliminate or severely truncate opening statements. It may be conceit, but judges typically believe that they can follow the evidence without the benefit of a preview. Counsel, however, should be reluctant to give up opening statements. It is just as important and valuable to capture the judge's imagination as it is to begin creating a mental picture for a jury. Indeed, it may be more important to impress your image of the case upon the judge, since the court eventually will render its verdict without the benefit of deliberations. Even in the absence of opening statements, a jury will be composed of at least six people, all of whom will enter the jury room with different predispositions and experiences. A judge will have only her own background to rely on, and the opening statement may be your best opportunity to begin to persuade the court to see the case your way.

Nonetheless, in most jurisdictions the court has the right to forego opening statements in bench trials. The surest way to be certain that opening statements will be allowed is not to abuse the privilege when it is granted. Your opening statement to the court should be particularly short, well focused, and to the point. Many of the conventions and techniques that are aimed at juries should be eliminated when trying a case to the bench.

Judges hate long opening statements. You must do everything that you can to shorten your presentation. For example, while repetition is effective in making a point to a jury, it can be deadly when opening to the court. There is seldom a need to repeat points, or to drive them home through a series of incremental steps, when your audience is a single judge. Do not omit significant details, but do not build them up in the same way that you would before a jury.

Similarly, there is certainly never any reason to go through a list of witnesses for the court. This technique has limited value in a jury trial, but it has absolutely no function in a bench trial. The judge will be able to understand who the witnesses are as they appear.

On the other hand, chronology and the ordering of facts continue to be important in bench trials. A clear picture of the occurrences will always help the judge's understanding. This applies not only to the sequence of events, but also to relationships among the various facts. If certain facts cast doubt on the credibility of a witness, tell that to the court. If a certain document will bolster or contradict a witness's testimony, tell that to the court.

Perhaps the most important consideration in opening to the court is to stress the legal issues. You should have much greater latitude in discussing legal issues

382

in a bench trial. Tell the court what the claims and defenses are. Explain exactly how the principal facts and supporting details relate to the legal issues in the case. The judge will eventually arrive at a verdict by applying the applicable law to the proven facts. Your opening statement can be most effective if it presages this process.

C. Timing

1. When to Open

The plaintiff always opens at the very beginning of the case. The defendant, at least as a technical matter, usually has the option of either opening immediately after the plaintiff, or waiting until the plaintiff has rested and the defense case is about to begin.

The overwhelming consensus view is that the defense should never delay opening. The plaintiff's (or prosecutor's) will portray their case in its strongest possible form. The defense can undermine that portrayal, and also create some discontinuity between the plaintiff's opening and the beginning of their evidence, by presenting their opening statement immediately after the plaintiff's. Delaying the defense opening will give the impression that the plaintiff's claims have gone unrebutted. On the other hand, opening at the outset of the trial will allow the jury to consider the defense position even while listening to the plaintiff's evidence. It will also create a context for defense counsel's cross examinations.

There are only a few possible justifications for delaying the defense opening until after the plaintiff has rested. It is remotely conceivable that you might have some surprise up your sleeve that you don't want to reveal before the plaintiff has concluded its case. Alternatively, criminal defense counsel sometimes prefer to evaluate the strength of the prosecution witnesses before deciding whether to present a defense. In these situations there may be some theoretical benefit to delaying the opening statement, although the same advantage can often be obtained by structuring an initial opening to achieve the same goals.

2. Multiple Parties

In cases with more than one plaintiff or defendant, the court will generally determine the order of opening statements. The plaintiff with the most at stake will typically be allowed to open first, followed by the others in descending order of potential recovery. Similarly, the defendant with the greatest exposure will usually be afforded the first opening statement. Other factors may also be considered, and the parties are customarily free to stipulate to some other order.

In a case with multiple defendants it may be possible for one to open immediately after the plaintiff, and for another to reserve opening until the beginning of the defense case. This approach provides the best of both worlds, although it obviously requires a fair level of cooperation among defendants. The court has discretion to grant or deny such a request.

— CHAPTER TEN —
Final Argument

I. THE ROLE AND FUNCTION OF THE FINAL ARGUMENT
A. The Whole Story

Final argument is the advocate's only opportunity to tell the story of the case in its entirety, without interruption, free from most constraining formalities. Unlike witness examinations, the final argument is delivered in counsel's own words, and without the need intermittently to cede the stage to the opposition; unlike the opening statement, it is not bound by strict rules governing proper and improper content. In other words, final argument is the moment for pure advocacy, when all of the lawyer's organizational, analytic, interpretive, and forensic skills are brought to bear on the task of persuading the trier of fact.

Final argument is the conclusion of the battle for the jury's imagination. Recall that opening statement marks the beginning of the attorney's efforts to help the jurors construct a mental image of occurrences, locations, objects, and transactions at issue in the case. This mental image, in turn, influences the way in which the jurors receive and interpret the evidence. At the close of the case, counsel returns to strengthen and explain the significance of those mental images.

Understanding this process should tell us something about final arguments. If counsel has been successful, the opening statement painted a picture that the jury began to accept and internalize. The witnesses, documents, and exhibits fit neatly into that picture, reinforcing the image that counsel created. At final argument the attorney can then nail down the image by pointing out the crucial details, weaving together with witnesses' accounts, and explaining the significant connections. All three aspects of the trial — opening, witness examinations, and closing — should combine to evoke a single conception of events.

Thus, the final argument cannot be fully successful unless the preceding stages of the trial were also successful. The opening statement's mental image will not stay with the jury unless it is sustained by evidence from the witness stand. More to the point, the final argument cannot paint a picture that is contrary to, or unsupported by, the evidence. While final argument can and should be the capstone of a well-tried case, it is unlikely to be the saving grace of a poor one.

In sum, the final argument must tell the whole story of the case, but it cannot tell just any story. The final argument has to complement the portrait begun during the opening statement, and, even more importantly, must reflect and encompass the evidence in the case. This goal can be best accomplished only when the case is presented according to a well-defined theory.

B. Use of Theory and Theme

1. Theory

If nothing else, the final argument must communicate the advocate's theory of the case. Some witnesses can be disregarded, some details can be omitted, some legal issues can be overlooked, but the theory of the case is absolutely essential.

The final argument, therefore, must be used to illuminate your theory. This means that you must tell the jury, or the court, why your client is entitled to a verdict. A simple recitation of facts is not sufficient. Rather, the argument should bring together information from the various witnesses and exhibits in a way that creates only one result.

To be successful, the theory presented in a final argument must be logical, believable, and legally sufficient.

a. Logical

A trial theory, and consequently a final argument, must be logical in the sense that the component facts lead to the desired conclusions. It is often helpful, therefore, to reason backward, starting with the end result and then providing supportive facts. In the fire engine case the plaintiff's goal is to prove negligence. The starting point for her theory, then, is to ask which facts most strongly contribute to the conclusion that the defendant was negligent. Those facts will form the basis of the theory.

Reasoning in this manner, plaintiff's counsel will probably conclude that her strongest "theory" facts are: (1) the nature of the collision itself; (2) the presence of the fire truck; and (3) the defendant's hurried morning. Note that each fact has a logical connection to the conclusion of negligence: the collision was a classic "rear-ender," which shows that the defendant either failed to keep a proper interval or was driving too fast just before the accident. The presence of the fire truck explains why the plaintiff stopped her car, and also demonstrates that the defendant failed to keep a proper lookout. The defendant's hurried morning adds proof that he was inattentive to the road.

Logic, however, is only the starting point for the final argument.

b. Believable

The most logical theory in the world will not win a case if the jury doesn't believe it. For a theory to be sound it must be based on facts that are likely to be accepted.

Returning to the fire engine case, we recognize that plaintiff's theory must explain why the defendant should have stopped his car. The obvious answer is the fire truck. Now, however, imagine that only the plaintiff testified that the fire truck sounded its siren. All of the other witnesses, including the firefighters, testified that there had been no siren. As certain as the plaintiff might be, the use of the siren will be a poor fact on which to ground her theory of the case; it simply will not be believed in the face of the overwhelming testimony to the contrary.

Plaintiff's counsel will have to arrive at an alternative theory to explain why the defendant should have known to stop his car. Several possibilities are immediately apparent: The defendant should have stopped once he saw the fire truck, whether it was sounding its siren or not. The defendant should have stopped because the car in front of him stopped, even if there had been no fire engine at all.

Use of the siren would certainly make the story more compelling. It enhances the defendant's negligence to imagine him ignoring the blaring alarm of a fire engine. The theory loses more than it gains, however, if it is based on an unproven or tenuous fact. There is a very real risk that the jury, having rejected one part of the plaintiff's theory, will go on to reject some or all of the rest.

There is no way to guarantee that the jury will accept your final argument; the purpose of the trial, after all, is to allow the judge or jury to decide which theory is more believable. It is possible, however, to construct a rough hierarchy of reliability that will assist you in evaluating the value of evidence for the purpose of the final argument. As is detailed below, the most believable evidence commonly takes the form of admissions from the opposing party, followed by the undisputed evidence that you produced. Concerning disputed evidence, it is generally best to rely first upon the common-sense value of the evidence, and finally upon the credibility of witnesses.

i. Admissions

For the purpose of final argument, the most "believable" information is often that which was produced by the other side. The opposing party obviously would not offer self-damaging testimony unless it were unavoidably true. Consequently, it is particularly effective to argue against a party using his or her own words and documents. The defendant in the fire engine case, for instance, makes an admission when he testifies that he was late for a meeting at the time of the accident. This fact passes every test of believability when used in the plaintiff's final argument:

How do we know that the defendant was running late that morning? He said so himself. Just remember his own words. He said, "I woke up late that morning and I knew that I would have to hurry up to get to my meeting."

This type of argument can continue, taking advantage of points that were scored on cross examination precisely for this purpose:

The defendant's own words also tell us how preoccupied he was. After all, it was the defendant who testified about the importance of new clients. I'm sure you remember how he answered when I asked him if new clients mean money. He said, "Yes, that's what we're in business for." And then I asked him whether this particular new client was a valuable one, and he said, "Every new client is valuable." So there he was, late for his meeting with a valuable new client, worrying about how much money he might stand to lose.

Note that for the purpose of believability analysis, admissions need not be direct concessions, nor do they need to come in the form of testimony from the actual party. Anything can be exploited as an admission so long as it was produced by the other side. A strong closing argument can therefore make use of the opposition's witness testimony, exhibits, charts or graphs, tangible objects, or even comments made by the opposing counsel during the opening statement.

ii. Undisputed Facts

Undisputed facts consist of the testimony, exhibits, and other evidence that you have offered, and which the other side has not controverted. The opposition's decision not to produce contrary evidence greatly enhances the value of such undisputed facts.

While not quite so powerful as admissions from the other side, undisputed facts can provide a sturdy cornerstone for case theory and final argument:

It is undisputed that there was a fire truck at the corner of Touhy and Sheridan. It is undisputed that the engine was answering a call. It is undisputed that other drivers slowed down or pulled over for the fire truck. It is undisputed that Lieutenant Bonnie Middleton was driving the fire truck. And it is undisputed that fire department policy requires the siren to be used whenever an engine company is responding to a call. The defendant may claim that there was no siren, but he hasn't even tried to deny these uncontroverted facts.

Thus, undisputed facts are helpful not only in their own right, but also because they can be marshalled to cast light on disputed evidence.

iii. Common Sense and Experience

Admissions and undisputed facts are valuable precisely because it is impossible for the other side to take issue with them. Every trial, however, involves a core of facts and issues that are in dispute. It will be the rare final argument that can avoid entirely the necessity of explaining why the jury should prefer one version of contested facts over the other.

When key events or occurrences are in dispute, an effective final argument will first make use of common sense. As between any two stories or accounts, a jury is likely to choose the one that most closely comports with its own experience. In structuring an argument, then, it is essential to bear in mind the relationship between your theory of the case and the jury's sense of what will or will not ring true.

A common-sense argument can be extremely helpful, as when defense counsel argues damages in the fire truck case:

> The plaintiff claims that her life's activities have been severely limited. Now pain is a subjective thing, so no one can step inside of the plaintiff's body to see whether or not she is exaggerating. But we can look at her actions, and we can interpret them in the light of our own common sense. The plaintiff went camping last Memorial Day at Eagle River Falls. She carried a backpack and slept on the ground for four straight nights. Is this the action of someone who is in constant pain? Is this the action of someone whose life's activities are severely limited? Can you imagine how the plaintiff might have thought about such a trip: "Well, things are difficult here at home; I guess I'll go sleep on the ground for a long week-end." I don't want to minimize the plaintiff's real injuries, but common sense certainly tells us that someone in as much pain as she claims just wouldn't go camping.

iv. Credibility

The final method of establishing believability is to rely upon the credibility of the witnesses. While credibility is important, in relative terms it is probably the weakest method of proving your version of disputed facts.

There are two problems with credibility arguments. First, they rest almost entirely on subjective impressions. While an advocate may regard one witness as enormously more credible than another, there is no way to be sure that the jury, or judge, perceived the testimony in the same way. Second, credibility arguments ask the jury to think ill of a person; to conclude that she has omitted something, exaggerated, or even lied. Most lawyers consider it to be particularly difficult to persuade a jury to draw such adverse conclusions about any but the most disreputable witnesses. In the following example defense counsel in the fire truck case has decided to attack the plaintiff's credibility:

The plaintiff claims that she was wearing her glasses on the morning of the accident, but you should not believe her. She has everything to gain from her own testimony. She wants to take thousands and thousands of dollars away from this case, so she obviously will tend to remember facts in the way that is the most helpful to her. If she had been wearing her glasses she wouldn't have stopped so abruptly, and the accident never would have happened.

The above argument is ineffective. The plaintiff's interest in the outcome of the case seems insufficient to persuade us that she would lie about wearing her glasses.

This is not to say that counsel should always avoid credibility arguments, but only that they should be supported through the use of admissions, undisputed evidence, or invocations of common sense. For example:

In addition to everything else, we know that the defendant didn't bother to have his brakes fixed just a week before the accident. Nate Lipton, a mechanic who operates his own garage, testified that he told the defendant that it was time to have his brakes relined. The defendant claims that Nate only suggested that he take care of the brakes within the next 10,000 miles. Well, who are we going to believe? Nate Lipton certainly has no reason to embellish his testimony. Unlike the defendant, Nate has no stake in the outcome of this case. But there is another reason to believe Nate Lipton. The defendant admits that Nate mentioned the worn brakes, and it is undisputed that Nate Lipton has 20 years experience as a mechanic. Our common sense tells us that no competent mechanic would open a brake drum, look at worn brakes, and then tell a driver that he could wait 10,000 miles to have them fixed. Why would Nate Lipton risk his own liability by suggesting that a customer drive out of the garage with badly worn brakes?

This credibility argument works because it is founded on the defendant's own admission as well as on common sense. In other words, the argument provides the jury with a reason to prefer the mechanic's testimony over the defendant's.

c. Legally Sufficient

The final component of a solid theory is legal sufficiency. The logic and believability of a final argument must lead to the desired legal result. In other words, a final argument must address the law as well as the facts.

A trial theory may be defined as the application of proven facts to legal issues. In the fire truck case, for example, the central legal issue is whether or not the defendant was negligent. The following might serve as an abbreviated statement of the plaintiff's trial theory:

We have proven that the defendant was distracted and rushed on the morning of the accident. He was negligent because he failed to pay sufficient attention to the road.

A lengthier theory statement would include a definition of negligence:

Under the law, a driver must always exercise due care and caution when operating a motor vehicle. We have proven that the defendant failed to meet that standard on the morning of the accident. A driver exercising due care wouldn't rush down the road just because he was late to a meeting. A driver exercising ordinary caution wouldn't allow himself to become so distracted that he would miss seeing and hearing a fire engine. At a bare minimum, the standard of due care and caution must call for a driver to keep his eye on the traffic around him, but the defendant didn't slow down, even though every other car on the road either pulled over or came to a stop.

In either case, the thrust of the argument is to explain not only that the defendant was wrong, but that the defendant was wrong in a way that should result in a legal consequence.

Lawyers commonly use jury instructions as a framework for discussing legal issues during final argument. [1]

2. Theme

A good trial theme provides an incentive for the entry of a verdict in your client's favor. In addition to being logical and believable, a trial theme invokes shared beliefs and common precepts. Just as a theory explains why the verdict is legally necessary, the theme explains why the verdict is morally desirable.

Your trial theme should be a constant presence throughout the final argument. Unlike opening statement and witness examinations, where a theme can only be used intermittently, the entire final argument can be organized so as to emphasize your theme. You can begin with a statement of the theme and constantly return to it in each segment of the argument.

In the fire engine case, for instance, plaintiff's counsel's first words on final argument could be, "This accident occurred because the defendant was too busy to be careful." Plaintiff's attorney might then proceed through the argument by discussing issues such as the defendant's morning preparations, the accident itself, defendant's post-accident conduct, defendant's shoddy brake-repair record, and finally plaintiff's damages. At each stage of the argument, plaintiff's attorney would find a way to advert to the theme. In some situations the usage would be obvious:

---

1 The uses, and occasional misuses, of jury instructions are discussed below in Section IV F, *infra* at p. 426.

"The defendant didn't bother to have his brakes repaired because he was just too busy." At other points in the argument the reference might be somewhat more subtle. Consider the question of the siren:

> The defendant claims that the fire engine was not sounding its siren. But the defendant's claim cannot be believed. Remember that the fire truck was being driven by Lieutenant Bonnie Middleton. Lieutenant Middleton, as we heard, is a decorated firefighter, and the first woman ever to be promoted to lieutenant in this city. Not only is she well trained, but she now teaches courses at the fire academy. Lieutenant Middleton knows full well that fire trucks are required to sound their sirens whenever responding to a call. It is part of her job to comply with that regulation. For Lieutenant Middleton, being busy and being careful are the same thing. We know that she was careful because she was busy.

The value of the theme is its use as a moral persuader. It provides the jury a reason to want to enter the appropriate verdict. Consequently, the theme can be employed in the damages section of an argument, even if its principal thrust goes to liability. Thus, the plaintiff in the fire truck case can argue damages at length, describing all of the plaintiff's injuries, disabilities, and attendant costs and expenses. Having established the nature and devastating scope of the plaintiff's damages, counsel can conclude by noting, "And all because the defendant was too busy to be careful."

As effective as the recurrent use of a theme can be on final argument, take care not to overdo it. No matter how compelling it is the first time, any single-sentence statement can become trite or bothersome if it is repeated *ad nauseam*. For this reason, it is often wise to utilize the spirit of the theme in place of the mantra itself. For example, plaintiff's counsel in the fire truck case might describe the plaintiff's own attentiveness to the road by saying something like the following:

> She was not in a hurry that morning. She was on her way to the Art Institute, but she had over an hour until it opened. She had no reason to speed, and every reason to stop as soon as she saw and heard the fire truck. There was nothing on her mind to distract her from her careful driving.

This argument employs the trial theme but does not repeat it, thus taking advantage of its moral force while avoiding an annoying echo.

C. What Makes It Argument

Recall the cardinal rule of opening statements that you may not argue. In final argument, on the other hand, you may, should, and must argue if you are serious about winning your case. The gloves are off, and the limitations are removed, but what precisely distinguishes argument from mere presentation of the facts? The following are some of the most useful elements of "argument."

1. Conclusions

The attorney in final argument is free to draw and urge conclusions based upon the evidence. A conclusion is a result, consequence, or repercussion that follows from the evidence in the case.

In our fire engine case, for example, the plaintiff will no doubt offer this evidence: the defendant woke up late on the morning of the accident; he had an important meeting to attend that morning; he did not have sufficient time to get to the meeting; he stood to lose a potential new client (and therefore a lot of money) if he arrived late.

From this evidence, several conclusions *may* be drawn: The defendant was in a hurry. The defendant was preoccupied. The defendant was trying to plan for his meeting while driving, because he wouldn't have time to plan for it after he arrived at the office. The defendant allowed his thoughts to drift to the point that he became careless and inattentive to the road.

All of the above conclusions would be permissible in argument, even though there is unlikely to be direct proof of any of them. That is what makes them conclusions; they follow logically, although not necessarily, from admitted evidence. In other words, the conclusion might or might not be accurate. It is possible for a driver to be exceptionally careful, even though late for a meeting. It is the force of advocacy, advanced through argument, that can lead the trier of fact to draw one conclusion as opposed to another.

Thus, it is not sufficient for a final argument to draw, or even urge, conclusions. The argument must go on to explain why the desired conclusions are the correct ones.

2. Inferences

While a final argument can and should include broad conclusions, it may also include the sort of narrow conclusions commonly known as inferences. An inference is a deduction drawn from the existence of a known fact. In other words, the inferred fact need not be proven, so long as it is a common-sense consequence of some established fact.

Turning again to the fire engine case, assume that the defendant testified that his parking garage was located two blocks from his office. From that known fact it could be inferred that it would take him at least five minutes to walk from the garage to his office. It could further be inferred that the defendant knew how long it would take him to reach his office. Such inferences, based upon a combination of proven fact and everyday experience, could be used to support the larger conclusion that the defendant was in a rush at the time of the accident.

An inference will be accepted only if it is well-grounded in common understanding. For that reason, it is often necessary or desirable to explain the basis of all but the most obvious inferences. For example, everyone will be willing to infer a child's age from knowledge of her grade in school. There is no need to explain that third graders are typically eight or nine years old. Other inferences, however, may be more complicated.

Recall the evidence in the fire truck case that the engine was being driven by veteran firefighter Bonnie Middleton. It can be inferred from this fact that the truck's siren was sounding just before the accident, but the inference will profit from some explanation:

> The fire truck was being driven by Lieutenant Bonnie Middleton, a ten-year veteran of the force. The first woman ever to be promoted to that rank, Lieutenant Middleton did not get where she is today by being careless or by ignoring departmental rules. A fire truck is required to sound its alarm whenever it is responding to a call. This is a simple safety precaution that alerts other vehicles to clear the way. It just doesn't make sense to argue, as the defendant claims, that Lieutenant Middleton would have carelessly neglected to use her siren that day at the intersection of Sheridan and Touhy.

The proven facts include Lieutenant Middleton's background and the departmental rules. The inference is that she sounded her siren on the date in question. The explanation — that the siren is a necessary safety precaution — bolsters the inference.

3. Details and Circumstantial Evidence

Final argument is counsel's only opportunity to explain the relevance and consequences of circumstantial evidence. Much of the art of direct and cross examination consists of the accumulation of details that lead to a certain conclusion or result. The knowledge of the individual witnesses, not to mention trial strategy and luck, may result in the scattering of such details throughout the trial. It is during final argument that the attorney can reassemble the details so that they lead to the desired result.

In a burglary prosecution, for example, there may have been no eyewitnesses to give direct evidence against the defendant. A number of witnesses, however, might provide detailed circumstantial evidence. Perhaps one witness saw the defendant running from the scene of the crime, while another found a single shoe in the doorway of the burglarized house. Yet a third witness might have heard the defendant complaining about her need for a new radio. The crime victim could testify that an expensive radio was taken in the burglary. Finally, on cross examination the defendant could be asked to try on the shoe, to show that it fits.

None of these circumstantial details constitute direct evidence of the defendant's guilt, particularly when they are adduced individually through the testimony of four or five different witnesses. They can, however, be organized into a powerful narrative leading irresistibly to conviction. Moreover, the circumstantial evidence becomes even more persuasive when all of the connections are explained in argument:

> No one saw the defendant commit the burglary, but the surrounding details point in only one direction. She was seen running, not walking, from the crime scene just after the house was robbed. That alone does not make her guilty, but it does tell us that she had a reason to run away from that house. Now consider all of the other evidence. She wanted a new radio so badly that she complained about it to her friends, and the largest item taken in the burglary was a brand new radio. It seems as though the burglar left a shoe behind that was caught in the door, and that shoe just happens to fit perfectly on the defendant's foot. It all falls together: The house was robbed, the defendant ran; she wanted a radio, a radio was stolen; the burglar left a shoe behind, the shoe fits the defendant. Perhaps one of these facts could be a coincidence, but all together they add up to guilt.

Trial lawyers understand that circumstantial evidence is probative and reliable. In the popular mind, however, the term "circumstantial" is often equated with doubtful or equivocal. It is therefore desirable to use final argument to explain the value and credibility of circumstantial evidence. This is frequently done through the use of an analogy, some of which have virtually become "standards":

> While no one saw the defendant commit the burglary, the circumstantial evidence is overwhelming. As the court will instruct you, circumstantial evidence can be just as credible as eyewitness testimony. We can all recognize the value of circumstantial evidence, based on our experiences in everyday life. For example, think of the last time that it snowed in the night. If you looked out on your front yard in the morning and saw footprints in the snow, then you knew for sure that someone had walked across your lawn. Even if you didn't actually see anybody, the footprints were circumstantial — and absolutely reliable — evidence that someone had been there. In this case, even though no one saw the defendant, there is no doubt that she left her footprints for everyone to see.

Analogies have many other uses at trial, some of which are detailed in the next section.

4. Analogies, Allusions, and Stories

a. Analogies

An analogy can explain human conduct through reference to everyday human behavior. A witness's testimony can be strengthened or diminished by comparing her version of events to some widely understood experience or activity.

Suppose that the defendant in the fire engine case testified that he saw the fire truck, but that he did not slow down because the siren was not sounding. Plaintiff's attorney will want to characterize this conduct as unreasonable. Counsel can, of course, simply say as much: the defendant should have slowed down, and it was unreasonable to keep driving once he saw the fire truck. From a purely legal perspective, that should be sufficient to establish negligence. It could be more persuasive, however, to use an analogy:

> The defendant admits that he saw the fire truck, but says that there was no siren, and so he did not feel it necessary to stop. Even if you believe him that he didn't hear the siren, there is nothing reasonable about conduct like that. By continuing to drive at the same speed he was playing Russian roulette with the safety of every other driver on the road. Simple attentiveness to safety tells us that we should slow down when we see an emergency vehicle. Just because he didn't hear the siren doesn't mean that it wasn't sounding. You wouldn't expect someone to pick up a gun and fire it at somebody, claiming, "Well, I didn't see any bullets." Of course not. A gun is dangerous, and simple prudence means that you should always treat it as though it is loaded. Well, cars can be dangerous, too. As soon as he saw that fire truck, the defendant should have recognized the possibility that traffic would slow or stop. He should have recognized the possibility that it was answering a call, whether he heard the siren or not. Continuing to drive, without at least slowing down, was the equivalent of pointing a loaded gun down the road.

The above excerpt takes conduct that everyone will recognize as unreasonable and explains why the defendant's conduct falls into the same category.

Analogies can support testimony as well as deride it, and they can be short as well as extended. Consider the following example from defense counsel's final argument:

> Fire trucks use their sirens to tell traffic to stop. We have all seen fire engines on the street that weren't responding to calls. Without their sirens, they are just part of traffic. If you look up into the sky and see an airplane flying by, you don't say, "I'd better take cover; it's going to crash."

While analogies can be very powerful, there is always the danger that they can be inverted and exploited by the other side. Thus, so long as the opposing counsel has yet to argue, care must be taken to ensure that any analogies are "airtight." For the same reason, plaintiff's counsel often reserves the use of analogies until rebuttal, when the defendant will no longer be able to reply.[2]

b. Allusions

An allusion is a literary or similar reference that adds persuasive force to an argument. In earlier days, before the advent of mass culture, trial lawyers' allusions were most commonly drawn from Shakespeare or the Bible. Perhaps the most frequently used quotation from Shakespeare is the suggestion that a witness "doth protest too much."[3]

Today references are just as likely to be taken from motion pictures, television, popular songs, fairy tales, or, alas, advertisements. Defense counsel in the fire engine case might disparage the plaintiff's injury claim with a reference to "The Princess and the Pea":

> The plaintiff claims that her life's activities are severely limited. She says that sometimes she can't even sleep. But last Memorial Day she went camping at Eagle River Falls where she slept on the ground for four nights. Now that her case is on trial she claims that she was in pain, but the truth is that she stayed at the campground for the whole weekend. We all know the story about the princess who could feel a pea even though it was underneath a stack of mattresses. But our law doesn't allow recovery for that sort of super-sensitivity. And this plaintiff, who had no hesitation about sleeping on the ground, certainly can't complain about peas under the mattress today. You can't be a backpacker when you want to, and then a princess when the time comes to try for damages.

Advertising slogans are commonly used during final argument. For all that they lack in elegance and literary merit, they have the advantage of familiarity and catchiness.

c. Stories

Stories, in the form of either hypotheticals or anecdotes, can be used effectively in final argument. It is permissible to illustrate an argument with a hypothetical story, so long as the story is based on facts that are in evidence. Again, from the plaintiff's argument in the fire engine case:

---

2   Regarding the uses of rebuttal argument, see Section II C, *infra* at p. 407.

3   "The lady doth protest too much, methinks." William Shakespeare, *Hamlet,* Act III, scene 2, line 242.

Imagine what the defendant's morning was like. His alarm clock didn't go off. He woke up, looked at the clock and began to panic. He was late, and if he missed the meeting with this new client he would lose money and damage his position with his firm. He rushed into the bathroom to shower and shave. Maybe he cut himself, as happens so often when you hurry. Think of all the things that people do when they are rushed in the morning. No time to read the newspaper. No time to eat breakfast. No time to stop for gas, even if the tank is low. You can be sure that the defendant hurried to his car that morning. This was not the day for a leisurely drive. This was a day to push the speed limit and to run yellow lights.

This reconstruction of the defendant's morning is hypothetical in that the details are all suppositions. It is proper argument because the entire story is derived from the defendant's own testimony.

Another form of argumentative storytelling is the illustrative anecdote. An anecdote is a sort of litigator's fable or folk tale, again used to elaborate on a theme in the case. Attorneys frequently draw upon real or imagined family wisdom:

My grandfather was a modest man who cared very little for life's material rewards. Although he loved other people's celebrations, he never wanted anything for himself. Especially birthday presents. "Please don't give me anything," he would say, "because every day is my birthday." When I got a little older I asked my mother why Grandpa always said that. She told me that Grandpa once almost died from a heart attack, and after that he considered every day to be a brand new gift from God; in other words, a birthday. I always thought that Grandpa was the happiest man in the world, because every day was his birthday.

I think that we would all like to view life the way that Grandpa did, but the plaintiff will never be able to. She wakes up every morning in pain. Every movement must be measured and gauged. One wrong move and she risks having to spend the day in bed, or even going to the hospital. She can't think of every day as her birthday, because each day is hell.

My grandfather had a joy in life and peace of mind that was an inspiration to everyone who new him. More than anything else, that is the possibility that the defendant has taken from the plaintiff. She will never know simple pleasures again.

The use of the story serves to humanize the plaintiff. It is always difficult to ask for money, but to compare the plaintiff with the kindly, unassuming grandfather demonstrates both the severity of her loss and the relatively modest nature of her claim.

5. Credibility and Motive

Counsel may also use the final argument to comment on, and compare, the motive and credibility of witnesses. Many, perhaps most, trials involve competing renditions of past events, which the trier of fact must resolve in order to reach a verdict. Final argument is the only time when the attorney may confront directly the character of the witnesses and explain why some should be believed and others discounted.

Perhaps a witness for the opposing party was impeached through the use of a prior inconsistent statement[4] or omission.[5] While the inconsistency will to one degree or another speak for itself, the final argument can underscore just exactly how it undermines the witness's credibility. The following example is taken from the defense argument in a robbery prosecution:

> We all heard the victim claim that the robber was easily recognizable by his long hair and moustache. But just thirty minutes after the robbery he was interviewed by Officer Ravid. At that time the robber was still at large, and the victim had every reason to give Officer Ravid the best description he could. That description is right here in the police report. Officer Ravid got height, weight, age, race, clothing — but not one word about long hair and a moustache. That's right, a short thirty minutes after the crime, the victim didn't have a word to say about long hair or a moustache.
>
> What happened? How did long hair and a moustache get added to the description? Unfortunately, the police made a suggestion. They drove the victim around the neighborhood, pointing out "possible suspects." And to his misfortune, my client was one of the people they pointed out. He had long hair and a moustache, so those facts were added to the description at that time. I am not saying that the victim is lying, but that second description is not reliable; it was suggested by the police. If the robber really did have long hair and moustache, the victim would have told that to Officer Ravid right off the bat.

Witness examinations can bring out impeaching facts, and the opening statement can use apposition to contrast the credibility of different witnesses. But only on closing argument can counsel make direct comparisons. Consider the question of the siren as plaintiff's counsel might argue it in the fire truck case:

---

4   *See* Chapter Four, Section II, *supra* at p. 119.

5   *See* Chapter Four, Section III A, *supra* at p. 144.

The plaintiff told you that she stopped because she saw a fire truck, which was flashing its warning lights and sounding its siren. The defendant has to concede that the truck was there, but he claims that it was not using its warning signals. Well, was there a siren or wasn't there? Who should you believe?

The defendant's story just isn't credible. Everyone agrees that the fire truck entered the intersection on its way to answer a fire scene. You have even seen the transcript of the 911 call that the truck was responding to. A fire truck would have to be using its siren under those circumstances. Only the most negligent firefighter would speed toward an intersection without sounding the siren, but this truck was being driven by Lieutenant Bonnie Middleton, one of the most decorated firefighters on the force. Which is more likely, that Lieutenant Middleton neglected such an elementary duty, or that the defendant is wrong about the siren?

The plaintiff heard the siren and stopped her car. The other drivers must have heard it as well, since all of the other traffic pulled over. Of course, it is possible that the defendant testified the way he did because he simply didn't hear the siren, but that is another story. Why didn't he hear the siren? Why didn't he stop his car? For the answers to those questions we have to look at the events of his day and why he was "too busy to be careful."

Finally, motive can be argued on the basis either of proven facts or logical inferences. Counsel may tell the jury why a witness would exaggerate, waffle, conceal information, quibble, or lie. The suggested reasons need not be based on outright admissions, so long as they follow rationally from the testimony in the case.

6. Weight of the Evidence

While the opening statement is limited to a recitation of the expected evidence, the final argument can be used to assert the weight of the evidence. Why is one version preferable to another? Why should some facts be accepted and others rejected? Why is one case stronger than the other? Consider the way in which the defense counsel in the fire truck case might argue the weight of the evidence regarding plaintiff's damages:

The plaintiff claims extreme disability, almost all of it based on pain. But pain is an elusive concept. It cannot be seen or measured; all we have is the plaintiff's own description.

But we can also look at the plaintiff's activities, to see the extent of her alleged disability. We know, for example, that she went camping last

Memorial Day at Eagle River Falls. She put all of her gear into a backpack and stayed in a tent, sleeping on the ground for four nights. She wasn't in so much pain that she canceled the trip. She wasn't in so much pain that she couldn't carry a pack. She wasn't in so much pain that she had to come home early.

Now she says that the camping trip was a mistake, and that she was in agony the whole time. But look at the other, objective evidence. We have seen the records from her doctor; she didn't visit the doctor, or even call, until over a month after the camping trip. We have seen the records from the pharmacy; she didn't change her medication, or even renew it for more than two months after the camping trip. What did she do? She took aspirin.

To judge the extent of the plaintiff's alleged disability you must weigh the evidence. Evaluate the claims that she made in her testimony against the proof of her own actions and the records of her own physician and pharmacist. It is easy to claim pain, and I don't want to minimize the plaintiff's discomfort, but her own conduct makes it clear that nothing happened to limit her life's activities.

7. Demeanor

It is fair game in final argument to comment on a witness's demeanor. Demeanor arguments are usually negative in nature, since it is easier to characterize untrustworthy conduct. An argument that counsel's own witness "looked like he was telling the truth" will tend to seem insincere or over-protective. Negative comments, on the other hand, can be effective so long as they are adequately based on observable fact.

It is not uncommon, for instance, to remark upon a witness's refusal to give a simple answer or to make an obvious concession. Similarly, counsel might mention that a witness averted his eyes or fidgeted on the stand, as though hiding something. Comparable points can be made about witnesses who sneer, lose their tempers, scowl, or become impatient.

One caveat: Demeanor argument is based strictly on perception, and there is little way to ensure that counsel's perception of the witness will be the same as the judge's or jury's. Conduct that the attorney sees as evidence of deception might be regarded by a juror as a reasonable response to unfair questioning. Be careful. Demeanor argument should be used only when the witness's behavior has been blatant and unambiguous.

8. Refutation

Another distinguishing feature of argument is refutation of opposing positions. Opening statements and witness examinations may recite and elicit facts that are contrary to the opposition case, but final argument can refute it directly by pointing out errors, inconsistencies, implausibilities, and contradictions. Consider this extract from the plaintiff's final argument in the fire engine case:

The defendant claims that he was not distracted on the morning of the accident, but that cannot be true. We know that he woke up late and that he had an important meeting to attend with a potential new client. New clients mean money, so missing the meeting, or even being late, could have had a devastating impact on the defendant's job.

By the time that he got ready for work and got to his car, he was already at least 30 minutes behind schedule. By the time he reached the corner of Sheridan and Touhy he was still running over 20 minutes late — he still had to drive downtown, get to his garage, park his car, and proceed to his office, all within 20 minutes.

There is no plausible way for the defendant to deny that he was preoccupied and in a hurry. His mind must have been elsewhere; certainly it wasn't on his driving. Every driver saw and heard the fire truck, but not the defendant. Every driver stopped or pulled over, but not the defendant. Those were not the acts of a careful man.

One last fact shows just how absorbed the defendant was. Right after the accident he jumped out of his car and ran to a telephone. He called his office. That meeting was so important to him that he didn't even check to see if the other driver was hurt. That meeting was more important to him than a possible injury. No wonder it was more important to him than safe, careful driving.

9. Application of Law

Final argument provides the attorney an occasion to apply the law to the facts of the case. Discussion of law is extremely limited during the opening statement and all but forbidden during witness examinations, but it is a staple of the final argument. In most jurisdictions counsel may read from the jury instructions[6] and explain exactly how the relevant law dictates a verdict for her client.

---

6   *See* Section IV F, *infra* at p. 426.

10. Moral Appeal

Final argument allows counsel to elaborate on the moral theme of the case. Recall that a trial theme states, usually in a single sentence, a compelling moral basis for a verdict in your client's favor. The theme invokes shared values, civic virtues, or common motivations. The theme can be stated during the opening statement and alluded to in witness examinations, but it can be hammered home in the final argument. Again, consider the plaintiff's final argument in the fire truck case:

> The defendant was "too busy to be careful." We know that from his actions and their consequences. But what was he busy doing? He was rushing to a meeting for the sole purpose of increasing his income. He was worrying about money, not about safety. It is true that he was late, but that was no one's fault but his own. And once he was late he was so obsessed with getting to the meeting that he threw caution out the window. He was so "busy" that he didn't even care to see whether or not the plaintiff was injured. No, that business meeting was all that mattered. Well, everyone is at risk when drivers behave that way. No one is safe on the road when people care more about their meetings than they do about the way they are driving. You cannot allow someone to think that it is all right to be "too busy to be careful."

Admittedly, the moral dimension of an intersection accident is not overpowering. Cases involving crimes, frauds, civil rights violations, child custody, reckless conduct, and even breach of contract will provide more fertile ground for the assertion of a moral theme. Nonetheless, even the most mundane case can be approached from the perspective of rectitude, by explaining how and why your client's position makes sense for reasons other than strict legality.

II. FORMAT

In most jurisdictions the parties' final arguments are divided into three distinct segments, which are presented in the following order: the plaintiff's (or prosecutor's) argument in chief, the defendant's argument in chief, and plaintiff's rebuttal.[7] While general principles of argument apply to all three, each segment also has its own unique set of uses, applications, and special techniques.

---

7   In a few jurisdictions the plaintiff is not allowed to argue first; thus, there are only two components: defendant's argument and plaintiff's rebuttal. The terms used to describe the components of final argument also vary from jurisdiction to jurisdiction. What we have called plaintiff's argument in chief, for example, is often called plaintiff's "opening," notwithstanding the potential for confusion with the opening statement. Final argument itself is also frequently referred to as closing argument, summation, or, in the United Kingdom, final address.

A. Plaintiff's Argument in Chief

The plaintiff (or prosecutor) must use argument in chief to define the issues and lay out the entire theory of the case. The plaintiff's argument in chief will not be successful unless it provides the jury with compelling reasons to find for the plaintiff on every necessary issue.

Because of the nature of our litigation system, the plaintiff's or prosecutor's initial argument must be comprehensive. The plaintiff in a civil case must usually prevail by a preponderance of the evidence, and the prosecutor in a criminal case must present proof beyond a reasonable doubt. In either situation, the burdened party must establish all of the elements of her cause of action. Thus, a civil plaintiff must establish all of the elements of the particular tort or contract action and a prosecutor must prove all of the elements of the charged crime. Failing to address an element can be fatal.

In contrast, and as will be discussed below in more detail, the defendant may often be considerably more selective during final argument. The defense can frequently prevail simply by disproving a single element of the plaintiff's case, and therefore need not address issues as comprehensively as the plaintiff.

To counterbalance this advantage, a plaintiff's attorneys will often use the final argument to issue a series of challenges to the defendant, thus drawing the defense into a discussion of issues that they might prefer to leave alone. A prime example of such a challenge commonly arises in tort litigation, as in this abbreviated example from the plaintiff's argument in the fire engine case:

> We have seen that the defendant had a duty to drive safely on the public roadway, and that he breached that duty by failing to look where he was going. There is no doubt that he struck the plaintiff's car from behind, and that the accident severely injured the plaintiff. We have discussed her injuries at length, so you know just how crippling they have been.
>
> The defendant, of course, is going to tell you that the accident wasn't his fault. But the one thing he cannot deny is how much harm he caused to the plaintiff. I invite the defendant's attorney to stand before you to discuss damages. If he thinks that the plaintiff wasn't hurt, let him come forward and say so.

The plaintiff can win only by establishing all of the elements of the specific tort; in negligence cases the classical elements are duty, breach of duty, cause in fact, proximate cause, and damages. The defendant, on the other hand, can win by disproving any single element. For that reason, defendants in many cases prefer to emphasize the issues of breach of duty or proximate cause (where they think they can win) and to avoid discussing damages (where the only result might be sympathy for the plaintiff). Plaintiff's counsel in the above example sought to cut off that route by issuing a specific challenge to address damages.

B. Defendant's Argument in Chief

The defendant generally has substantially more latitude than the plaintiff in determining the content of the argument in chief. While the plaintiff must address every element, the defendant is usually free to "cherry pick," selecting only those elements or issues in which counsel has the most confidence. The defense theory, of course, must be comprehensive in the sense that it explains all of the relevant evidence, but its legal thrust may be significantly more pointed than the plaintiff's.[8]

The defining characteristic of the defendant's argument in chief is that it is sandwiched between the two plaintiff's arguments. Defense counsel must respond to the plaintiff's argument in chief, but will not be able to respond to rebuttal.

1. Responding to the Plaintiff's Argument in Chief

It is essential that the defense reply directly to the plaintiff's argument in chief. After listening to the plaintiff's prolonged excoriation of the defendant, every reasonable jury will immediately want to know what the defendant has to say in return. This does not mean that defense counsel should adopt the plaintiff's organization or respond point by point, but the defendant's argument cannot be entirely divorced from the structure that the plaintiff creates.

At a minimum, the defendant should deny the specific charges leveled in the plaintiff's argument. It is a natural human response to deny unfair or untrue accusations. The jury will expect as much from a wrongly blamed defendant. Unless there is a good reason for doing otherwise, the denial should come early in the defendant's argument.

In a more general vein, the defendant should usually devote some time to debunking the plaintiff's case. While the defense may well have an extremely strong affirmative case of its own, it is quite risky to allow the plaintiff's assertions to stand unrebutted. The precise handling of the various arguments will be discussed below in the section on organization.

Finally, the watchword for the defendant's argument in chief is flexibility. While the plaintiff may have the luxury of composing her entire final argument,[9]

---

8   A defendant is certainly not required to focus on a single element or issue. The plaintiff's case may be vulnerable in many areas, and the defendant may wish to address them all. Furthermore, concentration on one element can be risky, as that approach may concentrate too many eggs in a single basket.

9   The plaintiff, of course, will not make final preparations for the final argument until the very end of the trial. However well-prepared you may be beforehand, it is still necessary to hear all of the evidence and to know which jury instructions will be given.

the defendant must always be alert to new issues and nuances raised once the arguments have begun. It simply will not do for defense counsel to deliver a set piece, because the defendant's argument is most effective to the extent that it rebuts the plaintiff's case as presented at the end of the trial. A particularly effective device is the "reverse analogy." In the following example, assume that plaintiff's counsel used her argument in chief to tell a story about her modest grandfather, who took such delight in life's simple pleasures.[10] The defense attorney can attempt to turn the story around:

> The plaintiff's lawyer spoke to us at some length about his grandfather, and it was a moving story about a straightforward man who regarded every day as his birthday. But you have to wonder what Grandpa would have thought about the plaintiff's case, which is anything but straight-forward. Don't you think that Grandpa would say that anyone who goes camping for four days can't be in too much pain? And don't you think that Grandpa would say that anyone who sleeps on the ground and carries a backpack can't be too limited? And, most of all, don't you think that Grandpa would say that no one would wait two months to see her doctor if she were really experiencing medical difficulties?

The defendant's attorney had no way of anticipating the grandfather story, but was nonetheless able to use it as an effective reverse analogy. This is not to say that defense counsel should defer preparation until the end of the plaintiff's argument, but rather that good preparation includes the ability to modify one's original plan in order to accommodate the plaintiff's remarks.

2. Anticipating Rebuttal

The greatest difficulty for defense counsel is knowing that she cannot speak again following the plaintiff's rebuttal. The plaintiff may comment on, criticize or even ridicule defendant's argument, but the defendant may not respond. Defense counsel may have perfectly good answers for everything that the plaintiff says on rebuttal, but no matter. The rule is that the defense may argue only once.

Under these circumstances, it is extremely important that counsel do what-ever is possible to blunt the rebuttal in advance. One approach is to anticipate and reply specifically to the plaintiff's possible rebuttal arguments, as in this example from the defendant's argument in the fire engine case:

> This entire accident could have been avoided if the plaintiff had only pulled over instead of slamming on her brakes in the middle of the street. If she didn't cause the accident, she at least contributed to it. Now when plaintiff's counsel argues again, she may claim that there

---

10 An example of the plaintiff's use of the "modest grandfather" story is found in Section I C(4)(c), *supra* at p. 398.

was no time to pull over. Don't believe it. There was really plenty of time to pull over. Let's look at the evidence . . . .

This approach has its drawbacks, not the least of which is the necessity of suggesting that, in fact, the plaintiff may not have had enough time to pull her car to the side. In any event, it may be just as effective to make the argument without referring to rebuttal.

Most lawyers choose to anticipate rebuttal only in the general sense, making sure to explain the phenomenon of rebuttal to the jury:

When I am done speaking, the plaintiff's attorney will have another opportunity to argue. That is called rebuttal. Following rebuttal, however, I will not be allowed to stand before you again. The rules of procedure only allow me to speak to you once. It is not that I don't want to speak again, or that I will have no responses to what plaintiff's counsel says, but only that I will not have the opportunity to give you my responses.

I have only one request to make of you. When plaintiff's counsel returns to argue, please bear in mind that, whatever she says, I will not be able to answer. I think you know from the evidence that I will have answers to her rebuttal argument. So please keep what I have said in mind, and provide those answers for me.

The timing of this aspect of the argument is important. Because it relates solely to the rebuttal, it obviously is preferable to make these remarks near the end of the defendant's argument in chief. On the other hand, placing them at the very end would deprive the argument of a strong finish. Thus, it is generally best to use the discussion of rebuttal as the penultimate point, saving the final moment for the most compelling substantive argument.

C.   Plaintiff's Rebuttal

The plaintiff or prosecutor, as the burdened party, is generally afforded the opportunity to present the last argument. Rebuttal, therefore, is a powerful tool. The plaintiff can reply to all of the defendant's arguments and contentions, but the defendant must stand mute in response. Everyone likes to have the last word, and the rules of procedure in most jurisdictions guarantee that right to the plaintiff.

Effective use of rebuttal can be elusive. While the plaintiff's argument in chief can be completely planned in advance, and the defendant's argument in chief can be mostly planned, rebuttal must generally be delivered extemporaneously. Preparation for rebuttal typically takes place while plaintiff's counsel listens to the defendant's argument in chief. Nonetheless, there are certain principles that can be applied to make rebuttal more forceful and compelling. The most important principle of rebuttal is to organize it according to the plaintiff's own theory of the case.

A common approach to rebuttal is simply to make notes of the defense arguments, and then to reply to the most important of them in the order in which they were delivered. This technique is easy to use, and it has the virtue of minimizing the potential for overlooking arguments. Its vice, however, is that it organizes the rebuttal according to the defendant's agenda, rather than the plaintiff's. It also tends to promote a boring delivery, since a rebuttal that follows this approach is likely to fall into a repetitive cadence of short paragraphs, each one beginning, "The defendant also argued . . . ."

A more effective technique involves matching the defendant's arguments to the major propositions in the plaintiff's own case. To do this, plaintiff's counsel needs only to prepare a truncated outline of the three or four most important, or hotly contested, issues in the case, leaving a blank half-page or so under each heading. In this manner, four major arguments can be spread over two sheets of paper, and can be arranged in the order most advantageous to the plaintiff. Then, as defense counsel argues, plaintiff's attorney can write her notes under the appropriate heading. When it comes time to deliver rebuttal, plaintiff's counsel will have automatically organized her notes of the defendant's remarks according to the plaintiff's own structure. The rebuttal can then be delivered topically, without regard to the order of argument used by the defendant.

A second principle of rebuttal is to present the plaintiff's case in an affirmative light. Even when it is well organized, rebuttal is weakened if it becomes nothing more than a series of retorts. As with all argument, it is more effective to present the positive side of your own case, and this is particularly important when you represent the burdened party. Consequently, even in rebuttal, every position should be framed as a constructive statement of the plaintiff's own theory, with the refutation of the defense being used to explain further or elaborate on the plaintiff's case. Consider this short example from the rebuttal in the fire engine case:

> I would like to talk to you once again about damages. I'm sure that you remember the plaintiff's own testimony about her efforts to cope with her injuries. She has done everything possible to bring her life back to normal. She is a courageous woman who won't give up. That is why it is particularly unfair to see defense counsel trying to exploit the plaintiff's camping trip to Eagle River Falls. Of course she tried to go camping. What does the defendant want her to do, give up on life and just sit at home? Unfortunately, her efforts didn't work out. As she told you, the camping trip was pure hell. She suffered every day, and she had to stay on her back in the tent for hours at a time. Why didn't she come home early? Because she and her family had all come in the same car, and she didn't want to ruin the trip for everyone else. Sure she tried

to enjoy camping. But that only proves how brave and determined she is, not that she wasn't injured.

Many lawyers attempt to save a single, devastating argument for rebuttal, on the assumption that it will be even more effective if it stands unanswered. There is, no doubt, a great deal of truth to this theory, as it deprives the defendant of all opportunity to respond. One caveat, however, is necessary. Rebuttal is technically limited to issues that were addressed during the defense argument in chief. If, for whatever reason, defense counsel does not raise a particular issue, then it is possible that the court will sustain an objection to its coverage on rebuttal.

Thus, it is inherently risky for the plaintiff to "sandbag" by completely omitting a subject from the argument in chief. Suppose, for example, the plaintiff in the fire engine case decided to defer all discussion of damages until rebuttal, thereby precluding the defendant from replying to the plaintiff's specific arguments. The defendant, in turn, could decide not to address damages at all. Some courts, then, would refuse to allow the plaintiff to raise damages for the first time on rebuttal, and the plaintiff would be entirely precluded from presenting any argument on damages.[11]

The rule requiring rebuttal to be within the scope of the defendant's argument is enforced with varying degrees of strictness from court to court. It is generally safe to assume, however, that the rule will be applied more rigidly to topics (such as damages) than to lines of argument (such as elaboration on a theme). Consequently, it usually is not risky to withhold the use of an analogy or story until rebuttal, thereby preventing the defendant from "reversing" it.

D. Variations

It is always within the discretion of the court to alter the usual order of argument so as to reflect the actual burden of proof in the particular case. In cases involving counterclaims or affirmative defenses, the defendant may be allowed to present the first and last arguments, or may be given a surrebuttal to follow the plaintiff's rebuttal. In multi-party cases the court will determine the order in which the various plaintiffs and defendants will proceed.

It is also the judge's prerogative to apportion the time for argument, although the court may not effectively deny a party the opportunity to argue its case. Finally,

---

11 Note that the rule is that rebuttal may be used only to respond to issues covered during the defendant's argument in chief. Thus, even if the plaintiff had addressed damages during her argument in chief, the omission of the issue from the defendant's argument in chief would still technically rule out damages as a subject for rebuttal. Unlike the "sandbagging" situation, however, the plaintiff in this supposition did not forego the opportunity to discuss damages at the outset.

some courts do not provide automatically for rebuttal, but rather require the plaintiff affirmatively to reserve time from the argument in chief.

III. STRUCTURE

The structure of the final argument must be developed for maximum persuasive weight. The central thrust of the final argument must always be to provide reasons — logical, moral, legal, emotional — for the entry of a verdict in your client's favor. Every aspect of the final argument should contribute in some way to the completion of the sentence "We win because . . . ." In the broadest sense, of course, the desired conclusion should simply follow from the facts and law of the case. Few cases, however, will go to trial unless the facts are capable of multiple interpretations. Effective argument therefore places a premium on arrangement and explanation.

The use of topical organization is the guiding principle in the structure of final arguments. The following section will discuss the various methods of employing topical organization, as well as the drawbacks and advantages of alternative structures.

A. Topical Organization

The importance of topical organization in final argument cannot be overemphasized. Seemingly natural methods of organization, such as chronology and witness listing, will not present the evidence in its most persuasive form. Topical organization, on the other hand, allows counsel to determine the best way to address the issues in the case. Topical organization can use, or combine, any of the following strategies.

1. Issues

One of the simplest and most effective forms of organization is to divide the case into a series of discrete factual or legal issues. Large issues, such as liability and damages, are obvious, but they are also so broad as to provide relatively little help in ordering an argument. It is more useful to think of issues as narrower propositions of fact or law.

In the fire engine case, for example, the plaintiff might organize the liability section of her argument according to these *factual* issues: (1) The defendant's hurried morning; (2) The siren; and (3) The events of the accident. The first section of the argument would emphasize the reasons for the defendant's inattention, the second segment would explain why all of the other traffic stopped for the fire truck (and why the jury should not believe the defendant's claim that there was no siren), and the third segment would finally describe the actual collision.

A fourth portion of the argument could be devoted to the *legal* issue of comparative negligence. Plaintiff's counsel can thereby isolate and explain all of the factors that made the plaintiff's own actions reasonable and non-negligent.

Note that this format, as opposed to strict chronology,[12] will allow plaintiff's counsel to plan the discussions of motivation and credibility in a coherent and logical fashion. All of the considerations pointing to the defendant's preoccupation can be addressed at once, including events that occurred both before (being late for the meeting) and after (rushing to call the office) the accident. Similarly, the entire "siren question" can be resolved, making it clear that the siren was sounding, before discussing the collision. Finally, counsel can address the question of comparative negligence without interrupting or detracting from the drama of the collision.

These strategies, of course, are open to question and reevaluation. Perhaps the use of the siren should be raised within the scope of the events, leaving the defendant's credibility to be addressed later. The point is that only the use of issue-based organization allows counsel to make such tactical decisions.

2. Elements

A second form of topical organization revolves around elements and claims. Every legal cause or defense is composed of various discrete elements. A claim of negligence, for instance, must be supported by proof of duty, breach of duty, cause in fact, proximate cause, and damages. A plaintiff can therefore develop her final argument by discussing the evidence as it supports each of the distinct elements of her cause of action. A defendant, who needs to challenge only a single element in order to win, can use the same form of organization, but can truncate it by focusing only on those elements that are truly likely to be negated.

3. Jury Instructions

In most jurisdictions an "instructions conference" is held immediately prior to the final arguments.[13] Armed with advance knowledge of the instructions that the court will give to the jury, counsel can use them to organize all, or more likely part, of the final argument.

Jury instructions must be used selectively as an organizing device. They are boring enough when read by the judge, and there is no reason to repeat them fully in their typically mind-numbing length as part of your argument to the jury. Rather,

---

12 The uses and pitfalls of chronological organization are discussed at Section III A(5)(a), *infra* at p. 413.

13 In most jurisdictions the final arguments are given before the court instructs the jury as to the law. In a few jurisdictions, however, final arguments follow the court's charge. In either situation, the attorneys know what the instructions will be before they deliver their arguments.

counsel should pick out several of the most important instructions and use those to develop the central points of the final argument. Thus, the plaintiff in the fire engine case might focus on the instructions dealing with due care and credibility, while the defendant might choose to utilize the instructions on comparative negligence and damages.

4. Turning Points

Modern cognitive theory tells us that jurors are likely to regard the information in a case as a series of turning points or problems. Rather than resolving the truth or falsity of every distinct fact, they are far more likely to focus on a limited number of contested issues. Once a juror decides those issues, she will be inclined to fit the individual facts into a picture that fits in with that view of reality. Thus, an attorney can persuade a jury by identifying the key turning points in the trial and explaining them in a way that comports with the jurors' life experience and sense of reality.

Assume that the defendant in the fire engine case has raised the defense of comparative negligence, and has also challenged the plaintiff's claim of damages. Defense counsel's final argument could easily be organized around turning points such as the plaintiff's failure to pull over (as opposed to merely stopping in the middle of the road) or the plaintiff's weekend-long camping trip.

Note how the turning-point approach tends to work. Defense counsel can argue (although with more details and at greater length) to the following effect:

> Everyone knows that you are supposed to pull over to the right when you see or hear an emergency vehicle. If the plaintiff stopped but did not pull over, it must have been because she didn't have enough time to do so. That means that the fire engine's warning devices must have become noticeable only at the last moment, since the plaintiff herself would have pulled over if she had seen or heard the truck sooner. This must mean that the siren was silent, or at least inaudible, since the siren can be heard long before the fire truck can be seen.

By persuading the jury that the plaintiff stopped in the middle of the road, defense counsel can also make progress in persuading them of the defendant's position on the siren issue. A juror who believes that the plaintiff did not pull over will look to her own life's experience for a reason or explanation, and will tend to embrace other facts that make sense in that context. An inaudible or non-operating siren provides such contextual support for the juror's conclusion that the plaintiff did not pull over. Thus, once a juror accepts that the plaintiff did not hear a siren, she will be far more likely to credit the defendant's claim that he had insufficient warning to stop his car.

5. Alternative Structures

a. Chronological Organization

Chronology is the most obvious alternative structure for a final argument. Since the events in a case manifestly occurred in a chronological order, it seems obvious to replay them in the same progression during final argument.

While chronology certainly plays an important role in final argument, it is usually not the best approach to overall structure. The difficulty with chronology is that events are unlikely to have occurred in the most persuasive possible sequence. Early events can frequently be illuminated by their subsequent consequences. In the preceding section, for example, we saw the forensic relationship in the defendant's argument between proof of the plaintiff's failure to pull over and the fire engine's use (or non-use) of its siren. Told in chronological order, an argument would address the siren first; the use of warning signals obviously must have preceded the plaintiff's response. This structure, however, deprives the story of its persuasive weight, since it is the failure to pull over that tends to prove the absence of a siren.

Consider, then, the following two snippets of defense argument. The first is in chronological order:

As the fire truck approached the intersection, it flashed its lights but it did not use its siren. The plaintiff saw the fire truck and stopped for it, but she did not have time to pull over. That is why the accident occurred. She saw the fire truck only at the last moment.

Now, the same argument presented topically:

The plaintiff stopped her car in the middle of the street. She didn't pull over. This can only mean that the fire truck was not using its siren. Everyone knows that you must pull over as soon as you become aware of an emergency vehicle, and a siren can be heard blocks away. The location of the plaintiff's car tells us that she saw that fire truck only at the last moment.

While both arguments make the same point, the discussion is clearly more persuasive once it is freed of the chronological strait jacket. It then becomes possible to move both backward and forward in time, in order to place events in the most compelling order.

There can be no doubt, of course, that chronology is an essential tool in the structure of a final argument. There will come a time, or several times, in every argument when key occurrences will have to be time-ordered. Indeed, the precise sequence of events can often be the central issue in a case.

Chronology often fails, however, when it is used as the primary organizational device, as though the entire story of the case can be presented in a single order. Rather, it is best to think of the case as consisting of a series of discrete sub-stories. Each sub-story can be set out in chronological order, while maintaining an overall format of topical organization.

b. Witness Listing

Some lawyers persist in presenting final argument as a series of witness descriptions and accounts, essentially recapitulating the testimony of each person who took the stand. This approach is unlikely to succeed, as it diminishes the argument's logical coherence and force. Where topical organization focuses on the importance of issues and chronological organization focuses on the real-life sequence of events, witness listing depends on nothing more than the serendipity of which witness said what. It is a lazy, and usually ineffective, method of organization.

To be sure, it will often be necessary to compare witness accounts in the course of a final argument. You may wish to demonstrate the consistency of your own witnesses as opposed to the contradictions among the opposition's. You may want to dwell on the integrity and credibility of your witnesses. Or you might want to point out the bias and self-interest of opposing witnesses. All of this can be accomplished through topical organization.

B. Other Organizing Tools

1. Start Strong and End Strong

The principles of primacy and recency apply with full force to the final argument. In presenting a final argument, counsel has a limited window in which to attempt to shape the jury's imagination of the acts, events, and circumstances at issue in the case. Anything that bores the jury, or that distracts them from the task at hand, must be eliminated from the final argument. And it is certain that prime time — the very beginning and the very end of the argument — must be devoted to the most important considerations in the case.[14]

The strength of a starting point can be measured against a number of standards such as theory value, thematic value, dramatic impact, or undeniability. What is the central proposition of your client's theory? What aspect of the evidence best

---

14 Accordingly, it is a mistake to begin the final argument with a lengthy introduction on the virtues of the jury system. It is also usually unnecessary to reintroduce counsel and clients to the jury, or to dwell on your gratitude for their faithful attention to the evidence. It is sufficient to thank the jury in simple language, and then to proceed to the heart of the argument. Remember that the final argument is a story. No best-seller begins with a paean to the publishing industry, and no motion picture ever starts by thanking the audience for attending.

evokes your theme? What is the most emotional or memorable factor in the case? What is the opposing party's greatest concession?

In the fire engine case, plaintiff's counsel might choose to begin the final argument with a compelling restatement of her theory:

The plaintiff was driving safely in the southbound lane of Sheridan Road. A fire truck approached the intersection from the west. It was flashing its lights and sounding its siren, so, as the law requires and as every high school student understands, she stopped her car. All of the other traffic stopped as well, with one awful exception. The defendant kept his foot on the accelerator, never slowing down and never swerving, and he crashed his car right into the plaintiff's automobile.

Alternatively, plaintiff's counsel could start with her theme:

This accident happened because the defendant was too busy to be careful. He was so preoccupied with his thoughts of a new client that he failed to notice what every other driver on the road saw and heard. He was so late, and so rushed, and so distracted that he paid no attention to the traffic all around him. He was in such a hurry to get to his office that the fire truck's emergency lights and sirens had no impact on him at all. He was so busy that getting to work became more important than ordinary caution. And make no mistake — ordinary caution would have been enough to avoid this accident completely.

Dramatic impact also works:

In a single instant the defendant's carelessness changed the plaintiff's life forever. In one moment, she went from being an ordinary, healthy, active individual, to being a person who cannot take a step, or lift a child, or even prepare a meal without pain.

As does undeniability:

The one thing the defendant cannot deny is that he failed to stop for a fire engine. There is no doubt that the fire truck was there, there is no doubt that it was answering a call, there is no doubt that the other cars stopped, and there is no doubt that the defendant kept driving right into the back of the plaintiff's automobile.

The most important point is that the opening salvo in the final argument should be directed at making the jury *want* to decide the case in your favor.

The last few minutes of the final argument should serve the same function, either summarizing the theory, utilizing the theme, driving home the strongest evidence, or painting the most compelling picture. Note that ending on a strong and memorable note is particularly important to the defendant, who will not be able to argue again following the plaintiff's rebuttal.

2. Affirmative Case First

Most final arguments will consist of two distinct components: developing the affirmative case and debunking the opposing party's claims and/or defenses. As a general rule, it is preferable to build up your own case first, and then proceed to debunk the opposition.

Plaintiffs in particular should resist the temptation to begin by criticizing the defense case. No matter how weak or ridiculous the defenses, it is usually best to begin with the strong points of your own case. The plaintiff, after all, bears the burden of proof, and can not win without establishing all of the elements of an affirmative case. Thus, there is little to be gained by refuting the defense if you can not prove your own case first. Moreover, a plaintiff who launches immediately into an assault on the defendant's case may be seen as confessing a lack of confidence in her own position. And if the jury does not jump immediately to that conclusion, you can be sure that defense counsel will argue that precise inference: "If plaintiff's case is so strong, why did counsel begin by attacking the defense; they must be worried."

The defendant has more latitude. Having just heard the plaintiff's or prosecutor's argument, a jury is unlikely to draw any adverse inference should defense counsel begin by refuting the plaintiff's case. Indeed, most juries will be waiting to hear the defendant's denial. Therefore, the defendant should almost always begin with a denial. After all, that is the natural response to an hour or so of the plaintiff's accusations.

Once a strong denial has been made, however, the defendant should, if possible, proceed to support it through the development of an affirmative case. That is, the defendant should usually explain why she is right before going on to explain why the plaintiff is wrong. Thus, the defendant's argument in the fire truck case might — in extremely skeletal form — proceed as follows:

> The defendant was not the cause of this accident. It was the plaintiff's fault. The defendant was driving safely and carefully; well within the speed limit. The fire engine was not sounding its siren, but as soon as he saw it, he hit his brakes and started to pull over. Unfortunately, the plaintiff chose to stop dead in the middle of the road, instead of pulling to the side as the traffic laws require.

The real argument, of course, would be much longer, but the organization of the above paragraph holds true. Counsel began with a denial, demonstrated that the defendant's actions were reasonable, and went on to explain the plaintiff's own negligence.

The most frequent exception to the "affirmative case first" rule is found in criminal cases. Since a criminal defendant is not required to present an affirmative case, it is not uncommon for a defense argument to focus solely (or primarily) on the deficiencies in the prosecution's proof.

The plaintiff's (or prosecutor's) rebuttal, of course, is technically limited to refutation of the defense. Within this stricture, however, it is still advisable to frame the argument in as affirmative a light as possible.

Note finally that the "affirmative case first" rule does not mean "affirmative case only." A substantial part of most final arguments should be devoted to the weaknesses in the opposition case. But not the first part.

3. Cluster Circumstantial Evidence and Accumulate Details

We have seen that details can give texture and support to a theory of the case, and that circumstantial evidence can establish major propositions. These small, constituent facts are often presented at different times during the testimonial phase of the trial. One witness may testify to several details, the importance of which will become apparent only in light of other evidence supplied by other witnesses. Moreover, on cross examination counsel may deliberately separate details, so as not to alert the witness to the intended thrust of the examination.

Final argument is the time for gathering details. Although the particulars may have occurred at widely different times, and have been testified to by several witnesses, they can and should be aggregated to make a single point in final argument. So, for example, the plaintiff in the fire engine case will want to collect all of the details, both direct and circumstantial, that support her proposition that the defendant was preoccupied with thoughts of his important meeting:

We know that his mind was not on his driving. Look at the details. He was late for work. He had an important meeting scheduled for 9:00 a.m., and he was still eleven miles from downtown. He had to park his car, leave the garage, walk over two blocks to his office, and get up to the fourteenth floor. And look at what would happen if he was late. The defendant himself testified that he was meeting with a potential new client, and that he hoped to land a valuable account. New clients mean advancement and raises. Losing a new client means losing money. You can't land a new client if you don't make it to the meeting. That meeting must have been the only thing on the defendant's mind. It was so important to him that the first thing that he did after the accident was run to a phone and call his office. He didn't call an ambulance, he didn't call the police, and he didn't even check to see if the other driver was injured. No, first and foremost he cared about that new client. Everything else — driving, traffic, safety — was unimportant compared to his need to get to that meeting.

Note that the details in the above passage could have come from as many as three different witnesses, and that they do not strictly follow the chronology of the accident. The argument makes coordinated use of both direct (the phone call after the accident) and circumstantial (the distance from the garage to his office) evidence. The argument also utilizes both positive (a new client means money) and negative (he didn't call an ambulance) inferences. It is the clustering or accumulation of all of these points that gives the argument its persuasive weight.

4. Bury Your Concessions

In the course of almost every argument it will be necessary to concede certain of the opposition's claims or facts, if only to minimize or discount them. As a corollary to the "start and end strong" rule, such concessions should usually be "buried" in the middle of your argument.

Suppose, for example, that your client was impeached on cross examination with a prior inconsistent statement. At some point in your argument you may well want to concede the inconsistency, but explain why it should be of no consequence to the outcome of the case. That is a fine strategy, but do not do it at either the beginning or the end of your argument. There are sure to be many facts that you want the jury to remember more vividly than your client's inconsistent statements, no matter how adeptly you are able to downplay their significance. In other words, bury the concessions.

5. Weave In Witness Credibility

We noted above that witness listing is an ineffective format for final argument. Witness credibility, on the other hand, is often a subject that must be addressed. The solution is to weave discussion of the witnesses, and their relative credibility, into the fabric of the story.

In most cases it will be sufficient to discuss witnesses only at the point that they become important to the theory of the case. So, for example, the credibility of the fire truck defendant should not form a separate section of the plaintiff's argument. There will be relatively little value to a freestanding attack on the defendant's credibility; it will seem like just that, an attack. On the other hand, the jury will be most receptive to a credibility argument at a moment when its significance is apparent:

Let us turn to the question of the siren. There is no doubt that a fire engine's siren is a signal that traffic must stop. Ignoring a siren is definite negligence. The defendant claims that there was no siren, but he cannot be believed. He has too much at stake in this case, and he knows that the siren is a vital piece of evidence against him. And remember that Lieutenant Bonnie Middleton testified that she always used her siren when answering a call. She has absolutely no stake in this case, and no reason to tell you anything but the truth. So it comes down to this: either you believe the defendant or you believe Lieutenant Middleton.

While the defendant might be unsavory, and Lieutenant Middleton upstanding, it makes no sense to discuss their character traits in the abstract. By weaving the witnesses into the story, however, counsel can make full use of their disparate believability.

6. Damages

A special problem is raised by the issue of damages in civil cases, and especially in personal injury cases.

Most authorities agree that plaintiff's counsel should argue liability before proceeding to damages. Particularly where the damages are great or inchoate, a jury will be more inclined to accept the plaintiff's argument once they have been convinced of liability. Stated otherwise, the desire to award damages flows naturally from a conclusion of liability. The converse, however, is not true. Proof of damages does not necessarily imply that the defendant was at fault.

For the same reason, defendants are often advised to address damages first, if at all. It is discordant to argue, "The defendant was not at fault, but even if he was, the damages were not so great as the plaintiff claims." The subsequent discussion of damages may be taken as a concession of liability.

Of course, many defense cases are based primarily, if not exclusively, on the issue of damages. In these cases it should be obvious that damages should form the first, last, and most important part of the argument.

IV. CONTENT

The specific content of any final argument will obviously be determined by the facts and issues in the case. It is possible, however, to enumerate certain sorts of information that should be considered for inclusion in every final argument.

A. Tell a Persuasive Story

Virtually every final argument should contain all of the elements of a persuasive story. The argument should detail the evidentiary support for counsel's theory of the case and should consistently invoke the trial theme.

We have previously discussed five substantive elements[15] to a persuasive story: It explains all of the known facts. It is told about people who have reasons for their actions. It is told by credible witnesses. It is supported by details. And it accords with common sense. These elements should be present at some point in all final arguments.

---

15 The sixth, non-substantive, element to a persuasive story is organization.

1. Known Facts — What Happened

A persuasive story accounts for all of the known facts. It is not premised on incomplete information, and it does not glide over or ignore inconvenient occurrences. This is not to say that a final argument must mention every minor detail in the case, but rather that it should, in some fashion, accommodate all of the established facts.

The final argument must, of course, cover the central facts of counsel's case, taking care to provide support for all of the legally necessary elements. It must also take into consideration the evidence produced by the opposing party.

Assume that the fire engine case has been tried along the lines that we have discussed in previous sections. The plaintiff has used "Too busy to be careful" as a trial theme, introducing evidence of the defendant's hurried morning. Since there was no dispute as to details such as the defendant's scheduled meeting and various travel times, these have become "known facts" in the sense that the jury is not likely to regard them with doubt or disbelief. Defense counsel might believe that these facts are inconsequential to the issue of liability; after all, people can be late for work and still drive carefully. Nonetheless, the defendant's final argument should account for these facts either by refuting them or by explaining their irrelevance.

2. Reasons — Why Did It Happen

Explain the reasons for the actions of the parties and other witnesses. It is not enough to state that an individual did something. Rather, counsel should go on to reveal why those activities were consistent with that individual's self-interest, announced intentions, past behavior, life style, or other understandable motivations.

The articulation of reasons gives logical weight to the argument, and can transform it from an attorney's assertion into an acceptable statement of fact.

3. Credible Witnesses — Who Should Be Believed

The credibility of witnesses should always be addressed on final argument. At a minimum, this means that the credibility of counsel's own witnesses should be developed in the course of establishing an affirmative case. This can usually be done subtly and indirectly, simply by providing the background information that tends to render your witnesses believable.

In cases where credibility is seriously in issue, it will be necessary to take a more frontal approach.

4. Supportive Details — How Can We Be Sure

As we have seen throughout, persuasion often rests on the accumulation of supportive details. An essential aspect of final argument is the marshalling of details that give weight to counsel's argument.

The inclusion or exclusion of details is a tricky problem. While the right details at the right time can add an airtight quality to your case, the use of too many details (or their use in support of unimportant propositions) can drag a final argument into the depths of boredom and despair. There is no single key to making judgments in this area, but it is safe to look to the following guidelines:

- Use details when important facts are in dispute. Whenever there is a disagreement as to an occurrence or incident, details can be used effectively to support your client's version of events.

- Use details when motivations are in issue. The presence (or absence) of motive can frequently be established through recourse to constituent facts. Explain why a party would want to act in a certain way. Look at the details that show the benefits of the actions' consequences.

- Use details to support an interpretation of the evidence. The meaning of certain evidence is often contested even when the underlying facts are not in dispute. Regarding damages in the fire engine case, for example, both parties will agree to the fact that the plaintiff went camping at Eagle River Falls. But how should that fact be interpreted? Does it mean that she was not really injured in the accident? Or does it mean that she is a brave woman trying to make the best of a difficult situation? Constituent details — Did she stay in the tent? Did she organize daily hikes? Did she express reluctance about going in the first place? — may help provide the answer.

- Do not use details for unimportant reasons. The judge or jury will have a limited tolerance for details. Every time you use one detail, you are diminishing the effectiveness of those that you will use later. It is therefore necessary to reserve your use of details for truly important situations. For example, you will not want to use details, even if they are available, to attack the credibility of a witness whose testimony was not damaging to your case.

- Do not use details to establish uncontested facts.

5. Common Sense — Is It Plausible

Perhaps the ultimate test of every final argument is plausibility. Even if an argument accounts for the known facts, gives reasons for every action, is supported by credible witnesses, and might be replete with convincing details, it still will not be accepted if it does not make sense to the jury. Almost every other failing can be overcome or forgiven. You cannot, however, win with an implausible argument.

It is essential, therefore, that every closing argument address the subject of common sense. Explain why your theory is realistic, using examples and analogies from everyday life. Plaintiff's counsel in the fire truck case, for instance, will need to explain why the plaintiff, who claimed crippling injuries, went camping at Eagle River Falls. The argument, of course, is that she did not want to be defeated by her disabilities. This argument can be strengthened by drawing on the jury's own observations and experiences:

> It is easy to understand why someone would not want to give in to her injuries. We all know, or have seen, people who refuse to be house-bound just because they are disabled. I read a story in the newspaper yesterday about a young boy who lost his right arm to cancer — but he still tried out for his high school baseball team. I'm sure that he went through a lot of pain and disappointment, but he never would have made the team if he hadn't tried. That is what the plaintiff did at Eagle River Falls. She tried to live a normal life.

"Common sense" arguments can also be used to belittle or even ridicule the opposition case. It is every lawyer's dream that the jury will retire to the deliberation room and immediately conclude that the opposition case just doesn't stack up.

B. Tie Up Cross Examinations

Final argument is the time to tie up the issues that were intentionally left unaddressed during cross examination. Recall the questions that are forbidden to the prudent cross examiner: Never ask a witness to explain; never ask a witness to fill in a gap; never ask a witness to agree with a characterization or conclusion. These questions, and others like them, all risk losing control of the witness. All authorities agree that it is better to refrain from asking the ultimate question, and to make the point instead during the final argument.

Thus, if your cross examinations were artful and effective, you should be able to spend some portion of the final argument drawing the previously unspoken conclusions.

Assume that you represent the prosecution in a burglary case involving an alibi defense. The defendant, on direct examination, recited his alibi, but left an apparent gap during the crucial window when the burglary was most likely to have occurred. As a skilled trial lawyer, you knew not to go into those gaps on cross examination, for fear that the defendant would fill them in with additional information as to his whereabouts. Final argument, however, is another matter:

> We know that this burglary occurred some time during the evening of November 7. The defendant claims that he was at work that entire time. He even produced his time card, showing that he punched in at 4:00 p.m. and punched out at midnight. Other witnesses testified that they

saw him at work at various times that night. But no one testified that they were with him during his dinner break. We know that he must have taken a break, or at least that he is entitled to one. It is the law in this state that no employee can be required to work for eight hours without a meal break of at least 30 minutes. So we have a full half hour that is unaccounted for. We know that the defendant could have slipped away, and absolutely no one testified that they were with him.

Confronted with this gap on cross examination, a clever defendant might come up with numerous explanations as to why he didn't take a break or why he went alone. By the time of final argument, however, it is too late. The gap stands unfilled, ready to be exploited by the prosecution.[16]

The same approach can be used with regard to explanations and characterizations. You did not ask a witness why something happened; be sure to use the final argument to tell the jury why it happened. You did not ask a witness to agree with a conclusion or characterization; be sure to use the final argument to draw the conclusion yourself.

C. Comment on Promises

Attorneys on both sides of a case will inevitably make various promises and commitments to the jury during the course of the trial. These promises may be overt, as is often the case during opening statements: "We will produce a series of documents and work records that prove that the defendant was nowhere near the scene of the crime." Or the commitments may be implicit in the theory of the case. When a plaintiff claims damages for personal injury, there is obviously an implied promise of certain proof.

Whatever the case, final argument is the time for counsel to comment on promises made, kept, or broken. Point out the ways in which you fulfilled your commitments. Perhaps more importantly, and certainly more dramatically, underscore the ways in which the opposition failed to live up to their own promises. Consider the explicit promise in the alibi example used above:

---

16 Is it unethical to use the final argument to lie in wait for a witness? Is a prosecutor entitled to obtain a conviction by depriving the defendant of an opportunity to explain himself during cross examination? The answer lies in understanding the adversary system. The decision to refrain from asking a question on cross examination does not deprive the witness of all opportunity to explain. The witness was free to provide whatever information he wanted during the direct examination, and opposing counsel had at least one additional opportunity to cure any defects during redirect examination. The prosecutor, or any lawyer, can fairly assume that the decision to omit a fact from direct examination means that the fact does not exist. The decision not to inquire further during cross examination, then, at most deprives the witness of yet a third chance to elaborate. It is at least possible, if not likely, that the witness would use that chance to invent facts or obfuscate the truth.

I am sure you remember defense counsel's opening statement. She told you that she would produce documentary evidence — work records — that would prove that the defendant was nowhere near the scene of the crime. Well the trial is now over and all of the evidence is in. We have not seen any documentary evidence; there were no work records.

The approach needs to be modified only slightly for use with implicit commitments:

When a plaintiff comes before you claiming injury, she makes a commitment about the proof that she will offer. You have the right to expect that she will produce evidence of the nature of the injury, that you will hear from doctors about her medical condition, or at least that you will hear from friends and neighbors about the changes in the plaintiff's life. In this case, however, there was no such proof. Of course, the plaintiff testified. But beyond her words there was absolutely no disinterested evidence that she was truly injured in any way.

Of course, the most effective final arguments are often those in which counsel is able to state that "We kept our promises and they broke theirs."

D.   Resolve Problems and Weaknesses

Final argument can be used to solve problems and confront weaknesses. No matter how well the evidentiary phase of the trial proceeded, you are sure to be left with a number of difficult or troublesome issues. Once identified, these issues can be addressed and resolved in the course of final argument.

A classic instance of such a weakness is the government's reliance on informers in drug prosecutions. Informers are assailable witnesses to begin with, and in drug cases they are often further sullied with histories of their own substance abuse. Recognizing the problems created by reliance on such witnesses, prosecutors have developed over the years an almost standardized, and extremely effective, final argument approach. In its barest form, it goes something like this:

It is true that a number of the prosecution witnesses were informers and former drug users. They aren't the most upstanding citizens in the world. It was not the prosecution, however, who chose them as witnesses. The defendants chose these people as witnesses when they set out to sell illegal and dangerous drugs. Who can we expect to serve as witnesses to drug deals? Not clergymen, not doctors, not solid citizens or civic leaders. No, drug deals take place in a shadowy world that is populated by petty criminals and addicts. Those were the people who were present for this transaction, and those were the witnesses whom we had to call to the stand.

There are several schools of thought as to the best timing for addressing weaknesses or problems. Some authorities believe that weaknesses should never be addressed unless the opposing side raises them first. Others believe that at least certain weaknesses should be dealt with "defensively," on the theory that the sting can be preempted by discussing the issue first.

The decision is not always simple. Plaintiffs' attorneys have the choice of dealing with weaknesses during either argument in chief or rebuttal. Thus, they can either initiate the discussion, or they can wait to see whether the defense brings up the issue during its argument in chief. Defendants, on the other hand, must be more wary. Even if the plaintiff (or prosecutor) omits a problem area from the argument in chief, it can still be exploited mercilessly on rebuttal.

Because the jury's deliberation does not depend solely upon the final arguments, there may ultimately be some weaknesses that must be addressed whether the opposition mentions them or not. Assume that the plaintiff's attorney in the fire engine case delivered the entire final argument without mentioning the plaintiff's camping trip, and that the subject was also omitted from the defense argument. Should the plaintiff's counsel rejoice and refrain from mentioning the subject in her rebuttal argument? The jury, after all, heard the evidence, which was damaging to the plaintiff's case. There is no guarantee that they will not consider it, or even base their verdict upon it, once they retire to the jury room. Because the evidence was both harmful and easily counteracted, it is probably wisest for plaintiff's counsel to make sure that the topic is covered during final argument. Since counsel's ability to discuss the issue on rebuttal is limited by the scope of the defense argument, the best approach might well have been to address the issue during the plaintiff's argument in chief.

E.   Discuss Damages

The trial of a civil case can usually be divided into the conceptual areas of liability and damages. Although liability is the threshold issue, it is a mistake to underestimate the importance of damages. Unless the trial has been bifurcated, plaintiffs in particular should devote a significant portion of the final argument to the development of damages.

It may be helpful to think of damages as comprising a "second persuasive story" in the case. Once liability has been established, damages can be addressed using all of the persuasive story elements that we have discussed above. Counsel should account for the known facts that bear on damages, give the reasons for the actions of the people involved, address the credibility of the specific witnesses, delineate the crucial details, and explain why the requested damage award accords with common sense.

There are two significant aspects involved in most arguments for damages: method and amount. It is important to explain to the jury precisely how damages have been (or should be) calculated. It is also usually important to request a specific amount, rather than leaving the award to the jury's guesswork.

Some defense attorneys prefer to avoid or minimize the issue of damages, reasoning that any discussion may be seen as an implicit admission of liability.[17] Most lawyers, however, choose not to "roll the dice" on liability, concluding that a reduced damage award is the next best thing to winning the case outright. When discussing damages, defense lawyers have a choice. You may simply rebut the plaintiff's damage claim, or you may present a competing estimate of your own. The decision will rest upon the circumstances of the particular case. Note, however, that the presentation of a competing damage estimate does run a greater risk of seeming to concede liability.

F. Use Jury Instructions

Some part of every final argument should be devoted to the court's forthcoming jury instructions, as well as to the elements of the claims and defenses in the case. Jury instructions can be extremely important in the way that the jurors decide the case, and it is to counsel's advantage to invoke some of the instructions during argument.

Care must be taken, however, not to overuse or dwell on the instructions. The charge to the jury is universally regarded as one of the most boring parts of the trial, and there is little to be gained by simply giving the jurors a lengthy advance notice of the instructions to come. The instructions should be used strategically, as further evidence of your client's right to prevail on key issues in the case. Thus, discussion of the instructions should not form a single, extended part of the final argument. Rather, they should be used throughout the argument, read or referred to at the points where they can accomplish the most good.

Assume, for example, that the plaintiff in the fire engine case called an expert economist to testify to the plaintiff's expected future losses. The defense, on the other hand, did not produce expert testimony, for fear of crediting the plaintiff's claim to damages. Assume also that the court agreed to give the standard expert witness instruction to the jury: they may reject all, or any part, of the testimony of expert witnesses, and the credibility of experts should be judged in the same manner as any other witness. As defense counsel approaches the issue of damages during her final argument, she will therefore want to make use of the expert witness instruction. The defendant's final argument, then, might go as follows:

---

17   Defense lawyers often seek bifurcated trials to avoid this problem.

It is true that the plaintiff offered the testimony of Dr. Krebs, an economist. But, as the court will instruct you, you may discount or reject any part of Dr. Krebs' testimony. You do not need to accept what he said just because he is an expert, and the facts of this case show that the plaintiff was not really injured that severely. As the court's instructions will make clear, expert witnesses can make mistakes, or even be biased, just like any other witness.

Thus, counsel can use the instruction to place the court's imprimatur on her position discounting the value of the expert witness.

Jury instructions are particularly useful when it comes to discussing the elements of the various claims and defenses. It is imperative that the plaintiff persuade the jury that she has established all of the legal elements of her claim. Since the concept of "legal elements" can often be confusing, it is frequently quite helpful simply to run through the court's instruction on elements, explaining at the same time the manner in which each requirement has been satisfied.

In similar fashion, the defendant can use the court's instruction to focus on one or more elements to show that they have not been satisfied by the evidence.

G.   Use Verdict Forms

In addition to jury instructions, the court will also provide the jurors with a set of alternate verdict forms. One of these forms will be the paper that the jury actually fills out as its official verdict in the case.

Use the verdict forms in your final argument. Show the jury the form that you want them to use, and explain how you want them to fill it out. You may persuade the jury that you are entitled to win the case, but that will do you little good if, by mistake, they end up entering the wrong verdict.

H.   Introductions and Thanks

By the time of final argument it should be unnecessary to reintroduce yourself and your co-counsel to the jury. If, for some reason, you believe that renewed introductions are called for, make them short.

You should, at some point, thank the jury for their time and attention. They have truly fulfilled an important civic duty, sometimes at considerable personal cost or inconvenience, and their importance should be recognized. It is, on the other hand, all too easy to overdo the acknowledgements. Lengthy encomiums to the jury system will quickly become cloying. Even worse are declarations of abject gratitude where counsel feels compelled to confess that the trial has been a boring ordeal. A simple statement of thanks, on behalf of yourself and your client, is usually sufficient.

V.   DELIVERY AND TECHNIQUE

Final argument is generally regarded as the advocate's finest hour. It is the time when all of the skills — no, the arts — of persuasion are marshalled on behalf of the client's cause. While a polished delivery will not rescue a lost cause, a forceful presentation can certainly reinforce the merits of your case.

Most of the persuasive techniques that we have discussed previously, and especially those used in opening statements, also have their applications in final argument.

A.   Do Not Read or Memorize

It is a mistake to write and read your final argument. As we noted in the chapter on opening statements,[18] only the most skilled actors can truly appear natural while reading from a script. Memorization is only slightly more likely to yield an unaffected presentation, and it carries the extreme additional risk that you will forget your place or leave out a crucial part of the argument.

In addition to the purely forensic drawbacks of reading and memorization, the advance scripting of a final argument deprives you of the ability to respond to opposing counsel, or to last minute rulings by the court.

The most effective final arguments are those that are delivered from an outline. The use of an outline allows you to plan your final argument, to deliver it with an air of spontaneity, and to adapt to the arguments of the opposition.

Do not be reticent to use notes during final argument. It is all well and good to speak without notes if you are able to do so, but it is far better to refer to a page or two on your pad than it is to omit a crucial argument. Even if you are capable of arguing without notes, you should still use the outline method of preparation, rather than writing out and memorizing a speech.

B.   Movement

A certain amount of body and hand movement will enliven your final argument and increase the attentiveness of the jurors. Gestures can be used to emphasize important points or to accent differences between your case and the opposition's.

Body movement can also be used for emphasis or transition. Pausing and taking a step or two will alert the jury that you are about to change subjects. Moving toward the jury will underscore the importance of what you are about to say. Moving away from the jury will signal the conclusion of a line of argument. Note that body movement can only be used effectively if you avoid aimless pacing.

---

18   *See* Chapter Nine, Section V A, *supra* at p. 375.

Constant movement is not only distracting to the jury, but it also deprives you of the ability to use movements purposefully.

Some courts require counsel to stand planted at a lectern, or even seated at a table, but most allow the attorney to move fairly freely about the courtroom. Many authorities suggest that the use of a lectern places an obstacle between counsel and the jury. While this may be true, it is easily possible to overstate the importance of abandoning the lectern. Use it if you need it.

C.   Verbal Pacing

The speed, tone, inflection and volume of your speech can be important persuasive tools. Changes in speed, tone, inflection and volume can be used to signal transitions and to maintain the jury's attention. It is important, of course, to avoid speaking to quickly or too loudly.

The pacing of your speech can be used to convey perceptions of time, distance, and intensity. If you describe an event rapidly, it will seem to have taken place very quickly. If you describe it at a more leisurely pace, the time frame will expand. In similar fashion, rapid speech will tend to magnify intensity and reduce distance. Slower delivery will reduce intensity and increase distance.

D.   Emotion

There are different schools of thought regarding the use of emotion in final argument. Many lawyers believe that emotion has little place at any point during the trial, while others believe that emotion can communicate as effectively as logic or reason. There is a strong concensus, however, that false emotion will backfire. Insincerity has a way of showing through, and there is little that is less persuasive than an overtly insincere attorney.

The best approach to emotion is to save it for the times when you are discussing the moral dimension of your case. There is no reason to wax passionate over the date on which a contract was signed. It is understandable, however, to show outrage or resentment toward a party who intentionally breached a contract, knowing that it would cause great harm to another.

The absence of emotion may be taken as a lack of belief in the righteousness of your case. What reasonable person would be unmoved when discussing crippling injuries to a child or perjury by the opposing party? There will be points in many trials that virtually call out for an outward display of feeling, and a flat presentation may be regarded as an absence of conviction.

E.   Visuals

As with opening statements, visual aids can be extremely valuable during final argument. Counsel is generally free to use any exhibit that has been admitted into evidence, and also to create visual displays solely for the purpose of final argument.

Any item that has been admitted into evidence may be utilized during final argument. Thus, documents may be read out loud, displayed, or enlarged. Counsel can underline key passages in important documents, or can array various documents side by side. This last technique is particularly useful to demonstrate relational concepts such as contradiction or continuity.

Physical evidence other than documents may also be used during final argument. It is permissible to exhibit items such as weapons, models, photographs, samples, and anything else that has been admitted by the court. It is also permissible to use the evidence to conduct demonstrations and re-enactments, so long as they are consistent with the testimony in the case. In criminal cases, for example, it is common for the prosecutor to show the jury precisely how a weapon was held and used.

Counsel has wide latitude to create visual aids specifically for use during final argument. The only restriction on the use of such materials is that they must be fairly derived from the actual evidence. Visual aids may be "argumentative." In fact, it may be best to think of them as argument in graphic or physical form.

Thus, it is perfectly legitimate for an attorney to use a blackboard or marking pen to write in large letters "THREE REASONS NOT TO BELIEVE THE PLAINTIFF," and then to fill in three columns of reasons for discounting the plaintiff's testimony. Since counsel could obviously tell the jury the reasons not to believe the plaintiff, she may also write them down. In other words, anything that could be spoken may also be illustrated.

More sophisticated visual aids can take the form of charts, graphs, overlays, and enlargements.

F. Headlines

A headline announces where the argument is going next. Just as newspapers use headlines to pique the interest of readers, so can they be used to focus the attention of jurors during final argument.

A headline can take the form of a simple statement, a rhetorical question, or a short "enumeration." The defendant in the fire truck case, for example, might use a headline as brief as the following headline when turning from liability to damages:

Now let us look at the plaintiff's claim for damages.

Alternatively, defense counsel might choose to make the transition more argumentative:

> Having seen how weak the plaintiff's position is on liability, let's turn to her damages claim.

Or the headline can be used to emphasize the importance of the coming subject:

> As I told you during the opening statement, the real heart of this case is damages. I want to show you now just how inflated the plaintiff's claim really is.

Rhetorical questions can also be useful, as in this example from the plaintiff's argument in the fire engine case:

> What could lead a person to drive so carelessly?

Or, more elaborately:

> How could the defendant have missed seeing the fire engine, when every other car on the road saw it and stopped?

Finally, the technique of "enumeration" might be the most effective of all. Every teacher, and probably most students, will recognize this phenomenon. As soon as the lecturer announces that there are "three reasons" or "four rules" or "six characteristics," every person in the room picks up a pen and begins to take notes. It seems that little serves to concentrate the mind more than the onset of a numbered list. This approach can also be used in final argument:

> The defendant was negligent in three different ways.

Or,

> There are four basic flaws in the plaintiff's claim for damages.

Or,

> There were three different moments at which the defendant could have avoided this accident. Let me explain them to you.

The technique of enumeration is particularly effective when it is used in conjunction with a visual aid. Do not simply tell the jury that the defendant violated three "rules of the road." Write the numbered headlines down in bold letters or project them on a screen.

G. Simple, Active Language

The chapter on opening statements contains a substantial discussion of the persuasive use of simple, active language.[19] The same rules apply equally to final

---

19 *See* Chapter Nine, Section IV B(1), *supra* at p. 363.

arguments, with the additional proviso that simple, active language may be applied in argumentative form.

One further point should be made. There is a strong temptation during final argument to use judgmental or conclusory terms such as heinous, brutal, deceptive, unfair, virtuous, naive, and the like. Although usually not permitted during opening statements, such language is allowed on final argument. Nonetheless, counsel would do well to remember that conclusory adjectives and adverbs are almost always less persuasive than are active nouns and verbs. It is one thing to assert that a crime was heinous, and quite another to describe its awful, vivid details.

VI. ETHICS AND OBJECTIONS

The rules of ethics, evidence, and procedure combine to place a number of very real, though definitely manageable, limits on what can be said during final argument.

A. Impermissible Argument

1. Statements of Personal Belief

It is improper and unethical for an attorney to "assert personal knowledge of facts in issue . . . or state a personal opinion as to the justness of a cause, the credibility of a witness, the culpability of a civil litigant or the guilt or innocence of an accused."[20]

The purpose of this rule is twofold. First, it prevents lawyers from putting their own credibility at issue in a case. The jury is required to decide a case on the basis of the law and evidence, not on their affinity for or faith in a particular lawyer. While every advocate strives to be trusted and believed, it subverts the jury system to make an overt, personal pitch.

Moreover, a statement of personal belief inevitably suggests that the lawyer has access to off-the-record information, and therefore invites the jury to decide the case on the basis of non-record evidence. Consider the following:

> I have investigated this case thoroughly. I have spent hours with my client, and I have visited the scene of the accident. I could tell, just from talking with her, how seriously she has been injured. Believe me, I would not take up your time if my client were not telling the truth. I have handled many other cases of this type, and I can honestly say that this is one of the strongest plaintiff's cases that I have ever seen.

---

20 *See* Rule 3.4(e), Model Rules of Professional Conduct.

Here, the lawyer has not merely asked for the jury's confidence. Counsel has impliedly asked the jury to enter a verdict on the basis of out-of-court interviews and previously tried cases.

The rule against statements of personal belief is an important one. It should not be demeaned by a too-literal interpretation. It is difficult to purge your speech entirely of terms such as "I think" or "I believe." While good lawyers will strive to avoid these terms, it is not unethical to fall occasionally into first person references. Similarly, it is unnecessary to preface every assertion with statements such as "the evidence has shown," "we have proven," or the like.

It is unethical to ask the jury to decide the case, or any issue in the case, on the basis of its trust in counsel. Thus, the following argument for the plaintiff in the fire truck case is permissible, though some of its language would better be avoided:

> The defendant must have been worried about how late he was for his meeting. We have heard from the defendant's own mouth that his parking garage is three blocks from his office. It would take an average person about ten minutes to park his car and walk that far. I think that he also had at least another half hour or so of driving to do. Put the times together and you will see that he was at least twenty minutes late. That was enough to distract him from his driving.

The personal statement in the above example is really nothing more than an inference from the evidence. Of course, things would be different if counsel used an exaggerated tone of voice or series of gestures to emphasize personal belief as opposed to a conclusion drawn from the trial evidence.

On the other hand, this argument is definitely improper:

> I know that it would take at least ten minutes to walk from the defendant's parking garage to his office. I work downtown, and I have walked that distance many times myself. Believe me, it is at least a ten-minute walk.

Here it is clear that counsel is asserting personal knowledge, not admitted evidence, as a basis for the desired conclusion.

2. Appeals to Prejudice or Bigotry

It is unethical to attempt to persuade a jury through appeals to racial, religious, ethnic, gender, or other forms of prejudice. It is a sad fact of life that juries can be swayed by their own biases, but lawyers cannot and should not seek to take advantage of this unfortunate phenomenon.

An appeal to prejudice asks the jury to disregard the evidence, and to substitute an unreasonable stereotype or preconception. Thus, such arguments violate the rule against alluding to "any matter the lawyer does not reasonably believe is relevant or that will not be supported by admissible evidence."[21]

The mention of race, gender, or ethnicity is not always improper. It may, for example, be permissible to refer to a party's race if it is relevant to identification by an eyewitness.

On the other hand, it is definitely unethical to make racial or similar appeals implicitly or through the use of code words. An argument based on bigotry cannot be saved through subtle language.

3. Misstating the Evidence

While it is permissible to draw inferences and conclusions, it is improper intentionally to misstate or mischaracterize evidence in the course of final argument. Accordingly, defense counsel in the fire truck case could portray the plaintiff's camping trip as follows:

> The plaintiff admits that she went camping at Eagle River Falls. She did all of the things that ordinary campers do. She carried a pack, she slept on the ground, she went hiking. In other words, she willingly undertook all of the strains, exertions, and activities of backpacking. No one made her take that trip; she did it for recreation. Of course, she told a different story here on the witness stand. The only possible conclusion is that she has exaggerated her claim for injuries.

To be sure, the above example is replete with characterizations, but they are fair characterizations. Even if no witness actually testified that the plaintiff went camping voluntarily, it is a reasonable inference that "no one made her take that trip."

The following argument, on the other hand, definitely appears to misstate the evidence:

> The plaintiff was an enthusiastic and carefree camper. She carried the heaviest pack in the family and she insisted on chopping the wood and pitching the tent. She would have gone camping again the next weekend, but her family couldn't keep up with her.

These are, by and large, assertions of fact, not simply inferences. (While the statement that the plaintiff was an "enthusiastic" camper might be seen as an inference, the statements concerning the "heaviest pack" and the plaintiff's desire to go camping the next weekend are clearly presented as proven facts.) They may not be made in final argument unless they are supported by the record.

---

21 *See* Rule 3.4(e), Model Rules of Professional Conduct.

Although the rule against misstatements and mischaracterizations is plain enough, judges, for obvious reasons, are usually loath to invoke it. No one is capable of remembering all of the evidence that was admitted at trial, and the line between allowable inferences and forbidden mischaracterizations is difficult to draw. Opposing counsel are, after all, retained to disagree about the content and interpretation of evidence. Thus, judges often try to refrain from ruling on objections based upon the misstatement rule. Instead, the court's typical response to an objection is merely to remind the jury that they are the sole judges of the evidence, and that they should rely upon their own memories, rather than upon counsel's presentation.

Nonetheless, in truly egregious situations a judge can and will sustain an objection to argument that misstates the evidence. What's more, appellate courts have been known to reverse judgments in situations where the prevailing attorney's argument strayed too far beyond the record.

Two lessons should be drawn concerning the "misstatement" rule. First, evidence should not be misstated. The courts' general reluctance to resolve questions raised by the rule should not be taken as license to ignore the rule. Second, the "misstatement" rule should not be used as an excuse to make spurious objections, to interrupt opposing counsel's argument, or to quibble over the meaning of the evidence. Objections should be made, but only when opposing counsel has seriously and prejudicially departed from the record.

4. Misstating the Law

In most jurisdictions attorneys may use final argument to explain the relevant law, to discuss the jury instructions, and to apply the law to the facts of the case. Counsel may not, however, misstate the law, or argue for legal interpretations that are contrary to the court's decisions and instructions.

Thus, defense counsel in a criminal case could not argue that the jury must acquit the defendant "if there is any doubt whatsoever, no matter how insignificant or far-fetched it might be." By the same token, the prosecutor could not argue that a reasonable doubt only exists if the jury "is persuaded that there is a good chance that the defendant is not guilty." In both of these examples the attorneys offered definitions of reasonable doubt that are not found in any jurisdiction.

Courts vary in the degree to which they allow lawyers to paraphrase or summarize the law. Attorneys in some jurisdictions are given relatively free rein to argue, while others permit counsel only to read the jury instructions.[22]

---

22 In yet other jurisdictions counsel is *not* permitted to read the jury instructions, but may paraphrase them.

Counsel is never free, however, to ask a jury to ignore or disregard the law. Although the potential for jury nullification plays an important role in both our civil and criminal justice systems, it is not a device that can be actively invoked by counsel. You may hope that the jury will refuse to apply a harsh, unfair or inequitable law, but you may not urge them to do so.

5. Misusing Evidence

When evidence has been admitted only for a limited or restricted use, it is improper to attempt to use it for any other purpose. Suppose, for example, that the ownership of an automobile is at issue in a case. The court has allowed evidence that the defendant maintained insurance on the vehicle, ruling that while the existence of liability insurance is generally inadmissible, it can be received to show agency, ownership, or control.[23] Thus, the following argument is permissible, in keeping with the limited admissibility of the evidence:

> We know that the defendant owned the automobile, because she paid for the insurance on it. You have seen the policy, signed in her own handwriting. No one would sign up and pay for insurance on a car that she did not own.

This argument, on the other hand, is improper:

> We have all seen the insurance policy. The defendant in this case carried over $100,000 in liability insurance — you can see it right there in black and white. She can afford to pay for the damages, and she should pay for the damages.

The Federal Rules of Evidence contain many examples of the limited admissibility doctrine. Rule 404 provides that character evidence may not be admitted to prove actions in conformity with a person's character, but that it may be used to prove motive, opportunity, intent, or preparation. Subsequent remedial measures, under Rule 407, cannot be admitted as proof of negligence, but they may be offered to prove the feasibility of precautionary measures. Offers of settlement or compromise are generally inadmissible, but Rule 408 does not require their exclusion if offered to prove the bias or prejudice of a witness.

In each of these situations, final argument should only employ the evidence for the purpose for which it was admitted. Finally, it should go without saying that counsel may not use, or attempt to use, evidence that was excluded by the court.

6. Appeals to the Jurors' Personal Interests

An appeal to the jurors' personal interests invites the jury to decide the case on a basis other than the law and evidence. So, for instance, it is improper for

---

23 *See* Rule 411, Federal Rules of Evidence.

defense counsel to tell a jury that a large verdict will raise taxes or insurance rates. Similarly, plaintiff's counsel cannot argue that an inadequate verdict will result in increased welfare payments. Other predictions as to the potential consequences of a verdict may be equally objectionable. Thus, a prosecutor cannot argue that an acquittal will increase the crime rate or endanger the citizenry.

A specific form of this principle is the so-called "Golden Rule," which prohibits counsel from asking the jurors to envision themselves in the position of one of the litigants. The following is an excerpt from a classic forbidden argument:

> The plaintiff in this case lost his right arm in an industrial accident. You must now determine how much money is necessary to compensate him for his loss. Let me ask you this question: How much money would you want if it had been your right arm? If someone offered you $1,000,000 to have your arm crushed, would you take it? Would you accept $2,000,000?

Such arguments obviously appeal to the jury's sympathy. They also ask the jurors to decide the case on the basis of their own self-interest, as though they were the people actually affected by the outcome of the case.

For much the same reason, counsel cannot refer to the possibility of reversal on appeal, pardon, parole, or other potentially curative measures. Such arguments appeal to the jurors' self-interest by inviting them to avoid making the hard decisions themselves.

7. Appeals to Emotion, Sympathy, and Passion

While there is an emotional side to virtually every trial, counsel may not use final argument to ask the jury to decide the case on the basis of sympathy or passion. Impermissible appeals to passion are often found when counsel dwells upon some dramatic but barely relevant aspect of the case, such as the nature of a plaintiff's extreme injuries when only liability is at stake.

We have already discussed the unethical nature of inflammatory arguments based on racial, religious, ethnic, and gender prejudice.[24] Equally objectionable, although perhaps slightly less offensive, are arguments that appeal to local chauvinism or stereotypical concepts of wealth, education, political affiliation, physical appearance, and the like.

8. Comments on Privilege

It is unethical for the prosecutor in a criminal case to comment on the defendant's invocation of the privilege against self-incrimination. The prosecutor

---

24   *See* Section VI A(2), *supra* at p. 433.

can neither point out, nor ask the jury to draw any adverse inference from, the defendant's decision not to testify or present evidence.

Jurisdictions are divided as to the rule in civil cases. In some states it is permissible to ask the jury to draw an adverse inference from a party's invocation of a privilege. Here is an example of such an argument:

> I am sure that you remember the cross examination of the plaintiff. I asked him where he was going on the morning of the incident, and he said that he was on his way to see the doctor. But he refused to answer when I asked why he was going to the doctor. He invoked what is called the physician-patient privilege. Now, the plaintiff had the right to invoke that privilege, and the court ruled that he did not have to answer my question. But I ask you, why was the defendant afraid of telling us the reason that he needed to see a doctor? What was he hiding? What is the awful secret? If it had just been an ordinary visit — a sore throat or the flu — you can be sure that he would have told us. So there must have been something about the visit that hurt his case.

In other states, however, the above argument would not be allowed, since it would be regarded as infringing on the party's right to assert the privilege in question. Whichever approach a jurisdiction takes, the same rule will usually apply to all privileges: attorney-client, physician-patient, husband-wife, clergy-penitent, and others. It is conceivable, however, that a court would allow counsel to comment on the assertion of one privilege, but forbid it concerning the invocation of another. Familiarity with local practice is therefore essential.

9. Exceeding the Scope of Rebuttal

The proper scope of rebuttal was discussed previously.[25] It is objectionable to attempt to argue new matters on rebuttal.

B. The Protocol of Objections

1. Making Objections

Objections during final argument follow the same general pattern as objections during witness examinations. Counsel should stand (unless local practice differs) and state succinctly the ground for the objection. There is usually no need to present argument unless requested by the court.

Some attorneys believe that so-called speaking objections should be employed during final argument, to ensure that the jury understands why counsel is objecting.

---

25 *See* Section II C, *supra* at p. 407.

Following this approach, you would not simply say, "I object, Your Honor, counsel is mis-stating the evidence." Instead, the objection might go as follows:

> I object, Your Honor. There was absolutely no evidence to the effect that the plaintiff carried the heaviest pack on that camping trip. In fact, she testified that her children had to help her with her pack every day.

This is not good form, and it may draw a rebuke from the court. Speaking objections should not be used to score substantive points with the jury. A far better approach is simply to make the identical point during counsel's own argument. There is some justification for defense counsel to make extremely limited use of speaking objections during the plaintiff's rebuttal, since the defense attorney will not have the opportunity to argue again.

In any event, most attorneys attempt to avoid objecting during opposing counsel's final argument. It is considered a common courtesy to allow opposing counsel to speak uninterrupted. Moreover, the overuse of objections may result in the interruption of one's own final argument. This does not mean, of course, that seriously improper arguments should be tolerated.

It is unethical to make spurious objections simply for the purpose of interfering with opposing counsel's argument.

2. Responding to Objections

The best response to an objection is often no response. An objection disrupts the flow of final argument, and an extended colloquy with the court will only prolong the interruption. A dignified silence will usually be sufficient to allow the court to rule, and to impress the jury with the basic rudeness of the interruption.

Once the court rules, whether favorably, unfavorably, or inscrutably, counsel should simply proceed by adapting the argument to the court's ruling.

3. Cautionary Instructions

When an objection to final argument has been sustained, the judge will usually caution the jury to disregard the offending remarks. If the court does not give such an instruction on its own motion, objecting counsel should consider asking for one. The downside, of course, is that a cautionary instruction may only serve to emphasize the content of the objectionable argument. Nonetheless, some jurisdictions require that counsel request such an instruction in order to preserve the issue for appeal.[26]

In extreme cases, and especially where a cautionary instruction may only exacerbate the situation, a motion for a mistrial may be appropriate.

---

26 Paradoxically, appellate courts often hold that a cautionary instruction has cured the negative impact of an improper argument.

VII. BENCH TRIALS

Most of the techniques discussed above can be used in both bench and jury trials. Judges, however, are famously impatient with long final arguments. Counsel should therefore strive to keep final arguments as short as possible in bench trials. Most of the adaptations discussed in the chapter on opening statements apply equally to final arguments.[27] In brief, counsel should be particularly alert to legal issues and standards when arguing to the court. The judge is likely to have followed and understood the evidence, but will still want to know how the law should be applied to the facts of the case. It is permissible to cite case law during final argument to the bench. Finally, be prepared for the court to ask questions.

---

27   *See* Chapter Nine, Section VI B, *supra* at p. 382.

— CHAPTER ELEVEN —
Jury Selection

I. INTRODUCTION

Jury selection is one of the least uniform aspects of trial advocacy. The procedures used to select and qualify jurors differ widely from jurisdiction to jurisdiction. In some courts the attorneys are little more than observers, while in others they are given wide latitude to question the panel of potential jurors. The trend for many years, however, has been to restrict, if not eliminate, attorney participation. While this is most often done in the name of efficiency, it is also a response to perceived abuses. Many lawyers have seen jury selection as an opportunity to begin arguing the case, or even to introduce evidence surreptitiously. Others have engaged in all manner of obsequious behavior aimed at currying favor with the jurors. In consequence, the heyday of jury selection is now past. In a few highly publicized trials the process may still occasionally consume weeks or months, but the reality is that jury selection has been de-emphasized in most parts of the country. It is likely that this will continue to be the case.

In truth, it was never really possible to "select" a jury. Even in the most lenient jurisdictions, the best that counsel could generally accomplish was to de-select or disqualify a certain number of potential jurors. Today, the goals of jury selection can probably be summarized as: (1) eliminating jurors who are biased or disposed against your case; (2) gathering information about the eventual jurors, in order to present your case effectively; and (3) beginning to introduce yourself, your client, and certain key concepts to the jury.

As restricted as jury selection may have become, however, it does remain the one aspect of the trial when counsel can interact with, and obtain direct feedback from, the jury. At all other moments in the trial, one can only observe and infer the jurors' reactions. During jury selection, even when it is conducted solely by the court, it is possible to learn directly from the jurors themselves. If this precious opportunity is to be preserved, lawyers must use it wisely and fairly.

II. MECHANICS OF JURY SELECTION

A. Terminology

Jury selection is markedly different from other aspects of the trial, and has developed a lexicon of its own.

The "venire" or venire panel is the group of citizens from which juries are to be chosen. The venire, also called the jury pool, is typically assembled from lists of registered voters, licensed drivers, or other adults. Jurisdictions vary widely as to an individual's term of service on the venire. Some courts utilize a "one day or one trial" system, in which potential jurors are released after one day unless they are seated on a jury. The more traditional approach, still employed by many courts, is to require potential jurors to be available for a set period of time, ranging from a week to a month.

"Voir dire"[1] is the process of questioning venire members, by either the court or the attorneys, in order to select those who will serve on a jury.

In the course of voir dire counsel may seek to disqualify potential jurors. This is done by making a "challenge." A "challenge for cause" is an objection to the venire member's qualifications to sit on the jury, either because she does not meet certain statutory requirements or because she has revealed significant bias or prejudice in the course of questioning. A challenge for cause must be ruled upon by the court, and may be objected to by opposing counsel. There is no limit on the number of potential jurors who may be challenged for cause.

"Peremptory challenges," sometimes known as strikes, may be exercised without cause. The parties are typically allowed to excuse a certain number of potential jurors without stating their reasons. Except in the case of apparent racial motivation, peremptory challenges must be allowed. The number of peremptory challenges available to each party is determined by statute or court rule.

In most states there are statutory "exemptions" that allow individuals to decline jury service. Traditionally, many occupational groups were exempt, including lawyers, physicians, dentists, clergy, and even embalmers. In many states most of these automatic exemptions have been eliminated. Note that an exemption does not disqualify a person from serving on a jury, but only allows her the privilege to opt out. Even in the absence of an exemption, venire members can request to be excused from service on the basis of hardship.

There are also minimal statutory "qualifications" for jury service. While these differ from state to state, they typically include the ability to understand English, as well as an age requirement. Convicted felons are also frequently disqualified from jury service.

---

1   Juror voir dire should not be confused with witness voir dire.

B. Questioning Formats

The voir dire of potential jurors may be conducted by the judge, the attorneys, or both. As noted above, the right of counsel to participate in jury voir dire has been greatly limited in many jurisdictions. Nonetheless, some state systems still permit wide-ranging attorney voir dire. In a few the judge is not even present for the questioning of potential jurors, unless one of the parties so requests.

In a large number of federal courts the current practice is for the judge to conduct the entire voir dire, allowing counsel only to submit written questions which the court may use or discard. This model saves time and avoids abuses, but it is subject to the criticism that a judge's questions will necessarily be fairly superficial. The judge, after all, cannot possibly know as much about a case as the attorneys, and is unlikely to be attuned to all of the possibilities for uncovering subtle prejudices.

Finally, a growing number of courts have adopted a mixed approach in which the judge conducts the primary voir dire, but where the attorneys are allowed to ask supplemental questions. This format attempts to accommodate both the court's need for efficiency and counsel's interest in participating in the voir dire.

C. Timing and Order of Voir Dire

The timing and exercise of challenges is determined in large part by the format for questioning the venire members.

1. Preliminary Statements

In all three questioning formats it is typical for the judge to make a preliminary statement to the entire venire panel, describing the voir dire process, the nature of the case and the issues involved, and perhaps introducing the parties and their attorneys. In systems where attorney questioning is permitted, the lawyers may also be allowed to make preliminary remarks, or at least to introduce themselves and their clients if the judge has not already done so.

2. Size of the Venire Panel

The number of venire members brought to the courtroom should exceed the total needed for the jury as well as the total number of peremptory challenges available to all of the parties. Assume, for example, that our fire engine case is to be tried by a jury of six, with two alternates, and that the local rules of court allow three peremptory challenges for each party. Thus, the minimum size for the venire would be 14. It is possible, however, that some venire members will be challenged for cause; others may request to be excused for reasons of hardship or personal convenience. Consequently, it is likely that the voir dire will begin with a panel of 20 or 24. In controversial or highly publicized cases, the initial panel may need to be much larger.

3. Questions to the Entire Panel

Many courts begin the voir dire with a series of inquiries to the entire venire panel. These questions typically require only "yes" or "no" responses, and seek to develop information relevant to the particular case. Some judges have a standard set of questions, but most will also accept suggestions from counsel.

Venire members are asked to raise their hands if the answer to any question is "yes." Are you related to any of the attorneys or parties?[2] Do you or members of your immediate family work in the aerospace industry? Have you ever been the victim of a crime? Have you ever been asked to co-sign for a loan? Venire members who raise their hands may be asked follow-up questions by the court. In jurisdictions where the attorneys participate, the follow-up questions may come during the lawyers' voir dire.

The court may also ask the entire panel whether anyone requests to be excused by reason of hardship, or whether any of the potential jurors falls under a statutory exemption.

Jury questionnaires may also be used to direct questions to the entire venire panel. In a large number of jurisdictions every venire member is asked to fill out a card providing information such as address, occupation, age, marital status, and the like. In some courts the attorneys are also allowed to fashion a more detailed questionnaire containing questions relating to the specific case. Such questionnaires are subject to court approval.

4. Questions to Individual Jurors

The questioning of individual jurors, either by the court or by counsel, may follow several models.

The jurors may be questioned one by one, with the exercise of challenges following immediately. In extremely sensitive or highly publicized cases, such questioning may take place in the judge's chambers.

It is more common for the venire to be questioned in groups. Frequently, twelve prospective jurors are seated in the jury box for voir dire. Sometimes smaller groups, of four or six, are questioned at one time.

5. Exercising Challenges

The timing for the exercise of challenges is governed by the approach used for questioning the venire members. When jurors are questioned singly, as noted

---

2   The court, of course, will name the attorneys and parties, perhaps also asking them to stand at this point. In addition, the court may also ask whether any of the potential jurors are related to certain named witnesses.

above, challenges (either peremptory or for cause) are usually expected to follow immediately.

A variety of challenge sequences can be used when potential jurors are questioned as a group.

One approach is to question the venire in groups of four. Once the questioning is finished, either by the court or by the attorneys, counsel is first asked whether there are any challenges for cause.[3] The plaintiff (or prosecutor) is usually asked to make her challenges first. Defense counsel may object to the challenge, and may also ask to conduct additional voir dire aimed at demonstrating that the juror can be fair. The judge will rule, either excusing or retaining the juror. Then the procedure is reversed, with the defense challenging and the plaintiff being given the opportunity to object.

If a challenge for cause is allowed, the excused juror will be replaced by another member of the pool, who will then be questioned in like fashion.

Once all challenges for cause have been ruled upon, the attorneys will then have the opportunity to exercise peremptory challenges. Again, the plaintiff and defendant will alternate, although except in rare circumstances there can be no objections to peremptory challenges.[4] Excused jurors will be replaced from the pool, and the new jurors will be questioned. This process continues until there are no further challenges and the applicable number of jurors have been seated.[5] The questioning will then begin again with another group of four. Variations on this approach are also used with groups of six or twelve.

Most lawyers prefer to make their challenges at a sidebar conference, in order to avoid offending the remaining members of the panel. If the judge requires challenges to be announced in open court, this should be done as politely as possible. Peremptory challenges can be made quite obliquely: "Your Honor, we request that Mr. Roth be thanked for his time and excused from further service." Challenges for cause will require more explanation, but they should still be courteous.

Note that courts vary as to the finality of an attorney's statement that she does not wish to exercise a challenge. In some jurisdictions counsel must present a challenge at the earliest possible time; otherwise it is waived forever. In other courts it may be permissible to "re-invade" the panel, usually because opposing

---

3   In some jurisdictions the plaintiff questions the jurors and must then present any challenges for cause, followed by the defendant's questions and challenges. In other jurisdictions both parties complete their questioning before either is given an opportunity to raise challenges.

4   Concerning the impermissible use of peremptory challenges, see Section IV C, *infra* at page 450.

5   Depending upon the jurisdiction, jurors who are not challenged are referred to as having been seated, accepted or "passed."

counsel subsequently exercised a challenge. Following this approach, if plaintiff's counsel "passes" a group of jurors, she may only challenge one later if defense counsel has challenged a member of the same group.

An alternative approach, widely used in federal courts, is the "strike" system. Under this method the entire venire panel is questioned before any challenges are heard. The attorneys and the judge then meet out of the presence of the venire. The court first hears challenges for cause. Once these are decided, the attorneys take turns stating their peremptory challenges. The first twelve (or six) unchallenged panel members will constitute the jury. The necessary number of alternates will be selected in the same fashion. In some jurisdictions the attorneys will simultaneously submit written strikes, rather than alternating.

6. Preserving Error

What happens when the court erroneously denies a challenge for cause? In most jurisdictions, the denial of a challenge for cause cannot be the basis of an appeal unless the challenging party has exhausted its peremptory challenges.

III. PLANNING AND CONDUCTING VOIR DIRE

In systems where lawyer participation is permitted, voir dire must be planned as carefully as any other aspect of the trial. Your areas of inquiry must be designed to obtain the maximum amount of useful information without overstepping the boundaries set by the court.

Bear in mind that a successful voir dire will accomplish at least three goals. First, it will allow you to uncover grounds to challenge jurors for cause. Second, it will provide you with enough information to make wise use of your peremptory challenges.

Finally, a well-conducted voir dire will give you a basis for adapting your trial strategy so as best to appeal to the jurors in the case. For example, suppose that voir dire in the fire truck case disclosed that one of the jurors had worked her way through college as an electrical inspector. While this information is unlikely to cause either party to want to challenge her, it does suggest that she will probably be receptive to arguments based on precision or safety standards. Thus, the plaintiff might want to use an analogy in her final argument to the effect that the defendant "broke the rules" when he failed to have his brakes repaired.

A. Permissible Inquiries

It is almost always permissible to question potential jurors on their backgrounds, work histories, and life experiences. In this vein, it is common to ask jurors about their past involvement with the legal system; their membership in civic, political, social and other organizations; their hobbies, reading interests, and other pastimes; their families and education; their business experience; and other similar topics.

It is also permissible to inquire as to the jurors' knowledge of or relationship to the parties, lawyers, and witnesses involved in the case. It is fair to ask about family relationships, friendships, business arrangements, debtor-creditor relationships, professional acquaintances, employment, or investment relationships.

Many courts likewise allow counsel to ask jurors about their attitudes and possible preconceptions or prejudices concerning legal and factual issues in the case. Thus, assuming relevance to the case, jurors can be questioned about their attitudes toward issues such as capital punishment, welfare, seat belt laws, or medical treatment. It is expected, for example, that defense counsel in criminal cases will ask potential jurors whether they understand the concepts of the presumption of innocence and proof beyond a reasonable doubt. Most courts draw the line, however, when purported questions about jurors' attitudes spill over into indoctrination or argument.[6]

Finally, it is almost always proper to inquire into an individual's exposure to pretrial publicity.

B. Question Form

Most authorities suggest that voir dire questions be asked in open, non-leading form. Leading questions circumscribe the potential jurors' answer and are therefore unlikely to result in much usable information. Open questions, on the other hand, have the potential to open a window on the juror's outlook or point of view. Consider the following examples. First, a leading question:

COUNSEL: Do you get the morning paper?

JUROR: Yes, I read it every day.

Now an open question:

COUNSEL: What magazines or newspapers to you read?

JUROR: I get the morning paper, and I also subscribe to *MotorSport*, *Car and Driver*, and *Automotive News*.

By the same token, narrow questions are unlikely to uncover much about a potential juror's true attitudes. Consider these scenarios:

COUNSEL: Are you prejudiced against people who receive public assistance?

---

6   *See* Section IV B, *infra* at page 449.

JUROR: No, I'm not prejudiced against anybody.

As apposed to:

COUNSEL: What do you think about public assistance?

JUROR: I suppose that it's necessary, but an awful lot of people get it just because it's easier than working.

Another reason to avoid leading questions is that they are almost certain to make the venire members uncomfortable. No one likes to be cross examined. And no matter how gentle we think we are, leading questions will probably feel like cross examination to potential jurors.

C.   Stereotypes

The early literature on jury selection was typified by its reliance on ethnic, class, and racial stereotypes. North Europeans were considered to be conservative and prosecution-oriented in criminal cases. Latins and Mediterraneans were thought to be emotional and therefore sympathetic to plaintiffs in personal injury cases.

Most of this thinking has long since been abandoned. Virtually all modern research indicates that there is far more diversity within ethnic groups than there is between groups, and that ethnicity is a poor predictor of complex attitudes.

This is not to say, however, that characteristics such as race, class, or gender are entirely irrelevant to jury selection. Recall from the discussion of opening statements that every advocate seeks to have the jury create a mental image that is helpful to her case.[7] That task is made far easier when at least some of the jurors have had personal experiences similar to those that counsel wishes to evoke.

A fact of contemporary life is that group identity can often be used as a proxy for certain life experiences. One obvious example is discrimination. While most Americans will say that they object to discrimination, members of minorities are far more likely to have seen or felt it directly. Thus, a lawyer whose case depends upon proof of discrimination will probably want minorities on the jury. This is not because minorities are inherently generous or sympathetic, but rather because it is more likely that they will comprehend the proof.

The use of group identification as a proxy for experience is not limited to minority groups. Union members, for example, will be more likely to understand concepts such as going on strike or the importance of paying dues, should those issues be relevant to a trial. Older people may have more experience with certain

---

7   *See* Chapter Nine, Section I A, *supra* at page 335.

types of medical treatment; parents can be expected to have more relevant knowledge in cases involving children.

Closely related is a concept that might be called "affinity selection." Much psychological research suggests that jurors will be more likely to credit the testimony of persons who are like themselves. Following this theory, lawyers will want to seek to empanel jurors who most resemble their clients and principal witnesses. To the extent possible, counsel would also want to exclude jurors who might be the counterparts of the opposing party or significant adverse witnesses. Tactical advantages notwithstanding, it is improper to use peremptory challenges to exclude minorities from juries.[8]

D. Jury Consultants

It is now possible to retain a consultant to assist with jury selection. There is a broad range of available services. Some consultants are professional psychologists who will sit at counsel table during voir dire in order to assess the venire members' responses and body language. Others are social scientists who will conduct surveys to determine the ideal juror profile. Some will assemble "shadow juries" for pretrial preparation, so that various arguments can be tried out on demographically representative samples.

Whatever their specialty, jury consultants are usually expensive. As a consequence, they are generally used only in big-budget cases.

IV. ETHICS AND OBJECTIONABLE CONDUCT

As was noted above, the conduct of voir dire has been subjected to increasing supervision by the courts. Here follows a survey of behavior that has been held unethical or improper.

A. Contact with Venire

Direct or indirect contact with the venire panel is unethical.[9] This is true when the contact is made for the purpose of gathering information, and it is doubly true when it is done in order to influence their opinions.

B. Improper Questioning

Many courts consider it improper to use voir dire as a means of arguing the case or indoctrinating the jury. While such a "persuasive" approach was once widely advocated, it is now generally frowned upon by most judges.

8　*See* Section IV C, *infra* at page 450.

9　*See* Rule 3.5(b), Model Rules of Professional Conduct.

It is particularly objectionable to use voir dire as a means of presenting inadmissible evidence. For example, it would be wrong for plaintiff's counsel in a personal injury case to proceed in this manner:

COUNSEL: Could you be fair to the defendant even though he is a business broker who earns over $100,000 a year?

Or,

COUNSEL: Would you be influenced by the fact that the defendant is heavily insured?

While each of these questions is ostensibly designed to ascertain the juror's ability to be fair, in reality they are intended to exert improper influence on the outcome of the case.

It is permissible to inquire as to jurors' understanding and acceptance of the law, but counsel cannot use voir dire to misstate the law or to suggest an improper standard. Thus, defense counsel in a criminal case could not ask this question:

COUNSEL: Do you understand that the defendant cannot be convicted if you hesitate, even for half a second, to believe that he committed the crime?

Similarly, the prosecutor could not make this inquiry concerning the burden of proof:

COUNSEL: Do you understand that hundreds of defendants are convicted in this courtroom every year, so the standard cannot be that hard to satisfy?

C.   Impermissible Use of Peremptory Challenges

Peremptory challenges cannot be used to exclude racial minorities from jury service. This rule applies to both the prosecution[10] and defense[11] in criminal cases, and to all parties in civil cases.[12]

If it appears that peremptories are being used in a racially discriminatory manner, the court must hold a *Batson* hearing to determine whether there is a legitimate, non-racial basis for the challenge.

The question of gender discrimination and peremptory challenges has not yet been firmly resolved.

---

10   *Batson v. Kentucky,* 476 U.S. 79 (1986).

11   *Georgia v. McCollum,* __ U.S. __, 112 S.Ct. 2348 (1992).

12   *Edmonson v. Leesville Concrete Co.,* __ U.S. __, 111 S.Ct. 2077 (1991).

— Index —

A

The Environment and International Relations

This exciting textbook introduces students to the ways in which the theories and tools of International Relations can be used to analyse and address global environmental problems. Kate O'Neill develops an innovative historical and analytical framework for understanding global environmental issues, integrating insights from different disciplines, and thereby encouraging readers to engage with the issues and equip themselves with the knowledge they need to apply their own critical insights. This book will be invaluable for students of environmental issues both from political science and environmental studies perspectives.

New to this edition
* Updated coverage to include the latest developments in the field, incorporating new perspectives and recent thinking up to the December 2015 Paris Climate Agreement.
* Includes new examples, textboxes and figures throughout to explain key concepts and debates, enabling readers to connect theory with practice.
* Features a new chapter examining the emergence and politics of market mechanisms as a new mode of global environmental governance.

Kate O'Neill is Associate Professor in the Department of Environmental Science, Policy and Management at the University of California at Berkeley.

Themes in international Relations

This new series of textbooks aims to provide students with authoritative surveys of central topics in the study of International Relations. Intended for upper-level undergraduates and graduates, the books will be concise, accessible, and comprehensive. Each volume will examine the main theoretical and empirical aspects of the subject concerned, and its relation to wider debates in International Relations, and will also include chapter-by-chapter guides to further reading and discussion questions.

The Environment and International Relations

Kate O'Neill

University of California at Berkeley

CAMBRIDGE
UNIVERSITY PRESS

CAMBRIDGE
UNIVERSITY PRESS

University Printing House, Cambridge CB2 8BS, United Kingdom

One Liberty Plaza, 20th Floor, New York, NY 10006, USA

477 Williamstown Road, Port Melbourne, VIC 3207, Australia

4843/24, 2nd Floor, Ansari Road, Daryaganj, Delhi – 110002, India

79 Anson Road, #06–04/06, Singapore 079906

Cambridge University Press is part of the University of Cambridge.

It furthers the University's mission by disseminating knowledge in the pursuit of education, learning, and research at the highest international levels of excellence.

www.cambridge.org
Information on this title: www.cambridge.org/9781107061675
DOI: 10.1017/9781107448087

© Kate O'Neill 2017

First published 2009
Second edition 2017

Printed in the United Kingdom by Clays, St Ives plc

A catalogue record for this publication is available from the British Library.

ISBN 978-1-107-06167-5 Hardback
ISBN 978-1-107-67171-3 Paperback

Additional resources for this publication at www.cambridge.org/9781107061675

Contents

Preface

Studying the global politics of the environment is a complex, sometimes challenging, but always illuminating task. Those who study this area approach it from many different directions: political science, economics, sociology, law, and ecology, to name but a few. For my own part, I first heard about climate change from my high school biology teacher in the mid-1980s; shortly thereafter, we all found out about the ozone layer as all the hairsprays, deodorants, and other aerosol products containing ozone-destroying chlorofluorocarbons (or CFCs) vanished from store shelves. As an undergraduate studying economics, I learned about "externalities," "public goods," and other ways that unregulated capitalism leads, in the absence of intervention, to environmental damage – including damage that travels across national borders. I carried these interests on to graduate school and Ph.D. work in political science, without really expecting to be able to study them in the context of an advanced degree in international relations theory. This all changed following the 1992 United Nations Conference on Environment and Development (UNCED), held in Rio de Janeiro. The Earth Summit, as it is often called, brought into focus a whole network of international treaties and agreements set up to manage international environmental problems – and proved to be a watershed moment for an emerging academic field of international environmental politics, particularly the study of international cooperation among nation states for global environmental protection. These days, as a professor in an interdisciplinary environmental studies department, and an active participant in the academic field of global environmental politics, I encounter perspectives outside the political science field that explain the deeply pervasive nature of global environmental change and advocate a range of political solutions above and beyond international diplomacy.

Today's students were born into a world with serious and widespread environmental challenges, with literally thousands of international agreements, organizations, partnerships, networks, and initiatives attempting to meet these challenges. They also know that many global environmental trends are in the wrong direction, and serious structural and institutional changes are likely to be needed in order to address them. There are no optimal solutions to global environmental degradation, and many will be grappling with these problems for decades to come. All who work in the field of international environmental politics face a constant tension between the normative aspects of our work – we do, after all, want to save the world and the world's environment for future generations – and the analytical: the need to understand and explain real-world political dynamics, which often fall short of anyone's ideal. This book is informed by the idea that in order to move forward we must understand the shape and dynamics of the governance systems we have now, and it is inspired by the efforts of my students to marry hope to political realities.

Acknowledgments

Attempting to distill a vast and ever-changing body of literature into a single volume is no easy task. Doing the same thing for a second edition of a book about an ever-changing field is even harder. Many people helped me along this journey. I would like to thank John Haslam and others from Cambridge University Press for their patience, encouragement, and enthusiasm. For reading drafts, helping with last-minute edits, and general support, special thanks to Erin Bergren and Laura Driscoll. In addition, thank you to Erika Weinthal, Stacy VanDeveer, and Susan Altman for support, Ben Cashore, Jane Dawson, and Sikina Jinnah – among many others – for using the first edition in their courses and encouraging me to write the second. I truly appreciated all feedback from users and readers. Particular thanks to Wil Burns for his patience and support during this whole process, as well as willingness to work through many seemingly minor details as the text progressed.

I began work on this edition during an immensely difficult transition in my life. I owe an immeasurable debt to my friends and colleagues in the broader Global Environmental Politics community for their support. It is good to belong to such a vibrant – and prolific – academic field.

Abbreviations

AOSIS	Alliance of Small Island States
BASIC	Brazil, South Africa, India, and China
BINGO	Business International Non-Governmental Organization
BRICs	Brazil, Russia, India, China, and South Africa
CBD	Convention on Biological Diversity
CDM	Clean Development Mechanism
CER	Certified Emissions Reduction
CFCs	chlorofluorocarbons
CITES	Convention on International Trade in Endangered Species
COP	Conference of the Parties
CSA	Canadian Standards Association
CSD	Commission on Sustainable Development
CSR	corporate social responsibility
CTE	Committee on Trade and the Environment
ENB	Earth Negotiations Bulletin
ESS	ecosystem services
ETS	emissions trading system/scheme
EU	European Union
EUA	European Union Allowance
FAO	UN Food and Agriculture Organization
FDI	foreign direct investment
FSC	Forest Stewardship Council
G77	Group of 77 Developing Countries
GATS	General Agreement on Trade in Services
GATT	General Agreement on Tariffs and Trade
GDP	gross domestic product
GEF	Global Environment Facility
GEG	global environmental governance
GEP	global environmental politics
GHG	greenhouse gas
GIS	Geographic Information System

GMO	genetically modified organism
HCFCs	hydrochlorofluorocarbons
HFCs	hydrofluorocarbons
HIPCs	highly indebted poorer countries
IAEA	International Atomic Energy Agency
IAM	Integrated Assessment Model
IBRD	International Bank for Reconstruction and Development
ICC	International Chamber of Commerce
IEP	international environmental politics
IGO	inter-governmental organization
IMF	International Monetary Fund
IMO	International Maritime Organization
INDC	Intended Nationally Determined Contribution
IPBES	Intergovernmental Science-Policy Platform on Biodiversity and Ecosystem Services
IPCC	Intergovernmental Panel on Climate Change
IPE	international political economy
ISO	International Organization for Standardization
IUCN	International Union for the Conservation of Nature
IWC	International Whaling Convention
LRTAP	long-range transboundary air pollution
MRV	monitoring, reporting, and verification
MEA	Multilateral Environmental Agreement
MNC	multinational corporation
NAFTA	North American Free Trade Agreement
NGO	non-governmental organization
NIEO	New International Economic Order
NOAA	National Oceanic and Atmospheric Administration
NSMD	non-state, market-driven (governance)
NTB	non-tariff barrier
OECD	Organization for Economic Cooperation and Development
PEFC	Programme for the Endorsement of Forest Certification Schemes
PES	payment for ecosystem services
POPs	persistent organic pollutants
RDB	regional development bank
REDD	Reducing Emissions from Deforestation and Forest Degradation
RGGI	Regional Greenhouse Gas Initiative
RTA	regional trade agreement
SAP	Structural Adjustment Program

SBSTTA	Subsidiary Body for Scientific, Technical, and Technological Advice
SCC	Social Cost of Carbon
SFI	Sustainable Forests Initiative
SIR	system for implementation review
SPS	Sanitary and Phytosanitary Standards
SRI	socially responsible investment
STS	science and technology studies
TAN	Transnational Advocacy Network
TEEB	The Economics of Ecosystems and Biodiversity
TRIPS	Trade-Related Intellectual Property Rights
TWG	technical working group
UN	United Nations
UNCCD	UN Convention to Combat Desertification
UNCED	UN Conference on Environment and Development
UNCHE	UN Conference on Humans and the Environment
UNCTAD	UN Conference on Trade and Development
UNDP	UN Development Programme
UNEP	UN Environment Programme
UNESCO	UN Educational, Scientific, and Cultural Organization
UNFCCC	UN Framework Convention on Climate Change
VCLT	Vienna Convention on the Law of Treaties
WBSCD	World Business Council for Sustainable Development
WCD	World Commission on Dams
WEO	World Environment Organization
WHO	World Health Organization
WMO	World Meteorological Organization
WSSD	World Summit on Sustainable Development
WTO	World Trade Organization
WWF	Worldwide Fund for Nature/World Wildlife Fund

1 Introduction: The Environment and International Relations

In December 2015 the official representatives of nearly 200 countries met in Paris to negotiate an agreement that would govern the global response to climate change and its impacts well into the twenty-first century. Climate change is among the most serious problems facing the international community. Rising global temperatures are threatening livelihoods and lives worldwide, through changing weather patterns, drought, and sea-level rise that threatens the very existence of the world's small island nation states. Even so, global action to date had proven deeply disappointing. The world's largest economy, the United States, had pulled out of negotiations. Others – even the member states of the European Union (EU), usually considered a strong supporter of environmental action – were barely meeting the low targets they had agreed to, and the new engines of the global economy – China, India, and Brazil – were rapidly increasing greenhouse gas (GHG) emissions without any obligation to act. The science behind climate change continued to come under fierce attack from skeptics. Activist groups and even business actors felt excluded from the governance arena, despite the ideas and initiatives they were offering.

Global climate politics reached a nadir after the 2009 Conference of the Parties (COP) to the United Nations Framework Convention on Climate Change (UNFCCC) in Copenhagen. Much hope and optimism in the lead-up suggested that this would be the time the international community broke through and came up with a strong, binding legal agreement to meet commitments. Instead, the meeting almost foundered on the rock of national interests, and the resulting Copenhagen Accord – not even a formal agreement – was deeply disappointing to many, setting only weak goals and vague commitments to a new global fund.

The Paris meeting – the twenty-first COP to the UNFCCC – was different. On the last day of the conference nation-states announced an agreement where, rather than being allocated targets they had to meet, they had crafted individual plans of action for reducing emission, called Intended Nationally Determined Contributions (INDCs). The agreement also contained processes for monitoring (and perhaps strengthening) those commitments over time, and general commitments to help the weakest states adapt, to encourage carbon storage, and to aspire to keep the global temperature rise to 1.5 degrees Celsius. The exhausted delegates, officials, and other observers stood to applaud at the conclusion of the meeting and the creation of the Paris Agreement.

The Paris Agreement has been hailed as a turning point, a success in the fight against climate change (Light 2015; Busby 2016). Previously uncommitted countries – the USA as well as China and other emerging major powers – have joined, and non-traditional actors, such as non-governmental organizations (NGOs), have new roles to play. Best estimates suggest that if the targets states have already set are met, we will avoid the worst impacts of global temperature rise. Paris also represents a major shift in how climate change is governed globally. It represents a more diffuse, "bottom-up" approach to global governance, which, as we shall see, is not how global environmental governance (GEG) is usually carried out. At the same time, many criticized the agreement, including many scientists, arguing that commitments are still far weaker than needed, and questioned the will of nation-states to maintain and strengthen commitments over time in the absence of strong monitoring and transparency rules, as yet to be negotiated (Sethi 2015; Geden 2015).

The outcome of the Paris meeting illustrates a major theme of this book, which directly addresses the relationship between international relations theory and the politics of GEG. From an environmentalist perspective, international actions around climate change and many other environmental problems are inadequate: they are too slow, and possibly too weak, to manage the problems we face. They do not challenge the basic global economic and political structures that drive unconstrained growth regardless of ecological limits.

From the perspective of a political scientist, especially from international relations, however, these steps represent significant progress. Given a world with a history of conflict and failed cooperation, the steps we have taken, and the extent of global environmental cooperation over the past five decades, are tremendous. We have built new organizations and institutions, empowered new actors, fostered science, knowledge building and new technology, and have nearly 200 vastly different nation-states working together in unprecedented ways. This particular tension – between environmentalist and political science views of the world – motivates this work, and much of my own thinking about global environmental politics (GEP), as a political scientist in an environmental studies department. The chapters that follow will, I hope, further illuminate this tension and suggest ways forward.

Outline and Themes

The question of when, if, and how well national governments cooperate to address shared environmental problems, from climate change to bio-diversity loss to international trade in hazardous wastes, drives much of the work that applies international relations theory to environmental problems. For many years now, the tools of political science, and specifically of the discipline of international relations, have been applied to the complex set of questions around global environmental change and GEG. At the same time, insights from this body of work have informed and shaped our broader understanding of the workings of international politics, and the emphases and directions of specific theoretical approaches within the academic discipline.

However, traditional political science and international relations approaches have limits when applied to problems of such political, scientific, and social complexity as those associated with global environmental change. A spectrum of perspectives, approaches, and tools from many different disciplines helps explain the nature of the global environmental crisis and offer possible solutions. Some of these perspectives have their origin in the world of practice and policy-making, others in other social science disciplines. Many of these perspectives lie well outside the traditional disciplinary parameters of international relations theory, but are becoming more central to debates within the field of global – or international – environmental politics.[1] This book, therefore, analyzes the politics of GEG – its shape, its history, its performance, and its possible future – through a broad theoretical lens. In the process, I identify a field of study that is shaping the way we understand international politics as a whole.

Three questions guide political science inquiry into the global environment.

- First, what are the political causes of global environmental change? Are they collective action problems, where states have little incentive to control the shift of pollution or resource depletion across national borders? Alternatively, are they shaped more by the structures of a global – and globalizing – capitalist economy, which prioritizes economic growth and free-market capitalism over environmental sustainability?

---

[1] The term "international environmental politics" (IEP) tends to be used when the work or approaches under investigation derive most directly from international relations theory; "global environmental politics" (GEP) is a broader, more interdisciplinary term, allowing for broader sets of theoretical and methodological approaches. GEP is becoming the more common term as the field evolves, and it is the term generally used throughout this text.

- Second, what factors account for the rise of global environmental concern and the ways in which critical actors perceive environmental problems? Why has such concern fluctuated over the years? How do we handle scientific and political uncertainties about global environmental change?
- Last but not least, what constitutes GEG, and what explains the shape, emergence, and effectiveness of such governance institutions and arrangements? It is this third question, informed by perspectives on the first two, that this book seeks to address.

International relations theory illuminates the answers to these questions in many ways. With its focus on the roles of power and national interests, of international institutions and rules, and of norms and ideas in international cooperation, it provides powerful leverage in explaining why and how we see the GEG institutions we do, and why some are more successful than others. In other respects, international relations theory (at least in conventional terms) is not enough. For example, the state-centric focus of much international relations theory has traditionally downplayed the roles and activities of non-state actors – of environmental movements, corporations, even scientists – in influencing existing, and even creating their own, governance institutions. This focus has now clearly changed.

As we shall see, some scholars question the viability and worth of existing GEG institutions, and argue for dismantling and rebuilding the ways in which the global community manages environmental problems. Others argue that we have been too blinkered in how we identify and categorize institutions and practices of GEG, and urge attention be paid to politics across scales and issue areas that have not traditionally been part of the global policy agenda. In short, studies of international environmental politics and governance are dynamic and evolving, creating an exciting field of study that is applied to the most urgent environmental, economic, and social challenges of our time. Understanding these dynamics offers critical insights into the opportunities for, and barriers to meeting, these challenges.

This book, therefore, traces the evolutionary arc of GEG since it first emerged as a coherent system in the early 1970s up to the more contested and disillusioned years of the early twenty-first century, focusing both on the evolution of governance institutions and on how the study of global governance has changed. It addresses how international relations theory has been analyzed and assessed, and has itself been challenged by the emergence of GEP as a serious arena of scholarship within – and outside – the discipline. In particular, this book identifies and assesses different *sites* and *modes* of GEG: state or government-led environmental cooperation and the creation of multilateral environmental agreements (MEAs); the emergence of a multitude of "non-state" governance initiatives, such as eco-certification schemes; and how global economic governance, from trade to development aid, has become a critical site of environmental governance. New modes of GEG include the deployment of information as a governance tool, and the rise of market mechanisms to create incentives for change.

This chapter introduces the various scholarly approaches within the broad field of international environmental politics. Chapters 2 and 3 introduce global environmental issues, or problems, and actors in international environmental politics respectively. Chapters 4 through 8 focus on the different sites and modes of global governance and its intersection with the environment. Chapters 4 and 5 address international environmental cooperation, or diplomacy: the negotiation, implementation, and impacts of MEAs. Chapter 6 turns to global economic governance – particularly of trade, finance, and aid – and how it increasingly engages with environmental issues. Chapter 7 describes "non-state" GEG: governance institutions and arrangements set up not by nation-states, but by non-state actors. Chapter 8 addresses the rise (and decline?) of market mechanisms as modes of GEG. Chapter 9 – the concluding chapter – addresses debates over where GEG is going, and how it can be best designed (if possible) to meet the challenges of the twenty-first century and beyond.

Global Environmental Governance: A Narrative Arc and Critical Debates

Defined most simply, GEG consists of efforts by the international community to manage and solve shared environmental problems. In an article published in 1970 in the influential policy journal *Foreign Affairs*, George Kennan – one of the architects of the post-World War Two world order – wrote about his own vision of GEG, then in its nascent stages (Kennan 1970). Recognizing that "the entire ecology of the planet is not arranged in national compartments; and whoever interferes seriously with it anywhere is doing something that is almost invariably of serious concern to the international community at large," he argued that the existing patchwork of national and international agencies were not up to the task of coordinating and managing the world's environment. He continues:

One can conceive, then, by an act of the imagination, of a small group of advanced nations, consisting of roughly the ten leading industrial nations of the world, including communist and non-communist ones alike ... constituting themselves something in the nature of a club for the preservation of natural environment, and resolving, then, in that capacity, to bring into being an entity – let us call it initially an International Environment Agency ... This entity, while naturally requiring the initiative of governments for its inception and their continued interest for its support, would have to be one in which the substantive decisions would be taken not on the basis of compromise among governmental representatives, but on the basis of collaboration among scholars, scientists, experts ... true international servants, bound by no national or political mandate, by nothing, in fact, other than dedication to the work at hand.

Kennan was writing with full knowledge of, and indeed in order to advise, the upcoming United Nations-sponsored Conference on Humans and the Environment (UNCHE), to be held in Stockholm in 1972. At that point in time the UN was looking to expand its role into managing global environmental problems. By bringing together government representatives from 113 countries, it hoped to lay the groundwork for an architecture of GEG that would serve the planet for decades to come.

Kennan's vision represents a highly technocratic form of GEG: governance through impartial expertise rather than through the politics of conflict and compromise. The system of GEG that emerged post-Stockholm, however, was far more political, and decentralized. Since 1972 GEG has consisted primarily of the negotiation and implementation by nation-states of international (multilateral) environmental treaties and agreements on an issue-by-issue basis, often coordinated by the United Nations Environment Programme (UNEP), established at Stockholm. In other words, the dominant driving force of GEG since 1972 has not been technocracy but international diplomacy.

The evolution of this system has been framed by three subsequent global summits. The UN Conference on Environment and Development (UNCED), held in Rio de Janeiro in 1992, marked the signing of two major international agreements on climate and biodiversity, and the creation of Agenda 21, a roadmap for global sustainable development (Gardner 1992). The World Summit on Sustainable Development (WSSD), held in Johannesburg in 2002, led to no major agreements, but rather, smaller-scale partnership initiatives and development-related goals. Held at a time of heightened global tension, it also reflected disillusionment with the pace of international environmental cooperation. Finally, in 2012, the Rio+20 summit was convened, in Rio de Janeiro. Its purpose was to define and generate strategies to implement a "green economy," a global economy that fully integrates environmental and social costs and benefits. This new norm of GEG represents the culmination of a shift toward a system that integrates environmental and economic priorities, which we will chart in subsequent chapters.

More than 400 MEAs and multilateral agreements with a strong environmental component have been created since 1920, most of them since 1973. Their creation and implementation is the subject of Chapters 4 and 5. Highlights include binding agreements over ozone-layer depletion, climate change, the protection of biological diversity, and the production and use of mercury.

The governance of each issue area has followed its own arc. Climate change, as outlined above, has been the most complex and contentious. Although countries were able to agree on goals in 1992, with the creation of the UN Framework Convention on Climate Change (UFCCC), the regime subsequently weakened as the USA withdrew in 2001, and commitments waned even as scientific evidence mounted. This trajectory has – potentially – changed with the signing of the Paris Agreement in 2015. Ozone-layer depletion is, by contrast, the success story of GEP. With 197 states on board and strong regulations in place to control the production and use of ozone-depleting substances, the "hole" in the ozone layer will mend by the end of this century. Global deforestation is another case that we discuss throughout this book. There is no formal international agreement around forests; too many governments objected to global restrictions on the use of their forests as a timber resource. Instead, forest governance arrangements have emerged in other arenas. Non-state actors have established certification initiatives for sustainably managed forests, while deforestation is now addressed under climate negotiations, as maintaining forest stocks is one way to store carbon and prevent it entering the atmosphere. This fragmentation of forest governance is also reflected in the climate arena, as initiatives emerge in cities and regions, managed by firms and NGOs. Finally, chemicals-related agreements – governing, for example, hazardous waste trading, persistent organic pollutants (POPs), and the production and use of mercury – have remained squarely the focus of intergovernmental cooperation, and have moved toward integration under a single "umbrella" organization.

These MEAs, or regimes, together comprise the dominant, state-led mode of contemporary GEG. Today two different narratives challenge the practice and the study of state-led GEG. The first is one of failure. James Gustave Speth, former director of the World Resources Institute, and Dean of Yale University's School of Forestry and Environmental Studies, offers a representative view:

[The] rates of environmental degradation that stirred the international community [a quarter century ago] continue essentially unabated today. The disturbing trends persist, and the problems have become deeper and truly urgent. The steps that governments took over the past two decades represent the first attempt at global environmental governance, an experiment that has largely failed. (Speth 2004, pp. 1–2)[2]

According to the second narrative, we have held too narrow a view of what counts as GEG, and we need to look beyond the standard international relations repertoire of inter-state cooperation and diplomacy (Bulkeley et al. 2014; Conca 2006; Newell and Paterson 2010; Wapner 2003). By examining non-traditional actors – activists, community groups, international organizations, multinational corporations – other modes of governance, such as forest certification or emissions trading, and actions across scales – from local to global – a picture of global governance emerges that is far more multi-faceted, contentious, and potentially more democratic than the dominant model of international diplomacy. This perspective challenges the position of nation-states as the sole agents of global governance and ultimately argues that a more democratic, or participatory, vision of global governance may help us reach a more environmentally sustainable world. By broadening our field of vision, as students, scholars, or practitioners, we can attain a more complete understanding of the various forces driving – or pushing against – effective GEG.

Sites and Modes of Global Environmental Governance

Following the insights from this second debate, this book focuses on existing and new sites and modes of GEG (see Box 1.1). These are: international environmental cooperation (state-led GEG; Chapters 4 and 5), the role of global economic institutions and GEG (Chapter 6), non-state GEG (Chapter 7), and market mechanisms (Chapter 8), which utilize prices and other economic instruments to shape behavior. "Sites" of governance are not literal locations, but rather arenas of governance within the broader structure of global governance in which actors interact and make decisions. "Modes" of governance are ways of crafting and implementing environmental regulations and initiatives – whether through the negotiation of treaties or the deployment of information in private-sector-led voluntary certification systems, which are designed to steer or change the behavior of relevant actors, from governments to firms to individuals (Rosenau 1995; Andonova et al. 2009).

We have already outlined the basic shape of state-led governance. The term "non-state governance" refers to a range of governance activities

---

[2] For examples of works that address this theme see Susskind 1994; VanDeveer 2003; Prins and Rayner 2007; and Victor 2011.

Box 1.1: Sites and Modes of Global Environmental Governance

1. Broadening Sites of Global Environmental Governance at the Global Level

Diplomatic Arena➔International Economic Arena➔Non–State Arena

- **State Led Governance:** Based on the primacy of international law and diplomacy and the negotiation of issue-based environmental regimes. Nation states are the lead actors. United Nations Environment Programme plays anchoring role, non-state actors are supporting players
- **International Economic Governance:** Lead actors include international economic organizations such as the World Trade Organization, the World Bank, and their member states. They exercise governance by coordinating capacity building and environmental aid, engaging in global conversations over the relationship between environment and development, and regulating and monitoring their own activities
- **Non-State Governance:** Lead actors are NGOs, corporations and other non-state actors who create, administer and maintain governance initiatives, such as certification systems or partnerships, often based on gathering and using information to steer behavior

2. Modes of Global Environmental Governance

- **International Cooperation:** The negotiation of commitments by nation states in a given issue area, often based on agreed targets and timetables. May include a threat of sanctions for non-compliance. Often contains capacity-building measures. International environmental governance as most people think of it.
- **Information Based Governance**: Gathering and using information to change or steer behavior of relevant actors, such as corporations. Most present in non-state governance initiatives, such as certification, but also in transparency mechanisms in state-led regimes. Can use formal (legal) or informal (normative or "shaming") means of enforcement
- **Market Mechanisms**: Global market mechanisms used by state and non-state actors to remedy market failures, e.g. by putting a price on carbon emissions or ecosystem services, allowing compensation for activities foregone or for buying and selling of emissions allowances They work by creating incentives for actors to meet goals, allowing them flexibility in decision-making

3. Deepening Sites: Global Environmental Governance across Scales

Global⟵ ⟶National ⟵ ⟶Local

- National influences on global processes, and global influences on national politics are well-understood: national interests shape

Box 1.1: (cont.)

international negotiations, while fulfilling international commitments involves political and policy changes at the domestic level
- Global-Local Connections are less well theorized and documented. Examples include regional centers under the chemicals regimes (global → local), cities and subnational jurisdictions and climate change (local → global), and knowledge, such as the take-up of local knowledge to the global level

created, implemented, and managed by non-state actors: civil society actors, such as NGOs, and private-sector actors – corporations and business associations – who may or may not work in partnership. In Chapter 7 we examine international transparency and certification regimes as leading examples of non-state governance. Given general disillusionment with the effectiveness of international environmental diplomacy, many activists, analysts, and members of the private sector have embraced these initiatives as a way to bypass the cumbersome process of international cooperation. Scholarly interest in these non-state regulatory regimes revolves around how they build authority and legitimacy, even while bypassing national governments – traditionally the sole holders of these governance properties (Cashore et al. 2004; Green 2014), and their ultimate effectiveness, especially given their voluntary nature.

Decisions and rules about trade, foreign investment and global capital movements, and development, particularly in an era of rapid globalization, have serious impacts on the state of the global environment. So, increasingly, forums such as the World Trade Organization (WTO) and the World Bank have had to take on issues of the environmental and social impacts of their decisions, and how to respond when their rules conflict with global rules and norms about environmental protection. Chapter 6 addresses these processes. Finally, and related to discourses of economic globalization, market mechanisms are increasingly used at national and now at global levels to create positive incentives and a degree of choice and flexibility for actors to meet global commitments, and to resolve market failures by creating prices and markets for environmental services and new "commodities" such as a tonne of carbon. Chapter 8 examines how this mode of governance, which differs from traditional "targets and timetables" approaches, has worked in global climate, biodiversity, and forests governance.

Box 1.1 depicts these sites and modes as processes, notably a broadening of sites, from the diplomatic arena out to economic and non-state arenas, and proliferation of modes of GEG. It also shows a deepening across scales of GEG, or the creation of vertical linkages between global, national, and local spheres of activity and governance (O'Neill 2014), a relatively new theme in GEP. We examine a case study in Chapter 8, of a program called REDD+ (Reducing Emissions from Deforestation and Forest Degradation), the initiative to preserve forest stocks in order to store carbon by paying forest owners and managers to maintain or enhance existing forests. Governed from the global level, it nonetheless directly shapes the lives and livelihoods of people on the ground, who have pushed to be included in its decision-making processes (Doherty and Schroeder 2011). Another example is that of cities and subnational governments becoming important players in global climate governance by developing and implementing their own climate initiatives, for both mitigation and adaptation, and creating transnational networks in order to work together and push global climate politics forward (Bulkeley et al. 2014; Gore and Robinson 2009).

I have chosen in this book to focus primarily on sites and modes of GEG. However, we return to matters of scale in Chapter 9. In the meantime, we begin this journey by sketching the scholarly perspectives and debates, both within and outside international relations theory, which guide our understanding of these developments.

Scholarly Perspectives on International Environmental Politics

The emergence of the environment as an area of study within international relations scholarship mirrored real world political developments. Works in the field appeared from the early 1970s on, but during the 1990s the field began to come into its own. Books, journals, university courses, list-serves, and conferences – all the hallmarks of a successful academic discipline – now provide forums for ongoing debates within the field. The field of GEP began as a subset of international relations theory, whereby the politics of the global environment provided a useful set of cases for developing and testing hypotheses about the nature and durability of international cooperation. GEP has now grown in scope to embrace many different social science perspectives and methodologies. The following sections of this chapter discuss the relationship between international relations theory, social science theory, and the global environment, addressing the following themes:

- How the basic tools and perspectives of international relations theory help us understand the dynamics of global environmental change and governance.

- How the study of GEG – and particularly the study of international environmental cooperation – has contributed to the study of international relations.
- How the study of global environmental problems and politics have generated new perspectives on GEG that draw on a full range of social science traditions.

International Relations Theory and Global Environmental Politics

Theory provides a way of thinking about and analyzing the world in systematic ways. It helps us describe, explain, and predict real world events. The broad field of international relations, with its focus on interactions among nation-states, has generated many theoretical approaches, concepts, and tools for understanding international environmental politics. In this section we examine three primary theoretical approaches in mainstream international relations theory that have been applied to GEP: (neo)realism, institutionalism, and constructivism. Historically, institutionalism has made the strongest contribution to understanding GEP. In recent years, however, realist and constructivist approaches have made significant gains in their theoretical utility.

An Introduction to International Relations Theory   Most essentially, international relations theory is concerned with the dynamics of international conflict and cooperation among nation-states. In the aftermath of World War Two many scholars in the field focused on the dynamics of the Cold War between the East (the Soviet Union) and the West (the United States and Western Europe). This period also saw a growing interest in international political economy (IPE) – the economic interactions among nation-states, including trade and financial relations, issues of debt and dependency, the role of international organizations and international law in managing both the global economy and collective security – and, ultimately, the global environment.[3]

Works on international politics and transboundary environmental problems first appeared in the 1970s (e.g. Pirages 1978; M'Gonigle and Zacher 1979). At first they connected more closely with international environmental law and legal scholarship. Over the 1980s and 1990s the field consolidated around two trends, becoming more closely allied with international relations and politics. First, the 1970s and 1980s were active decades on the international political scene. The 1972 Stockholm

---

[3] For general overviews of international relations theory see Baylis et al. 2014; Gilpin 2001; and Burchill and Linklater 2013. On theories of international cooperation see O'Neill et al. 2004.

Conference ushered in a flurry of diplomatic activity coordinated by the new United Nations Environment Programme (UNEP). Treaties – on trade in endangered species, ozone-depleting substances, hazardous waste trading, ocean dumping, biodiversity, climate change, and so on – were being mooted, signed, and ratified by nation-states, providing a new and fertile field of study for political scientists.

Second, many international relations theorists had shifted toward closer study of international cooperation – the intentional coordination of policies and adjustment of behaviors among nation-states to address collective problems – as a durable and influential phenomenon (e.g. Keohane 1984; Krasner 1983). These scholars questioned a dominant assumption of the discipline: that cooperation among rival states was purely transitory and reflective only of state interests. Interest surged in conditions facilitating the formation of international governance regimes, their functions, durability, and impact. In turn, emerging structures of GEG provided a rich set of cases for the study of international cooperation. Oran Young, one of the pivotal early GEP scholars (Young 1989, 1991), was soon joined by other existing and new scholars whose work continues to influence the field today (Benedick 1987; Haas 1990b; Haas, Keohane and Levy 1993; Lipschutz and Conca 1993; Mitchell 1994).[4]

To quote an early and influential statement of the global environmental problematique from an international relations perspective:

Can a fragmented and often highly conflictual political system made up of over 170 sovereign states and numerous other actors achieve the high (and historically unprecedented) levels of cooperation and policy coordination needed to manage environmental problems on a global scale? (Hurrell and Kingsbury 1992, p. 1)

Three traditions within the mainstream of the field – (neo)realism, (neo)liberal institutionalism, and constructivism, based respectively on power, institutions, and norms – provide insights into problems and politics of international environmental cooperation. They share certain perspectives on the international system, and the identity of key actors, but differ extensively in the emphasis they give to different explanatory variables. Realists and institutionalists agree that the international political system is anarchic, and that the primary actors within this system are sovereign nation states; constructivists may agree but do not take these conditions as given.[5] In international relations theory, "anarchy" means the absence of a sovereign world government: nation-states answer to no higher authority than themselves. It does not mean that the system is

---

[4] To name but a few. Early and recent overviews of the field tell this story. See Stevis et al. 1989; Mitchell 2003; Dauvergne and Clapp 2016.
[5] On anarchy and sovereignty see Milner 1991; Krasner 1988.

chaotic, nor is there a strong connection to classical political theories of anarchy, or self-governing communities. Within this system, states – or countries – are considered sovereign territories: governments rule over their citizens, territory, and resource base, and, except under limited circumstances, interference from other states is considered an act of war.

Realist and neorealist theorists of international politics hew most closely to these basic assumptions (Waltz 1979; Keohane 1986). For these theorists, international anarchy is unmitigated: states have little or no incentive to work together to solve joint problems, and their attitudes to each other have been conditioned by a history of international conflict, not one of international cooperation. They are motivated primarily by rivalry and the pursuit of relative power, most particularly power in military or economic terms. In fact, it is this pursuit of relative gains, vis-à-vis other states, that drives interactions between them. This makes lasting cooperation – other than the formation of strategic military alliances – extremely unlikely, except when cooperation is driven and maintained by one single, powerful state, or hegemony, for as long as it is willing and able to do so. For example, the USA in the post-World War Two years took on this role, setting up and maintaining the global free trade regime (Kindleberger 1973). For realists, state actors – being those that hold the reins of military and economic power – are the only actors who matter. Other types of international actor – international organizations, NGOs, etc. – are purely peripheral.

Liberal theorists – or, in their latter-day variant, neoliberal institutionalists – see a different sort of world, one that is more amenable to cooperation (Baldwin 1993; Keohane 1984; Krasner 1983).[6] They posit that states are, in fact, far more interdependent than most realists, or neorealists, recognize. In a world where countries depend on one another for mutual peace and prosperity, there is a strong incentive to work together to achieve joint, or absolute, gains for the international community. Strong variants on liberal theories in international relations do, in fact, see a very important role for international law in creating an international community of nation-states and other actors, rather than a world occupied by autonomous and rivalrous states (Bull 1977).

For theorists in the neoliberal institutionalist tradition, anarchy is a problem in that the absence of a sovereign authority makes it easy – and desirable – for states to cheat on mutual agreements. Thus, a single

---

[6] Note that "neoliberalism" in this context does not mean the same thing as "neoliberalism" in the context of neoliberal economic globalization, and it is not nearly as politically loaded. In international relations terms, it stems from a reworking of the classic Liberal tradition of political thought; in globalization theory, it stems from free market, laissez-faire economics.

state can free-ride on an international agreement, and receive the benefits from it without paying any costs of adjustment. Under this scenario, no state cooperates, hoping instead to free-ride on the actions of others. Therefore, neoliberal institutionalists look for ways to mitigate these problems. They see international cooperation succeeding when states can work together to realize joint gains, and when institutions are set up that can monitor compliance, increase transparency, reduce the transactions costs of cooperation, and prevent most, if not all, cheating. They assign non-state actors, such as the UN, or NGOs important roles in fostering such transparency, and making durable cooperative agreements much more likely.

Constructivism, the third approach, introduces ideational and normative elements into the equation. Over the past twenty-five years it has become a leading school of thought in international relations theory (Barnett 2014). Both realist and neoliberal institutionalist traditions tend to assume that states are out to maximize their individual utility (be that in relative or absolute terms), and that preferences, or interests, are predetermined and inflexible. Constructivism, instead, examines how states respond to, and how the global system is shaped by, ideas, knowledge, and norms, namely shared conceptions of appropriate behavior.[7] These approaches tend to assign a far more influential role in international politics to non-state actors than do realists or even institutionalists, arguing they are more than supporting players. Instead, non-state actors are frequently the shapers and carriers of these new ideas or norms.

Constructivism has weak and strong variants.[8] At one level, new ideas or norms may change the way states calculate costs and benefits of different courses of action. At another, these ideas and norms can work to change states' own perceptions of their interests or roles in the international system, or even transform the contours of the international system itself. Slavery is an example frequently used in the literature. At the start of the nineteenth century slavery was widely accepted as a legitimate practice by many nations. However, over the course of that century, political ideas about democracy and the intrinsic equality of human beings began to gain influence, promulgated by the Abolitionist movement, which had important roots in Great Britain, but soon spread

---

[7] See Nadelman 1990; Wendt 1992; Finnemore and Sikkink 1998; and Goldstein and Keohane 1993 for a sampling of influential constructivist approaches in international relations theory.

[8] Although they use the term "cognitivism," Hasenclever et al. 2000 capture this distinction. Weak constructivism "focuses on the role of causal beliefs in regime formation and change," strong constructivism focuses on how the same variables – knowledge, norms, and beliefs – may transform actors' conceptions of themselves, their roles in the international systems, and their relationship with other actors (pp. 10–11).

to become one of the world's first transnational social movements (Keck and Sikkink 1998). The moral pressure exerted by these activists, and their influential allies, gradually led to the abolition of the institution of slavery in the industrializing world (although not without the cost of a devastating civil war in the USA). These days, any state that legally permits slavery within its borders is considered a pariah, violating what has become an important international norm.

International Relations Paradigms and Global Environmental Politics
Each of these three mainstream traditions in international relations theory contributes to our understanding of international environmental cooperation in different ways.

The neoliberal institutionalist perspective has traditionally been the most influential in the GEP field, and many GEP theorists emerged from and speak to this tradition. Global environmental degradation, more than many international problems, highlights the interdependence of nation-states. However, international coordination needs to be strong and organized to realize mutual gains: why should one state voluntarily move to reduce its GHG emissions if others will not? To that end, international cooperation is not only desirable but also necessary to overcome collective action problems, and mitigate the negative effects of interdependence. International institutions, reinforced by environmental activist groups, play a critical role in raising international concern, reducing the transactions costs of cooperation, and monitoring and enforcing resultant agreements (Haas et al. 1993). Therefore, neoliberal institutionalist approaches make powerful contributions to understanding why states cooperate over environmental problems and why we see the sorts of cooperative agreements we do.

At the same time, with greater awareness of the institutional density, ideational and normative challenges, and new inter-state power dynamics that characterize modern global environmental politics, neoliberal institutionalism may have done as much as it can on its own. Once marginalized in this field, realist and constructivist theories have increasingly important roles to play in understanding these new dynamics.

Historically, realism and later traditions of neorealism, with their focus on the "high politics" of international peace and security, and their general skepticism about cooperation, may have had little to contribute to understanding the politics of the global environment. There certainly is no hegemonic state willing to create and maintain environmental cooperation. Yet this dismissal underestimated the importance of power politics in international environmental cooperation (Rowlands 2001; see also Jervis 1999). Certainly, military power in the strictest sense is a poor predictor of cooperative outcomes in the environmental arena. However, by adopting different perceptions of power, including control over natural resources or more intangible variables such as leadership and leverage, we can begin to understand particular patterns of bargaining and cooperative outcomes in GEP. Such outcomes include, for example, the influence of southern countries on environmental negotiations around terrestrial resources. More recently, it seems that climate change politics has entered the realm of high politics, ranking with the global security and economic issues that have dominated the international system. First, as climate change progresses, it is likely to deeply affect international economic and political stability, up to and including causing inter- or intra-state conflict (Gemenne et al. 2014; Center for Naval Analyses 2007). Second, with respect to the structure of the international system, climate change is one of the arenas where the emerging powers of India, China, and Brazil made their mark. As the BASIC alliance (with South Africa; see Chapter 4), they have been instrumental in shaping negotiating outcomes from 2009 onwards, just one of the ways they are gaining influence in the international system.

Finally, constructivist theories, focusing on the importance of ideas, knowledge, and norms, have also influenced our understanding of international environmental cooperation. For example, an influential approach developed by Peter Haas examines how transnational "epistemic communities" of scientists have been able to influence cooperative outcomes by transmitting shared ideas of causes and responses to problems to government representatives (Haas 1990a).[9] Work on norms – shared understandings of expected behavior, which work at a deeper level than ideas or knowledge necessarily do – is also becoming increasingly important (Bernstein 2013a). Norms shape the evolution of individual regimes. For example, the International Whaling Convention (IWC) shifted over time from a norm of sustainable exploitation to one of preservation, banning global whaling, in a contested process that pit countries against each other (Epstein 2006). In the climate regime, debates over the use of market mechanisms – which enable rich countries to reduce overall GHG emissions by investing in poorer countries rather than reducing themselves – has taken on strong normative content (see Chapter 8). At a meta-level, the norms governing sustainable development have shifted from a focus on distributive justice within and across generations to one that frames it as a balance between environmental/social protection and economic growth

---

[9] Other works that explicitly address the role of ideas and knowledge in GEP include Ringius 2001; Martello 2001a, 2001b; Williams 2012; Haas and Stevens 2011. See also Chapters 4 and 5.

(Bernstein 2002), finding its most recent incarnation in the notion of the Green Economy introduced at Rio+20 (Tienhaara 2014). Some works combine the realist emphasis on balance of power with the constructivist insight that norms and ideas can help socialize states in particular ways (Terhalle and Depledge 2013). Chapter 5 goes into more depth on approaches to transformational politics and learning within this tradition.

The Contributions of Global Environmental Politics to International Relations Theory

International environmental problems and politics have significantly informed and reshaped contemporary international relations theory.[10] First and foremost, international environmental negotiations constitute a rich set of cases for developing and testing hypotheses about the formation, durability, and impacts of international cooperation. In practice, international cooperation consists of the negotiation by nation-states – with or without coordination by an international body such as the UN – of international governance regimes, the basic building blocks of GEG. The term "regime" covers the rules, organizations, and basic norms and principles involved in the global governance of an individual issue area (Krasner 1983; Chapter 4). Therefore a regime includes, *inter alia*, treaties negotiated by states, the organizations set up to govern those treaties, and the decision-making processes that govern future negotiations within the issue area. It also includes norms, which, while they may not be written down on paper, often exert significant influence on the behavior of regime members.

Theories of regime formation examine the factors that contribute to successful or unsuccessful negotiating outcomes (see Chapter 4). The incorporation of environmental case studies into theories of regime formation brought a wealth of additional insights into why we get the international agreements that we do. Environmental issues are frequently characterized by complexity, uncertainties, and long time horizons (Young 1994). While some scholarly work examines how issue area characteristics affect bargaining (Miles et al. 2002), other scholars focus on the configuration and roles of domestic interests in influencing national bargaining positions (Schreurs and Economy 1997; DeSombre 2000), and their direct engagement with policy-making at the international bargaining table (Betsill and Corell 2001; Pulver 2002). Compared

[10] Direct analyses of this topic are rare. However, Morin and Orsini brought together a collection of articles in *International Studies Review* in 2014 that address how international relations can be/has been shaped by insights from environmental politics and law: Morin and Orsini 2014.

with other international issue areas, environmental negotiations have been far more open to non-state actor participation.

A second area in which the environment has made a critical contribution to understandings of international cooperation is through studies of the effectiveness and impacts of international regimes (Zürn 1998; see Chapter 5). This area of international cooperation – why and how international cooperation actually works – had been relatively under-studied in international relations theory. GEP has made great strides in defining effectiveness, developing methods for studying effectiveness, and building case studies that demonstrate when, how, and why international environmental regimes influence state behavior and environmental outcomes. In part, this work is driven by theoretical questions, and in part by normative concerns held by many in the field about whether or not international cooperation can help our planet. GEP scholars also examine how regimes evolve over time (Young 2010). Do they grow stronger or weaker as new amendments or protocols are negotiated? What individual tracks do they follow, and why?

Other research themes cut across these different phases of environmental cooperation. One analyzes the dimensions, relative power dynamics, and outcomes of disputes – or differences – between countries of the wealthy North and the poorer nations of the global South (Chapters 3 and 4; Najam 2015). Southern countries have found a powerful voice in international environmental negotiations, and have utilized sources of bargaining leverage that do not exist to the same extent in other negotiating forums. These include powerful alliances and a critical role in protecting existing natural resources or preventing future pollution. Southern countries have also been able to make powerful normative claims against the North, which has historically been responsible for most global pollution and resource consumption. They have been instrumental in turning international attention away from purely environmentalist goals toward adopting sustainable development as the main underlying norm of international environmental negotiations. They have also been successful in including measures for environmental aid and technology transfer in most international environmental agreements. Thus, work in this area examines North–South differences at the bargaining table, differential obligations under environmental treaties, and the politics of international environmental aid and building national capacity to address global environmental problems, as well as recent changes in Southern coalitions and relationships.

Non-state actors have taken on significant new roles in GEG, often influencing its shape and outcomes (Chapters 3, 4, and 7; Park 2013), challenging the assumption that nation-states are the only important actors on the international political scene. While states retain sole voting and implementation powers under international law, non-state actors have found an active voice in the negotiation and implementation of "traditional" GEG regimes, and, as we shall see, are beginning to construct governance regimes of their own. From NGOs and activist groups, such as Greenpeace or the Third World Network, to multinational corporations such as Royal Dutch Shell or Chevron-Texaco, and international organizations such as the United Nations or the World Bank, the field of international environmental politics has proven fertile ground for examining a wide range of questions (O'Neill 2015). To what extent are international organizations and non-state actors actually supplanting state actors in performing key global governance roles, from shaping through to the implementation of policy programs? How has the rise of transnational activist and business networks changed the ways in which international politics is conducted – or even understood? How do we understand the influence of non-state actors on GEG?

Scientific, technical, and other forms of knowledge fundamentally shape our understandings of, and responses to, environmental problems (see Chapters 3 and 4; Haas 1990a, 1990b; Lidskog and Sundqvist 2002). GEP has taken a lead role within international relations theory in examining the role of knowledge, ideas, and experts (often scientific) in international politics. Scientific understandings of the causes, impacts, and range of solutions for global environmental problems – particularly those not easily seen in the short term – have been critical in galvanizing political concern and shaping particular policy outcomes. But the need for scientific knowledge and expert opinion is by no means unique to the environmental arena. Other international policy regimes – from the global economy to arms control, and even human rights – have been built on input from different expert communities, including economists and legal experts as well as scientists. Writers in this field have asked who these "experts" are, how they affect the international policy process, and the implications of the politicization of science for scientific communities. International policymakers have also turned to "local" (indigenous, traditional) knowledge, and local knowledge holders for input into policy decisions, with further implications for how we understand the role of knowledge in GEG.

Finally, in recent years GEP scholarship has turned to conceptualizing and analyzing the architecture of GEG as a whole (Biermann et al. 2009). Rather than viewing it as a collection of individual regimes, scholars are now examining whether, and to what extent, this dense set of international institutions is more than the sum of its parts. Studies of fragmentation examine how governance of certain issues – notably climate change, but also biodiversity protection – is becoming more decentralized, showing up in other regimes, or within smaller-scale (e.g. regional) governance institutions, within or without the state-led system (Zelli and Van Asselt 2013). Studies of regime complexes (Keohane and Victor 2011) focus on linkages across these fragments and the borders that delineate them. Other studies look at how cross-regime linkages are managed and by whom (Jinnah 2014; Oberthür and Stokke 2011). Finally, some scholars analyze and assess a possible World Environment Organization (WEO), which could bring all these piecemeal governance regimes under a single organizational roof (Biermann 2001). We return to these questions in Chapter 9.

Critical Theory in International Environmental Politics: Political Economy, Globalization, and Political Ecology

The field of global environmental politics cannot be defined by international relations theory alone. Theoretical approaches from other social science fields, from sociology to science and technology studies (STS) to political ecology, challenge key assumptions of mainstream understandings of GEG. They offer a broader range of explanations of causes and impacts of global environmental change and the politics of the global environment.

Realist, institutionalist and weak constructivist approaches within international relations theory are commonly referred to as "problem-solving" or "explanatory" theories: they take the shape of the world or the basic structures of world politics as given, and explain outcomes or make policy prescriptions within that framework. By contrast, the approaches examined here are often referred to as "critical," or "normative," a characteristic they share with constructivist traditions. Critical theories challenge the notion that existing world orders are immutable, and ask instead how they came into existence, and how they may be changing. Normative theories posit a particular point of view: they seek to show how the world ought to be.[11] Critical theories have a strong tradition in environmental studies (Wapner 2008). What follows is a brief discussion of these approaches, to be expanded on in later chapters.

First, political economy theorists – in neo-Marxist, historical materialist, and neo-Gramscian traditions – challenge both the centrality of the nation-state and the underlying principle of anarchy in understanding and explaining international politics (Cox 1986; Levy and Newell 2002).

---

[11] For an overview of these approaches see Burchill and Linklater 2013, particularly the introduction, and chapters by Linklater ("Marxism") and Paterson ("Green Politics").

Instead, they see international politics shaped by the forces of global capital, often in alliance with the state. World systems theorists posit a bifurcated international system (Wallerstein 1974). While some states form the wealthy core, others (often formerly colonized states) are relegated to the far poorer periphery. In this approach, state interests are subservient to those of global capital (and, by extension, global capitalists, including transnational corporations). To that end, international cooperation, and other forms of GEG, serve mainly the interests of the wealthy capitalist nations, and the corporate interests they depend on, a constellation of power and interests, creating a form of global hegemony (Linklater 2013, p. 131, citing the works of Robert Cox). Against the global hegemony, social and political movements (e.g. environmental or labor activists) form opposing "counter-hegemonic" forces (Linklater 2013; see also McAfee forthcoming).

Neo-Gramscian approaches are gaining traction in studies of global environmental politics, as, using specific empirical cases, they can identify specific coalitions of interests in forms of GEG that might seem open and participatory but in fact may serve particular, powerful interests (Levy and Newell 2002; Newell 2014; Matt and Okereke 2015). This lens is often applied to areas where business interests play a role – as in certification systems or the application of market mechanisms. Likewise, global political ecologists scale the central concerns of political ecologists working at the local level – access to resources, inequalities, violence, and human rights – up to the global stage (Peet et al. 2011), with particular implications for cross-scale institutions such as REDD+ that are hard to analyze from a traditional international relations perspective.

By contrast, globalization theorists often decentralize the role of states in international politics.[12] One variant focuses on the rise of global civil society – "politics above and below the state" – as a democratizing force in international politics (Wapner 1996, 2000; Khagram et al. 2002). Another centers its analysis more squarely on the agents of global capitalism, or neoliberal globalization, including international financial institutions such as the WTO, the World Bank, and the International Monetary Fund (IMF). In this framework, these have in effect supplanted sovereign nation-states as the central actors in international politics, controlling critical financial and knowledge resources, with profound implications for the global environment (Goldman 2001; McCarthy and Prudham 2004).

---

[12] For an overview of perspectives on globalization and the environment see Clapp and Dauvergne 2011.

Finally, other approaches draw inspiration from green political theory (Paterson 2013). Green political theorists, like many globalization theorists and historical materialists, challenge the existing structures of the international system, but, in this case, posit alternatives based on ethics of sustainability, justice, and ecosystem harmony (e.g. Low and Gleason 1998). Creating "green states" by integrating ecological concerns into state structures and institutions, rather like the emergence of welfare states in the 1950s, is posited as a way forward that bypasses or reshapes the exigencies of current world politics (Eckersley 2005; Meadowcraft 2012). Other scholars put issues of global justice and inequality first and foremost in addressing environmental inequities (e.g. Shiva 1993; Sachs 1993).

These perspectives challenge the mainstream international relations understanding of GEG in specific ways. For example, mainstream international relations theorists tend to classify global environmental problems specifically as those that cross international borders or affect the global commons. Globalization theorists do not make the same distinction between domestic and global environmental problems. Rather, they are concerned with environmental problems that are driven by forces of globalization and global capital, at whatever level they occur. These two broad approaches also differ in their framing of the political causes of global environmental degradation, whether as a collective action problem resulting from an anarchic international system, or as a set of problems arising from a deeply embedded system of global capitalism. This debate in turn leads to differences over the sorts of solutions that best address global environmental degradation, and the most effective sites of GEG. Should we continue to rely on inter-state diplomacy, or should we instead address the actions of international economic institutions or multinational corporations directly? Should action be located primarily at the global level, or should it reach down to include local communities and actors?

Within the mainstream of international relations, the global environment is framed as a set of collective action problems. In the absence of an international sovereign authority, states have little incentive to curb behavior that affects the environment of other states or the global commons. Thus framed, the central problem for policy-makers is to create cooperative mechanisms that will overcome the incentive to cheat or free-ride on collective agreements, create enough incentive for states to participate in international negotiations, and protect the principle of state sovereignty over their own natural resources, while at the same time making environmental progress.

By contrast, critical theorists posit alternative framings of the causes of global environmental problems. Environmental problems are also strongly rooted in the emergence since the 1950s of a system of global capitalism (and, until the late 1980s, its mirror opposite, global socialism) that is both deeply politically embedded and inimical to social and environmental concerns (Paterson 2001b; Vogler 2005). Leading states (national governments) are deeply implicated in the development and maintenance of this system, and, to at least some degree, have shifted control over the economic processes that most significantly affect the global environment to the agents of global capital. Therefore, solutions that merely involve cooperation between nation-states are unlikely to be more than superficial (akin to rearranging the deckchairs on the *Titanic*). Not surprisingly, this analysis yields a different set of solutions to the problem of GEG. These include the radical decentralization of GEG (building initiatives from the ground up); harnessing the transformative potential of transnational activism and global civil society; and the construction of alliances between civil society and global capital to create private governance regimes. Sometimes these solutions propose active contestation of the status quo, at other times, working with existing players, but most involve bypassing the state, and other intergovernmental actors.

Are international relations and global political economy/ecology perspectives mutually exclusive? They certainly start from very different views of the world. One centers on nation-states and their interactions, structured by the anarchic nature and conflictual history of the international system, the other on the broad structures of global capitalism, the set of power relations they foster, and the actors they empower. Both do, however, focus our attention on global institutions – environmental, political, and economic – and on the dynamics of underlying power relations among different international constituencies. Focusing on one to the exclusion of the other runs the risk of missing important aspects of global environmental politics.

Next Steps

In the early years of the twenty-first century both the theory and practice of GEG entered a state of flux. Many have expressed disappointment with the failure of mainstream GEG – international environmental diplomacy – to meet the hopes and expectations of the early 1970s. Even supporters of MEAs and international environmental law began to look for ways to create linkages and new institutional arrangements to strengthen existing GEG, up to and including a new WEO. The outcome of the 2015 Paris climate conference has breathed new life into this process, but also represents a significant shift from how things have been done previously.

Other actors have begun looking beyond the convention halls and meeting rooms, to potentially new, perhaps more participatory modes of governance. The emergence of a transnational protest movement in the late 1990s, which focused its attention first of all on the international financial institutions, but soon extended its tactics to the 2000 climate change negotiations in The Hague, put issues of social legitimacy, accountability, and participation front and center in discussions of global governance (O'Neill 2004; Fisher and Green 2004). This movement has found voice in both the parallel conferences of NGOs and civil society groups around world environmental summits. Many of the civil society actors who engaged in protests against the WTO or the World Bank began also to target large, highly visible multinational corporations, not simply to express outrage or to expose environmental or labor standard violations, but to work with them, to take advantage of their desire to be seen as good environmental citizens. This process of cooperation has led to the creation of voluntary, non-state governance initiatives (such as forest or chemicals certification) that have received a lot of recent attention.

Further attention is focused on local sites of activity and resistance around global environmental issues. From communities facing down multinational mining or oil companies to Inuit and Pacific Island peoples fighting to add a loss and damages protocol to the UNFCCC, to cities around the world implementing programs to reduce GHG emissions, it is clear that global and local environmental politics are becoming increasingly connected. An important discourse that links global environmental politics to basic human rights has emerged that challenges the technocratic notion that sustainable development is best achieved through technological innovation and economic efficiency.

In the light of the above arguments, what utility does a focus on international environmental diplomacy and regimes continue to have, and what can international relations theory say about these new developments? Will existing modes of GEG continue to coexist, and what other forms might emerge to compete? First, theory, including international relations theories, remains important. In the years since the first edition of this book, international relations theory has maintained its relevance in supplying concepts and tools that help us understand global governance dilemmas. GEP has also become much more multidimensional, incorporating diverse perspectives and insights from the fields discussed here. Ultimately, however, in a field such as this, where real problem solving and applied research really matters, the complexity and unpredictability of many current global environmental problems requires nimble and interdisciplinary approaches. This is one of the challenges future generations of GEP will face.

The arguments presented in this book recognize that we are currently in an era where global governance is hybridized: there is no one way in which GEG occurs. It is also hard to predict when, how, or if the international system will settle again into a primary mode of global governance. However, following Vogler (2005), I argue that the network of international regimes and organizations established by national governments have an essential role to play in GEG. Not in the sense that they are the predominant route to effectively address problems of global environmental degradation, but that they provide a normative, legal, and organizational framework that has the potential to ground and unify all the different components of GEG in the twenty-first century. In this story, international relations theory plays a central role in helping us understand how, and how well, efforts to address global environmental degradation are working. However, it needs to listen to the various voices, scholarly and otherwise, which urge a broad, multisited, and multilevel approach to understanding the realities of GEG in the twenty-first century.

Discussion Questions

- What do you consider the main global environmental problems, and what are their causes? Particularly, what are the political and socio-economic factors that have contributed to them?
- What do the various theoretical perspectives outlined in this chapter tell us about why effective global environmental governance is such a challenge?
- What groups of actors does this chapter identify? What roles do they play in global environmental politics?

SUGGESTIONS FOR FURTHER READING

Haas, Peter M., Robert O. Keohane, and Marc A. Levy, eds. 1993. *Institutions for the Earth: Sources of Effective International Environmental Protection.* Cambridge, MA: MIT Press: an early and influential study of effective institution building for the environment; relies on detailed and authoritative empirical case studies.

Jinnah, Sikina. 2014. *Post-Treaty Politics: Secretariat Influence in Global Environmental Governance.* Cambridge, MA: MIT Press: an award-winning study of how secretariats – often overlooked in global environmental and economic governance – are becoming drivers of political change.

Morin, Jean-Frédéric, and Amandine Orsini, eds. 2015. *Essential Concepts of Global Environmental Governance.* London: Earthscan: very useful short pieces covering nearly one hundred topics in global environmental politics and governance, linking to key thinkers and literatures.

Nicholson, Simon, and Paul Wapner, eds. 2015. *Global Environmental Politics: From Person to Planet*. Boulder: Paradigm Publishers: a diverse collection of essays on global environmental challenges and steps we can take to address them, as individuals and global citizens, from some of the leading authors in this field.

Speth, James Gustave. 2004. *Red Sky at Morning: America and the Crisis of the Global Environment*. New Haven: Yale University Press: a leading, and eminently readable, critique from a highly regarded practitioner-academic of the way that GEG has been managed to date.

In addition, several major journals focus on global environmental politics and governance, and cover recent empirical developments and theoretical debates. Especially recommended are *Global Environmental Politics, International Environmental Agreements, Environmental Politics,* and *Global Governance.*

2   Global Environmental Problems

As with many other global issues – managing the global economy, protecting human rights, combating diseases such as Ebola and HIV/AIDS, controlling terrorism and the proliferation of weapons of mass destruction – global environmental problems are so complex and widespread that unilateral measures – measures undertaken by countries acting on their own initiative – are not enough. This is an interdependent world: even if a country the size of the USA acted to unilaterally reduce its greenhouse gas (GHG) emissions by a significant amount, we would not forestall the impacts of climate change without other countries doing likewise.

Global problems are not new, but over the past decades they have increased in scale, scope, visibility, and complexity. The international community itself has changed as well. Membership of the UN has grown by 370 percent since 1945; NGOs, corporations, and expert groups are seeking a voice in international affairs, economic globalization has increased the complexity of global management, and new technology has vastly increased the speed and quantity of information traversing the globe. Many global problems are environmental in nature, or have environmental side effects.

This chapter explains how, and why, environmental change became a matter of global concern and political action in the late twentieth century. We examine ways to think about framing and comparing environmental issue areas, and how to find out more about global environmental trends. The first part of this chapter charts the globalization of environmental concern and action, focusing on awareness of the expanding scope and scale of environmental problems from the Industrial Revolution onwards, and the role of the environmental movement and the UN in transforming new knowledge and concern into political action at the international level. Second, we examine different types and examples of international environmental issues, how one might track them, and how they change over time. We focus specifically on how environmental problems are framed at the global level – generating distinct forms of political action. The third part shifts the analysis to global problems with strong environmental dimensions – such as population growth, consumption, and nuclear power – that are not addressed as environmental issues or by environmental agencies and organizations at the international level. Throughout, we examine how many of these issues are linked.

The Globalization of Environmental Concern and Political Action

Scale, Scope, Ideas and Imagination

The environment truly emerged onto the international political agenda at the UN Conference on Humans and the Environment (UNCHE), held in Stockholm in 1972. However, bilateral and multilateral cooperation over the environment can be traced further back in time (Bernauer 1997, p. 158). In 1616 Austria and Turkey concluded an agreement regulating navigation rights on the Danube, and in 1815 the Congress of Vienna established the right of free navigation of international rivers. In 1900 another treaty established controls over transport of corrosive and poisonous substances on the River Rhine (Bernauer 1997). Yet, it was only in the latter decades of the twentieth century that environmental problems became recognized as more than local or even regional.

This realization mobilized first concern, and then action on the part of the international community. Environmental historians demonstrate clear links between industrialization, globalization, and environmental degradation, all processes that increased exponentially during the twentieth century.[1] Dominant models of industrial development (both capitalist and state socialist) paid little attention to rates of resource extraction or to the externalities imposed by pollution and other activities. Environmental problems over this time frame expanded in scale, spreading over ever-larger territorial regions, and scope, extending to new (or hitherto unrecognized) problem areas.

The twentieth century saw a rapid increase in the scale of many environmental problems. Local problems became regional or transnational, as firms exported hazardous wastes for disposal abroad, or as winds carried sulfur dioxide from the tall smokestacks of England to fall as acid rain in northern Europe, killing local forests. As human population and industrial and agricultural production increased, transboundary rivers and virgin forests became focal points for conflict over water scarcity and resource access. As developing countries industrialized, they began to experience many of the same problems as their industrialized counterparts.

---

[1] See, for example, McNeill 2000; Guha 2000.

The same time frame also saw greater realization, especially on the part of the scientific community, of the changing scope of global environmental problems. Theories of human-induced climate change date back to the late nineteenth century and the work of scientists such as Swedish chemist Svante Arrhenius (whose most significant works on climate change were published between 1896 and 1908). With the advent of new sensory and modeling technologies in the twentieth century, scientists increased their capacity to measure and predict the extent of human impact on the atmosphere, whether caused by the burning of fossil fuels, the emission of ozone-depleting substances, or long-range air pollution (Edwards 2001). Ozone-layer depletion and climate change are invisible to the naked eye, but their impacts are very real, and, in a sense, represent the "tragedy of the commons" writ large (Hardin 1968).

Economic globalization, too, has accelerated and transformed processes of environmental degradation. In the nineteenth and first half of the twentieth centuries globalization took on the form of colonization. European countries used raw materials extracted from their colonies in Asia and Africa to drive their ever-expanding economies. After World War Two, as many of these colonies emerged into independence, globalization changed shape. A new economic order, based on economic growth and free movement of goods and capital, came into existence. While this accelerated global economic growth, it also accelerated resource depletion and pollution generation. The environmental impact of the transportation of goods around the world is also significant, increasing pollution en route, and transporting invasive organisms to new ecosystems. These are deeply pervasive externalities of globalization, and very difficult to address.

The emergence of the environment as a global political issue cannot, however, be explained merely as a function of scientific and technological insights into the causes, scale, and scope of global environmental degradation. Ideas and images are important too. In the late 1960s the global environment began to capture the imagination of environmentalists, especially in the North. Photographs taken from space of the earth, a tiny globe characterized not by the artificial demarcation of national borders, but by glimpses of blue and green hidden by clouds, galvanized a growing movement to address environmental problems beyond the confines of the nation-state (Brand 2003; Jasanoff 2001, 2004). Earth Day 1970, the Save the Whales campaign, and education campaigns about threatened species and areas of biological diversity such as the Amazon rainforest got many activists "thinking globally." At around the same time, prominent scholars published work that highlighted the threats of population growth and economic development to the continued sustainability of life on earth.[2] Other areas of global politics around this time – the threat of global destruction through nuclear war, for example – provided other reasons for thinking in terms of global risks, and global, rather than national, solutions. In other words, at the same time as humanity was realizing the benefits of technological progress, we also began to realize that some of these technologies carried serious risks on a scale that could threaten the planet (Beck 1992). Triggering imagination matters up to this day, as Paul Wapner's short but powerful essay on climate suffering demonstrates (Wapner 2014).

The UN, the Stockholm Conference, and the Emerging Global Environmental Governance Agenda

The UN's role as political entrepreneur, catalyzing inter-state concern and action around the global environment in this early period of global environmental governance (GEG), cannot be understated. The UN, by sponsoring critical international and interdisciplinary research on the atmosphere and biosphere, played a key role in generating research about the changing state of the global environment, its causes, and likely impacts. In the late 1960s and early 1970s it set up the main architecture of global governance that underpins international environmental politics (IEP) today, which provides the empirical foundation for much scholarly work on the politics of the global environment. In addition to sponsoring multiple multilateral environmental agreements (MEAs), the UN and its agencies have convened four global summits. The UNCHE (Stockholm, 1972) was followed by the 1992 UN Conference on Environment and Development (UNCED), held in Rio de Janeiro, Brazil, the 2002 World Summit on Sustainable Development (WSSD), held in Johannesburg, South Africa, and the Rio+20 Summit, held in Rio de Janeiro in 2012. Such mega-conferences raise international awareness, set important principles and long-term goals, and establish procedural and normative frameworks in order to meet them (Seyfang 2003).[3]

The Stockholm Conference marked the start of the modern era of global environmental cooperation. Attended by representatives from 113 countries, it established environmental goals and priorities for the international community, and a coordinated legal and political framework through which to meet them (Sohn 1973; Ivanova 2010). First, in terms of global environmental goals and priorities, Stockholm helped

---

[2] These include Paul Ehrlich, *The Population Bomb* (1968), Donella H. Meadows, *Limits of Growth* (1972), and E. F. Schumacher, *Small is Beautiful* (1973).

[3] For contrasting views of UN mega-conferences see Friedman et al. 2005; Death 2011; and Falkner 2012.

place the environment squarely on the international political agenda, and made it part of the UN's official agenda. States agreed on a Declaration of Twenty-six (non-binding) Guiding Principles, and an Action Plan, which set forth 109 recommendations for more specific international action (Peel 2015, p. 59).[4]

Second, the countries meeting at Stockholm set up procedures through which to meet collective environmental goals, integrating the existing body of international environmental laws and treaties. In addition to establishing the United Nations Environment Programme (UNEP; see Chapter 3), the Stockholm Declaration called for multilateral cooperation based on sound scientific knowledge, coordinated by international organizations, and governed by international law. Thus, the governance system established at Stockholm essentially ratified existing practices of international environmental diplomacy. It accorded the highest priority to the negotiation of multilateral treaties, on an issue-by-issue basis. Utilizing established channels of global governance would maximize participation by states and grant the process greater legitimacy in the eyes of national governments, protecting and elevating the principle of national sovereignty.

Stockholm also marked the beginning of a debate over the relationship between environmental protection and economic development. Initially, lead negotiators had approached the problem of global environmental protection in purely environmental terms (hence the title of the meeting). However, Southern countries – beginning at this time to discover their collective voice in international politics (Najam 2015) – injected a different note into this incipient debate, later to find full voice at the 1992 Rio conference. Southern representatives argued that environmental goals needed to be balanced with development goals, and that global environmental protection could not be achieved at the expense of inhibiting the ability of poorer nations (or future generations) to meet development goals. These concerns were reflected in the Stockholm Declaration, in calls for respecting the needs of developing countries, and for technical and financial assistance institutions. They were further developed as an underlying norm of GEG – sustainable development – and in individual governance regimes as the principle of common but differentiated responsibility (See Chapter 4; Najam 2015).

The concept of sustainable development provides a normative framework for all forms of global environmental politics (GEP) (and, increasingly, global economic and development politics too), linking causes of environmentalism, economic development, and human

---

[4] The Stockholm Declaration is available at www.unep.org.

health and well-being. From the 1987 report of the World Commission on Environment and Development (also known as the Brundtland Report), through Agenda 21, published at the Rio Summit, to the seventeen Sustainable Development Goals adopted by the UN in 2015, the concept has been used by activists, policy-makers, philanthropists, and the corporate sector to signal their intentions.

Sustainable development's great strength, and its great weakness as a rhetorical framework or "meta-norm," is that, like many sweeping ideas, it is vague enough to be open to multiple interpretations (Bernstein 2000). On the one hand, it focuses attention on incorporating notions of equity into environmental protection, and intergenerational sustainability into concepts of development. On the other, it justifies a turn toward using the tools of economic development – free trade, private sector initiatives, and other economic incentives – for environmental protection, a process which many see as related more to "sustained" development than to true protection of natural resources (Sachs 1999, and later chapters in this volume). Further, it is not particularly helpful in understanding the micro-level politics around identifying and acting on individual environmental problems, the process to which we now turn.

Global Environmental Problems

At the most basic level, an environmental problem becomes international, or global, in a political sense, when it crosses national borders or affects the global commons: the atmosphere, the ocean, or other global resources not subject to rule by sovereign states. In fact, a good case can be made that all environmental problems are international: even if they don't literally spill over national borders, then they are likely to occur in many, if not all, countries. This section examines the environmental problems that have been the object of GEG, and how the process of framing environmental problems can make them more (or less) amenable to international cooperation. It introduces a typology of global environmental issues: global commons, transboundary, and local–cumulative problems. This is not the only possible categorization of global environmental issues.[5] However, it is useful for identifying where global environmental problems are similar or different, and the political complexities of dealing with certain kinds of problems in multilateral settings.

Box 2.1 lists and defines some important examples of problems associated with different political processes, along with their primary impacts. All have been the subject of GEG efforts, and nearly all have one or more

---

[5] For alternative typologies and critiques see Young 1994; Turner et al. 1990.

Box 2.1: Definitions and impacts of major international environmental problems

Climate Change
- Increased atmospheric concentration of GHGs including carbon dioxide, methane, nitrous oxide, hydrofluorocarbons (HFCs), and water vapor, as a result of human activity, notably the burning of fossil fuels; expected to lead to a rise in overall global temperatures, with regional variations.
- Impacts: sea-level rise and coastal zone flooding as polar ice-caps melt, possible violent weather patterns, widespread ecosystems and land-use change, food insecurity and biodiversity loss, and human health impacts.

Stratospheric Ozone Depletion
- Thinning of the stratospheric ozone layer caused by the emission of chlorofluorocarbons (CFCs) and other widely used chemicals into the atmosphere, leading to increased infiltration of ultraviolet rays to ground level.
- Impacts: degradation of terrestrial and aquatic ecosystems and human health impacts, including increased incidence of skin cancer, and cataracts.

Long-Range Transboundary Air Pollution
- Air pollution – notably emissions of sulfur dioxide and oxides of nitrogen – that originates in one country but is carried, often long distances, into another.
- Impacts: particularly a problem when it falls as acid rain, causing forest damage, damage to buildings, and water pollution.

Biodiversity Loss and Conservation
- Loss not only of animal and plant species, but also of genetic diversity and habitats, caused by human activity, including economic exploitation of particular species and land use change.
- Impacts: intrinsic value of lost or threatened species, plus wider impacts on ecosystems; economic impacts due to loss of valuable resources and ecosystems services.

Deforestation and Unsustainable Use of Forest Resources
- Clearing or destruction and degradation of global forest cover through human activity.
- Impacts: disruption to ecosystem health and biodiversity, forest dwellers' livelihoods, and increased atmospheric GHG concentrations.

Box 2.1: (cont.)

Desertification
- Land degradation through drought, climate change, overuse, caused by complex mix of human actions and environmental change.
- Impacts: loss of livelihood (especially in already marginal rural communities), famine.

Persistent Organic Pollutants and Other Harmful Chemicals
- Manufacture, use, circulation, and disposal of chemicals, including dioxins, the pesticide DDT, and mercury, which are highly toxic and do not break down easily in the environment. They are often transported long distances by wind and ocean currents.
- Impacts: bio-accumulation (within one individual) and bio-magnification (along the food chain) in humans and animals, causing cancer, reproductive-system damage, and nervous system and brain damage over short and longer terms.

Hazardous Waste Trading
- Transfer, for disposal or recycling, of wastes that are toxic, flammable, corrosive, explosive, or otherwise hazardous from one country to another, particularly from Northern to Southern countries.
- Impacts: severe, localized impacts on recipient communities, ecosystems, up to and including reported deaths.

Rivers and Lakes
- More than 200 river or lake basins are shared by more than one country, areas that include 40% of the world's population. Transboundary water flows are subject to diversion, overuse, and other flow disruptions.
- Impacts: flow disruptions and river pollution often disproportionately affect downstream states, but also disrupt regional navigation, agriculture, and so on.

Whaling
- Overexploitation of whale stocks worldwide.
- Impact: many whale species on the brink of collapse by the mid-twentieth century.

Marine Environment and Resource Degradation
- Overfishing, ocean dumping, oil pollution at sea, ocean acidification, coastal-zone pollution.
- Impacts: fish-stock collapse, loss of marine biodiversity, coastal and ocean pollution, and coral reef destruction.

associated MEAs. An exception is deforestation, where treaty-building attempts failed in the early 1990s.

Without a classification scheme, the proliferation of international environmental problems can be overwhelming and confusing, and the resultant solutions can be ad hoc. The following section addresses the ways relevant actors – international officials, state actors, NGOs, and others have sought to frame global environmental problems to elicit action at the international level. These issue area definitions are critical in informing the shape of international negotiations in each area, and as we shall see in Chapters 4 and 5, the outcomes and overall effectiveness of international cooperation.

Framing the Global Environment: Galvanizing Political Action

Given the complexities of international diplomacy and state sovereignty, international actors have focused on problems that are explicitly global or transboundary, or worked to isolate the transboundary or global aspects of particular problems. The UN and other organizations concerned with environmental problems have approached GEG by breaking down the broader issue of global environmental change or degradation into individual issue areas, often starting with the ones that seem most amenable to international cooperation. This process is known as issue or problem framing. In some cases – such as climate change, stratospheric ozone depletion, or trade in endangered species – the rationale for international action has been clear, even if turning it into acceptable policy has been less easy. Other cases, such as deforestation or biodiversity loss, have proved more complex to define as an issue of common international concern.

Formally, framing behavior consists of "conscious and strategic efforts by groups of people to fashion shared understandings of the world and of themselves that legitimate and motivate collective action" (David Snow, cited in McAdam et al. 1996, p. 6). Framing processes help draw the boundaries of a given problem, outlining its causes, and most importantly, what can and needs to be done to solve it (and who should do it). They focus and mobilize action and concern. In the context of IEP, framing frequently means demonstrating why the problem is best dealt with at the international level (or not). UNEP officials, scientific bodies, environmental NGOs, and government actors, all engage in framing actions. Problem-framing processes are particularly important during agenda-setting phases of policy-making, getting actors around the table, and giving them a course of action when they do. Classifying problems in terms of shared characteristics may also provide a roadmap for traversing unknown political territory. Understanding how problems are framed also helps explain the particular site or sites of global governance in which they are addressed.

Global environmental problems may be framed in a variety of ways, and to different strategic purposes. In this section we discuss problem framing as a way to justify particular types of international action. None of these categories are immutable. Rather, they provide frameworks to enable us to think about, categorize, and compare problems in politically salient ways. Sometimes, however, as explained below, they can obscure more than reveal in international negotiations and their outcomes.

Some perspectives in the scientific literature urge us to think of the entire planet as a single ecosystem or biosphere, or as a set of interlocking ecosystems.[6] If the balance in one ecosystem is disrupted, this is likely to have knock-on effects on others. Recent work that develops the concept of a new geological era driven by human action – the Anthropocene – highlights entire Earth System outcomes and effects of human-driven environmental change, including tipping points and feedback loops that are becoming evident over time (Steffen et al. 2011; Biermann 2014). Such a grand concept evokes large-scale crises, and (human) species-wide responsibility, galvanizing political action at the highest levels. The problem, however, with all-encompassing definitions of global environmental change is that they do not generate politically feasible policy options.

To that end, breaking down global environmental change (or indeed any large, complex global problem area) into manageable pieces is an effective strategy to bring nation-states and other actors to the negotiating table. Some divide environmental issues by medium: water, air, and land. UNEP's Global Environmental Outlook series (UNEP 2012) separates environmental data and trends into five categories: atmosphere (climate, ozone-layer depletion, and air pollution, both transboundary and local); land (forests, desertification, land-use change, and soils); water (inland, coastal, and marine ecosystems); biodiversity; and chemicals and wastes. While such classifications provide sound frameworks for analyzing the state of the global environment, and identifying courses of action and particular problems, they do not provide guidance as to whether such action should be taken at national, local, or international levels.

A Typology of Global Environmental Problems

One way to start thinking about global environmental problems and their solutions is to break them down according to their relationship to a global system made up of nation-states: in other words, how they relate to

---

[6] An early iteration of an integrated approach to a global ecological system is the Gaia Hypothesis, associated with James Lovelock (e.g. Lovelock 2000).

territories and borders. The following sections discuss categories of global commons, transboundary, and local–cumulative problems: a political framing that provides a starting point but, as we shall see, by no means an end point for discussing problem characterization.

a.   Global Commons Issues We start with problems that affect the global commons: the atmosphere, the high seas, and Antarctica. Following the metaphor of the tragedy of the commons (Hardin 1968), these resources are vulnerable to overexploitation or overpollution precisely because they belong to no one: to no state, no individual, and no corporation. In the absence of rationing, allocation of property rights, or use quotas, economic actors (individuals, firms, or governments)continue to exploit the commons for their own benefit, up to the point of resource or ecosystem collapses. Any country can emit GHGs into the atmosphere, or harvest fish from the high seas, without itself tipping the balance of the system's sustainability. However, once we examine the collective impact over time of all states treating the atmosphere or the oceans as their own private sink or source, we can see that these seemingly limitless resources are, in fact, vulnerable.

One of the complicating factors in addressing global commons problems is that there are many perpetrators and many victims, and it is very difficult to allocate responsibility among them. At the same time, the structure of international law around the commons and their lack of sovereign rule has meant that problems of ocean dumping, climate change, or ozone-layer depletion are particularly likely to be addressed at the international level – i.e. through multilateral cooperation. However, the contrast in terms of political outcomes between two of the major global commons issues – climate change and stratospheric ozone-layer depletion – demonstrates the limits of this classification when broader issue-area characteristics come into play (Young 2010).

While international cooperation over ozone-layer depletion is one of the success stories of GEG, climate change politics have long been mired in national differences and conflicts of interest. Climate change has been described as a "wicked" or "unstructured" problem (Levin et al. 2012; Hoppe et al. 2013). A wicked policy problem is one that defies easy description or objective solution (Rittel and Webber 1973). It requires difficult social negotiations to reach an outcome – and there may be no outcome considered wholly equitable. By contrast, stratospheric ozone-layer depletion resolved itself into a far more straightforward problem: replacing one set of chemicals – CFCs, produced by only a handful of companies – with another, less harmful set. Despite early and ongoing efforts to apply lessons from ozone negotiations to climate politics (Morrisette 1991; Broder 2010), the sheer complexity of climate change as a political problem, the interests of many different sorts of actors, and the depth of action required stands in sharp contrast to a simpler structure of ozone-layer depletion as a political problem. Arguably, early efforts to frame climate change as a global atmospheric problem, while galvanizing international action, may have hampered the international community's ability to come to terms with a problem fraught with complexity, uncertainties, and high levels of value conflict.

b.   *Transboundary Environmental Problems*   Transboundary environmental problems are those that cross, or spill over, from one country to another. Classic examples include long-range transboundary air pollution (LRTAP) including acid rain; river pollution; and the global trade in hazardous wastes or in endangered species. The transfer of pollution from one country to another may be unintentional (pollutants blown by prevailing wind patterns across national borders) or intentional (shipping wastes from one country to another).

These sorts of problems are sometimes considered simpler than global commons problems, if only because they can involve a smaller, and identifiable, number of victims and perpetrators. In some cases – for example, shared rivers – they can be addressed through bilateral or regional agreements, and in other cases by multilateral agreements. For instance, global efforts to address LRTAP are governed by a broad framework convention – the 1979 Convention on Long Range Transboundary Air Pollution – that provides controls on all such pollutants, regardless of their point of origin or ultimate destination. There is also a long history of international intervention in the movement of goods – and "bads," such as wastes or endangered species – across borders, therefore providing greater justification for intervention.

Framing a complex environmental problem as transboundary, or focusing on the transboundary aspects of a given problem, has been an effective tool in galvanizing international action. Take the international trade in hazardous wastes. A plausible case can be made that the underlying cause of the waste trade is that growth in global generation of hazardous wastes has outstripped that of waste-disposal capacity in many countries. Politically, however, it is difficult to get nation-states to agree collectively to reduce or minimize waste generation. Therefore, UNEP decided to tackle the most visible and easily tackled international aspect of the hazardous waste problem: waste dumping ("trading") from wealthy Northern countries to poorer communities in Southern countries. A similar rationale applies to global controls on trade in endangered species, which originated in the early 1970s, and to the ways that chemicals agreements specifically address trade, use and manufacture of persistent organic pollutants (POPs) or mercury.

c.   *Local–Cumulative Problems*   Local–cumulative environmental problems are those that occur within national borders but have cumulative global effects. They have been harder to define explicitly as international environmental issues, and have, therefore, been less often addressed by formal treaty arrangements (Conca 2006). While the effects of local–cumulative environmental problems tend to be felt most immediately within national borders, their ultimate impact reaches far beyond, often affecting global processes, such as the climate, in a significant way. They are also often exacerbated or transformed by processes of globalization. Examples of local–cumulative issues include biodiversity loss, deforestation, and fresh-water management and provision.

Biodiversity loss is one of the few such issues to be addressed at the global level through inter-state cooperation beginning with the negotiation of the 1992 Convention on Biological Diversity (CBD). While most areas of natural biodiversity are located within national boundaries and are therefore primarily subject to national rules and legislation, this issue became "international" for a number of reasons. First, the conservation biology community made a pressing scientific case for the global impacts of species and ecosystems loss. Second, biodiversity preservation has great (potential and actual) economic value, as in, for example, the hypothetical cure for cancer residing in a patch of threatened rainforest. More recently, this argument has found its voice in calls to protect biodiversity for its broader ecosystem services, such as food provision and regulation of air and water. Third, many have made the case that biodiversity has great cultural value for much of the world's population, regardless of whether they would ever see the Amazon, or a panda bear in the wild. Negotiations over the CBD initially sought to define biodiversity as a global commons issue. This turned out to be controversial, as many Southern countries objected to their own resources being defined this way and feared the international interventions that might bring. The final wording in the CBD thus states that biodiversity is part of the "common concern," rather than the "common heritage" of humanity.

Other local–cumulative issues, such as deforestation or watershed management, have been far less amenable to standard treaty-making approaches. For one, states are unwilling to cede their sovereign rights over managing and developing these resources. For another, these issues are complex and multi-scalar, affecting stakeholders and communities who do not have a voice at the global level, or involving local institutions that have no global standing. In later chapters we shall see how these issues have been more easily addressed in non-state governance arenas, or through international economic organizations such as the World Bank.

Global Environmental Problems: Identifying and Assessing Changes over Time

The state of the global environment constantly changes: some environmental problems worsen, while others improve over time. Rates of change in environmental quality may also slow down or speed up. Most global environmental trends, when measured in absolute terms, are more negative than positive. However, areas of positive change include the reduction of air pollution in many large cities (especially in the developed world), the successful preservation of some threatened areas and species, and the high likelihood that the ozone layer will return to its pre-1950s state by 2065. At the same time, new aspects of existing problems continue to emerge or be recognized, and entirely new problems are starting to become salient on international political agendas.

a.   Global Environmental Trends: Data Gathering and Assessment
There are many ways of tracking how the global environment is changing. Many publicly available sources, often updated annually, provide data and indicators across major environmental problems, across countries, and over time. Box 2.2 lists a few of the main online sources of global environmental data from NGOs and UN and US agencies that cover a broad swath of global environmental issues, but it is by no means exhaustive.

Other more specialized research-based organizations include the International Renewable Energy Agency (IRENA), TRAFFIC, a wildlife monitoring program run by the World Wildlife Fund and the International Union for the Conservation of Nature (IUCN), and Oceana, a Washington DC-based NGO that provides knowledge and recommendations on many ocean-related issues. Treaty secretariats associated with most international environmental agreements publish relevant data on their websites.

Online news services such as Grist.org provide daily updates on and links to environmental stories around the world, and the websites of many leading newspapers and organizations have environmental sections where stories are archived across different media platforms. Blogs, Twitter, Facebook and other social media platforms have all added to the number of venues where people can obtain information and engage with others who share the same concerns. Finally, journalistic writing, books, and

---

Box 2.2: The State of the Global Environment: Sources of Information, Trends, and Data

United Nations Environment Programme
- Global Environment Outlook series: provides integrated assessments of the state of, trends in, and outlook for the global environment and its governance. GEO 5, published in 2012 and running to over 500 pages, is online at www.unep.org/geo/geo5.asp.
- Vital Graphics: in collaboration with GRID-Arendal, a compilation of user-friendly data and graphics on various international environmental issues, at www.grida.no/publications/vg/.

UN Food and Agriculture Organization (FAO)
- The FAO provides extensive local, national, and global data on forests, world agriculture, fisheries, and sustainable development, at www.fao.org.

US National Oceanic and Atmospheric Administration (NOAA)
- NOAA (www.noaa.gov), a US government agency, monitors and provides data on weather, climate, fisheries conditions, and marine and coastal environmental conditions. Data, graphs, and images on the state of the global atmosphere, including the ozone layer, is also provided by the US National Atmospheric and Space Administration (www.nasa.gov).

World Resources Institute
- An independent, not-for-profit think tank, based in Washington, DC. Publishes *World Resources*, a biennial publication, covering the state of the global environment and global environmental governance. Maintains online database of relevant information, at www.wri.org/.

World Watch Institute
- An independent, not-for-profit think tank, based in Washington, DC. Publishes *State of the World* and *Vital Signs* on an annual or biennial basis, at www.worldwatch.org/.

---

documentaries are another rich source of information, providing narratives and images that put a human face on global environmental change.[7] Former US Vice President Al Gore's award-winning documentary about

---

[7] See, for example, Flannery 2006; Kolbert 2006; McKibben 2011.

climate change, *An Inconvenient Truth*, was widely released in summer 2006, and other documentaries have followed suit, though perhaps none with such a wide impact.[8]

Our ability to track trends in the state of individual issues has improved dramatically over the past decades. Modeling and scenario building and analysis have become important tools for scientists and policy-makers, extending into the future – what might happen under certain conditions – and back into the past – what would have happened had certain actions not been taken or conditions prevailed (Pulver and VanDeveer 2009).[9] Many of these now operate on a vast scale. Integrated Assessment Models (IAMs) incorporate both scientific and human-related variables to generate predictions and recommendations (Stanton et al. 2009). Such tools are now able to take into account many different variables in assessing different pathways of complex environmental change, although they still struggle with the contingencies of social science variables, including human actions and motivations (O'Neill et al. 2013).

The growing availability of satellite images, mapping, and data techniques, including methods such as geographic imaging system (GIS) mapping, and visualization tools such as Tableau that render complex data into maps and infographics, have made the state of the global environment far more accessible than ever before. Anyone with a smart phone or a tablet can download apps that allow them both to view existing ecological data and to report data to an NGO or an agency, if, for example, they see a rare bird or marine specimen. In 2013 an NGO, Project Seahorse, launched an application, iSeahorse, enabling users to record and report seahorse sightings worldwide.

A controversial but high-profile problem in studying global environmental trends is that of data use and interpretation. In 2001 Danish scientist Bjorn Lomborg published *The Skeptical Environmentalist* (Lomborg 2001), in which he argued that the state of the global environment was not nearly as bad as some believed. A firestorm of criticism over his selection and use of available data followed (Schneider et al. 2002). The continued strength of the climate denial community – those groups,

---

[8] Examples include *Climate Refugees* (2012), *The Cove* (2009, on dolphin culls in Japan), *Chasing Ice* (2012, on the changing face of the Arctic), *Darwin's Nightmare* (2004, on invasive species in Lake Victoria), and *Food Inc.* (2008, on industrial agriculture and fast food).

[9] Fiction can help us imagine alternative scenarios. Recommended are John Brunner's 1970 novel *The Sheep Look Up*, a richly imagined alternative world without any environmental or health and safety regulations, and well-known science fiction author Kim Stanley Robinson's (*Red Mars, Forty Signs of Rain*) essay on the use of imagination in combating climate change, "Imagining Abrupt Climate Change: Terraforming Earth," available online.

including scientists, who fervently deny that climate change exists as a phenomenon driven by human activity (Jacques et al. 2008) – demonstrates how data can continue to be disputed, even after the mainstream scientific community has reached as close as a consensus as it is likely to. We explore these disputes and their implications in Chapters 3 and 4. For now, the main implication is that care must be taken when identifying and using different data sources on the global environment, and when assessing their reliability and credibility.

b.   *New Dimensions, New Problems, New Linkages*   Over time, impacts – actual or likely – of global environmental problems of which we were not aware, which were not considered politically salient, or which did not exist when the problems were first identified, come to the fore in global environmental governance. These dimensions of change often pose problems for policy-making, especially in cases where the existing policy process is not flexible enough to respond quickly to emerging information, or to incorporate new aspects of existing problems.

For example, global efforts to halt the destruction of the stratospheric ozone layer are widely considered successful, but they are far from over. The major substitutes for CFCs – HCFCs (hydrochlorofluorocarbons) and HFCs – turned out to be highly potent GHGs. Despite the fact that both substitutes are effective and require relatively little technological change when switched with CFCs, ozone negotiations have recently had to take these impacts into account and start to explore ways of developing coolants that are beneficial for both the ozone layer and the climate (Young 2010). These new chemicals will require significant adaptation of production processes and incur more costs than earlier substances, and industry and NGOs are already pitted against each other in offering alternatives.

To take other examples, consumer electronic wastes (or e-wastes), such as cell phones or iPods, when shipped to countries such as China or India for disposal in large quantities, pose a complex set of new problems to a governance regime more used to addressing trade in larger quantities of industrial wastes (Lepawsky and McNabb 2010). Similarly, ocean acidification resulting from growing carbon dioxide concentrations in the atmosphere (not a symptom of climate change but caused by the same phenomenon) is considered a new global environmental problem. It threatens coral reefs such as Australia's Great Barrier Reef, and many forms of ocean life, including calciferous organisms such as mollusks, and vital parts of oceanic food chains, including critical prey species (Doney et al. 2009).

Global climate governance has expanded its scope as efforts to slow climate change have proven inadequate. In 2007 negotiators moved to make adaptation measures a central plank of climate governance. By 2015 even adaptation measures seemed inadequate, with the most vulnerable regions of the world calling for provision for damages and compensation, recognizing that coastal regions, low-lying islands, and glacial and polar ice may soon be lost forever, displacing communities permanently and destroying ecosystems. Island nations in the southern Pacific are already taking steps to ensure that their populations and cultures can be transplanted in the very likely event that their homelands will be submerged by rising oceans, although many developed countries are resisting formal arrangements for climate refugees (Biermann and Boas 2008; McAdam 2011).

Nonetheless, the potential for millions of climate refugees displaced from submerged or drought-ridden lands has exercised both military establishments in the US (Center for Naval Analyses 2007), and humanitarian and development agencies. The United Nations Security Council recognizad in a 2011 statement that climate change could be a leading cause of conflict, and the US White House's 2015 National Security Strategy has an entire section on climate change and conflict. Climate change could be one of the biggest security threats in years to come, although identifying and isolating the ways in which these threats will play out on the ground in different parts of the world poses significant challenges (Gemenne et al. 2014).

As the above examples demonstrate, the global environment does not exist in isolation from other areas of international politics and human activity. Global environmental problems themselves often intersect. Climate change, for example, is a leading cause of biodiversity loss, desertification, and other changes in terrestrial and marine ecosystems. Substitutes for ozone-depleting substances themselves are potent GHGs. The recognition of these linkages alters the terms, and often the venues, of global governance efforts. Efforts to reduce the use of CFC replacements because of their global warming potential are ongoing within the ozone regime. The controversial UN program Reducing Emissions from Deforestation and Forest Degradation (REDD or REDD+) connects initiatives that help preserve existing forests as carbon sinks for GHGs by paying forest owners to maintain and improve forest cover (see Chapter 8). Chapter 4 discusses how regime actors forge such linkages across individual areas of environmental governance. Chapter 6 addressess how linkages have been made between global economic growth and development, on the one hand, and environmental change, on the other.

Why Some Global Problems are Not on the International
Environmental Policy Agenda

The above sections discuss global environmental problems that are on, or are proposed for, the international environmental policy agenda. We have seen that the definition, or framing, of these problems is a political process. Another angle that sheds light on how global environmental problems are defined and acted upon is to examine the issues that clearly have both global and environmental implications, but that have not entered the traditional international environmental policy process. Examples include supplies of, and access to, fresh water for household, agricultural, and industrial use; the environmental impacts of industrialized agriculture and food production, mining, and oil exploration by multinational corporations; invasive species prevention; and nuclear issues (transport, storage, and disposal of nuclear waste, and nuclear accident prevention). They also include what many see as major drivers of global environmental change: population and consumption.

In some of these cases the issue is dealt with in other global policy arenas. The International Atomic Energy Agency (IAEA) has the greatest global jurisdiction over nuclear issues – both weapons and power generation – as a means of reducing the threat of nuclear-weapons proliferation. The irony of the nuclear case is that one of the most frequently cited examples of transboundary environmental interdependence is the 1986 Chernobyl disaster, when a nuclear power plant in what is now Ukraine broke down, sending waves of radiation right across Europe. Yet, dealing with issues of nuclear safety is usually seen as the responsibility of individual countries, and a prerogative often jealously guarded by states, particularly states with nuclear weapons.

Access to and provision of fresh water, including drinking water, have largely been the domain of the international aid and development agencies – including the UN Development Programme (UNDP) and the World Bank. Over 750 million people worldwide currently lack access to clean water according to UN data, a number likely to increase as climate change and associated processes of desertification worsen. As issues of environment and development become more and more entwined, so too do water-access issues become more part of the global environmental agenda. The setting of international goals for access to safe drinking water was a major result of the 2002 WSSD. Global water-governance institutions that do exist are complex, multiscalar, and piecemeal. They all address important aspects of the problem but fail to connect across global development and environment regimes (J. Gupta 2013).

The environmental impacts of industrialized agriculture and food production – including land clearance, pesticide run-off, and land degradation, in addition to issues of food security and access to land – appear only tangentially on the international environmental agenda. Biodiversity negotiations address genetically modified organisms, including seeds, and climate negotiations attempt to address land use and forest clearance. Other international organizations – such as the FAO – have responsibility for this sector. However, while international environmental regimes can provide alternate venues for agriculture-related disputes, they remain secondary to the global economic arena, including the World Trade Organization (WTO) and its associated agreements.

In many respects, the theoretical lens of globalization studies has made problems such as water and energy provision, food security, and resource extraction visible as global environmental issues, as opposed to being problems that are shared by many countries but fall largely within the jurisdiction of national or local authorities. The activist community has also played a central role in linking environmental issues to broader questions of human rights and global justice. Take, for example, indigenous or community resistance to oil exploration or mining activities by multinational corporations, or to the construction of large dams. In the latter case, activists have pointed to the role of international finance – particularly from the World Bank, but also (and increasingly) from the private sector – in supporting dam construction projects from Costa Rica to India to Laos (Conca 2006; Khagram 2004). In the former, activists from poorer parts of the world have been able to tap into networks of partners in other countries, and also into a growing body of international law that addresses the rights of indigenous communities who are often marginalized in their own countries (McAteer and Pulver 2009). Farmer, peasant, and landless movements have mobilized against international trade rules that encourage socially and environmentally harmful farming practices (Martinez-Torres and Rosset 2010).

These issues do not easily lend themselves to the traditional model of treaty-based GEG (Conca 2006). Either national interests are too strong and too much in conflict, or economic interests are able to fight environmental regulations. Sometimes activists decide to fight in the global human rights arena, rather than the environmental. These issues are also often too heterogeneous in their form and impacts across, and even within, different countries to be neatly packaged as a manageable global issue. This does not mean that forms of global governance are entirely absent from these arenas: these are exactly the sorts of issues that the scholars who are seeking to broaden our perspective on what constitutes global environmental governance address.

Finally, few international agreements or negotiations tackle head-on what many see as two fundamental environmental issues of the twenty-first century: overpopulation and overconsumption (UNEP 2012). These are both, for different but overlapping reasons, very difficult or even explosive, issues for politicians to address (Crane 1993; Princen et al. 2002). Global population reached 7.2 billion in 2014, and could reach 9 billion by 2050. Certainly, many international, often non-governmental, programs and agencies address issues of birth rates, birth control, and women's health and education. However, several fundamental obstacles – including religious and other cultural and/or individual values – stand in the way of setting any sort of international goals or standards regarding population. Instead, major international programs, such as the UN's Millennium Development Goals, focus on maternal health, poverty reduction, and education as ways to indirectly reduce population growth while improving the overall quality of human life, especially in developing countries.

Issues of consumption – particularly in the global North – have long been seen as the "third rail" of global environmental politics.[10] Further, rising global consumption rates are driven by both population growth and rising per capita income, especially in countries such as India and China. Telling people that they need to sacrifice for the good of a nebulous global community, or future generations, tends not to get politicians re-elected. Further, there are splits within the community advocating changing consumption practices, particularly between those who focus on structural causes of consumption – ranging from social alienation to the growth of a vast global advertising industry – and those who focus on reducing individual ecological footprints through substitution (e.g. driving hybrid cars) or recycling.

As writers in the global environmental politics field argue, incremental or individual approaches to reducing the environmental impacts of consumption do not address core problems arising from the distancing of production networks and supply chains from people making consumption decisions (Princen 2002; Maniates 2002; Dauvergne 2008). Consumers have also become (or been made to become) dependent on modes of consumption, such as the automobile in the absence of public transit or other alternatives (Dauvergne 2008), or on plastic grocery bags (Clapp and Swanston 2009). We discuss steps that have been taken to make global supply chains more sustainable, often initiated by non-state actors, in

---

[10] The "third rail" is the live rail in many urban subway transit systems that supplies power to the trains. Such systems carry prominent warnings to stay away from it, given the electrocution danger.

Chapter 7. Generally, these framings suggest that consumers should act as citizens, figuring out appropriate points of intervention, from campuses and local planning boards on upwards, to change the institutional structures that facilitate or require overconsumption.[11]

Next Steps

This chapter has demonstrated how the global environment contains multiple complex and dynamic issues and problems. It has also emphasized that the ways in which global environmental issues are framed are by no means immutable, and have important consequences for how they are governed, at local, national, and global levels. From the UN to national governments, activists and scientists, many different sorts of actors are engaged in processes of environmental problem identification, assessment, and framing for the purposes of global governance. It is to these actors – and their roles, activities, and interactions – to which we turn in Chapter 3.

Discussion Questions

- How would you identify and evaluate different sources of information about the state of the global environment or specific environmental problems? What distinguishes a reliable source of information from one that is not?
- This chapter distinguishes between global commons, transboundary, and local–cumulative environmental problems. Taking complex problems such as climate change or biodiversity protection as examples, when is such a distinction helpful, and when does it oversimplify? What different prescriptions for action emerge from this typology?
- Population growth and consumption both help drive many environmental problems, yet they are very difficult problems to deal with at the international level. Why is this? What would you suggest as appropriate ways for the global community to address population and consumption problems?

SUGGESTIONS FOR FURTHER READING

Falkner, Robert, ed. 2013. *The Handbook of Global Climate Change and Environment Policy*. London: John Wiley & Sons: an authoritative overview of the politics and process of global environmental governance, with many

[11] See Maniates 2002; Steinberg 2014; Grady-Benson and Sarathy 2015.

chapters focusing on the characteristics and governance of specific environmental problems.

Jasanoff, Sheila. 2001. "Image and Imagination: The Formation of Global Environmental Consciousness." *Changing the Atmosphere: Expert Knowledge and Environmental Governance.* Eds. Clark A. Miller and Paul N. Edwards. Cambridge, MA: MIT Press: discusses how the image of the earth from space and the "spaceship earth" metaphor have been framed and used in political and cultural discourse.

McKibben, Bill. 2010. *Eaarth: Making a Life on a Tough New Planet.* New York: Henry Holt & Company: one of the leading environmental writers of our age takes on the damage humans are inflicting on the planet in the Anthropocene era, and implications of this damage for our society.

Princen, Thomas, Michael F. Maniates, and Ken Conca, eds. 2002. *Confronting Consumption.* Cambridge, MA: MIT Press: this collection of essays explores the dynamics of consumption and the global environment, discussing why consumption is the "third rail" of international environmental politics.

United Nations Environment Programme. 2012. *GEO 5: Environment for the Future we Want.* Nairobi: United Nations Environment Programme, available at www.unep.org/geo/geo5.asp: a highly authoritative source of data and analysis on the state of the global environment and future trends. The website gives free access to all available editions. Expect *GEO 6* in 2017.

3   Actors in Global Environmental Politics

This chapter introduces the large and complex cast of characters active across different sites and modes of global environmental politics (GEP) and governance. We examine five types of actors: nation-states; international organizations; the global environmental movement; the corporate sector; and experts. The latter three groups are often referred to collectively as "non-state actors," but they differ significantly from each other. We look at each group's participants, how they engage in GEP and global environmental governance (GEG), and the critical questions around their participation in and influence on the politics of the global environment.

The roles these groups of actors play in GEG and GEP has changed significantly over time and across issue areas, partly because of changing governance structures and opportunities to participate but also because of entrepreneurialism on the part of the actors themselves. In the case of the dominant mode of international environmental diplomacy, states take the lead, with non-state actors in supporting roles. For non-state modes of governance, their roles are reversed. Across the modes and sites of GEG we examine in this book, there is also strong variation in how groups of actors interact with each other. For example, civil society actors, including environmental groups, have been far more confrontational in dealing with international economic institutions than in their engagement in international environmental cooperation, employing tactics from repertoires of contentious politics.

In turn, these observations raise questions of influence and agency. Does wider participation in GEG signal greater influence on the part of non-traditional actors, or is it still the case that states and their representatives wield the most power in governance decisions? Within actor groups, are some more influential than others? For example, are certain types of expertise, and therefore experts, more privileged than others in international environmental politics (IEP)? As we proceed in later chapters to discuss different sites and modes of GEG, these questions remain front and center.

51

Nation-States and Global Environmental Politics

Nation-states, or, more accurately, their governments, are the primary actors in the international system: the only actors with decision-making authority under international law. There are nearly 200 nation-states in the international system: 193 states are members of the UN, and 197 government entities (including the European Union [EU], which has its own vote on top of those of its member states) have signed the main UN convention that governs ozone-layer depletion, which is considered to have universal membership.[1] Only official state representatives are authorized to vote on, sign, and enforce international treaties. Only governments, through their sovereign authority, are empowered to make environmental regulations enforceable on their own populations. States can also draw on an impressive array of resources, from military and economic power to political and social legitimacy to further their goals. This section examines three major topics: what states, and their interests, are; the impact of one of the major global fault lines in GEP – the divide between rich and poor states of the North and South; and challenges to the continued, central role of the state in world politics.

a.   States and their Interests

What states' goals and interests are and where they come from are the topics of some debate. In mainstream international relations theory, a Realist perspective posits that states engage in international cooperation only when they see a chance of relative gains for themselves over others in the international system. This point of view contrasts with the Institutionalist perspective – that states are interested in absolute gains for the entire international community, regardless of how their relative position changes. Constructivists argue that states' goals and interests are not predetermined, and can, in fact, be changed through engagement in international politics, particularly through cooperation: states become socialized through interaction with others, and come to share common norms and goals. Either way, national interests – the goals states pursue in international bargaining – play a critical role in determining the course and outcomes of GEP, as we shall see in Chapter 4. In Chapter 5, we shall see that such concepts as national will and capacity are very important in determining levels of compliance with, and effectiveness of, multilateral environmental agreements (MEAs).

---

[1] Neither Taiwan nor Kosovo, both independent nation-states, have sufficient recognition from other countries to join the UN, while the Holy See chooses to remain an observer state, although with the right to sign treaties. At this time of writing, Palestine remains in international legal limbo, maintaining observer status.

Despite the importance of national interests, preferences, and capacity in determining how and why states act, nation-states are not unitary actors. Governments are made up of multiple agencies, and decision-makers are subject to multiple pressures, which all help sway international outcomes. Many agencies or ministries may play a role in global environmental negotiations. At the 1997 Kyoto Protocol negotiations, the USA delegation included members of the State Department, the Department of Commerce, and the Environmental Protection Agency, and members of the executive branch, notably Vice President Al Gore. These agencies had significantly different positions on how negotiations should proceed. Decision-makers, too, especially in democracies, are subject to pressure from various domestic interest groups. Environmental groups, industry groups, and others all have interests in the outcomes of IEP, which often conflict. They can use multiple channels of access to the political process, with varying levels of success, to influence decision-makers either directly or indirectly, via shaping public opinion. In Chapter 4 we examine ways in which these domestic political factors help shape international policy outcomes.

Many different sorts of states inhabit the international system. As the most powerful state in the international system, the USA played a pivotal role at Stockholm in establishing the state-led system of GEG (Sohn 1973). Its participation in international environmental negotiations is often considered critical, yet in the 1990s and 2000s it became more of a laggard state. It has been, for a variety of reasons (see Chapter 4), reluctant to participate in international environmental diplomacy, although it keeps the commitments it makes (DeSombre 2015).

The EU is a major supporter of GEG, although there is still considerable variation in environmental performance and attitudes across its member states (Bretherton and Vogler 2006; Oberthür and Rabitz 2013). Established in 1958 as the European Economic Community to foster free trade within its borders, the EU has widened and deepened the scope of its activities to become a quasi-federal union, a unique entity in global politics. As of 2016 it had twenty-eight member states. The prevalence of environmental interdependence and environmental problems within Europe made environment and sustainable development an obvious choice for European governance institutions to take the lead, and most important environmental assessments and directives in Europe come from Brussels (Selin and VanDeveer 2015). In terms of international environmental law, the EU can sign treaties as a regional economic organization. Its member states also sign individually, although usually following the lead of the EU and taking a unified position.

China has emerged as a complex actor in GEP. It has, as the world's largest country in terms of population, greenhouse gas (GHG) emissions, and other indicators, a considerable global ecological footprint. As an official leader of the global South (see below) it has been able to take full advantage of the various aid and capacity-building initiatives that accompany different regimes but avoid the commitments that Western nations have taken on. As this situation changes, and as China's domestic environmental conditions worsen, it is emerging as an environmental player in its own way (Compagnon et al. 2012). The central government in Beijing is taking on commitments and actions such as developing its own emissions-trading system (Lo and Howes 2015; see Chapter 8), and allows a domestic environmental movement, but it is also continuing development funding in Africa and other parts of the world.

Smaller states take on a variety of roles, often punching above their weight in GEG. The Scandinavian nations, for instance, have often taken strong positions on the global environment, encouraging others to join negotiations and often taking unilateral measures above and beyond their basic commitments (Chasek et al. 2014, pp. 49–51). As we shall see in Chapter 4, states often form coalitions in different issue areas to help achieve common goals. These coalitions may change over time (Wagner et al. 2012), but stable examples include the Alliance of Small Island States (AOSIS) in climate negotiations, and the "Miami Group" in biodiversity negotiations, consisting of the main states producing genetically modified seeds and crops, including the USA, Canada, Australia, and Argentina.

Finally, the international system has expanded since World War Two, with two major waves of states joining or rejoining the international community. The first occurred as the European nations dismantled their colonial empires after the war, and the second followed the end of the Cold War in the early 1990s, when states part of or closely allied with the Soviet Union gained their independence. The larger number of states participating in multilateral institutions has increased the complexity of negotiations, but has also meant wider participation across the international community. It has also meant that the global South has been able to take on a bigger role in GEP.

b.   *North–South Politics and the Global Environment*

Under most circumstances, it would be a vast oversimplification to divide the world into two camps: the wealthy "haves" of the North (or "First World"), including North America, Europe, and other industrialized nations; and the poorer "have-nots" of the global South (or "Third

World"), consisting of countries in Asia, Africa, and Latin America. Many of these countries only emerged into independence and economic development in the second half of the twentieth century, and have suffered from their peripheral role in the global economy. The "North–South" distinction obscures the countries of what used to be called the "Second World" – those countries that spent decades in the orbit of the Soviet Union. It fails to differentiate between the relatively developed economies of Brazil, India, and China and the "Fourth World" of highly indebted poorer countries (HIPCs), many in Africa, so torn by war, disease, and economic misfortune that they are moving backwards, not forwards. Finally, it obscures inequalities within rich and poor countries, what Doyle (2005) calls "minority" and "majority" worlds that are not so easily defined by national borders.

However, in the context of international environmental negotiations the distinction has had considerable utility, for the primary reason that the Southern countries have explicitly argued to be recognized as a voting bloc, which articulates specific interests, positions, and ideas. These states have, in a sense, adopted a collective identity, despite the very real differences between them (Najam 2015; Williams 2005; Miller 1995). Thus, until recently the "Southern" label effectively encompassed countries as diverse as China, Brazil, Chad, and Somalia, at least for the purpose of international environmental negotiations. In turn, distinctions between rich and poor countries have been formalized in treaty texts, as the principle of "common but differentiated responsibilities" has allowed Southern countries more time and/or more resources to meet environmental commitments.

The South as a group has its roots in the Non-Aligned Movement (NAM) of the 1950s and 1960s and the movement for a New International Economic Order (NIEO; Najam 2015). NAM was a coalition of countries led by India and Indonesia that wished to take a neutral stance in the ongoing Cold War. The NIEO, formed in the 1970s, sought to break the South of its economic dependency on the North. The organizational form of NIEO movement is the Group of 77 (G77, now consisting of over 130 member states), which began as an alliance within the UN's General Assembly, and has taken on an organizational identity of its own, including articulating and representing Southern interests at international environmental negotiations.

Starting at the 1972 Stockholm Conference, Southern governments have led in linking environmental protection and economic development under the rubric of sustainable development and stressing the environmental degradation caused by poverty. They have also successfully challenged the environmental priorities and problem frames set out by the international community, arguing that they have focused on problems of greater concern to the North (climate change, ozone depletion) while underplaying the environmental problems of most concern to people in poorer nations, including desertification and fresh water availability.[2] These debates have influenced the choice of issues over which to negotiate in recent decades, as well as the shape of international environmental agreements and national commitments. In particular, they successfully incorporated the principle of common but differentiated responsibilities into international agreements, giving the South additional time or resources to meet (often lower) targets.

Given the skepticism with which many Southern leaders approached the Stockholm Conference (Najam 2005), the environmental arena seems a surprising one for the South to have taken so influential a stand. However, there are good reasons for this. First, unlike key arenas of GEG – international trade and finance – environmental negotiations operate under a more open, "one-member, one vote" process, rather than through closed-door meetings of major regime donors. Second, in addition to finding a collective negotiating voice, Southern countries have critical sources of power and leverage in environmental issues. Given that over half the world's population already lives in the developing world, and that it is in the South that the bulk of the world's industrial and population growth will occur in the twenty-first century, their participation at this stage was recognized as critical to future global sustainability. In specific issue areas, too, the South has been able to exert material leverage (e.g. biodiversity) or moral leadership (e.g. the hazardous waste trade).

Without explicit recognition of the roles and needs of Southern countries in international environmental negotiations, GEG would be far less extensive and accepted than it is today. However, the North–South distinction is breaking down with the rise of China, India, and Brazil – and, to a lesser extent, Russia and South Africa – as global economic leaders. These countries are already or will shortly be world leaders in GHG emissions. Brazil, India, and China are tipped to be the world's leading

---

[2] A powerful example of how Southern activists were able to challenge problem framing arose when the Centre for Science and Environment (CSE), an Indian NGO, issued a stinging rebuttal of an influential report by the USA-based World Resources Institute (WRI) on national GHG emissions, a rebuttal that received a lot of attention in international forums (Agarwal and Narain 1991). Among other arguments, the CSE noted that the WRI report had, when it allocated relatively high emissions figures to India and other Southern countries, failed to distinguish between the "survival" emissions of poorer countries (e.g. methane from rice fields) and the "luxury" emissions of richer countries, such as high automobile ownership, in allocating responsibility for GHG emissions.

economies, as they grow and the traditional economic superpowers (the USA and the EU) shrink in relative terms.

Two coalitions of states have emerged as players in the global economic and environmental arenas, notably climate politics: BRICS and BASIC. BRICS consists of Brazil, Russia, India, China, and South Africa, and is considered an economic alliance, with its own development funds and economic identity. BASIC, consisting of Brazil, South Africa, India, and China, is by contrast an active alliance specifically in global climate politics since 2009, somewhat to the cost of the G77 alliance (Hochstetler 2012; Qi 2011). They have made commitments to reduce GHG emissions and provide assistance to other G77 countries. In so doing, they have responded to pressure from the USA and other developed countries, but in the process have forced recognition of their ascendant role in a changing global political system. We examine the implications of this shift in Chapter 4. At the other end of the continuum, the least developed countries (including many in Africa) that are the most vulnerable to global change remain marginalized in international environmental negotiations. Even the small island states, despite their moral standing, have been unable to gain their desired results, including funding and plans for displaced communities as a result of climate change.

c.   *Are Nation-States in Decline?*

Studies of GEP grapple with the question of whether or not states are in decline as the most powerful actors on the international scene (Falkner 2012, 2013; Compagnon et al. 2012), mirroring a general debate in international relations theory (Spruyt 2002). Some have argued that pressures of globalization have limited the ability of individual governments to form and shape their own policies, especially economic policies, powers that have shifted to the global economic and financial institutions (Robinson 2001; Sassen 1999). Others argue that the "center of gravity" in GEG is shifting to powerful non-state actors, including global civil society, corporate actors, or international economic institutions, and that state-led modes of governance may increasingly share the stage with other sorts of non-state or hybrid initiatives (Speth 2004; Hoffmann 2011). Many believe that the global system of territorially sovereign nation-states is deeply dysfunctional for addressing global and transboundary ecological interdependence and should be reformed (Falkner 2013, p. 252, and Chapter 1).

The implications for GEP, if this shift is occurring, are that global governance could increasingly come from the non-state arena, including the private sector, civil society, and sub-state political actors (see Chapter 7) – unless governments push back to maintain their sovereign rights over global governance. At the extreme, it implies that the state and the arena of inter-state politics are the wrong target for environmental activists, and that they should be targeting forces of global capitalism instead.

On the other hand, there is little evidence that the international system of nation-states is going away (Falkner 2013). States still fulfill many functions that only they can provide in the international system: forces of law and order, a legitimacy grounded in years of political practice, financial aid and policy tools that make them essential to effective global governance, even in partnership with other actors (Vogler 2005). This does not mean that states are immune to change. General scholarship on state sovereignty points out that state structures and organization have changed and evolved over time (Spruyt 1994). Autocracies became liberal democracies (providing civil liberties), then social democracies (providing social welfare). Hence, the possibility that environmental exigencies and pressures from multilateral governance institutions could lead to the "greening" of states – where ecological functions are put at the core of their activities – is a subject of real debate around the future of the nation-state.[3]

Shifting notions of authority and the hybridization and fragmentation of GEG, and their implications for state-led GEG, are recurring themes throughout this book. Chapters 4 and 5 examine the processes, strengths and weaknesses, and Chapters 6, 7 and 8 all examine challenges and alternatives to this dominant model of GEG. Chapter 9 takes up the question of transformation of the international system raised here.

International Organizations

Intergovernmental organizations (IGOs), also known as international governmental organizations, are set up by states to manage international problems, provide a forum for collective decision-making, and bear responsibility for managing and implementing global policies, including the allocation of international financial loans and aid. They are called governmental organizations because they were established by and represent the collective interests of the governments that founded them, and that make up their membership.

Currently around 250 IGOs operate in the international system (Mingst 2012), a number that has remained relatively stable since the early 1980s.[4]

---

[3] See Falkner 2013; Barry and Eckersley 2005; Meadowcraft 2012.

[4] According to the *International Yearbook of International Organizations*, conventional IGOs are those whose operations and membership cover at least three countries, which have formal operating and financial structures, and which have been active in the past four years.

The current system of IGOs dates back to the years immediately following World War Two. The UN, the World Bank, the International Monetary Fund (IMF), and the General Agreement on Tariffs and Trade (GATT) were all established in the late 1940s, with the goals of maintaining international peace and stability, encouraging reconstruction and economic growth following the devastation of the war, and helping numerous former colonized nations navigate their way into independence. The World Trade Organization (WTO), set up as the organizational embodiment of the GATT and related trade agreements, was established in 1995. Regional economic organizations include the EU, the North American Free Trade Agreement (NAFTA), and the Association of South East Asian Nations (ASEAN, which also has an important security component).

IGOs tread the border between categories of "state" and "non-state" actors. While they are supposed to represent the collective will of their member states, they have also been able, on many occasions, to adopt their own agendas and activities, and certainly have been very influential in setting international policy agendas (O'Neill 2015). These activities have raised important questions about their autonomy and influence independent of their member states, which, for some organizations, appears to be relatively high (Barnett and Finnemore 1999, 2004). In terms of actual material resources (budget, staff, office space), IGOs tend to be small (Blackhurst 1998). They gain legitimacy and wield influence through their mission, through work "on the ground" in different countries, and the standing granted to them by member states. In recent years IGOs have sought to expand the basis for their legitimacy, in part responding to global pressures for more accountability, and in part to assert themselves above and beyond conflicts among their member states. Two sets of IGOs are particularly important for GEG: the UN and associated agencies, and international economic institutions, such as the WTO, the World Bank, and the IMF.

The United Nations System

The UN and its associated agencies play the largest direct role in GEG. It has sponsored four global summits on environment and development, and is most active in setting the global environmental policy agenda, and providing a forum for international environmental negotiations. It has, however, been criticized for a piecemeal approach to environmental issues, driven by its politics and institutional structures, that does not fully address their seriousness or interconnectedness (Conca 2015).

The UN Charter was signed in San Francisco in October 1945 by fifty nations; today the UN has 193 member states.[5] Its primary mandate is to promote international peace and security. To fulfill this mission, it has been active in peacekeeping, conflict prevention and arms control, international human rights protection, social and economic development, human health – and global environmental protection. The main governing body of the UN, the Security Council, is made up of five permanent members (the USA, the United Kingdom, Russia, China, and France), each of whom has the ability to veto any proposal brought before the council, and ten members elected by the General Assembly. Proposals to reform the Security Council include changing or expanding the roster of permanent members. Each member state has a seat, and a vote, in the General Assembly, the UN's deliberative body, which provides a forum to discuss – and potentially resolve – pressing international issues and crises.

The UN manages a dense network of specialized agencies, programs, funds, and other bodies. Its main organs include the General Assembly, the Security Council, the Secretariat (office of the Secretary General), the Economic and Social Council, and the International Court of Justice. The World Bank, the World Health Organization (WHO), the IMF, and the Food and Agriculture Organization (FAO) count as "specialized agencies" of the UN: autonomous bodies linked to the UN through special agreements. The programs most directly involved in GEG, UNEP (UN Environment Programme) and UNDP (UN Development Programme) are directly under the UN's umbrella, with organization, employees, and budget managed by the UN Secretariat and the General Assembly.

UNEP is based in Nairobi, Kenya, with offices also in Geneva. Its primary function is to oversee the development of international environmental agreements and initiatives, to provide a forum for negotiations, to gather information and promote research on environmental problems, and to serve as the central body monitoring, and overseeing funding for, states' international environmental commitments: an "anchor institution" for the global environment (Ivanova 2007, 2010).

UNEP's beginnings, at the 1972 Stockholm Conference, were inauspicious: there was little support for an international environment agency among developed countries, and developing countries were suspicious of what it might entail. UNEP owes its existence, to a large part, to the entrepreneurial leadership of Maurice Strong, the Secretary General of the Stockholm Conference, and to the political contingencies prevailing

---

[5] For an overview of the UN and its activities see Hanhimäki 2008.

at the time (Ivanova 2010). Its eventual institutional form, as a UN "program," rather than a specialized agency, with limited resources and autonomy, has made it a target for reform, particularly by those who favor a stronger, more centralized form of GEG. In 2012, following the Rio+20 Summit, the UN General Assembly upgraded and strengthened UNEP. Its governing council, previously restricted to fifty-eight UN member states, is now open to all member states, and it has the promise of enhanced funding and strengthened capacity.

UNEP oversees many of the treaty-specific secretariats and agencies responsible for the day-to-day running of international environmental governance regimes. These secretariats are located in many different parts of the world – Geneva, Bonn, Nairobi, and other cities. Treaty secretariats report to the parties to different conventions, and have often been dismissed as mere functional bureaucracies, collecting paperwork and managing meetings. Recent studies demonstrate that this perspective is far from reality. There is growing evidence that they are taking on larger, and more autonomous, roles, guiding the development of their issue areas, and managing linkages and overlaps that have inevitably emerged in the complex and piecemeal system of GEG (Jinnah 2012a, 2014; Biermann and Siebenhüner 2009). Additionally, most treaty-based environmental regimes also contain subsidiary bodies for scientific and technological advice, for managing funding, or for other regime functions.

Together with UNDP and the World Bank, UNEP also helps manage the primary global institution designed to fund projects directly related to global environmental problems, the Global Environment Facility (GEF; see Chapter 5). The GEF, founded in 1991, coordinates funding and capacity-building projects to do with climate change, ozone depletion, biodiversity, oceans, persistent organic pollutants (POPs), and desertification. The inclusion of the latter two problems in its mandate has to do with direct lobbying from Southern countries. It funds projects that help fulfill global environmental goals, providing assistance for those parts of the project that incur the additional costs of meeting a global goal, playing an important role in helping meet capacity-building goals in less-developed and transitioning countries.

Other non-environmental IGOs have taken on roles in GEG. The International Maritime Organization (IMO) oversees the International Convention for the Prevention of Pollution from Ships (MARPOL). The World Meteorological Organization (WMO) helped set up the Intergovernmental Panel on Climate Change (IPCC; see below) in 1988. There are numerous other examples, but none are as significant as the economic IGOs, which had to be dragged, unwillingly, into the environmental arena.

IGOs for the Global Economy

International economic organizations, such as the World Bank, the WTO, and, to a lesser extent, the IMF, are also important actors in GEP, as we shall see in Chapter 6. Although they are not directly involved in global environmental negotiations, their policies, according to their critics, have helped exacerbate global environmental problems. Others have pointed out the role they play in forging sustainable solutions to problems associated with economic growth.

The World Bank's chief mission, following the immediate process of post-World War Two economic reconstruction, is to provide aid and loans to developing countries. It has come under fire from environmental and human rights activists because it has been the chief funding agency for numerous projects – dams, roads, etc. – that have been implemented without regard for their environmental or social costs (Fox and Brown 1998; Gutner 2012). Since protests led to its withdrawal from such controversial projects as the Narmada Dam project in India in the late 1980s and early 1990s, it has invested time and energy in "greening" its approach to international development, including establishing an environmental unit and implementing environmental impact assessment procedures (Clapp and Dauvergne 2011). While these efforts have met with some acclaim, others claim that they represent mere "window dressing" – or that they represent a particularly technocratic approach to green governance that reinforces, rather than changes, the dominant international status quo.

The WTO has also been a target for protests by environmental, human rights, and labor activists. It was set up in 1995, in order to administer the increasingly unwieldy global trading rules contained in the GATT, first signed in 1948. The main purpose of the GATT was to liberalize international trade, through reducing tariffs and other barriers to the free movement of goods and services worldwide, with the goal of encouraging global economic growth, and, through prosperity and interdependence, global peace and stability. The WTO has a membership of over 160 states, and operates formally on a one member, one vote principle. All member states are committed to a strict and far-reaching set of rules aimed at further trade liberalization. The WTO's relationship to the global environment has engendered much debate. Some argue that gross domestic product (GDP) growth through trade has led to overuse of natural resources, while others argue that it is only through economic growth and prosperity that we can afford to protect the environment (Clapp and Dauvergne 2011). Others point to ways in which trade liberalization has struck down or stunted domestic environmental regulations (Jaspers and Falkner 2013), and could strike down MEAs (O'Neill and Burns 2005). We return to these debates in Chapter 6.

NGOs, Activist Groups, and the Global Environmental Movement

Environmental activist groups play a critical role in highlighting global environmental problems, and in influencing – directly or indirectly – the course of GEG. Many types of groups, representing many different interests, are active on the global political scene – from large, professionalized NGOs to small local groups networking with each other via e-mail, text, and social media. These broad types differ extensively in ideology, strategy, organizational form, and targets (not all of them would even define themselves as "environmental"), but share critical concerns over the state of the global environment and/or the role and rights of human communities within the environment, and over the need for different voices to be heard in global governance processes. They draw on moral resources, on membership, and on sheer passion to do the work that they do.

Environmental, human rights, indigenous rights, and other sorts of activist groups are often referred to as civil society actors. The term civil society has a long history in the study of social movements and their relationship with the state (Ehrenberg 1999; Wapner 2000). Most simply, civil society consists of voluntary associations and movements – religious, activist, and other collective groups that individuals choose to join: "the bonds and allegiances that arise through sustained, voluntary, noncommercial interaction" (Wapner 2000, p. 266). These relationships exist independently of the state, or government (or ruling party). Civil society can be an important counterbalance to overweening state power. Civil society actors may also be able to channel societal demands to the state more effectively than individual or mass actions.

Environmentalism as a form of social movement has a long history around the world (Guha 2000; O'Neill 2012).[6] Groups of individuals and communities have engaged in political struggles and protests, lobbying, and other strategies to save wilderness, rainforests, and whales, to close polluting factories, or prevent dam construction across the globe. Sometimes these groups have formed around a single issue, and then faded away. At other times they have built effective networks and

---

[6] Social movements are made up of groups of societal actors seeking to change key aspects of policy or governance. For a basic outline of social movement theory see McAdam et al. 1996.

organizations, and continued to campaign. It is not surprising that many different groups are playing an active role at the global level, seeking to influence the course and progress of international environmental negotiations. The nature and extent of this influence is one of the key areas of debate around the role of civil society groups in GEP (Betsill and Corell 2001, 2008). Another is the extent to which environmental groups can claim or maintain legitimacy, especially as they grow and professionalize away from their grass roots. Questions of representation and legitimacy come from both inside and outside social movements: in 2000, following the anti-WTO protests in Seattle of the previous year, an article in the influential periodical *The Economist* asked just who elected NGOs to take the positions that they do.[7]

Global environmental activism has manifested itself in several ways. First, many groups – Greenpeace, the Worldwide Fund for Nature (WWF), the Climate Action Network, the Third World Network, and others – have focused their attention on explicitly global problems. Greenpeace, for instance, has been instrumental in drawing international political attention to problems such as whaling or the international waste trade, using striking protest actions, garnering maximum media attention. Some organizations focus on providing data on the extent of global environmental degradation – the Washington DC-based World Resources Institute produces regular reports that cover all aspects of humanity's impact on the environment.

Second, while environmental groups continue to lobby their home governments, they have become a very active presence at international negotiations and at global summits (Princen and Finger 1994; Betsill and Corell 2008; Park 2013). The UN has accredited more than 3,000 NGOs with official observer status, and many others are admitted to individual negotiating processes (O'Neill 2015; Raustiala 2012). They include ENGOs (environmental NGOs) to IPOs (Indigenous Peoples' Organizations) and YOUNGOs (youth NGOs). More recently, representatives of cities – often their mayors – and other local government actors have been recognized as NGOs in their own right (despite, technically, being "government" organizations), known as LGMAs (local governments and municipal authorities).

From colorful protests to actively lobbying state representatives inside negotiating halls, publicizing the progress of negotiations, and holding "parallel summits" at the same time and place as major UN summits, NGOs in GEG have been hard to ignore. Chapter 4 examines their roles at all stages of the international negotiations process – from agenda-setting

---

[7] "Angry and Effective," *The Economist*, September 23, 2000.

to implementation, and the extent to which they actually influence regime outcomes, a somewhat contested idea (Betsill and Corell 2008).

Third, environmental organizations have actively engaged with each other across borders, creating transnational advocacy networks (TANs).[8] TANs are "sets of actors linked across country boundaries, bound together by shared values, dense exchange of information and services, and common discourses" (Khagram et al. 2002, p. 7). They may be coalitions of groups loosely allied across national borders for particular purposes, or tighter networks or movements that coordinate strategies and can mobilize in several different jurisdictions at once (Khagram et al. 2002, pp. 7–10). Connections between these groups may be horizontal (groups ally themselves on a relatively equal basis) or vertical (linked by a chain of command).

Environmental TANs engage in many different activities (see Park 2013). Many of the groups engaged in the international environmental negotiations process fall into this category: the Climate Action Network, an umbrella organization made up of climate-related NGOs, represents the collective position of its membership at international climate negotiations. Similar peak associations are engaged in POPs, hazardous waste trade, and other international environmental negotiating processes. TANs are starting to cut across environmental regimes. The climate negotiations now attract participation from gender, indigenous, and even waste-picker TANs, given the breadth and diversity of communities affected by climate change or the policies designed to remedy it (Ciplet 2014).

Local activist groups use TANs to target, publicize, and change the behavior of recalcitrant governments, IGOs, and multinational corporations, particularly in cases when domestic channels of access are not available.[9] For example, many of the communities most affected by large-scale projects funded by the World Bank (such as dam construction) have little recourse at the domestic level, given that these projects are usually initiated and supported by their own governments. In such cases, an alliance with a similar group in a different country – particularly in a country with a large share of votes in the World Bank Group – makes for good strategy, as these groups can then pressure their own governments to change World Bank actions (Fox and Brown 1998). Such

[8] See, for example, Khagram et al. 2002; Keck and Sikkink 1998; Fox and Brown 1998; Conca 2006; Park 2013.
[9] This is known as the "boomerang" model (Keck and Sikkink 1998): groups living under a repressive regime are able to work with groups in other countries, who are able to lobby their governments to put pressure on the repressive government to change their practices. This model is most closely linked with global human rights activism, and the activities of groups such as Amnesty International. For an example of how the boomerang model works with corporations as the targets, see McAteer and Pulver 2009.

coalitions have played an instrumental role in making the World Bank start taking the environmental and social impacts of its funding decisions into account. At the same time, questions of interactions and relationships within advocacy coalitions – especially those with membership from both Northern and Southern groups – raises questions of power dynamics, accountability, and learning (Fox and Brown 1998): do Northern groups dominate Southern partners? Do they learn from each other? Do internal dynamics undermine or enhance their attainment of immediate or longer-term goals?

One of the strategic decisions that transnational movements or networks must make is the extent to which they engage in confrontation with their targets, including states, IGOs, and the corporate sector. Protest actions have always been a key part of the social movement repertoire. The global protest movement that arose in the 1990s around meetings of the main international financial institutions has received a lot of attention in terms of its capacity to mobilize a broad activist coalition around issues of global justice (O'Neill 2004). The 1999 Ministerial Meeting of the WTO in Seattle drew around 30,000 protestors, a number that surprised organizers, who had not expected such breadth and depth of opposition to WTO activities. Protestors at global climate meetings at The Hague in 2000 built flood barriers made of sandbags around the convention halls. While it is often hard to draw a direct line between protests and policy change, the performative – and sometimes violent – actions of the protestors helped focus international attention on equity and justice issues around globalization – and helped many activists forge new transnational alliances. These actions have also been instrumental in raising awareness of the connections between environmental degradation and the international human rights agenda, and connecting local concerns with abstract global governance agendas (Conca 2005).

Many NGOs have adopted cooperative strategies, especially when targeting the corporate sector. Large, visible multinational corporations, such as Nike and Royal Dutch Shell, have made good focal points for protests and publicity. They have also been ready to engage with NGOs to build their reputations and develop corporate social responsibility (CSR) practices (Gallagher and Weinthal 2012). Examples include the Rainforest Action Network's partnership with Home Depot in the late 1990s to encourage the use of sustainably harvested timber, or Conservation International's work with Starbucks. More recently – and more controversially – the Environmental Defense Fund has representatives who work with Walmart, the world's largest retailer. In this way, NGOs can keep corporations accountable, and even get directly involved in corporate operations and production practices. These sorts of collaborative efforts also underpin the long-term non-state governance initiatives, such as the Forest Stewardship Council (FSC), which we examine in Chapter 7.

While such partnerships have delivered benefits, this path can be fraught with peril for NGOs, however, which face accusations, sometimes true, of cooptation (Baur and Schmitz 2012). NGOs involved in sustainable palm-oil certification have been criticized for accepting that palm-oil plantations, which often involve large-scale clearance of forested lands, can ever be considered sustainable (Oosterveer et al. 2014). Holmes (2011) points out how the revolving door between corporate and elite NGO boards has helped foster the emergence of an elite circle of highly professionalized conservation NGOs whose operations and ideas are increasingly distant from the communities they work with.

Even with these concerns in mind, environmental organizations have been major actors in highlighting the global environmental crisis and advocating for just solutions. We turn now to our other main set of non-state actors: the corporate sector.

Corporations and the Private Sector

Private economic actors – firms, corporations, and business lobbying groups – are perhaps the most controversial group of non-state actors in GEP. Critics argue that corporations, wielding undue political influence with little or no public accountability, are primarily responsible for today's environmental crises. Many corporations are currently working hard to prove the opposite: that instead, through adopting management standards and production practices, they can in fact be engines of environmentalism.

As with the NGO sector, the private sector is made up of many different types of actors, with varying interests, capacities, and activities. Of particular concern to environmental activists are multinational corporations (MNCs), that is, "any business corporation in which ownership, management, production and marketing extend over several national jurisdictions" (Gilpin 1975, p. 8), and firms in the manufacturing and raw-materials extraction sectors. However, firms of all sizes and types of production may have an impact on the state and politics of the global environment. Table 3.1 gives examples of primary and secondary industries associated with particular international environmental issues.

Even today, there are significant differences in MNC behavior. While some are good citizens, instituting practices of CSR, others are decidedly bad actors, refusing to engage in the sorts of environmental, social, and

Table 3.1 *Global Environmental Issues and Associated Industries*

Issue	Primary Industry	Secondary (User) Industries
Climate Change	Fossil fuels extraction/refining (e.g. Shell, Chevron-Texaco)	Transportation sector, Electric utilities, Other energy-intensive industries
Hazardous Waste Trade	Waste disposal industry, Scrap metal, Recycling	Numerous manufacturers
Biodiversity/ Biosafety	Agricultural biotechnology, Pharmaceuticals	Agriculture, Medicine
Ozone Depletion	Chemical manufacturers	Refrigeration, Electronics, Aerosols, Air conditioning
Persistent Organic Pollutants	Chemical manufacturers	Agriculture
Deforestation	Timber industry	Furniture, Hardware, Office supplies, Pulp and paper manufacturing
Ocean Pollution	Oil industry, Shipping (cruise ships and tankers)	Multiple industries relying on fuel, trade

labor practices that others have.[10] These differences are often most stark in resource-extraction sectors, including the mining, timber, and fishing industries (Dauvergne 2001; Webb 2012; Havice and Campling 2010; Watts 2001). The significance of these differences is that there remain major challenges in getting many MNCs, especially those from the leading developing countries, on board with certification, sustainable resource use, or labor practices at the global level. These are very similar to the problems nation-states have in bringing laggard states on board but with far fewer pressures that can be brought to bear in the corporate sector. Transparency measures, such as "naming and shaming" violating firms, are becoming an important mechanism for accomplishing this goal (Gupta and Mason 2014 and see Chapter 7).

Representative organizations such as trade associations and industry NGOs provide a vehicle for collective political action by corporate actors in the international arena. One of the broadest industry associations engaged in GEG, the World Business Council for Sustainable Development (WBCSD), was formed in 1991 just prior to the UN Conference on Environment and Development (UNCED: the 1992 Rio Conference). With roughly 200 members across multiple industrial

[10] There is a huge literature on CSR. See Carroll 1999 for a basic overview, Gallagher and Weinthal 2012 for a comparative perspective, and Hilson 2012 for specific applications to extractive industries in developing countries.

sectors and regions, it advocates constructive involvement of the business sector in sustainability issues. The International Chamber of Commerce (ICC), which also represents many different sectors, is another key industry player at international negotiations. In 2001 WBCSD and ICC formed the Business Alliance for Sustainable Development (BASD), to engage with policy-makers at Johannesburg in 2002 and subsequently at Rio+20 in 2012 (Clapp and Meckling 2013).

Direct private-sector attendance and involvement in international environmental negotiations, as we shall see in Chapter 4, is a relatively recent phenomenon, and they have lagged behind environmental NGOs in this. As is true at the domestic level, the corporate sector operates from a mixture of motives, and firms may often favor international regulations – for obtaining market advantage, a level playing field with global competitors, reducing uncertainty, or even out of genuine concern for the environment.

First, this involvement reflects the corporate sector's desire for uniform international standards (DeSombre 2000). Famously, the major US manufacturer of chlorofluorocarbons (CFCs), DuPont, faced with strict domestic restrictions on CFC generation, changed its position in 1986 to favor international regulation of ozone-depleting substances, thus leveling the international playing field for its products, and, given its leading position in developing substitutes for CFCs, strengthening its position against smaller competitors (Parson 2003, p. 127).

Second, for several key environmental issues, such as climate change, ozone depletion, and biodiversity protection, most political activity has been initiated and debated at the international level. Many industries now feel that they ignore international environmental negotiations at their peril, and that they may in fact benefit from them. The global oil industry, for example, has actively attended and participated in climate negotiations to the extent that they can (Pulver 2002). Some oil companies – notably the European-based corporations – have taken positions in favor of GHG limitations, while many others remain opposed. Industry groups have sought to frame debates around global environmental problems (Clapp and Meckling 2013), as oil companies have done quite successfully in funding research against climate change. They have also brought knowledge and expertise resources to bear, sometimes with political purpose, at technical stages of policy-making processes.

Finally, and especially with widespread disillusionment over the outcomes of global environmental diplomacy, more and more attention is being paid these days to the role that industry plays in developing its own governance regimes, or governance regimes in partnership with civil society actors. These private, or "hybrid," governance regimes, often

built around voluntary eco-labeling or certification processes, are particularly prevalent in the forestry and chemicals sectors, but are also present
in other sectors, including the fishing industry and other key commodities, such as coffee. Firms participating in these schemes agree to certify
that their products are produced according to predetermined environmental and/or labor standards. While some see these schemes as critical
to the future of environmental regulations, others are more skeptical,
pointing out that they are voluntary, and can often lack transparency or
legitimacy. We return to these discussions in Chapter 7.

Scientists, Expert Groups, and Knowledge Holders

Scientists and other experts and knowledge holders have, through their
authoritative claims to knowledge and expertise, played a critical role in
GEP, far more so than in other arenas of global governance. Given that
many of the environmental issues dealt with at the international level are
complex and fraught with uncertainties, "good science" has frequently
been called upon as the justification for particular paths of political action
(Jasanoff 1997). What constitutes "good science," or appropriate knowledge in the context of GEP, is a contested issue. It is apparent that the
boundaries between science and politics, and between "expert" and "lay"
knowledge, are becoming increasingly blurred.

From the 1960s through the 1980s, members of the natural science
community began to study what has come to be termed the human
dimensions of global environmental change. This initiative was led by
researchers in the atmospheric sciences, who began to focus on the
collective impact of human activity on the global environment as
a system, or set of closely interlocking systems (Miller and Edwards
2001). This new interdisciplinary science of the human dimensions of
global environmental change was driven in part by the emergence of
international collaborative research programs, including UNESCO's
Man and Biosphere Program (1971–84), the Scientific Committee on
Problems of the Environment (SCOPE), established by the International
Council of Scientific Unions (ICSU) in 1969, and the WMO.[11] The first
International Geophysical Year, 1957–8, sponsored by the ICSU, is
widely thought to have initiated serious international research on climate
change. These various initiatives brought together scientists across
national borders, and across different disciplines (although not, at first,

---

[11] For histories of international scientific collaboration around the global environment see
Price 1990 and Edwards 2001.

the social sciences), to examine the causes and impacts of global environmental change.

Scientists engaged in work related to GEG are found at universities, in think tanks, in NGOs and in government agencies. The pool of expertise for understanding and addressing international environmental problems is large, ranging from the atmospheric sciences to disciplines such as terrestrial or marine ecology, conservation biology, and more. The dominant group of scientific experts in these expert bodies consists of those who hold particular accreditations, usually academic, in their field or discipline of expertise ("people with Ph.D.s").

The best-known example of a scientific organization at the global level is the IPCC, which shared the 2007 Nobel Peace Prize with former US Vice President Al Gore. The IPCC is a transnational organization of 3,000 scientists, whose role is to gather, assess, and communicate scientific findings about the causes and impacts of global climate change. It was founded in 1988 by the WMO and UNEP, and operates independently of the UN Framework Convention on Climate Change (UNFCCC: Hulme and Mahony 2010). Between 1988 and 2014 it produced five Assessment Reports on the state of climate change knowledge, each of which revealed higher scientific consensus on the existence and human-driven causes of global climate change.[12] The nature of its role in a hotly contested international political issue has served both to push toward strong consensus that climate change is occurring and is driven by human activity, and to pull its members, often unwillingly, into political battles they had not sought.

Other places to look for scientific involvement in the international policy process include formal panels and ad hoc working groups associated with international environmental agreements, such as the Subsidiary Body on Scientific, Technical, and Technological Advice (SBSTTA) of the Convention on Biological Diversity (CBD), or other assessment processes. These panels assess and incorporate new scientific knowledge into regime negotiations, make policy recommendations, and assess the overall performance of the regime (Farrell and Jäger 2006). Experts from both atmospheric sciences and economics have taken the major role in developing a price on carbon, instrumental in the development of market mechanisms to reduce GHG emissions (see Chapter 8). The Intergovernmental Science-Policy Platform on Biodiversity and Ecosystem Services (IPBES) was established in 2012 as an IPCC equivalent for the biodiversity regime. As an example of a significant ad hoc process, the Millennium Ecosystem Assessment Report (2005) involved more than 1,300 authors from 95 countries.

---

[12] These reports are available at the IPCC's website, www.ipcc.ch.

For individual scientists the decision to engage in the political process can pose personal and professional dilemmas. While some individuals and organizations have managed to bridge the worlds of advocacy science and "pure" science – the late Professor Stephen Schneider of Stanford University, one of the world's leading climate scientists, for example – it is, for many, a difficult and potentially treacherous path to negotiate.

Given the critical role that scientific expertise and other forms of knowledge have played in framing global environmental issues and driving particular solutions, scholars from political science and science and technology studies (STS) focus on who these experts are, who counts as an expert, how they organize collectively, and how they relate to the political side of policy-making. We discuss the main perspectives on how scientific knowledge is taken up into the policy process in Chapter 4 (see also Lidskog and Sundqvist 2002; Gupta et al. 2012).

Early models of science–policy interaction posit a separation of science and politics: scientific knowledge, generated outside the political sphere, informs policy debates, but is not shaped by them. This perspective is sometimes referred to as "speaking truth to power." At the other extreme, some make an argument that all science is political: scientific goals, results, funding, and communications are all shaped by politics. More nuanced models posit that in fact the interaction between science, or scientists, and policy, or policy-makers, is neither wholly political nor wholly scientific, and varies over time, across issue areas, and according to who exactly is involved (Jasanoff 1997).

One of the more compelling approaches developed to study the collective impact of experts, and consensual expert opinion, on the international policy process is Peter Haas's epistemic communities model (Haas 1990a, 1992; see Chapter 4). This approach identifies transnational groups of scientific experts who are in a position to work with each other and to influence governments attempting to negotiate environmental agreements. Other studies (e.g. Litfin 1994) address how scientific knowledge can be effective under conditions of uncertainty, and which actors are able to straddle the worlds of science and politics, or under what conditions scientists can mediate outcomes under highly politicized circumstances (Gupta et al. 2012).

Restricting discussions about experts in GEP to the pool of "people with Ph.Ds" has generated critical reflection. Two issues in particular have stimulated debate. First, with the exception of economics, the natural sciences have tended to dominate the social sciences and humanities in terms of giving expert opinion on the causes and consequences of global environmental degradation. Second, official scientific panels and advisory groups associated with international negotiating processes have tended to be dominated by scientists trained and/or working in the global North (Kandlikar and Sagar 1999; Karlsson 2002; Hulme and Mahony 2010).

More broadly, the concept of "expert" has become more contested in recent years, with the incorporation of local knowledge perspectives into several international negotiating processes and the expansion of the category of "science" into a broader one of "knowledge" (Jasanoff 2005, p. 374). For example, the CBD and the UN Convention to Combat Desertification (UNCCD) both contain processes for direct participation by indigenous groups and other local knowledge holders (Martello 2004). "Citizen experts," "lay experts," "traditional" or "indigenous" "knowledge holders" – many of the actors within these categories are becoming sources of legitimate authority, holding as they do particular specialized knowledge, even if they have not passed through a traditional accreditation process (Smith and Sharp 2012). On the one hand, this recategorization of expertise and who "counts" as an expert brings a wider range of knowledge to the international policy process, and direct participation by a broader range of actors. On the other hand, established scientific bodies need to understand that their generalized findings may be received and assessed very differently in local and other settings and be prepared to work with these perspectives in order to gain support (Jasanoff and Martello 2004; Hulme and Mahony 2010).

Overall, however, the biggest challenge to scientists in the past decade has been how to respond to challenges to their credibility, and the legitimacy of the knowledge they provide. The IPCC has come under attack from powerful climate denialist groups, which used instances of mistakes in reports (such as how long it will take for the Himalayas to become ice-free) and informal use of language in communications among some climate scientists to undermine the organization's credibility.[13] In the latter case – known as "Climategate" – e-mails between climate scientists at the University of East Anglia in the UK that spoke, among many mundane things, of using "tricks" in data analysis were first hacked then leaked to the press in 2009 (Maibach et al. 2012). Subsequent investigation found no malfeasance – for example, "trick" was used in its other meaning of "neat solution" – but considerable damage was done, particularly in the USA, where the denial movement is strongest.

---

[13] The climate denial movement has been particularly strong in the USA, where it has received significant financial backing and press coverage. For an analysis of what brings scientists into the movement see Lahsen 2013. For an analysis of how "balanced coverage" leads to bias see Boykoff and Boykoff 2004. For an anatomy of the misuse of science to mislead the public see Oreskes and Conway 2010.

The scientific community and the IPCC in particular were caught off-guard by these responses, which seemed so out of proportion. In the Himalayan glaciers case the IPCC did not respond for a few days. The public-relations component of its organization is tiny, and navigating political waters such as these is not its strong suit. In the end, however, the Fifth Assessment Report (2014) in its breadth and findings and procedural thoroughness gained back lost ground. The Climategate scandal led to scientific bodies paying more attention to communicating with the public and engaging its trust (Maibach et al. 2012). Maintaining a process of communication and diversification in the global scientific community will be challenging but is essential for the legitimacy and influence of scientists and knowledge holders in GEP.

The Global Public and Individual Leaders

The global public – or, more broadly, global public opinion – is largely absent from the GEG stage, unless, perhaps, as a passive audience. This is to a large part because of the distancing of processes of global governance from popular participation. Decisions about how global governance is managed and who manages it are the prerogative of global policy elites. A frequent critique of international environmental cooperation is that it appears to have very little impact on people's everyday lives. Taking the argument one step further, many claim that we need a fundamental change in people's values and behaviors to achieve a more sustainable world – but identifying what those values are, and how that transition might be achieved, is a very difficult task (Leiserowitz et al. 2006).

There is, in fact, a substantial literature that examines public attitudes toward, and understanding of, various aspects of global environmental and sustainable development (Dunlap and York 2012; Leiserowitz et al. 2006). Many studies focus specifically on the factors shaping public opinion – and skepticism or uncertainty around – climate change (Engels et al. 2013; Scruggs and Benegal 2012; McCright and Dunlap 2011). Many analyze data that was gathered across a number of countries.[14] In their survey of existing polls, Leiserowitz et al. (2006) found growing public support for a cluster of values and behaviors around sustainable development, even placing environmental protection above economic prosperity in some cases.

---

[14] Organizations that carry out such international opinion polls include the Gallup organization, the Pew Research Center, and Eurobarometer.

It is, however, unclear how growing concern translates into political action: few respondents in one such poll had actually taken political action around the environment, though many agreed that they had changed or planned to change their individual behaviors (Leiserowitz et al. 2006, pp. 421–22). It is possible that these attitudes reflect a deeper normative shift, which, in combination with other actions, could lead to a transition toward a more sustainable global economy. It could also still be the case that a major global economic recession could reverse people's thinking. A constructivist theorist would argue for the former, while a realist would argue the latter. Either way, direct connections between GEG actions and institutions and global public opinion are weak, and a problem that may need to be addressed for global governance to be truly effective and legitimate.

Public opinion within different countries can sway representatives' actions, however. The 2007 election campaign in Australia hinged in part on the pledge of the then opposition leader, subsequently Prime Minister, Kevin Rudd, to ratify the Kyoto Protocol, a popular move (at that time) with the Australian electorate. Many NGOs and civil society organizations place great emphasis on popular support (through membership, or through changing public opinion, often through the media) and claim to represent the underrepresented in global politics. Specific communities too have become part of the global environmental narrative: the Inuit population, or the people of Tuvalu, for instance, or indigenous/tribal communities resisting dam construction or resource extraction. Some global governance processes – for example, the CBD and the FSC – reach out to specific communities – indigenous knowledge holders in the former case and forest-dwelling communities in the latter.

The role of particular individuals, especially charismatic leaders, in shaping the course of GEP and GEG gets short shrift in the theoretical literature. Notwithstanding this, there are people whose lives and works have left an indelible mark on how we think about environmental problems and about their political, social, and distributional effects. Rachel Carson's *Silent Spring* (1962) transformed thinking about chemicals' impacts on the environment. Al Gore and Stephen Schneider focused public and political attention on climate change. Sir Maurice Strong (first executive director of UNEP and strong advocate for global environmental action), Mustafa Tolba (executive director of UNEP during the critical years of negotiations, 1975–92), and Gro Harlem Brundtland (former Prime Minister of Norway and leader of the WHO, who chaired the global commission that defined sustainable development) all helped create global environmental institutions and norms.

Influential environmental activists include Rachel Carson (USA), Sunita Narain (India), Vandana Shiva (India), documentarian David Attenborough (UK), and the late Wangari Maathai (of Kenya's Green Belt Movement, and Nobel Peace Prize winner). Some celebrities such as Leonardo DiCaprio and Robert Redford have gone above and beyond their immediate star power for environmental causes. The Goldman Prize, established by the San Francisco-based Richard and Rhoda Goldman Foundation, has been awarded each year since 1990 to six grassroots activists from different regions of the world who have done outstanding environmental work. Its recipients have done, and continue to do, critical work. The prize not only highlights their achievements, it also brings attention that should serve to protect activist groups that face powerful opponents. This protection unfortunately is not always enough: in February 2016, Goldman Prize-winner and Honduran activist Berta Cáceres was murdered by unknown assailants. The NGO Global Witness reported that in 2014, 116 environmental activists were murdered worldwide (Global Witness 2015). Activists such as Ken Saro-Wiwa (leader of Nigeria's Movement for the Survival of the Ogoni People), Chico Mendes of the Brazilian rubber tapper movement, and Petra Kelly, of the German Green Party, helped forge environmental movements. As a reminder of the very real dangers and even personal challenges environmental activists face, all three died violently, well before their time.

Without the particular framing, communications, or negotiating abilities of these individuals and many others at specific times and in specific places, GEG would likely look very different. Yet, social science theory, in its quest for generalizations and widely applicable theories, has a hard time dealing with the "random variables" of individual psychology, skill, and leadership.[15] Detailed histories or narrative case studies of GEG are more likely to pay greater attention to specific individuals and their roles, and the definitive history of GEG in the twentieth and twenty-first centuries has yet to be written. Scholars in this field tend to heed lessons learned in the discipline of history: that "great men" are more often the products than the drivers of broader social, political, and economic forces. Still, the reasons why individuals enter into environmental activism and politics, how they reached the positions they did (and, in many cases, the price that they paid), and the impact they have had on GEG and institutions provide instructive reading, and important insights into the twists and turns of global politics.

---

[15] With the exception of international relations theory on the psychology of leaders and influential decision-makers' decision-making processes and influences. For an overview see McDermott 2004.

Next Steps

This chapter has introduced the different types of actors engaged in GEP. Each is deeply involved in global governance: in creating governance institutions, shaping their development, and assisting (or not) in their implementation. In Chapters 4 and 5 we examine the roles of states, IGOs, and non-state actors in state-led GEG: the formation and implementation of international environmental agreements and regimes. Chapter 6 extends this analysis to the critical institutions of the global economic order: the WTO, the World Bank, and the IMF. Chapter 7 examines how GEG institutions are emerging "beyond the state," in the form of certification schemes and other private sector–civil society initiatives. In Chapter 8 we examine the complex configurations of actors engaged in devising and implementing global market mechanisms. In all these cases we observe and assess the changing roles, alliances, and degrees of influence of state and non-state actors across different sites and modes of GEG.

Discussion Questions

- Governments' positions in international environmental negotiations are often affected by domestic political factors. Using examples from the country you live in or know best, what domestic political factors (and groups) shape its foreign environmental policy, and how?
- Why do Southern countries tend to have different positions from their Northern counterparts over global environmental politics? When is this "North–South" distinction useful, and when is it an oversimplification?
- Who counts as an "expert" with respect to the causes and impacts of climate change? Why? What factors would you look for to establish expert credibility?
- Choosing two or three large environmental NGOs, find their websites and examine their goals, activities, membership, and sources of financing. What factors do you think contribute to their success or lack of success? How do they compare? Repeat the exercise, this time with well-known IGOs.

SUGGESTIONS FOR FURTHER READING

Dauvergne, Peter, and Jane Lister. 2011. *Timber*. London: Polity Press: part of the Resources series from Polity Press, *Timber* examines the complex supply chains and corporate networks that make up the global timber sector, with implications for governance.

Ivanova, Maria. 2010. "UNEP in Global Environmental Governance: Design, Leadership, Location." *Global Environmental Politics* 10.1: 30–59: an account of the founding, and effectiveness, of the main global environmental agency by a leading expert.

Martello, Marybeth Long. 2001. "Local Knowledge: Global Change Science and the Arctic Citizen." *Science and Public Policy* 31.2: 107–15: covers both how Arctic communities are especially vulnerable to global environmental harm and how local knowledge is playing an increasingly important role in global policy deliberations.

Steinberg, Paul F., and Stacy VanDeveer, eds. 2012. *Comparative Environmental Politics: Theory, Practice and Prospects*. Cambridge, MA: MIT Press: an introduction to comparative environmental politics, actors and institutions.

4   State-Led Global Environmental Governance

The most significant way that the international community has sought to govern the global environment is through cooperation among nation-states, creating multilateral environmental agreements (MEAs) and international regimes. Some counts put the number of MEAs at more than 400, many of which have come into being since 1972.[1] This chapter introduces this state-led model of global environmental governance (GEG), its basic rules and principles, and the driving forces behind it. In so doing, we address a question that underlies the study of global environmental negotiations: Who, or what, shapes the negotiating outcomes we see in this system, and how?

Studying international environmental cooperation provides insights into exactly how nation-states succeed or fail to work together to address complex transboundary and global problems. International environmental negotiations have been fraught with difficulties, and conflicts of national interests, values, and priorities. These clashes have often led to compromises that have disappointed many. Environmental negotiations are, however, often remarkable for examples of political entrepreneurship, creative compromises, and last-minute solutions. They have attracted attention and participation from a wide range of actors, not only states and their representatives, but also scientists, activists, and business leaders. Despite frustrations and failures that have afflicted some recent negotiations, James Rosenau's description of global governance efforts being "marked less by despair over the past and present than by hope for the future" still resonates (Rosenau 1995, p. 21).

International relations theories of state-led bargaining and cooperation under anarchy have provided important insights into the complex factors that shape negotiation outcomes and regime formation. At the same time, the study of international environmental cooperation has brought to the

---

[1] Data from Ronald B. Mitchell, 2002–2014. *International Environmental Agreements Database Project (Version 2013.2)*. Available at http://iea.uoregon.edu/. Date accessed: June 19, 2015.

fore important dimensions of these processes that had hitherto been less visible in this field of study, but have gained in importance across most, if not all, types of global governance regime in recent years. In later sections of this chapter we examine the growing influence of the South in global governance, the role of scientific and technological expertise, and increasing demands for participation by non-state actors, notably civil society and corporate-sector actors. We finish by examining critiques of the state-led system of GEG, while noting the important changes that have happened or been instituted within this system. We begin with a description of the major building blocks of state-led GEG, and the formal (and informal) processes of international law and negotiation that lead to their creation.

International Regimes

Bargaining among nation-states toward the creation of binding agreements and international law has long been the preferred means for peacefully resolving international differences and achieving mutual goals. Chapter 1 related how the environment emerged onto the international policy agenda in the early 1970s as a collective action problem, whereby nation-states needed to cooperate in order to avoid or minimize transboundary and global impacts of pollution and resource depletion. Despite proposals to create a world environment organization that would operate outside the exigencies of "international politics as usual" (e.g. Kennan 1970), in 1972 at Stockholm the UN and its members chose (or perhaps had no other choice than) to adopt a governance framework based on intergovernmental cooperation. Building on existing international environmental laws and treaties, the model of issue-by-issue negotiation of MEAs by nation-states continues to dominate GEG, from the adoption of the International Whaling Convention (IWC) in 1946 to the newest international environmental agreement, the Minamata Mercury Convention, opened for signature in 2013 (see Table 4.1).

State-led GEG involves far more than states signing an agreement and meeting individual commitments. It involves developing and maintaining new rules, organizations, norms, and decision-making procedures that govern issue areas over time. We call these constellations of activities, actors, rules, and norms international regimes. Classically, regimes are "sets of implicit or explicit principles, norms, rules and decision-making procedures around which actors' expectations converge in a given area of international relations" (Krasner 1983, p. 2). They can also be understood as "rules of the game agreed upon by actors in the international arena (usually nation-states) and delimiting, for these actors, the range of

Table 4.1 *Major Multilateral Environmental Agreements*

Agreement and Major Associated Legal Instruments	Purpose	Date Adopted	Entry into Force (Date/ Requirements)	Agency in Charge	Parties (2008)	Parties (2016)
International Whaling Convention (IWC)	To provide for the proper conservation of whale stocks and thus make possible the orderly development of the whaling industry	1946	1946 (none)	International Whaling Commission	78	88
Convention on International Trade in Endangered Species (CITES)	To ensure that the international trade in wild plant and animal species does not threaten their survival	1973	1975 (90 days after 10th ratification or accession)	UNEP	172	182
International Convention for the Prevention of Pollution from Ships (MARPOL)	To prevent and minimize pollution from ships, both accidental and that from routine operations	1973	1983	International Maritime Organization	146	154
Protocol Related to MARPOL	*To strengthen regulations specific to oil tanker operations*	*1978*	*1983 (15 states with combined merchant fleet of at least 50% of gross tonnage of world shipping)*		*146*	*87*
UN Convention on the Law of the Seas (UNCLOS)	To establish a comprehensive legal order to promote peaceful use of the oceans and seas, equitable and efficient utilization of their resources; conservation of their living resources	1982	1994 (12 months after 60th ratification or accession)	United Nations	155	166

Table 4.1 (*cont.*)

Agreement and Major Associated Legal Instruments	Purpose	Date Adopted	Entry into Force (Date/ Requirements)	Agency in Charge	Parties (2008)	Parties (2016)
Agreement for the Implementation of UNCLOS related to the Conservation and Management of Straddling and Highly Migratory Fish Stocks		*1995*	*2001 (30 days after 30th ratification or accession)*		*67*	*83*
Vienna Convention on Substances that Deplete the Ozone Layer	To protect human health and the environment from the effects of stratospheric ozone	1985	1988 (90 days after 20th ratification or accession)	UNEP	191	197
Montreal Protocol	*To reduce and eventually eliminate emissions of man-made ozone-depleting substances*	*1987*	*1989 (January 1, 1989, if 11 parties had ratified the protocol)*		*191*	*197*
Basel Convention on the Control and Transboundary Movements of Hazardous Wastes and their Disposal	To ensure environmentally sound management of hazardous wastes by minimizing their generation, reducing their transboundary movement, and disposing of these wastes as close to their point of generation as possible	1989	1992 (90 days after 20th ratification or accession)	UNEP	170	183
Basel Ban Amendment (Decision III/1, COP 3)	*To ban the trade in hazardous wastes for disposal and recycling from OECD to non-OECD countries*	*1995*	*Not in force (75% of the parties accepting the amendment must ratify)*		*63*	*81*

Treaty	Objective	Adopted	Entered into force	Administering body		
UN Framework Convention on Climate Change (UNFCCC)	To stabilize (GHG) concentrations in the atmosphere at a level preventing dangerous human-caused interference with the climate system	1992	1994 (90 days after 50th ratification or accession)	United Nations	192	197
Kyoto Protocol	*To supplement the UNFCCC by establishing legally binding constraints on greenhouse gas emissions and encouraging economic and other incentives to reduce emissions*	*1997*	*2005 (90 days after at least 55 parties, including Annex 1 parties accounting for 55% of 1990 global carbon dioxide emissions)*	*UN Climate Secretariat*	*176*	*192*
Convention on Biological Diversity (CBD)	To conserve biodiversity and promote its sustainable use, and to encourage the equitable sharing of the benefits arising out of the use of genetic resources	1992	1993 (90 days after 30th ratification or accession)	UNEP	190	196
Cartagena Biosafety Protocol	*To promote biosafety by establishing practical rules and procedures for the safe transfer, handling and use of genetically modified organisms, especially as they move across national borders*	*2000*	*2004 (90 days after 50th ratification or accession)*		*143*	*170*
Nagoya Protocol on Access and Benefit Sharing	*To share the benefits arising from the utilization of genetic resources in a fair and equitable way, thereby contributing to the conservation of biological diversity and the sustainable use of its components.*	*2010*	*2014 (90 days after 50th ratification or accession)*		*n/a*	*78*

Table 4.1 (*cont.*)

Agreement and Major Associated Legal Instruments	Purpose	Date Adopted	Entry into Force (Date/ Requirements)	Agency in Charge	Parties (2008)	Parties (2016)
UN Convention to Combat Desertification (UNCCD)	To combat desertification in order to mitigate the effects of drought and ensure the long-term productivity of dry lands	1994	1996 (90 days after 50th ratification or accession)	UNEP	191	195
Stockholm Convention on Persistent Organic Pollutants (POPs)	To protect human health and the environment from POPs, by eliminating or reducing their release into the environment	2001	2004 (90 days after 50th ratification or accession)	United Nations	150	180
Minamata Convention on Mercury	To protect human health from production, use of and trade in mercury	2013	n/a (90 days after fiftieth ratification or accession)	UNEP	n/a	32

Sources: Treaty Websites

legitimate or admissible behavior in a specified context of activity" (Rittberger 1995, p. xii). Regimes are the basic building blocks of state-led GEG, and the establishment and maintenance of effective regimes are the goals of international environmental cooperation among nation-states. They are common across all areas of international politics, including international trade in goods and services, the control of nuclear proliferation, human rights protection, and the environment.

Most of the regimes examined in this chapter are anchored in a single negotiating process stemming from a single originating MEA. The climate regime is anchored by the 1992 UN Framework Convention on Climate Change (UNFCCC), the desertification regime by the 1994 UN Convention to Combat Desertification (UNCCD). It is not unusual, however, for a regime to encompass a number of different agreements. The biodiversity regime, for example, is often defined as including the 1992 Convention on Biological Diversity (CBD), the 1972 World Heritage Convention, the 1979 Convention on Migratory Species, the 1973 Convention on International Trade in Endangered Species (CITES), and others. A prominent exception is the forests regime: there is no global treaty governing the use of the world's forests, despite efforts to create one. However, the existence of a number of more informal governance institutions, such as the UN Intergovernmental Forum on Forests, along with numerous non-state governance initiatives suggests that there is a global forests regime, although it looks quite different from, and is less coherent than, mainstream treaty regimes (Gulbrandsen 2004; Humphreys 2013).

From an institutionalist perspective, the rules and practices embodied in an international regime reduce the transactions costs associated with international cooperation. They create a political arena in which as many states as possible can reach consensus on action to take over a specific issue, and deal, over time, with each other in a multilateral setting.[2] Reaching agreement over shared goals and the means through which to achieve them enables states to achieve mutual gains over time that would be impossible to attain in the absence of cooperation. Regimes, and the rules and practices embedded in them, also function to increase transparency (and thus reduce the chance of cheating, or free-riding, on the part of states). For example, most international environmental regimes contain mechanisms for national reporting and assessment. Some also contain formal sanction mechanisms for violators, although such sanctions have been used relatively rarely (see Chapter 5).

[2] Classic works on regimes and international cooperation include Rittberger 1995; Krasner 1983; and Baldwin 1993. On the general features of environmental agreements see Mitchell 2003.

From a constructivist perspective, the process of regime formation and strengthening over time helps create and spread shared norms of acceptable behavior among states, consensus over the significance and definition of a given problem, and knowledge about a given problem and its solutions (Bernstein 2013a; Conca 2006; Finnemore 1996). In turn, the practice of participating in regimes may come to change state preferences and identities themselves: the act of cooperation over time works to socialize states to a more cooperative international system. In the environmental context, the hope is that states come to accept international norms of environmental protection and sustainable development, as well as collective action. Often, an early act of many newly democratized (but often still unstable) governments is to sign on to environmental agreements, thus signaling their intent to be good global citizens.

Taking a cue from Realist and neo-Gramscian approaches, regimes are also forums for exercising power.[3] Intra-regime struggles over key guiding principles and decision-making procedures have real impacts not only in terms of defining and solving problems, but also in reaffirming or shifting the existing balance of power among key players. These arguments are particularly cogent from a Southern perspective. For example, the definition of biological diversity as sovereign property, as opposed to the "common heritage of humanity," in the CBD gave Southern countries important leverage in maintaining control over and the right to benefit from their own resources.

Environmental Treaties and International Law

This section introduces the basic components of the MEAs that anchor state-led GEG regimes. MEAs usually take the form of formal treaties.[4] Under international law, treaties are written documents concluded by state representatives or intergovernmental organizations (IGOs). They set out rights and obligations that are legally binding on signatory states, or parties, who must implement and enforce such law within their own jurisdictions (Birnie 1992, p. 53; see also Bodansky 2009; Birnie et al. 2009). By signing a treaty, a state is consenting to take on commitments to act in concert with other states; likewise, treaties obtain much of their legal force from the consent of member states (Bodansky 2013, p. 180). General ground rules for negotiating international treaties are laid

---

[3] See Jervis 1999; Levy and Newell 2002.

[4] In a generic sense, the term "agreement" refers to all international accords and legal instruments, including treaties. Specifically, it may refer to agreements that do not meet the formal standards of treaties. In this book "agreements" is used in the generic sense.

Box 4.1: Major Treaty Components

Preamble: As the treaty's introduction, it outlines the problem being addressed, and articulates how parties to the treaty have elected to frame that problem. It does not obligate states to particular courses of action, but can provide a normative framework for future actions.

Articles: Individual numbered paragraphs that make up the main body of the treaty text, containing the treaty's substantive elements, such as reporting requirements, emissions reduction targets and timetables, or funding and technology-transfer mechanisms. They establish the regime's organizational structure and procedural details, such as the number of ratifications needed for entry into force or dispute-settlement procedures.

Annexes and/or *Appendices*: These additions to the treaty text usually contain information (e.g. on different national obligations or the regulatory scope of the agreement) that is too lengthy or technical to include in the main body of the treaty. CITES (1973) has appendices that list plant and animal species that cannot be traded, and those that can be traded under limited circumstances. The 1997 Kyoto Protocol differentiates between (mostly developed) Annex I countries, which have obligations to reduce greenhouse gas (GHG) emissions, and (mostly developing) non-Annex I countries, which do not.

---

down in the 1969 and 1986 Vienna Conventions on the Law of Treaties (VCLT).

Many environmental treaties share a common structure, although they differ in terms of the institutions and procedures they set up, and the extent and nature of the commitments states undertake. Copies of most international environmental treaties are available online, either through the treaty's own website or through sites that collect and post instruments of international law; some are short (under ten pages), others far longer.[5] Box 4.1 briefly describes the major components of most treaties. It should be noted that all of these – from the preamble to the seemingly dull procedural details – are often hard-fought political compromises.

The commitments laid out in the treaty text in articles, annexes, and appendices make up what is called hard law, or the commitments and rules that are binding on members of international regimes (Birnie 1992). Hard law also includes measures for facilitating state compliance or

---

[5] See the UN Treaty Collection, a database of all international treaties deposited with the Secretary General's Office, and the above-cited International Environmental Agreements Database, developed by Professor Ronald Mitchell at the University of Oregon.

punishing non-compliance. By comparison, non-binding measures, norms, guidelines, and principles set out in a treaty text are referred to as soft law as they do not impose binding commitments on states (Bodansky 2013). They correspond to the norms and principles in the definition of a regime. Examples of soft law instruments or principles include the Precautionary Principle, which governs decision-making under conditions of uncertainty in a general sense, the Forest Principles, which came out of the 1992 Rio Summit in place of a forests convention, and the Principle of Prior Informed Consent, associated in particular with trade measures within the chemicals regimes.

Some legal scholars argue that it is more through soft than through hard law that international law has its greatest impacts, given how difficult it is for states to agree to – or enforce – sanctions and other disciplinary measures associated with hard law (Bodansky 2009, 2013). They argue that such principles are important in that they can lead to a gradual convergence in state behavior toward conforming to these guiding principles, and may even, over time, "harden" to become customary international law (Birnie 1992). The institutions and norms or rules of soft and hard law may also serve to reinforce each other (Skjaerseth et al. 2006).

Treaties establish the organizational entities that manage the regime. Environmental regimes are often housed within the UN Environment Programme (UNEP). Organizational components of a treaty regime include conferences of the parties, secretariats, subsidiary bodies such as technical or expert committees, and funding mechanisms. Conferences of the Parties (COPs), bodies that are unique to international environmental agreements (Bodansky 2013), bring signatory states to a given treaty together every one to five years.[6] COPs make the major policy decisions related to the regime, for example over amendments, and other future developments. Treaty secretariats, often based in Geneva, but also further afield, supervise the implementation of the agreement and ongoing negotiation processes, gathering, analyzing, and distributing information, maintaining convention records, and supporting the COPs (Jinnah 2010; Biermann and Siebenhüner 2009). When necessary, they coordinate with other international regimes, and manage any financial mechanism associated with the regime. Recently, secretariats have taken on a stronger and more assertive role with respect to implementing GEG (Jinnah 2014; see Chapter 5).

---

[6] The term "meeting of the parties" (MOP) refers to parties that belong to a sub-grouping of the regime. It is primarily for the Kyoto Protocol meetings, which happen at the same time as the UNFCCC COPs.

Negotiating Treaty-Based Regimes: Process and Politics

The construction of international environmental treaty regimes rests on a complex process of bargaining and negotiation among nation-states. Several factors complicate this process. States have different, frequently conflicting interests within a particular issue area. They may not always trust their negotiating partners to follow through on an agreement, or they may be unwilling to make concessions in cases where a rival state might do better than they do. Government representatives are concerned about the economic and political costs of signing on to any international agreement, especially one that might be unpopular with powerful domestic constituencies. Multiply all these factors by the number of states involved in negotiations, and it may seem surprising that any cooperative agreements are agreed upon in the first place. Global environmental problems create additional complications, as they are often characterized by a good deal of uncertainty over causes and impacts, long-time horizons, or a need to constrain powerful corporate actors.

For these reasons, international environmental cooperation is an ongoing process. Even after an agreement is negotiated and signed, regimes continue to evolve over time. In the initial phases, negotiators define a global environmental issue, establishing its basic parameters and the rationale for international action. Government representatives then meet to negotiate a treaty or other legal agreement, thereafter entering ongoing implementation and strengthening: putting the existing agreement into practice, and strengthening or modifying its initial obligations. Although some negotiating processes have faltered, to date no environmental treaty regime, once established, has ever been terminated.

Major Treaties, Regimes, and Regime Processes

Environmental agreements are usually negotiated in stages on an issue-by-issue basis. A common negotiating process for environmental treaties is the convention–protocol method (Susskind 1994, pp. 30–7). A framework convention sets out the nature, scope, and cause of the problem, directions for future negotiations, and minor obligations on states, such as reporting requirements. They establish regime-related organizations and committees. Framework conventions have been described as "soft law in hard law form," given that they rarely lay specific obligations on states (Hunter et al. 2002, p. 349) but remain binding. In subsequent stages of negotiation, member states negotiate protocols or amendments, both part of the same regime, setting up concrete goals and targets that are binding on signatory states. Protocols are nested within broader conventions, but are separate legal instruments that require independent ratification by signatory states. An umbrella convention brings together separate treaties under one organizational structure or creates an overarching institution under which sub-agreements can be negotiated.[7]

Table 4.1 lists the major MEAs, starting with the IWC, adopted in 1946, up to the newest environmental MEA: the Minamata Convention on Mercury, adopted in 2013, along with their associated protocols and/ or amendments. In addition to the title, purpose, and managing agency of each agreement, the table shows dates of adoption and entry into force, as well as the requirements for entry into force, and the number of parties in 2008 (when this table was first compiled) and 2016.

Table 4.1 clearly shows the Convention–Protocol negotiating model. For example, the Montreal Protocol on Substances that Deplete the Ozone Layer followed the 1985 Vienna Convention for the Protection of the Ozone Layer in 1987. The Vienna Convention laid out the general problem of ozone-layer depletion, in particular that chlorofluorocarbon (CFC) emissions were damaging the stratospheric ozone layer and must be reduced. The Montreal Protocol added specific targets for reducing the use and production of CFCs and other ozone-depleting substances worldwide. The agreement allowed additional time for developing countries to meet their goals and established a fund to help them meet commitments.

The climate change regime followed a similar pattern: while the 1992 UNFCCC does not contain specific targets or timetables for GHG reduction, the 1997 Kyoto Protocol imposed differential obligations on states to reach particular targets for GHG emissions. Developed countries needed to reduce their GHG emissions by an average of 5.2 percent below 1990 levels by 2012, while developing countries had no emissions reductions requirements. The 1992 CBD has two associated protocols: the 2000 Cartagena Protocol on Biosafety, which addresses trade in genetically modified organisms, and the 2010 Nagoya Protocol on Access and Benefit Sharing, neither of which is an obvious progression from the framework convention but reflects the concerns of member states at those times.

The Basel Convention and MARPOL have both been amended – the latter many times – by signatories. The 1990 London Amendments to the Montreal Protocol greatly strengthened the ozone regime, setting firm dates and a fast timetable for ending the production of CFCs altogether. Amendments have different entry into force requirements that can make a big difference in outcomes. Usually they must be ratified by a certain

---

[7] The Convention on Migratory Species (1979) is an example of an umbrella convention.

number of states, which takes time and may lead to more compromise (see below). In the case of the Montreal Protocol, however, amendments can be accepted by a majority vote at the meeting. This very easy amendment process has allowed for far stronger and faster regime development but has rarely, if ever, been replicated (Young 2010).

From PrepCom to Implementation

While there is no prescribed process for initiating treaty negotiations, various actors, including individual states, NGOs, and the UN have played this role (Hunter et al. 2002, p. 293). Once a call for international action has been issued, state representatives ("parties" to the negotiation) convene – often over a lengthy time frame – to discuss the content of the treaty. These discussions take place between government officials (usually bureaucrats), experts, and other interested or affected actors, including scientific organizations, industry and society representatives, via the convening of a preparatory committee, or PrepCom. PrepComs are where a lot of the basic negotiating work is done, including the creation of a draft agreement (Chasek 2001). They are where alliances are made and deals brokered. For example, in the run-up to the 1992 Rio Summit, PrepCom negotiations for the forests and biodiversity conventions led to significant changes in the negotiating texts and were, in the case of forests, where negotiations broke down.

Once agreement is reached on the draft text, high-level government representatives convene over a one-to-two-week period to negotiate the final text of the agreement. At this stage the process is highly vulnerable to last-minute disputes over exact language. Treaty drafts, even at this late stage, are usually a mess of bracketed text – text that has been disputed by one party or another, which must be agreed upon before moving forward.[8] Often, time constraints imposed by the convening organization (and the willingness of the official running the meeting to keep delegates

---

[8] Treaty text that is disputed appears in drafts in brackets. Even at a late stage, a treaty clause may look like this example taken from negotiations held in May 2009 in the lead-up to the December Copenhagen conference of the parties to the UNFCCC:

[Paragraph] 14. To this end, {developed country Parties} {Parties included in Annex I to the Convention (Annex I Parties)} {developed country Parties included in Annex II to the Convention (Annex II Parties)}, as a group, {shall} {should} reduce their GHG emissions: (a) {By at least 25–40} {By 25–40} {By more than 25–40} {In the order of 30} {By at least 40} {by 45} {by at least 45} per cent from 1990 levels by 2020, {with further reductions to be achieved through policies and measures that promote sustainable lifestyles}; (b) {And {by more than 95} {in the range of 75–85} percent by 2050} (see Andrew Revkin, "Bracket Time for Climate {Treaty} {Pact}," *The New York Times* DotEarth Blog, May 20 2009).

in the negotiating chamber till all hours) have proven decisive in reaching last-minute compromises.[9] When participants agree upon – adopt – a final text, the treaty is opened for signature by nation-states.

Next, signatory states must ratify agreements, including conventions, protocols, and sometimes amendments, by enacting them into domestic law. While sometimes this can be done by central government directive, often it entails formal approval by the national legislature, which can be time-consuming and may even fail. For example, in the USA treaties can only be ratified if they are voted for by two-thirds of the Senate (the Upper House of Congress), which usually necessitates bipartisan agreement. Senate opposition to the CBD and the Kyoto Protocol meant that neither treaty was ever submitted for ratification, making the US withdrawal from Kyoto in 2001 more of a dramatic gesture than a policy choice. In parliamentary democracies, such as the UK or Australia, ratification itself is an executive decision (by the cabinet and/or Prime Minister), although treaties are put before parliament for a number of weeks or days for comment in advance.

In some cases, states accept or approve a treaty without needing to go through formal ratification processes. For example, in late 2013 the USA became the first party to the Minamata Mercury Convention. The Obama Administration was able to do this because implementing the Convention would require no change in existing US domestic laws, therefore not requiring ratification by the Senate.

An MEA enters into force once it has been ratified or accepted by an agreed-upon number of states, both signatories of the original treaty and those states who have joined subsequently through accession. All conventions, protocols, and amendments associated with the treaty process are subject to individual ratification before they enter into force. States may also leave a treaty they have ratified without facing formal punishment. The number of ratifications or accessions required for a treaty to go into force varies, and sometimes the bar can be set extremely high. Table 4.1 shows entry-into-force requirements and times between treaty adoption and when it entered into force. For example, the MARPOL Convention of 1973/78 did not enter into force until 1983, as it required ratification by states representing more than half of the world's merchant shipping, by weight. While the UNFCCC took only two years to enter into force, the Kyoto Protocol took nearly nine years. Even when ratification thresholds are more straightforward, this process can take a comparatively long time, as with the Cartagena Protocol of the CBD, or the Basel Ban amendment,

---

[9] See Benedick 2007 for a first-hand account of tactics used to reach agreement at the final Montreal Protocol negotiations.

often blocked by intense lobbying by groups or countries opposed to the measure.

Some regimes may negotiate second, third, or fourth protocols, or amend core agreements several times. As parties to the UNFCCC moved toward final negotiations in 2015 to replace the Kyoto Protocol, they produced the 2007 Bali Road Map, the 2009 Copenhagen Accord, the 2011 Durban Platform and the 2013 Warsaw Mechanism, all of which inched them toward an agreement that would broaden obligations and allow states to set their own goals.

Regime membership usually rises over time, as Table 4.1 shows. New states, such as East Timor and South Sudan, join the international system. New members may be recruited for political reasons. The IWC, for instance, can attribute its sharp rise in membership (including several notably landlocked states such as the Czech Republic) to a competition between the EU (anti-whaling) and Japan (pro-whaling) to recruit states that would vote for them.[10] In other cases, the change in numbers reflects the time some countries take to ratify agreements, or changes in political priorities on the part of governments.

After a treaty has entered into force (or earlier if states are fully committed or anticipate that entry into force will occur), member states begin to implement the terms of the agreement. Such actions include passing new laws, transferring aid or technology to developing countries, or otherwise attempting to meet the treaty goals through changing actor behavior.

All of these features make up the narrative of each individual global environmental governance regime. The next section identifies and discusses the factors that contribute to the differences across these narratives.

Explaining the Outcomes of State-Led Global Environmental Negotiations

The course and outcomes of international negotiations are to a large part driven by the complex interplay of opposing national interests. They are also driven by the need to solve often highly complex – "wicked" – problems (Miles et al. 2002), characterized by long time horizons and considerable uncertainty (Young 1994). Environmental negotiations are, as Thomas Schelling (1960), one of the most influential theorists of bargaining, would note, characterized by the sorts of tactics and strategies

---

[10] On the other hand, Greece left the IWC in 2013, most likely because it could not pay its membership dues (applied because the IWC is independent of the UN).

that matter in any form of negotiation, from international conference rooms to corporate boardrooms to dorm rooms and living rooms. Brinksmanship, provision of side-payments, and issue-linkage are all tactics employed by negotiators seeking an outcome in their favor. In the discussion that follows we examine how different actor groups seek to influence regime outcomes, focusing primarily on the positive: the factors that enable agreements to transcend the lowest common denominator effect (Susskind 1994). This effect happens when regimes, in the absence of mediating factors, wind up conforming to the preferences of the most reluctant participants, in particular those who wield veto power over outcomes.

In the rare cases where national interests coincide, international negotiations are about coordinating goals that are already shared or agreed upon. Crises – environmental or otherwise – may be key in focusing negotiators' minds. In most cases, however, interests clash, and the bargaining process often results in winners and losers. Sometimes national differences are wholly intractable, and negotiations fail, as in the case of the global forests convention, when differences around what forests to regulate, and how to respect sovereign control over forest resources, led to the collapse of multilateral talks in the run-up to the Rio Earth Summit (Humphreys 2013). Other negotiating processes have teetered on the edge of failure, such as the climate or biodiversity conventions (Hoffmann 2013; Rosendal 2015). Still others – over ozone-layer depletion or long-range transboundary air pollution (LRTAP) – have proceeded relatively smoothly over time, even becoming progressively stronger (Young 2010). The ozone regime is considered the prime example of successful international environmental negotiations.

Influence is a complicated factor to assess, and goes beyond the exercise of leadership in negotiations.[11] For any given group, simply being present with an agenda at international negotiations does not necessarily translate into outcomes. The situation is complicated by potentially competing claims actors make about their own or each other's influence. However, the arguments presented in this chapter challenge the conventional wisdom that only the powerful actors – Northern states or corporate actors – wield influence, addressing also the roles small or poorer states, NGOs, and scientific groups play in this context.

---

[11] Betsill and Corell (2001, 2008) developed a methodological framework to assess NGO influence across the cases they examine using triangulation techniques, namely, applying several data-gathering approaches including interviews, participant-observation and primary and secondary documents to see what collective picture emerges of NGO goals and end effects. See also C. Downie 2014; Lund 2013, Witter et al. 2015.

1. Nation-States

If international environmental diplomacy is at its heart about reconciling different national interests, it makes sense to start with how states, their interests, and their interactions shape negotiating outcomes. Many factors influence states' negotiating interests, including domestic and international pressures, perceptions of vulnerability, economic incentives, and other factors (Downie 2014; Falkner 2013). How states interact, and how their interests change (or can be induced to change) over time, is a primary narrative of international environmental diplomacy.

a.   Domestic Influences on Foreign Environmental Policy Domestic political factors have shaped national interests over time and affected the course of international environmental negotiations in many ways. Such factors include perceptions of national vulnerability (small island states or the major oil-producing countries in climate negotiations), and structures and types of government (such as democracies versus non-democracies).[12]

For example, domestic lobbying groups push their governments to adopt particular positions at international negotiations. The choice to lobby at home or at the international level may depend on the country and its channels of access for environmental organizations and/or industry organizations in domestic politics. Climate NGOs in the US are very active, and arguably quite successful in lobbying their government representatives. They proved to be particularly influential during the 1990s, when the leading environmental NGOs had close ties to the Administration (Downie 2014). The EU deliberately fosters relationships with and input from non-state actors, including environmental groups (Selin and VanDeveer 2015, p. 61). In countries with weaker or less accessible governments and government delegations it may make more sense to work transnationally, although there are few studies that examine this question directly.

Opposition in the USA from its powerful fossil-fuel lobby damaged efforts to get on board with the climate regime. The petroleum industry not only targeted government officials but funded institutes and think-tanks

---

[12] For studies of the role of domestic politics in international environmental politics (IEP) see Schreurs and Economy 1997; Sprinz and Vaahtoranta 1994; DeSombre 2015. On how different government types participate in environmental negotiations see Recchia 2002; Elsig et al. 2011; Carbonell and Allison 2015. These studies examine participation in environmental negotiations by various government types, including democratic, authoritarian, and newly democratized regimes.

designed to perpetuate denialist "science."[13] Alliances between environmental and industry organizations can also be powerful. So-called
Baptist–Bootlegger coalitions were important in pushing the USA to take
international action on issues as diverse as endangered-species protection
and ozone-layer depletion (DeSombre 2000).[14]

Government representatives use domestic factors strategically at the
negotiating table. Because treaties always need to be ratified, negotiators
often pay particular attention to the interests and preferences of the
ratifying body, especially of elected legislatures, which may have a very
different set of priorities compared to national leadership, or government
officials. National representatives can use the preferences of their legislature as a reason not to support strong measures (the "two-level games"
strategy explored by Putnam 1988). Sometimes they have to bring home
an agreement that will never be ratified by the existing Congress or
Parliament. Either way, not only can the preferences of elected officials
affect the outcome of international negotiations, they can also help determine whether a country continues to actively participate in any given
regime.

b.   Coalitions, Leaders, and Laggards   Moving to state interactions at
the international level, the leader–laggard approach to understanding
how state interests shape regime outcomes examines how individual
states can push an agreement toward a better outcome or pull it back.
The USA and the EU are often cited in this context (Busby and Ochs
2005; Skjaerseth et al. 2013). The EU, for example, has tended to push
for stronger agreements over climate change, biosafety, and in other
areas, while the USA pushed back, to the point of withdrawing from the
Kyoto Protocol in 2001. By contrast, the USA took the lead role in
negotiating strong national commitments in the ozone regime while
Europe, then the European Community, opposed binding international
controls on CFC use and production (Kauffman 1997). In other
instances the EU has failed to achieve its goals, as in 2009 at the
Copenhagen COP, when it failed to achieve international commitment
to a new binding agreement. This failure has been ascribed variously to
a loss of intra-EU cohesion following the incorporation of states such as

[13] There is, however, some evidence they have recently stopped doing this, replaced instead
by private foundation and individual funding. Actual transactions are, however, very hard
to trace (Brulle 2014).

[14] The term "Baptist–Bootlegger coalition" comes out of the Prohibitionist era in the USA
in the 1920s. Although opposed to each other in so many ways, the temperance movement (the Baptists) and the organizations running the black market in alcohol (the
Bootleggers) both had a direct interest in maintaining Prohibition, hence the notion of
such coalitions.

Poland that do not support strong goals (Parker and Karlsson 2010), to setting overambitious goals (Bäckstrand and Elgström 2013), or simply to being outweighed as the USA and BASIC countries (Brazil, South Africa, India, and China) worked together to create a different deal.

States and their representatives also shape environmental negotiations by forming alliances or coalitions (Wagner et al. 2012; Chasek et al. 2014). Veto coalitions of states have often derailed or watered down treaty provisions. The pro-whaling states (Japan, Iceland, and Norway) have consistently fought against a total moratorium on global whaling, while the Miami Group of GMO (genetically modified organism)-exporting states (the USA, Canada, Argentina, and others) attempted to weaken the 2000 Cartagena Biosafety Protocol. On the other hand, many countries have helped to strengthen treaty regimes. Scandinavian countries helped establish a demanding form of "tote-board diplomacy" around acid rain (Levy 1993). Coalitions that represent the most vulnerable nations, such as the Alliance of Small Island States (AOSIS), may exercise strong moral leadership (Corneloup and Mol 2014). As coalitions shift, so can regime outcomes, as we see below with the emergence of the BASIC coalition in climate negotiations, which at Durban in 2011 helped set the stage for a new climate agreement reached in Paris in 2015.

c.   North–South Politics: From G77 to BASIC   The global South has powerfully influenced the shape and progress of state-led global environmental negotiations and of particular international environmental regimes within that system. In negotiations over the CBD, Southern country representatives effectively reframed the entire issue. While initial drafts of the Convention sought to define biodiversity as a "global commons" issue, Southern countries, concerned over the extent to which this designation might remove sovereign control over valuable resources, fought successfully to maintain sovereign jurisdiction over biodiversity. The 1994 UNCCD was proposed, negotiated by, and chiefly affects the world's poorest countries (Najam 2004), while Southern opposition – notably from Malaysia – helped derail international forest convention negotiations in the early 1990s (Agarwal et al. 1999). The 1995 Basel Ban Amendment would likely not have been proposed had it not been for the 1991 Bamako Convention and other regional agreements signed by countries in Africa and Central America that banned any waste imports under any circumstances. At the same time, developing country governments – India among them – are among the leading opponents of the ban, arguing that the Convention unfairly limits their right to import wastes for recycling in order to obtain valuable metals and other components.

Another area in which the South has wielded significant influence is through the incorporation of the principle of Common but Differentiated Responsibility into major MEAs (Najam 2015). In practice, this means the incorporation of different targets and obligations, for less developed countries, and the creation of mechanisms for the transfer of aid and technology for poorer countries, including the creation of the Global Environment Facility, or GEF (see Chapter 5). Under the 1987 Montreal Protocol, developing countries, listed under Article V, obtained a ten-year extension on the deadline for phasing out the production of CFCs, and pushed for and obtained a multilateral fund to aid adoption of less harmful substitutes. The principle of differential obligations under the 1997 Kyoto Protocol was far more contentious. The USA and its allies in this process (Australia, Japan, and Canada) argued that as countries such as Brazil, China, and India were likely to surpass them in global GHG emissions, they should not be given major concessions. Nonetheless, ultimately the Protocol called only for emissions-reduction commitments from industrialized countries, listed in Annex 1.

Obstacles remain to Southern participation at global environmental meetings, limiting their potential influence (Chasek 2001). The sheer number of international environmental meetings, conferences, working groups, and so on has put a strain on understaffed and underfunded Southern bureaucracies, as the title of Joyeeta Gupta's monograph *"On Behalf of my Delegation … ": A Survival Guide for Developing Country Negotiators* suggests (J. Gupta 2000). This lack of capacity particularly applies to the very poor and marginalized countries. Chad's delegation to Copenhagen numbered 10 individuals, while the USA sent a delegation of close to 200 people, which turned out to be well behind Brazil's tally, roughly 720 (a number that apparently raised eyebrows at the time). Uzbekistan and Vanuatu each sent 2 official delegates.[15]

As we saw in Chapter 3, North–South politics has, in recent years, been reshaped by greater differentiation among members of the Group of 77 Developing Countries (G77), with new coalitions, notably the BASIC group, making their mark on global climate politics. BASIC emerged as a negotiating coalition during UNFCCC COPs in Bali (2007) and Copenhagen (2009). It was particularly influential in creating the 2011 Durban Platform, which laid out basic structures for a formal replacement agreement for the Kyoto Protocol. As of December 2014, each BASIC country had pledged to significantly reduce GHG emissions by 2020, with Brazil's commitment the strongest and China's the weakest. Analysts differ

---

[15] The list of official delegates to UNFCCC COP 15 at Copenhagen can be found at http://unfccc.int/resource/docs/2009/cop15/eng/misc01p01.pdf.

on the likelihood of BASIC remaining a strong coalition (see Qi 2011 and Hochstetler 2012 for different opinions). The politics of identity – how each BASIC country sees its own changing identity in the world versus BASIC's identity as a group – are likely to be determinative as we move forward (Hochstetler and Milkoreit 2014).

Nonetheless, climate politics have transcended a binary North–South division, a shift that has significant implications for the climate regime as it moves forward. This reshaping of traditional political divides is making itself felt in other regimes – hazardous waste trading for one – but none as clearly as climate change. Coalitions remain relatively stable in arenas where North–South differences are less disputed, such as the chemicals or ozone regimes.

2.   The UN and UNEP: Architects and Entrepreneurs

The UN and, within it, UNEP shape the outcomes of environmental negotiations in many ways. Even though their roles are delegated to them by their member states, they still have the space to exercise significant leadership and influence (O'Neill 2015). First, they provide the forum and the negotiating rules, outlined earlier in this chapter, which create the institutional context for international cooperation. This has the effect of reducing transactions costs associated with regime participation over time (Haas et al. 1993). Earlier sections of this chapter gave specific examples of how IGOs such as UNEP created institutions to foster stronger regime outcomes, from specific voting rules, such as the Montreal Protocol amendment rule and including funding mechanisms from the Protocol's fund, to the GEF. They enable formal and informal participation by non-state actors in negotiating processes (Raustiala 2012), although as negotiations reflect higher stakes the less inclusive they become: the restriction on the number of observers accredited NGOs could bring to the Paris UNFCCC COP in 2015 reflects this shift in climate politics.

Second, individual leaders within the UN system have exercised effective charismatic or entrepreneurial leadership. Often-cited examples include Mustafa Tolba, who chaired the Montreal Protocol negotiations (Benedick 1987) or Tommy Koh, who chaired UN Law of the Sea negotiations in the late 1970s (Skodvin and Andresen 2006). Successful UNEP leaders, from Maurice Strong, UNEP's first director, to Achim Steiner, director from 2006 to 2016, have also been instrumental in setting agendas and maintaining regime momentum. The UNFCCC operates beyond the UNEP framework, possible in part because Tolba, at that time UNEP director, had been too successful in pushing other negotiations further along, worrying the more reluctant states. Its chairs, such as Yvo de Boer (2006–2010) and Christiana Figueres (2010–2016), are powerful individuals in their own right, navigating increasingly complex political interests and contexts to keep negotiations afloat and moving forward (Kolbert 2015).

Third, secretariats are the primary managerial actors in an increasingly crowded governance landscape. They shape regime development in important ways, even with more responsibilities and depleted budgets (Jinnah 2012a; Biermann and Siebenhüner 2009). They frame particular issue areas, set agendas for discussion, assist developing-country actors, and help bring new countries on board as regimes evolve over time. They also manage and run negotiations: how well the chair and the secretariat work together can have a major impact on the outcome of a particular negotiating session (Depledge 2007).

Over the past forty plus years, the UN, UNEP, and associated agencies have worked hard to establish a normative framework to underpin and guide a piecemeal system of GEG. Likewise, the Millennium Development Goals (2000) and the Sustainable Development Goals (2015) set broad agendas and targets for the global community to meet over the next decades. The UN's four "earth summits" – Stockholm 1972, Rio 1992, Johannesburg 2002, and Rio+20 2012 – were designed to initiate new eras of global governance for the environment and sustainability. In 1992, in addition to the biodiversity and climate conventions, governments also agreed to Agenda 21, an ambitious global action plan that remains a significant document in sustainability governance today. The 2002 Johannesburg Summit saw no such grand achievements, but rather smaller-scale initiatives and calls for broader participation from civil-society and private-sector actors (Von Frantzius 2004). Rio+20, despite being widely seen as a failure, reintroduced big but controversial ideas and goals, including the Green Economy, one that, as defined by UNEP, would meet social needs, while lowering environmental risks and creating a low-carbon but prosperous global economy (see also Chapter 6). It is unclear, however, what the implications are for traditional state-led GEG. The main documents coming out of Rio+20 recognize the role of other actors, particularly global economic actors, in shaping a more diffuse system of global governance in the future. We return to this theme in later chapters.

3.   Non-State Actors: Civil Society and Corporate Sectors

The number of non-state actors seeking to participate in international policy-making has increased exponentially since the 1972 Stockholm Conference. Focusing on the environmental NGO and corporate sectors, this section examines their role in and influence on the negotiation of environmental treaty regimes. Environmental NGOs have probably gained the greatest advantage from the relatively open nature of international environmental negotiations, where they have found a better venue than their home governments to express opinions and communicate with each other. Corporate interest groups were slower to engage directly at the international level. Both sectors have had to navigate the complexities of achieving formal observer status. Nonetheless, both groups have had opportunities to exercise moral, entrepreneurial, and (primarily in the case of the corporate sector) material leadership.

a.   Channels of Access to the International Policy Process   NGOs and corporate-sector actors utilize several channels of access to the international policy process, both domestic and transnational or international (Downie 2014). First, as we saw earlier, they lobby their government representatives to take a particular position at the negotiating table. Second, they attend and participate in international negotiating sessions, from the early PrepComs to the latest COPs. In many ways they seek to shape the terms of the debate, frame issues, open avenues of participation, and help direct policy responses.

Despite the legal primacy of nation-states, the structures and precepts of international law have created channels of access that non-state actors can use to target international negotiations (Raustiala 2012). The codification of international law through the creation of treaties and other written records and documents, starting in the 1920s, has given non-state actors the information they needed to engage with the proceedings. Second, the establishment of formal negotiation processes with their pre-arranged COPs, PrepComs, and so on provided meeting dates and venues, along with published agendas, working documents, and other materials to use to prepare a platform.

The UN has a process – which it controls – whereby NGOs, including business international non-governmental organizations (BINGOs), can apply to be accredited as official observers at international meetings.[16] Observer status gives registered NGOs access to the building in which negotiations are taking place, and the ability to sit in on most – but not all – deliberations. The UN has currently accredited more than 3,000 NGOs with observer status, with more accredited to different treaty

---

[16] To view a list of NGOs represented in the ongoing climate-change negotiations, see http://maindb.unfccc.int/public/ngo.pl. Under this system, individual firms cannot represent themselves at negotiations. Instead, they are represented by business associations (BINGOs), which advocate for a collective industry stance.

processes (Raustiala 2012). Particular treaties accord non-state actors explicit recognition: both CITES and the Convention on Migratory Species include (expert or issue-based) groups in their treaty texts. Non-state actors also sit on technical working groups (TWGs) and expert panels, submit policy briefs directly to UNEP or other negotiations – and sometimes serve on national delegations.

Finally, non-state actors of all types are present and active outside the actual negotiating halls. Side events, forums, protests, performances, and art installations designed to inform and attract the attention of delegates and the wider public provoke discussion and occasionally confrontation. All are hallmarks of non-state efforts to shape the course of international environmental diplomacy.

b.   *NGO Influence on International Negotiations*   First, environmental NGOs have without doubt brought environmental problems to the attention of the international community. NGOs such as Greenpeace used protest actions, political persuasion, and tactics of "witnessing" to highlight problems such as whaling and the hazardous waste trade (Wapner 1996). The International Union for the Conservation of Nature (IUCN) was instrumental in mobilizing international concern over biodiversity, even composing the first draft of the CBD. The influence they wield at early stages of the policy process is significant, and enhanced by their ability to be early, and more nimble, entrants into issue area politics (Lund 2013; Pulver 2002).

Second, by providing information and ideas to negotiators, NGOs have eased the course of some international negotiations. For example, environmental-health NGOs helped highlight the impacts of mercury on human health and the environment and pushed for controls on mercury throughout Minamata Convention negotiations. They lobby delegates to take particular positions, circulate, and propose draft treaty language (which, according to anecdotal evidence, may find its way into the final text). Where they can, they engage directly with delegates in the corridors, outside the buildings, and at formal and informal events.

Third, NGOs focus on the process of international environmental negotiations, often seeking to make them more transparent and inclusive. They produce daily – and even hourly – reports of meeting activities, which are quickly and widely disseminated via conventional and social media. NGOs also organize and participate in side events throughout the meeting. Side events are officially sanctioned panels, posters, performances, and other events that bring together participants from diverse states, IGOs, and other organizations to highlight and discuss specific topics relevant to those negotiations. The Climate Action Network

(CAN) is known for its popular "Fossil of the Day" Award, given to the country that is most obstructive on any given day of climate negotiations. Usually the award is accepted – with much fanfare – by NGO representatives from that country, but occasionally the delegates themselves appear. Big winners include Canada (winner of a "lifetime underachievement award" in 2013), Japan, and Australia. NGOs and advocacy networks may also seek to influence regime structures in order to open up participation and access rights for marginalized actors, although studies note limited degrees of success (Ciplet 2014).

NGO actions inside the conference halls are matched by equally committed but usually louder activity outside. At the UNFCCC COP in The Hague in 2000, protestors surrounded the conference hall with flood barriers. Organizations have marched, unfurled banners, staged "drown-ins," donned gas masks, dressed up as penguins, and installed highly creative art installations. Protests at COPs have had far less tendency toward violence or property damage than those at economic summits. Nonetheless, the size and frequency of protests outside the Bella Center at Copenhagen in 2009 prompted Danish authorities to remove most accredited NGO representatives from the negotiating halls where the official meetings were being held (Fisher 2010). The influence that the choice of protest tactics has on negotiation outcomes is debated (O'Neill 2004). Protestors do not necessarily influence immediate policy choices, but they may have indirect impacts on wider audiences and on wider problem-framings. For example, the concept of climate justice came out of protest movement action as a spillover of anti-globalization rhetoric. Protests can also cause backlash effects, including higher levels of policing and the continued exclusion of NGOs from convention halls (O'Neill 2004; Fisher 2010).

NGOs continue to face significant challenges in engaging in international environmental negotiations that diminish their potential influence, even as they become more important in the implementation of governance regimes (see Chapter 5). Many environmental NGOs have few resources – in terms of money and personnel – to meet all the commitments they would like to. This is particularly true of NGOs from Southern countries. Southern NGO representation increased at Johannesburg (La Viña et al. 2003), particularly as it attracted a wider spectrum of interests, including farmers and landless and indigenous movements, but remains problematic at most international meetings. Insider–outsider conflicts between professionalized and more radicalized NGOs, as happened at Copenhagen in 2009, can distract organizations from the main task and undermine their claim to represent a broader civil society. Finally, NGOs can be least effective when facing strong corporate opposition, which, as we shall see in the following section, can be significant but surmountable.

c.   *Corporate Influence on International Environmental Negotiations*
Corporate actors have important incentives to influence the outcomes of international environmental negotiations. Environmental agreements can be "market closing," cutting off economic opportunities via, for example, restricting trade in wastes, CFCs, or endangered species (Levy and Prakash 2003). MEAs also generate economic opportunities, which firms are anxious to realize. Despite these incentives, corporate actors were relative latecomers in the global environmental arena. They saw GEG at first as weak, not a threat, and far less important than other negotiating forums, such as the World Trade Organization (WTO) (Sell 1998). It took the signing of the Montreal Protocol in 1987, which had a powerful impact on the operations of a range of industries, to wake industry up to the potential of GEG as both a risk and an opportunity.

Just as with NGOs, industry representation at the global level is diverse (Clapp and Meckling 2013). As detailed in Chapter 3, most of the largest BINGOs, such as the World Business Council for Sustainable Development (WBCSD) and the International Chamber of Commerce (ICC), engage constructively with global environment and development politics. They engage in many of the same activities that environmental NGOs do, including lobbying delegates, providing information and other inputs, and participating in side events. Their participation in GEG has generated important innovations, including the development and implementation of market mechanisms (Meckling 2011). Famously, the decision by key US chemical producers, notably DuPont, to come out in favor of international controls on CFC production is seen by many as instrumental in the success of the Montreal Protocol (Parson 2003; Kauffman 1997).

It practically goes without saying that corporations occupy a "privileged place in the global hierarchy," with the resources, expertise, organizational capacity, and political leverage to achieve their goals (Tienhaara et al. 2012, p. 59). Therefore, some of the more illuminating cases in this literature are those where corporate interests have not prevailed. For example, the story of the global energy industry and climate change is complex (Levy and Kolk 2002; Downie 2014). Oil companies were at first united in opposing any global emissions reductions, led by the now defunct Global Climate Coalition (GCC). In the late 1990s, however, British Petroleum (BP) and Royal Dutch Shell both reversed their positions on climate negotiations in the late 1990s – a result of shareholder pressure and industry foresightedness in seeing strategic opportunities in renewable energy – while US firms, such as Chevron-Texaco and Exxon-Mobil, maintained their opposition (Pulver 2002). Since Kyoto, BINGOs opposed to global climate regulations have targeted their actions primarily at governments (notably the USA) and at public opinion. By contrast, BINGOs such as the International Emissions Trading Association (IETA) continue to engage constructively and innovatively in climate policy processes (Lund 2013).

Industry actors have been successful in gaining representation on the advisory panels and Technical Working Groups (TWGs) that do a lot of the behind-the-scenes, highly technical work that shapes important regime outcomes, including the Ozone Assessment Panels of the Montreal Protocol and others. Both the ICC and the Bureau of International Recycling (BIR), which strongly oppose the Basel Ban Amendment, participate in the TWG of the Convention, which decides which wastes are to count as hazardous, and therefore not to be traded. In September 1996, of the 159 representatives attending the TWG meeting, 49 were from industry organizations (Clapp 1999, p. 14), raising concerns about possible regulatory capture by industry of this area (O'Neill 2001). In negotiations over the Clean Development Mechanism (CDM) (see Chapter 8), corporate-sector actors were far more influential than NGOs, with a greater command of the intricacies and necessary tasks of such a mechanism (Lund 2013).

Corporate actors, despite the resources at their disposal, are still limited by differences within their ranks, strong competition from NGOs, and the need to navigate formal channels of access to negotiations. There is one major gap in studies of corporate-sector actors and GEG. Unlike environmental NGOs, there is next to no work so far on North–South dynamics in the BINGO sector. With the major corporations of China, India, and Brazil appearing on the international scene, it is going to be interesting to see how the possible synergies and conflicts from this development play out across many different regimes.

4.   *Scientists, Knowledge, and Environmental Diplomacy*

Scientific and technical experts play a critical role in defining global environmental problems and our responses to them: "It is through science that the scale of the problems, the ground for conflicts and the scope of solutions are defined" (Lidskog and Sundqvist 2002, p. 78). It is only through scientific research that we were even made aware of major global problems, such as climate change, the hole in the ozone layer, or the cumulative loss of biological diversity worldwide. Science has demonstrated complex cause-and-effect relationships across most, if not all, global environmental issues, especially when these relationships are hard to see on the ground.

While most scholars accord science – or, more broadly, expert knowledge – a vital role in the construction and ongoing development of international environmental regimes, there is considerable debate about how science and scientists actually shape these regimes, and under what conditions. In fact, many complex global problems have their own expert communities including scientists, economists, lawyers, and engineers. It is hard to ignore the role of these groups as actors in the policy process, or how perceived interactions between expert and policy communities shape regimes' legitimacy and effectiveness.

Science is incorporated into the negotiation of treaty regimes through a number of channels. In fact, the negotiation process – specifically, the iterated convention-protocol method – was designed to be able to consider new knowledge in later negotiating rounds (Williams 2005). First, science often plays a critical role during the process of issue definition and agenda setting. Scientists, by publishing research results, and advocating specific courses of action, can profoundly influence how, and when, particular problems make it onto the international policy agenda. Second, scientists have played formal advisory roles to international organizations, national governments, and even non-state actors, such as NGOs and corporations, during the process of regime construction, from draft conventions onwards. Chapter 3 details scientific groups and bodies found at different levels of governance, from national agencies through to international bodies such as the Intergovernmental Panel on Climate Change (IPCC) and assessment panels associated with different regimes.

The role of science in the international environmental policy process remains contested. Some argue that scientific knowledge shapes regimes: "environmental regimes are not only driven 'by state power, but by the application of scientific understanding about ecological systems to the management of environmental policy issues'" (Lidskog and Sundqvist 2002, p. 81, citing Haas 1997, p. 200). Scientific consensus, in particular, can override normative and political conflicts, and generate "legitimate" solutions to complex transboundary environmental problems (Gupta 2004, p. 130). Others argue that while scientists have a critical fact-finding role, their input into actual negotiations is minimal, and actual regime outcomes are driven by inter-state bargaining processes (Susskind 1994, p. 65). Science is only one input among many, and is open to political manipulation or subjugation to national interests.

The most influential model of the role of expert knowledge in regime construction is the epistemic community model, most closely associated with the work of Peter Haas (1990a, 1990b, 1992). Epistemic communities are "transnational networks of knowledge-based communities that are both politically empowered through their claims to exercise authoritative knowledge and motivated by shared causal and political beliefs" (Haas 1990a, p. 349). In Haas's model, scientists in policy positions in their respective countries work as a network to influence their governments to accept common solutions to a transboundary problem. By exercising their claims to authoritative knowledge, they are in a better position to resolve political conflicts among negotiating states, generate successful regime outcomes, and facilitate policy learning than are more politically motivated actors, such as NGOs. Epistemic communities have been identified in several environmental issue areas, for example around the Mediterranean pollution regime, the ozone regime, and others; in other cases, such as climate change, the absence of an epistemic community, particularly during critical early phases of negotiation, may have hampered the regime's evolution.

Some scholars, particularly in the science and technology studies (STS) community, criticize the epistemic communities model for its emphasis on consensual science that happens outside political processes, arguing that it glosses over the very real normative conflicts and uncertainties that characterize much of the science of global environmental change (Gupta et al. 2012; Forsyth 2003). Instead, they address how science mediates politics (and vice versa) under conditions of uncertainty, and how the legitimacy and salience of knowledge can matter more than its neutrality in different situations (Gupta et al. 2012, p. 72).

Karen Litfin developed the concept of knowledge brokers to explain how science influences regime construction even under conditions of uncertainty and conflict (Litfin 1994). Knowledge brokers, often lower-level government or IGO officials, function as "intermediaries between the original researchers or producers of knowledge, and the policymakers who consume that knowledge, but lack the time and training necessary to absorb the original research" (Litfin 1994, p. 4). Using the ozone regime as a case study, she challenges conventional wisdom that it emerged out of scientific consensus. Rather, a group of knowledge brokers with strong ties to UNEP and the US Environmental Protection Agency (EPA) were able to frame and interpret the relevant science and to identify an acceptable range of political outcomes under conditions of uncertainty.

Other analysts highlight the interaction of science and politics under conditions of higher or lower political conflict within regime negotiations (Gupta et al. 2012; Gehring and Ruffing 2008). Scientific understanding of whale stocks, for example, suggests that limited harvesting of particular species would be sustainable. However, the continued moratorium under the IWC speaks to the political support anti-whaling nations have maintained in the face of challenges from pro-whaling countries. In setting up its expert advisory body, the UNCCD, an agreement far less fraught by conflicts among its parties, has been able to emphasize a broader concept of "knowledge" that included local and traditional knowledge. Almost uniquely within the MEA universe, it has encouraged input from women farmers, nomadic pastoralists, and local NGOs in understanding the causes and consequences of land degradation as they are experienced and understood on the ground (Martello 2004).

The role of the IPCC in the climate regime shines a strong spotlight on the relationship between science and politics in state-led GEG. The IPCC is, to bring in another important STS concept, a boundary organization, an organization that straddles the difficult line between science and politics, trying to coordinate the imperatives of "speaking truth to power" as well as informing and enabling political choices (Hoppe et al. 2013). As an expert body established to be independent of the political process, the IPCC has managed to be dragged into the fray. Its Assessment Reports have been indispensable in furthering understanding of climate change and its impacts, and it has, according to some, used scientific uncertainty (and its ability to reduce it) to shore up its authority in public debate over climate change (Lidskog and Sundqvist 2015, p. 13). However, other studies agree that its enmeshment in politics and controversy has undermined its influence on actual policy-making (Gupta et al. 2012, p. 83). Chapter 3 discussed the general controversies in which climate scientists and the IPCC have been caught up in recent years, including the 2009 Climategate incident, which highlighted the very thin line between science and politics that members of boundary organizations – responsible for generating science in the public interest – must tread.

Disputes over the composition of the IPCC, which for many years consisted primarily of scientists from Northern countries, omitting scientists working in or trained in the South, have also taken center stage. The exclusion of Southern scientists has had the effect of weakening the profile, impact, and legitimacy of environmental treaty regimes in Southern countries (Biermann 2002). In India, once the IPCC expanded its representation of Indian scientists, the issue of climate change began to gain more currency in domestic political debates, feeding back into the government's negotiating position (Biermann 2002). Gender and disciplinary representation – especially in terms of who speaks for the IPCC at international meetings – have raised concern (O'Neill et al. 2010), as has the absence – except in a few forums such as the Arctic Climate Impact Assessment – of indigenous or other situated climate knowledges in UNFCCC deliberations and IPCC assessments (Smith and Sharp 2012).

In sum, to understand how science and scientists influence negotiation outcomes we need to look beyond those rare cases when "truth" can speak to "power," and engage with the often-messy realities of the science–politics interface across negotiating processes. On the positive side, Gupta et al. (2012) identify a participatory turn in the science surrounding certain issue areas, engaging different voices, disciplines, and topics of study. In the absence of the possibility (or even the desirability) of consensual science, this inclusive trend could increase the influence of scientific bodies on GEG through increasing their legitimacy to broader political constituencies, and their reach. These perspectives on the relationship between science and politics challenge the technocratic assumption that knowledge, or science, is universal, existing independently of who produces it and where, creating new avenues for understanding the relationship between science, scientists, and GEG.

Strengths and Weaknesses of the State-Led Negotiating Model

The state-led model of GEG, through inter-state cooperation and the construction of treaty-based regimes, has dominated GEG for as long as the system has existed. States remain the dominant actors, and reconciling their interests is often lead negotiators' primary task. It is a system that fits with perceived global political realities. It has generated an incredible amount of energy and attention, with many people and organizations committed to making it work effectively. As the above sections demonstrate, there are many different interests that intervene constructively (and others less so) to push outcomes well beyond lowest-common-denominator outcomes. It has also attracted intense criticism: James Gustave Speth, former head of Yale's School of Forestry and Environmental Studies and a founder of the World Resources Institute, has called it a "failed experiment" (Speth 2004).

The main advantage of the piecemeal, step-by-step process of international environmental diplomacy as it currently stands is that it eases collective action and commitment problems on the part of states, and allows participants to take account of new knowledge or information about the problem under negotiation (Joyner 2001; Bodansky 2013). It allows for the participation of many, and possibly all, nation-states, a feature important to the architects of state-led GEG. States do not have to sign on to a complex mix of potentially costly obligations all at once, but they may participate in the initial stages of the negotiations. Once a state has taken part in this first stage, treaty supporters hope that moral or other sorts of pressure can be exerted to ensure its participation in subsequent stages. An iterated process also allows opportunities for incorporating new knowledge – scientific or otherwise – into the regime, and enables signatories to learn from mistakes and assess progress (see Chapter 5).

There are also significant disadvantages to this system. First, as Table 4.1 clearly shows, the negotiation of framework conventions and successive protocols can be exceedingly slow. Negotiations themselves may often take more than ten years to get to the convention stage, then another several years for protocols to be negotiated, ratified, and enter into force, during which time environmental conditions are likely to have worsened. Second, renowned negotiations expert Lawrence Susskind argues, "in the final analysis, only agreements that are politically acceptable to national leaders will be approved" (Susskind 1994, p. 12). He also criticizes the dominant approach for its lack of imagination. International leaders have applied the same blueprint to issue after issue, without considering other more innovative forms of regime formation.

At a systemic level, there are many negotiation processes ongoing simultaneously – so many, in fact, that "treaty" or "summit fatigue" is a recognized problem (VanDeveer 2003). Muñoz et al. (2009) estimated that, counting only top-level meetings for ten large MEAs, the average number of meeting days per year rose from under 70 in the early 1990s to nearly 120 in 2008. Over the years the numbers of issues, numbers, and types of meetings (including subsidiary meetings and other gatherings), and their participants, proposals, and documents to read and discuss have snowballed (Depledge and Chasek 2012). While the Kyoto Protocol meeting in 1997 had 9,000 participants, considered huge at the time, 40,000 attended the 2009 Copenhagen COP. This heightened tempo of negotiations puts a disproportionate burden on Southern countries, with fewer resources and people to send, not to mention imposing a large carbon footprint on the planet, and strains on the lives of delegates themselves.

By reinforcing existing international structures, this system arguably maintains existing power relations and alliances in the international system (Levy and Newell 2002; Paterson 2001b). At the same time, engagement in global environmental politics (GEP) can in fact change the interests of powerful actors. We see this clearly in the early days of the ozone regime, when the EU changed its position on regulating CFCs, and in the climate regime, as non-Annex 1 countries, such as Brazil, China, and India, have taken on their own obligations. Therefore, the assumption that many mainstream international relations and other theorists make, that interests are fixed as states go into negotiations, is not the case, and, as interests have changed, so have the agreements that are subject to ongoing negotiation.

Over and above these questions, international environmental negotiation processes have importance in and of themselves. Without ongoing processes of environmental cooperation, which have seriously engaged many governments and other powerful actors and agencies, we would have made far less progress in learning about or combating global environmental problems over the past three decades. Arguably, we have also constructed networks and institutions that have strengthened global governance and international connections as a whole. However, whether or not this is enough to meet the environmental and social challenges the global community faces remains an open question.

Next Steps

The state-led mode of GEG – through cooperation and treaty negotiation – has its critics. To some it represents the art of the possible, reconciling as much as possible the interests of the most powerful players in the international system in order to make significant progress toward combating global environmental degradation. To others, to quote Shakespeare, it is all "sound and fury, signifying nothing." Renowned legal theorist Daniel Bodansky calls inter-state diplomacy a "Thirty Percent Solution" to problems of environmental governance (Bodansky 2010, p. 15). Treaties and treaty negotiation have a substantial role to play, especially in setting up international rules and norms, generating knowledge, and empowering institutions and actors to address these pressing issues.

As his argument, and the critiques above, imply, international law cannot be the only solution. One of the major themes of this book, as outlined in Chapter 1, is the way that GEG has become broader and more complex over time. Some issue areas – chemicals, for example – remain dominated by treaty processes, as the 2013 conclusion of the Minamata Mercury Convention demonstrates (Selin 2014). Others, such as climate change, are broadening beyond the UNFCCC process. The following chapters demonstrate changes in sites and modes of GEG that move beyond, but do not fully leave behind, this state-led model, which itself has changed in response to new pressures and challenges.

From an analytical perspective, studying international environmental cooperation has generated many new insights into international cooperation more broadly. Dynamics between countries of the North and of the South, the role of NGOs and corporations, and the take-up of science and other forms of expert knowledge into the international policy process are all significant contributions made by IEP analysis to our broader understandings of contemporary international politics. They touch on serious theoretical questions about power and influence, about access and equity, and about knowledge and policy. We move on now to questions that follow directly on from those that concluded this chapter: how effective are state-led GEG regimes, what broader impacts do they have, and how can we tell?

Discussion Questions

- This chapter has outlined the rules that govern international environmental negotiations, and ways in which they have been criticized. What changes would you suggest in order to make them work better?
- Discuss conditions under which scientists and/or environmental activists successfully influence environmental negotiation outcomes, and how. When are they less influential? How can you tell?
- Copies of environmental treaties are available at secretariat websites, or at www.untreaty.un.org. Choosing one of those listed in Table 4.1, read the full text and identify: (a) how the treaty defines the problem; (b) the obligations placed on signatory states; and (c) the institutional mechanisms set up in the treaty to manage the regime, and meet obligations, such as funding and technology transfer.

SUGGESTIONS FOR FURTHER READING

Benedick, Richard E. 2007. "Science, Diplomacy and the Montreal Protocol." *Encyclopedia of Earth.* Ed. Cleveland, Cutler J. Washington DC: Environmental Information Coalition, National Council for Science and the Environment: a first-hand account of the Montreal Protocol negotiations from the leader of the US negotiating team.

Chasek, Pamela S., and Lynn M. Wagner, eds. 2012. *The Roads from Rio: Lessons Learned from Twenty Years of Multilateral Environmental Negotiations.* New York: Routledge: a collection of essays on global environmental negotiations by past and present members of the *Earth Negotiations Bulletin* team, from their position at the front line of negotiations.

Kolbert, Elizabeth. 2015. "The Weight of the World: Can Christiana Figueres Persuade Humanity to Save Itself?" *New Yorker,* August 24: a fascinating study of the Chair of the UNFCCC, and her role during the critical negotiations prior to COP 21.

Selin, Henrik. 2014. "Global Environmental Law and Treaty-Making on Hazardous Substances: The Minamata Convention and Mercury Abatement." *Global Environmental Politics* 14.1: 1–19: a case study of the most recent international environmental treaty negotiations, including why mercury became the subject of international negotiations and the negotiation dynamics themselves.

Susskind, Lawrence E. 1994. *Environmental Diplomacy: Negotiating More Effective Global Environmental Agreements.* New York: Oxford University Press: a critique, with prescriptions for reform, of existing modes of negotiating multilateral agreements; remains the most authoritative study of this subject.

5   The Impacts and Effectiveness
of Global Environmental Governance

In Chapter 4 we examined the factors that influence the construction of state-led environmental governance regimes, ending with critiques of this model of global environmental governance (GEG). Now we address these critiques directly, turning to assessing the impacts and effectiveness of environmental treaty regimes, issues that apply to analysis of any policy or governance initiative.

In Chapter 1 I argued that a central problem for global policy-makers in creating effective regimes is how to alter states' willingness and capacity to comply with the terms of an international agreement. They must also ensure that the terms of this agreement are strong or designed well enough to address the environmental problem under negotiation, in other words that they contain a measure of problem-solving effectiveness. In turn, the ways these issues are addressed shape how regimes evolve and change, and whether they become progressively stronger, or falter with time (Young 2010).

In this chapter we discuss findings about environmental regime performance to date and define key terms and challenges in measuring regime impacts. We next examine how aspects of regime design create incentives – both positive and negative – that change state behavior over the short and long term. In this section we challenge the notion that international environmental regimes are weak because they lack full enforcement mechanisms or because they result from an unsatisfactory compromise of conflicting national interests. Finally, we delve into deeper changes regimes may bring about, including how they facilitate learning within regimes themselves and by the actors they seek to influence.

Half-Full or Half-Empty?

The field of international environmental politics (IEP) took an early lead within the discipline of international relations in generating research on the impacts and effectiveness of cooperation (Zürn 1998; O'Neill et al. 2004). Part of the reason for this is the problem-driven nature of the field.

However, it is also the case that with such a large number of environmental treaties, many of which have been in place for many years, scholars began moving beyond the question of what makes states cooperate in the first place to examining the impacts of environmental treaty regimes as they mature.

From a problem-solving perspective we want to know how, and to what extent, international environmental diplomacy slows down, halts, or even reverses global environmental degradation. If treaty regimes are ineffective, we want to know how to improve their performance. Some variables that have important causal impacts on regime effectiveness – such as the structure of the international system, or domestic political structures – are relatively fixed, and hard to change. Others are far more malleable, making for more effective policy recommendations. One such variable is regime design, or the specific institutional characteristics of treaty regimes. Thus, much work in this subfield has concentrated on these factors, aiming to influence the development of existing treaty regimes or the design of future ones, with additional implications for global governance regimes in other issue areas (Ohta and Ishii 2013).

This work also speaks to theoretical debates in international relations theory over the utility and impacts of international cooperation and institutions (Mearsheimer 1994/95). Does international cooperation work? Does it change the behavior of states over the long term? Under what conditions are global governance regimes effective, and how?

Many of the influential early works in this field – notably large-scale projects examining regime effectiveness across cases and time – were published in the 1990s or shortly after, with fewer in recent years (Andresen 2013, p. 304).[1] While researchers have focused more recently on different questions, such as those of linkages, learning, and fragmentation we look at in Chapter 9, the issue of regime effectiveness remains compelling. We still need to understand why and how some regimes work better than others – and the insights from this work are applicable to GEG initiatives of any sort.

Empirical findings on environmental quality tell a mixed story about regime effectiveness, but one that is more positive than some would suggest. There is strong consensus that regimes do matter, notably in that environmental conditions are likely to have become far worse in their absence (Andresen 2013). Their performance, however, varies considerably across regimes, across national contexts, and over time (Weiss and Jacobson 1998; Miles et al. 2002). The ozone regime is considered the

---

[1] Classic works include Weiss and Jacobson 1998; Haas et al. 1993; Victor et al. 1998; Young 1999; Miles et al. 2002.

most successful regime on many fronts (see Box 5.2). The Convention on International Trade in Endangered Species (CITES, 1973) is considered by many legal experts to be the most effective of the conservation regimes (Sand 2013), while the Convention on Long Range Transboundary Air Pollution (LRTAP, 1979) has made a significant difference to air quality in Northern Europe (Lidskog and Sundqvist 2011). Many smaller river and regional seas agreements (in terms of numbers of parties and/or geographical regions) are also highly effective (Young 2011). While the performance of the UN Framework Convention on Climate Change (UNFCCC) is, at the very least, disappointing, Oran Young and other experts deem fisheries-management regimes to be the most significant failure of international environmental cooperation (Cullis-Suzuki and Pauly 2012; Young 2010). Other regimes fall at different points along this continuum.

To some, these mixed results mean a glass that is half-empty, to others, a glass half-full (Simmons and Oudraat 2001, p. 719). Which perspective one chooses depends a good deal on one's expectations, how one defines the object and fields of study, and potential alternative actions and outcomes. On the one hand, the state of the global environment – particularly with respect to biodiversity and climate – is dire and getting worse. On the other, given the obstacles to effective environmental coop-eration – domestic intransigence, lack of capacity, scientific uncertainty and unpredictability, and an international political system that allows cheating or freeriding – the regimes we have seem all the more effective in context.

Defining and Measuring Regime Effectiveness

Regime effectiveness is a multi-faceted concept. It encompasses how, and how well, regimes work across different dimensions, and the impacts they have on a range of outcomes and variables. Discussions around identify-ing these different dimensions of effectiveness have been informed by perspectives from international relations and political science, legal the-ory, environmental studies, and policy-makers.

Two leading scholars offer definitions of effectiveness that capture the multiple dimensions of this concept. Thomas Bernauer identifies success-ful regimes as "those that 1. Change the behavior of states and other actors in the direction intended by the cooperating parties; 2. Solve the environmental problem they are designed to solve, and 3. Do so in an efficient and equitable manner" (Bernauer 1995, p. 358). Oran Young identifies no fewer than six distinct dimensions of regime effectiveness: problem-solving; goal attainment; and behavioral, process, constitutive,

Table 5.1 *Dimensions of Compliance (adapted from Weiss and Jacobson 1998, Table 1.1)*

Type of Compliance	Shallow Compliance	Deep Compliance
Procedural	States report in timely fashion	Reports are accurate and comprehensive
Substantive	States enact relevant laws	States enforce laws
Spirit of the Treaty	States include commitment in policy rhetoric	States exceed and extend commitments

and evaluative effectiveness. In sum, they take into account how regimes solve problems or reach their goals, change participants' behavior in meaningful ways, and whether regime outcomes meet criteria such as equity or efficiency (Young 1994, pp. 143–49).

Compliance, Problem-Solving, and Other Regime Impacts

In practice, scholars have focused on two main dimensions of regime effectiveness: compliance and problem-solving. Compliance is commonly defined as "the extent to which the behavior of a state – party to an international treaty – actually conforms to the conditions set out in this treaty" (Faure and Lefevere 2015, p. 111). Studies of compliance dominated early studies of regime effectiveness, and are common in international legal theory as well.[2] Behavioral and political changes are easier to identify and measure than other sorts of regime impacts. Further, this area of research conforms most closely to central questions in the study of international cooperation in international relations theory, in particular with its focus on the behavior of states as the central political units in the international system.

Table 5.1 outlines different dimensions of compliance and related state activities. Following Weiss and Jacobson (1998), the table notes three different types of compliance-related behavior. First, procedural compliance means that state actors fulfill their commitments to the treaty process, for example by preparing national reports. Second, substantive compliance refers to actions taken to fulfill treaty commitments. Finally, compliance with the spirit of the treaty refers to actions that fulfill the broad normative framework of the agreement, such as placing biodiversity protection in the context of broader goals of conservation or

---

[2] For international legal scholarship on compliance theory see Bodansky 2009, 2013; Treves et al. 2009. For early international relations works see Chayes and Chayes 1993; and Downs et al. 1996.

Box 5.1: Dimensions of Problem-Solving

a. *Absolute Change in Environmental Quality*
   - Has the problem been eliminated or solved?
   - If not, has relevant environmental quality improved to a measurable degree?
   - Has the overall pace of environmental degradation slowed?
b. *Relative Change in Environmental Quality*
   - Is the problem better than it would have been in the absence of the regime?
   - If there is no overall change, can absence of deterioration be ascribed to the regime?
   - If environmental quality has deteriorated, would it have deteriorated further in the regime's absence?

---

sustainable development. In each case, compliance may occur at any one of several levels. Shallow procedural compliance means, for example, states meet reporting deadlines, while a deep level of substantive compliance means they enforce laws that succeed in changing the behavior of target actors, such as polluting firms.

For many, however, using compliance as the critical dimension of regime effectiveness is not enough. For example, regimes with the highest rates of compliance may simply be the weakest ones, with the fewest binding commitments, or those that most closely mirror the existing status quo. Thus, they urge a focus on problem-solving effectiveness.[3] Do international environmental regimes actually help slow down, prevent, or even reverse processes of global environmental degradation? Do regime members meet the substantive goals of the regime? What would the state of the environment be like in its absence? Measuring changes in global environmental problems, and showing that at least part of that change is caused by the existence of the regime, are difficult but important tasks.

Less independent attention has been paid to the final element of both Bernauer and Young's definitions, namely the extent to which the regime fulfills criteria of efficiency (cost-effectiveness) and equity, and, related, that of feasibility. These aspects play an important role in both behavioral and problem-solving notions of effectiveness. Rates of compliance, for example, tend to be far lower if the regime is perceived as inequitable, imposes an unfair share of the costs on particular parties, or if the negotiations process is perceived as unfair (Young 2014; Pickering et al. 2012).

---

[3] See, for example, Bernauer 1995; Young 1999; Miles et al. 2002.

Box 5.2: Indicators of Effectiveness: The Ozone Regime

a. *Substantive Compliance*
   - As of 2005, production of ozone-depleting substances had fallen by 99% in developed countries and by 80% in developing countries (Vital Ozone Graphics website).
b. *Problem-Solving*
   - According to a 2014 assessment, the stratospheric ozone layer is expected to return to its 1980 baseline between 2040 and 2060 (WMO/UNEP 2014).
   - Earlier UN Environment Programme (UNEP) and World Meteorological Organization (WMO) studies suggest that while skin-cancer rates will increase due to ozone-layer depletion, in the absence of action, rates might have quadrupled by 2050 (Schiermeier 2009, p. 795).
c. *Progressive and Rapid Regime Development*
   - Accelerated phase-out schedules of major ozone-depleting substances (Young 2010).
   - Increased financial support of the Multilateral Fund for the Implementation of the Montreal Protocol (Multilateral Fund website).
d. *Global Acceptance*
   - In September 2009 the Vienna Convention and the Montreal Protocol, and associated amendments, became the only treaties in UN history to achieve universal ratification, with 197 parties (Ozone Secretariat website).

Box 5.2 uses the ozone regime to illustrate dimensions of regime effectiveness. Not only does the regime score highly in terms of substantive compliance and problem-solving effectiveness, its rapid and progressive development and global membership demonstrate its persistence and legitimacy. Despite ongoing issues in the negotiations, the ozone regime illustrates dimensions of effectiveness that may be lacking or less straightforward in other regimes, but indicate what to look for in assessing effectiveness or the lack thereof.

Next, independent regime impacts may ultimately shape regime effectiveness or have broader social or political effects. Regimes may generate distributive effects (changing wealth distribution between rich and poor countries), learning effects (new information and research that changes our view of the global environment), process effects (e.g. resolving existing, but not necessarily directly related, conflicts between parties), or unanticipated side effects (Young 2001, pp. 113–14). We look at learning effects later in this chapter.

As an example of a malign side effect of an international regime, the illegal trade in chlorofluorocarbons (CFCs) became an issue in the decade in which Southern countries were still allowed to manufacture CFCs under the provisions of the Montreal Protocol (Clapp 1997; Young 2010). At one point, illegal CFCs were the second-most-seized contraband at the port of Miami, after cocaine (Clapp 1997, p. 264). A regime may also have unanticipated consequences as governments enforce treaty commitments. For example, policies put in place by the Kenyan government in the 1980s ostensibly to meet commitments under CITES involved oppressive measures against local minority communities who were opposed to the government at the time (Peluso 1993).

More fundamentally, some argue that the construction of and participation in environmental regimes might, collectively, be changing, or transforming, wider structures of global politics and actor roles and identities (Falkner 2012). These sorts of questions are most closely associated with constructivist research agendas in international relations theory (O'Neill et al. 2004; Finnemore 1996). For example, does participating in international treaty regimes help change the basic interests and preferences of states themselves? These are difficult questions to answer, particularly as relevant empirical data is hard to acquire, and open to multiple interpretations, but important to consider in terms of the general evolution of global governance.

Studying Effectiveness: Methods and Measures

Generally, it is difficult to empirically and definitively assess the impacts and effectiveness of international regimes. Identifying causality is a complex task, given the range of dependent variables (what one is trying to explain), independent variables (competing explanations of observed changes), and intervening factors (Bernauer 1995). Both environmental systems and institutional responses change, often rapidly and unpredictably, over time (Young 2011; Bernstein and Cashore 2012). Finally, untangling and adjudicating between narratives of regime effectiveness is no easy task: stakeholders may make different claims according to their own interests (Bowman 2013). These challenges notwithstanding, the global environmental politics (GEP) field has made considerable progress in developing methodological tools to answer broader questions of regime effects and effectiveness (O'Neill et al. 2013).

Historically, the lack of adequate and reliable data on the state of the global environment has challenged scholars in this field, especially those interested in impacts of international regimes on environmental problems (Haas et al. 1993, p. 7). Recent advances in satellite and imaging technology, as well as emissions-measurement technology, have vastly increased experts' ability to measure environmental change, and, particularly through the internet, the public's access to environmental data and images. Geographic information systems (GIS) technology, which enables monitoring of changes in environmental quality at scales from regional to extremely local, is a highly effective tool for tracing environmental impacts over space and time. Large-scale, ongoing data-collection efforts help push and coordinate data collection. UNEP's data collection and dissemination programs, including Global Environmental Monitoring System (GEMS), Global Resource Information Database (GRID), and INFOTERRA, are cases in point (Ivanova 2010). The development of ever larger and more complex Integrated Assessment Models (IAMs) have also made it easier to predict environmental outcomes under a variety of scenarios (O'Neill et al. 2013).

Data unavailability is only one part of the problem (Seelarbokus 2014). Data may exist but not be reported or compiled for different reasons. Much of the available data relevant to environmental agreements is gathered by regime secretariats and relies on self-reporting by individual states, which may lack the capacity or will to accurately report results. Such data, too, is often not standardized across countries, making it hard to draw accurate comparisons. Hazardous-waste statistics are notorious in this respect, as countries define "hazardous wastes" very differently, making it hard to compare generation, import, and export data in the absence of a well-defined set of international standards (O'Neill 2000). Data held across many institutions and organizations is harder to gather, and proprietary data collected and analyzed by private firms or consulting agencies is hard to make public.

Even when data has been gathered, establishing the causal impacts of a regime can be hard, especially given lengthy time lags between regime implementation and change in the relevant environmental problem. First, how do we separate the effects of a treaty regime from exogenous factors that affect the state of the environment, such as economic shocks, natural changes in the environment, or technological changes (Young 2001, p. 100)? For example, the countries of the former Soviet Union were able to reach targets under the climate change and ozone regimes primarily because of the economic collapse the region experienced in the 1990s.

Second, studies of effectiveness have to establish counterfactual scenarios that estimate what might have happened had the regime never existed. Evidence from UNEP, the World Wildlife Fund (WWF), International Union for the Conservation of Nature (IUCN), and others

all demonstrate that many environmental problems are worsening globally in absolute terms. However, Andresen (2013) points out that
a common finding across the effectiveness literature is that environmental
quality would indeed have been worse without the rules, knowledge
bases, and normative force of existing environmental regimes. Bowman,
for example, argues that CITES should be considered a partial success,
even though the illegal wildlife trade still exists. Not only is it likely that
the trade would be far worse in the absence of an agreement, but there is
demonstrable evidence that it works better than the most likely alternative, incentivizing a "sustainable" trade (Bowman 2013, pp. 232–33).
The counterfactual problem has come to the fore in the design of climate
funding mechanisms, where funding or project approval depend on
establishing a baseline. Baseline methods, which are supposed to indicate
what would happen in the absence of a proposed project, have been
heavily criticized for being open to manipulation (see Chapter 8).

Despite the complexity of the subject matter, and the difficulties of
undertaking empirical analysis, we have made considerable progress in
identifying the factors that make regimes more effective, and under what
conditions. It is to these we now turn.

Designing Effective Regimes

Many factors shape the impacts of GEG regimes. If you are interested in
how a treaty regime changes the behavior of member states, you may
focus on factors associated with regime design. If you want to understand
broader issues of problem-solving and regime change over time, you
might focus more on how treaty regimes incorporate mechanisms to
assess performance, incorporate new information, and learn from past
experience. Such work is often motivated by scholars' own desire to help
improve regime performance in practice. Policy recommendations –
based on what fails to work about a given regime, or what has worked in
other similar situations – are important. In the following sections, we
focus on how institutions and regimes can be designed to improve rates
of compliance and problem-solving effectiveness.

Haas et al. (1993) argue that effective international regimes do three
things (what they term the "3Cs"): they raise intergovernmental concern;
they ameliorate the international contractual environment, making it
easier for states to cooperate and comply under anarchy; and they raise
the capacity of states to meet their commitments. Truly successful
regimes capture positive feedback from these three factors, and improve
compliance and problem-solving effectiveness over time. Evidence
demonstrates that in any given environmental regime, member states

exhibit a range of preferences for compliance, and a single state's performance often varies over time (Weiss and Jacobson 1998). When states perceive compliance with an international agreement as both in their direct interests and within their ability to meet, compliance is non-problematic. Such situations are relatively rare in world politics.

Non-compliance results from one (or more) of three factors: a lack of political will or intent to comply; a lack of capacity, or ability to comply; and inadvertent non-compliance (Mitchell 1994). While states may want to comply with an agreement, they may find themselves unable to do so, due to lack of resources or control over the actors whose behavior is the ultimate target of the regime. Alternatively, they may lack the political will to comply, and may have signed the treaty for other reasons (for example, to forestall criticism from domestic or international constituencies, or to shape the subsequent evolution of the regime). Therefore, many studies of regime compliance examine how measures such as limited sanctions, positive incentives (such as environmental aid), transparency-enhancing practices, and the scope and fit of regime obligations help alter states' will and capacity to comply with treaty commitments over time.

a.   Drafting Compliance: Treaty Characteristics Different treaties evoke different levels of compliance. Sometimes these variations can be directly related to the terms of an agreement and how it is perceived by signatory states. Here we focus on two characteristics of treaty commitments: their legitimacy and their precision.[4]

First, states are more likely to comply with an agreement, even when compliance is costly, when the obligations are seen as legitimate and fair and when the regime's decision-making processes are seen as open and equitable, fulfilling a shared understanding of appropriate behavior and expectations. For example, there was broad consensus during negotiations of the ozone regime that poorer countries should receive additional assistance from the international community (in terms of funding and an extended deadline for phasing out CFCs). Further, the ban on dumping hazardous wastes from North to South, especially for disposal, was widely supported on the basis of broad principles of environmental justice. Ideas of fairness have most clearly been explored in climate negotiations, where recent studies examine how output and procedural fairness shape regime effectiveness (Young 2014; Pickering et al. 2012). They suggest that, as hard as it is to reach a fair *and* effective agreement, fairness may be

---

[4] Other characteristics that have been identified as important in this context include a treaty's fit with problem or political characteristics, and its scope – the range of activities it covers. See Young 2002.

necessary (though not sufficient) for an effective regime. Related, the perceived lack of feasibility of the targets set under the Kyoto Protocol for many Annex 1 countries undermined compliance with that agreement (Barrett 2008).

There is some disagreement over how the precision of regime obligations affects compliance. Precision refers to the clarity of commitments: do states know exactly what they have to do, and by when, or are regime commitments relatively ambiguous? For example, while the Montreal Protocol set out exact targets and timetables for eliminating CFCs, other treaties, particularly framework conventions, offer no more than a set of criteria that countries should aim for. Certainly the greater the precision of treaty commitments, the easier it is to ascertain and measure compliance (Weiss and Jacobson 1998, p. 524). In their study of the relationship between the precision of commitments and compliance, Weiss and Jacobson (1998, pp. 524–25) do find that in general, where commitments are more precise, compliance rates are higher. Nonetheless, important qualifications apply, and precision cannot fully explain variation across regime cases. First, when states agree with the terms of an agreement, compliance tends to be high, even when the terms are ambiguous. Second, "precise and relatively simple commitments are easier to comply with than precise and complicated ones" (Weiss and Jacobson 1998, p. 524). Third, precision is not on its own sufficient to ensure regime compliance.

b.   Enforcing Compliance: Sanctions and Dispute-Settlement Mechanisms
Insights from studies of international trade and security suggest that non-compliant actors may respond to sanctions or other enforcement mechanisms. If the agencies in control of the regime or powerful member states have the ability to detect and punish non-compliant behavior, or at least can make a credible threat to do so, compliance is more likely. Sanctions and the threat of punishment are, of course, common under domestic law, and have been incorporated into other areas of global governance. Countries found to be in violation of trade or weapons-control regimes can be subjected to economic sanctions, for example. However, the impacts of international sanctions, be they economic, political, or military, are controversial at the best of times (Drezner 2011), and there is little international political will to apply them to the environmental arena, although some argue that this seriously undermines regime effectiveness (Jenkins 1995). Nor have there been moves to bring treaty violators in front of international courts.

However – contrary to some popular belief – "stick" measures are incorporated into, and used by, several environmental regimes. Sanctions tailored to particular regimes are sometimes used under international environmental law. CITES (1973) is a prominent example. The convention text did not originally contain sanctions mechanisms. With few financial resources to use positive incentives such as aid and capacity-building, regime actors started in 1985 to use trade suspensions for various forms of non-compliant behavior on the part of member states. There is considerable evidence that such suspensions, even if only partially enacted, have indeed changed the behavior of non-compliant actors (Reeve 2006; Sand 2013). For example, by 2013 eleven persistently non-compliant parties had their rights to trade in Appendix II-listed species (species which require special permits to be traded) suspended until they demonstrate, at least on paper, that they have met requirements: in nearly all of these cases, suspensions were lifted within a year (Sand 2013, pp. 255–56).

In the mid to late 2000s a huge escalation in illegal trade in ivory and other valuable wildlife commodities to fund wars in Africa (Milliken 2014) led CITES to work more directly with Interpol and international criminal agencies as part of direct global efforts to combat transnational environmental crime. Likewise, the growth in (or growth in awareness of) a range of transboundary environmental crimes also including trade in illegal timber, ozone-depleting substances, and hazardous wastes, including electronic wastes, has generated a multilevel and actor response, with partnerships across national and agency borders (Elliott 2007, 2014). Strictly speaking, private actors commit most of these crimes, and more often than not state compliance needs to be enhanced by capacity-building, not punishment. However, if state actors are complicit or seriously negligent, then potential sanctions could be more easily justified under international law.

Other regimes contain dispute-settlement procedures, including the Montreal and Kyoto Protocols. As with other such processes, they share due processes of evidence gathering, hearings, and rights to appeal. Although they strive first to use positive incentives and softer legal solutions to address compliance issues, punitive measures can be triggered by state intransigence, including suspension from treaty privileges. According to a recent study, they tend to be most used when NGOs or a secretariat, as well as member states, are able to initiate complaints, and work best when processes are clear and non-confrontational (Treves et al. 2009; Faure and Lefevere 2015). The Montreal Protocol's Implementation Committee is considered a good example of a successful non-compliance mechanism (Jacur 2009; Barrett 2008). Expectations of member states' behavior are clear, compliance is feasible, and therefore violations are easier to detect. The Kyoto Protocol, while having stronger measures on paper, suffers the opposite. The general conflict around its goals, the belief on the part of many Annex 1 countries that they cannot meet their targets anyway, and the lack of support for more general trade sanctions (such as the World Trade Organization [WTO]) has made their application unlikely (Barrett 2008).

Thus, many treaty regimes have sanctions and dispute-settlement procedures at their disposal, often allying with international enforcement agencies to catch and punish serious violators. Because, however, of the voluntary nature of state participation in international regimes and the prevalence of inadvertent non-compliance, most regimes rely primarily on positive incentives in cases of non-compliance, using direct sanctions as a last resort. It is to these "carrot" mechanisms that we now turn.

c.   *Eliciting Compliance: Transparency and Reputation*   Given the difficulty – and political infeasibility – of relying fully on punitive measures to enforce compliance, environmental treaty regimes have relied more often on a variety of "softer" mechanisms to elicit compliance from otherwise capable members. Some of these are direct mechanisms – such as exceptions clauses – that bring otherwise recalcitrant parties along. Others rely on normative force to exert their influence. For example, Scandinavian countries used "toteboard diplomacy" in LRTAP, where they set themselves higher emissions-reduction targets and essentially dared other countries to meet them (Levy 1993). In fact, the process of norm creation and diffusion ongoing in environmental negotiations creates (by definition) shared expectations and standards of behavior that many states are unwilling to breach (Bernstein 2013a). This approach is consonant with soft law or constructivist approaches in international cooperation studies, which posit that non-binding and less precise commitments (soft law) coupled with positive incentives to comply can be equally or more effective, particularly as they are less likely to deter states from participating in the regime in the first place (Downs et al. 1996; Bodansky 2009).

Members of any group are more likely to comply in a social setting when they perceive that they may suffer significant social sanctions or loss of reputation within that setting if they are seen not to comply. They may also want to comply, but need the regime to incorporate ways to ensure other states are also complying, and to reduce the transactions costs of enforcing and monitoring cooperation (Young 1999, p. 261). Thus, many environmental regimes contain procedural mechanisms that enhance the ability to tell if a state is fulfilling or reneging on its commitments. Such "sunshine" mechanisms include regular national reporting requirements, independent monitoring (by scientific bodies, NGOs and specially established agencies) of procedural compliance, environmental quality, media access, and public education programs (Weiss and Jacobson 1998, pp. 543–46). Many treaties require countries to submit annual reports on their progress. These reports are made available to the public, usually via the Convention's website. The main problem with relying solely on national reporting for creating transparency is that governments may misreport or simply fail to report their progress, and the information requirements may be too shallow to ascertain real progress.

Therefore, treaty secretariats employ additional mechanisms to enhance transparency (Gupta and Mason 2014). For example, some conventions require independent, on-site monitoring of progress. The World Heritage Convention is one example: independent international experts visit designated heritage sites to ensure that they are being managed in accordance with regime goals. Others, such as the Rotterdam Convention, mandate careful documentation of prior informed consent from recipient states before allowing exports of certain chemicals (Jansen and Dubois 2014). Independent and state-led commissions and organizations, such as the Extractive Industries Transparency Initiative (EITI) can hold state and corporate actors to account when norms and rules in a given issue area are violated (Haufler 2010).

NGOs, both transnational and local, have proven highly effective allies in the effort to enhance regime transparency, and to publicize policy failures or successes, playing a vital role as whistle-blowers as well as providing data and analysis on the scope of particular problems (O'Neill 2015). By monitoring state behavior, engaging in public education, and working with the media to publicize results, they have, in many cases, succeeded in changing state behavior in situations where regime officials would have little success. Princen (1995) highlights the role of NGOs in enforcing CITES provisions in Kenya and Zimbabwe. Other examples include the work of TRAFFIC, an anti-wildlife-trade NGO that works closely with CITES, or the Basel Action Network, which reports on instances of illegal hazardous waste trade, working with the Basel Convention Secretariat and other concerned organizations, such as the International Maritime Organization (IMO). The NGO Sea Shepherd has utilized direct-action tactics and media to expose Japan's whaling practices that violate the terms of the IWC, although, as the Japanese response illustrates, such "naming and shaming" does not always have the desired effect (Hoek 2010). Therefore, adopting these strategies – by any global actor – requires consideration of the conditions under which they are likely to work. As with the corporate sector, some state actors are simply immune, while others care more deeply about their standing.

d.   Creating Compliance: Capacity-Building Measures   Much effort to enhance regime compliance and effectiveness has centered on building the capacity of state and other actors, particularly in the global South, to meet international goals. Mechanisms such as environmental aid and technology transfer not only improve capacity, they may also alter the will to comply on the part of recipient nations, and over the longer term enhance environmental problem-solving. Many environmental treaties contain measures to provide financial aid and technology to poorer countries, as we saw in Chapter 4, such as the Multilateral Fund of the Montreal Protocol. NGOs have taken on important roles in monitoring and implementing the terms of international environmental agreements. They provide an invaluable assisting role to UNEP and other IGOs, who are often overstretched. The Global Environment Facility (GEF)-funded International POPs Elimination Project has assisted more than 350 NGOs in 65 countries to work with local communities on education about, identification, and reduction of persistent organic pollutants (POPs) in local communities (Sow et al. 2012). For Northern countries, market mechanisms, such as emissions-trading schemes or carbon offset mechanisms in the climate regime, are also means for encouraging compliance, by allowing such countries to balance or spread the costs of adjustment. Chapter 8 addresses such mechanisms in detail.

Capacity has multiple dimensions (VanDeveer and Dabelko 2001). The first is material. Do government or private-sector organizations have adequate financial resources at hand to meet their commitments? Do they have access to trained personnel, expertise, and technology? Is there adequate physical infrastructure (roads, electricity, etc.) to support environmental projects? Organizational capacity refers to the way individual organizations and agencies are run, their leadership or management style, their organizational culture, and the incentives provided to personnel (employees, agents, volunteers) to carry out their jobs. At a broader, institutional level, capacity-building activities are also targeted at the basic political institutions of the country: improving the government's ability to make policy work through strengthening or reforming key institutions and agencies. High societal capacity connotes a strong network of NGOs and other civil society organizations that help a government carry out policy, or effectively criticize it if it does not (Weinthal and Parag 2003).

A lack of capacity across some or all the above dimensions is a major obstacle to regime effectiveness (Weiss and Jacobson 1998), and it became abundantly clear during the negotiation of early multilateral environmental agreements (MEAs) that meeting commitments would be costly, particularly for countries with the fewest resources to adjust to new rules. The 1987 Montreal Protocol was the first agreement to establish a Fund to provide developing countries with financial and technological assistance to end the production and use of CFCs. Operating independently of the financial arrangements discussed below, it is widely considered a success (Downie 2014; see Box 5.2).

Funding targeted at environmental capacity-building is both bilateral and multilateral. Norway, through its Sovereign Fund (which redistributes its oil revenues), has been one of the bigger providers of bilateral aid targeted specifically at environmental projects. In 1991 the UN approved a three-year pilot program, the Global Environment Facility (GEF), with the mandate of funding developing-country projects with global environmental benefits. Following reforms in 1993 that enhanced the influence of recipient countries and the role of NGOs, it became the main multilateral agency to coordinate financial commitments associated with international treaty regimes (Streck 2001; Lattanzio 2013). The GEF is funded by the World Bank, and administered by UNEP and the UN Development Programme (UNDP), in an unusual example of interagency cooperation. It provides aid or loans on favorable terms for small-scale projects that combat particular global environmental problems: ozone depletion, greenhouse-gas (GHG) emissions, biodiversity loss, and pollution of transnational waters. In 2002 projects related to land degradation (or desertification) and POPs were added to the GEF portfolio. As of early 2015 the GEF had provided $13.5 billion in grants and leveraged $65 billion in co-financing for 3,900 projects in over 165 developing countries. It has provided more than $653 million in small grants to civil-society and community-based organizations worldwide, totaling around 16,000 projects. GEF has, to give just a few examples, funded projects to develop renewable-energy sources in Mexico and the Philippines, to reduce pollution in marine ecosystems in East Asia, to deploy environmentally sound alternatives to DDT across sub-Saharan Africa to combat malaria, to conserve heirloom seed varieties in Jordan and Vietnam, and to bring clean-fuel-cell buses to Beijing.

The GEF also pioneered the principle of additionality in global environmental aid and lending. It funds only the additional or incremental costs incurred in the course of a project: those costs that take a project from having merely local benefits to one that has global benefits in at least one of the GEF's programmatic areas. For example, GEF funds could be used to cover the additional costs of building a biomass power plant rather than a coal-fired plant, given that it generates global benefits in terms of fewer GHG emissions. This principle is also used in the application of the UNFCCC's Clean Development Mechanism (CDM; see Chapter 8).

GEF aid is, however, project-based and therefore does not fund crosscutting or infrastructural initiatives that would enhance overall environmental capacities. Nor is it integrated (mainstreamed) into broader development initiatives of the World Bank. GEF funding remains a mere drop in the bucket compared to estimated needs, global development funding, or military expenditures. More recently, traditional capacity-building mechanisms, based on aid and direct low-cost lending to recipient actors, have been crowded out of the market by more complex market mechanisms, almost exclusively in the climate-change arena. The GEF is becoming a minor player in a complex, public–private climate funding architecture (© Nakhooda et al. 2015). As a public funding agency that funds projects that address environmental problems beyond climate change, it has an important niche in global funding networks, but it is not clear whether that niche will expand or contract in years to come.

Finally, the concept of additionality is highly problematic. Some argue it is overly technocratic, taking a strictly quantitative approach to project evaluation (Horta et al. 2001). Others suggest that quantification masks the imprecision and even dishonesty in evaluating what additional costs actually are. The need for counterfactual analysis (e.g. would the project have gone ahead anyway?) makes an accurate assessment of additional costs next to impossible (Streck 2011). At the relatively small scale at which the GEF operates, these problems are less significant than they are for larger mechanisms such as the CDM, but they still pose a challenge for its supporters.

Capacity-building efforts on the part of international environmental regimes have been critical to the successes to date of several international regimes – including ozone, biodiversity, and climate change. The global capacity-building infrastructure is, however, rapidly changing. As the private sector enters the global environmental funding arena, and market mechanisms, sometimes coupled with profit-based motives, become the tool of choice, straightforward funding that addresses an array of different problems in the global South is becoming more rare (Matt and Okereke 2015). Climate financing and capacity-building initiatives have become more complex and fragmented (Nakhooda et al. 2015). Certain capacity initiatives – such as "readiness initiatives" targeted at countries that will receive Reducing Emissions from Deforestation and Forest Degradation (REDD+) funding – reflect a more targeted, and conditional, approach to capacity-building. Climate negotiators are struggling to find the resources needed to fund adaptation and mitigation measures in developing countries, given studies that suggest that very large amounts are needed. One 2011 overview estimates that climate finance of "at least US$200 billion per year is needed by 2030, roughly balanced between mitigation and adaptation. To put this in perspective, official development assistance currently totals about US$120 billion per year" (Haites 2011, pp. 966–67). The Green Climate Fund, formally established in 2011 under UNFCCC auspices, struggles to meet its goal of $100 billion per year from Annex 1 countries. The search is on to find creative new ways of raising the needed funds, from leveraging private finance through sales of carbon credits (see Chapter 8) to imposing a tax on international financial transactions.[5]

Beyond Compliance: Learning, Socialization, and Transformative Effects

Regimes also have broader political impacts that go beyond compliance by shaping actors' interests, roles, and opportunities. Over time, such shifts have the potential to significantly improve the overall effectiveness of GEG. First, regimes can foster learning and, indeed, assess their own performance and learn from experience, thus enhancing or undermining a regime's problem-solving effectiveness. Second, the act of engaging in global governance can transform actors' interests, their roles, and even their identities in a changing global system.

These perspectives sit somewhat uneasily with the dominant approaches to IEP and the pragmatic, problem-solving perspective of many in scholarly and policy-making communities. They do not generate easy policy recommendations, are hard to operationalize and measure, and certainly do not occur within most political time frames. Yet, their implications are quite profound. The impacts of regimes – in this case, environmental treaty regimes – suggest that the shape of the international system of nation-states and the balances of power within that system are not immutable.

Regimes as Engines of Learning

An important way in which environmental regimes have impact is through the fostering of scientific research and other forms of knowledge, such as policy knowledge, targeted at policy-makers, NGOs, and other actors. In other words, effective regimes are able to enhance scientific and social knowledge about the problems the global community is trying to address,

---

[5] One such proposal, the so-called Tobin Tax, could potentially raise billions for climate financing by placing a small levy on global currency transactions, but remains controversial. See Sandbu 2011.

as well as knowledge about how best to address them. This extra-regime learning may lead to behavioral, preference, or interest adjustments outside the immediate boundaries of the regime and its obligations, allowing the spread of knowledge within states and across different constituencies (Haas and McCabe 2001, pp. 340–42). If such impacts occur, they are generally positive in terms of improving problem-solving effectiveness, and can change perceptions of problem structures, potentially ameliorating wicked problems (Miles et al. 2002). Therefore, they are not direct, goal-attaining regime impacts, but could be considered a critical part of the infrastructure of GEG if it is to be successful over the longer term.

The sorts of activities that can foster such learning include global environmental assessments at the regime level, including the Intergovernmental Panel on Climate Change (IPCC) or the Subsidiary Body for Scientific, Technical, and Technological Advice (SBSTTA) of the Convention on Biological Diversity (CBD) (Farrell and Jäger 2006). Larger-scale studies, such as the UN-sponsored Millennium Ecosystem Assessment (2005), drew on the expertise and support of many national and international agencies and scientific bodies to provide perspective on the state of the global environment. Many of the initiatives mentioned in the previous section on capacity-building are carried out by regime or cross-regime bodies with the goal of facilitating policy learning and knowledge-building on the ground in developing countries. Training initiatives help build knowledge and expertise on the ground in Southern countries. The UN Institute for Training and Research (UNITAR) provides training issue areas such as chemicals and waste management, climate change, and more generally in environmental governance and international diplomacy. The Green Customs Initiative, sponsored by UNEP, Interpol, and other international agencies, trains customs officials in Southern countries to recognize transboundary environmental crime and smuggled goods. These examples highlight the importance of forging linkages across regimes, pooling and augmenting knowledge and learning capacities, a topic we return to in the final section of this chapter.

Many regimes provide databases and knowledge banks for actors to use as needed. Regime actors also disseminate knowledge to state and other relevant actors. These actions are frequently the result of secretariat activism (Biermann and Siebenhüner 2009). The CBD Secretariat has been an effective knowledge builder: the regime has a number of expert committees, and publishes well-read and respected reports (such as *Global Biodiversity Outlook*). It has been less successful in terms of outreach and influence (Siebenhüner 2009). The same study identifies the small and decidedly underresourced Secretariat of the UN Convention to Combat Desertification (UNCCD) as having a strong discursive influence in shaping how desertification is talked about as a global issue, shifting it from a local-cumulative issue to more a problem of the global commons (Bauer 2009). UNEP, as an anchor organization for the whole system, is widely considered successful in terms of providing knowledge, information, and resources to states (per its mandate) and the regimes under its auspices, despite the capacity constraints it operates under (Ivanova 2010).

Learning within Regimes

Given the complexities of global environmental problems and international politics, it would be wrong to assume that regime participants "get it right" at the outset. Instead, most treaty regimes provide mechanisms to assess their progress, incorporate new information, learn from experience, and adjust policies, practices, and goals accordingly. The ability to incorporate new information or learn from experience is a crucial component of treaty regimes if they are to be effective over the long term.

Oran Young distinguishes between two different types of learning that can be applied to regimes. On one level, learning is "fundamentally a matter of devising new means through which to pursue unchanging objectives." On another, "a more far-reaching form of social learning . . . occurs in cases where the operation of a regime leads to major changes in how the problem a regime addresses is understood, and as a result, ideas about how to cope with it" (Young 1999, p. 262). Joanna Depledge identifies three important dimensions of intra-regime learning in environmental regimes (Depledge 2006, p. 2): the input and processing of new technological information; the evolution of concepts and ideas (some of which may be incorporated, others discarded); and the strengthening of relationships among participants. As governments continue to interact, they learn more about each other's motives and concerns, developing a shared collective perspective, and new individual outlooks on the world. She contrasts learning with regime ossification: the failure to learn or evolve across all three of these dimensions, a condition she argues afflicts large parts of the UNFCCC process.

Many regimes have internal and external self-assessment processes. Receptive individuals within regimes may play a role too, as can a positive extra-regime context (including strong relationships with UNEP, NGOs, or the research world). High conflicts of interest among states tend to militate against learning, as the climate example appears to show. Just because new knowledge, whether scientific data about a problem, or new insights on how to design policy, exists does not mean it is going to be taken up and used by the actors who should (Haas and Stevens 2011).

For an example of intra-regime learning, take the case of the major agreements governing intentional oil pollution at sea: OILPOL (1954) and its successor, MARPOL (1973) (Mitchell 1994; Mitchell et al. 1999). Both were created with the intention of preventing or controlling the deliberate discharge of oil and other pollutants by marine vessels. Amendments to these regimes have both widened the scope of the marine pollution regime (from oil to a range of other pollutants) and substantially improved compliance by shipping companies (and their home governments), following earlier failures in controlling ballast discharges. Moving away from discharge limits toward equipment standards (the installation of double hulls on ships, which keep dirty ballast water separate from a ship's cargo of oil), beginning in the 1970s, is credited with a good deal of the improvement in compliance rates. Rather than having to ascertain whether a ship has illegally discharged its ballast in coastal waters, regulatory agencies can instead check whether ships are adhering to equipment standards. Ships violating MARPOL standards can be barred from entering ports.

In a study of how different regimes manage the task of reviewing performance in the context of implementation, Victor et al. (1998) find that many regimes in fact contain active systems for implementation review (SIRs), operating through formal and informal channels. SIRs are "institutions through which the parties share information, compare activities, review performance, handle noncompliance, and adjust commitments" (Victor et al. 1998, p. 3). They include the basic decision-making processes of the regime: protocols and amendments, and conferences of the parties (COPs); rules for submitting reports and carrying out on-site inspections; the work of scientific and technical bodies associated with the regime; and, at a more informal level, work carried out by NGOs and similar actors on the ground. The ozone regime is a case of a successful SIR process (Greene 1998). Its SIR operates both through dedicated regime-review processes (e.g. the formal reporting process) and through agencies and institutions that have taken on these functions over time, even though some, including various NGOs, are not directly part of the regime. Greene notes that the most important part of this process is that these disparate actors and processes began at a certain point to operate as a "system," with an allocation of responsibilities and mechanisms for coordinating tasks and passing on information from one branch to another, greatly enhancing problem-solving effectiveness in this particular case.

Other studies focus on why some regimes or international organizations are better at learning or at fostering learning than others. The GEF is often cited as an example of an intergovernmental organization (IGO) that has exhibited successful learning, while the CDM is also praised as a market mechanism that has learned and adapted (Jacur 2010; see also Chapter 8). On the other hand, the IPCC has had a harder time both fostering learning on the part of the global climate regime and learning as an organization itself (Haas and Stevens 2011; Hulme and Mahony 2010). Intense inter-state politics of the climate negotiations have inhibited the smooth uptake of the IPCC's findings into regime negotiations (Depledge 2006). In terms of its own learning, the IPCC has faced continued attacks on its credibility, whether via the Climategate e-mail scandal or because of (inevitable) errors in its lengthy reports – yet it has been slow to take the offensive against such attacks.

Yet, as scholars working in science and technology studies (STS) and local knowledge traditions argue, learning per se is not always good if it privileges particular sources of information or problem-framing over others or attempts to "impose known truths onto recalcitrant or dissident actors" (Jasanoff 1998, p. 86). In this perspective, successful regimes are those that "leave room for negotiation among competing views of the world – a negotiated and networked compliance, promoting a horizontal politics of the global environment" rather than those relying on "a compliance that is too firmly imposed and monitored from above" (Jasanoff 1998, p. 86). In part this is a call to integrate different voices, and knowledge holders, into GEG, and in part it is a call to recognize that processes of learning are open-ended, and that regime goals should not be fixed according to any one particular worldview or frame.[6]

Transformative Effects of Global Environmental Regimes

Environmental governance regimes may have deeper impacts on participants and political institutions. Rather than state and other actor preferences, roles, and even identities being given, they can be shaped by the process of engaging in global governance (VanDeveer 1997; O'Neill et al. 2004). Although these changes can be hard to identify and trace empirically, it is possible to identify important regime impacts in these areas that can shape both regime effectiveness and actors' roles in global politics and governance more generally. This section sketches out relevant examples.

First, GEG regimes have led to role redefinition with respect to state and non-state actors in the international system. Processes of state-led environmental governance may also reshape power relations in the existing anarchic international system. Climate change has entered the realm of international "high politics" previously occupied only by economic and

---

[6] See also Jasanoff and Martello 2004.

security issues. The rise of the BASIC countries (Brazil, South Africa, India, and China) within the climate regime suggests that this changing balance of power might spill over into other issue areas, helping to disrupt, for example, the longstanding international economic order. As we saw in Chapter 4 and throughout this chapter, non-state actors have been allocated or taken on increasingly significant roles at different stages of the diplomatic process. In terms of regime implementation, for example, NGOs have been more formally incorporated into roles of monitoring compliance and receiving and channeling environmental aid. This practice relieves states of some immediate burdens, though it may expose them to more scrutiny than they might have expected.

Second, transformative pressures are evident in states' domestic politics and interactions. Regimes "affect behavior by creating new constituencies or shifting the balance among factions or subgroups vying for influence within individual states or other actors" (Young and Levy 1999, p. 26). Such impacts already exist, even in the USA, where, for example, agencies such as the State Department's Bureau of Oceans, Environmental and Scientific Affairs deal specifically with international environmental problems and negotiations. US NGOs and business international non-governmental organization (BINGOs) have nearly all established international campaigns. Beyond the Beltway, US state governments and cities are taking climate action into their own hands. California and the North Eastern states have taken action to reduce GHG emissions, while many US cities belong to international networks such as C40 or the International Council of Local Environmental Initiatives (ICLEI) that encourage action at the local level (Gore and Robinson 2009).

Third, at the level of the nation-state, participation in regimes may help socialize individual states (Terhalle and Depledge 2013). Scholars who study socialization processes in international relations theory are interested in how, as states and their leaders develop deeper links with international institutions and regimes, "these interactions help shape their perceptions of the world, and their role within it" (Cronin 2002, p. 138; Finnemore 1996). This process involves the internalization by states of international norms, both procedural (e.g. problems are best solved through cooperation rather than conflict) and substantive (e.g. sustainable development supplanting environmental protection). While socialization processes are often discussed with respect to states new to the international system, such as the former Soviet bloc, they can also apply to states that have long participated in the mainstream of international diplomacy. In a study of US and Chinese engagement in climate negotiations, Terhalle and Depledge (2013) illustrate the conditions under which socialization does or does not occur.

Finally, GEG regimes are arenas for the emergence and contestation of global norms and ideas (Bernstein 2002; Okereke 2006). Notions of inter- and intra-generational equity as embodied in some conceptualizations of sustainable development emerged from and have shaped environmental negotiations. Likewise, market-based environmentalism – the use of economic liberalization and economic instruments to combat the market failures associated with problems such as climate change – have gained traction through the UNFCCC process, as well as at major international meetings such as Rio+20 in 2012. These norms and principles are often contested in international forums. For example, the Precautionary Principle – which suggests a "go-slow" approach in the face of scientific uncertainty and risks over the long term in cases such as genetically modified organisms (GMOs) or certain chemicals, supported by the EU, has faced off against principles of "sound science." These principles suggest that in the absence of positive evidence of harm, development and use of GMOs or chemicals should proceed so that we may reap benefits now. Strong advocacy by the EU and its allies have introduced the Precautionary Principle into agreements such as the Cartagena Protocol of the CBD, in turn empowering actors facing similar struggles in other political arenas, domestic and international (Gupta 2014). These are important impacts, as ideas and norms help shape actors' (including states') interests and preferences as they continue to engage in GEP.

Ultimately, environmentalist goals and politics may be reshaping fundamental institutions of the global system, including that of territorial sovereignty (Eckersley 2005). Robert Falkner calls this the "greening of international society" whereby "environmental ideas and norms have gradually been woven into the normative fabric of the states system," a process that started in the early twentieth century (Falkner 2012, p. 503). It is, at this point of writing, too early, and too difficult, to assess this trend, but the environment may well be a major force reshaping the international system in the twenty-first century.

Next Steps

Identifying when and how international environmental regimes are effective raises difficult – but interesting – questions about how to design and assess effective GEG regimes. With more than forty years' experience with some regimes, the international community has learned a lot about what makes regimes work, or fail to work. This process has both deepened our understanding of the workings of international cooperation over time and generated numerous policy recommendations.

Assessments of regime effectiveness have also generated prescriptions for making the existing state-led system of GEG work better. Yet, while results to date are far from ideal from an environmentalist viewpoint, the progress that has been made in terms of setting up international institutions, creating mechanisms that enhance transparency and accountability, and creating mechanisms that encourage reflection and learning within regimes has been impressive.

Even so, we must not forget remaining challenges, of maintaining and building levels of compliance over time, of maintaining legitimacy and fairness – and learning to build in institutional agility to deal with unpredictable, non-linear problems (Bernstein and Cashore 2012; Young 2011). Questions of learning and assessment remain critical, and the insights written about in this chapter are equally applicable to the different sites and modes of governance we examine in the rest of this book. Efforts to improve the performance of state-led GEG also underpin movements toward creating and exploiting linkages and interaction across environmental regimes and a more comprehensive GEG architecture, as addressed in Chapter 9.

Next, in Chapter 6, we turn to another critical site of GEG, one that has only recently been recognized as critical to the global environment: the international economic order, and the institutions that govern international trade, finance, and development aid, more generally, economic globalization.

Discussion Questions

- Discuss and give examples of the differences between "problem-solving" and "compliance" dimensions of effectiveness. What are the challenges involved in measuring each? Using examples from specific regimes and agreements, what would you expect problem-solving and compliance to look like in those regimes?
- What are the arguments for and against incorporating more punishment or enforcement mechanisms into international environmental regimes? Are we better off relying on soft law or positive incentives, such as capacity-building, to enhance compliance?
- Many countries fail to meet their international commitments because they lack the capacity to meet them. What does "capacity" mean in this context? What are the criticisms of capacity-building initiatives, both as they are practiced in GEG and more generally?

SUGGESTIONS FOR FURTHER READING

Bernauer, Thomas. 1995. "The Effect of International Environmental Institutions: How we Might Learn More." *International Organization* 49.2: 351–77: this article describes the conceptual and methodological challenges in measuring the effectiveness of environmental regimes.

Falkner, Robert. 2012. "Global Environmentalism and the Greening of International Society." *International Affairs* 88.3: 503–22: thought-provoking reading on the deeper currents of the international system and global governance.

Gupta, Aarti, and Michael Mason, eds. 2014. *Transparency in Global Environmental Governance: Critical Perspectives*. Cambridge, MA: MIT Press: analysis and case studies about transparency as a global governance principle, its applications, and its strengths and weaknesses in both state-led and non-state GEG.

Weiss, Edith Brown, and Harold K. Jacobson, eds. 1998. *Engaging Countries: Strengthening Compliance with International Environmental Accords*. Cambridge, MA: MIT Press: a classic study of compliance that examines state behavior across five treaties and ten countries.

Young, Oran R., ed. 1999. *The Effectiveness of International Environmental Regimes: Causal Connections and Behavioral Mechanisms*. Cambridge, MA: MIT Press: a qualitative comparative analysis of regime effectiveness that identifies causal pathways through which regimes may exert a range of influences, applied to empirical cases. This is only one of Oran Young's many contributions to the field of GEP and the study of regime effectiveness.

6   Global Economic Governance and the Environment

The relationship between economic globalization and the environment has spurred debate across the fields of economics, international relations, law, geography, and other social science disciplines (Clapp and Dauvergne 2011). Is economic globalization, and the political structures that support it, intrinsically bad for the global environment? Is it a net positive for the environment, as the additional wealth generated by globalization is channeled into environmental protection and technological innovation? Alternatively, is globalization compatible with a sustainable future as long as we build in institutions and processes that enable environmental – and social – protections? As Clapp and Dauvergne point out, there are no definitive answers to these questions. However, they continue to inform how scholars, activists, and policy-makers address the ways in which the global economic order intersects with global environmental politics (GEP).

In this chapter we focus on the three main international economic governance institutions identified in Chapter 3 as sites of global governance: the World Trade Organization (WTO), the World Bank, and the International Monetary Fund (IMF), known collectively as the Bretton Woods institutions, after the 1944 conference where they were founded. We examine how they have created rules and institutions that steer and shape environmental governance at all levels, including governing the impacts of their own activities. Further, we focus on how they manage this transition, including the linkages and overlap between their work and that of the global environmental governance (GEG) arena.

As the main international organizations governing trade, finance, and development assistance, the Bretton Woods institutions have been critical in defining the path of economic globalization in the decades since World War Two. More recently, they have become focal points for critics of the environmental and social impacts of capitalist, or neoliberal, globalization. We examine the origins and trajectory of the post-war global economic order, and how trade, aid, and global finance are seen both as causes of global environmental change, and – potentially – as part of a transition to a more sustainable global economy.

Scholars give different weight to the role of the international economic order in global environmental politics. In Chapter 1 we discussed the difference between scholars who approach the global environment from a collective-action perspective and those who argue, by contrast, that global environmental degradation needs to be seen in the context of global capitalism. For the first group, largely associated with mainstream international relations theory, the problem is one of issue linkage. The Bretton Woods institutions are an uneasy fit with GEG norms and practices. The linkages that exist between the global economy and the environment and between their respective governance regimes are important and potentially conflict-laden. For either economic or environmental regimes to be effective, these linkages must be recognized and addressed.

For critical theorists, the way economic globalization drives environmental and social change and inequities is a central problem, and its omission from much of the mainstream GEP literature is a problem:

> Unless international relations theory sets out explicitly to tackle the set of questions that arise for the interaction between the economy and the ecosystem, it will instead merely find itself co-opting environmental analysis and accommodating 'green' issues within the prevailing conception of international relations. (Williams 1996, p. 43)

In this account, the WTO, the World Bank, and the IMF, as sites of global governance, are where powerful states and corporate actors work to maintain and reproduce the norms and structures of global capitalism, with corresponding pressures on the global environment and social justice concerns. Rather than focusing on environmental treaty regimes, we need to pay more attention to harnessing international economic institutions to a more environmentally and socially responsible agenda, or on the potential for restructuring the global economy to one that is (perhaps) more localized and (certainly) recognizes environmental and societal sustainability.

Thus, the visibility of and the political responses to linkages between the global economy and the global environment have galvanized new lines of inquiry into the relationship between international relations and the environment. This chapter begins by outlining the emergence of the global economic order and its basic trajectory since World War Two. We turn then to a discussion of three major GEG issues that have had a major impact on environmental politics and change: trade liberalization, development funding and debt, and how the WTO, World Bank, and IMF respectively have responded to environmental criticisms. The final section analyzes their emergence as sites of GEG, and their continued existence as sites of global contestation.

The Post-World War Two Economic Order and the Bretton Woods Institutions

In July 1944, 750 representatives from 45 Allied nations met in Bretton Woods, New Hampshire, to discuss the creation of a post-war economic order. At that point in time, World War Two had left much of Europe and Asia in ruins. Although the war was not to end for another year, Allied leaders had already begun plans for reconstruction, for easing the transition to independence of many colonized nations, and, over the long term, for providing a framework for stable, and peaceful, economic growth and development worldwide.

The ideational underpinnings of the new economic order born at the Bretton Woods Conference were clear. Allied leaders were intent on avoiding the economic mistakes made in the years following World War One, which led to the Great Depression of the late 1920s and early 1930s, and contributed to the rise of totalitarian and extreme nationalist ideologies in Europe and Japan (Hobsbawm 1995; Wood 1986). They saw economic growth, an open global economy, a system of safeguards to protect against financial crisis, and open cooperation among nation-states as essential to a more peaceful world.

The delegates to the Bretton Woods Conference were concerned with three main areas of the global economy: trade; economic reconstruction and development; and international financial stability. To those ends, delegates agreed to establish the International Bank for Reconstruction and Development (IBRD), which became the World Bank, and the IMF. The IBRD's role was to funnel money into post-war reconstruction, and, later, to the development of poorer or newly independent countries. The IMF was designed to aid countries with severe balance-of-payments problems, and underwrite the stability of the new international fixed-exchange-rate monetary system. In 1947 twenty-three countries, meeting in Havana, Cuba, signed the General Agreement on Tariffs and Trade (GATT), an agreement mooted at Bretton Woods, and designed to lower barriers to global trade in goods and services. Only in 1995 did a formal international trade organization, the WTO, come into being.

Three general points about the evolution of this new global economic order are worth noting. First, in 1944 environmental concerns were not part of the political or economic agenda. With the exception of one article of the GATT, the environment is not mentioned in any of the founding documents of the World Bank, the GATT, or the IMF. This is not surprising: awareness of resource limitations and global environmental degradation did not emerge in a real, political sense at the global level until the late 1960s.

Second, the period from the 1940s through to the 1970s marks an era of US leadership in underwriting and maintaining international cooperation, and building international economic regimes. This was a period of US hegemony, when the USA was both willing and able to support the global economic order (Keohane 1984). US leadership after the immediate post-war recovery period was driven by the Cold War, when halting the spread of global communism and containing the Soviet Union were central among Western concerns. Many decisions about development aid, in particular, were made with the aim of keeping newly independent nations out of the Soviet sphere of influence. In the same way, aid decisions in the modern era are driven by geopolitical concerns, including maintaining democracies or repelling terrorist organizations, which sometimes sit uneasily with environmental or social concerns.

Third, the story told here, of a liberal global economic order set up to foster worldwide peace and prosperity, looks quite different from the neoliberal globalization that has caused so much outrage today, even though the cast of characters remains the same. In fact, the Bretton Woods leaders – and their post-war successors – were quite aware that an open global economy, while carrying the promise of greater economic growth and international interconnectedness, also carried risks. Open economies are vulnerable economies. Whole economic sectors can be destroyed as domestic buyers shift to cheaper imports. In other cases, countries can become dependent on producing one or a few raw materials, which are then shipped overseas for sale or processing. In practice, the post-1945 settlements were more aware of economic vulnerability than of dependency. The GATT had built into it, for example, safeguards that allowed countries to protect certain industries, but little to protect against global price volatility. This era also marked the rise of welfare states in North America and Western Europe: governments took on responsibility for their populations by providing pensions, unemployment insurance, and health care. John Ruggie refers to this bargain – an open global economy backed up by international and domestic safeguards to protect the vulnerable – as the "compromise of embedded liberalism" (Ruggie 1983).

By the early 1990s the terms of this bargain had changed (Stiglitz 2002), with significant social and environmental impacts (Clapp and Dauvergne 2011; Liverman and Vilas 2006). Many factors contributed to the rise of a far more free-market type of global capitalism that stressed economic efficiency, small government (and small welfare states), and privatization. These principles dominated the economic policies of the USA and UK under Prime Minister Margaret Thatcher and President Ronald Reagan throughout the 1980s, spreading globally by the end of the decade. Both leaders embarked on vigorous programs of privatization, increasing efficiency, and dismantling welfare states in their own countries – with positive results for economic growth, but negative impacts on many sectors of society, certainly increasing income inequality in the USA and the UK. During the 1990s the IMF applied many of the same ideas to the emerging, post-Soviet democracies in Central and Eastern Europe – with an ideological clarity, but decidedly mixed economic and environmental results.

It did not take long for these ideas to permeate international financial and development organizations. Following the Latin American debt crises of the 1980s, leading economic policy-makers in the USA and at the IMF and World Bank contributed to formulating the so-called Washington Consensus, a set of guiding economic principles that has come to underpin contemporary neoliberal globalization, and described by some as "market fundamentalism" (Stiglitz 2002; Gore 2000). As part of their lending programs, both the IMF and the World Bank promoted a series of policy adjustments, including privatization, market liberalization, open economies (to trade and foreign direct investment), the allocation of property rights, tax reform, fiscal discipline, and the elimination of many government support programs and subsidies. Combined, these are known as Structural Adjustment Programs (SAPs). Loan recipients have to agree to implement these reforms as a condition for receiving aid. From Latin America in the 1980s, to the emerging democracies of Central and Eastern Europe in the 1990s, to struggling governments in Africa today, rapid adjustment and market reforms have become a feature of political and economic life, affecting all sectors of society.

As the ideas of neoliberal globalization spread, criticism of the impacts of these reforms became more systematic and widespread (Stiglitz 2002). Critics focused on how these reforms were undertaken (too rapidly, and with little account taken of different national contexts), their impacts on poverty, debt, and income inequality, and their impacts on key indicators of environmental quality. By the late 1990s tens of thousands of protestors were showing up at meetings of international financial institutions, and many more individuals and groups – from Nobel Prize winners to rock stars – were voicing their concern about the social and environmental impacts of globalization, targeting the WTO, the World Bank, and the IMF in particular.

Perhaps surprisingly, these institutions began to listen – in their own fashion, but listening nonetheless. In this process, environmental concerns have emerged as focal points in calls for global economic reform, aiding a push towards a "post-Washington Consensus," whereby the tools of neoliberalism can be used to create a more sustainable (and equitable) global economy. What this actually means in practice, and whether it can be achieved, remains unclear. The 2008 global financial crisis muddied the waters even further. Certainly, the economic downturn led to less pollution (and to more countries reaching their Kyoto Protocol targets by 2012 than were expected). The recession, however, pushed environmental quality and policy issues to the bottom of political agendas in developed and developing countries (Cha 2008). Incentives to invest in costly environmental technologies were lost.

Opportunities for new synergies emerged at the global level as the concept of the Green Economy took hold at Rio+20, and global economic institutions began to shift their gaze to large-scale, public–private climate mitigation and adaptation funding as ways to create new avenues for development, markets, and economic growth. A global Green Economy is defined by the UN Environment Programme (UNEP) as "one that results in improved human well-being and social equity, while significantly reducing environmental risks and ecological scarcities. In its simplest expression, a green economy can be thought of as one that is low carbon, resource efficient and socially inclusive."[1] Along with earlier framings of sustainable development and green growth, the Green Economy concept focuses on positive interactions between environmental, sustainable development, and economic priorities (Tienhaara 2014). Representing the latest incarnation of this overarching global norm, it has been heavily criticized by some and lauded by others, but reinforces the arena of global economic governance as a site of global environmental governance as well. We now move to tracing these political and normative shifts, and the ongoing challenges facing first, the international financial institutions and second, the international trade regime.

Global Development, Finance, and the Environment: The World Bank and the International Monetary Fund

The participants at the 1944 Bretton Woods Conference recognized that post-war recovery, stability, and development would depend on global flows of development aid and loans, and that these large capital transfers would require careful coordination and governance. This section examines how the World Bank and the IMF operate, the debate over the environmental (and social) impacts of their activities, and the extent to which each has responded to criticisms. The World Bank is best known for funding government-led development projects in developing and emerging economies, and the IMF for structural adjustment lending, again to governments. Of the two, the World Bank has been more of

[1] See www.unep.org/greeneconomy/AboutGEI/WhatisGEI/tabid/29784/Default.aspx.

a focal point for critics and opponents. It has also been more responsive to criticism from environmentalist constituencies. Many still wonder, however, if either organization has fully taken on board the implications of the full range of their activities for environmental protection and sustainability worldwide.

The World Bank, the IMF, and Post-War Development

Both the World Bank and the IMF are funded and directed by, and lend almost wholly to, national governments. Both are membership organizations, operating under weighted voting systems (compared with the "one member, one vote" operating principles of the WTO and the UN), and funded by a combination of member contributions and financing on international capital markets. Voting rights in the World Bank governing council are allocated according to financial contribution to the Bank. Thus, the USA, Japan, and the EU control over half the vote in the World Bank, with the USA alone holding between 16 and 17 percent of the total votes.[2] Voting power in the IMF is allocated according to countries' relative gross domestic product (GDP).

The Bank and the IMF are not the only sources of international development aid and lending. Most developed countries have bilateral aid agencies and programs in place, although almost all fall below the 0.7 percent of GDP level established as a baseline for developed countries' giving levels established by the UN in 1970. Regional development banks (RDBs) supplement the World Bank's activities, including the African Development Bank, the Asian Development Bank, the Interamerican Development Bank, and others. Governments also borrow money from private financial institutions and from other governments. However, the World Bank and the IMF are often the main port of call for large-scale loans or financing or refinancing once countries are in financial crisis. Their decisions often influence directions taken by other global financial institutions, and they are an authoritative source of information on the state of the world's economy.[3]

The World Bank's chief mandate is global poverty alleviation. Along with other RDBs in Asia, Africa, and elsewhere, it makes loans and channels aid and development assistance from developed to less-developed countries. Its two largest agencies lend or grant money to governments. The IBRD issues loans at market rates and raises its own capital through investing in international financial markets. It accounts

---

[2] See the World Bank's website, www.worldbank.org.
[3] See www.worldbank.org. The World Bank's *World Development Indicators*, published annually.

for roughly 80 percent of World Bank lending. The International Development Association (IDA) issues loans at zero or low interest, and is funded by donations from member countries. A third arm of the Bank, the International Finance Corporation (IFC), engages in private-sector lending, while the International Center for Settlement of Investment Disputes and the Multilateral Investment Guarantee Agency engage in risk-reduction and insurance activities in order to incentivize foreign direct investment (FDI).[4]

The World Bank is best known for funding large-scale development projects. It has, historically, funded large dams, roads, power plants, large-scale agriculture, and other sorts of projects aimed at national infrastructure development. In recent years it has shifted its project portfolio more toward environmental aid (partly through the Global Environment Facility [GEF]) and smaller-scale development projects, such as micro-lending initiatives.

The IMF was created to supervise the international monetary system and engage in short- to medium-term lending to countries experiencing temporary balance-of-payments problems arising from the fixed-exchange-rate system set up after the war. When the international monetary order switched from fixed to floating exchange rates in 1973, this part of the IMF's mandate was undercut. During the Latin American debt crises of the 1980s several countries threatened to default on loans issued by private lenders, with a potentially devastating knock-on effect on private lending institutions in developed countries (Gilpin 2001, pp. 313–16). This threat led to a new role for the IMF as the main proponent of structural adjustment lending programs, as outlined above, to forestall future economic crises. Increasingly, the IMF and World Bank have coordinated their activities, with the Bank taking on a wider role in structural adjustment lending.

Although they are far from the only agencies engaged in development assistance, the World Bank and the IMF have always been at the forefront of development debates. In the following section we focus on two types of development assistance that have been highlighted in debates about the relationship between global finance, development, and the environment: the funding of large-scale development projects, such as big dams; and debt relief in the form of structural adjustment lending, practiced by both the IMF and the Bank. We then move on to examine how the international financial institutions have addressed critics, then the more complex contemporary global economic and environmental landscape they face today.

---

[4] Collectively, these five agencies are called the World Bank Group; the term World Bank usually (and as used here) refers to the IBRD and the IDA.

Environmental and Social Impacts of Development Institutions

International development institutions took the first steps toward becoming a site of GEG in response to criticisms of lending practices and their negative environmental and social impacts. This section investigates those practices before moving on to collective responses – especially on the part of the World Bank – and newer challenges to the fragile equilibrium between development and environment that emerged during the 2000s.

a.   *Project Lending and the World Bank*   Large-scale infrastructure and development projects, proposed by governments and frequently funded by the World Bank, emerged in the 1980s as a flashpoint for debate around the Bank's development goals and trajectories. From Egypt's huge Aswan Dam project, begun in the 1950s, onwards, projects such as large dams (providing hydroelectric power and irrigation), modern highways, coal and nuclear power plants, and the expansion of industrialized agriculture were designed to meet goals of rapid development and to enhance the strength and prestige of governments of newly independent nations and their leaders. The environmental and social impacts of these massive projects – from relocating affected communities (more often than not marginalized or indigenous peoples), to the destruction of valuable ecosystems, to the waste of many resources for a far smaller gain than anticipated – were frequently devastating. International attention has focused specifically on large (mega) dam projects around the world, as they have been among the most visible of these projects (McCully 2001). Starting in 1949, the Bank's first loans to fifteen developing countries were to fund the construction of large dams, and the funding of dams remains a large part of the Bank's portfolio even today, with one of the highest-profile current projects being the Inga 3 Project on the Congo River. In 2000 the World Commission on Dams (WCD) estimated that 20–80 million people had been displaced by large dam projects globally, many of those funded by the World Bank, with concomitant negative impacts on biodiversity and environmental health.[5]

In the 1980s emerging transnational activist coalitions began specifically targeting the World Bank. A series of such projects – notably the Polonoroeste resettlement project in Brazil, begun in 1981 and which included the construction of a major highway through the Amazon rainforest, the Narmada Dam project in India, first authorized in 1978, and the Arun III Dam project in Nepal – came under particular scrutiny (Clapp and Dauvergne 2011, p. 202; Fox and Brown 1998). Two factors

---

[5] Recent data and analysis can be found at www.internationalrivers.org, the website of International Rivers, a leading anti-dam NGO.

made World Bank-funded projects attractive targets for opposition. First, activists could point to visible and persuasive evidence of social and environmental harm, particularly the impacts on relocated communities, often forcibly moved to substandard (even non-existent) housing in lands that barely suited their skills. Second, the political structure of the Bank made it an especially vulnerable target. Because of the preponderance of power held by the USA and other Organization for Economic Cooperation and Development (OECD) countries in World Bank decision-making processes, activist groups were able to lobby elected representatives in these countries to get them to withhold funding to the Bank until it became more accountable to these constituencies. Often, Northern activist groups were able to work on behalf of, or in coalition with, partners in the affected areas (Fox and Brown 1998). As a result in part of activist engagement, the US International Financial Institutions Act (1986) contained an amendment that required the USA to withhold funding from the World Bank if any of its projects did not release an impact assessment within a given time period. This action helped galvanize a series of reforms on the part of the Bank, detailed below.

b.   *Debt, Structural Adjustment Lending, and the Environment*   Harder to address has been the problem of national indebtedness to global institutions – and the social and environmental impacts of their lending programs. Notably, structural adjustment lending programs implemented by the IMF and, more recently, the World Bank, developed in part to get countries out of serious fiscal crises, instead generated a cycle of unsustainable payment schedules and a financial morass that highly indebted countries could not pull themselves out of. Debt sustainability and/or forgiveness were targeted in the UN Millennium Development Goals as part of a sustainable future. In its own policies and publications, the IMF has maintained general support of environmental objectives, especially when directly affected by macroeconomic policies, but has not gone nearly as far as the World Bank in terms of implementing reforms. As part of broader critiques of neoliberal development and structural adjustment lending, and in specific issue areas, such as debates over water privatization or deforestation, its impacts have increasingly come under scrutiny.

A country's external debt includes money owed to governments, to the World Bank and the IMF, and to private financial institutions. Loan amounts are compounded by the interest payable on that debt, known as debt-servicing payments. While the debt crises of the 1970s and 1980s led to increased attention by leading governments and multilateral institutions to the external debt challenge, by the 1990s the ratio of private and official debt to national income in low- and middle-income countries had risen sharply. For the poorest countries, their debt peaked at 200 percent of their national income in the mid-1990s (United Nations Department of Economic and Social Affairs 2005, Figure 12.1), and the most indebted countries were, on average, only paying 40 percent of their debt-service obligations annually. In order to meet these obligations, many countries have been obliged to channel other sorts of financial assistance into debt-service payments, drastically reducing the amount of money available for development goals. Further, large external debt encourages deforestation, mining, and other economic activities designed to raise hard currency through export.

Most agree that high external debt has an adverse impact on sustainability and environmental protection programs at national and local levels. There is less agreement over the impact of neoliberal reforms through SAPs (and neoliberalism in general) on the environment (Liverman and Vilas 2006; Clapp and Dauvergne 2011). On the one hand, the impacts of marketizing (thereby pricing) natural resources, such as water, forests, and land, might be positive for the environment, in that they lead to more efficient use of those resources, or help reform and restructure agricultural and land management and practices (Hecht et al. 2006). Likewise, FDI might improve environmental quality if developed-country multinational corporations import better technology and hold more closely to the standards of their home countries.

On the other hand, by reducing accountability and oversight programs and creating incentives for rapid resource exploitation and industrialization, particularly for export, many argue that these reforms are just as likely to lead to severe environmental damage (Friends of the Earth 1999). For example, one study of Bank/IMF-led restructuring of the energy sector in Bolivia finds that the facilitation of the entry of multinational corporations, such as Enron and Shell, into the national market had a detrimental effect on local environments and communities, impacts that the Bank and the IMF failed to take into account (Hindery 2004). In the wake of the 2008 financial crisis, the bailout agreements that the EU and other actors have imposed on highly indebted developed countries have generated significant environmental impacts. Greece, for example, faces higher air pollution and deforestation as people switch to gathering and burning wood in the wake of higher energy taxes, the environmental costs associated with increased gold-mining activity, and a crumbling environmental regulatory system (Lekakis and Kousis 2013).

c.   *Responses and Reforms* The World Bank began addressing its environmental and social impacts in the 1980s. In 1985 it pulled out of the Polonoroeste project, and in 1987 it established an Environment Department, which undertakes considerable research and assessment, but does not have lending decision-making capacity. In 1991 the Bank set up an independent panel – the Morse Commission – to investigate the Narmada Dam project. The 1992 report of the Commission was highly critical of both the project itself and the World Bank's efforts to ensure environmental and social protections. The Bank withdrew from the project, and in 1993 it established an Inspections Panel, an independent appeals process that allows citizens adversely affected by Bank projects to file claims regarding Bank policies. This important external accountability mechanism has subsequently been adopted by other arms of the World Bank Group (Park 2010). All projects the Bank now funds are required to submit an environmental impact assessment, and the Bank has increased its portfolio of "good" projects, namely those related to environmental protection, small-scale projects, and greener production or energy generation.

The World Bank's commitment to environmental reform can also be seen in its commitments – old and new – to global environmental funding and capacity-building. Since 1991 the Bank has administered the finances of the GEF and the Montreal Protocol Fund (see Chapter 5), and plays a leading role in the complex world of global climate funding (Nakhooda and Norman 2014). In the latter arena, it has fostered a mix of market-based financial mechanisms (in part to raise money for funding over and above member contributions) along with "old-school" aid and loans. It funds both mitigation and adaptation activities. Through the Forest Carbon Partnership Facility, the Bank funds developing countries that are implementing preparatory – "readiness" – plans to be able to receive funding under the Reducing Emissions from Deforestation and (forest) Degradation (REDD+) initiative, in order to preserve forest stocks as carbon sinks. In early 2015 it had total contributions of $850 million, with forty-seven recipient countries chosen.[6] The Bank is also the (temporary) trustee of the Green Climate Fund, set up in the 2010 UN Framework Convention on Climate Change (UNFCCC) Conference of the Parties (COP), held in Cancun, to be a long-term source of climate financing. In addition to pledges of $100 billion per year by developed countries by 2020 (so far, slow getting off the ground), the Fund is also supposed to be supported by money raised from global private capital markets – a move that is controversial, and considered risky.[7]

---

[6] See www.forestcarbonpartnership.org.
[7] The Berlin-based Heinrich Böll Institute maintains data and analysis of the complex architecture of global climate financing. See www.climatefundsupdate.org.

Arguably, one of the most significant things the IFIs can do to minimize global environmental impacts is to forgive debt owed to them by poorer countries. The combined social and environmental impacts of national indebtedness (real and perceived) galvanized enough political opposition to these actions that both the IMF and the World Bank have had to rethink debt-amelioration strategies. In 2006 the Bank announced a Multilateral Debt Relief Initiative (MDRI), which would cancel all debt owed by the highly indebted poorer countries (HIPCs) to the IDA, and would institute debt-sustainability initiatives for low-income countries. A 2014 study showed that debt ratios have indeed declined among HIPCs, from an average of 145% of gross national income in 2000 to 35% in 2011, and, due in part to less exposure to the 2008 financial crisis, are lower than in many developed countries (Prizzoni and Mustapha 2014). This decline can be traced directly to the MDRI.

However, the likely positive impacts of this initiative may be outweighed by the environmental costs associated with austerity financing of European and other developed countries in the wake of the global financial crisis. Further, IFI resources have been stretched addressing these crises and, despite the success of the HIPC debt-forgiveness initiative in meeting its goals, there is little evidence of comprehensive attention to the truly complex nature and sources of debt across the international system today (Soederberg 2013).

d.   Ongoing   and   Emerging   Challenges Despite implementing a number of significant reforms in a short period, the World Bank remains a target for criticism. As a large international institution with many stakeholders, interested observers, and a variety of mandates, the Bank has been subject to different preferences and incentive structures at different phases of its policy process – from defining objectives to implementing specific projects and policies on the ground – making it hard to translate environmental goals into outcomes (Gutner 2002). The Bank has struggled to mainstream environmental concerns into all of its activities: several critical sectors of Bank activity, including structural adjustment lending and drawing up country-assistance strategies, have yet to incorporate environmental concerns (Clapp and Dauvergne 2011). Its own 2014 review of its safeguards process revealed major flaws in its implementation, on top of standards that had not been changed in decades (Yukhanov 2014).

The overall portfolio of Bank projects remains biased toward large-scale and environmentally damaging projects (especially energy projects with large greenhouse-gas [GHG] emissions), and environmental lending remains a tiny fraction of overall lending. Without a direct mandate to address climate change, one of the most critical threats to development, it finds itself floundering to keep up amidst the intense politics of global climate governance (Birdsall 2012). The World Resources Institute has estimated that in the 2000s less than 20 percent, on average, of its energy projects considered climate impacts. In 2009, reports indicated that World Bank investment in coal-plant construction remained high (Clapp and Dauvergne 2011, p. 205). Critics noted its reengagement in funding large dams, without properly auditing its processes for preventing social displacement (Broussard 2015). There is also a huge gap between what is pledged to address climate-change impacts and what will be needed: "estimates of the costs of addressing climate change in developing countries vary substantially from $480 billion to $1.5 trillion per year" (Nakhooda 2012). Even the lowest number vastly exceeds the amount pledged to date by developed countries.

Further, while the Bank has been praised for pulling out of, or refusing to fund, certain big, environmentally damaging projects, such as China's Three Gorges Dam, the loss of Bank funding does not always mean that governments cancel the projects. Instead, they often turn to bilateral or private-sector alternatives, from export credit agencies to venture-capital funds. Export credit agencies from Canada, Germany, Sweden, and Switzerland have all funded the Three Gorges Dam (Clapp and Dauvergne 2011, p. 216). These sources of funding are considerably less transparent and accountable than the World Bank, and offer far fewer opportunities for international review. Even when the Bank has implemented a "mixed" funding model, as in projects to build a dam on the Mekong, evidence suggests that stakeholders prefer private funding (Hirsch and Wilson 2011). China has taken advantage of these preferences, funding development projects in Africa in return for access to oil and other resources. Its actions, and African countries' acceptance of this aid, has worried the international community (Peh and Eyal 2010; Mol 2011).

Some argue that the "greening" of the World Bank and other IFIs has led to the development and implementation of a new ideology of development, a sort of "green neoliberalism" (Goldman 2005; see also Park 2012). Goldman argues that in responding to critics and setting up organizational and policy structures to cope with environmental and societal demands, the Bank, relying on its vast financial resources and on a transnational network of experts and government employees, has reshaped the architecture, substance, and trajectory of the environment/development policies of many of its recipient states. This argument is echoed across the more critical literature on global financing and development and the Green Economy, and speaks to both constructivist and neo-Gramscian perspectives on GEG (Newell 2014; Bernstein 2013b; see Chapter 1).

Finally, the Bank faces significant fragmentation challenges, as does the WTO (see below). RDBs remain strong, and have proliferated over the years. The rise of non-traditional Southern-led development banks operating outside the multilateral system has caused more concern in recent years (Wihtol 2014). The New Development Bank of the BRICS countries (Brazil, Russia, India, China, and South Africa), and China's Asian Infrastructure Investment Bank add to the fragmentation of global development financing, and could lead to a dilution of social and environmental safeguards, even those maintained by the World Bank.

Trade, the GATT/WTO, and the Global Environment

Debates over links and conflicts between global trade rules and environmental laws and quality began in the early 1990s, engaging economists, political scientists, scholars of international law, and many others. At first, the primary concern was the extent to which free, or liberalized, trade harmed environmental quality. The debate rapidly moved on to the question of whether or not the rules associated with the GATT/WTO regime could be used to undermine domestic environmental regulations. Many have raised the possibility that the rules associated with environmental treaty regimes could themselves conflict with WTO rules, and others are concerned with the environmental impacts of the broader agreements contained within the overall WTO structure.[8]

From GATT to the WTO: The International Trade Regime

The main agreement governing international trade is the GATT, subsumed by the WTO in 1995. The GATT coexists (sometimes uneasily) with an increasingly large number of regional trading agreements, including the 1994 North American Free Trade Agreement (NAFTA), the European Union (EU), and bilateral agreements. These more focused agreements often go beyond GATT rules in eliminating barriers to free trade. Some contain advanced arrangements to address environmental or labor-related impacts, others do not (Jinnah 2012b).

The GATT entered into force in 1948. It established a rules-based international trade regime, designed around principles of trade liberalization, non-discrimination, and reciprocity among member states, and transparency in trade rules and practices (Gilpin 2001, p. 219). Trade liberalization under GATT rules means the gradual reduction and ultimate elimination of tariffs, taxes (or duties) imposed by an importing

---

[8] For more information on specific aspects of the WTO and its politics see Daunton et al. 2012.

country on other countries' goods, allowing global welfare and efficiency to improve, trade volumes to expand – and (in theory) all countries to benefit from economic growth.

By institutionalizing the principle of reciprocity, the GATT required all signatory states to agree to not discriminate among other countries through trade controls or import decisions (Article I of the GATT), nor to discriminate between goods produced domestically and the same goods produced by other countries (the "national treatment" rule). The GATT also built in a system of dispute adjudication, in the event of disagreements among member states over the application of national laws or GATT rules.

In addition to these principles of trade liberalization and reciprocity, the GATT also had built into it certain safeguards, or circumstances where tariffs or other trade restrictions could be justified. Most important for subsequent conflicts over environmental protection, Article XX of the GATT contains "general exceptions," which allow for trade discrimination or trade restrictions under a number of scenarios: to protect "public morals," when goods are produced by prison labor or are "national treasures." Most pertinently for the relationship between economic and environmental governance, two subsections of Article XX allow actions "necessary to protect human, animal or plant life or health" (Article XXb) or actions "relating to the conservation of exhaustible natural resources if such measures are made effective in conjunction with restrictions on domestic production or consumption" (Article XXg), as long as they "are not applied in a manner which would constitute a means of arbitrary or unjustifiable discrimination between countries where the same conditions prevail, or a disguised restriction on international trade."

From 1948 to 1994 the GATT achieved significant successes. In the 1950s and 1960s global trade volumes grew an average of 8 percent per year, due at least in part to tariff reductions. By early 1995 GATT membership had grown to 124 nation-states. Over that time the GATT ran into a number of serious challenges. Run by a tiny secretariat based in Geneva, it had little organizational capacity or autonomy. Second, the agreement did not address non-tariff barriers to trade (NTBs), which limited the gains made by tariff reductions. Common forms of NTBs include import quotas and government subsidies. Less obviously protectionist are national rules on labeling or packaging, or health and safety requirements (Dicken 1998, p. 93). These requirements may have a practical rationale in the home country, but can also function as a barrier to trade if a country's trade partners cannot, or will not, comply due to costs or for other reasons. Not surprisingly, NTBs soon became the subject of bitter disputes between member states, including forming the basis of the trade–environment disputes we examine in the following sections.

In order to address these and other flaws, members negotiated a new and stronger trade regime. On January 1, 1995 the World Trade Organization came into being. It brought together a range of trade-related treaties under a single organizational roof (Krueger 1998). It incorporated the GATT, and expanded it to include agriculture, textiles, and clothing, and a number of new or recently concluded agreements, in total approximately 26,000 pages of agreement text. These new agreements include the General Agreement on Trade in Services (GATS), and agreements on Trade-Related Aspects of Intellectual Property Rights (TRIPs), Trade-Related Investment Measures (TRIMs), Technical Barriers to Trade (TBT), and the Application of Sanitary and Phytosanitary Standards (SPS). Members, and potential members, must implement the full package of WTO agreements into national law in order to join the organization. Despite the more extensive conditions, membership in the GATT/WTO grew to 161 by 2015.

The WTO administers the trade agreements that make up the WTO, provides a forum for multilateral trade negotiations, administers arrangements for dispute-settlement among member states, and reviews national trade policies, with the overall goal of maintaining predictable, rules-based governance of international trade. As an actual organization, the WTO has the same legal and organizational standing as the World Bank and the IMF, and a permanent staff of roughly 700. The highest authority within the WTO is the Ministerial Conference. It is made up of trade ministers from each member country and meets at least every two years. Ongoing decisions are made by the General Council, which is made up of delegates from each member state.

Another area that saw substantial reform in the shift from the GATT to the WTO that has proven particularly important for environmental concerns is the organization's dispute-settlement procedure. Under GATT, if a country wished to dispute another's trade practices, it was able to lodge a complaint before a panel of experts (usually three to five experts in trade law, from different countries). The WTO maintained the basic panel system, but instituted several reforms. Perhaps most critically, it instituted automaticity, whereby the panel's report must be adopted unless it is rejected by a consensus of the membership, and, to balance this, an Appellate Body to oversee the disputes procedure and hear appeals from parties that had been ruled against.

Finally, the WTO's Committee on Trade and the Environment (CTE) has a mandate to study the impacts of environmental policies on trade, and make relevant recommendations to the organization. As a consulting forum rather than a regulatory body it is not a rule-making component of the trading order, and has remained marginalized in political debates over managing trade–environment overlap (Jinnah 2014, pp. 126–27).

The expansion of the WTO agenda to include issues such as intellectual property rights appeared to many to represent a victory for the forces of global capital, and for the economic superpowers – notably the USA and the EU – who were certainly the most powerful voices within the organization. The WTO's enforcement powers are far superior to those of, say, international environmental treaties, and it appears to be backed by more powerful, and often anti-environmental, interests. Yet, the WTO's trajectory since 1995 has been far from smooth. First, Southern countries have pushed for a greater voice within the organization, and, in particular, for the WTO to confront developed countries over issues such as agricultural subsidies, which have acted as effective barriers to trade for their agricultural goods. Second, criticism of the WTO's apparent disregard for social and environmental issues led the organizers of the Doha Round of negotiations, launched in 1999, to focus more on using trade to achieve social and sustainable development – although so far to little effect. Finally, its resources have been severely stretched, in part by a series of disputes between the USA and the EU, most critically over the EU's refusal to accept imports of genetically modified organisms (GMOs) from the USA. Some argue that the WTO is facing a serious legitimacy crisis, which it will need to overcome if it is to maintain its identity, or even its existence (Wilkinson 2012). How the WTO confronts issues of environmental change and sustainable development are key in these debates. We turn, therefore, to examine how the global trade agenda intersects with the global environment.

Trade and the Environment: The Contours of the Debate

a.   Trade Liberalization and Environmental Quality Economists have noted both positive and negative impacts of trade liberalization on environmental quality. One set of arguments concerns the impact of economic growth – the primary goal of trade liberalization. Economic growth leads to more resource exploitation and more pollution. On the other hand, some studies have noted the possibility of an ultimately positive relationship between GDP growth and environmental quality, or dispute the link between trade liberalization and environmental damage (Bhagwati 1993). GDP growth may enable countries to enact and implement effective systems of environmental regulation. Related, as countries grow, they are able to afford more environmentally friendly technologies, or even to shift their economic base away from harmful production.[9] Some claim that environmental problems arise from the global trading system not being liberal enough, pointing, for example, to agricultural subsidies in developed countries, which lead to environmentally damaging overproduction (Esty 2000, p. 250).

Other studies isolate the specific impacts of higher trade volumes on environmental quality. For example, export-oriented countries such as China have experienced higher levels of pollution as exports of pollution-intensive products have increased (Jaspers and Falkner 2013, p. 413; Economy 2004). A recent study (Lin et al. 2014) found that in 2006 around 21 percent of China's overall emissions of air pollutants results from production for export to the USA alone – and much of that flows back to the USA. On a daily basis, they estimated that around 12–24 percent of sulfate concentrations in the western USA could be attributed to export-related Chinese production.

The actual transportation of goods, often thousands of miles across the globe, by ship, plane, truck, and (to a lesser extent) rail, has environmental impacts, through additional pollution, including GHG emissions. An unanticipated side effect of greater trade volumes has been an exponential increase in the number of invasive species arriving in new ports, often with drastic impacts on local ecosystems (Tzankova 2009). Further, the liberalization of global trade has helped enable various forms of "toxic" trade, including the global trade in hazardous wastes and dangerous chemicals, partly through lower transportation costs and partly through the assumption that such trades were "goods" unless proven otherwise (Strohm 1993; O'Neill 2001).

b.   Trade Liberalization and Environmental Regulations Second, there are significant controversies over the impact of trade liberalization and GATT/WTO rules on national standards of environmental protection. Such impacts can be direct (in the sense that the GATT/WTO has the power to directly overrule national environmental rules if they are deemed a non-tariff barrier to trade) or indirect (shaping the development and implementation of national environmental regulation). Higher levels of environmental regulation typically raise the costs of production for the average firm, making their products less competitive than the same goods produced under lower standards abroad. This can lead to a "race to the

---

[9] These arguments are associated with the "environmental Kuznets curve," which posits an inverse U-shaped relationship between GDP growth (x-axis) and pollution levels: as income grows, pollution levels rise, then level off and start falling at a certain point. This hypothesis has generated significant empirical research, which has found that while this relationship works in certain cases – air pollution being one example – it otherwise does not hold, or its effects are quite weak. See Grossman and Krueger 1995 and Stern 2014.

bottom," as countries dismantle regulations to maintain even a narrow advantage, or to countries getting "stuck at the bottom" (Porter 1999), unable to implement environmental or other regulations. By contrast, others argue that under certain conditions – for example, when the market is dominated by a region with high environmental standards – free trade can lead to higher environmental regulations, as firms in other countries or parts of the region decide to meet the standards of the largest market (Vogel 1995).

Concerns that the GATT/WTO has the power to strike down national environmental regulations arise from several high-profile cases brought before GATT/WTO dispute-settlement panels in the 1990s and 2000s, most brought by Southern countries as a response to what they saw as "green protectionism" by the North. In 1991 Mexico accused the USA of discrimination when the USA banned imports of Mexican tuna, because the Mexican tuna-fishing industry did not take adequate measures to prevent dolphin by-catch when harvesting tuna. Dolphin-unsafe fishing practices had been banned in US waters under the Marine Mammals Protection Act 1972, following extensive lobbying by environmental groups. In ruling for Mexico, the GATT panel argued that the USA had unfairly discriminated between like products – thus reinforcing the product–process distinction, namely that how goods are produced is irrelevant if the product is to all intents and purposes the same. Further, the panel concluded that the USA had not exhausted "all possible options" to protect dolphins prior to banning Mexican tuna (a narrow interpretation of Article XX).

The *Shrimp–Turtle* case, brought by several Southeast Asian countries against the USA in 1996 (this time under WTO dispute-settlement procedures), was sparked by a similar problem: the USA had banned shrimp imports from these countries due to excessive turtle by-catch. Again, the disputes settlement panel ruled against the USA in 1997, on the grounds that it had not offered the same assistance to Southeast Asian countries in implementing turtle-friendly shrimp-harvesting practices as it had to countries in the Western hemisphere.

Other important trade–environment cases over this time frame include one brought by Venezuela in 1995 against the USA over gasoline additives, and another initiated in 2005 by the EU against Brazil's ban (on environment and health grounds) of imports of retreaded tires.[10] In 2003, in one of the most high-profile cases, the USA, Canada, and Argentina

---

[10] For updates see the WTO's disputes-settlements portal, at www.wto.org/english/tra top_e/dispu_e/dispu_e.htm.

brought a case against the EU in order to strike down its moratorium on imports of GMOs, which was based on a precautionary approach to scientific uncertainty on the long term-impacts of biotechnology. The 2006 ruling in the *EU-Biotech* case found primarily in favor of the USA but did not strike down the EU's application of the Precautionary Principle (Jaspers and Falkner 2013, p. 419).

These cases alarmed environmentalists and those concerned about the ability of the GATT/WTO to strike down domestic laws without considering environmental impacts (Conca 2000). The implications of the product–process distinction were also potentially serious: if countries could not, except under the most narrow of circumstances, restrict imports of goods produced in environmentally damaging ways, then one major weapon to change environmental (and other) behaviors in other countries would be gone.

However, the ultimate outcomes of both the *Tuna–Dolphin* and the *Shrimp–Turtle* cases are more complex. First, the *Tuna–Dolphin* decision was never enforced, because Mexico did not press for its adoption, as was required under the GATT. It also played a key role in prompting companies to adopt voluntary labeling practices – in this case, the well-known "dolphin-safe" label, enabling consumers to decide what they wanted to buy, without governments – the target of GATT/WTO rules – entering into the equation (Murphy 2006). Second, the Appellate Body ruling on *Shrimp–Turtle* effectively overturned the initial decision, provided the USA made a "good faith effort" to work toward multilateral measures to protect sea turtles (O'Neill and Burns 2005, p. 326; DeSombre and Barkin 2002). Not only did the WTO in this case effectively recognize that how something is produced matters, it also acknowledged that it has a role in protecting the environment – and, in the course of the appeal, accepted for the first time an amicus curiae ("Friend of the Court") brief, submitted, in this case, by the World Wildlife Fund (WWF).[11] Likewise, in the Venezuelan *Gasoline* and the Brazilian *Retreaded Tires* cases, the WTO ruled against the USA in the former, and Brazil in the latter, less for environmental protectionism than for misapplying them in ways that could be considered "arbitrary or discriminating" (Jaspers and Falkner 2013, p. 420).

These developments are worth bearing in mind as countries consider trade measures to combat climate change. Currently, some economists advocate trade measures to bolster domestic GHG-emissions-reductions policies, and such proposals have appeared in legislative drafts such as the

---

[11] An amicus curiae brief is an informational document submitted to a court case by a third party, sometimes an advocacy organization, not directly connected to the case.

proposed 2009 American Clean Energy and Security Act, which passed in the House of Representatives but failed in the Senate. For example, in a country or region (such as the EU) where firms must buy emissions credits or pay a carbon tax, those firms face higher costs, making them less competitive than cheaper goods from countries without such policies in place. Under these conditions, production may also shift to less-regulated economies, effectively counteracting the global emissions reductions achieved by the country with unilateral measures. This problem is known as carbon leakage (Jaspers and Falkner 2013, p. 420; see also Chapter 8). One way to address this problem and keep domestic firms on board with emissions reductions policies is to apply border-tax adjustments, whereby imports are taxed to redress the imbalance in production costs. On the face of it, such tax adjustments are not consistent with WTO rules. WTO and UNEP statements have, however, left the door open for such adjustments, and trade–environment experts have speculated that carefully designed proposals that do not violate the WTO's non-discrimination principle should not be struck down (Pauwelyn 2012).

c.   *The WTO and Multilateral Environmental Agreements*   Trade restrictions have played a critical role in environmental diplomacy. At least two agreements – the Basel Convention on the Control and Transboundary Movements of Hazardous Wastes and their Disposal and the Convention on International Trade in Endangered Species (CITES) – are almost wholly based on trade restrictions. Many other agreements, including the Montreal Protocol, the Kyoto Protocol, the Cartagena Protocol of the Convention on Biological Diversity (CBD), and others contain trade-restrictive measures. The possibility that these restrictions might conflict with WTO rules has given rise to a good deal of concern in policy-making and academic circles (O'Neill and Burns 2005; Conca 2000), especially given that the WTO has a greater legal and enforcement capacity than most, if not all, multilateral environmental agreements (MEAs).

Most immediately, countries negatively affected by any of these measures might bring a complaint to the WTO, and may well win, especially given the GATT/WTO's track record and general perceptions that it is much more powerful than environmental counterparts, with the support of significant states and private-sector actors. Over the longer term, the threat of trade disputes might lead to a "chilling effect" on ongoing and new environmental negotiations (Conca 2000; Eckersley 2004). Trade measures have traditionally been a successful means of enforcing environmental agreements, and their loss would undermine the overall effectiveness of international environmental cooperation.

As of early 2016 no direct challenge to an environmental agreement had been issued. However, analysts agree that several agreements are vulnerable, including CITES, the Basel Convention, the Cartagena Protocol of the CBD, and even the Kyoto Protocol. The Ban Amendment to the Basel Convention, for example, bans all imports of hazardous wastes – for both disposal and recycling – by non-OECD countries and non-members of the Convention, and is strongly opposed by several governments and the international recycling industry. The Amendment relies on a closed list of importing countries. There are no criteria established by which a country could join this list. A WTO panel could quite easily interpret this as an unfair trade restriction.

If such a challenge were brought, it is not clear what the outcome would be. The WTO's dispute-settlement process is geared more toward trade law than environmental law, making the WTO an attractive venue for bringing such a dispute. On the other hand, several practical and legal obstacles militate against such a challenge succeeding. From a legal perspective, it is unclear what the WTO's jurisdiction over other multilateral treaties would be. In *Tuna–Dolphin* and *Shrimp–Turtle*, it ruled specifically against unilateral measures by the USA, while a decision about an MEA would affect an agreement with at least as many members as the WTO.

International law also contains measures and procedures for dealing with inter-treaty conflicts, notably provisions of the 1969 Vienna Convention on the Law of Treaties (VCLT), which also guides WTO dispute-settlement procedures (Hudec 1999). MEA supporters could, in some cases, invoke the principle of *lex posterior*, which states that the later treaty supplants an earlier one unless specified, or that of *lex specialis*, which states that the treaties more specific to the subject matter at hand should prevail (Sinclair 1984). Under international law, both principles are open to interpretation, but the chances are that the combination of these principles of the VCLT and the multilateral nature of environmental treaty regimes could provide adequate legal protection.

Yet, indirect evidence suggests that the WTO has a significant advantage in certain respects. First, empirical studies have found evidence for the chilling effect of global trade rules on MEAs. Mark Axelrod (2011) examines the use of savings clauses – clauses that defer to other, usually preceding, international instruments – across a sample of all international agreements. He found that while savings clauses are fairly uniformly common across all agreements, MEAs are more likely to contain "strongly" deferential savings clauses – namely, ones that defer to agreements outside their own policy field.

A direct dispute between global trade and environment rules could prove damaging to both MEAs and the WTO. Both UNEP and WTO officials have expressed a desire to avoid or mitigate lengthy, and costly, disputes, and have set up several formal and ad hoc procedures to do this. Trade–environment issues were prominent at both the Doha Ministerial Meeting of the WTO in 2001 and at the World Summit on Sustainable Development (WSSD) in Johannesburg in 2002, with participants declaring the need to find ways to make trade liberalization and sustainable development more compatible (O'Neill and Burns 2005). However, the WTO Secretariat is fraught with internal differences on the role of the environment in trade politics (Jinnah 2014). MEAs have moved, for their part, toward adopting more WTO-friendly market mechanisms (incentives rather than rules), in part to avoid conflicting with the trade regime.

d.   Environmental Impacts of Broadening the WTO: TRIPS, SPS, and Other Agreements   Finally, the broader agreements clustered within the WTO have environmental impacts, over and above those of the liberalization and growth of global trade in goods. The WTO "family" of treaties includes agreements over trade-related intellectual property rights (TRIPS), sanitary and phytosanitary standards (SPS), and trade in services (GATS). These agreements in particular present concerns for environmentalists, many of which have crystallized in global debates over patent issues, biotechnology, and trade in GMOs, the use of the Precautionary Principle in international law, and the privatization of historically commonly held resources.

One of the main motives for setting up an international framework for the adoption and protection of intellectual property rights under the WTO was to end "piracy" of patented products – from medicine to computer software – in countries where domestic legal frameworks are inadequate to prevent such infringements. The TRIPS Agreement requires signatory states to adopt a model of patent development and enforcement, whereby rights to develop and market a product are restricted for a number of years to a single individual or corporation. A side effect of this set of rules is that patent rights are open to anyone able to claim them, generating two related concerns. First, this system trumps other sorts of property rights systems, such as communal or customary property rights, in force in many parts of the world for centuries. Second, it grants a huge advantage to large corporations, often based in the North, with the financial and legal resources to file a patent application. These concerns underpinned discussions around access and benefit-sharing agreements under the 2010 Nagoya Protocol to the CBD, which laid out conditions under which (Western) corporations could gain access to biodiverse resources in (developing) countries.

The issue of biotechnology and trade in GMOs has cropped up across a number of international regimes, including the CBD, and the WTO, specifically its SPS Agreement, which addresses differences in national public health standards with respect to imported produce and meats (Kastner and Powell 2002). Concerns that GMOs might have long-term impacts on ecosystems and human health that have not yet been adequately explored or quantified have led many consumers, civil society groups, and even governments to call for moratoriua on their use, including imports of GM seeds and agricultural produce. The SPS Agreement allows countries to maintain different health and food safety standards as long as they are justified by scientific risk assessment and data (Winickoff et al. 2005). In the eyes of GMO supporters, the Precautionary Principle does not meet that standard. The 2003 *EU-Biotech* case described above is at the center of these disputes. As this case made its way through the decision and appeals process, arguments focused on how, and what sort of, scientific risk assessments were necessary to justify restrictions on GMO imports – thrusting the WTO into one of the major scientific/environmental controversies of the early twenty-first century (A. Gupta 2014).

The agreements associated with the WTO have also opened up opportunities for environmental protection that did not exist under the original GATT framework. Under the GATS agreement, which addresses trade in services, the international community has the opportunity to "hyperliberalize" trade in environmental goods and services, enabling faster and cheaper transfer of environmentally friendly technologies across national borders (Esty 2000; Carpentier et al. 2005). While "environmental goods and services" is a category yet to be fully defined under international law, it could include waste-disposal facilities and services, solar panels and other renewable energy components, air pollution control technology, and other products and services designed to reduce pollution and conserve resources (Carpentier et al. 2005, pp. 228–29). Eliminating barriers to this trade could be a win–win–win situation for the corporate sector, consumers, and the environment, but is not without potential political pitfalls as countries such as China take over particular sectors (e.g. solar panel manufacture), undermining renewable energy enterprises in developed countries.

The GATT/WTO and the Environment: Ongoing Challenges

Over the past fifteen years the WTO has faced significant challenges, from huge street protests at its meetings, to deep splits between its two most powerful members, the USA and the EU, to staunch opposition from

Group of 77 Developing Countries (G77) members, to continued agricultural subsidies in Northern member states. Across the board, activists, policy-makers (especially from the South), and academics decry its lack of transparency in its decision-making processes.

To counter suggestions that it has lost both momentum and legitimacy, the WTO has embraced the concept of sustainable development as part of its mandate, and it maintained a significant presence at WSSD in Johannesburg in 2002 and at Rio+20 in 2012. Yet, the 2001 Doha Declaration that kicked off the most recent – and still ongoing – round of WTO negotiations remains unfulfilled.[12] The WTO is struggling to move forward on issues of agriculture, biotechnology, intellectual property rights, and sustainable development as the balance of power shifts within its membership, and developing countries challenge the long-dominant powers of the USA and the EU (Collins 2014).

Arguably, the WTO is facing an identity conflict as it tries to take on sustainable-development priorities (Wilkinson 2012). It is not a development agency. Rather, its role is to set trade rules. Similarly, the WTO remains uncomfortable with its environmental governance role, with divisions within its Secretariat and across its membership on this issue (Jinnah 2014, p. 122). Southern member states are the strongest opponents of incorporating environmental concerns into the WTO's agenda, given development implications and fears of green protectionism on the part of Northern states.

Finally, the WTO faces growing fragmentation of the world trade regime. Regional and bilateral free-trade agreements (RTAs) are increasingly taking the lead as engines of economic liberalization as the WTO remains stalled (Powell and Low 2011), including taking on integration of environmental provisions that often, but not always, outstrip those of the WTO (Jinnah 2012b). The OECD notes that as of February 2015 more than 250 RTAs have been reported to the WTO, with more under negotiation, most of which are part of a strong second wave of RTA negotiation since the start of the Doha Round (Lejárraga 2014). Nearly every WTO member belongs to at least one. Around 31 percent are South–South agreements, and 59 percent are North–South (Lejárraga 2014, p. 17). Most RTAs concluded since 2000 go beyond WTO commitments in many ways, and whether the WTO will subsume, be subsumed by, or simply coordinate this group remains an open question.

---

[12] The full text of the Doha Declaration can be found at www.wto.org/english/thewto _e/minist_e/min01_e/mindecl_e.htm.

Situating Global Economic Governance and the Environment

In this chapter we have seen how discussions about global environmental change and governance must take into account the workings of the global economic order. It is impossible to avoid the extent to which trade liberalization, development finance and debt, and the ways they have been managed by the Bretton Woods institutions have considerable environmental impacts. This final section explores how the global economic governance arena has itself become a site of GEG, while remaining a site of global contention.

A New Site of Global Environmental Governance . . .

In 1945 environmental concerns were barely on the radar screen of the post-war economic order. By the 1990s they were impossible to ignore, in large part due to the rise of GEG, and the emergence of transnational expert and activist communities with an interest in environmental protection. Environmental problems were recognized as significant market failures associated with global free markets, notably with liberalizing trade. Discourses of sustainable development, too, became central to critiques of models of external development aid and lending based purely on facilitating economic growth.

As we have seen above, a variety of pressures were brought to bear on the WTO, the World Bank, and the IMF to reform their practices to take social and environmental impacts of trade liberalization, project lending, and structural adjustment lending into account. Transnational NGO activism throughout the 1980s was one influential factor (Park 2012). The design and impact of SAPs catalyzed strong alliances between environment and human rights (or social justice) groups and local communities whose livelihoods have been particularly affected by these changes. For example, IMF-driven water-privatization programs generated fierce opposition at the local level (including the "water wars" of Cochabama, Bolivia) and a nascent transnational activist network (Conca 2006).

Government pressures were also important. The US Congress was able to use the threat of cutting off funding to the World Bank to get it to implement reforms. Disputes brought before the GATT/WTO on environmental protection pushed the WTO to take seriously links between trade liberalization and environmental impacts. There was also a role for expertise. Leading economists, such as Nobel Prize winner Joseph Stiglitz, advocated departing from the Washington Consensus (Stiglitz 2002). Interventions in trade disputes (Winickoff et al. 2005) helped define the application of the Precautionary Principle across economic and environmental governance arenas.

Therefore, somewhat unwillingly, the leading economic governance IGOs found themselves becoming a new site of GEG, for good or ill. First, in a practical sense, the sheer scale of some World Bank-funded projects and the growth in global trade under the GATT/WTO requires regulation and oversight of their environmental and social impacts. Second, the creation of institutions for assessment and monitoring of impacts within the WTO and the World Bank integrates global sustainability concerns into their policy agendas. These actions are further reflected in the creation and support of environmental funds, and in efforts to use trade measures to enhance movement of environmental goods and services. Whether one considers these steps real, greenwash, or merely ineffective, they have reshaped the terms of global economic governance.

Third, others argue that the economic IGOs have driven a normative shift that has come to dominate the rhetoric and practice of GEG and sustainability. Bernstein (2002) argues that global institutions – the WTO, the Bank, and the UN – have internalized a series of ideas that integrate environmental protection and a liberal economic order, and that have altered the course of both economic and environmental governance at the global level. He refers to this process as the "compromise of liberal environmentalism," a norm that has been reflected in various incarnations of green capitalism, most recently in the concept of a Green Economy (Tienhaara 2014). There are different perspectives on whether economic IGOs shape or are shaped by this norm. Goldman (2005) would argue they are the prime movers. By contrast, Park (2012) argues that they themselves have been shaped as well, internalizing – to differing extents – norms of sustainable development.

Finally, the economic IGOs are important sites of GEG because of the ways the WTO and the World Bank have recognized conflicts and forged linkages with GEG organizations and regimes. These linkages and conflicts have been most clear-cut in disputes over trade rules and environmental regulations, but have also emerged in discussions over global environmental financing, the GEF, and new climate-funding architectures, including carbon partnerships such as REDD+ (see Chapter 8).

... But Still a Site of Contestation

As might be evident by now, the global governance world is not one of smooth trajectories and predictable processes. The global economic institutions exist in a complex and changing landscape, with roles that remain objects of contestation. Global economic volatility remains a big issue: it would have been hard to imagine in the late 1990s that SAP-based rescue policies – and vast amounts of money – would be targeted at members of the EU such as Greece and Spain. These and other problems are stretching the large but still limited capacity of the development agencies, whose mandates are not yet compatible with demands for sustainable development and, increasingly, climate action.

International economic regimes are challenged by the stagnation of state-led negotiation processes (in the case of the WTO) and evidence of their failure to fully implement environmental reforms (in the case of the World Bank). They are confronted with growing fragmentation of trade and finance regimes, with the emergence of new regional RTAs and regional development banks, which operate outside the mainstream norms of global economic governance.

Efforts by the IFIs and other IGOs to connect economic, environmental, and sustainable development at the global level continue to face societal contestation. The Peoples' Summit, held in parallel to Rio+20, produced a document, *Another Future is Possible*, which promoted alternatives to the Green Economy lauded in the official conference document, *The Future We Want*. Academic and other commentators point out the flaws of a union between environmental and economic imperatives in its latest incarnation (Mueller and Passadakis 2009; Tienhaara 2014). Although the large, transnational protest movements that targeted the Bretton Woods institutions during the 1990s and early 2000s have died down, they played a crucial role in highlighting issues, such as dam construction or mining, that have clear, adverse, and visible impacts on particular (and often indigenous or already marginalized) communities across the planet. Transboundary activists across political scales continue to carry the torch, applying notions of global justice to issues such as food sovereignty and security, community and indigenous rights in the wake of REDD+, and climate justice for the world's most vulnerable populations (Broussard 2015; Hiraldo and Tanner 2011; McMichael 2014).

The challenges facing the Bretton Woods institutions also highlight central questions in global governance theory: how do IGOs achieve and maintain legitimacy, and to whom are they accountable (Smythe and Smith 2006)? Until recently, these questions were considered relatively unproblematic. IGOs were accountable only to, and their legitimacy depended solely on, their member states. Now, as their authority and effectiveness is challenged by transnational activist networks calling for more transparency and participation, and by growing rifts among their member governments, they are looking for ways of addressing these problems (Park 2012; Jinnah 2014).

Next Steps

The extent to which global environmental governance and global economic governance have become intertwined was unanticipated by the architects of either governance order. Now, however, environmental and social issues are quite firmly on the agendas of the Bretton Woods institutions, and UNEP and other environmental governance institutions are looking for ways to work with, and not against, global trade and finance regimes.

Even though strong disagreements remain as to whether the Bretton Woods institutions can be effective engines of environmentalism, or whether they should be thoroughly restructured (even dismantled), there is little argument that they have become important sites of GEG. Their actions strongly affect the state of the environment as well as the welfare of many communities and the policies of many governments, and they have the financial capacity and legal force to implement national- and local-level change quite quickly. At the same time, they are perceived (and perceive themselves) to be suffering from a loss of legitimacy, particularly in the wake of transnational protest, and criticism from many leaders and scholars. At both the 2002 Johannesburg and 2012 Rio+20 conferences, leading IGOs asserted the need for collaboration between the global environment, economic, and development institutions, in effect recognizing this new site of GEG. Despite ongoing challenges, this relationship remains strong. In Chapters 7 and 8 we move on to broader sites and modes of GEG, which face many of the same questions and critiques: the emergence of non-state governance regimes, and the increased integration of market mechanisms into GEG.

Discussion Questions

- Summarize arguments for and against the proposition that economic globalization is bad for the environment. What sorts of evidence would you look for on both sides of the argument?
- Why and how are MEAs vulnerable to challenges under global trade rules? In what ways could such challenges be avoided?
- In what ways do international development institutions such as the World Bank address the negative environmental and social impacts of their activities? Do you think it is possible for them to fully incorporate sustainability into their mandate?

SUGGESTIONS FOR FURTHER READING

Clapp, Jennifer, and Peter Dauvergne. 2011. *Paths to a Green World: The Political Economy of the Global Environment*, 2nd edition. Cambridge, MA: MIT Press: a highly accessible text on the relationship between economic globalization and the environment that assesses these debates from four different perspectives.

Hicks, Robert L., Bradley C. Parks, J. Timmons Roberts, and Michael J. Tierney. 2008. *Greening Aid? Understanding the Environmental Impact of Development Assistance*. Oxford: Oxford University Press: this book uses a database of development projects to examine the tension between development and the environment, and how and why international development aid became more environmentally conscious between 1980 and 1999.

Stiglitz, Joseph E. *Globalization and its Discontents*. 2002. New York: W. W. Norton & Company: from a Nobel Prize-winning economist, why the IMF went so wrong in the 1990s, and a strong critique of neoliberal globalization.

Tienhaara, Kyla. 2014. "Varieties of Green Capitalism: Economy and Environment in the Wake of the Global Financial Crisis." *Environmental Politics* 23.2: 187–204: this piece defines and compares different dimensions of "green capitalism" and their deployment in the contemporary global economy.

7 Non-State Global Environmental Governance

In October 1993, 130 representatives from 26 countries met in Toronto, Canada, to inaugurate a governance regime designed to protect the world's forests. Participants agreed on ten principles for sustainable forest management, from controlling harvests to ensure steady timber yields over time, to protecting fragile ecosystems, to protecting the rights of local forest-dwellers. The implementation of these principles would not be cost-free, and monitoring compliance hard to achieve. Nonetheless, participants agreed that this program represented a significant step forward in global forest conservation, while still allowing forest owners to benefit economically.

This governance institution – the Forest Stewardship Council (FSC) – now covers over 180 million hectares of forest across eighty-one countries, according to 2015 data. In some ways it looks like the intergovernmental regimes we have examined in previous chapters. In others it is very different. First, none of the participants at the Toronto meeting were government representatives. Instead, the driving force behind the establishment of the FSC was a coalition of NGOs, forest owners and timber companies, and forest-dwelling communities, led by the World Wildlife Fund (WWF), a leading international NGO. Second, FSC achieves its goals through the transmission of information and the power of the market. If a timber-producing firm signs up to its standards, it agrees to allow an independent auditor to certify its compliance with FSC's principles. If it qualifies, the firm can then affix an eco-label to its products, which tells purchasers and consumers further down the supply chain that the wood they are buying was grown and harvested sustainably. Purchasers can then signal their support for these measures by buying products with the FSC logo – often at a significant price premium, providing an additional incentive for firms to participate in this governance initiative.

The recognition of failures across current state-led efforts to regulate environmental problems has encouraged the decentralization and diversification of traditional sites and modes of governance, shifting regulatory

170

action to markets and to the non-state sector. In Chapter 6 we saw how economic globalization has at best complicated and at worst harmed the state of the global environment. In this chapter we highlight a contrasting dimension of globalization: the increased ability of civil society actors worldwide to ally with each other, exchange information, and engage the public in their activities, in ways that make environmentally damaging corporate practices more visible and make the actors behind them more accountable to a broader audience. FSC is one of the best-known examples of private (or non-state) global environmental governance (GEG): governance initiatives and institutions that are created and operated by NGO and private-sector actors outside the state-led system of GEG.

This chapter examines how the non-state sector has emerged as another important site of GEG, often using the production and dissemination of information as a mode of governance. We examine the factors underlying growing demand for non-state governance, which have increased the capacity of civil society and industry to work together in this area. We then assess the impacts of these initiatives from normative and theoretical perspectives. Many of the questions asked about FSC, or socially responsible investment (SRI) or other sorts of non-state or hybrid initiatives, mirror those asked about intergovernmental regimes. Do they actually solve large-scale environmental problems? Who participates and who does not? Are private-sector–civil-society partnerships enough, or is official, governmental development and enforcement of environmental regulation still necessary?

Most generally, non-state governance represents devolution of authority to non-state actors, and raises new issues about accountability and legitimacy in GEG. Literature on private authority in global governance sees global governance not purely as a realm of intergovernmental action, but as a hybrid mix of new and not-so-new initiatives and institutions existing – sometimes uneasily – alongside each other.[1] It identifies a wide range of actors – from corporations and financial market institutions to NGOs, transnational religious organizations and even organized crime – who are taking on authoritative roles in global politics (Green 2014). They claim to be, perform as, and are recognized as legitimate by larger publics (including states themselves) as authors of policies, of practices, of rules, and of norms. They set agendas, establish boundaries or limits for action, certify, offer salvation, guarantee contracts, and provide order and security. In short, they do many of the

---

[1] For overviews see Hall and Biersteker 2002; Cutler et al. 1999; Falkner 2003; and Green 2014.

things traditionally associated exclusively with the state (Hall and Biersteker 2002, p. 4).

In this chapter we ask what the emergence of these new sites and modes of GEG means for it, and for global governance writ large. Are they supplanting or reinforcing existing intergovernmental modes of international environmental politics (IEP), and what do they mean for the role of the state, and inter-state cooperation, in the international system? How do they fit into broader discussions of linkages and fragmentation in GEG? While we cannot answer these questions definitively in this one chapter, it is clear that non-state governance initiatives have injected new energy and ideas into the theory and practice of global environmental politics (GEP). They carry their own problems, but have become a durable component of global governance, and are an important part of a new, more hybridized perspective on the part of scholars as to what constitutes this field of study.

This chapter first examines the emergence of non-state governance, and then goes into more depth on specific cases. We look at hybrid partnerships and the use of market discipline – e.g. through insurance markets or SRI mechanisms – before focusing on the two main forms of information-based governance: transparency and certification initiatives. We follow with an assessment of the strengths and weaknesses of non-state GEG, and its implications for theoretical debates in studies of GEG.

Explaining the Emergence of Non-State Governance

In essence, non-state GEG initiatives are established, implemented, and maintained not by governments, but by civil-society and private-sector actors, behaving as agents of governance in their own right, establishing and enforcing their own rules. They thus exercise their own authority. Jessica Green defines private authority as "situations in which non-state actors make rules or set standards that other actors in world politics adopt" (Green 2014, p. 6). This universe also includes hybrid initiatives – where non-state actors work in partnership with governments and IGOs. As we shall see in later examples, it is rare that states and non-state actors are fully decoupled in this arena.

The state of GEP has proved particularly amenable to the emergence of non-state governance. For many, especially those frustrated with the slow pace and obstructive politics of international treaty negotiation, these developments are highly welcome, and represent a wide and exciting array of new, and experimental, governance tools and techniques. Turning to the private sector to regulate itself (with or without the aid of global civil society) may overcome major drawbacks of state-led governance of global production in the twenty-first century. In this section we examine the reasons why demand has increased for non-state environmental governance initiatives, focusing on structural changes in the global economy, and on the reasons why specific groups of actors favor new directions in global governance.[2]

Frustration with State-Led Global Environmental Governance

Many non-state actors have expressed a high level of dissatisfaction with the pace and extent of traditional, intergovernmental cooperation and regime formation. Private-sector actors, especially multinational corporations (MNCs), feel excluded from the direct decision-making process, and unhappy with the extent to which national interests trump their own commercial interests. As Haufler puts it, "the process of negotiating intergovernmental agreements can be slow, clumsy, often wrong-headed, and highly political, which means the design of rules – even rules that the private sector desires – can be fraught with risk" (Haufler 2001, p. 22). Furthermore, NGOs and other activist groups heavily involved in IEP are also highly dissatisfied with the pace and direction of international cooperation, and with governance vacuums in important and high-profile issue areas such as deforestation and extractive resources. For example, during negotiations on a global forests convention in the lead-up to the 1992 Earth Summit, NGOs expressed dissatisfaction both with the content of the draft text, as excluding local communities in favor of state interests, and with the ways in which international negotiations in general led to such outcomes (Humphreys 2005).

The challenges posed by particularly complex and politically fraught issue areas, including forests, climate, and extractive industries (mining, including gold, gemstone, oil, and gas extraction) have made them far less amenable to governmental regulation. Both firms and NGOs, on the other hand, have been able to step in and fill those governance vacuums, at least to an extent. Likewise, non-state actors have played an important role in global governance efforts to reduce resource exploitation in weak states and war zones – helping to certify non-conflict-zone diamonds and other minerals (Haufler 2009) and even providing logistical support – and sometimes personnel – to police endangered species threatened with poaching, for example (Duffy 2014).

---

[2] See also Bartley 2003 and Auld 2014 for accounts of the emergence of non-state governance, particularly certification systems.

A Changing Global Economy

The challenges of regulating corporate activity worldwide have grown more complex at a time when the will and capacity of states to engage in such regulation has waned, again creating windows for non-state intervention, especially in the governance of production and of extractive resources. Foreign direct investment (FDI) has increased exponentially since the 1970s. In 2014 the UN Conference on Trade and Development (UNCTAD) reported global FDI inflows at $1.23 trillion, compared with closer to $450 billion in 1995 (United Nations Conference on Trade and Development 2015). Ensuring that foreign investors and MNCs maintain adequate environmental and social protection in vastly different national contexts and in situations where they can use exit threats if regulations change (or are enforced) can be difficult.

Moreover, as corporate activity has globalized, corporate structures have become more complex, with ownership and control often highly diffused across global supply chains, making governance of global investment and production by governmental or intergovernmental actors far more challenging (Haufler 2003; Dauvergne and Lister 2012). These models are based on flexible, contract-based production. Contracts can be rapidly switched from one vendor to another, and compliance and monitoring along the production chain may be weak if purchasing firms lack the ability or will to gather necessary information about the environmental or social activities of vendor firms. This growing flexibility of contemporary production means that the obstacles for well-meaning firms to fulfill social or environmental goals can be formidable, and the opportunities for less well-inclined firms to avoid regulation are greater.

Multilateral and bilateral agreements governing corporate activity and FDI have always been weak in terms of environmental or social protection. They are generally designed to encourage or protect FDI, rather than control it, although voluntary guidelines for MNCs issued by the OECD call for implementation of the 1992 Rio Declaration on Environment and Development (Clapp and Dauvergne 2011, p. 189). NGOs and related organizations have been able to help fill this gap. The growing availability of global communications tools and technologies have made it much easier for them to gather and disseminate information about how goods are produced, and what needs to change to make that production more sustainable and equitable. These include multi-stakeholder transparency initiatives discussed below, such as the Extractive Industries Transparency Initiative (EITI), Global Witness, and GoodGuide.

New Opportunities, Changing Motives

For new sites and modes of governance to emerge, there must be supply as well as demand (Green 2014). In the case of non-state GEG, we clearly see strong motives on the part of NGO, corporate, and other actors in the international system, as well as the entrepreneurialism and technology to create and implement new governance initiatives and institutions.

The prime corporate movers in non-state environmental governance initiatives are industrialized country MNCs. These firms are particularly prone to transnational activist pressures, and operate across multiple jurisdictions, facing regulation from host countries, their home countries, and from the international level (Haufler 2001, p. 10). By embracing environmental and social governance principles, they protect or enhance their brand-name reputation and minimize risks and uncertainties associated with multiple and shifting governmental and intergovernmental rules. Many corporate entities, large and small, have moved to establish their own corporate social responsibility (CSR) policies. They may also reduce transaction costs by creating explicit external standards, providing information that is clearly understood from firm to firm that would, on an individual basis, be costly to obtain and unreliable (Cutler et al. 1999, p. 336). Firms may also look to take advantage of existing vacuums in GEG. Where international environmental law is almost wholly absent, as in the case of global deforestation and the international trade in tropical timbers, firms seek to populate the area with regulatory schemes, and thus shape (or possibly replace) future governmental action.

In other cases, NGOs may use both stick and carrot techniques (such as threats of consumer boycotts, targeting shareholders and investment companies, or working directly with corporations) to provide incentives for firms to start greening their activities. Many NGOs now work with major corporations to improve environmental performance: WWF has worked with the Coca-Cola Company to assess its water-use practices worldwide, the Sierra Club has advised Ford Motors, and Environmental Defense, another US-based NGO, has worked with McDonalds to pressure chicken suppliers to cut antibiotic use in poultry (Deutsch 2006).

Beyond individual initiatives, NGOs have worked hard to establish broader systems of environmental governance, shaping the forms of governance that have emerged, their transparency, and their perceived legitimacy. NGOs have established and now help run certification and labeling schemes, identifying which products meet certain social or environmental standards, from clothing to timber and wood products to coffee, seafood, gold, and diamonds. This level of collaboration with the corporate sector can pose a dilemma for civil-society actors (Falkner

2003). On the one hand, there are many advantages to working directly with corporations, the source of many environmental problems. On the other hand, they run the risk of being co-opted into corporate agendas with which they, and their supporters, do not agree.

Finally, many governments and intergovernmental organizations (IGOs) support these forms of environmental governance. States, rather than feeling threatened by possible usurpation of their authority, often benefit by avoiding the political and economic costs of imposing government regulation on key sectors of the economy, especially transnational sectors where control is difficult. For IGOs there is an emerging consensus that voluntary forms of regulation are more consonant with the overall goals of a liberalized world economy than compulsory regulations. The World Trade Organization (WTO), for example, has so far not opposed voluntary eco-labeling schemes, although similar schemes applied by governments could violate its rules on not differentiating among products on the basis of how they were produced. The UN Environment Programme (UNEP) and other UN agencies are, for their part, moving toward a "partnership" model for environmental protection, as evidenced at the 2002 World Summit on Sustainable Development (WSSD).

Varieties of Non-State Global Environmental Governance

Non-state initiatives in GEG began in the 1980s, with not wholly successful experiments in debt-for-nature swaps engineered between financial institutions, NGOs, and developing countries.[3] Despite these relatively inauspicious beginnings, there currently exists a wide array of non-state governance mechanisms and initiatives. As with inter-state cooperation, participation in non-state GEG is voluntary. Unlike traditional inter-state cooperation, these governance regimes aim for broader participation by a range of actors in important governance decisions.

Non-state governance now encompasses a wide range of activities, some more institutionally complex and durable than others. In addition, these initiatives employ a range of different modes of governance to steer the behavior of the actors they seek to govern. In the following sections we examine three major categories: multi-stakeholder public–private partnerships; insurance and investment strategies, which

---

[3] Debt-for-nature swaps, at their most simple, involved NGOs buying a portion of a (biodiversity-rich, developing) country's debt in return for pledges to, for example, create reserves or other forms of conservation (see Jakobeit 1996). They are receiving more attention these days in the context of global payment for ecosystem services initiatives (see Chapter 8).

utilize tools of financial market discipline; and certification and transparency initiatives and regimes, which employ information collection and distribution as their major governance mode. As we shall see, the difference between these forms of non-state governance is less clear-cut than these categories suggest. However, such classifications are useful in understanding the different ways in which they operate. Private governance initiatives are also present in the arena of market-based mechanisms in GEG, especially in the form of carbon-offset schemes (see Chapter 8; Peters-Stanley and Yin 2013).

Multi-Stakeholder Partnerships in Global Decision-Making

One way in which non-state actors are participating at higher levels in global decision-making is through the adoption by IGOs of multi-stakeholder participation, or partnership, models of governance. Based on principles of deliberative democracy (Dryzek 2014), the idea is to foster greater participation, and hence more legitimacy (Bäckstrand and Kylsäter 2014). The 2000 World Commission on Dams (WCD) is one example of this phenomenon. Convened by the World Bank, it brought together government, dam and hydropower industry, and civil-society actors to assess experience with and impacts of large dams, and to make (non-binding) recommendations for future development.

On a smaller scale, delegates and UN officials at the 2002 Johannesburg Summit supported the creation of Type 2 partnerships for sustainable development, a model already used by the Global Environment Facility (GEF) (Joyner 2005; Andonova and Levy 2004). Such partnerships, usually realized at the local level, could receive funds to engage in small-scale conservation and development projects, and display a nimbleness or creativity not usually associated with large-scale government-led initiatives. Examples unveiled in Johannesburg included a bicycle-refurbishing initiative led by a Dutch NGO, a forest-management and conservation initiative for the Congo Basin led by South Africa, and the Andean BIOTRADE program led by UNCTAD (Andonova and Levy 2004, p. 24). By 2012 348 such partnerships had been identified (Bäckstrand and Kylsäter 2014).

Partnerships between IGO, government, industry, and civil-society representatives have a role in the implementation of international environmental agreements, as they are likely to be more effective, and more sensitive to local impacts and concerns (Joyner 2005). Joyner cites the International Coral Reef Action Network (led by the governments of the UK, France, and the Seychelles, and including many NGOs and UN groups, as well as leading philanthropic foundations as partners) as just one example of a diverse partnership engaged in sharing knowledge and policy ideas while building capacity for coral reef protection (Joyner 2005, p. 110). The International Union for the Conservation of Nature (IUCN) is another such example. More recently, a voluntary partnership including state and non-state actors engaged in activities to maintain forest stocks as a means of storing carbon under the Reducing Emissions from Deforestation and Degradation initiative (REDD+, see Chapter 8) brought together national, local, and global interests in the formation and implementation of this complex initiative. The REDD+ Partnership has the potential to serve as a bridging organization between fragmented stakeholders, organizations, and institutions in this emerging field (Gupta et al. forthcoming).

While partnership initiatives and multi-stakeholder commissions may increase participation in important global decision-making processes, this approach has its critics. Same NGOs have criticized the Type 2 partnership model as a way for governments to avoid the responsibilities inherent to international environmental agreements (Friends of the Earth Australia 2002). Others challenge the extent to which partnerships have achieved their own goals or met expectations (Bäckstrand and Kylsäter 2014). There are other questions about how groups or actors are chosen or left out of these processes, and about the extent to which their recommendations can be translated into policies and actions. In fact, although the "eminent persons" commission as pioneered by the WCD at the global level is modeled on similar processes that have been effective at national levels, it has not been repeated at the same scale. Despite, therefore, continued rhetoric from the UN and other global actors in support of partnership approaches, such arrangements more often than not display a promise that has remained unfulfilled.

Financial Market Discipline: Insurance and Investment

A second set of private governance mechanisms involves harnessing the disciplinary power of the insurance and investment industries to change corporate – and sometimes government – behavior. As powerful transnational networks, these industries have considerable potential to steer behavior but remain understudied (MacLeod and Park 2011). Members of activist and scientific communities have targeted the insurance industry as a potentially powerful force in changing firms' behaviors, arguing that the destruction wrought by climate change could bankrupt the entire industry, giving them a strong incentive to encourage mitigation (Leggett 1996). Similar arguments apply to investment. SRI firms are under a mandate to direct funds under their care to companies that satisfy particular ethical requirements, such as environmental responsibility or employee welfare. Green venture capital and "cleantech" investment firms are looking for ways to improve the environment while still maintaining a high rate of return on investments. They are, for example, playing a large role in developing alternative energy technologies, from solar power to biofuels (Randjelovic et al. 2003). These activities, aimed at directing basic choices by firms about investment and production, have been met with both enthusiasm and skepticism.

Advocates of using the insurance industry to help mitigate the impacts of climate change define climate change as a problem that is both preventable and political, resulting in "losses due to actions, or inactions by governments or other political entities" (Haufler 1999, p. 204; Mills 2012). To that end, activists argue, by changing its requirements for adequate coverage or switching investments away from fossil fuels, the insurance industry could bring about changes in company behavior that could help ameliorate global warming. It could also lobby governments to enact regulations limiting greenhouse gas (GHG) emissions, a political clout amplified by the fact that the insurance industry is among the world's largest economic sectors, accounting for $4.7 trillion of revenue and 7 percent of the global economy (Mills 2012, p. 1424).

Studies of the insurance industry have demonstrated that neither private nor government-run insurance firms have lived up to environmentalists' expectations in terms of persuading governments to mitigate emissions, although leading actors have voiced concern and encouraged adaptation actions.[4] While the industry has worked with scientists to improve long-term climate-change prediction models and to quantify risks, attempts to harness its market power have been relatively ineffective. For example, some insurers, particularly US companies, have remained more skeptical than their European counterparts over the risks posed by climate change, and government lobbying by the industry has been minimal.

The industry as a whole has also moved to protect itself, rather than change the behavior of its clients (Paterson 2001a). Insurance firms have withdrawn coverage or raised premiums in coastal areas. Reinsurance markets, by developing innovative mechanisms such as catastrophe bonds, have also helped minimize the insurance market's exposure to risk. At the same time, interest has grown in funding micro-insurance schemes that could serve, if not the world's poorest, then those who could pay modest premiums to offset all but the most major disasters, which are currently covered by government or international donor agencies

[4] As well as Paterson 2001a and Mills 2012, see Brieger et al. 2001 and Phelan et al. 2011.

(Linnerooth-Bayer and Hochrainer-Stigler 2015). They are also encouraging corporate transparency around carbon emissions and exposure to climate risk, as with the development of the Carbon Disclosure Project (see below).[5]

Discussion of how SRI can help redirect firms' choices has been dominated by debates over how criteria for social responsibility are determined, and how that information actually translates into positive social and financial outcomes. Important players in this field include large-scale institutional investors (such as universities or large mutual funds) and ratings firms, who supply information and assessments of CSR across the corporate sector. For example, the MSCI KLD Social Index, in existence since 1990, ranks the top 400 US companies based on social or environmental performance.

SRI covers a broad range of screens and indices of corporate behavior. Many funds screen out any firms engaged in the production of arms, alcohol, or tobacco products, for instance. After that, any or all of a broad range of criteria may be used to assess corporate performance, such as community relations, hiring practices, human rights, and environmental performance. According to the 2014 Report of the US Forum for Sustainable and Responsible Investment, a leading SRI research and advocacy organization, nearly $1 out of every $6 under professional management in the United States is invested using SRI management strategies, a total of $6.57 trillion, continuing a significant growth trend.[6]

Some question whether this amount is enough to change the behavior of corporate actors, especially those excluded from SRI funds – for example, the success of SRI so far could be due to "cherry-picking" of corporate actors that can easily comply with CSR requirements. Others doubt the link between corporate social and financial performance.[7] After all, the point is still to make a healthy rate of return for investors. Finally, some question how ratings firms actually determine which firms are "in" and which are not, and whether or not these decisions represent an objective set of ethics or are, instead, paternalistic and subjective (Entine 2003). Nonetheless, the growth of SRI funds demonstrates that there is a high demand for such methods of ensuring responsibility at this fundamental stage of firms' decision-making.

These governance approaches – using financial market discipline exercised by insurance and investment companies – have their origin in the 1980s civil-society movement that pushed for divestment from the

---

[5] Many of the large insurance companies are also moving to reduce or eliminate their own carbon footprints, a small but telling detail (Mills 2012).
[6] See www.ussif.org/trends.
[7] For a meta-analysis of SRI studies see Revelli and Viviani 2015.

apartheid regime in South Africa. Frustration with how these methods have been relatively weak in combating GHG emissions has helped generate a similar transnational activist movement, also strong on college campuses, pushing large institutional investors to divest funds from fossil-fuel companies (Ayling and Gunningham 2015). It has to date met with both some success and considerable pushback, a sign that it is hitting a nerve with particular interests. It is also part of a portfolio of more radical measures that civil-society actors are adopting across different sites of governance in order to address the particular urgency of taking action against climate change.

Information-Based Governance Strategies: Transparency and Certification

The generation and distribution of information is another widely deployed mode of governance that has become far more prevalent in GEG over the past twenty years. Information is a powerful tool for non-state actors, who often lack other means of eliciting behavioral change. The use of information-based governance in these cases can be distinguished from coercion or regulatory power, usually the domain of state actors, and incentive-based governance, as in market mechanisms or capacity-building initiatives (Bullock 2015, p. 48). It relies on the powers of education and persuasion, and depends on its completeness and credibility to be effective. In this section we examine two modes of information-based GEG: transparency initiatives and certification systems, while noting that there is often considerable overlap between them.

Transparency Initiatives   As we saw in Chapter 5, creating and maintaining transparency in environmental regimes, in particular making public the extent to which states are meeting commitments, is considered a key tool in making intergovernmental regimes more effective. Likewise, transparency initiatives are another way that non-state actors, often working with governments, can keep corporate and state actors, as well as IGOs such as the World Bank, accountable through the disclosure of relevant information to interested publics (Gupta and Mason 2014, p. 6). Such disclosure (ideally) steers or shapes the behavior of corporate and government actors in desired directions. Transparency is also a component of the labeling and certification initiatives discussed in the next section, but these initiatives go a step further, by directly encouraging premium pricing and creating a consumer market for sustainably produced goods.

Box 7.1: International Transparency Initiatives

- *The Extractive Industries Transparency Initiative (EITI):* First proposed in 2002 by (then) UK Prime Minister Tony Blair, EITI seeks to improve the social and environmental performance of extractive industries by encouraging transparency both on the part of firms and the governments in whose countries these resources are located. It includes a capacity-building component, and is a multi-stakeholder initiative with state, corporate, and NGO actors working together in forty-nine countries (developed and developing) to implement its standards (Haufler 2010). Companies are expected to disclose resource-extraction data and revenues, as well as social and environmental impacts. Countries need to meet particular criteria for admission, and are suspended if they fall out of compliance. Benefits of membership include better government infrastructure and a more stable investment climate in member countries.
- *The Carbon Disclosure Project (CDP):* Founded in 2001, CDP, an investor consortium, requests information from leading firms on an annual basis about their GHG emissions, the risks they perceive from climate change, and the measures they are taking to avoid them (Newell and Paterson 2010, p. 65). Compliant companies cut across sectors, including fossil fuels, agriculture, food production, high-tech, and construction. Cities and other government entities also report to CDP. In 2015 CDP received responses from nearly 2,000 companies in 51 countries, representing 55 percent of the global market capitalization of listed companies (Carbon Disclosure Project 2015). It is now a leading source of data on what companies across the board are doing to address climate change risks.
- *GoodGuide*: GoodGuide, launched in the San Francisco Bay Area in 2007, is the smallest of these examples but one that has had considerable impact in aggregating and disseminating information about how products are made from the various labels and disclosure information available. Members of the public can log onto the website or smart-phone application and find out the health, social, and environmental impacts of over 250,000 basic products, as well as the conditions under which they are produced. Maintaining and updating this information is a considerable challenge. One of GoodGuide's advantages is that consumers can look up this information exactly when they are making their purchase choices. Although it has been found to have a significant impact on the choices of these direct users, its founders agree that ways need to be found to get this information to others (O'Rourke and Ringer 2015).

Box 7.1 provides examples of international transparency and disclosure-based initiatives.[8] They do face challenges. Maintaining current and credible information is a challenge, especially with multiple sites of

---

[8] See also Gupta and Mason 2014.

production and long commodity chains. Transparency should also not be seen as an end in itself, but rather as a mobilizing device to steer consumer and producer behavior (Haufler 2010).

Certification and Eco-Labeling Initiatives   Since the 1990s a wide variety of certification or labeling initiatives has emerged, significantly bolstering the visibility and impact of private environmental governance. In essence, firms voluntarily adopt environmental (and labor) standards and practices, often created by a third-party organization, which they then broadcast to investors, shareholders, and consumers via the use of an eco-label. These labels are not restricted to the environmental arena. Clothing retailers claim that their products are not manufactured under sweatshop conditions. Vegetables, milk, and other foods may be labeled natural, hormone-free, or organic, and coffee and tea may receive fair trade or shade-grown labels, and so on. These labels and standards are usually not mandated by government rules or regulations. Instead, firms themselves voluntarily undergo certification, often accepting significant costs in the process, but also benefiting from consumers and investors who place a premium on ethically produced goods.

Many of these initiatives are transnational, even global, in membership. They can be adopted across a variety of national contexts. Certification schemes can be found across forestry, chemicals production, agricultural production, fishery, eco-tourism, coffee and tea, and even the bamboo and palm-oil sectors.[9] These cases are examples of non-state initiatives, but other schemes, such as EnergyStar in the USA, are government-run. They trade in information and reputation. By participating, firms signal their environmental commitment to potential customers and investors, using their own reputation and often that of an independent certifying body to provide credibility.

Table 7.1, as a representative sample of leading non-state or hybrid certification organizations, demonstrates that this field is complex and continuing to expand.[10] Organizations range extensively in coverage and

---

[9] Leading empirical studies of certification systems that reflect the complexities of this realm include Cashore et al. 2004; Gulbrandsen 2010; Auld 2014; Prakash and Potoski 2014; Richardson 2015.

[10] For brevity, Table 7.1 omits older, broader organizations – such as Fairtrade or the British charity Oxfam – that are, however, important for pioneering awareness of labor and social issues in production, creating the foundation for eco-labels. Likewise, "meta-governance" NGOs – such as the International Social and Environmental Accreditation and Labeling Alliance (now simply the ISEAL Alliance) – provide common standards for the standard-setting organizations themselves, an additional layer of governance complexity in this field.

Table 7.1 *Major Standard–Setting, Certification, and Accreditation Organizations*

Organization	Focus	Date Founded	Scope
Forest Stewardship Council (FSC)	Forests and timber products	1993	190m hectares of forest across 79 countries
Programme for the Endorsement of Forest Certification Schemes (PEFC)	Forests and timber products	1999	267m hectares; 90% in Europe and North America
Marine Stewardship Council (MSC)	Seafood and fisheries	1995	231 certified fisheries (19 in developing countries); chain of custody certificates in 72 countries; 10% of wild-caught fish
International Organization for Standardization (ISO)	Management standards across industry, notably 14000 series (environmental management standards)	1947 (ISO 14001 in 1996)	Over 300,000 ISO 14001 certificates in 171 countries
Responsible Care	Chemicals production	1985	Member associations in 58 countries
Rainforest Alliance – Sustainable Agriculture Network (RA-SAN)	Coffee, tea, bananas, cocoa, cut flowers and other agricultural commodities (101 in total)	1987	1.2m farms in 42 countries; 15% global tea production, 13% cocoa, 5% coffee and bananas
Roundtable on Sustainable Biomaterials (RSB)	Biofuels (liquid, gas, and solid) and other biomass-based products[11]	2007	24 certified entities in 18 countries

---

[11] RSB defines biomaterials as "material from biological origin produced through agricultural processes and forestry, as well as by-products and residues from the food, feed, timber, paper and other industries" (RSB website). Biofuels are important as possible replacements for fossil fuels, and biomass products as replacements for petroleum-based plastics. They are controversial as they may shift grain production away from food, causing price rises, as well as other adverse impacts.

International Sustainability and Carbon Certification (ISCC)	Biomass and bioenergy	2010	More than 10,000 certificates in 100 countries
Roundtable for Sustainable Palm Oil (RSPO)	Palm-oil production (plantation-based)	2004	3.34m hectares certified (primarily Indonesia and Malaysia), covering 20% of global palm oil; 2,614 global members
Smithsonian Migratory Birds Center (SMBC)	Shade-grown (bird-friendly) coffee	1998	32 farms in 13 countries, around 6,000 hectares

Sources: Organization website data available as of early 2016

size – some are huge (such as FSC and PEFC), others – such as the SMBC and RSB – are small, or even tiny in the case of SMBC. In forestry and biofuels, organizations are in direct competition (Ponte 2014). Deeper investigation reveals wide differences in standards and support: RSB has a more socially and ecologically aware certification, while ISCC is faster to obtain and more industry-oriented (Ponte 2014). One of the cases cited – RSPO, endorsed by the WWF – has come under fire for certifying large plantations, which, for some, can never be considered sustainable. Another argument about RSPO (and other certifications for new products) is that it actually helped create a market for palm oil that did not previously exist at the same scale by legitimizing sectors of that market (Richardson 2015). Likewise, FSC certification of bamboo also raises questions about the acceptability of plantation agriculture (Buckingham and Jepson 2015).

Labeling and certification initiatives share three main components: the development of standards; certification (the process firms go through to show that they meet the required standard); and accreditation (ensuring organizations that carry out certification are competent and credible). Most of the best-known organizations, including many of those in Table 7.1, set standards but outsource certification activities to specialized firms that they have accredited. Nearly all have sophisticated governance structures: in addition to main offices, they have governing councils or assemblies made up of members and other representatives which oversee the overall implementation and evolution of the institution.

Some certifications apply to individual firms, facilities, farms, forests, and other sites of production. Others are chain-of-custody certifications, which certify a product as it moves from firm to firm along the supply chain, from extraction to final consumption. They verify that the product, timber, for example, has not been replaced by or mixed with non-certified timber products or components. Within these two categories, management system standards require firms to establish processes and management systems to ensure that environmental goals are developed, assessed, and met. Performance standards, by contrast, specify the level of performance required across various criteria, including level of environmental protection.

Certification schemes also vary according to the degree of independent monitoring. Under first party certification, corporations themselves make their own claims about their products and standards, backed by their own reputation and credibility, and not verified by an independent authority. Corporate codes of conduct, for example, proclaim a firm's commitment to social or environmental stewardship (Haufler 2003, p. 238). Under second- and third-party certification, industry actions are monitored and verified by outside actors. Second-party certification is conducted by industry-related entities, such as trade associations, while third-party certification "is performed by either a governmental agency, a non-profit group, a for-profit company, or an organization representing some combination of these three" (Lipschutz and Fogel 2002, p. 134).

In the forestry sector, two global accreditation organizations dominate a crowded field of smaller labels. The FSC, governed by a council consisting of NGO, timber industry, and forest community representatives, serves as one, and the PEFC, which was initiated by the timber industry, is the second. Each reflects different perceptions of the scope and role of sustainable forest management, and represents different constituencies and competing visions of balancing environmental protection with economic development. Because of the relative absence of international law on forest management, the range of existing schemes (and the competition between them), and the size and importance of forest ecosystems from environmental, economic, and sociological perspectives, forest certification has generated significant interest from academics, activists, and international organizations.

The FSC was founded to be a more effective way of protecting tropical forests than NGO-led boycotts of timber products. Firms seeking FSC certification must adhere to ten performance-based principles of sustainable forest management (including respecting the rights of forest-dwellers). The FSC also offers chain-of-custody certification, allowing products to be verified along the supply chain. As of 2015, 190 million hectares of forest across seventy-nine countries had been certified under FSC standards, mostly in industrialized countries (FSC website). It scores highly across several criteria, including ecosystem-based science, representation in decision-making, accountability, and transparency (Gale 2002), and has served as the model for other NGO-run certification regimes, including the Marine Stewardship Council and the Sustainable Tourism Stewardship Council (Gulbrandsen 2010).

Given the breadth and stringency of its standards, the FSC is unpopular with dominant firms in the timber industry, who saw its entry as a "declaration of war" on large-scale tropical forest logging operations (Smouts 2003, p. 205). The PEFC, originally an umbrella organization for smaller European firms, was founded in 1999. Based more on management-system standards, the PEFC accredits national certification systems, and has expanded its reach well beyond Europe. In 2005 it endorsed the two main North American, industry-led schemes, the Sustainable Forests Initiative (SFI) and Canadian Standards Association (CSA). In total, industry-dominated forest certification schemes claim a greater share of this market, primarily in developed countries and plantation areas. In 2015 PEFC certifications covered nearly 270 million hectares of forestland, 90 percent of that in Europe and North America.

Adoption and choice of certification systems varies by national context (Cashore et al. 2004; Espach 2006). Corporations in some countries are more willing to participate in transnational certification than others. Export-dependence is one critical factor, especially when products are sent to developed-country markets. So are structural factors, such as the strength of the domestic economy, the capacity of governments to monitor corporate behavior, and the ways that companies at a very local level perceive the costs and benefits of membership. One study found Argentinian companies far less likely than their Brazilian counterparts to participate in FSC and similar plans, despite similar incentives. The answer lies in part in the relative absence of strong national corporate and NGO networks in Argentina that can help support firms' participation in transnational private governance schemes (Espach 2006). Prakash and Potoski (2014) find that the stronger the state infrastructure, the stronger voluntary regulations, such as ISO 14001, are likely to be, an observation that highlights the hybridity of modern environmental governance structures.

Over the past ten years, market consolidation has shaped the evolution of both the PEFC and FSC. The PEFC remains larger, but both cover significant portions of global forests, albeit primarily in developed countries. Analysts have noted, however, that in this process the PEFC has moved to adopt more socially oriented policies, opening up to wider range of stakeholders, while the FSC has been criticized for, for example, seeking to certify plantations potentially downplaying their social and ecological impacts (Ponte 2014; Overdevest 2010).

Further work in this field examines how certification and labeling schemes are evolving as they grow and gain in stature (Auld 2014; Bernstein and Cashore 2007), and why they sometimes fail (Schleifer and Bloomfield 2015). Are they becoming more like traditional treaty regimes, or are they a very different form of global governance? Are they learning and responding to pressures for change? How are certification organizations responding to greater fragmentation and complexity within their domain? We move on to these questions in subsequent sections.

The Effectiveness of Non-State Global Environmental Governance

The generation and dissemination of information as a mode of GEG started to gain traction in the 1990s, and has continued to maintain a strong presence in the arena of non-state governance, with the proliferation of new governance organizations and the expansion of existing ones. Information as a tool to steer consumers and producers toward particular decisions is, however, fallible, and this approach has been called into question on a number of fronts. This section discusses these critiques of both information-led governance and non-state GEG more generally.

Strengths: Speed, Flexibility, and Support

The strengths of the non-state sector as a site of GEG are significant. First, harnessing private-sector actors as partners in developing and implementing environmental governance schemes potentially creates a "win-win" situation, where firms can continue to benefit economically while working to make production more sustainable. Corporations bring considerable knowledge and expertise to environmental governance that would not be available if they were merely the objects of regulation. If they engage stakeholders excluded from state-led negotiations, such as NGOs and community groups, these initiatives may generate broader support, arguably allowing more to be accomplished, and far more efficiently than otherwise.

Second, transnational non-state governance regimes have emerged in areas where significant gaps exist in regulatory coverage – in the gaps between negotiation and implementation of multilateral environmental agreements, and in areas such as forestry, where international regimes have failed to converge on a set of legally binding international rules. These mechanisms are faster than MEAs to set up and to implement, and are significantly more flexible and adaptable to changes in business or environmental conditions (Detomasi 2002). They also emerge when state and international regulatory authorities have low capacity or when they are unwilling to intervene in industry practices. Garcia-Johnson's study of the positive impacts of Responsible Care in Mexico and Brazil bears this out (Garcia-Johnson 2000). Economic globalization has aided, rather than hindered, the diffusion of private environmental standards (Prakash and Potoski 2006). In fact, standards developed by certification regimes have found their way into national legislation. South Africa and Mexico, for example, have developed national forestry policies that draw heavily on FSC principles and practices (Pattberg 2006).

Third, multi-stakeholder information-led governance mechanisms have been relatively successful at reaching across scales, including to local community levels, as Gupta et al. (forthcoming) point out with respect to the REDD+ Partnership. Organizations work with IGOs to achieve mutual goals. Responsible Care, for example, works with the

Strategic Approach to International Chemicals Management (SAICM), an intergovernmental forum implemented by UNEP that develops safe-management programs and policies for chemicals around the world. Many certification systems may have, indeed, helped ratchet up global standards (Cashore et al. 2007).

Limitations: Participation, Information, and Effectiveness

Non-state governance mechanisms also demonstrate significant limitations. Some are general. Others are specific to existing initiatives. Many are, in fact, similar to the challenges faced by state-led governance regimes. Are standards implemented? How are they monitored? Do actors comply, or can they cheat on their commitments? Finally, do these schemes actually result in sustainable resource use and/or environmental protection? Many of the points below refer to certification and transparency initiatives, but they also apply to other forms of non-state governance.

First, participation, especially in voluntary, and costly, initiatives such as forest certification can be problematic. This is important, as persistent patterns of exclusion lead to perceptions of inequity among potential participants, which may undermine the legitimacy and effectiveness of the regime. Participation by firms across an industry may vary extensively. Firms whose practices are most environmentally damaging do not participate in these regimes. Peter Dauvergne, in a study of the logging industry in the Asia-Pacific region, finds that "timber firms weave themselves into webs of financial and trade ties that obscure environmental accountability. These corporate ties also contribute to widespread illegal activities ... Intricate and obscure connections among firms ... have also made it extremely difficult to hold companies accountable for environmental mismanagement" (Dauvergne 2001, p. 107). The intractable problem of how to capture and change behavior of the worst offenders in the context of voluntary governance has contributed to interest in supplementing certification systems with monitoring and legality-verification techniques to stem illegal logging. This new direction involves harnessing certification to existing laws and regulations regarding logging, a hybrid approach that may address this serious issue (Cashore and Stone 2012).

Second, smaller firms and firms in poorer countries may find themselves excluded from regime participation (and therefore access to more lucrative markets), mainly due to costs of certification. An earlier estimate puts costs of ISO 14001 certification at $50,000 for smaller firms, to over $200,000 for larger firms (Delmas 2002, p. 95). Little progress has been made in expanding forest certification to tropical forests, located in the poorest countries, and considered the most highly threatened. In the mid-2000s "the share of certified forestland in developing countries in the world's total certified area [was] only about 10 percent" (Gulbrandsen 2004, p. 90). FSC data from 2012 puts this figure at close to 15 percent, primarily in Latin America but also in Africa (3 percent) and Asia-Pacific (4 percent), but these certificates count for only a tiny fraction of forest areas in those parts of the world.

In terms of the main currency of certification and transparency regimes – information – questions remain about how audiences – purchasers, consumers, and/or a wider public – acquire, assess, and act upon this information. Given the proliferation of eco-labeling and certification schemes, how do consumers gain enough information to decide which to support? How can we tell when information is complete and fully credible? These are serious problems. Often, not much differentiates one label from another, although they may represent very different standards. It is complex and time-consuming for consumers to look for the relevant information to enable them to choose. Once they have that information, it is also unclear what they may do with it. Also, consumers' preferences – whether for local, organic, fair trade and/or ecologically sustainable – may combine to send conflicting or weak signals to producers.

Evidence on consumer willingness to pay a premium for labeled products is mixed, as recent studies – based on experiments and on actual behavior – suggest (Grolleau et al. 2016; Gulbrandsen 2004). In some cases – child-labor prevention or wild-caught seafood – the certification effect is strong, but in others far less so.[12] A study of consumers in Germany in the 1990s, at the height of public enthusiasm for eco-labels, found that while "half of German consumers pay attention to eco-labeled products, only a third would pay 5 percent more for them," inadequate to effect changes required for sustainable forest use (Freris and Laschefski 2001, p. 6, citing Brockmann et al. 1996).

More concerning is the gap between what consumers want and how they actually behave: "studies have shown that 30% to 70% of consumers say they want to buy greener, healthier, more socially responsible products, but only 1% to 5% actually do" (O'Rourke and Ringer 2015, p. 2, citing a range of studies). This concern extends to transparency initiatives as well. Simply putting the information out on the internet or on smart phones is not enough to change behavior – of either consumers or producers – in desirable ways (Haufler 2010; O'Rourke and Ringer 2015). In recognition of these problems of demand-side penetration, the FSC,

---

[12] See, for example, Fonner and Sylvia 2015; Veisten 2002.

for example, has targeted high-profile purchasing firms, such the companies that buy wood products to manufacture or process in order to sell to the general public, as well as governments, who can accept or even mandate such certifications for state procurement practices.

As with state-led governance regimes, there is little hard data on the direct impact of private governance regimes on environmental, social, and economic conditions. Data collection is challenging, especially when comparing certified entities against those that have chosen not to disclose that data. Many certification systems themselves have not been designed to incorporate assessment mechanisms (Blackman and Rivera 2010). Relevant meta-analyses are not exactly encouraging. Most significant have been environmental and biodiversity impacts of organic farming and sustainable-forest-management practices (Ibanez and Blackman 2015; van Kuijk et al. 2009). Economic impacts are hard to measure because of a selection effect: those farmers who choose to undertake certification are often wealthier to start with. Social impacts are also hard to measure, as they are often less tangible, occurring in the form of learning over the years or in the creation of networks of farmers and growers (Elder et al. 2013). More work is needed on these impacts, and the broader conditions under which certification initiatives create positive differences.

Overall, however, nothing harms an information-based government mechanism more than a loss of credibility. As we saw in discussions of the Intergovernmental Panel on Climate Change (IPCC) in earlier chapters, a successful challenge to an organization's credibility, regardless of its veracity, can have crippling effects. In the arena of information-led governance, there are strong concerns about greenwashing – the extent to which firms are able to manipulate data or undertake activities that make them appear greener than they actually are. That big corporations – such as Walmart – are jumping into this field, getting certified, or contributing to the CDP – has made some people more suspicious of weakened information, or regulatory capture (Dauvergne and Lister 2012). Some NGOs may be co-opted by industry interests (Baur and Schmitz 2012). As certification and transparency systems extend into sectors with higher stakes – extractive resources, biofuels – the ability to critically assess how information is supplied, by whom, and to what ends, is paramount.

Transforming Global Environmental Governance? Theoretical Insights

As a site of GEG, non-state governance remains vibrant, despite the caveats above. Over time, many certification and transparency initiatives have become strong and highly institutionalized – in effect mirroring the state-led regimes and IGOs they are often compared against (Bernstein and Cashore 2007). They have been able to maintain their legitimacy in the eyes of key constituencies. These successes do not happen in a vacuum. Information-based governance initiatives depend on a number of factors: the political salience of the issue area, the existence of other allies and networks, and in many cases their relationship with states, IGOs, and other governmental actors. We pick up on this debate as part of this section, which examines the theoretical contributions of non-state GEG to the field.

Governing Global Production: Bringing Commodity-Chain Analysis into International Relations Theory

Many forms of non-state global governance put the governance of production front and center. Traditionally, multilateral controls on FDI and production of goods and services have been weak, designed more to facilitate economic growth through investment and production than to minimize environmental and social impacts. Early activism, in the form of awareness campaigns and boycotts, helped highlight these impacts. Calls to govern global production focused both on the actions and intentions of individual corporations – particularly large multinationals – and on the ever longer and more complex commodity, or supply, chains that carry raw materials and goods around the world. They have highlighted the circumstances under which raw materials and primary commodities – diamonds, timber, fish – are extracted, and the conditions under which they are refined, manufactured, and sold, particularly to consumers in the global North.

Under contemporary global capitalism, vast distances – geographical and cultural – separate decisions about resource extraction, production, and consumption (Princen 2002). Technology has created a lightning-fast commodity system, where a dress can be designed one day in New York, produced the next day in China, and in Mexico the day after that (O'Rourke 2014). Commodity-chain analysis "brings into focus the technological, commercial and organizational networks that link the various stages of production and exchange for a particular commodity, be it an automobile, an orange, or a pair of tennis shoes" (Conca 2002, p. 139). All these different stages, including packaging, marketing, advertising, and so on, create a set of linkages that are increasingly globalized, and increasingly complex. It is rare that the same corporate entity can exert control across the entire chain, and harder to govern from the outside (Conca 2002; Gereffi et al. 2005).

Commodity-chain analysis helps us understand the complexities of global production, and the long shadows that Western consumers cast on the global economy (Dauvergne 2008). It also demonstrates opportunities to change – or govern – production decisions, the role that certification and transparency initiatives are designed to play (VanDeveer 2015). Exerting pressure on key points along the supply chain can have both upstream and downstream impacts on the entire chain, and providing consumers with information about the extent and impacts of distancing can help shape their own decisions, sending signals back along the chain. This logic underlies the approach of many certification and labeling schemes, thus generating new possibilities for GEG. For example, if a large buyer of wood products, such as Home Depot, starts preferring certified wood, producers will pay attention, and pass this information back to forest owners. As so many commodity chains cross national borders, it may well be easier for non-state actors than it is for governments to push for these sorts of controls.

These extended commodity chains generate asymmetries of information and power, helping to obscure environmental and social impacts of production. Traditional policy/political science analysis has found it challenging to recognize and suggest solutions for these governance issues, which is why scholars of GEP have turned to this literature as a way to move forward. At the same time, an analysis that draws on political science and international relations can remain attentive to continuing power dynamics that may shape governance relations within commodity chains, and the extent to which information-based governance can be backed up by traditional regulatory frameworks.

Non-State-Actor Authority and the Role of the State

The emergence of civil-society and corporate-sector actors as agents in their own right in setting up and managing governance schemes challenges state-centric perspectives on IEP. No longer just lobbying from the sidelines, non-state actors have proved that they have significant autonomy and influence on the extent and shape of GEG. Some argue that this hybridization of global governance is not new. Rather, the theoretical frames employed by many analysts simply excluded it from the overall picture (Conca 2005).

The interrelationships between corporate and civil-society actors are often quite complex, and possibly conflictual. Sometimes, as in the case of PEFC, private governance emerges in an antagonistic context – in this case, in competition with the more civil-society-based FSC. Relationships may break down: even after endorsing Ford Motors' new hybrid vehicles, the Sierra Club strongly condemned their overall efforts to curb GHG emissions in 2005, though the two continue to work together (Deutsch 2006). In 2013 WWF came under intense criticism for supporting RSPO and palm-oil certification.[13] Over the longer term, more studies are needed as to how industry–NGO partnerships work, and why some actors (corporate or civil society) stay out of them, or leave. Another area in which more work is needed is how corporate and environmental groups change as they work together (Holmes 2011). Do NGOs become more "corporate" in ideology and practice? Do corporations internalize norms and practices from the NGO sector? The environmental movement is itself split over the desirability of cooperation with industry, with some groups maintaining that confrontation remains the most effective strategy.

Questions continue to be asked over whether and how non-state actors acquire the legitimacy and authority – internal and external – to maintain and broaden GEG regimes. Internal authority or legitimacy is the extent to which the regime members view it as legitimate. It determines whether members will comply with their commitments or remain within the regime. External authority or legitimacy is the extent to which the regime is perceived as legitimate, or authoritative, by outside actors: states, civil-society actors, international organizations, and the court of public opinion. A lack of external legitimacy will lead to other actors seeking to remove or replace the regime, undermine confidence in the effectiveness of the regime, and ultimately threaten its survival. Some worry that democratic accountability is far harder to maintain in the private governance spheres than in public, for NGOs as well as corporations (Cutler 2002, p. 4). Firms not wishing to comply may simply exit the regime. NGOs question the accountability of industry-led schemes, while industry actors question that of NGO-led schemes (Gulbrandsen 2004, p. 92).

Evidence on internal legitimacy within private governance schemes shows that it is quite high, perhaps not surprisingly, as participation is entirely voluntary (see, for example, Raines 2003 on ISO 14001). External legitimacy is more complex, and tied up with issues of credibility, efficacy, and transparency. Benjamin Cashore argues, in effect, that the legitimacy of non-state governance regimes is measured by their actions (Cashore 2002): How credible are certification processes over time? How well do they reflect societal values, and encourage participation? He suggests that regimes that include a wider range of stakeholders, such as the FSC, are more likely to achieve external legitimacy. However,

---

[13] "Memo to WWF: Destroying Rainforests and Peatland for Palm Oil is not 'Sustainable'," REDD-Monitor, May 14, 2013 at www.redd-monitor.org.

these may be the schemes most likely to be rejected by industry actors if alternatives exist. Finally, legitimacy and authority also derive from efficacy. If these regimes actually "get the job done" in terms of protecting forest areas and communities, for example, they will derive further standing in the eyes of other actors. So far the data suggests that this is not yet the case, but that many are gaining ground.

Turning to the role of governments, just because many of the governance initiatives examined in this chapter are "private," this does not imply that the state is entirely absent. Strictly speaking, very few of the initiatives we have examined in this chapter are wholly private, in the sense that they occur entirely outside the sphere of state influence (Falkner 2003). Government actors are frequently involved in the development, uptake, and implementation of standards, and, as we have seen, national contexts matter in explaining why some firms participate and others do not (Espach 2006).

Nonetheless, the emergence and institutionalization of non-state governance challenges the role of the state in international politics. Does the emergence of these forms of governance undermine state sovereignty? Does it imply that states have diminished capacity or will to manage a globalized world order? In other words, are these new governance regimes in competition with the nation-state for global authority, or are they stepping into a political vacuum? There are no simple answers to these questions, as Green (2014) suggests. If there could be said to be a majority consensus in the GEP literature, it is that non-state governance regimes are essentially complementary to state and inter-state activity in the environmental arena, in that they have emerged in areas largely not covered by international and national legislation (Falkner 2003). The relationship between non-state governance and state capacity is more complex, however: third-party certification schemes have sometimes emerged not where state capacity is considered low, but where it is high. The standards regimes considered in this chapter have taken hold not in the South, where governments are weaker, but in the North, notably in the EU, where states and the EU itself are quite strong.

Finally, critical analyses of state–corporate–civil society relations ask whether corporate actors have crowded out ("chilled") state action, with complicity from states themselves. This neo-Gramscian perspective on the role of private interests in international politics (see Levy and Newell 2002) holds that "capitalist forces are seen to be engaging in alliance building processes with a variety of state and civil society actors in an effort to realign the ideological and material bases of the dominant hegemonic order" (Falkner 2003, citing Cox 1987). In other words, corporate interests are reshaping GEG in a way that co-opts other actors, and reinforces the ideology of market liberalism in this sphere, a perspective that contrasts significantly with one that views non-state governance as creating more, rather than less, participation in global governance.

Finally, how transformative, or disruptive, are strategies of harnessing environmental and social protection to consumer choice? Environmental problems are also a consequence of structures of globalization and corporate power. To rely on individual choices in the absence of a strategy targeting these structures is likely to fail, especially given resources at the disposal of corporations through advertising and pricing to combat environmentalists' efforts. Consumption decisions soothe the conscience, but may have little further effect (Maniates 2002). Perhaps, in the absence of more fundamental transformations, the legal frameworks of state-led GEG may be able to shore up these weaknesses.

Linking Non-State and State-Led Global Environmental Governance

The GEG arena clearly now encompasses different sites and modes, including the private sector and information-led governance. How do non-state governance initiatives compare with international treaty regimes? How do they interact with each other? Some analysts contrast one with the other, and suggest that treaty regimes could be replaced by more decentralized, hybrid governance activities (Speth 2004). Others point to how non-state governance contributes to the growing fragmentation of GEG (see Gupta et al. forthcoming). In many instances governmental and non-governmental governance initiatives coexist, and even work to strengthen each other.

There are strong points of comparison between the two. Several of the non-state governance initiatives listed in this chapter fit the definition of international regimes applied primarily to intergovernmental arrangements: "principles, norms, rules and decision-making procedures around which actors' expectations converge" (Krasner 1983, p. 2, cited in Cutler et al. 1999, p. 13). First, they transcend short-term or strategic cooperative arrangements among firms or between firms and NGOs, instead representing "interaction that is institutionalized and of a more permanent nature" (Falkner 2003, p. 73; Pattberg 2006, p. 245). Second, as with international cooperation, participation is voluntary – but anchored in, and institutionalized by, a range of transnational organizations, particularly certification and accreditation bodies. Finally, many of these regimes are transnational, or global, bringing together participants across national borders, and addressing global environmental problems, such as deforestation.

At the same time, non-state governance regimes can allow for participation by a broader range of stakeholders, and use different steering mechanisms: market forces and distribution of information, rather than the force of law. They also have a tactical advantage, in that they are far less likely to conflict with global economic regimes. So far, for example, the WTO has remained friendly to voluntary eco-labeling practices, while legal restrictions designed to achieve the same goal could fall foul of global trade rules. Finally, non-state initiatives move beyond the relatively narrow framing of global environmental issues as collective action problems, embracing instead the complexities of a globalization frame on environmental problems. As these systems mature, however, they are coming up against the problems that have plagued their governmental counterparts. These include proving that they have made significant inroads in solving difficult environmental problems, engaging actors who strongly resist efforts to change their behavior, and ensuring equity between Northern and Southern participants.

Some analysts argue that particular forms of non-state global governance – particularly "non-state, market driven" (NSMD) governance regimes, such as the FSC – are becoming a real soft-law alternative to traditional international treaty regimes, in a way that other forms of private environmental governance are not (Bernstein and Cashore 2007). NSMD governance differs from traditional intergovernmental governance in several key respects (Cashore et al. 2004). First, governments are not involved in policy-making or enforcement; authority instead rests in actors within the global marketplace. Second, this authority is diffuse: producers and consumers along the supply chain grant it as the product moves from production or extraction to end-use. Legitimacy is derived not only from the active participation in and support of the regime by various stakeholders, but also from the extent to which the regime draws on, or fits with, authoritative international norms. In essence, NSMD is unique – and challenging – because it not only uses market mechanisms to enforce compliance, it also contains "purposeful social steering efforts," in Rosenau's terms (Rosenau 1995), whereby "actors purposely guide themselves towards collective goals or values" through participatory decision-making and active learning (Bernstein and Cashore 2007).

Others point out that intergovernmental regimes and cooperative arrangements are able to accomplish tasks beyond the scope and authority of non-state regimes (Vogler 2005). They have a greater capacity to finance large-scale scientific research, to help build the capacity of poorer states to meet environmental goals, and, if necessary, to threaten rule violators with sanctions (and, potentially, force). Intergovernmental meetings, notably the environmental mega-conferences, drove the early generation and diffusion of global environmental norms. Many of the norms that underpin forest certification systems were generated through intergovernmental consultative processes (Gulbrandsen 2004).

Rather than one dominating the other, it is likely that these governance forms will continue to coexist in a hybrid system of GEG. The important lesson to learn is how to use these different sorts of initiatives to strengthen each other, working together rather than competitively. Certain issue areas, such as global chemicals regulation and trade in wastes and endangered species, remain more firmly in the state-led arena. Others, such as water, forests, and conservation, which have resisted efforts to craft inter-state regimes, are amenable to mixed forms of global governance (Conca 2006). Increasingly, climate governance is becoming more hybrid, as well as fragmented (Bulkeley et al. 2014). Intentional efforts to bring these initiatives together – even if only loosely – may create a more effective framework in the short and longer term to develop more effective climate governance.

Next Steps

It is clear that the emergence of non-state GEG challenges traditional state-centric perceptions of the architecture of global governance. An overview of the state of GEG at the start of the twenty-first century demonstrates considerable hybridity, with various non-state, multi-stakeholder, and state-led governance regimes and initiatives all laying claim to effective environmental protection and pathways to sustainability. In sum, these all add up to the creation of a new site of GEG, one where actors often deploy information generation and disclosure as a governance mode. Others deploy market discipline, and yet others, norms and practices of deliberative democracy.

The emergence of non-state governance is part of the narrative of fragmentation and hybridity within the arena of GEG as a whole (Bulkeley et al. 2014), a question we will pick up in Chapter 9. In Chapter 8 we move on to the emergence of market mechanisms as a governance mode, one that cuts across the sites of GEG – states, economic regimes, and the non-state sectors – we have examined so far.

Discussion Questions

• Take a look around your local supermarket and see what different labels on food products tell you, beyond the nutritional values. Do you find them credible? If so, why? If not, why not? What steps should be taken to make information-based governance work better for consumers?

- Non-state environmental governance regimes face many of the same problems as state-led regimes. What are the problems they share? Are there major differences in the way either type of regime can overcome these problems?
- What challenges do non-state governance regimes face in establishing legitimacy and authority? In what ways does their emergence challenge the centrality of states in global governance?

SUGGESTIONS FOR FURTHER READING

Auld, Graeme. 2014. *Constructing Private Governance: The Rise and Evolution of Forest, Coffee, and Fisheries Certification*. New Haven: Yale University Press: a comparative analysis and history of certification and private governance, telling their story across three common commodities.

Cashore, Benjamin, Graeme Auld, and Deanna Newsom. 2004. *Governing through Markets: Forest Certification and the Emergence of Non-State Authority*. New Haven: Yale University Press: a prize-winning book that examines factors explaining where and how FSC standards are taken up in different developed countries, with a critical discussion of issues of legitimacy and authority in NSMD.

Garcia-Johnson, Ronie. 2000. *Exporting Environmentalism: US Multinational Chemical Corporations in Brazil and Mexico*. Cambridge, MA: MIT Press: Garcia-Johnson's path-breaking study of when multinational corporations are able to improve environmental performance in the countries where they locate, comparing Mexico and Brazil.

Green, Jessica. *Rethinking Private Authority: Agents and Entrepreneurs in Global Environmental Governance*. 2014. Princeton: Princeton University Press: another prize-winning book that breaks new ground in thinking rigorously about what private authority looks like, how it works, and who supports it.

8   The Global Politics of Market Mechanisms

This chapter examines the emergence of market mechanisms as new modes of global environmental governance (GEG). As tools of governance, market mechanisms create or correct markets for environmental "goods" such as avoided greenhouse gas (GHG) emissions or ecosystem services. Actions to create prices and markets for environmental goods or services create incentives for actors to conserve or use them sustainably, hence steering toward better outcomes. From relatively abstract beginnings in economic theory, market mechanisms first took hold in domestic environmental policies of developed countries, and have now gained traction at the global level. Carbon markets and taxes, emissions-trading schemes (ETSs), payment for ecosystem services: all these terms are now commonplace, and are reflected in the activities of expansive networks of NGO and corporate organizations, private market exchanges, and national and intergovernmental organization (IGO) agencies and funds. They have displaced command and control modes of governance across large-scale and complex issues, particularly deforestation, biodiversity and climate change, both within and outside of state-led governance regimes, and have cropped up in unlikely places, such as the People's Republic of China, which launched its own ETS in 2013.

Studying market mechanisms as new modes of GEG generates significant insights into how modern global governance is changing, and how new ideas and interests are injected into these political processes. They are part of the growing fragmentation and hybridity of twenty-first-century GEG. While market mechanisms emerged suddenly and diffused quickly across regulatory jurisdictions, political science (including international relations) analysis of their emergence and impact has lagged considerably. This chapter represents one attempt to redress this, focusing on governance and political implications of global market mechanisms in relevant governance regimes. States and IGOs remain central through most of this chapter. Private market mechanisms do exist (and we discuss them as they come up), but the impetus and infrastructural support for creating prices and markets for carbon and ecosystem services tends to come from government coffers.

201

Markets are human-constructed institutions, not a natural logic of economic organization. While they are powerful tools for changing behavior, they are highly fallible. One of the major contributions of a political-science-based analysis of market mechanisms is in understanding why, in fact, market mechanisms in GEG have been far less successful than their advocates expected, but persist as governance institutions. For example, the 1997 Kyoto Protocol surprised many by introducing emissions trading and offset mechanisms as a way to make it easier for Annex 1 countries – and their industries – to meet their obligations. The 2015 Paris Agreement, however, does not refer to them explicitly at all, although in many articles it advocates "voluntary" approaches.

The following sections focus on understanding the conditions under which market mechanisms for GEG have been established, and under which they succeed or fail. I describe the main market mechanisms that have come to the fore so far, including emissions trading, carbon taxes, offset mechanisms, and payment for ecosystem service initiatives. Final sections offer a threefold assessment typology of market mechanisms, based on the design of specific schemes and mechanisms and their political contexts; social justice and equity concerns; and broader normative and political critiques about the compatibility of market mechanisms with real goals of environmentalism and sustainability.

From Command and Control to Market Mechanisms

In responding to environmental harm, governments have historically employed command and control regulatory techniques, whereby agencies set targets and standards for regulated actors to meet, timetables to meet them, and sanctions for failing (Helm and Pearce 1990). These techniques have been readily and successfully applied in international environmental regimes. The ozone regime, with its targets and timetables for phasing out ozone-depleting substances has been, as we have seen, highly successful. Likewise, the chemicals regimes, up to and including the Minamata Convention on mercury, have had few problems applying command and control techniques.

In the 1980s, command and control modes of environmental regulation came under intensifying criticism from politicians and economists (Helm 2010).[1] Such criticism centered first and foremost on the likelihood and costs of government failure. Governments are not always capable of protecting the environment – or even willing to do so – even

---

[1] For good overviews of environmental economics see Helm and Pearce 1990; Pearce 2002; and Smith 2011.

when failure generates significant economic costs. They may not have the capacity to gather and assess the information they need to formulate successful rules. Governments may also be subject to regulatory influence, or even capture, by the powerful economic interests they are supposed to regulate. Second, command and control approaches do not take into account the costs and economic inefficiencies imposed on firms required to meet inflexible targets. Some firms may face far higher costs than others in the same sector in meeting the same standards, with additional costs imposed on the economy should that firm cut back, fail, or relocate to a jurisdiction with less costly rules. Finally, it is argued, there are few financial incentives under command and control approaches. Firms lose through adjustment costs, and governments lose through lack of additional revenues and the costs of enforcing existing laws. Market mechanisms, on the other hand, may generate revenue for firms and governments, while minimizing overall costs to the economy.

Two approaches underlie the most widely used market mechanisms for global climate governance (Meckling and Hepburn 2013, p. 469): price and quantity-based mechanisms. For example, carbon taxes create a fixed price that firms pay to emit GHGs, while emissions trading or cap and trade set overall quantities of emissions and allow firms to meet targets in the ways most efficient for them. Such tactics might include the creation or purchase of offsets, whereby firms invest in outside projects which meet their targets, but more cheaply. Finally, valuation of, for example, ecosystem services enables resource owners to be compensated if they forgo their rights to fully exploit those resources. Not all of these tools require the creation of an actual market, where goods and services are exchanged. Government and private-sector actors also use them as valuation tools in cost–benefit analysis of investment and/or policy decisions, or to assess how much money is needed to preserve a given ecological asset.

Box 8.1 outlines the main types of market mechanisms designed and implemented for the purposes of GEG. These mechanisms may be regulatory (compliance based), aimed at meeting targets imposed by a government authority or under an international agreement such as the Kyoto Protocol, or voluntary. They may be established and operated by governments, IGOs, and/or non-state actors.

Global market mechanisms have hit more obstacles in their design and implementation than similar initiatives at national or local levels, not least because they have been targeted toward the thorniest issue areas with the most complex global politics: climate change, biodiversity, and deforestation. Linking decentralized initiatives across borders to create larger, more stable markets has proven a difficult task. These challenges are particularly apparent in the cases we go on to examine in the rest of this

Box 8.1: Primary Market Mechanisms for Global Environmental Governance

Taxes: By increasing the price of an activity, good, or service that contributes to environmental degradation, taxes limit their production or consumption and raise revenues for governments. Carbon-emissions taxes can be imposed on point-source polluters. Consumers pay fuel (gasoline) taxes at the pump. Border-tax adjustments allow countries with strong mitigation policies to tax cheaper imports from countries that have laxer policies.

Emissions Trading: Also referred to as cap and trade, these mechanisms set a cap within a given area for pollution emissions, allocate permits to emitting entities, and allow them to trade these permits with each other. Firms with lower reductions costs can sell permits to higher-cost firms, reaching the goal of the cap at a lower overall economic cost. Tradable fishing quotas work in a similar way.

Offsets: Offset mechanisms allow firms or governments to reach targets by investing in emissions-reductions projects in other jurisdictions. The Clean Development Mechanism (CDM) under the Kyoto Protocol allows Annex 1 (developed) countries to invest in non-Annex 1 counterparts. Joint Implementation allows investment in other Annex 1 countries. Other offset schemes allow individuals to purchase offsets to counterbalance carbon emissions from air travel, through, for example, tree-planting programs.

Payment for Ecosystem Services: PES allows for the maintenance of ecosystem services by providing financial support for owners or users, based on an estimated value of these services over time. While not usually a form of exchange, PES provides valuable incentives to landowners and users. Reducing Emissions from Deforestation and Degradation (REDD+) is an example of a targeted PES program, where payments are made to conserve or enhance existing forest stocks as carbon-storage repositories.

chapter. Governments and IGOs continue to play a role, as we shall see, in shoring up faltering environmental markets, creating institutions and rules to support well-functioning markets and ameliorate the inequitable impacts of market mechanisms.

The Rise of Market Mechanisms in Global Environmental Governance

The first concerted effort to introduce market mechanisms to GEG came during the 1997 Kyoto Protocol negotiations (see Box 8.1). Originally they were not part of negotiators' plan for a binding emissions-reduction agreement, but were introduced in order to keep the USA on board with the negotiations, and to help break the North–South deadlock over relative responsibility and technology transfer (Forsyth 1998). From these early steps emerged the vast and complex network of actors, organizations, and initiatives that comprise today's global carbon markets and ecosystem services initiatives. These networks emerged across many jurisdictions over a short time frame (Paterson et al. 2014). Payment for ecosystem services arose more slowly as an international policy idea, first in climate talks as part of conserving forests as carbon stocks, and then in Convention on Biological Diversity (CBD) negotiations, reaching full voice at COP 10 of the CBD in Nagoya in 2010.

The political appeal of market mechanisms is underscored by a compelling set of ideas expertly advocated for by scientific and academic communities – particularly economists, but also climatologists, whose modeling work has played a crucial role in enabling and shaping conceptions of carbon and ecosystem services costs and benefits. They proved to be a fit with the political interests of critical actors: states, corporate actors, and NGOs at a time when neoliberal ideas about the role of government in regulation were fully in play in the global system. For example, ecological economist Robert Costanza has pioneered the process of assigning value to ecosystem services (Costanza et al. 1997, 2014). Michael Grubb, then of the Royal Institute of International Affairs at Chatham House in London, was an instigator of using cap and trade mechanisms as part of the climate regime (Newell and Paterson 2010, p. 94).

Within the IGO sector, the World Bank has been particularly important, producing publications and recommendations for general audiences as well as policy-makers. Units such as its Carbon Finance Unit and Forest Carbon Partnership Facility provide basic research and policy platforms, as well as coordinating funding. Climatologists have developed large-scale models that allow for increasingly sophisticated assessment of the costs of carbon, and the ever larger amount of data and research on both climate change and ecosystem loss have bolstered economists' ever-increasing valuations of their costs. Other IGOs – such as the UN Environment Programme (UNEP) – have followed suit.

Business elites support market mechanisms as they provide both efficient means of carrying out environmental regulations and potentially profitable business opportunities. "Carbon coalitions" of business actors supported market mechanisms in the Kyoto Protocol (Meckling 2011), and they have been supportive ever since, reflecting the important shift in their thinking about environmental threats and governance charted in earlier chapters. Business thinking with respect to climate change, even that of many fossil-fuel-producing companies, has moved from seeing it as a threat, then to a risk, and now a business opportunity (Newell and

Paterson 2010). A huge array of businesses and consultancies has emerged precisely in response to market mechanisms. They develop activities that offset fossil-fuel emissions, they sell offset credits to individuals and corporations, broker sales of emissions credits, and provide consulting services to CDM applicants. Even sectors likely to be most negatively affected by efforts to mitigate climate change – fossil-fuel companies or the aviation industry – are embracing pricing mechanisms as a way to avoid stricter government intervention, costly changes in production processes, and, as we see below, a way to quantify risk in internal decision-making processes.

Parts of the NGO sector, especially large, highly professionalized Northern-based NGOs, have embraced market mechanisms. Conservation International and the World Wildlife Fund (WWF), for example, are strong advocates of market-based mechanisms. They have the funding and other resources to run their own programs or to assist other organizations and agencies to set up and implement market-based initiatives. Conservation International has partnered with the World Bank and other agencies to implement local PES schemes in countries such as Madagascar and Colombia, as has WWF. They are active in developing and implementing global offset projects. The International Emissions Trading Association (IETA) is a leading business international non-governmental organization (BINGO) in the world of carbon markets. They are involved in monitoring and verifying existing projects or generating proposals for funding or assistance, forming part of the world of consultancies and other businesses that have arisen in carbon and other environmental markets. At the same time, NGOs have pushed for stringent standards and oversight of carbon and ecosystem services markets. Some are highly critical of the use of mechanisms such as climate offsets to meet regime goals (Paterson 2012, p. 93), and argue that elite conservation groups are allying too closely with corporate and state interests, losing track of more fundamental concerns at the local level (Holmes 2011). REDD+ and PES initiatives have been of particular concern to NGOs representing indigenous and other local resource-dependent communities (Humphreys 2013).

Finally, today's complex global market mechanisms depend on the leaps and bounds made in communications, data processing and gathering, and visualization technologies over the past decades. Their credibility in the marketplace depends on effective monitoring (or measurement), reporting and verification (MRV) tools.[2] For example, offset projects in

---

[2] Usually, the "M" in MRV stands for "monitoring," except for the UN Framework Convention on Climate Change (UNFCCC) and REDD+ who use "measurement" to refer to the first step in the MRV process.

developing countries must undergo extensive evaluation to determine if they really do deliver climate benefits that would not have been achieved in their absence. To address these needs, centralized repositories store data, to be analyzed and released. Modeling techniques help estimate carbon savings over time. Satellite technology enables visualization of landscape use changes over time. Even crowd-sourcing (data collection by individuals and communities using mobile phone technologies, for example) can play an important role on the ground (Tran 2015).

Global Carbon Markets: Taxes, Emissions Trading, and Offsets

Market mechanisms as a mode of GEG thus emerged rapidly and decisively onto the political stage. The phrase "carbon market" barely existed outside elite circles a decade ago. Now it is routinely used in mainstream media reports and political discourse. Carbon has become a commodity, bought and sold on international markets, although, at this time of writing, at a catastrophically low price. The theoretical principle behind carbon markets is this: the more expensive it becomes to emit a tonne of carbon (or CO_2e), and the more alternative technologies that are available at lower cost, the higher the rate of decarbonization of the economy, thus mitigating the risks of climate change.

The structure and sophistication of these markets, despite the challenges they face, lead Newell and Paterson to argue that we are witnessing the emergence of an embryonic form of "climate capitalism" – "a model which squares capitalism's need for continual economic growth with substantial shifts away from carbon-based industrial development" (Newell and Paterson 2010, p. 1). The 2014 edition of the World Bank's annual report on the *State and Trends of Carbon Pricing* established that carbon markets continued to grow despite the global financial crisis, changing political alliances, and stalled global climate negotiations (World Bank 2014). According to the Bank report, "about 40 national and over 20 sub-national jurisdictions are putting a price on carbon. Together these carbon pricing instruments cover almost 6 $GtCO_2e$ or about 12% of the annual global GHG emissions" (World Bank 2014, p. 15). In mid-2015 the Bank estimated the value of the world's carbon-pricing initiatives to be worth close to $50 billion (World Bank and Ecofys 2015).

Global carbon markets, as established under the Kyoto Protocol, remain the largest, longest-lasting example of the use of market mechanisms in GEG. As Box 8.2 shows, they have also generated a unique and sometimes confusing set of acronyms, including at least three separate

---

Box 8.2: Carbon Market Alphabet Soup

AAU: Assigned Amount Unit, a tonne of carbon as designated
          by the UNFCCC
CCX: Chicago Climate Exchange
CDM: Clean Development Mechanism
CER: Certified Emissions Reduction, a tonne of carbon as
          designated by the CDM
CO_2e: Carbon Dioxide Equivalent
ETS: Emissions Trading System or Scheme
EUA: European Union Allowance, a tonne of carbon as
          designed by the EU
JI: Joint Implementation (also known as AIJ, Activities
          Implemented Jointly
MCA: Marginal Cost of Abatement of one tonne of CO_2e
MRV: Monitoring (or Measurement), Reporting and Verification
REDD: Reducing Emissions from Deforestation and Forest
          Degradation
RGGI: Regional Greenhouse Gas Initiative
SCC: Social Cost of Carbon

---

terms used by different entities for a tonne of CO_2e, adding complexity to already challenging market structures.

Setting a Price on Carbon

One of the reasons global carbon markets have rapidly diffused across national borders is that they are based on a single unit of exchange that is fungible, standardized, and compatible across markets: tonnes of carbon dioxide equivalent (CO_2e).[3] In real terms, we are talking about a tonne of avoided emissions, CO_2e kept out of the atmosphere either through emissions reductions or carbon storage. Despite the common unit of exchange, arriving at the "right" price for this invisible commodity is no

---

[3] CO_2e depicts the global warming potential of all GHGs using their global warming potential (GWP) as a base, with CO_2 having a GWP of 1. For example, methane has a GWP twenty-five times higher than that of CO_2. Therefore, each tonne of methane avoided is the equivalent of removing 25 tonnes of CO_2 from the atmosphere.

Box 8.3: What *Should* the Price of Carbon Be?

There are different ways of thinking about what the price of carbon ought to be in order to prevent or minimize damage, or to change behavior without imposing too high a cost on the economy (Bowen 2011; Price et al. 2007). These, however, rarely correspond to actual market prices of carbon at any given time.

1. The *marginal cost of abatement* is the cost of eliminating each additional tonne of carbon. It represents the costs of reducing emissions rather than the costs of future damages.

2. Carbon prices can be set to meet a particular *goal*, such as spurring innovation or to meet a target, or not exceeding a 2° Celsius temperature rise or a 450 ppm atmospheric concentration of CO_2. Studies suggest that a price of around \$35–40 per tonne is the right level to spur innovation.

3. The *Social Cost of Carbon* (SCC) is the most comprehensive measure. It "measures the full global cost today of an incremental unit of carbon (or equivalent amount of other greenhouse gases) emitted now, summing the full global cost of the damage it imposes over the whole of its time in the atmosphere" (Price et al. 2007, p. 1). In 2009 a US government study estimated a range of SCC values from \$5 to \$65 per tonne. At about the same time the UK came up with a range of \$41 to \$124 per tonne of CO_2. In 2015 a study published in *Nature Climate Change* argued that a more accurate value would be close to \$220 per tonne (Moore and Diaz 2015). Estimates differ because economists use different models to achieve results, and because they reflect the different values policy-makers place on the welfare of future generations (Pizer et al. 2014; Grady 2015).

4. *The Economist* reported in 2013 that leading oil companies, including Exxon-Mobil and ConocoPhillips, apply *internal* carbon prices of up to \$60 per tonne to estimate of the costs of future projects, identify high-emissions projects, and spur innovation.[4] Such costs used for planning purposes are assuming that governments are likely to impose a real price on carbon by the time projects are enacted.

---

simple matter, and carbon prices vary widely across jurisdictions and programs, and fluctuate substantially over time.

For example, there are very real questions about why carbon prices vary so radically across different contexts as well as from the "ideal" prices outlined in Box 8.3. For example, at the same time that Certified

---

[4] "Carbon Copy: Some Firms are Preparing for a Carbon Price That Would Make a Big Difference," *The Economist*, December 14, 2013.

Emissions Reductions (CERs) issued by the CDM were priced at less than $2 a tonne, companies such as Royal Dutch Shell were placing an internal value of carbon at up to $40 per tonne. The World Bank (2014, p. 17, Figure 2) shows carbon prices varying from a tax rate of $168 per tonne in Sweden to $1 per tonne in the New Zealand ETS.

Carbon prices are, therefore, not mechanistic values reached by a freely operating market. Their differences and inconsistencies reflect the impossibility of correctly internalizing all the different signals and information related to future impacts of GHG emissions, and the political and other pressures that all markets are prone to. Although carbon prices reflect the state of climate science and the knowledge about likely impacts and risks from "business as usual" emissions, concrete values – $5 per tonne, or $220 – actually mask a wide range of assumptions, trade-offs, and decisions in the face of uncertainty and other pressures, including political pressures (Bell and Callan 2011). An oversupply of carbon permits or certificates in emissions-trading systems has, for example, been one of the major causes of falling prices. The next sections address the major economic instruments used at the global level to combat global GHG emissions, demonstrating how variations in carbon prices across instruments and jurisdictions and over time have been one of the major obstacles to their success.

Carbon Taxes

Environmental taxes – such as taxes on gasoline purchased at the pump, or on carbon emissions – are a pricing mechanism. They shift prices of a given activity to a higher level to more accurately reflect its total social and environmental costs, ideally changing consumer or company behavior in desirable ways.[5] A high tax on gasoline will encourage consumers to drive less, or purchase fuel-efficient vehicles, operating in a similar way to "sin taxes" on cigarettes or alcohol. A high enough tax on carbon emissions from large power plants and other stationary sources will encourage affected firms to invest in new technology to lower emissions and avoid the tax. Environmental taxes also generate significant government revenue, although for reasons we discuss below, this revenue is often redistributed back to tax payers.

Despite strong political opposition to new taxes in many parts of the world, many jurisdictions have carbon-related taxes in place.[6] The World

---

[5] The theory and practice of environmental taxation is often seen as deriving from the work of economist Arthur Pigou (e.g. 1920).

[6] Carbon- or fossil-fuel-related taxes are not the only forms of environmental tax. The UK, for example, enacted a landfill tax in the 1990s. Congestion charges in cities such as London, Singapore, and Milan have helped ease traffic conditions in those cities while raising revenue for local authorities.

Bank (2014) identified twelve national and subnational tax schemes that explicitly put a price on carbon or CO_2e (as opposed to more general energy taxes). Most existing schemes are in Europe, but Japan, Mexico, and British Columbia also have tax schemes in place. Australia scrapped its tax in 2014, but carbon taxes are being enacted in another four countries (South Africa, Brazil, Chile, and the Republic of Korea), as well as in the US state of Oregon. The Scandinavian countries were the first to enact such taxes, starting in the early 1990s. They vary in terms of their rates and scope. Australia taxed a specific group of largest emitters. France and most others target particular fuels across uses (with exceptions, such as fuels covered by emissions-trading schemes, targeted for particular uses such as agriculture, or exported). Norway's tax applies to all consumption of mineral oil, gasoline, and natural gas. Tax rates vary widely: at the low end, Japan and Mexico have set rates between $1 and $4 per tonne of CO_2e, while Norway's rates go up to $69. The rest hover around $10–$15, although France has plans to increase its tax from $10 to $30 per tonne by 2016.

Typically, carbon taxes have been introduced most successfully in countries that already had fuel taxes. By fixing the price of carbon, they send direct signals to corporations and consumers about the consequences of their actions, and are less vulnerable to rent-seeking behavior. They are a transparent and predictable pricing mechanism as long as they remain in place. As they are usually built onto an existing infrastructure, carbon taxes tend to have lower administrative costs than the emissions-trading schemes discussed next, which need to be set up from scratch (Meckling and Hepburn 2013, p. 474).

They also come with specific disadvantages. First, carbon and energy taxes are regressive. Energy companies will pass the cost of the tax on to consumers, both households and businesses, with the burden of the tax falling disproportionately on lower- or fixed-income consumers. Therefore, most carbon-tax initiatives contain measures for redistribution of revenues through tax credits or business subsidies. Many are revenue neutral, in that all revenues received are redistributed to offset these regressive impacts on consumers and small business.

As a fixed-price mechanism, they can be slow to adjust as market conditions change. Governments can fix the price at the wrong level for the economy: too low, and firms do not innovate; too high, and governments face opposition and potential exit threats from powerful firms. As a state-led initiative, taxes are particularly vulnerable to changes in government make-up or policy. Australia's controversial carbon tax, enacted in 2012 by the Labor Government under Prime Minister Julia Gillard, was unceremoniously scrapped by her successor, the Liberal Prime Minister

Tony Abbott in 2014, despite public support and some evidence of success (Baird 2014).

Carbon taxes are harder than other market mechanisms to scale up to the global level. Fiscal structures differ significantly across nation-states, making taxes hard to harmonize efficiently. Carbon taxes are especially problematic when it comes to taxing goods or services that cross borders. For example, the EU faced heavy opposition from international airlines when it attempted to impose an aviation fuel tax on planes flying to or from EU destinations in the late 1990s. Planned border taxes to redress differences in emissions-reductions programs may run up against World Trade Organization (WTO) rules (see Chapter 6).

Emissions-Trading Systems

The idea of emissions trading, or "cap and trade" as a way to control pollution – carbon or otherwise – is highly persuasive from an environmental economics perspective.[7] First, authorities establish a geographical area (often termed a bubble) in which emissions are to be regulated. They then set a maximum amount – quantity – of emissions levels within that bubble, often with a schedule to reduce levels over time: the cap. Firms within the bubble are then allocated permits to emit a certain fraction of the cap. These may be auctioned or allocated freely at the outset, with many firms grandfathered in, meaning they are allocated enough permits to start at the emissions levels they entered the system with. After the initial allocation, firms are allowed to start selling – trading – permits.

Firms that can meet the targets at lower cost can sell extra permits to firms that find reductions more costly, or choose not to make them. Over time, permits can be withdrawn from the system to reduce overall emissions levels within the bubble. The practice of allocating tradable permits to emit pollutants – or emissions trading – goes back to the 1990 amendments to the US Clean Air Act, which regulated sulfur dioxide and other pollutants. The advantage of this system is its cost efficiency and flexibility. The ETS model is also easier than carbon taxes to scale up to national, regional, or even global levels, as planned under the Kyoto Protocol.

According to the World Bank (2014), ETSs cover around 7 percent of global GHG emissions (using 2010 emissions figures), and have expanded in the 2010s, despite global economic challenges and declining carbon prices (Betsill and Hoffmann 2011). The EU operates the first, largest, and most well-known transboundary ETS. It includes all EU

---

[7] This approach – essentially advocating the allocation of property rights, and the right to buy and sell these rights – is associated with economist Ronald Coase (e.g. 1960).

members plus Iceland, Liechtenstein, and Norway, covering 12,000 installations and just over 40 percent of EU GHG emissions (Talberg and Swoboda 2013). Kazakhstan, Switzerland, Japan, and New Zealand have national ETSs, and the Republic of Korea launched its ETS in 2015. North American schemes are regional or at state/province level. The US-based Regional Greenhouse Gas Initiative (RGGI) includes the states of Connecticut, Delaware, Maine, Maryland, Massachusetts, New Hampshire, New York, Rhode Island, and Vermont (New Jersey pulled out in 2011). California, Quebec, and Alberta have their own cap and trade programs in place. Up-and-coming ETSs include Brazil, Chile, Thailand, Turkey, Ukraine, Russia, and the Pacific Northwest on both the US and Canadian sides of the border. Vietnam is due to begin its program in 2020.[8]

China's emergent ETS has captured intense interest since it was established in 2013 with seven regional or city-based pilot programs in Beijing, Chongqing, Guangdong, Hubei, Shanghai, Shenzen, and Tianjin and plans to scale up to the national level in 2016. It is the first ETS that has expanded from the bottom up. It links local schemes that are, as of time of writing, quite different from each other in terms of prices, emissions covered, and other important features (CDC and IETA 2015). China is the world's largest overall emitter of GHGs, and one of the world's most rapidly growing economies. Despite the legacy of communist rule and a centrally planned economy, business and political leaders have embraced the ETS model, a puzzle for explanations of carbon trading driven by neoliberal economics. Lo and Howes (2015) relate this enthusiasm to Chinese leaders' desire to gain sovereign autonomy in global carbon markets by influencing "the terms by which [carbon] reductions are defined, credited and traded" (Lo and Howes 2015, p. 61).

As the Chinese example demonstrates, national and subnational ETSs vary significantly. They differ in terms of sectors covered, initial allocation methods, and how they allow covered entities to use offsets toward their emissions-reduction totals. Most systems have an absolute cap, based on overall emissions-reductions targets. China, by contrast, bases its scheme on carbon intensity-reduction targets, which allows for continued

---

[8] Experiments in private cap and trade schemes have been limited. The most well known, the Chicago Climate Exchange (CCX), was established in 2003. It was a membership organization: firms paid fees to join, and agreed to binding emissions-reductions targets reaching through trading permits among CCX members or engaging in offset activities. Despite demonstrating some positive returns for members (Gans and Hintermann 2013), it closed in 2010, in large part due to the failure of the US federal government to enact a national ETS.

economic growth during a boom period and can limit price crashes as growth rates decline (CDC and IETA 2015).[9]

Subnational cap and trade systems in the USA remain strong despite (or perhaps because of) the lack of federal action (Selin and VanDeveer 2009). In 2014 the parties to the RGGI in the northeastern USA reduced their cap by 45 percent from previous levels. California's cap and trade scheme began in 2013, implemented under the 2006 California Global Warming Solutions Act (known as Assembly Bill [AB] 32), and administered by the California Air Resources Board. Despite the delay in implementation, the system has significant support from key California stakeholders (Gillis 2014), and permit auctions have raised significant revenue for the state. It has become known for paying careful attention to design features, such as sectoral coverage and the measurability of offsets (Arup and Zhang 2015), evidently learning lessons from its larger counterparts.

The tumultuous experience of the European Union Emissions Trading Scheme (EU ETS) helps illuminate the promise and perils of designing and implementing a trading scheme on a regional scale. First established in 2005, it has weathered significant ups and downs (see Box 8.4). Its biggest challenges stem from design flaws (overallocation of permits and a slow schedule for drawing down the cap) resulting from political pressures at the time the ETS was first constructed, and external market conditions – both the global economy and global carbon markets – helping cause the crashing price of permits. The oversupply of permits in the market has been estimated as moving up to 2.5 billion tonnes of CO_2e by 2020 (Carbon Market Watch 2014), over one year's worth of the EU's total emissions. It has also had a hard time extending into new sectors, such as aviation, where firms have argued that EU carbon regulations would diminish their international competitiveness. Its successes are indirect, and evidence of positive impacts of the EU ETS before the 2008 crash is limited (Branger et al. 2015, p. 10; Martin et al. 2012). It has succeeded in creating a durable mechanism in one of the world's largest markets and a cross-EU acceptance that a carbon price is necessary (Tavone 2015). It has certainly learned by doing, as the reforms in each successive phase demonstrate. The EU's GHG emissions have fallen during the ten years of the ETS's operation to date, although direct causality is hard to trace. Finally, a 2015 report from Cambridge University's Institute for Sustainability Leadership finds it has support from significant members of the corporate community, in a way that

[9] China's emissions-intensity target is based on reducing its GHG emissions per additional unit of GDP, as opposed to an absolute GHG emissions reduction.

Box 8.4: The EU Emissions Trading System, Phases I–IV

Phase I (2005–2008): Established with the goal of meeting the EU's targets under the Kyoto Protocol. Permits were allocated free of charge, EU members set their own caps. At this stage the scope of the pilot was limited to particular energy-intensive industries, such as refineries, cement, steel, and pulp and paper, and to CO_2 emissions only.

Phase II (2008–2012): Introduced permit auctions and expanded the scope of the ETS to allow companies to use credits from offset programs in non-EU countries, including the CDM. At the outset of Phase II the ETS was confronted with its first major challenge: studies revealed that Phase I permits had been overallocated, depressing the prices of EU Allowances (EUA) from a peak of nearly €30 in 2005 to €6 in late 2006 (Newell and Paterson 2010, 102). Prices rallied again during the first couple of years of Phase II, only to crash at the onset of the global financial crisis in 2008.

Phase III (2013–2020): Despite the highly unfavorable economic context, Phase III reforms tightened up the system considerably. The EU took over responsibility from the member states in setting the cap. The number of permits that had to be auctioned (rather than given away) was increased. More specific conditions and restrictions were set regarding the use of offsets, including requirements for purchasing offset credits only from the least developed countries. Finally, the new cap was calculated from the 2008–2012 median emissions, and set to decrease by 1.74 percent annually to reach 21 percent below 1990 levels by 2020.

EU ETS in Crisis, April 2013: The huge surplus of permits caused the greatest political crisis in the ETS to date, when the EU proposed backloading EUAs, keeping 900 billion off the market from 2013 to 2015, in order to stabilize prices at a higher level. The European Parliament voted this proposal down in April 2013, leading to plummeting EUA prices and a political crisis for the ETS. Although that decision was reversed the following July, the incident suggests continued political problems within the EU ETS. As of December 2015 EUA prices were higher – close to €6.3– but remain volatile.

Phase IV (2021–2028): The EU announced further restructuring, raising the annual reduction of the cap on the total number of permits to 2.2 percent, and introducing a set-aside mechanism that could set a price floor by pulling permits off the market as needed. It has also set ambitious new targets for emissions reductions, to 40 percent below 1990 levels by 2030 and 80 percent by 2050, by domestic means alone, cutting out the option for most offset opportunities.

indicates they are taking the need to price carbon and embrace efficiency seriously (Duggan 2015).

The overall outlook for the EU ETS depends on a number of factors. Unless the EU musters the political will and capacity to substantially reduce the cap and pull permits off the market permanently and quickly, the price of EUAs will remain low. Permits will remain in such oversupply that firms have little incentive to reduce emissions at all through fuel switching or other innovations, with knock-on effects on companies that supply those innovations. There is some doubt as to whether these reduction targets will be enough, and whether the EU will be able to draw down the cap enough to make a difference. Newer member states, such as Poland, that are heavily dependent on coal, have resisted any efforts to price carbon. These political constituencies and the pressure they put on the wider EU help explain why EU reform is so complicated (Wettestad 2014). The projected Phase IV reforms recognize and address these problems, but will need to be effectively implemented even in the face of political opposition.

Another part of the problem for the EU has been the failure of the global carbon markets envisaged under Kyoto to materialize. This means there has been little additional capacity in the form of other, linked markets that would allow market imperfections within the EU to be ironed out in a broader system. Some analysts are more optimistic: Marcacci (2013) points to emerging markets in China, California, and elsewhere as part of a market that could extend beyond its current bounds, creating a more stable and durable global market. The long-term prospects for such an outcome depend to no small extent on the state of the global economy and the results of UNFCCC negotiations beyond 2015.

Carbon Offsets and the Clean Development Mechanism: A Failed Experiment?

The third and final category of carbon market mechanisms are offset, or crediting, mechanisms, where individuals, firms, or countries can get credits toward emissions-reductions goals by investing in projects that reduce GHG emissions on their behalf. These take several forms:

- Under the Clean Development Mechanism (CDM) established by the Kyoto Protocol, Annex 1 countries or firms could meet official targets by funding emissions-reducing projects in other countries for less money than the project would have cost at home.[10] These projects have an extra benefit in terms of providing development benefits to host countries.
- Under private offset schemes, corporations invest directly in projects, or through a private intermediary, to offset emissions in order to meet

[10] They may also partner with other Annex 1 countries (including the former Soviet Bloc countries) through a similar mechanism called Joint Implementation (JI).

their own goals or improve their image.[11] Offsets are verified and monitored by private-sector bodies. Several certification bodies (see Chapter 7) play instrumental roles in this arena, particularly as the CDM has weakened. Among the best known are Gold Standard, Verified Carbon Standard, and Social Carbon.

- Individuals may also purchase offsets, for example paying an NGO to plant trees to offset emissions from air travel, although they account for only a small fraction of the overall offset market.

The CDM has dominated global offset initiatives. It has, however, become an archetype of what happens when an elegant economic idea is pasted onto a messy, uncertain, and contested global political terrain. At the end of 2015 its future is uncertain, and it faces, at the very least, significant reform (Arup and Zhang 2015).

The CDM, sometimes referred to as the "Kyoto Surprise" (Werksman 1998), was designed to help Annex 1 countries meet their Kyoto commitments, and non-Annex 1 countries meet development goals. It does this by leveraging foreign direct investment (FDI) from wealthy Annex 1 countries toward emissions-reduction projects in poorer, non-Annex 1 countries that might have trouble reducing emissions using only their own financial resources. The program does not fund projects directly, but serves as a certification and verification mechanism. Projects registered with the CDM are expected to bring in emissions reductions that must be "real, measurable, long-lasting and additional" (Jacur 2010, p. 30). Box 8.5 outlines its complex structure and activities.[12]

Despite its achievements, the CDM was clearly in serious trouble by the 2015 Paris COP. Significantly, the price of CERs, which had peaked at €25 in 2008, had collapsed, from €14 in early 2011 to close to zero in 2013, where it remained at the end of 2015. In response, the number of newly registered projects dropped precipitously – from 1,119 in 2011 and 3,428 in 2012 to a mere 338 in 2013. Other projects were canceled. March 2014 saw the lowest monthly CER issuance for the previous three years (World Bank 2014, p. 39).

The most proximate cause of the CDM's near-collapse lies with changes in the EU ETS system, as CDM Chair Hugh Sealy bluntly stated in interviews in Lima during the 2014 climate talks.[13] The EU started restricting the number of international offsets that could be used by EU

---

[11] See Peters-Stanley and Yin 2013; Newell and Paterson 2010; and Chapter 7.

[12] For other straightforward descriptions of the CDM pipeline see Paulsson 2009 and Sutic 2010.

[13] Wambi Michael, "Q&A: Why Kyoto's Clean Development Mechanism is at a Crossroads," Inter Press Service News Agency, December 4, 2014.

Box 8.5: CDM Structure and Activities

- Projects submitted for CDM approval must be backed by financial commitments from Annex 1 countries, where the investment is coming from, and approved by the appropriate authorities in the non-Annex 1 host country.
- Before they are registered with (accepted by) the CDM they go through a complex validation procedure. Projects must demonstrate that they are additional, contributing more GHG emissions reductions than would have occurred in the absence of CDM registration.
- Once the project is implemented, it goes through cycles of monitoring and verification of the emissions reductions. A third-party actor, different from the validating agency, carries out verification.
- If successful, credits are issued in the form of CERs, which reflect the estimated amount emissions were lowered below the baseline. Most of these CERs, minus fees taken out to support the CDM, are added to the accounting ledgers of Annex 1 parties. Some are also sold on open markets, directly from registries, or on secondary markets.
- Since it came online in 2004 the CDM has, according to its own data, registered over 8,000 projects in 107 countries, reducing or avoiding, at least at face value, 1.5 gigatonnes of CO_2e. Most CDM projects are in renewable energy, with 30 percent wind power and another 28 percent hydropower. Biomass projects, methane avoidance, and hydrofluorocarbon (HFC) substitution are also significant, as are projects related to lowering CO_2 emissions in cement production, which generates 5 percent of human-made CO_2 emissions worldwide.

---

installations. CER prices were also affected by the same forces that caused the crash in price of EU carbon credits, but the fact that the CDM had to rely almost wholly on the EU as its main source of demand for CERs made it uniquely vulnerable to both economic and political changes in Europe.

The CDM had, however, been under fire. First, one of the biggest questions is the extent to which CDM projects are truly additional.[14] There are different ways of measuring additionality, but they come down to two questions. First, would the project have gone ahead without CDM registration and associated foreign investment? Second, have GHG emissions come down because of the project's attention to emissions reductions? To show additionality, the CDM set out to provide rigorous definitions, baselines, and methodologies to establish actual GHG

---

[14] See Paulsson 2009; Haya et al. 2009; Erickson et al. 2014.

emissions, even in far-flung parts of the least developed countries. Efforts to achieve rigor, however, undermined clarity. Baselines and measurements that seemed appropriate in a boardroom were often based on best possible, rather than realistic, conditions. For example, benefits from cooking-stove projects were estimated based on assumptions of use – such as perfect operation – that were not borne out in communities, nor was it possible to measure these in real time (Tran 2015). Approved methodologies used to assess additionality have proliferated, with 217 in existence at this time of writing.

Another major question is whether the CDM truly delivered planned development benefits to non-Annex 1 countries, particularly the least developed countries. CDM projects have a notoriously uneven geographic distribution that favors countries that already have a strong business climate or other sources of leverage. Three countries – China, India, and Brazil (a distant third) – host or have hosted 75 percent of registered projects (World Bank 2014, p. 46), not countries typically thought of as needing large-scale development assistance. Project developers have typically prioritized so-called "low-hanging fruit": low-cost, quick-return projects rather than bolder ones that might deliver significant co-benefits at higher cost (Paulsson 2009, pp. 70–71). Finally, although the CDM does not encompass nuclear power, other renewable-energy projects under its remit, including hydropower, come with considerable social and environmental costs not encompassed under carbon methodologies (Haya 2007).

The CDM thus faces significant challenges as the international community moved to create new agreements on climate change. Suggested reforms include measures that make it simpler, more transparent, and more economically stable, including streamlining assessment methodologies, and encouraging investments on a larger scale, such as by sector.[15] Another option is to broaden the CDM's portfolio to include carbon capture and storage projects (such as REDD+) or nuclear-energy-related activities, or to create additional demand by allowing CDM offsets to be credited across all ETSs, not just those associated with Kyoto Protocol obligations. Overall, however, despite design flaws, offset initiatives, be they CDM or voluntary, have to address the big question of whether Northern firms are simply "buying their way out of trouble" without changing their own behavior or even making a real difference to global GHG emissions. We turn to this and other critiques in the final sections of this chapter.

---

[15] See Jacur 2010; Arup and Zhang 2015; World Bank 2014.

Assigning Value to Nature: PES and REDD+

In 1997 an article by environmental economist Robert Costanza and colleagues (Costanza et al. 1997) caused waves in political, scientific, and activist circles by putting the total value of the world's ecosystem services (ESS) at $33 trillion per year. An updated version of the same study, published in 2014, more than tripled that estimate, to $125 trillion per year (Costanza et al. 2014). These huge global numbers have served to focus political attention on what we stand to lose by eroding the world's stocks of natural capital. They point, at a macroeconomic level, to a need to incorporate environmental costs and externalities into measures of GDP, an idea long championed by ecological economists such as Herman Daly (1977). At a microeconomic level they imply that ecosystems and biodiversity resources could be individually priced to reduce overexploitation.

The assignment of value to ESS is a prime example of pricing goods or services characterized by missing markets. Ecologists and conservation biologists use the term "ecosystem services" to describe everything ecosystems and the creatures that live in them provide us, and the world around us, over time. The Millennium Ecosystem Assessment (2005) identifies four main categories of ESS:

- provisioning services (the provision of food, fresh water, fuel, fiber, and other goods);
- regulating services (such as climate, water, and disease regulation as well as pollination);
- supporting services (such as soil formation and nutrient cycling);
- cultural services (educational, aesthetic, and cultural heritage values, recreation and tourism).

Placing a monetary value on the services provided by particular ecosystems, from coral reefs to old-growth forests, performs two functions from an environmental perspective. First, it sends signals to policy-makers as to what it might cost the economy were that ecosystem to be lost, or to potential donors as to what level of investment might be needed to save it. Second, it opens up the possibility for actual payment for ecosystem services (PES), a significant shift in thinking about global biodiversity conservation, but also controversial (McAfee 1999; Redford and Adams 2011). PES schemes involve resource or land owners receiving payment from government, IGO, or private actors in order to conserve or maintain particular ESS.

ESS values are hard to determine. In fact, creating a standardized and fungible currency across ESS has proven a far harder task than with carbon markets, given the vast differentiation of resources that could be encompassed under this framework, and the more complex trade-offs that need to be made (Reid 2013, p. 222). For example, should a destroyed wetland be replaced by another wetland that may be of lesser value, or by the preservation or restoration of a different ecosystem deemed to be of equal value? Often, PES schemes use contingent valuation as a pricing tool: the amount relevant individuals would be willing to pay in order to protect ESS against alternate use (Venkatachalam 2004).

Such payments may come as direct compensation to land owners for forgoing resource use and/or as subsidies or payment rendered for particular work, such as engaging in eco-tourism, sustainable agriculture, or watershed restoration. They may also offset environmentally damaging activity elsewhere, as in a mining company paying to preserve an area of biodiversity or wetland away from its mines. While more PES schemes are implemented in developed countries (Wunder 2005), they are also being piloted in the developing world. Although an exact count is hard to find, the GEF, WWF and other IGOs, NGOs, and national and regional agencies provide data and assessments of the PES projects they support around the world, from Romania to Costa Rica to Uganda.[16] One study identifies four major market-oriented funding systems relevant to biodiversity that are deployed in low- to middle-income countries: eco-tourism; green commodities (e.g. forest certification); hydrological services (e.g. watershed protection); and REDD/REDD+, which we examine below (Hein et al. 2013). They find an estimated total flow of funds from developed to developing countries of $3.5–4.5bn per year, over half of which is in green commodities (Hein et al. 2013, p. 90).

The notion of ESS/PES has gained increased traction in international biodiversity negotiations, most notably at the tenth conference of the parties of the CBD, held in Nagoya in 2010 (Suarez and Corson 2013). It marks the latest chapter in efforts to find effective modes of biodiversity conservation from the global level, following on the heels of protected areas creation and decentralized governance. There are many initiatives at the international level (state, non-state, and hybrid) that push for an ESS/PES approach to global biodiversity conservation, in addition to the Millennium Ecosystem Assessment (Gómez-Baggethun and Pérez 2011). In 2010 The Economics of Ecosystems and Biodiversity (TEEB) report, released at the Nagoya COP and which strongly advocated the use of PES measures, successfully framed the issue for global, national, and local agencies, as well as for business and NGO

---

[16] See Global Environment Facility 2014 and NGO websites. The International Institute for Environment and Development (iied.org) publishes reports and assessments of PES schemes it is involved with. Grima et al. (2016) analyze forty PES case studies they identified in Latin America.

constituencies (even producing specific executive summaries for each group). Likewise, the recently established Intergovernmental Science-Policy Platform on Biodiversity and Ecosystem Services (IPBES; see Chapter 3) puts an ESS framing for biodiversity conservation policies front and center.

The Reducing Emissions from Deforestation and (forest) Degradation (REDD/REDD+) initiative is one of the primary global PES systems in operation today, and one of the most controversial. REDD+ serves as an umbrella term for a set of initiatives – bilateral, multilateral, and non-state operated – that combat both climate change and deforestation, linking the two areas, by providing payments for a specific ESS.[17] Trees – especially in mature/old-growth stands – store carbon, keeping it out of the atmosphere, and land-use change, particularly through deforestation, is responsible for 12–20 percent of global GHG emissions (Norman and Nakhooda 2014). By placing financial value on that carbon, forest owners or authorities in developing countries can be paid by developed-country agencies to maintain those stocks rather than cut them down. Developed countries may then receive offsets. REDD+ is an advance over earlier inclusion of forest stocks as carbon sinks in the Kyoto Protocol, which created perverse incentives for governments to cut down old-growth forests and replace them with plantations to claim net emissions reductions via creating sinks. It is also a tremendously challenging institution – or set of institutions – to grasp from a global environmental politics (GEP) perspective, as well as highly complex to understand and implement on the ground. This short discussion will cover the points most relevant to this chapter.[18]

REDD+ as a possible plank of the international climate regime first came up in 2005 at COP 11 of the UNFCCC, proposed by Costa Rica and Papua New Guinea. It was formally integrated into draft negotiations in Copenhagen in 2009. In 2015, at the Paris COP, it became a formal part of the final Agreement. Article 5 specifically recommends parties taking action to create and maintain carbon sinks, emphasizing forests in developing countries. As of December 2015 REDD+ mechanisms were managed by a group of multilateral funds and donor countries (Norman and Nakhooda 2014). In total, $2.89 billion had been pledged to multilateral funds that focus on REDD+, including the World Bank's Forest

---

[17] REDD+ goes beyond REDD in that it includes the role of conservation, sustainable management of forests, and enhancement of carbon stocks within existing forests and tree stands.

[18] On REDD and REDD+ see, for example, Doherty and Schroeder 2011; Lederer 2012; Humphreys 2013; Gupta et al. forthcoming; the UN-REDD Program at http://www.un-redd.org; and REDD-Monitor at http://www.redd-monitor.org.

Carbon Partnership, the UN-REDD Program, the Amazon Fund, and the African Development Bank's Congo Basin Forest Fund. The major donor countries are Norway (by a long way), the UK, the USA, and Germany.[19] Australia also provides bilateral donations to Indonesia. The largest single country recipients are Brazil and Indonesia, but 22 percent of multilateral REDD+ funding has gone to sub-Saharan Africa. Private entities are active in REDD+ too – Conservation International runs projects and the Brazilian oil company Petrobras is a large contributor to the Amazon Fund. These funds go toward specific projects in developing countries as well as to more general "readiness" and capacity-building projects. Largely, they are allocated to national governments to implement specific programs and projects, ultimately reaching landholders and/or communities at the local level. So far, donors do not receive offset credits, as they do with CDM projects, but this may happen as a REDD+ mechanism is formalized under the climate regime.

REDD+ initiatives have particular strengths. They link the need to combat forest degradation with that to mitigate climate change, through identifying and quantifying a specific and important ecosystem service that forests perform: carbon storage. They may be important tools to prevent further GHG emissions in the short term before emissions are stabilized or reduced. REDD+ is also representative of the way thinking around environment–development issues has evolved, connecting environmental (in this case, climate and forests) gain with development gains on the ground. Finally, it is an important recent effort to create a cross-scale institution in GEG (Doherty and Schroeder 2011), also one of the reasons it is complex and hard to recognize from an international relations theory perspective.

As a forest/climate-governance institution, REDD+ is highly controversial, as reports from NGOs such as Carbon Trade Watch and REDD Monitor bear out. First and foremost, particularly in initial proposals, it did not take into account the potential impacts, and marginalization, of forest-dwelling communities, who could easily face dispossession from their lands and livelihoods as forests were enclosed as carbon sinks, especially in cases of customary property rights, when forest-dwellers' right to access resources is not codified under law and enforced. Indigenous-rights groups have strongly contested the implementation of REDD+ projects in the absence of social safeguards or without their positive inclusion in decision-making.

---

[19] Norway is able to be the largest contributor to global environmental aid programs – REDD+ and otherwise – because of its oil wealth, part of which is dedicated to global development through its Sovereign Wealth Fund.

On a practical level, there are concerns about MRV: forest preservation has to be, to all intent and purposes, permanent if carbon storage is going to work, hence the need to protect from logging, fires, future political change, or change in the opportunity cost of land use (Humphreys 2013, p. 83). Carbon stocks have to be accurately measured and accounted for. Finally, handing over money in this way to governments or local actors may lead to corruption or mismanagement.

All these challenges have played into REDD+'s evolution as a global mechanism. "REDD Readiness" programs have been a large component of multilateral funding, especially from UN-REDD. Countries receive aid, training, and other capacity-building resources so that they can ensure the effective functioning of projects. The multilateral funding agencies have built-in mechanisms for consultation with indigenous and local communities, creating social as well as technical safeguards, and the REDD+ partnership has created a bridging organization for all stakeholders to foster transparency. What meaningful participation in complex and abstract decision-making might mean for marginalized, poor communities in practice is another point that analysts of international institutions make (Goldman 2005), and one that REDD+ proponents have yet to adequately address. We pick up on this and other critiques of market mechanisms in the following section.

Assessing Market-Based Modes of Global Environmental Governance: Three Perspectives

In this section we analyze common critiques of and challenges facing market mechanisms as a new mode of GEG, and consider the implications for GEG in theory and in practice. Market mechanisms have only recently become a serious object of analysis for international relations and GEP scholars, but the political-science perspectives reflected in this chapter illuminate how market mechanisms work, their strengths, and their weaknesses. Market mechanisms may be tools of governance, but experience is proving that they need significant governance themselves (Newell and Paterson 2010, p. 142).

Newell and Paterson (2010) take a critical but pragmatic approach to analyzing market mechanisms, arguing that they are most likely here to stay, whether as a dominant mode of governance, or part of a portfolio of measures to address complex issues that traditional intergovernmental approaches cannot reach. The support, the sunk costs, and the extensive networks of actors, organizations, and agencies engaged in this work suggest that dismantling this system could be very costly. That does not mean that market mechanisms are unproblematic. As Paterson points out, they are being implemented despite high levels of criticism, resistance, and a sense that they lack legitimacy (Paterson 2012; Matt and Okereke 2015). They are also replete with glitches – more, apparently, than the "targets and timetables" of traditional regimes. Perhaps they are just under higher scrutiny, or being applied to the most difficult problems, but much ink has been spilled on the specific problems these initiatives experience, their costs, and their impacts.

Here we examine three perspectives from which to critique market mechanisms as a mode of GEG, which build on each other. The first accepts the utility (or at least potential) of market mechanisms but notes the design flaws, the political failures, and broader vulnerabilities that beset them. The second focuses on justice and distributional concerns: for example, do market mechanisms disproportionately affect communities that have no voice in the decision-making processes? The third stems from perspectives that do not believe that market mechanisms can solve the critical problems of GEG, given structural conditions in the global economy, and the very big, complex, and immediate threat a problem such as climate change poses.

Designing Market Mechanisms

In some ways this first perspective could be seen as technocratic, finding fixes for easily identifiable problems, such as reconfiguring baselines within the CDM or creating price floors in ETSs. In fact, the questions it raises are deeply relevant to political science, and can be addressed using tools of political science. They include issues of institutional choice and design, reform and learning, of political interests and pressures, and wider contexts – such as the 2008 recession – that reveal vulnerabilities that need to be reduced as much by political will and capacity as by re-design (Newell and Peterson 2010; Meckling 2014).

Starting with carbon markets, carbon leakage is a problem common across single-country or regional regulatory regimes. It happens when demand for carbon-intense goods or energy does not decrease as mechanisms are put in place. Business actors can relocate, or actors outside the system can increase production and use of fossil fuels, undermining goals of reducing overall global emissions. Regional emissions-trading systems, carbon taxes, CDM projects, and avoided deforestation under REDD+ are all prone to this problem in the absence of efforts to reduce demand and/or broaden the scope of the schemes. Carbon leakage under the CDM occurs when a conservation project displaces activity, such as timber harvesting to unprotected forests, leading to an increase in carbon emissions beyond the boundaries of the project, potentially erasing its benefits (Paulsson 2009, pp. 69–70). Carbon-storage projects also have to take into account leakage effects over time. Afforestation projects, for example, have to remain intact for an indefinite but lengthy period for their climate benefits to be maintained. If a forest is harvested or burns, the benefits are lost.

Second, ensuring additionality, especially of offset or storage projects (or of any of the projects managed under the Global Environment Facility [GEF] – see Chapter 5) is a constant issue, as the above discussion of the CDM demonstrates. Additionality is hard to measure on the ground, requiring complex calculations of counterfactuals and baselines. Incentives for investors or project managers to make their projects appear additional – even if they might have gone ahead anyway – are high. Solutions are not easy, though simplification of methodologies and tightening of measurement has been suggested (Arup and Zhang 2015; Jacur 2010). In a similar vein, so-called hot-air credits also undermine the overall effectiveness of an ETS. Specifically, the term is used to refer to credits issued to Russia as part of an incentive package to ratify the Kyoto Protocol, credits that represented reductions targets that had already been met due to its post-Soviet economic collapse, but that have been traded on international markets nonetheless.

Third, there are significant transactions costs associated with establishing, administering, and participating in an ETS, the CDM, or REDD+. Participation costs are disproportionately high for smaller businesses (Jaraité et al. 2010; Meckling and Hepburn 2013). One analysis suggests "projects must reduce emissions by around 30–40 thousand [tonnes CO_2e] at a minimum before it is worth bothering with the costly and lengthy validation, registration, and verification process" (Meckling and Hepburn 2013, p. 474). Further, any system that generates income for participants is vulnerable to fraud: in 2011 hackers got into the EU ETS computer system and stole $40 million worth of credits for re-sale (Branger et al. 2015, p. 11).

Fourth, carbon and PES market systems are growing more complex. They have diversified to include derivative markets, including futures, options, and certificate swaps (Paterson 2014, p. 59). Results-based financing programs often link other project outcomes – such as public-health benefits from the adoption of solar-powered cooking stoves – to global carbon-removal goals. Blue carbon (oceans and marine systems), green carbon (carbon sequestration in forests), and gold carbon (projects linked to broader outcomes, as in the cooking-stove example) are expanding and differentiating carbon markets (Newell 2014, pp. 415–416). This diversification – and complication – of markets for environmental goods and services demonstrates how the governance of carbon – and therefore climate change – has been enmeshed in the global capitalist system, but poses further complications for effective governance (Newell and Paterson 2010).

Finally, simply stabilizing carbon and other "green" markets over a long time frame is a challenge. Short-term fixes, such as holding back permits in the EU or the purchase of CERs by the Norwegian government at a higher than market price, are smart but not enough. Carbon markets will need to be broadened globally and – if possible – integrated if they are to work over the longer term, and include better MRV – to assess values and to detect fraud – and other stabilization mechanisms and safeguards. Ultimately, the vast global differences among carbon prices, from taxes to EUAs to CERs to internal calculations, may need to be reconciled. Ultimately, this system will most likely shift to one of results-based financing, where funding will be allocated primarily after the project's goals are reached, a path called for in Article 5 of the 2015 Paris Agreement.

One way to understand how to design effective mechanisms is to identify the conditions under which they are successful. Grima et al. (2016), in a study of forty PES initiatives in Latin America, examine the focus of each project (deforestation etc.), its geographic scale and time frame, the form of compensation used, and the actors involved (government, NGO, private). They find that medium- to long-term projects, on a local scale, with private sector actors and compensation in kind (infrastructure, education, materials) rather than cash tend to be more successful. This sort of study is needed across this field, especially as REDD+ initiatives multiply.

Justice and Equity

Despite being couched in apparently neutral economic language and theory, the implementation and operation of market mechanisms have very real distributive impacts on people's lives and livelihoods. They often fail to connect to or reflect the interests of local communities or the public in general. At the very least, the political and technical complexity of market mechanisms – not to mention the alphabet soup they swim in – contributes to a general lack of transparency and accessibility for the non-expert public, underscoring the primacy of particular sorts of expertise in this political realm. These kinds of connections, however, matter particularly for mechanisms and institutions that reach across scales and directly affect or involve communities, NGOs, financial institutions, states, and IGOs (Newell 2014, p. 417).

Neo-Gramscian critiques point out that the market mechanisms we have serve powerful interests (Matt and Okereke 2015). While the EU initially wanted a carbon tax, business interests pushed for an emissions-trading scheme. While developing countries proposed technology transfer via a global fund in the run-up to Kyoto, the Clean Development Mechanism created instead a market where Northern firms could accumulate returns from investments in the South, undercutting Southern countries' opportunities to benefit fully from climate-friendly technologies (Matt and Okereke 2015, pp. 122–24).

Distributional issues come into focus when there is cross-scalar conflict, which has been particularly the case with respect to the CDM and REDD+. The CDM has a local community feedback participation component, but it is very weak. Local communities – for example waste pickers, communities living next to methane storage sites, and forest-dweller communities – have organized across borders to protest the loss of rights of access to – and use and ownership of – resources, and of community health and safety (Newell and Bumpus 2012; Vilella 2012). Adaptation funding has been significantly downplayed in the rush to finance what are chiefly mitigation mechanisms. Designing mechanisms that enable real public deliberation and participation is time-consuming, difficult, and often expensive. It works best very early in the institutional design process (Burns and Flegal 2015). Unfortunately, in these cases public input is more an afterthought than an integral component.

In terms of broader carbon markets, California's ETS may have produced one of the stronger processes for building in justice and procedural concerns, particularly with respect to offsets. Implementation of AB 32, California's Global Warming Solutions Act (2006), was halted early on when environmental justice groups took the legislation to court for its likely serious effects on minority and poor communities, particularly because if energy companies offset their emissions, poorer communities around refineries and power plants would remain exposed to the co-pollutants produced there. While litigated in California, this issue has implications for global ETSs (Pastor et al. 2013).[20] AB 32 also has put measures in place to monitor and verify offset projects over time, and to ensure that they operate to the advantage of local communities. Offsets are restricted to 8 percent of a covered entity's obligations, and must be sourced from within North America, although it has plans to include REDD+ projects in Brazil (Arup and Zhang 2015, pp. 90–92).

---

[20] Even though environmental justice groups ultimately lost in their effort to halt AB 32's implementation, the California Air Resources Board built in measures that would allow for adaptive management of the system and addressed production of short-lived GHGs, such as black carbon, methane, and hydrocarbons, which would serve to reduce pollution in areas immediately around power plants. See Pastor et al. 2013; Kaswan 2014.

PES mechanisms and REDD+ also generate strong concerns about equity. Particular concerns exist over the dispossession of local communities from their land, and their loss of access to resources, with the concomitant failure to benefit from resulting revenues. "Land-grabbing" is the purchase of land in the global South for agriculture or other reasons by countries such as China or Saudi Arabia. Critical analysts have extended this notion to discuss "green-grabbing" – the acquisition and enclosure of land, often by NGOs or other interests, to maintain its forests or other resources often justified as conserving ESS or creating carbon sinks or biofuels (Fairhead et al. 2012).

ESS/PES approaches raise questions too that touch on ethics and philosophical questions. What happens when values placed by different actors on ESS diverge over time? Or the value of a single ecosystem grows so high that wealthy actors compete, to the detriment of the system and its inhabitants (Redford and Adams 2011)? Can non-human use and values be included in calculations? What about the interests of future generations? These questions challenge a pricing- or market-based approach to ecosystem conservation.

Critical Perspectives on Market-Based Governance

Perspectives that are profoundly critical of market mechanisms are grounded in both practical experience and social theory. First, with careful attention to design, broader political and economic contexts, and to enhancing political will and capacity, many of these problems could, at least in part, be addressed. However, they may be costly diversions given the urgency with which many political constituencies now view the speed and impacts of climate change. The contribution of market mechanisms to resolving climate issues could remain too small, with the costs of establishing and maintaining them outweighing benefits. For example, given that emissions reductions in the EU can be attributed to other factors, the costs of establishing and running an ETS might be better spent on other policies, such as fully incentivizing a switch to renewable energy sources. It is doubtful to what extent market mechanisms could contribute to offsetting the costs of mitigating GHG emissions, let alone what contribution they might make to the big problems of adaptation and disaster management as the climate becomes more and more perturbed. Analysts suggest that energy market reform and a transition to renewables is a more effective path (Pearse 2015).

Second, from a critical-theory perspective, market mechanisms remain highly contested. Arguments that they represent detrimental forms of carbon capitalism or new environmental colonialisms raise questions of power, justice, and the impacts of broader economic ideologies on policy choice (Lohmann 2012; Bumpus and Liverman 2011; Monbiot 2012). Others remind us that full-blooded capitalism, as the cause of the problems, should not be seen as the tool for saving us (Klein 2014). Using the tools of neoliberal economics creates fundamental contradictions, serving only narrow issues and interests. "Market fundamentalism" cannot be sustained as the underlying ideology of sustainable development or ecological protection, as the title of McAfee's highly cited essay "Selling Nature to Save it" suggests (McAfee 1999). Nor can processes of commodification capture all elements and values of natural/human systems and societies (Paterson 2014).

These perspectives also encompass moral arguments. Carbon offsets, for example, have been likened to "indulgences" issued by the Catholic Church, essentially a way of offsetting sins before committing them, through good deeds or through payment. In other words, firms or individuals pay for their carbon emissions and are therefore still allowed to continue their behavior (Monbiot 2006). Countries such as Bolivia and Venezuela heavily opposed mention of carbon pricing in the Paris Agreement as it implies Northern countries shifting the actual burden of adjustment to the South.

Next Steps

Market mechanisms for GEG have operated since the late 1990s. They have, however, been subject to considerable, and often deserved, criticism, as the previous section outlined. It is hard to say, particularly given the extent to which they were underplayed in the 2015 Paris Agreement, what their future is. Important interests, however, remain committed at the very least to pricing mechanisms, for both carbon and ESS. Setting a price on environmental goods and services sends a signal that they have value and should therefore be used sparingly, which (if a suitable price can be maintained) is an important policy component. Real problems seem to come from setting up a market and allowing prices for these invisible, contested commodities to be set through transactions that are essentially not backed by a credible product. It is possible that momentum will shift to the private sector, as the continued efforts of organizations such as Gold Standard attest.

This chapter has demonstrated that political-science perspectives provide clues to the emergence, rise and fall, and remaining persistence of global market mechanisms for environmental governance. It has also attempted to cut through the alphabet soup and complex economic theory that characterizes this subject area. As we move forward to this book's concluding chapter, it is worth noting that market mechanisms still represent growing hybridity in systems of GEG, and, as with other sites and modes examined in this book, raises fascinating questions about complexity, scale, and linkages across this complex field of political activity.

Discussion Questions

- What are the differences between price- and quantity-based market mechanisms? What are their relative strengths and weaknesses?
- Going back to the three perspectives on assessing market mechanisms, discuss how these apply to specific examples of such mechanisms, from taxes to PES. How would you ground your assessment in empirical evidence?
- What do you think the mechanisms identified here might look like ten years from now? Will they still exist? What are the reasons for your answer?

SUGGESTIONS FOR FURTHER READING

Costanza, Robert, et al. 1997. "The Value of the World's Ecosystem Services and Natural Capital." *Nature* 387: 253–60: the article that opened global conversations about ESS as a drastically undervalued component of the global economy.

Helm, Dieter, and David Pearce. 1990. "Economic Policy towards the Environment." *Oxford Review of Economic Policy* 7.4: 1–16: a brief but thorough introduction to related topics in environmental economics, and how market mechanisms might be translated to the global level.

Klein, Naomi. 2014. *This Changes Everything: Capitalism vs. the Climate.* New York: Simon & Schuster: global justice activist, writer, and scholar Naomi Klein discusses why we need to leave capitalism behind in order to redress climate change, offering directions as to how we can accomplish this transformation of the global system.

Newell, Peter, and Matthew Paterson. 2010. *Climate Capitalism: Global Warming and the Transformation of the Global Economy.* Cambridge: Cambridge University Press: pragmatic yet critical, this book carefully addresses many of the major themes in the history and development of carbon markets from a governance perspective.

9 Conclusions: The Environment and International Relations in the Twenty-First Century

This book opened with the outcome of the twenty-first Conference of the Parties (COP) to the UN Framework Convention on Climate Change (UNFCCC) held in Paris in December 2015. Notably, after years of stalemate on crafting a post-Kyoto agreement, states had finally decided a course of action. International relations theory and the theories of inter-state bargaining and cooperation we studied in Chapter 4 are critical in enabling us to follow and understand this outcome. Several elements of international cooperation theory are present. The interests of a powerful "laggard" state (the USA) had changed, at least at the executive level: President Obama had crafted a US plan based on actions the Executive Branch could take without the approval of Congress, which remained opposed. The French, by all accounts, ran a tight meeting, pushing delegates toward agreement on a number of difficult issues. Perhaps most importantly in explaining the immediate outcome, a huge part of the negotiations – the part that had stymied negotiations in previous years – was bypassed. By submitting individual national plans the negotiations were able to start with commitments in place, allowing delegates to focus on other issues in the regime, such as finance and monitoring. For many reasons, the ultimate agreement deserved the standing ovation it received on the final day of the COP, representing a significant political advance over earlier efforts.

However, the issue pushed most strongly by the least developed countries – the need for a Loss and Damage Protocol to compensate for unavoidable climate-related damage – failed. Nor were significant transparency, monitoring, and verification measures put in place: that decision was put off for three years. Further, while the "bottom-up" approach was hailed as a way to break through negotiating deadlocks, concerns remain about the big differences among plans, which allowed some countries (such as Russia) to commit to very little. Still, according to studies, while we are well past meeting the 1.5° Celsius goal parties agreed on, if all individual national plans are fulfilled (a big if), we may be on target to a rise of less than 3°, less than earlier studies predicted and low enough to avoid disaster.[1] Parties will meet every three years to review – and strengthen – their commitments.

Institutionalist theory only goes so far in understanding the Paris outcome. Realist arguments, focusing on changes in the balance of power, note the rising role of the new "great powers," notably China, in pushing for new climate agreements, starting at Copenhagen in 2009. Constructivist arguments matter significantly in understanding the shift Paris represented. At long last, the knowledge generated through the Intergovernmental Panel on Climate Change (IPCC) and other expert communities has been taken up and internalized by leading nation-states. Climate change is increasingly accepted as reality – driven in part by the experience of extreme weather patterns around the world since 2010, and evidence of year after year of record-breaking temperatures. Norms long advocated in climate negotiations, often by non-state actors, such as ensuring engagement of local communities and other civil society actors in decision-making, were internalized in the agreement. Perhaps it is also the case that new understandings of climate change and attendant global challenges are helping transform how the international community works together to address shared problems.

How the climate regime evolves in the post-Paris era will be a central concern for scholars and practitioners of global environmental governance (GEG). Climate change is not the only global environmental problem, nor is climate governance the focus for all theorists of global environmental politics. The most salient point to arise out of the Paris negotiations is that GEG is complex, and beyond the control of any one set of actors. It is not easy to predict paths of change in GEG, except that in the absence of a fundamental shock to the international system, it is likely to be shaped by its path so far. This final chapter pulls together the main narrative threads that have guided this book, and examines new frontiers of research and practice in GEG. The focus is on the book's findings about the changing architecture of GEG, and the emergence of new sites and modes of GEG.

International Relations and the Environment: Analytical Themes

Theoretical Pluralism: The Need for a Broader Theoretical Lens

The emergence of the environment onto the international political agenda has provided a rich set of cases for scholars of international

---

[1] See http://climateactiontracker.org/news/224/indcs-lower-projected-warming-to-2.7c-significant-progress-but-still-above-2c-.html.

relations, and particularly for the study of international cooperation. We have seen how the study of state-led GEG through the negotiation and implementation of treaty regimes has led analysts to highlight factors that had been marginalized or overlooked in mainstream international relations theory. These include North–South relations, the role of science and expertise in international politics, and the role of non-state actors. The study of regime impacts and effectiveness recognizes the fact that international regimes are a durable international phenomenon, and has led to the development of tools and methods to understand their impacts, and how well they work. Trade–environment debates have helped foster a shift away from examining different global governance processes in isolation. Rather, how global governance orders interact with each other has, as with regime effectiveness, come to the fore as global governance institutions mature and grow in density and complexity. The rise of private authority in the international system is a relatively new frontier in international relations theory: the fact that so many instances of such authority occur in the environmental arena has helped push these research agendas further than they might otherwise have gone. Finally, the appearance of global market mechanisms – tools of environmental economics – challenged political scientists to analyze and contest non-legal solutions to global environmental problems, mechanisms described as "neutral," but in practice decidedly not.

International relations theory in turn provides a helpful set of tools for understanding the dynamics of GEG. Insights over the nature and scope of international interdependence in the absence of an overarching sovereign international authority highlight a particular set of causes of global environmental degradation, and the pervasiveness of collective-action problems in a world of territorially sovereign nation-states where environmental problems refuse to stay within national borders.

Theories of international regimes and institution-building help us understand the conditions that make international cooperation possible, and the ways in which institutional design can help overcome divergent national interests and collective action problems. They provide tools for assessing how well different modes of GEG are working, and what broader impacts they have.

Realist insights about the ways in which power is exercised in international politics, and how climate change may be one pressure moving the international system toward a change in its balance of power. Constructivist insights about the role of norms, ideas, and knowledge, and how they move around the international system, help us understand particular outcomes and the ideational or knowledge-driven components of global governance regimes. Similarly, insights about how actors' interests, identities, and roles in international politics may change over time provide a foundation for understanding the deeper impacts and practices of GEG, beyond the immediate concern of effective problem-solving. Mainstream international relations theory has moved in recent years to encompass these and broader theoretical perspectives.

A full appreciation of global environmental politics, however, necessitates utilizing a broader range of theoretical insights from different fields, including sociology, globalization studies, science and technology studies, even ecology. These fields yield different – even conflicting – questions and findings to those we would expect from more mainstream international relations approaches. They direct the eye to different driving forces, actors, and levels and units of analysis. There is a strong case from both analytical and normative perspectives on GEG for theoretical pluralism. Not only does it enhance our knowledge and understanding of critical forces in global politics, it also increases the range of actions that can be taken to address global environmental degradation.

To illustrate, Chapter 1 highlighted how theories that come out of a focus on economic globalization and the structures of global capitalism generate very different insights as to the political causes of global environmental degradation, what counts as a global environmental problem, and the primary sites and targets of global governance. For example, an institutionalist approach from international relations theory tends to view World Trade Organization (WTO)–environment relations as a problem of linkages, but a global political economy approach adds the perspective that many global environmental problems are in fact a function of neoliberal globalization, of which the WTO is a key component. Similarly, a neo-Gramscian perspective on corporate involvement in GEG highlights the importance of delving further into questions of whose interests are served by a voluntary, non-state approach to environmental regulation, and the power relations that underlie such a system. As a final example, science and technology studies (STS) approaches to the incorporation and sources of knowledge and expertise in GEG has opened up the academic field to an appreciation of the role of local and contingent (or lay) knowledge in achieving effective GEG. Such knowledge holders are already playing an important role in international environmental regimes. At least two international regimes – the Convention on Biological Diversity (CBD) and the UN Convention to Combat Desertification (UNCCD) – formally incorporate indigenous and local knowledge holders in regime decision-making processes, and there are signs that local forms of expertise and understandings (for example, among the Inuit) are being taken increasingly seriously in global efforts to combat climate change.

Sites, Modes, and the Changing Architecture of Global Environmental Governance

Focusing solely on state-led GEG – the negotiation and implementation of multilateral environmental agreements – fails to capture the full picture of GEG existing in the world today. However, simply embracing the plurality of governance initiatives lacks theoretical rigor. In this book I have argued that there are, in fact, several different sites and modes of GEG. From an analytical standpoint, their coexistence tells us that global governance is far more vibrant and multidimensional than might ever have been assumed. It is also a durable and complex phenomenon. If nothing else, this book has demonstrated the sheer number of international environmental institutions, many of which have been in existence for several decades, and which often operate well beyond their state-determined mandates. Global governance is also capable of changing, particularly as new participants enter a field traditionally reserved for government actors and take on new roles, even creating their own governance regimes and initiatives.

I have focused on three sites: state-led governance through the negotiation and implementation of international cooperative agreements; the emergence of the global economic order – particularly trade and finance regime – as a critical site of GEG; and the emergence of non-state GEG initiatives and regimes. Matching that, the leading traditional mode of governance – via creation of international law and cooperative agreements – has been supplemented by information-based governance and market mechanisms. This theoretical framework helps us see both institutional structures and dynamic change in environmental governance at the international level.

More broadly, this discussion speaks to growing debates about the overall architecture of GEG and global governance more generally (Biermann et al. 2009). Several developments have encouraged this focus on a more macro level of global governance. First, regime theory has advanced beyond the study of individual regimes to include regime linkages and networks of various kinds, including, for example, trade–environment linkages, or the way deforestation is now linked to the climate regime (Jinnah 2014; Young 1996). Second, the emergence and recognition of different arenas of GEG has broadened theoretical perceptions of the range of governance types and participants. The fragmentation of climate governance, for example, beyond the UNFCCC to non-state, cross-regional, and local forums has driven theory about fragmentation in global governance more generally, what drives it, and what its implications are (Zelli and van Asselt 2013). Studies of "regime complexes" focus on the links between these fragmented governance institutions (Keohane and Victor 2011).

A focus on macro-level analyses of governance architectures has several advantages. First, it allows us to ask whether existing global governance practices in fact add up to more than the sum of their parts (Orsini et al. 2013). Are they adequate to cope with global interdependence and the complexities of many problems facing the international community? Second, it enables us to ask questions about issues of deeper structural change and adaptation in the international system. Does the involvement of non-state actors as agents, not merely subjects or supporters, of global governance initiatives or the apparent growing autonomy of international organizations signal a shift away from an international system dominated by nation-states?

The various components of the GEG architecture presented in this book have more in common than might at first appear. They share a similar cast of characters – albeit with the actors playing different roles – and a shared normative commitment to global action through established organizations and rules and to sustainable development (albeit with slightly different interpretations in practice). It is hard, however, to argue that they are working together as a system of GEG. Conflicts remain – particularly at the intersection of global environmental and economic regimes.

It is also not certain which direction this set of institutions is taking. Some argue that GEG is moving (and should move) away from the dominant state-led models that have been so important to date (e.g. Speth 2004). As many point out, the international cooperation model is not always appropriate for solving some problems, such as deforestation or fresh water management (Conca 2006). Nor is it necessarily effective, in the problem-solving sense, or even equitable: GEG is still largely the province of global political and economic elites.

Nonetheless, governments and their interests and priorities are not going away. A critical question for the future will be how best to use the strengths of the international system of sovereign states to foster and improve GEG in all its forms, a position supported by scholars of international law (Bodansky 2009). John Vogler (2005) observes that national governments hold significant resources that no other actor on the international stage has. Over and above the legitimate use of coercion to enforce international law (as yet, not a major factor in GEG), these include the legitimacy granted to most governments as the elected representatives of their peoples, a legitimacy that NGOs, corporations, and even intergovernmental organizations (IGOs) cannot yet approach, and the capacity to make rules and implement change at the domestic level.

Governments are also the primary funding agencies for scientific research, particularly for science for its own sake. For these reasons, a rapid shift away from involving governments as central actors in GEG would be a mistake, even if it were possible.

Similarly, the existing network of negotiated international environmental regimes, especially when viewed as a totality, is a flawed but invaluable support system for all efforts to protect the global environment that at least provides a normative and institutional framework for moving forward. When looked at from this perspective, the loss of the organizations, expertise and knowledge, and rules and decision-making procedures embedded in international environmental agreements if this system were to change radically would be a tremendous blow.

It is also a mistake to assume that the state-led system of GEG has remained unchanged in the decades since the 1972 Stockholm meeting. In fact, the international environmental establishment has been receptive to the involvement of non-state actors and the adoption of new tools and methods of regulating the environment. It has been particularly receptive to ideas for utilizing and encouraging positive linkages across existing regimes, and for creating partnerships between states, IGOs, and non-state actors of different types, often informal. The Paris COP marked the first time a negotiating process had, rather than spend the time fighting over top-down national targets, started by accepting countries' own, self-determined targets, although this strategy may remain confined to the climate regime.

From Stockholm to Rio+20, shifts are evident at the macro level. First, a normative shift occurred quite early on, away from environmental protection, toward sustainable development, and now the even more contentious notion of the Green Economy, as the underlying norm of GEG. Second, IGOs, notably the international economic organizations, are far more strongly engaged, as is the corporate sector (see Chapter 4). Third, the number of non-state actors attending major summits has grown exponentially, from a mere 255 accredited NGOs at Stockholm, to 1,420 at Rio in 1992, with another 17,000 representatives at a parallel NGO forum. At Rio+20, 44,000 name badges were issued for official events, a number that does not include participation outside the convention hall (O'Neill 2015, Table 2.1). As we saw in Chapter 4, attendance does not necessarily mean influence, but nonetheless, civil society voices are growing louder and remain contentious (Reitan and Gibson 2012). Civil society's frustration with the state-led process also fed into the evolution of state-led GEG and a devolution of climate governance following the disappointment of the 2009 Copenhagen summit.

At the level of individual regimes, paths have diverged. The climate regime has fragmented far more than others – perhaps not surprising, given the import, complexity, and politics of the issue. At the other end of the spectrum, the ozone and chemicals regimes have remained squarely – and successfully – inside the state-led system of international cooperation. In fact, the chemicals regimes, including the Stockholm Convention (on persistent organic pollutants [POPs]) and the Basel Convention, have formally integrated into a system that will ultimately become a "cradle-to-grave" global chemicals regulatory process. Further, the most recently negotiated international treaty – the 2013 Minamata Mercury Convention – is also part of the chemicals regime.

There are many forces driving these changes, as this book has shown. Different actors have pushed for change across governance arenas, some more influential than others. Normative change, plus the impact of new knowledge and ideas, has been effective. Many institutional responses are shaped by path dependence – where institutional change is steered by historical experience, perhaps problematic when the problems we face are unpredictable and certainly not guided by what has gone before (Bernstein and Cashore 2012). These are good questions for the reader to think through. One thing is certain: the complexity of these interlinked political, social, economic, and ecological systems means that deliberate large-scale reform may not be enough to push GEG onto a determined course.

Wider Changes in Global Environmental Governance

As concern over global environmental degradation remains high, and as efforts to date to govern the global environment remain imperfect, new sites and modes of GEG are likely to emerge. One proposal, on the table for a while but unlikely to be adopted in the near future, is for a World Environment Organization (WEO). The central argument for a WEO is that it could unify the existing, very piecemeal system of global environmental regimes and governance initiatives, in a way that would enhance efficiency and effectiveness, and allow GEG to compete on an equal footing with other powerful international orders, such as the WTO (Biermann 2001). However, both the will and capacity on the part of the UN, key supporters of a WEO, and national governments to create another international bureaucracy is low, and likely to remain so.

Second, as referred to in Box 1.1 (see Chapter 1), the broadening of sites of GEG has been accompanied by a "deepening" of governance across scales, or levels, of governance, where ideas, rules, and institutions move from global down to local, or up, from local to global. This notion of vertical linkages, or multilevel governance, has been understudied, with some important exceptions (as O'Neill et al. 2013 note). The development and functioning of regional centers under the global chemicals treaties are a good example of a multilevel governance initiative (Selin 2010). Cases of the incorporation of local or indigenous knowledge in biodiversity negotiations have highlighted how ideas, knowledge, and expertise may flow not only downwards, from the global level, but also upwards, informing how global policies are created and strengthened (Martello 2001; Jasanoff and Martello 2004). The growing role of cities, local governments, and other sub-state entities in encouraging greenhouse gas (GHG) mitigation and building transnational networks for sustainable development illustrates the emergence of such actors in global political spaces, especially when national governments are absent or weak (Betsill and Bulkeley 2006; Gore and Robinson 2009).

Further, the "new regionalism" in GEG (Balsiger and VanDeveer 2012) and new political initiatives such as REDD+ (Reducing Emissions from Deforestation and [forest] Degradation) have drawn attention to vertical linkages in GEG. These cases may be nested (such as regional centers nested within a broader chemicals regime), or separate institutions focusing on the same problem at different scales (Cities for Climate Protection and the UNFCCC), or indeed a single institution operating simultaneously across multiple scales (REDD+).

Although works that think systematically about these initiatives' implications for GEG remain rare, the concept of transnational climate change governance (TCCG) developed by Bulkeley et al. (2014) gets at the hybridity and multi-scalar possibilities for climate governance. Based on a huge database of climate governance initiatives, it analyzes state, non-state, and below-state initiatives as a collective, and the extent to which they work – or not – to achieve their goals. Discussion of climate adaptation (e.g. Shi et al. 2016) often focus at local levels – such as cities – to ground empirical analysis in the choices facing real communities.

Conca (2015) builds on work that looks at systemic issues of GEG. In a book that raises serious questions about the will and capacity of the UN system as a whole to take on environmental challenges, one of the themes he highlights is the failure to make substantive connections between conflict, environmental change, and peace-building (Homer-Dixon 1994; Peluso and Watts 2001). Climate change may be the driving issue, but others of the issue areas where global governance is weakest or most contested are also the most conflict-ridden: mining, water provision, food sovereignty, and land access. For example, growing concern over the privatization of fresh-water resources worldwide, often putting them in the hands of large multinational corporations, and imposing greater costs (actual and environmental) on already impoverished communities, has generated its own transnational resistance movement (Conca 2006). Rob Nixon, in a path-breaking work, introduces the concept of "slow violence" (Nixon 2011): how climate change, toxic exposure, deforestation, and other global problems wreak forms of violence slowly – in some cases almost imperceptibly – on the world's most vulnerable, and far less obviously than a conflict or war would do. Making this violence visible, and galvanizing action, is a difficult task, but one that scholars have a role in.

New Imperatives for Global Environmental Politics Scholarship

GEG scholars, broadly defined, should pay attention to two particular issues as we move forward. These are both issues that international relations theorists are well positioned to analyze too. The first is to push for attention to effectiveness issues – improving compliance, problem-solving and learning capacities of regimes, and the actors within them. Second, we have a role to play in highlighting dilemmas of justice, equity, and democracy in contemporary global governance choices.

As Steinar Andresen (2013) has pointed out, the field has left studies of regime effectiveness on the sidelines recently, instead focusing on issues of linkage and fragmentation (see Chapter 5). However, studies of how regimes – of any sort – can become more effective remain needed, given the critical nature of their work over the short to long term. The final text of the 2015 Paris Agreement, for example, put off deciding how to talk about transparency and monitoring for several years down the road. The 2013 Minamata Convention tackles contentious and hard-to-monitor problems around the use of mercury in small-scale gold mining. Chapters 5, 7, and 8 of this book discuss frameworks for assessing governance initiatives and regimes, their strengths, and their flaws, and suggest paths for incorporating learning as well as compliance-related mechanisms. GEP scholarship needs to keep informing these debates – in the academic literature and in policy circles.

Second, this book has occasionally touched on the thorny question of how the global community's governance choices themselves are governed. Many of the regimes and policy choices outlined in this book have potential "side effects," perhaps most explicitly discussed in the context of REDD+. Under REDD+ most initiatives are now actively seeking the participation of affected local communities, although what that means in practice is open to question (Burns and Flegal 2015). Other cases clearly fall into this category. Large-scale geoengineering – the use of technologies to remove carbon dioxide from the atmosphere, or to prevent solar radiation reaching the atmosphere to warm it – poses particular dilemmas (Burns and Strauss

2013). Its advocates say that techniques such as injecting huge quantities of sulfur dioxide particles into the atmosphere will slow global warming down enough for countries to take action. Opponents, however, argue that there will be serious side effects, such as shutting down the monsoon, affecting millions of people in South Asia. This is a classic example of a trade-off. To what extent are we willing to accept a certain amount of global warming in order to protect the livelihoods of millions of the planet's poorest peoples? What if that comes at the cost of losing small island states? Science cannot answer these questions. They require careful political deliberation and choices based on individually or collectively held values. While we cannot offer yes or no answers, as scholars who are concerned about the state of the world we need to weigh in, at the very least to illuminate the choices and real dilemmas the global community faces, framed in the context of political theory.

Final Words

It is hard to end a book like this with a few pithy words designed to send the reader off to explore these fascinating and complex issues of global environmental politics on her or his own. At a round-table discussion at the Annual Meeting of the International Studies Association a number of years back, on the Future of Environmentalism, one of the topics of discussion was how to engender a sense of optimism in our courses, particularly in the last lecture of the term or semester. There was no real consensus among the panelists – all professors – as to how to do this. After fifteen weeks or so of doom and gloom, efforts to strike a positive note tend to fall a bit flat. Global environmental challenges remain serious and complex, and sometimes we all feel that political efforts to address these at the global level are too small, too slow, and too late.

Still, there are positive messages to convey. First, the emergence of the environment as an area of study in international relations theory has challenged many of the traditional assumptions of the discipline, bringing in new actors, new types of decision-making processes, rules and norms, and offering potential for transforming the ways that global governance is done. Second, this book has provided an analytical framework for understanding why GEG has evolved in the way that it has, and the diverse forms it has taken on; understanding the lessons of the past can only help guide us in the future. Third, societies can turn around quickly on important issues. In the early 2000s, for example, gay marriage seemed an impossible goal in the USA; now it is legal across all fifty states – and in many other countries, accompanied by a major shift in public opinion. Finally, in this book I hope to have broken down "politics" for the reader, discussing instead a dynamic – if vast – collection of institutions and organizations, some of which are open to public intervention. I try to tell – as a political scientist – a story of political transformation in the international system that will stand us in good stead, even as we face challenges that we failed to forestall. I write this second edition of *The Environment and International Relations* with greater concern about the extent and pace of environmental challenges facing the world, but also with more optimism about how our governance institutions can change and become stronger. Nonetheless, the road is long and fraught with obstacles, although I hope this book has demonstrated some of the ways they can be circumvented or overcome.

Discussion Question

• What do you think are the most important forces and actors driving changes in GEG in the twenty-first century? What do you believe these changes might – or ought to – look like in practice?

SUGGESTIONS FOR FURTHER READING

Bulkeley, Harriet, Liliana B. Andonova, Michele M. Betsill, Daniel Compagnon, Thomas Hale, Matthew J. Hoffmann, Peter Newell, Matthew Paterson, Charles Rogers, and Stacy VanDeveer. 2014. *Transnational Climate Change Governance.* Cambridge: Cambridge University Press: a book that represents a major global survey of climate governance regimes and initiatives, developing an innovative theoretical framework for understanding how hybrid, multi-scalar global governance works in modern times.

Conca, Ken. 2015. *An Unfinished Foundation: The United Nations and Global Environmental Governance.* Oxford: Oxford University Press: a vital read for people in other fields to gain insight into the big questions around global environment and development politics, and the structure, successes, and failures of the world's largest and most important governance organization.

Nixon, Rob. 2011. *Slow Violence: The Environmentalism of the Poor.* Cambridge, MA: Harvard University Press: from a global political ecology perspective, how climate change, toxic exposure, deforestation, and other global problems harm the world's most vulnerable communities, and far less obviously and far more slowly than a conflict or war would do. Making this violence visible, and galvanizing action, is a difficult task, but one in which scholars play a role.

References

Agarwal, Anil, and Sunita Narain. 1991. *Global Warming in an Unequal World: A Case of Environmental Colonialism.* New Delhi: Centre for Science and Environment.

Agarwal, Anil, Sunita Narain, and Anju Sharma, eds. 1999. *Green Politics.* New Delhi: Center for Science and Environment.

Andonova, Liliana B., Michele M. Betsill, and Harriet Bulkeley. 2009. "Transnational Climate Governance." *Global Environmental Politics* 9.2: 52–73.

Andonova, Liliana B., and Marc A. Levy. 2004. "Franchising Global Governance: Making Sense of the Johannesburg Type II Partnerships." *Yearbook of International Cooperation on Environment and Development 2003/04.* Eds. Stokke, Olav Schram and Øystein B. Thommessen. London: Earthscan.

Andresen, Steinar. 2013. "International Regime Effectiveness." *The Handbook of Global Climate and Environmental Policy.* Ed. Falkner, Robert. London: John Wiley & Sons Ltd.

Arup, Christopher, and Hao Zhang. 2015. "Lessons from Regulating Carbon Offset Markets." *Transnational Environmental Law* 4.1: 69–100.

Auld, Graeme. 2014. *Constructing Private Governance: The Rise and Evolution of Forest, Coffee, and Fisheries Certification.* New Haven: Yale University Press.

Axelrod, Mark. 2011. "Savings Clauses and the 'Chilling Effect': Regime Interplay as Constraints on International Governance." *Managing Institutional Complexity: Regime Interplay and Global Environmental Change.* Eds. Oberthür, Sebastian and Olav Schram Stokke. Cambridge, MA: MIT Press.

Ayling, Julie, and Neil Gunningham. 2015. "Non-State Governance and Climate Policy: The Fossil Fuel Divestment Movement." *Climate Policy*: DOI:10.1080/14693062.2015.1094729.

Bäckstrand, Karin, and Ole Elgström. 2013. "The EU's Role in Climate Change Negotiations: From Leader to 'Leadiator'." *Journal of European Public Policy* 20.10: 1369–86.

Bäckstrand, Karin, and Mikael Kylsäter. 2014. "Old Wine in New Bottles? The Legitimation and Delegitimation of UN Public–Private Partnerships for Sustainable Development from the Johannesburg Summit to the Rio+20 Summit." *Globalizations* 11.3: 331–47.

Baird, Julia. 2014. "A Carbon Tax's Ignoble End: Why Tony Abbott Axed Australia's Carbon Tax." *New York Times*, July 24.

Baldwin, David A., ed. 1993. *Neorealism and Neoliberalism: The Contemporary Debate*. New York: Columbia University Press.

Balsiger, Jörg, and Stacy VanDeveer. 2012. "Navigating Regional Environmental Governance." *Global Environmental Politics* 12.3: 1–17.

Barnett, Michael. 2014. "Social Constructivism." *The Globalization of World Politics: An Introduction to International Relations*, 6th edition. Eds. Baylis, John, Steve Smith, and Patricia Owens. Oxford: Oxford University Press.

Barnett, Michael N., and Martha Finnemore. 1999. "The Politics, Power, and Pathologies of International Organizations." *International Organization* 53.4: 699–732.

2004. *Rules for the World: International Organizations in World Politics*. Ithaca: Cornell University Press.

Barrett, Scott. 2008. "Climate Treaties and the Imperative of Enforcement." *Oxford Review of Economic Policy* 24.2: 239–58.

Barry, John, and Robyn Eckersley, eds. 2005. *The State and the Global Ecological Crisis*. Cambridge, MA: MIT Press.

Bartley, Tim. 2003. "Certifying Forests and Factories: States, Social Movements, and the Rise of Private Regulation in the Apparel and Forest Products Fields." *Politics and Society* 31.3: 433–64.

Bauer, Steffen. 2009. "The Desertification Secretariat: A Castle Made of Sand." *Managers of Global Change: The Influence of International Environmental Bureaucracies*. Eds. Biermann, Frank and Bernd Siebenhüner. Cambridge, MA: MIT Press.

Baur, Dorothea, and Hans Peter Schmitz. 2012. "Corporations and NGOs: When Accountability Leads to Co-Optation." *Journal of Business Ethics* 106: 9–21.

Baylis, John, Steve Smith, and Patricia Owens, eds. 2014. *The Globalization of World Politics: An Introduction to International Relations*, 6th edition. Oxford: Oxford University Press.

Beck, Ulrich. 1992. *Risk Society: Towards a New Modernity*. London: Sage.

Bell, Ruth Greenspan, and Dianne Callan. 2011. "More Than Meets the Eye: The Social Cost of Carbon in US Climate Policy in Plain English." World Resources Institute Policy Brief. Available at www.researchgate.net/publica tion/266853598_More_than_Meets_the_Eye_The_Social_Cost_of_Carbon_ in_US_Climate_Policy_in_Plain_English.

Benedick, Richard. 1987. *Ozone Diplomacy*. Cambridge, MA: Harvard University Press.

2007. "Science, Diplomacy and the Montreal Protocol." *Encyclopedia of Earth*. Ed. Cleveland, Cutler J. Washington DC: Environmental Information Coalition, National Council for Science and the Environment.

Bernauer, Thomas. 1995. "The Effect of International Environmental Institutions: How we Might Learn More." *International Organization* 49.2: 351–77.

1997. "Managing International Rivers." *Global Governance: Drawing Insights from the Environmental Experience*. Ed. Young, Oran R. Cambridge, MA: MIT Press.

Bernstein, Steven. 2000. "Ideas, Social Structure and the Compromise of Liberal Environmentalism." *European Journal of International Relations* 6.4: 464–512.

2002. *The Compromise of Liberal Environmentalism.* New York: Columbia University Press.

2013a. "Global Environmental Norms." *The Handbook of Global Climate and Environment Policy.* Ed. Falkner, Robert. London: Wiley.

2013b. "Rio+20: Sustainable Development in a Time of Multilateral Decline." *Global Environmental Politics* 13.4: 12–21.

Bernstein, Steven, and Benjamin Cashore. 2007. "Can Non-State Global Governance Be Legitimate? An Analytical Framework." *Regulation and Governance* 1.4: 347–71.

2012. "Complex Global Governance and Domestic Politics: Four Pathways of Influence." *International Affairs* 88.3: 585–604.

Betsill, Michele M., and Harriet Bulkeley. 2006. "Cities and the Multilevel Governance of Global Climate Change." *Global Governance* 12.2: 141–59.

Betsill, Michele M., and Elisabeth Corell. 2001. "NGO Influence in International Environmental Negotiations: A Framework for Analysis." *Global Environmental Politics* 1.4: 65–85.

eds. 2008. *NGO Diplomacy: The Influence of Nongovernmental Organizations in International Environmental Negotiations.* Cambridge, MA: MIT Press.

Betsill, Michele M., and Matthew J. Hoffmann. 2011. "The Contours of 'Cap and Trade': The Evolution of Emissions Trading Systems for Greenhouse Gases." *Review of Policy Research* 28.1: 83–106.

Bhagwati, Jagdish. 1993. "Trade and the Environment: A False Conflict?" *Trade and the Environment: Law, Economics and Policy.* Eds. Zaelke, D., P. Orbuch, and R. F. Housman. Washington DC: Island Press.

Biermann, Frank. 2001. "The Emerging Debate on the Need for a World Environment Organization: A Commentary." *Global Environmental Politics* 1.1: 45–55.

2002. "Institutions for Scientific Advice: Global Environmental Assessments and Their Influence in Developing Countries." *Global Governance* 8: 195–219.

2014. *Earth System Governance: World Politics in the Anthropocene.* Cambridge, MA: MIT Press.

Biermann, Frank, and Ingrid Boas. 2008. "Protecting Climate Refugees: The Case for a Global Protocol." *Environment. November–December*: 8–16.

Biermann, Frank, Philipp Pattberg, Harro van Asselt, and Fariborz Zelli. 2009. "The Fragmentation of Global Governance Architectures: A Framework for Analysis." *Global Environmental Politics* 9.4: 14–40.

Biermann, Frank, and Bernd Siebenhüner, eds. 2009. *Managers of Global Change: The Influence of International Environmental Bureaucracies.* Cambridge, MA: MIT Press.

Birdsall, Nancy. 2012. *The World Bank and Climate Change: Forever a Big Fish in a Small Pond?* CGD Policy Paper 007. Washington DC: Center for Global Development.

Birnie, Patricia. 1992. "International Environmental Law: Its Adequacy for Present and Future Needs." *The International Politics of the Environment: Actors, Interests, Institutions.* Eds. Hurrell, Andrew and Benedict Kingsbury. Oxford: Clarendon Press.

Birnie, Patricia, Alan E. Boyle, and Catherine Redgwell. 2009. *International Law and the Environment,* 3rd edition. Oxford: Oxford University Press.

Blackhurst, Richard. "The Capacity of the WTO to Fulfill its Mandate." 1998. *The WTO as an International Organization.* Ed. Krueger, Anne O. Chicago: University of Chicago Press.

Blackman, Allen, and Jorge Rivera. 2010. "The Evidence Base for Environmental and Socioeconomic Impacts of 'Sustainable Certification'." Resources for the Future Discussion Paper 20.17. Available at www.rff.org/research/publications/evidence-base-environmental-and-socioeconomic-impacts-sustainable-0.

Bodansky, Daniel. 2009. *The Art and Craft of International Environmental Law.* Cambridge, MA: Harvard University Press.

2010. "The Copenhagen Climate Change Accord." *ASIL Insight* 14.3. Available at www.asil.org/insights/volume/14/issue/3/copenhagen-climate-change-accord.

2013. "International Environmental Law." *The Handbook of Global Climate and Environment Policy.* Ed. Falkner, Robert. London: John Wiley & Sons.

Bowen, Alex. 2011. *The Case for Carbon Pricing.* London: Grantham Research Institute on Climate Change and the Environment.

Bowman, Michael. 2013. "A Tale of Two CITES: Divergent Perspectives upon the Effectiveness of the Wildlife Trade Convention." *RECIEL* 22.3: 228–38.

Boykoff, Maxwell T., and Jules M. Boykoff. 2004. "Balance as Bias: Global Warming and the US Prestige Press." *Global Environmental Change* 14: 125–36.

Brand, Stewart. 2003. "The Earth from Space." *Rolling Stone,* May 15.

Branger, Frédéric, Oskar Lecuyer, and Philippe Quirion. 2015. "The European Union Emissions Trading Scheme: Should we Throw the Flagship out with the Bathwater?" *WIRES Climate Change* 6: 9–16.

Bretherton, Charlotte, and John Vogler. 2006. *The European Union as a Global Actor,* 2nd edition. London: Routledge.

Brieger, Tracey, Trevor Fleck, and Douglas MacDonald. 2001. "Political Action by the Canadian Insurance Industry on Climate Change." *Environmental Politics* 10.3: 111–26.

Brockmann, Karl L., Jens Hemmelskamp, and Olav Hohmeyer. 1996. *Certified Tropical Timber and Consumer Behavior: The Impact of a Certification Scheme for Tropical Timber from Sustainable Forest Management on German Demand.* Heidelberg: Physica-Verlag.

Broder, John. 2010. "A Novel Tactic in Climate Fight Gains Some Traction." *New York Times,* November 6.

Broussard, Peter. 2015. "Dammed, Displaced and Forgotten." *Huffington Post,* March 27.

Brulle, Robert J. 2014. "Institutionalizing Delay: Foundation Funding and the Creation of US Climate Change Counter-Movement Organizations." *Climatic Change* 122: 681–94.

Buckingham, Kathleen, and Paul Jepson. 2015. "The Legitimacy of Bamboo Certification: Unpacking the Controversy and the Implications for a 'Tree-Like' Grass." *Society & Natural Resources* 28.6: 575–92.

Bulkeley, Harriet, Liliana B. Andonova, Michele M. Betsill, Daniel Compagnon, Thomas Hale, Matthew J. Hoffmann, Peter Newell, Matthew Paterson, Charles Rogers, and Stacy VanDeveer. 2014. *Transnational Climate Change Governance*. Cambridge: Cambridge University Press.

Bull, Hedley. 1977. *The Anarchical Society: A Study of Order in World Politics*. London: Macmillan.

Bullock, Graham. 2015. "Independent Labels? The Power behind Environmental Information about Products and Companies." *Political Research Quarterly* 68.1: 46–62.

Bumpus, Adam, and Diana M. Liverman. 2011. "Carbon Colonialism? Offsets, Greenhouse Gas Reductions, and Sustainable Development." *Global Political Ecology*. Eds. Peet, Richard, Paul Robbins, and Michael J. Watts. London: Routledge.

Burchill, Scott, and Andrew Linklater, eds. 2013. *Theories of International Relations*, 5th edition. London: Palgrave Macmillan.

Burns, William C. G., and Jane Flegal. 2015. "Climate Geoengineering and the Role of Public Deliberation: A Comment on the US National Academy of Sciences' Recommendations on Public Participation." *Climate Law* 5: 252–94.

Burns, William C., and Andrew L. Strauss, eds. 2013. *Climate Change Geoengineering: Philosophical Perspectives, Legal Issues, and Governance Frameworks*. Cambridge: Cambridge University Press.

Busby, Joshua. 2016. "After Paris: Good Enough Climate Governance." *Current History*, January.

Busby, Josh, and Alexander Ochs. 2005. "From Mars and Venus Down to Earth: Understanding the Transatlantic Climate Divide." *Climate Policy for the 21st Century: Meeting the Long-Term Challenge of Global Warming*. Ed. Michel, David. Washington: Brookings Institution.

Carbon Disclosure Project. 2015. *CDP Global Climate Change Report 2015: At the Tipping Point?* London: Carbon Disclosure Project.

Carbonell, Joel, and Juliann E. Allison. 2015. "Democracy and State Environmental Commitment to International Environmental Treaties." *International Environmental Agreements* 15: 79–104.

Carbon Market Watch. 2014. "What's Needed to Fix the EU's Carbon Market: Recommendations for the Market Stability Reserve and Future ETS Reform Proposals." Carbon Market Watch policy briefing, July. Available at http://carbonmarketwatch.org/whats-needed-to-fix-the-eus-carbon-market-recommendations-for-the-market-stability-reserve-and-future-ets-reform-proposals/.

Carpentier, Chantal Line, Kevin P. Gallagher, and Scott Vaughan. 2005. "Environmental Goods and Services in the World Trade Organization." *Journal of Environment and Development* 14.2: 225–51.

Carroll, Archie B. 1999. "Corporate Social Responsibility: Evolution of a Definitional Concept." *Business and Society* 38.3: 268–95.

Cashore, Benjamin. 2002. "Legitimacy and the Privatization of Environmental Governance: How Non-State Market Driven (NSMD) Governance Systems Gain Rule-Making Authority." *Governance: An International Journal of Policy and Administration* 15.4: 503–29.

Cashore, Benjamin, Graeme Auld, Steven Bernstein, and Constance McDermott. 2007. "Can Non-State Governance 'Ratchet up' Global Environmental Standards? Lessons from the Forest Sector." *RECIEL* 16.2: 158–72.

Cashore, Benjamin, Graeme Auld, and Deanna Newsom. 2004. *Governing through Markets: Forest Certification and the Emergence of Non-State Authority.* New Haven: Yale University Press.

Cashore, Benjamin, and Michael W. Stone. 2012. "Can Legality Verification Rescue Global Forest Management? Analyzing the Potential of Public and Private Policy Intersection to Ameliorate Forest Challenges in Southeast Asia." *Forest Policy and Economics* 18: 13–22.

CDC Climat Research and IETA. 2015. "China: An Emissions Trading Case Study." Available at www.ieta.org/resources/Resources/Case_Studies_Worl ds_Carbon_Markets/china-emissions-trading-case%20study_cdc_clima t_ieta%20march_2015.pdf.

Center for Naval Analyses, Military Advisory Board. 2007. *National Security and the Threat of Climate Change.* Washington DC: CNA Corporation.

Cha, Ariana Eunjung. 2008. "China's Environmental Retreat: In Tough Economic Times, Promises Fall by Wayside." *Washington Post,* November 19.

Chasek, Pamela S. 2001. *Earth Negotiations: Analyzing Thirty Years of Environmental Diplomacy.* Tokyo: United Nations University Press.

Chasek, Pamela S., David L. Downie, and Janet Welsh Brown. 2014. *Global Environmental Politics,* 6th edition. Boulder, CO: Westview Press.

Chasek, Pamela S., and Lynn M. Wagner, eds. *The Roads from Rio: Lessons Learned from Twenty Years of Multilateral Environmental Negotiations.* New York: Routledge, 2012.

Chayes, Abram, and Antonia H. Chayes. 1993. "On Compliance." *International Organization* 47.2: 175–205.

Ciplet, David. 2014. "Contesting Climate Injustice: Transnational Advocacy Network Struggles for Rights in UN Climate Politics." *Global Environmental Politics* 14.4: 75–96.

Clapp, Jennifer. 1997. "The Illegal CFC Trade: An Unexpected Wrinkle in the Ozone Protection Regime." *International Environmental Affairs* 9.4: 259–73.

1999. "The Global Recycling Industry and Hazardous Waste Trade Facilities." Paper presented at the 1999 Annual Meeting of the International Studies Association, Washington DC.

Clapp, Jennifer, and Peter Dauvergne. 2011. *Paths to a Green World: The Political Economy of the Global Environment,* 2nd edition. Cambridge, MA: MIT Press.

Clapp, Jennifer, and Jonas Meckling. 2013. "Business as a Global Actor." *The Handbook of Global Climate and Environment Policy.* Ed. Falkner, Robert. London: John Wiley & Sons.

Clapp, Jennifer, and Linda Swanston. 2009. "Doing Away with Plastic Shopping Bags: International Patterns of Norm Emergence and Policy Implementation." *Environmental Politics* 18.3: 315–32.

Coase, Ronald H. 1960. "The Problem of Social Cost." *Journal of Law and Economics* 3: 1–44.

Collins, David. 2014. "The Chaos Machine: The WTO in a Social Entropy Model of the World Trading System." *Oxford Journal of Legal Studies* 34.2: 353–74.

Compagnon, Daniel, Sander Chan, and Aysem Mert. 2012. "The Changing Role of the State." *Global Environmental Governance Reconsidered.* Eds. Biermann, Frank and Philipp Pattberg. Cambridge, MA: MIT Press.

Conca, Ken. 2000. "The WTO and the Undermining of Global Environmental Governance." *Review of International Political Economy* 7.3: 484–94.

——— 2002. "Consumption and Environment in a Global Economy." *Confronting Consumption.* Eds. Princen, Thomas, Michael F. Maniates, and Ken Conca. Cambridge, MA: MIT Press.

——— 2005. "Environmental Governance after Johannesburg: From Stalled Legalization to Environmental Human Rights?" *Journal of International Law & International Relations* 1.1–2: 121–38.

——— 2006. *Governing Water: Contentious Transnational Politics and Global Institution Building.* Cambridge, MA: MIT Press.

——— 2015. *An Unfinished Foundation: The United Nations and Global Environmental Governance.* Oxford: Oxford University Press.

Corneloup, Inés de Aguéda, and Arthur P. J. Mol. 2014. "Small Island Developing States and International Climate Change Negotiations: The Power of Moral 'Leadership'." *International Environmental Agreements* 14: 281–97.

Costanza, Robert, Ralph d'Arge, Rudolf de Groot, Stephen Farber, Monica Grasso, Bruce Hannon, Karin Limburg, Shahid Naeem, Robert V. O'Neill, Jose Paruelo, Robert G. Raskin, Paul Sutton, and Marjan van den Belt. 1997. "The Value of the World's Ecosystem Services and Natural Capital." *Nature* 387: 253–60.

Costanza, Robert, Rudolf de Groot, Paul Sutton, Sander van der Ploeg, Sharolyn J. Anderson, Ida Kubiszewski, Stephen Farber, and R. Kerry Turner. 2014. "Change in the Global Value of Ecosystem Services." *Global Environmental Change* 26: 152–58.

Cox, Robert W. 1986. "Social Forces, States and World Orders: Beyond International Relations Theory." *Neorealism and its Critics.* Ed. Keohane, R. New York: Columbia University Press.

——— 1987. *Production, Power and World Order: Social Forces in the Making of History.* New York: Columbia University Press.

Crane, Barbara B. 1993. "International Population Institutions: Adaptation to a Changing World Order." *Institutions for the Earth: Sources of Effective International Environmental Protection.* Eds. Haas, Peter, Robert O. Keohane, and Marc A. Levy. Cambridge, MA: MIT Press.

Cronin, Bruce. 2002. "Creating Stability in the New Europe: The OSCE High Commissioner on National Minorities and the Socialization of Risky States." *Security Studies* 12.1: 132–63.

Cullis-Suzuki, Sairka, and Daniel Pauly. 2012. "Failing the High Seas: A Global Evaluation of Regional Fisheries Management Organizations." *Marine Policy* 34: 1036–42.

Cutler, A. Claire. 2002. "Private International Regimes and Interfirm Cooperation." *The Emergence of Private Authority in Global Governance*. Eds. Hall, Rodney Bruce and Thomas J. Biersteker. Cambridge: Cambridge University Press.

Cutler, A. Claire, Virginia Haufler, and Tony Porter, eds. 1999. *Private Authority and International Affairs*. Albany: SUNY Press.

Daly, Herman E. 1977. *Steady State Economics*. Toronto: University of Toronto Press.

Daunton, Martin, Amrita Narlikar, and Robert M. Stern, eds. 2012. *The Oxford Handbook on the World Trade Organization*. Oxford: Oxford University Press.

Dauvergne, Peter. 2001. *Loggers and Degradation in the Asia-Pacific: Corporations and Environmental Management*. Cambridge: Cambridge University Press.

2008. *The Shadows of Consumption: Consequences for the Global Environment*. Cambridge, MA: MIT Press.

Dauvergne, Peter, and Jennifer Clapp. 2016. "Researching Global Environmental Politics in the 21st Century." *Global Environmental Politics* 16.1: 1–13.

Dauvergne, Peter, and Jane Lister. 2011. *Timber*. London: Polity Press.

2012. "Big Brand Sustainability: Governance Prospects and Environmental Limits." *Global Environmental Change* 22: 36–45.

Death, Carl. 2011. "Summit Theatre: Exemplary Governmentality and Environmental Diplomacy in Johannesburg and Copenhagen." *Environmental Politics* 20.1: 1–19.

Delmas, Magali. 2002. "The Diffusion of Environmental Management Standards in Europe and the United States: An Institutional Perspective." *Policy Sciences* 35: 91–119.

Depledge, Joanna. 2006. "The Opposite of Learning: Ossification in the Climate Change Regime." *Global Environmental Politics* 6.1: 1–22.

2007. "A Special Relationship: Chairpersons and the Secretariat in the Climate Change Negotiations." *Global Environmental Politics* 7.1: 45–68.

Depledge, Joanna, and Pamela S. Chasek. 2012. "Raising the Tempo: The Escalating Pace and Intensity of Environmental Negotiations." *The Roads from Rio: Lessons Learned from Twenty Years of Multilateral Environmental Negotiations*. Eds. Chasek, Pamela S. and Lynn M. Wagner. New York: Routledge.

DeSombre, Elizabeth R. 2000. *Domestic Sources of International Environmental Policy: Industry, Environmentalists, and US Power*. Cambridge, MA: MIT Press.

2015. "Domestic Sources of US Unilateralism." *The Global Environment: Institutions, Law, and Policy*, 4th edition. Eds. Axelrod, Regina S. and Stacy D. VanDeveer. Los Angeles and Washington DC: Sage/CQ Press.

DeSombre, Elizabeth R., and Samuel J. Barkin. 2002. "Turtles and Trade: The WTO's Acceptance of Environmental Trade Restrictions." *Global Environmental Politics* 2.1: 12–18.

Detomasi, David. 2002. "International Institutions and the Case for Corporate Governance: Towards a Distributive Governance Framework?" *Global Governance* 8: 421–42.

Deutsch, Claudia. 2006. "Companies and Critics Try Collaboration." *New York Times*, May 17.

Dicken, Peter. 1998. *Global Shift: Transforming the World Economy*, 3rd edition. New York: Guilford Press.

Doherty, Emma, and Heike Schroeder. 2011. "Forest Tenure and Multi-Level Governance in Avoiding Deforestation under REDD+." *Global Environmental Politics* 11.4: 66–88.

Doney, Scott C., Victoria J. Fabry, Richard A. Feely, and Joan A. Kleypas. 2009. "Ocean Acidification: The Other CO2 Problem." *Annual Review of Marine Science* 1: 169–92.

Downie, Christian. 2014. "Transnational Actors in Environmental Politics: Strategies and Influence in Long Negotiations." *Environmental Politics* 23.3: 376–94.

Downs, George W., David M. Rocke, and Peter N. Barsoom. 1996. "Is the Good News about Compliance Good News about Cooperation?" *International Organization* 50.3: 379–406.

Doyle, Timothy. 2005. *Environmental Movements in Majority and Minority Worlds: A Global Perspective*. New Brunswick: Rutgers University Press.

Drezner, Daniel W. 2011. "Sanctions Sometimes Smart: Targeted Sanctions in Theory and Practice." *International Studies Review* 13.1: 96–108.

Dryzek, John. 2014. "Global Deliberative Democracy." *Essential Concepts of Global Environmental Governance*. Eds. Morin, Jean-Frédéric and Amandine Orsini. London: Earthscan.

Duffy, Rosaleen. 2014. "Waging a War to Save Biodiversity: The Rise of Militarized Conservation." *International Affairs* 99.4: 819–34.

Duggan, Jill. 2015. "Ten Years of Carbon Pricing in Europe: A Business Perspective." Cambridge Institute for Sustainability Leadership. Available at www.cisl.cam.ac.uk/publications/publication-pdfs/10-years-carbon-pricing-europe.pdf.

Dunlap, Riley E., and Richard York. 2012. "The Globalization of Environmental Concern." *Comparative Environmental Politics: Theory, Politics and Practice*. Eds. Steinberg, Paul F. and Stacy VanDeveer. Cambridge, MA: MIT Press.

Eckersley, Robyn. 2004. "The Big Chill: The WTO and Multilateral Environmental Agreements." *Global Environmental Politics* 4.2: 24–50.

——. 2005. "Greening the Nation-State: From Exclusive to Inclusive Sovereignty." *The State and the Global Ecological Crisis*. Eds. Eckersley, Robyn and John Barry. Cambridge, MA: MIT Press.

Economy, Elizabeth C. 2004. *The River Runs Black: The Environmental Challenge to China's Future*. Ithaca: Cornell University Press.

Edwards, Paul N. 2001. "Representing the Global Atmosphere: Computer Models, Data, and Knowledge about Climate Change." *Changing the Atmosphere: Expert Knowledge and Environmental Governance*. Eds. Miller, Clark A. and Paul N. Edwards. Cambridge, MA: MIT Press.

Ehrenberg, John. 1999. *Civil Society: The Critical History of an Idea*. New York: New York University Press.

Elder, Sara D., Hisham Zerreffi, and Philippe Le Billon. 2013. "Is Fairtrade Certification Greening Agricultural Practices? An Analysis of Fairtrade Environmental Standards in Rwanda." *Journal of Rural Studies* 32: 264–74.

Elliott, Lorraine. 2007. "Transnational Environmental Crime in the Asia-Pacific: An 'Un(der)Securitized Problem?" *Pacific Review* 20.4: 499–522.

2014. "Governing the International Political Economy of Transnational Environmental Crime." *Handbook of the International Political Economy of Governance*. Eds. Payne, Anthony and Nicola Phillips. Cheltenham: Edward Elgar.

Elsig, Manfried, Karolina Milewicz, and Nikolas Stürchler. 2011. "Who is in Love with Multilateralism? Treaty Commitment in the Post-Cold War Era." *European Union Politics* 12.4: 529–50.

Engels, Anita, Otto Hüther, Mike Schäfer, and Hermann Held. 2013. "Public Climate-Change Skepticism, Energy Preferences and Political Participation." *Global Environmental Change* 23: 1018–27.

Entine, Jon. 2003. "The Myth of Social Investing: A Critique of its Practice and Consequences for Corporate Social Performance Research." *Organization and Environment* 16.3: 352–68.

Epstein, Charlotte. 2006. "The Making of Global Environmental Norms: Endangered Species Protection." *Global Environmental Politics* 6.2: 32–54.

Erickson, Peter, Michael Lazarus, and Randall Spalding-Fecher. 2014. "Net Climate Change Mitigation of the Clean Development Mechanism." *Energy Policy* 72: 146–54.

Espach, Ralph. 2006. "When is Sustainable Forestry Sustainable? The Forest Stewardship Council in Brazil and Argentina." *Global Environmental Politics* 6.2: 55–84.

Esty, Daniel C. 2000. "Environment and the Trading System: Picking up the Post-Seattle Pieces." *The WTO after Seattle*. Ed. Schott, Jeffrey J. Washington DC: Institute for International Economics.

Fairhead, James, Melissa Leach, and Ian Scoones. 2012. "Green Grabbing: A New Appropriation of Nature?" *Journal of Peasant Studies* 39.2: 237–61.

Falkner, Robert. 2003. "Private Environmental Governance and International Relations." *Global Environmental Politics* 3.2: 72–87.

2012. "Global Environmentalism and the Greening of International Society." *International Affairs* 88.3: 503–22.

ed. 2013. *The Handbook of Global Climate Change and Environment Policy*. London: John Wiley & Sons.

Farrell, Alexander E., and Jill Jäger, eds. 2006. *Assessments of Regional and Global Environmental Risks: Designing Processes for the Effective Use of Science in Decisionmaking*. Cambridge, MA: MIT Press.

Faure, Michael, and Jürgen Lefevere. 2015. "Compliance with Global Environmental Policy: Climate Change and Ozone Layer Cases." *The Global Environment: Institutions, Law, and Policy*, 4th edition. Eds. Axelrod, Regina S. and Stacy VanDeveer. Los Angeles and Washington DC: Sage/CQ Press.

Finnemore, Martha. 1996. *National Interests in International Society*. Ithaca: Cornell University Press.

Finnemore, Martha, and Kathryn Sikkink. 1998. "International Norm Dynamics and Political Change." *International Organization* 52.4: 887–917.

Fisher, Dana R. 2010. "Cop-15 in Copenhagen: How the Merging of Movements Left Civil Society out in the Cold." *Global Environmental Politics* 10.2: 11–17.

Fisher, Dana R., and Jessica F. Green. 2004. "Understanding Disenfranchisement: Civil Society and Developing Countries' Influence and Participation in Global Governance for Sustainable Development." *Global Environmental Politics* 4.3: 65–84.

Flannery, Tim. 2006. *The Weather Makers: How Man is Changing the Climate and What it Means for Life on Earth*. New York: Atlantic Monthly Press.

Fonner, Robert and Gil Sylvia. 2015. "Willingness to Pay for Multiple Seafood Labels in a Niche Market." *Marine Resource Economics* 30.1 (January): 51–70.

Forsyth, Tim. 1998. "Technology Transfer and the Climate Change Debate." *Environment* 40.9: 16–20, 39–43.

   2003. *Critical Political Ecology: The Politics of Environmental Science*. London: Routledge.

Fox, Jonathan A., and L. David Brown, eds. 1998. *The Struggle for Accountability: The World Bank, NGOs and Grassroots Movements*. Cambridge, MA: MIT Press.

Freris, Nicole, and Klemens Laschefski. 2001. "Seeing the Wood from the Trees." *The Ecologist* 31.6. Available at www.wald.org/fscamaz/ecol_eng .htm.

Friedman, Elizabeth J., Kathryn Hochstetler, and Ann Marie Clark. 2005. *Sovereignty, Democracy, and Global Civil Society*. Albany: SUNY Press.

Friends of the Earth. 1999. *The IMF: Selling the Environment Short*. Washington DC: Friends of the Earth.

Friends of the Earth Australia. 2002. "Voluntary Partnerships Not Enough." Available at www.foe.org.au/media-releases/2002-media-release/voluntary-partnerships-not-enough.

Gale, Fred. 2002. "Caveat Certificatum: The Case of Forest Certification." *Confronting Consumption*. Eds. Princen, Thomas, Michael F. Maniates, and Ken Conca. Cambridge, MA: MIT Press.

Gallagher, Deborah Ringling and Erika Weinthal. 2012. "Business–State Relations and the Environment: The Evolving Role of Corporate Social Responsibility." *Comparative Environmental Politics: Theory, Practice and Prospects*. Eds. Steinberg, Paul F. and Stacy VanDeveer. Cambridge, MA: MIT Press.

Gans, Will, and Beat Hintermann. 2013. "Market Effects of Voluntary Climate Action by Firms: Evidence from the Chicago Climate Exchange." *Environmental Resource Economics* 55: 291–308.

Garcia-Johnson, Ronie. 2000. *Exporting Environmentalism: US Multinational Chemical Corporations in Brazil and Mexico*. Cambridge, MA: MIT Press.

Gardner, Richard N. 1992. *Negotiating Survival: Four Priorities after Rio*. New York: Council on Foreign Relations Press.

Geden, Oliver. 2015. "Paris Climate Deal: The Trouble with Targetism." *The Guardian*, December 14.

Gehring, Thomas, and Eva Ruffing. 2008. "When Arguments Prevail over Power: The CITES Procedure for the Listing of Endangered Species." *Global Environmental Politics* 8.2: 123–48.

Gemenne, François, Jon Barnett, W. Neil Adger, and Geoffrey D. Dabelko. 2014. "Climate and Security: Evidence, Emerging Risks, and a New Agenda." *Climatic Change* 123: 1–9.

Gereffi, Gary, John Humphrey, and Timothy Sturgeon. 2005. "The Governance of Global Value Chains." *Review of International Political Economy* 12.1: 78–104.

Gillis, Justin. 2014. "A Price Tag on Carbon as a Climate Rescue Plan." *New York Times*, May 30.

Gilpin, Robert. 1975. *US Power and the Multinational Corporation: The Political Economy of Foreign Direct Investment*. New York: Basic Books.

2001. *Global Political Economy: Understanding the International Economic Order*. Princeton: Princeton University Press.

Global Environment Facility. 2014. *GEF Investments on Payment for Ecosystem Services*. Geneva: Global Environment Facility.

Global Witness. 2015. "How Many More? 2014's Deadly Environment: The Killing and Intimidation of Environmental and Land Activists, with a Spotlight on Honduras." Available at www.globalwitness.org/documents/17882/how_many_more_pages.pdf

Goldman, Michael. 2001. "The Birth of a Discipline: Producing Authoritative Green Knowledge, World Bank-Style." *Ethnography* 2.2: 191–217.

2005. *Imperial Nature: The World Bank and Struggles for Social Justice in the Age of Globalization*. New Haven: Yale University Press.

Goldstein, Judith, and Robert O. Keohane, eds. 1993. *Ideas and Foreign Policy: Beliefs, Institutions and Political Change*. Ithaca: Cornell University Press.

Gómez-Baggethun, Erik, and Manuel Ruiz Pérez. 2011. "Economic Valuation and the Commodification of Ecosystem Services." *Progress in Physical Geography* 35.5: 613–28.

Gore, Charles. 2000. "The Rise and Fall of the Washington Consensus as a Paradigm for Developing Countries." *World Development* 28.5: 789–804.

Gore, Christopher, and Pamela Robinson. 2009. "Local Government Response to Climate Change: Our Last, Best Hope?" *Changing Climates in North American Politics: Institutions, Policymaking and Multilevel Governance*. Eds. Selin, Henrik and Stacy VanDeveer. Cambridge, MA: MIT Press.

Grady, Barbara. 2015. "The Real Social Cost of Carbon: $220 per Ton, Report Finds." *Greenbiz*, January 15.

Grady-Benson, Jessica, and Brinda Sarathy. 2015. "Fossil Fuel Divestment in US Higher Education: Student-Led Organizing for Climate Justice." *Local*

Environment: The International Journal of Justice and Sustainability: DOI 10.1080/13549839.2015.1009825.

Green, Jessica. 2014. *Rethinking Private Authority: Agents and Entrepreneurs in Global Environmental Governance*. Princeton: Princeton University Press.

Greene, Owen. 1998. "The System for Implementation Review in the Ozone Regime." *The Implementation and Effectiveness of International Environmental Commitments: Theory and Practice*. Eds. Victor, David G., Kal Raustiala, and Eugene B. Skolnikoff. Cambridge, MA: MIT Press.

Grima, Nelson, Simron J. Singh, Barbara Smetschka, and Lisa Ronghofer. 2016. "Payment for Ecosystem Services (PES) in Latin America: Analyzing the Performance of 40 Case Studies." *Ecosystem Services* 17: 24–32.

Grolleau, Gilles, Lisette Ibanez, Naoufel Mzoughi, and Mario Teisl. 2016. "Helping Eco-Labels to Fulfil their Promises." *Climate Policy* 16.6: 792–802.

Grossman, Gene M., and Alan B. Krueger. 1995. "Economic Growth and the Environment." *Quarterly Journal of Economics* 110: 393–96.

Guha, Ramachandra. 2000. *Environmentalism: A Global History*. New York: Longman.

Gulbrandsen, Lars H. 2004. "Overlapping Public and Private Governance: Can Forest Certification Fill the Gaps in the Global Forest Regime?" *Global Environmental Politics* 4.2: 75–99.

2010. *Transnational Environmental Governance: The Emergence and Effects of the Certification of Forests and Fisheries*. Northampton, MA: Edward Elgar.

Gupta, Aarti. 2004. "When Global is Local: Negotiating Safe Use of Biotechnology." *Earthly Politics: Local and Global in Environmental Governance*. Eds. Jasanoff, Sheila and Marybeth Long Martello. Cambridge, MA: MIT Press.

2014. "Risk Governance through Transparency: Information Disclosure and the Global Trade in Transgenic Crops." *Transparency in Global Environmental Governance: Critical Perspectives*. Eds. Gupta, Aarti and Michael Mason. Cambridge, MA: MIT Press.

Gupta, Aarti, Steinar Andresen, Bernd Siebenhüner, and Frank Biermann. 2012. "Science Networks." *Global Environmental Governance Reconsidered*. Eds. Biermann, Frank and Philipp Pattberg. Cambridge, MA: MIT Press.

Gupta, Aarti, and Michael Mason, eds. 2014. *Transparency in Global Environmental Governance: Critical Perspectives*. Cambridge, MA: MIT Press.

Gupta, Aarti, Till Pistorius, and Marjanneke J. Vilge. Forthcoming. "Managing Fragmentation in Global Environmental Governance: The REDD+ Partnership as Bridge Organization." *International Environmental Agreements*.

Gupta, Joyeeta. 2000. *"On Behalf of my Delegation … ": A Survival Guide for Developing Country Climate Negotiators*. Washington DC: Center for Sustainable Development of the Americas.

2013. "Global Water Governance." *The Handbook of Global Climate and Environment Policy*. Ed. Falkner, Robert. London: John Wiley & Sons.

Gutner, Tamar. 2002. *Banking on the Environment: Multilateral Development Banks and their Environmental Performance in Central and Eastern Europe*. Cambridge, MA: MIT Press.

2012. "Evaluating World Bank Environmental Performance." *Handbook of Global Environmental Politics*, 2nd edition. Ed. Dauvergne, Peter. London: Edward Elgar.

Haas, Peter M. 1990a. "Obtaining Environmental Protection through Epistemic Consensus." *Millennium* 19.3: 347–63.

1990b. *Saving the Mediterranean: The Politics of International Environmental Cooperation*. New York: Columbia University Press.

1992. "Introduction: Epistemic Communities and International Policy Coordination." *International Organization* 46.1: 1–35.

1997. "Scientific Communities and Multiple Paths to Environmental Management." *Saving the Seas: Values, Scientists and International Governance*. Eds. Brooks, L. Anathea and Stacy D. VanDeveer. College Park: Maryland Sea Grant.

Haas, Peter M., Robert O. Keohane, and Marc A. Levy, eds. 1993. *Institutions for the Earth: Sources of Effective International Environmental Protection*. Cambridge, MA: MIT Press.

Haas, Peter M., and David McCabe. 2001. "Amplifiers or Dampeners: International Institutions and Social Learning in the Management of Global Environmental Risks." *Learning to Manage Global Environmental Risks*. Ed. The Social Learning Group, vol. I: *A Comparative History of Social Responses to Climate Change, Ozone Depletion, and Acid Rain*. Cambridge, MA: MIT Press.

Haas, Peter M., and Casey Stevens. 2011. "Organized Science, Usable Knowledge, and Multilateral Environmental Governance." *Governing the Air: The Dynamics of Science, Policy, and Citizen Interaction*. Eds. Lidskog, Rolf and Göran Sundqvist. Cambridge, MA: MIT Press.

Haites, Erik. 2011. "Climate Change Finance." *Climate Policy* 11: 963–69.

Hall, Rodney Bruce, and Thomas J. Biersteker, eds. 2002. *The Emergence of Private Authority in Global Governance*. Cambridge: Cambridge University Press.

Hanhimäki, Jussi. *The United Nations: A Very Short Introduction*. Oxford: Oxford University Press, 2008.

Hardin, Garrett. 1968. "The Tragedy of the Commons." *Science* 162: 1243–48.

Hasenclever, Andreas, Peter Mayer, and Volker Rittberger. 2000. "Integrating Theories of International Regimes." *Review of International Studies* 26: 3–33.

Haufler, Virginia. 1999. "Self-Regulation and Business Norms: Political Risk, Political Activism." *Private Authority and International Affairs*. Eds. Cutler, A. Claire, Virginia Haufler, and Tony Porter. Albany: SUNY Press.

2001. *A Public Role for the Private Sector: Industry Self-Regulation in a Global Economy*. New York: Carnegie Endowment for International Peace.

2003. "New Forms of Governance: Certification Regimes as Social Regulations of the Global Market." *Social and Political Dimensions of Forest Certification*. Eds. Meidinger, Errol E., Chris Elliott, and Gerhard Oesten. Remagen: www.forstbuch.de.

2009. "Insurance and Reinsurance in a Changing Climate." *Changing Climates in North American Politics: Institutions, Policymaking, and Multilevel Governance*. Eds. Selin, Henrik and Stacy VanDeveer. Cambridge, MA: MIT Press.

2010. "Disclosure as Governance: The Extractive Industries Transparency Initiative and Resource Management in the Developing World." *Global Environmental Politics* 10.3: 53–73.

Havice, Elizabeth, and Liam Campling. 2010. "Shifting Tides in the Western and Central Pacific Ocean Tuna Fishery: The Political Economy of Regulation and Industry Responses." *Global Environmental Politics* 10.1: 89–114.

Haya, Barbara. 2007. *How the Clean Development Mechanism is Subsidizing Hydro Developers and Harming the Kyoto Protocol*. Berkeley: International Rivers.

Haya, Barbara, Malini Ranganathan, and Sujit Kirpekar. 2009. "Barriers to Sugar Mill Cogeneration in India: Insights into the Structure of Post-2012 Climate Financing Instruments." *Climate and Development* 1: 66–81.

Hecht, Susanna B., Susan Kandel, Ileana Gomes, Nelson Cuellar, and Herman Rosa. 2006. "Globalization, Forest Resurgence, and Environmental Politics in El Salvador." *World Development* 34.2: 308–23.

Hein, Lars, Daniel C. Miller, and Rudolf de Groot. 2013. "Payments for Ecosystem Services and the Financing of Global Biodiversity Conservation." *Current Opinion in Environmental Sustainability* 5: 87–93.

Helm, Dieter. 2010. "Government Failure, Rent-Seeking, and Capture: The Design of Climate Change Policy." *Oxford Review of Economic Policy* 26.2: 182–96.

Helm, Dieter, and David Pearce. 1990. "Economic Policy towards the Environment." *Oxford Review of Economic Policy* 7.4: 1–16.

Hilson, Gavin. 2012. "Corporate Social Responsibility in the Extractive Industries: Experiences from Developing Countries." *Resources Policy* 37: 131–37.

Hindery, Derrick. 2004. "Social and Environmental Impacts of World Bank/IMF-Funded Economic Restructuring in Bolivia: An Analysis of Enron and Shell's Hydrocarbons Projects." *Singapore Journal of Tropical Geography* 25.3: 281–303.

Hiraldo, Rocio, and Thomas Tanner. 2011. "Forest Voices: Competing Narratives over REDD+." *IDS Bulletin* 42.3: 42–51.

Hirsch, Philip, and Katherine Wilson. 2011. "Ebbs and Flows: Megaproject Politics on the Mekong." *Engineering Earth*. Ed. Brunn, S. D. Berlin: Springer Science and Business.

Hobsbawm, Eric J. 1995. *Age of Extremes: 1914–1991*. New York: Pantheon Press.

Hochstetler, Kathryn. 2012. "Democracy and the Environment in Latin America and Eastern Europe." *The Comparative Politics of the Environment*. Eds. Steinberg, Paul F. and Stacy VanDeveer. Cambridge, MA: MIT Press.

Hochstetler, Kathryn, and Manjana Milkoreit. 2014. "Emerging Powers in the Climate Negotiations: Shifting Identity Conceptions." *Political Research Quarterly* 67.1: 224–35.

Hoek, Andrew. 2010. "Sea Shepherd Conservation Society v. Japanese Whalers, the Showdown: Who is the Real Villain?" *Stanford Journal of Animal Law and Policy* 3: 159–94.

Hoffmann, Matthew J. 2011. *Climate Governance at the Crossroads: Experimenting with a Global Response after Kyoto*. Oxford: Oxford University Press.

2013. "Global Climate Change." *The Handbook of Global Climate and Environment Policy*. Ed. Falkner, Robert. London: John Wiley & Sons.

Holmes, George. 2011. "Conservation's Friends in High Places: Neoliberalism, Networks and the Transnational Conservation Elite." *Global Environmental Politics* 11.4: 1–21.

Homer-Dixon, Thomas F. 1994. "Environmental Scarcities and Violent Conflict: Evidence from Cases." *International Security* 19.1: 5–40.

Hoppe, Rob, Anna Wesselink, and Rose Carins. 2013. "Lost in the Problem: The Role of Boundary Organizations in the Governance of Climate Change." *WIREs Climate Change* 4: 283–300.

Horta, Korinna, Robin Round, and Zoe Young. 2002. *The Global Environment Facility: The First Ten Years – Growing Pains or Inherent Flaws?* Washington DC and Ottawa: Environmental Defense Fund/Halifax Initiative.

Hudec, Robert E. 1999. "The New WTO Dispute Settlement Procedure: An Overview of the First Three Years." *Minnesota Journal of Global Trade* 8: 2–50.

Hulme, Mike, and Martin Mahony. 2010. "Climate Change: What do we Know about the IPCC?" *Progress in Physical Geography* 34.5: 705–18.

Humphreys, David. 2005. "The Elusive Quest for a Global Forests Convention." *RECIEL* 14.1: 1–10.

2013. "Deforestation." *The Handbook of Global Climate and Environment Policy.* Ed. Falkner, Robert. London: John Wiley & Sons.

Hunter, David, James Salzman, and Durwood Zaelke, eds. 2002. *International Environmental Law and Policy*, 2nd edition. New York: Foundation Press.

Hurrell, Andrew, and Benedict Kingsbury, eds. 1992. *The International Politics of the Environment*. Oxford: Oxford University Press.

Ibanez, Marcela, and Allen Blackman. 2015. "Environmental and Economic Impacts of Growing Certified Organic Coffee in Colombia." Resources for the Future Discussion Paper 15.03. Available at www.rff.org/research/publica tions/environmental-and-economic-impacts-growing-certified-organic-cof fee-colombia.

Ivanova, Maria. 2007. "Designing the United Nations Environment Programme: A Story of Compromise and Confrontation." *International Environmental Agreements* 7: 337–61.

2010. "UNEP in Global Environmental Governance: Design, Leadership, Location." *Global Environmental Politics* 10.1: 30–59.

Jacques, Peter J., Riley E. Dunlap, and Mark Freeman. 2008. "The Organization of Denial: Conservative Think Tanks and Environmental Skepticism." *Environmental Politics* 17.3: 349–85.

Jacur, Francesca Romanin. 2009. "The Non-Compliance Procedure of the 1987 Montreal Protocol to the 1985 Vienna Convention on Substances that Deplete the Ozone Layer." *Non-Compliance Procedures and Mechanisms and the Effectiveness of International Environmental Agreements.* Eds. Treves, Tullio, et al. The Hague: T. M. C. Asser Press.

2010. "An Assessment of CDM: Lessons Learned and the Way Forward." *Developing CDM Projects in the Western Balkans: Legal and Technical Issues Compared.* Ed. Montini, Massimiliano. Dordrecht: Springer.

Jakobeit, Cord. 1996. "Non-State Actors Leading the Way: Debt-for-Nature Swaps." *Institutions for Environmental Aid: Pitfalls and Promise.* Eds. Keohane, Robert O. and Marc A. Levy. Cambridge, MA: MIT Press.

Jansen, Kees, and Milou Dubois. 2014. "Global Pesticide Governance by Disclosure: Prior Informed Consent and the Rotterdam Convention." *Transparency in Global Environmental Governance: Critical Perspectives.* Eds. Gupta, Aarti and Michael Mason. Cambridge, MA: MIT Press.

Jaraitė, Jūratė, Frank Convery, and Corrado Di Maria. 2010. "Transaction Costs for Firms in the EU ETS: Lessons from Ireland." *Climate Policy* 10.2: 190–215.

Jasanoff, Sheila. 1997. "Compelling Knowledge in Public Decisions." *Saving the Seas: Values, Scientists and International Governance.* Eds. Brooks, L. Anathea and Stacy VanDeveer. College Park: Maryland Sea Grant.

    1998. "Contingent Knowledge: Implications for Implementation and Compliance." *Engaging Countries: Strengthening Compliance with International Environmental Accords.* Eds. Weiss, Edith Brown and Harold K. Jacobson. Cambridge, MA: MIT Press.

    2001. "Image and Imagination: The Formation of Global Environmental Consciousness." *Changing the Atmosphere: Expert Knowledge and Environmental Governance.* Eds. Miller, Clark A. and Paul N. Edwards. Cambridge, MA: MIT Press.

    2004. "Heaven and Earth: The Politics of Environmental Images." *Earthly Politics: Local and Global in Environmental Governance.* Eds. Jasanoff, Sheila and Marybeth Long Martello. Cambridge, MA: MIT Press.

    2005. "Science and Environmental Citizenship." *Handbook of Global Environmental Politics.* Ed. Dauvergne, Peter. Cheltenham: Edward Elgar.

Jasanoff, Sheila, and Marybeth Long Martello, eds. 2004. *Earthly Politics: Local and Global in Environmental Governance.* Cambridge, MA: MIT Press.

Jaspers, Nico, and Robert Falkner. 2013. "International Trade, the Environment, and Climate Change." *The Handbook of Global Climate and Environment Policy.* Ed. Falkner, Robert. London: John Wiley & Sons.

Jenkins, Leesteffy. 1995. "Trade Sanctions: Effective Enforcement Tools." *Improving Compliance with International Environmental Law.* Eds. Cameron, James, Jacob Werksman, and Peter Roderick. London: Earthscan.

Jervis, Robert. 1999. "Realism, Neoliberalism, and Cooperation: Understanding the Debate." *International Security* 24.1: 42–63.

Jinnah, Sikina. 2010. "Overlap Management in the World Trade Organization: Secretariat Influence on Trade–Environment Politics." *Global Environmental Politics* 10.2: 54–79.

    2012a. "Singing the Unsung: Secretariats in Global Environmental Politics." *The Roads from Rio: Lessons Learned from Twenty Years of Multilateral Environmental Negotiations.* Eds. Chasek, Pamela S. and Lynn M. Wagner. New York: Routledge.

    2012b. "Trade–Environment Politics: The Emerging Role of Regional Trade Agreements." *The Handbook of Global Environmental Politics,* 2nd edn. Ed. Dauvergne, Peter. New York: Edward Elgar.

    2014. *Post-Treaty Politics: Secretariat Influence in Global Environmental Governance.* Cambridge, MA: MIT Press.

Joyner, Christopher C. 2001. "Global Commons: The Oceans, Antarctica, the Atmosphere and Outer Space." *Managing Global Issues: Lessons Learned.* Eds.

Simmons, P. J. and Chantal de Jonge Oudraat. Washington DC: Carnegie Endowment for International Peace.

2005. "Rethinking International Environmental Regimes: What Role for Partnership Coalitions?" *Journal of International Law and International Relations* 1.1–2: 89–119.

Kandlikar, Milind, and Ambuj Sagar. 1999. "Climate Change Research and Analysis in India: An Integrated Assessment of a South–North Divide." *Global Environmental Change* 9: 119–38.

Karlsson, Sylvia. 2002. "The North–South Knowledge Divide: Consequences for Global Environmental Governance." *Global Environmental Governance: Options and Opportunities*. Eds. Esty, Daniel C. and Maria H. Ivanova. New Haven: Yale School of Forestry and Environmental Studies.

Kastner, Justin, and Douglas Powell. 2002. "The SPS Agreement: Addressing Historical Factors in Trade Dispute Resolution." *Agriculture and Human Values* 19: 282–92.

Kaswan, Alice. 2014. "Climate Change and Environmental Justice: Lessons from the California Lawsuits." *San Diego Journal of Climate and Energy Law* 5.1; University of San Francisco Law Research Paper No. 2015–03. Available at SSRN: http://ssrn.com/abstract=2471155.

Kauffman, Joanne M. 1997. "Domestic and International Linkages in Global Environmental Politics: A Case-Study of the Montreal Protocol." *The Internationalization of Environmental Protection*. Eds. Schreurs, Miranda A. and Elizabeth Economy. Cambridge: Cambridge University Press.

Keck, Margaret E., and Kathryn Sikkink. 1998. *Activists beyond Borders: Advocacy Networks in International Politics*. Ithaca: Cornell University Press.

Kennan, George F. 1970. "To Prevent a World Wasteland: A Proposal." *Foreign Affairs* 48.3: 401–13.

Keohane, Robert O. 1984. *After Hegemony: Cooperation and Discord in the World Economy*. Princeton: Princeton University Press.

ed. 1986. *Neorealism and its Critics*. New York: Columbia University Press.

Keohane, Robert O., and David G. Victor. 2011. "The Regime Complex for Climate Change." *Perspectives on Politics* 9.1: 7–23.

Khagram, Sanjeev. 2004. *Dams and Development: Transnational Struggles for Water and Power*. Ithaca: Cornell University Press.

Khagram, Sanjeev, James V. Riker, and Kathryn Sikkink, eds. 2002. *Restructuring World Politics: Transnational Social Movements, Networks, and Norms*. Minneapolis: University of Minnesota Press.

Kindleberger, Charles P. 1973. *The World in Depression, 1929–1939*. Berkeley: University of California Press.

Klein, Naomi. 2014. *This Changes Everything: Capitalism vs. the Climate*. New York: Simon & Schuster.

Kolbert, Elizabeth. 2006. *Fieldnotes from a Catastrophe*. New York: Bloomsbury USA.

2015. "The Weight of the World: Can Christiana Figueres Persuade Humanity to Save Itself?" *New Yorker*, August 24.

Krasner, Stephen D., ed. 1983. *International Regimes*. Ithaca: Cornell University Press.

1988. "Sovereignty: An Institutional Perspective." *Comparative Political Studies* 21.1: 66–94.

Krueger, Anne O., ed. 1998. *The WTO as an International Organization.* Chicago: University of Chicago Press.

Lahsen, Myanna. 2013. "Anatomy of Dissent: A Cultural Analysis of Climate Skepticism." *American Behavioral Scientist* 57.6: 732–53.

La Viña, Antonio G. M., Gretchen Hoff, and Anne Marie DeRose. 2003. "The Outcomes of Johannesburg: Assessing the World Summit on Sustainable Development." *SAIS Review* 23.1: 53–70.

Lattanzio, Richard K. 2013. *International Environmental Financing: The Global Environment Facility (GEF).* Washington DC: Congressional Research Service.

Lederer, Markus. 2012. "REDD+ Governance." *WIREs Climate Change* 3: 107–13.

Leggett, Jeremy. 1996. *Climate Change and the Financial Sector.* Munich: Gerling Akademie Verlag.

Leiserowitz, Anthony A., Robert W. Kates, and Thomas M. Parris. 2006. "Sustainability Values, Attitudes, and Behaviors: A Review of Multinational and Global Trends." *Annual Review of Environment and Resources* 31: 413–44.

Lejárraga, Iza. 2014. "Deep Provisions in Regional Trade Agreements: How Multilateral-Friendly? An Overview of OECD Findings." OECD Trade Policy Papers No. 168. Paris: OECD Publishing. DOI: http://dx.doi.org/10.1787/5jxvgfn4bjf0-en.

Lekakis, Joseph N., and Maria Kousis. 2013. "Economic Crisis, Troika and the Environment in Greece." *South European Society and Politics* 18.3: 305–31.

Lepawsky, Josh, and Chris McNabb. 2010. "Mapping International Flows of Electronic Waste." *The Canadian Geographer* 54.2: 177–95.

Levin, Kelly, Benjamin Cashore, Steven Bernstein, and Graeme Auld. 2012. "Overcoming the Tragedy of Super Wicked Problems: Constraining our Future Selves to Ameliorate Global Climate Change." *Policy Sciences* 45.2: 123–52.

Levy, David L., and Ans Kolk. 2002. "Strategic Responses to Global Climate Change: Conflicting Pressures on Multinationals in the Oil Industry." *Business and Politics* 4.3: 275–300.

Levy, David L., and Peter J. Newell. 2002. "Business Strategy and International Environmental Governance: Toward a Neo-Gramscian Synthesis." *Global Environmental Politics* 2.4: 84–101.

Levy, David L., and Aseem Prakash. 2003. "Bargains Old and New: Multinational Corporations in Global Governance." *Business and Politics* 5.2: 131–50.

Levy, Marc A. 1993. "European Acid Rain: The Power of Tote-Board Diplomacy." *Institutions for the Earth: Sources of Effective International Environmental Protection.* Eds. Haas, Peter M., Robert O. Keohane, and Marc A. Levy. Cambridge, MA: MIT Press.

Lidskog, Rolf, and Göran Sundqvist. 2002. "The Role of Science in Environmental Regimes: The Case of LRTAP." *European Journal of International Relations* 8.1: 77–101.

eds. 2011. *Governing the Air: The Dynamics of Science, Policy, and Citizen Interaction*. Cambridge, MA: MIT Press.

2015. "When Does Science Matter? International Relations Meets Science and Technology Studies." *Global Environmental Politics* 15.1: 1–20.

Light, Sarah E. 2015. "Reasons for Optimism in the Paris Agreement." *RegBlog*, December 24. Available at www.regblog.org/2015/12/24/light-reasons-for-optimism-in-the-paris-agreement/.

Lin, Jintai, Da Pan, Steven J. Davis, Qiang Zhang, Kebin He, Can Wang, David G. Streets, Donald J. Wuebbles, and Dabo Guan. 2014. "China's International Trade and Air Pollution in the United States." *PNAS* 111.5: 1736–41.

Linklater, Andrew. 2013. "Marx and Marxism." *Theories of International Relations*, 5th edition. Eds. Burchill, Scott and Andrew Linklater. London: Palgrave Macmillan.

Linnerooth-Bayer, Joanne, and Stefan Hochrainer-Stigler. 2015. "Financial Instruments for Disaster Risk Management and Climate Change Adaptation." *Climatic Change* 133: 85–100.

Lipschutz, Ronnie D., and Ken Conca, eds. 1993. *The State and Social Power in Global Environmental Politics*. New York: Columbia University Press.

Lipschutz, Ronnie D., and Cathleen Fogel. 2002. "'Regulation for the Rest of us?' Global Civil Society and the Privatization of International Relations." *The Emergence of Private Authority in Global Governance*. Eds. Hall, Rodney Bruce and Thomas J. Biersteker. Cambridge: Cambridge University Press.

Litfin, Karen T. 1994. *Ozone Discourses: Science and Politics in Global Environmental Cooperation*. New York: Columbia University Press.

Liverman, Diana M., and Silvina Vilas. 2006. "Neoliberalism and the Environment in Latin America." *Annual Review of Environment and Resources* 31: 327–63.

Lo, Alex Y., and Michael Howes. 2015. "Power and Carbon Sovereignty in a Non-Traditional Capitalist State: Discourses of Carbon Trading in China." *Global Environmental Politics* 15.1: 60–82.

Lohmann, Larry. 2012. "Financialization, Commodification and Carbon: The Contradictions of Neoliberal Climate Policy." *Socialist Register* 48: 85–107.

Lomborg, Bjorn. 2001. *The Skeptical Environmentalist: Measuring the Real State of the World*. Cambridge: Cambridge University Press.

Lovelock, James. 2000. *Gaia: A New Look at Life on Earth*. Oxford: Oxford University Press.

Low, Nicholas, and Brendan Gleeson. 1998. *Justice, Society and Nature: An Exploration of Political Ecology*. London: Routledge.

Lund, Emma. 2013. "Environmental Diplomacy: Comparing the Influence of Business and Environmental NGOs in Negotiations on Reform of the Clean Development Mechanism." *Environmental Politics* 22.5: 739–59.

M'Gonigle, R. M., and M. W. Zacher. 1979. *Pollution, Politics and International Law: Tankers at Sea*. Berkeley: University of California Press.

MacLeod, Michael, and Jacob Park. 2011. "Financial Activism and Global Climate Change: The Rise of Investor-Driven Governance Networks." *Global Environmental Politics* 11.2: 54–74.

Maibach, Edward, Anthony A. Leiserowitz, Sara Cobb, Michael Shank, Kim M. Cobb, and Jay Gulledge. 2012. "The Legacy of Climategate: Undermining or Revitalizing Climate Science and Policy?" *WIRES Climate Change* 3: 289–95.

Maniates, Michael F. 2002. "Individualization: Buy a Bike, Plant a Tree, Save the World?" *Confronting Consumption*. Eds. Princen, Thomas, Michael F. Maniates, and Ken Conca. Cambridge, MA: MIT Press.

Marcacci, Silvio. 2013. "Why Europe's Carbon Market Collapse Won't Kill Cap and Trade." Energy Collective Blog post, April 22. Available at http://cleantech nica.com/2013/04/19/why-europes-carbon-market-collapse-wont-kill-cap-and -trade/.

Martello, Marybeth Long. 2001. "A Paradox of Virtue? 'Other' Knowledges and Environment-Development Politics." *Global Environmental Politics* 1.3: 114–41.

———. 2001. "Local Knowledge: Global Change Science and the Arctic Citizen." *Science and Public Policy* 31.2: 107–15.

———. 2004. "Expert Advice and Desertification Policy: Past Experience and Current Challenges." *Global Environmental Politics* 4.3: 85–106.

Martin, Ralf, Mirabelle Muuls, and Ulrich Wagner. 2012. *An Evidence Review of the EU Emissions Trading System, Focusing on Effectiveness of the System in Driving Industrial Abatement*. London: Department of Energy and Climate Change.

Martinez-Torres, Maria Elena, and Peter M. Rosset. 2010. "La Vía Campesina: The Birth and Evolution of a Transnational Social Movement." *Journal of Peasant Studies* 37.1: 149–75.

Matt, Elah, and Chukwumerije Okereke. 2015. "A Neo-Gramscian Account of Carbon Markets: The Cases of the European Union Emissions Trading Scheme and the Clean Development Mechanism." *The Politics of Carbon Markets*. Eds. Stephan, Benjamin and Richard Lane. London: Routledge.

McAdam, Doug, John D. McCarthy, and Mayer N. Zald, eds. 1996. *Comparative Perspectives on Social Movements: Political Opportunities, Mobilizing Structures, and Cultural Framings*. Cambridge: Cambridge University Press.

McAdam, Jane. 2011. "Swimming against the Tide: Why a Climate Change Displacement Treaty is Not the Answer." *International Journal of Refugee Law* 23.1: 2–27.

McAfee, Kathleen. 1999. "Selling Nature to Save it? Biodiversity and Green Developmentalism." *Environment and Planning D: Society and Space* 17: 133–54.

———. forthcoming. "Green Economy and Carbon Markets for Conservation and Development: A Critical View." *International Environmental Agreements*.

McAteer, Emily, and Simone Pulver. 2009. "The Corporate Boomerang: Shareholder Transnational Advocacy Networks Targeting Oil Companies in the Ecuadorian Amazon." *Global Environmental Politics* 9.1: 1–30.

McCarthy, James, and Scott Prudham. 2004. "Neoliberal Nature and the Nature of Neoliberalism." *Geoforum* 35: 275–83.

McCright, Aaron M., and Riley E. Dunlap. 2011. "The Politicization of Climate Change and Polarization in the American Public's View of Global Warming, 2001–2010." *Sociological Quarterly* 52: 155–94.

McCully, Patrick. 2001. *Silenced Rivers: The Ecology and Politics of Large Dams*, updated edition. London: Zed Books.

McDermott, Rose. 2004. *Political Psychology in International Relations*. Ann Arbor: University of Michigan Press.

McKibben, Bill. 2011. *Eaarth: Making a Life on a Tough New Planet*. London: St. Martin's Griffin.

McMichael, Philip. 2014. "Historicizing Food Sovereignty." *Journal of Peasant Studies* 41.6: 933–57.

McNeill, J. R. 2000. *Something New under the Sun: An Environmental History of the Twentieth-Century World*. New York: W. W. Norton & Company.

Meadowcraft, James. 2012. "Greening the State?" *Comparative Environmental Politics: Theory, Politics and Practice*. Eds. Steinberg, Paul F. and Stacy VanDeveer. Cambridge, MA: MIT Press.

Mearsheimer, John. 1994/95. "The False Promise of International Institutions." *International Security* 19: 5–49.

Meckling, Jonas. 2011. *Carbon Coalitions: Business, Climate Politics, and the Rise of Emissions Trading*. Cambridge, MA: MIT Press.

2014. "The Future of Emissions Trading." *WIRES Climate Change* 5: 569–76.

Meckling, Jonas, and Cameron Hepburn. 2013. "Economic Instruments for Climate Change." *The Handbook of Global Climate and Environment Policy*. Ed. Falkner, Robert. London: John Wiley & Sons.

Miles, Edward L., Arild Underdal, Steinar Andresen, Jorgen Wettestad, Jon Birger Skjaerseth, and Elaine M. Carlin. 2002. *Environmental Regime Effectiveness: Confronting Theory with Evidence*. Cambridge, MA: MIT Press.

Miller, Clark A., and Paul N. Edwards, eds. 2001. *Changing the Atmosphere: Expert Knowledge and Environmental Governance*. Cambridge, MA: MIT Press.

Miller, Marian A. L. 1995. *The Third World in Global Environmental Politics*. Boulder: Lynne Rienner.

Milliken, Tom. 2014. *Illegal Trade in Ivory and Rhino Horn: An Assessment Report to Improve Law Enforcement under the Wildlife TRAPS Project*. Cambridge: USAID and TRAFFIC International.

Mills, Evan. 2012. "The Greening of Insurance." *Science* 338: 1424–25.

Milner, Helen V. 1991. "The Assumption of Anarchy in International Relations Theory: A Critique." *Review of International Studies* 17: 67–85.

Mingst, Karen A. 2012. "International Organization." Encyclopaedia Britannica Online. London: Encyclopaedia Britannica Inc.

Mitchell, Ronald B. 1994. *Intentional Oil Pollution at Sea: Environmental Policy and Treaty Compliance*. Cambridge, MA: MIT Press.

2003. "International Environmental Agreements: A Survey of their Features, Formation and Effects." *Annual Review of Environment and Resources* 28: 429–61.

Mitchell, Ronald B., Moira L. McConnell, Alexei Roginko, and Ann Barrett. 1999. "International Vessel-Source Pollution." *The Effectiveness of International Environmental Regimes: Causal Connections and Behavioral Mechanisms*. Ed. Young, Oran R. Cambridge, MA: MIT Press.

Mol, Arthur P. J. 2011. "China's Ascent and Africa's Environment." *Global Environmental Change* 21: 785–94.

Monbiot, George. 2006. "Selling Indulgences." *The Guardian*, October 18.

——— 2012. "Putting a Price on the Rivers and Rain Diminishes us All." *The Guardian*, August 6.

Moore, Frances C., and Delavane B. Diaz. 2015. "Temperature Impacts on Economic Growth Warrant Stringent Mitigation Policy." *Nature Climate Change* 5: 127–31.

Morin, Jean-Frédéric, and Amandine Orsini. 2014. "Insights from Global Environmental Governance: An Edited Symposium." *International Studies Review* 15: 562–89.

Morin, Jean-Frédéric, and Amandine Orsini, eds. 2015. *Essential Concepts of Global Environmental Governance*. London: Earthscan.

Morrisette, Peter M. 1991. "The Montreal Protocol: Lessons for Formulating Policies for Global Warming." *Policy Studies Journal* 19.2: 152–61.

Mueller, Tadzio, and Alexis Passadakis. 2009. "Green Capitalism and the Climate: It's Economic Growth, Stupid!" *Critical Currents* 6: 54–61.

Muñoz, Miquel, Rachel Thrasher, and Adil Najam. 2009. "Measuring the Negotiation Burden of Multilateral Environmental Agreements." *Global Environmental Politics* 9.4: 1–13.

Murphy, Dale D. 2006. "The Tuna–Dolphin Wars." *Journal of World Trade* 40.4: 597–617.

Nadelmann, Ethan A. 1990. "Global Prohibition Regimes: The Evolution of Norms in International Society." *International Organization* 44.4: 479–526.

Najam, Adil. 2004. "Dynamics of the Southern Collective: Developing Countries in Desertification Negotiations." *Global Environmental Politics* 4.3: 128–54.

——— 2005. "Developing Countries and Global Environmental Governance: From Contestation to Participation to Engagement." *International Environmental Agreements* 5: 303–21.

——— 2015. "The View from the South: Developing Countries in Global Environmental Politics." *The Global Environment: Institutions, Law, and Policy*, 4th edition. Eds. Axelrod, Regina S. and Stacy D. VanDeveer. Los Angeles and Washington DC: Sage/CQ Press.

Nakhooda, Smita. 2012. "How Much Money is Needed to Deal with Climate Change?" Thompson Reuters Foundation, August 1. Available at http://news.trust.org/item/20120801162300-9keti.

Nakhooda, Smita, and Marigold Norman. 2014. *Climate Finance: Is it Making a Difference? A Review of the Effectiveness of Multilateral Climate Funds*. London: Overseas Development Institute.

Nakhooda, Smita, Charlene Watson, and Liane Schalatek. 2015. *The Global Climate Finance Architecture*. Washington DC: Heinrich Böll Stiftung North America.

Newell, Peter. 2014. "The International Political Economy of Governing Carbon." *Handbook of the International Political Economy of Governance*. Eds. Payne, Anthony and Nicola Phillips. London: Edward Elgar.

Newell, Peter, and Adam Bumpus. 2012. "The Global Political Ecology of the Clean Development Mechanism." *Global Environmental Politics* 12.4: 49–67.

Newell, Peter, and Matthew Paterson. 2010. *Climate Capitalism: Global Warming and the Transformation of the Global Economy*. Cambridge: Cambridge University Press.

Nicholson, Simon, and Paul Wapner, eds. 2015. *Global Environmental Politics: From Person to Planet*. Boulder: Paradigm Publishers.

Nixon, Rob. 2011. *Slow Violence: The Environmentalism of the Poor*. Cambridge, MA: Harvard University Press.

Norman, Marigold, and Smita Nakhooda. 2014. "The State of REDD+ Finance." CGD Working Paper 378. Washington DC: Center for Global Development. Available at www.cgdev.org/publication/state-redd-finance-working-paper-378.

O'Neill, Kate. 2000. *Waste Trading among Rich Nations: Building a New Theory of Environmental Regulation*. Cambridge, MA: MIT Press.

2001. "The Changing Nature of Global Waste Management for the 21st Century: A Mixed Blessing?" *Global Environmental Politics* 1.1: 77–98.

2004. "Transnational Protest: States, Circuses, and Conflict at the Frontline of Global Politics." *International Studies Review* 6: 233–51.

2012. "The Comparative Study of Environmental Movements." *Comparative Environmental Politics*. Eds. Steinberg, Paul F. and Stacy VanDeveer. Cambridge, MA: MIT Press.

2014. "Vertical Scale and Linkages." *International Studies Review* 15: 571–73.

2015. "Architects, Agitators, and Entrepreneurs: International and Nongovernmental Organizations in Global Environmental Politics." *The Global Environment: Institutions, Law, and Policy*, 4th edition. Eds. Axelrod, Regina S. and Stacy D. VanDeveer. Los Angeles and Washington DC: Sage/CQ Press.

O'Neill, Kate, Jörg Balsiger, and Stacy VanDeveer. 2004. "Actors, Norms and Impact: Recent International Cooperation Theory and the Influence of the Agent–Structure Debate." *Annual Review of Political Science* 7: 149–75.

O'Neill, Kate, and William C. G. Burns. 2005. "Trade Liberalization and Global Environmental Governance: The Potential for Conflict." *Handbook of Global Environmental Governance*. Ed. Dauvergne, Peter. Cheltenham: Edward Elgar.

O'Neill, Kate, Erika Weinthal, Kimberly R. Marion Suiseeya, Steven Bernstein, Avery S. Cohn, Michael W. Stone, and Benjamin Cashore. 2013. "Methods and Global Environmental Governance." *Annual Review of Environment and Resources* 38: 441–71.

O'Neill, Saffron J., Mike Hulme, John Turnpenny, and James A. Screen. 2010. "Disciplines, Geography, and Gender in the Framing of Climate Change." *Bulletin of the American Meteorological Society* 91: 997–1002.

O'Rourke, Dara. 2014. "The Science of Sustainable Supply Chains." *Science* 344.6188: 1124–27.

O'Rourke, Dara, and Abraham Ringer. 2015. "The Impact of Sustainability Information on Consumer Decision Making." *Journal of Industrial Ecology*: DOI 10.1111/jiec.12310View.

Oberthür, Sebastian, and Florian Rabitz. 2013. "On the EU's Performance and Leadership in Global Environmental Governance: The Case of the Nagoya Protocol." *Journal of European Public Policy* 21.1: 39–57.

Oberthür, Sebastian, and Olav Schram Stokke, eds. 2011. *Managing Institutional Complexity: Regime Interplay and Global Environmental Change*. Cambridge, MA: MIT Press.

Ohta, Hiroshi, and Atsushi Ishii. 2013. "Disaggregating Effectiveness." *International Studies Review* 37: 581–83.

Okereke, Chukwumerije. 2006. "Global Environmental Sustainability: Intragenerational Equity and Conceptions of Justice in Multilateral Environmental Agreements." *Geoforum* 37: 725–38.

Oosterveer, Peter, Betty E. Adjei, Sietze Vellema, and Maja Slingerland. 2014. "Global Sustainability Standards and Food Security: Exploring Unintended Effects of Voluntary Certification in Palm Oil." *Global Food Security* 3: 220–26.

Oreskes, Naomi, and Erik M. Conway. 2010. *Merchants of Doubt*. New York: Bloomsbury Publishing.

Orsini, Amandine, Jean-Frédéric Morin, and Oran Young. 2013. "Regime Complexes: A Buzz, a Boom or a Boost for Global Governance?" *Global Governance* 19: 27–39.

Overdevest, Christine. 2010. "Comparing Forest Certification Schemes: The Case of Ratcheting Standards in the Forest Sector." *Socio-Economic Review* 8: 47–76.

Park, Susan. 2010. *World Bank Group Interactions with Environmentalists: Changing International Organization Identities*. Manchester: Manchester University Press.

2012. "Greening Development Finance: Cases from the World Bank Group." *Handbook of Global Environmental Politics*, 2nd edition. Ed. Dauvergne, Peter. New York: Edward Elgar.

2013. "Transnational Environmental Activism." *The Handbook of Global Climate and Environment Policy*. Ed. Falkner, Robert. London: John Wiley & Sons.

Parker, Charles F., and Christer Karlsson. 2010. "Climate Change and the European Union's Leadership Moment: An Inconvenient Truth?" *Journal of Common Market Studies* 48.4: 923–43.

Parson, Edward A. 2003. *Protecting the Ozone Layer: Science and Strategy*. Oxford: Oxford University Press.

Pastor, Manuel, Rachel Morello-Frosch, James Sadd, and Justin Scoggins. 2013. "Risky Business: Cap-and-Trade, Public Health, and Environmental Justice." *Urbanization and Sustainability: Linking Urban Ecology, Environmental Justice and Global Environmental Change*. Eds. Boone, Christopher G. and Michael Fragkias. New York: Springer.

Paterson, Matthew. 2001a. "Risky Business: Insurance Companies in Global Warming Politics." *Global Environmental Politics* 1.4: 18–43.

2001b. *Understanding Global Environmental Politics: Domination, Accumulation, Resistance*. Basingstoke: Palgrave.

2012. "Who and What are Carbon Markets for? Politics and the Development of Climate Policy." *Climate Policy* 12.1: 82–97.

2013. "Green Politics." *Theories of International Relations*, 5th edition. Eds. Burchill, Scott and Andrew Linklater. London: Palgrave Macmillan.

2014. "Commodification." *Critical Environmental Politics*. Ed. Death, Carl. London: Routledge.

Paterson, Matthew, Matthew Hoffman, Michele M. Betsill, and Steven Bernstein. 2014. "The Micro Foundations of Policy Diffusion towards Complex Global Governance: An Analysis of the Transnational Carbon Emission Trading Network." *Comparative Political Studies* 47.3: 420–49.

Pattberg, Philipp. 2006. "The Influence of Global Business Regulation: Beyond Good Corporate Conduct." *Business and Society Review* 111.3: 241–68.

Paulsson, Emma. 2009. "A Review of the CDM Literature: From Fine-Tuning to Critical Scrutiny?" *International Environmental Agreements* 9: 63–80.

Pauwelyn, Joost. 2012. "Carbon Leakage Measures and Border Tax Adjustments under WTO Law." Available at http://papers.ssrn.com/sol3/papers.cfm?abstract_id=2026879.

Pearce, David. 2002. "An Intellectual History of Environmental Economics." *Annual Review of Energy and the Environment* 27: 57–81.

Pearse, Rebecca. 2015. "After Paris: Where Now for Carbon Pricing?" *Inside Story*, December 21.

Peel, Jacqueline. 2015. "International Law and the Protection of the Global Environment." *The Global Environment: Institutions, Law, and Policy*, 4th edition. Eds. Axelrod, Regina S. and Stacy D. VanDeveer. Los Angeles and Washington DC: Sage/CQ Press.

Peet, Richard, Paul Robbins, and Michael J. Watts, eds. 2011. *Global Political Ecology*. London: Routledge.

Peh, Kelvin S.-H., and Jonathan Eyal. 2010. "Unveiling China's Influence on African Environment." *Energy Policy* 38: 4729–30.

Peluso, Nancy Lee. 1993. "Coercing Conservation: The Politics of State Resource Control." *The State and Social Power in Global Environmental Politics*. Eds. Lipschutz, Ronnie D. and Ken Conca. New York: Columbia University Press.

Peluso, Nancy Lee, and Michael Watts, eds. 2001. *Violent Environments*. Ithaca: Cornell University Press.

Peters-Stanley, Molly, and Daphne Yin. 2013. *Maneuvering the Mosaic: State of the Voluntary Carbon Markets 2013*. Washington DC: Forest Trends' Ecosystem Marketplace and Bloomberg New Energy Finance.

Phelan, Liam, Ros Taplin, Ann Henderson-Sellers, and Glenn Albrecht. 2011. "Ecological Viability or Liability? Insurance System Responses to Climate Risk." *Environmental Policy and Governance* 21.2: 112–30.

Pickering, Jonathan, Steve Venderheiden, and Seumas Miller. 2012. "'If Equity's in, We're Out': Scope for Fairness in the Next Global Climate Agreement." *Ethics and International Affairs* 26.4: 423–43.

Pigou, Arthur. *The Economics of Welfare*. 1920. London: Macmillan.

Pirages, Dennis. 1978. *The New Context for International Relations: Global Ecopolitics*. North Scituate, MA: Duxbury Press.

Pizer, William, Matthew Adler, Joseph E. Aldy, David Anthoff, Maureen Cropper, Kenneth Gillingham, Michael Greenstone, Brian Murray, Richard Newell, Richard Richels, Arden Rowell, Stephane Waldhoff, and Jonathan Wiener. 2014. "Using and Improving the Social Cost of Carbon." *Science* 346.6214: 1189–90.

Ponte, Stefano. 2014. "'Roundtabling' Sustainability: Lessons from the Biofuel Industry." *Geoforum* 54: 261–71.

Porter, Gareth. 1999. "Trade Competition and Pollution Standards: 'Race to the Bottom' or 'Stuck at the Bottom'?" *Journal of Environment and Development* 8.2: 133–51.

Powell, Stephen Joseph, and Trisha Low. 2011. "Is the WTO Quietly Fading Away? The New Regionalism and Global Trade Rules." *The Georgetown Journal of Law and Public Policy* 9: 261–82.

Prakash, Aseem, and Matthew Potoski. 2006. "Racing to the Bottom? Trade, Environmental Governance, and ISO 14001." *American Journal of Political Science* 50.2: 350–64.

2014. "Global Private Regimes, Domestic Public Law: ISO 14001 and Pollution Reduction." *Comparative Political Studies* 47.369–394. DOI 10.1177/0010414013509573000-00.

Price, Martin F. 1990. "Humankind in the Biosphere: The Evolution of International Interdisciplinary Research." *Global Environmental Change* 1.1: 3–13.

Price, Richard, Simeon Thornton, and Stephen Nelson. 2007. *The Social Cost of Carbon and the Shadow Price of Carbon: What they are, and How to Use them in Economic Appraisal in the UK.* London: DEFRA.

Princen, Thomas. 1995. "Ivory, Conservation and Environmental Transnational Coalitions." *Bringing Transnational Relations Back in: Non-State Actors, Domestic Structures and International Institutions.* Ed. Risse-Kappen, Thomas. Cambridge: Cambridge University Press.

2002. "Distancing: Consumption and the Severing of Feedback." *Confronting Consumption.* Eds. Princen, Thomas, Michael F. Maniates and Ken Conca. Cambridge, MA: MIT Press.

Princen, Thomas, and Matthias Finger. 1994. *Environmental NGOs in World Politics: Linking the Local and the Global.* London: Routledge.

Princen, Thomas, Michael F. Maniates, and Ken Conca, eds. 2002. *Confronting Consumption.* Cambridge, MA: MIT Press.

Prins, Gwyn, and Steve Rayner. 2007. "Time to Ditch Kyoto." *Nature* 449.25: 973–75.

Prizzoni, Annalisa, and Shakira Mustapha. 2014. "Debt Sustainability in HIPCs in a New Age of Choice." Overseas Development Institute Working Papers, No. 397. Available at www.odi.org/publications/8476-debt-sustainability-hipcs-new-age-choice.

Pulver, Simone. 2002. "Organizing Business: Industry NGOs in the Climate Debates." *Greener Management International* 39: 55–67.

Pulver, Simone, and Stacy VanDeveer. 2009. "'Thinking About Tomorrows': Scenarios, Global Environmental Politics and Social Science Scholarship." *Global Environmental Politics* 9.2: 1–13.

Putnam, Robert D. 1988. "Diplomacy and Domestic Politics: The Logic of Two-Level Games." *International Organization* 42.3: 427–60.

Qi, Xinran. 2011. "The Rise of BASIC in UN Climate Change Negotiations." *South African Journal of International Affairs* 18.3: 295–318.

Raines, Susan Summers. 2003. "Perceptions of Legitimacy and Efficacy in International Environmental Management Standards: The Impact of the Participation Gap." *Global Environmental Politics* 3.3: 47–73.

Randjelovic, Jelena, Anastasia R. O"Rourke, and Renato J. Orsato. 2003. "The Emergence of Green Venture Capital." *Business Strategy and the Environment* 12.4: 240–53.

Raustiala, Kal. 2012. "NGOs in International Treatymaking." *The Oxford Guide to Treaties*. Ed. Hollis, Duncan B. Oxford: Oxford University Press.

Recchia, Steven P. 2002. "International Environmental Treaty Engagement in 19 Democracies." *Policy Studies Journal* 30.4: 470–94.

Redford, Kent H., and William M. Adams. 2011. "Payment for Ecosystem Services and the Challenge of Saving Nature." *Conservation Biology* 23.4: 785–87.

Reeve, Rosalind. 2006. "Wildlife Trade, Sanctions and Compliance: Lessons from the CITES Regime." *International Affairs* 82.5: 881–97.

Reid, Colin T. 2013. "Between Priceless and Worthless: Challenges in Using Market Mechanisms for Conserving Biodiversity." *Transnational Environmental Law* 2.2: 217–33.

Reitan, Ruth, and Shannon Gibson. 2012. "Environmental Praxis, Climate Activism and the UNFCCC: A Participatory Action Research Agenda." *Globalizations* 9.3: 395–410.

Revelli, Christophe, and Jean-Laurent Viviani. 2015. "Financial Performance of Socially Responsible Investing (SRI): What Have we Learned? A Meta-Analysis." *Business Ethics: A European Review* 4.2: 156–85.

Richardson, Ben. 2015. "Making a Market for Sustainability: The Commodification of Certified Palm Oil." *New Political Economy* 20.4: 545–68.

Ringius, Lasse. 2001. *Radioactive Waste Disposal at Sea: Public Ideas, Transnational Policy Entrepreneurs, and Environmental Regimes*. Cambridge, MA: MIT Press.

Rittberger, Volker, ed. 1995. *Regime Theory and International Relations*. Oxford: Oxford University Press.

Rittel, Horst W. J., and Melvin M. Webber. 1973. "Dilemmas in a General Theory of Planning." *Policy Sciences* 4: 155–69.

Robinson, William I. 2001. "Social Theory and Globalization: The Rise of a Transnational State." *Theory and Society* 30: 157–200.

Rosenau, James N. 1995. "Governance in the Twenty-First Century." *Global Governance* 1.1: 13–43.

Rosendal, G. Kristin. 2015. "Global Biodiversity Governance: Genetic Resources, Species and Ecosystems." *The Global Environment: Institutions, Law and Policy*, 4th edition. Eds. Axelrod, Regina S. and Stacy VanDeveer. Los Angeles and Washington DC: Sage/CQ Press.

Rowlands, Ian H. 2001. "Classical Theories of International Relations." *International Relations and Global Climate Change*. Eds. Luterbacher, Urs and Detlef F. Sprinz. Cambridge, MA: MIT Press.

Ruggie, John Gerard. 1983. "International Regimes, Transactions and Change: Embedded Liberalism in the Postwar Economic Order." *International Regimes*. Ed. Krasner, Stephen D. Ithaca: Cornell University Press.

Sachs, Wolfgang, ed. 1993. *Global Ecology: A New Arena of Political Conflict*. London: Zed Books.

1999. *Planet Dialectics: Explorations in Environment and Development*. London: Zed Books.

Sand, Peter H. 2013. "Enforcing CITES: The Rise and Fall of Trade Sanctions." *RECIEL* 22.3: 251–63.

Sandbu, Martin. 2011. "The Tobin Tax Explained." *Financial Times*, September 28.

Sassen, Saskia. 1999. "Embedding the Global in the National: Implications for the Role of the Nation State." *States and Sovereignty in the Global Economy.* Eds. Smith, David A., Dorothy J. Solinger, and Steven C. Topik. London: Routledge.

Schelling, Thomas. 1960. *The Strategy of Conflict.* Cambridge, MA: Harvard University Press.

Schiermeier, Quirin. 2009. "Fixing the Sky." *Nature* 460: 792–95.

Schleifer, Philip, and Michael Bloomfield. 2015. "When Institutions Fail: Legitimacy, (De)Legitimation, and the Failure of Private Governance Systems." EUI Working Papers, RSCAS 2015/36.

Schneider, Steven, John P. Holdren, J. Bongaarts, and T. Lovejoy. 2002. "Misleading Math about the Earth: Science Defends Itself against the Skeptical Environmentalist." *Scientific American* 286.1: 59–69.

Schreurs, Miranda A., and Elizabeth C. Economy, eds. 1997. *The Internationalization of Environmental Protection.* Cambridge: Cambridge University Press.

Scruggs, Lyle, and Salil Benegal. 2012. "Declining Public Concern about Climate Change: Can we Blame the Great Recession." *Global Environmental Change* 22: 505–15.

Seelarbokus, Chenaz B. 2014. "Assessing the Effectiveness of International Environmental Agreements (IEAs): Demystifying the Issue of Data Unavailability." *SAGE Open* 4: 1–18.

Selin, Henrik. 2010. *Global Governance of Hazardous Chemicals: Challenges of Multilevel Management.* Cambridge, MA: MIT Press.

Selin, Henrik. 2014. "Global Environmental Law and Treaty-Making on Hazardous Substances: The Minamata Convention and Mercury Abatement." *Global Environmental Politics* 14.1: 1–19.

Selin, Henrik, and Stacy VanDeveer, eds. 2009. *Changing Climates in North American Politics: Institutions, Policymaking and Multilevel Governance.* Cambridge, MA: MIT Press.

2015. *European Union and Environmental Governance.* London: Routledge.

Sell, Susan K. 1998. *Power and Ideas: North–South Politics of Intellectual Property and Antitrust.* Albany: SUNY Press.

Sethi, Surya P. 2015. "Ten Inconvenient Truths about the Paris Climate Accord." *The Wire*, December 16.

Seyfang, Gill. 2003. "Environmental Mega-Conferences: From Stockholm to Johannesburg and Beyond." *Global Environmental Change* 13: 223–28.

Shi, Linda, Eric Chu, Isabelle Anguelovski, Alexander Aylett, Jessica Debats, Kian Goh, Todd Schenk, Karen C. Seto, David Dodman, Debra Roberts, J. Timmons Roberts, and Stacy VanDeveer. 2016. "Roadmap towards Justice in Urban Climate Adaptation Research." *Nature Climate Change* 6: 131–37.

Shiva, Vandana. 1993. "The Greening of the Global Reach." *Global Ecology: A New Arena of Political Conflict.* Ed. Sachs, Wolfgang. London: Zed Books.

Siebenhüner, Bernd. 2009. "The Biodiversity Secretariat: Lean Shark in Troubled Waters." *Managers of Global Change: The Influence of International Environmental Bureaucracies.* Eds. Biermann, Frank and Bernd Siebenhüner. Cambridge, MA: MIT Press.

Simmons, P. J., and Chantal de Jonge Oudraat, eds. 2001. *Managing Global Issues: Lessons Learned.* Washington DC: Carnegie Endowment for International Peace.

Sinclair, I. 1984. *The Vienna Convention on the Law of Treaties.* Manchester: Manchester University Press.

Skjaerseth, Jon Birger, Guri Bang, and Miranda A. Schreurs. 2013. "Explaining Growing Climate Policy Differences between the European Union and the United States." *Global Environmental Politics* 13.4: 61–80.

Skjaerseth, Jon Birger, Olav Schram Stokke, and Jorgen Wettestad. 2006. "Soft Law, Hard Law, and Effective Implementation of International Environmental Norms." *Global Environmental Politics* 6.3: 104–20.

Skodvin, Tora, and Steinar Andresen. 2006. "Leadership Revisited." *Global Environmental Politics* 6.3: 13–27.

Smith, Heather A., and Karyn Sharp. 2012. "Indigenous Climate Knowledges." *WIREs Climate Change* 3: 467–76.

Smith, Stephen. 2011. *Environmental Economics: A Very Short Introduction.* Oxford: Oxford University Press.

Smouts, Marie-Claude. 2003. *Tropical Forests, International Jungle: The Underside of Global Ecopolitics.* Trans. Schoch, Cynthia. New York: Palgrave Macmillan.

Smythe, Elizabeth, and Peter J. Smith. 2006. "Legitimacy, Transparency, and Information Technology: The World Trade Organization in an Era of Contentious Trade Politics." *Global Governance* 12: 31–53.

Soederberg, Susanne. 2013. "The Politics of Debt and Development in the New Millennium: An Introduction." *Third World Quarterly* 34.4: 535–46.

Sohn, Louis B. 1973. "The Stockholm Declaration on the Human Environment." *Harvard International Law Journal* 14: 423–515.

Sow, Ibrahima, Robert K. Dixon, Hie Pan, Anil Sookden, Evelyn Swain, and Laurent Granier. 2012. "Financing for Innovative Technologies and Best Practices to Reduce Persistent Organic Pollutants." *Mitigation and Adaptation Strategies for Global Change* 19.1: 93–106.

Speth, James Gustave. 2004. *Red Sky at Morning: America and the Crisis of the Global Environment.* New Haven: Yale University Press.

Sprinz, Detlef, and Tapani Vaahtoranta. 1994. "The Interest-Based Explanation of International Environmental Policy." *International Organization* 48.1: 77–105.

Spruyt, Hendrik. 1994. *The Sovereign State and its Competitors.* Princeton: Princeton University Press.

2002. "The Origins, Development and Possible Decline of the Modern State." *Annual Review of Political Science* 5: 127–49.

Stanton, Elizabeth, Frank Ackerman, and Sivan Kartha. 2009. "Inside the Integrated Assessment Models: Four Issues in Climate Economics." *Climate and Development* 1.2: 166–84.

Steffen, Will, Asa Persson, Lisa Deutsch, Jan Zalasiewicz, Mark Williams, Katherine Richardson, Carole Crumley, Paul Crutzen, Carl Folke, Line Gordon, Mario Molina, Veerabhadron Ramanathan, Johan Rockström, Marten Scheffer, Hans Joachim Schellnhuber, and Uno Svedin. 2011. "The Anthropocene: From Global Change to Planetary Stewardship." *AMBIO* 40: 739–61.

Steinberg, Paul F. 2014. *Who Rules the Earth? How Social Rules Shape our Planet and our Lives*. Oxford: Oxford University Press.

Steinberg, Paul F., and Stacy VanDeveer, eds. 2012. *Comparative Environmental Politics: Theory, Practice and Prospects*. Cambridge, MA: MIT Press.

Stern, David I. 2014. "The Environmental Kuznets Curve: A Primer." CCEP Working Paper 1404, Crawford School of Public Policy, Australian National University, June.

Stevis, Dimitris, Valerie J. Assetto, and Stephen P. Mumme. 1989. "International Environmental Politics: A Review of the Literature." *Environmental Politics and Policy: Theories and Evidence*. Ed. Lester, James P. Durham: Duke University Press.

Stiglitz, Joseph E. 2002. *Globalization and its Discontents*. New York: W. W. Norton & Company.

Streck, Charlotte. 2001. "The Global Environment Facility – a Role Model for International Governance?" *Global Environmental Politics* 1.2: 71–94.

2011. "Ensuring New Finance and Real Emission Reduction: A Critical Review of the Additionality Concept." *Carbon and Climate Law Review* 2: 158–68.

Strohm, Laura. 1993. "The Environmental Politics of the International Waste Trade." *Journal of Environment and Development* 2.2: 129–53.

Suarez, Daniel, and Catherine Corson. 2013. "Seizing Center Stage: Ecosystem Services, Live, at the Convention on Biological Diversity!" *Human Geography* 6.1: 64–79.

Susskind, Lawrence E. 1994. *Environmental Diplomacy: Negotiating More Effective Global Environmental Agreements*. New York: Oxford University Press.

Sutic, Radmila Vlastelica. 2010. "The CDM Project Cycle." *Developing CDM Projects in the Western Balkans: Legal and Technical Issues Compared*. Ed. Montini, Massimiliano. Dordrecht: Springer.

Talberg, Anita, and Kai Swoboda. 2013. "Emissions Trading Schemes around the World." Parliamentary Library (Australia). Available at http://apo.org.au /node/34458.

Tavone, Jonathan. 2015. "Evaluating the EU ETS – Policy Failure or Relative Success: Where Does it Go from Here?" Blog post at Global Conversations, January 26. Available at https://munkglobalconversations.wordpress.com/20 15/01/26/evaluating-the-eu-ets-policy-failure-or-relative-success-where-does-it-go-from-here/.

Terhalle, Maximilian, and Joanna Depledge. 2013. "Great-Power Politics, Order Transition, and Climate Governance: Insights from International Relations Theory." *Climate Policy* 13.5: 572–86.

Tienhaara, Kyla. 2014. "Varieties of Green Capitalism: Economy and Environment in the Wake of the Global Financial Crisis." *Environmental Politics* 23.2: 187–204.

Tienhaara, Kyla, Amandine Orsini, and Robert Falkner. 2012. "Corporations." *Global Environmental Governance Reconsidered.* Eds. Biermann, Frank and Philipp Pattberg. Cambridge, MA: MIT Press.

Tran, Jimmy H. 2015. "An Evaluation of Market Based Policy Instruments for Clean Energy in the Global South." Ph.D. thesis, Department of Environmental Science, Policy and Management, University of California at Berkeley.

Treves, Tullio, Laura Pineschi, Attila Tanzi, Cesare Pitea, Chiara Ragni, and Francesca Romanin Jacur. 2009. *Non-Compliance Procedures and Mechanisms and the Effectiveness of International Environmental Agreements.* The Hague: T. M. C. Asser Press.

Turner, B. L. II, Roger Kasperson, William. B. Meyer, and Kristin M. Dow. 1990. "Two Types of Global Environmental Change: Definitional and Spatial-Scale Issues in their Human Dimensions." *Global Environmental Change* 1.1: 14–22.

Tzankova, Zdravka. 2009. "The Science and Politics of Ecological Risk: Bioinvasions Policies in the US and Australia." *Environmental Politics* 18.3: 333–50.

United Nations Conference on Trade and Development. 2015. *World Investment Report 2015.* New York and Geneva: United Nations.

United Nations Department of Economic and Social Affairs. 2005. *World Economic and Social Affairs 2005: Financing for Development.* New York: United Nations.

United Nations Environment Programme. 2012. *GEO 5: Environment for the Future we Want.* Nairobi: United Nations Environment Programme.

van Kuijk, Marijke, Jack Putz, and Roderick Zagt. 2009. *Effects of Forest Certification on Biodiversity.* Wageningen: Netherlands Environmental Assessment Agency, Tropenos International.

VanDeveer, Stacy. 1997. "Sea Changes and State Sovereignty." *Saving the Seas: Values, Scientists, and International Governance.* Eds. Brooks, L. Anathea and Stacy VanDeveer. College Park: Maryland Sea Grant.

2003. "Green Fatigue." *Wilson Quarterly* 27.4: 55–59.

2015. "Consumption and Commodity Chains, and Global and Local Environments." *The Global Environment: Institutions, Law, and Policy*, 4th edition. Eds. Axelrod, Regina and Stacy D. VanDeveer. Los Angeles and Washington DC: Sage/CQ Press.

VanDeveer, Stacy D., and Geoffrey D. Dabelko. 2001. "It's Capacity, Stupid: International Assistance and National Implementation." *Global Environmental Politics* 1.2: 18–29.

Veisten, Knut. 2002. "Potential Demand for Certified Wood Products in the United Kingdom and Norway." *Forest Science* 48.4: 767–78.

Venkatachalam, L. 2004. "The Contingent Valuation Method: A Review." *Environmental Impact Assessment Review* 24: 89–124.

Victor, David G. 2011. "Why the UN Can Never Stop Climate Change." *The Guardian*, April 4.

Victor, David G., Kal Raustiala, and Eugene B. Skolnikoff, eds. 1998. *The Implementation and Effectiveness of International Environmental Commitments: Theory and Practice.* Cambridge, MA: MIT Press.

Vilella, Mariel. 2012. "The European Union's Double Standards on Waste Management and Climate Policy: Why the EU Should Stop Buying CDM Carbon Credits from Incinerators and Landfills in the Global South." Global Alliance for Incinerator Alternatives. Available at www.no-burn.org/down loads/15%20May%20Mariel%20Vilella.pdf.

Vogel, David. 1995. *Trading Up: Consumer and Environmental Regulation in a Global Economy*. Cambridge, MA: Harvard University Press.

Vogler, John. 2005. "In Defense of International Environmental Cooperation." *The State and the Global Ecological Crisis*. Eds. Barry, John and Robyn Eckersley. Cambridge, MA: MIT Press.

von Frantzius, Ina. 2004. "World Summit on Sustainable Development Johannesburg 2002: A Critical Analysis and Assessment of the Outcomes." *Environmental Politics* 13.2: 467–73.

Wagner, Lynn M., Reem Hajjar, and Asheline Appleton. 2012. "Global Alliances to Strange Bedfellows: The Ebb and Flow of Negotiating Coalitions." *The Roads from Rio: Lessons Learned from Twenty Years of Multilateral Environmental Negotiations*. Eds. Chasek, Pamela S. and Lynn M. Wagner. New York: Routledge.

Wallerstein, Immanuel. 1974. "The Rise and Future Demise of the World Capitalist System: Concepts for Comparative Analysis." *Comparative Studies in Society and History* 16.4: 387–415.

Waltz, Kenneth N. 1979. *Theory of International Politics*. Reading: Addison-Wesley.

Wapner, Paul. 1996. *Environmental Activism and World Civic Politics*. Albany: SUNY Press.

 2000. "The Normative Promise of Non-State Actors: A Theoretical Account of Global Civil Society." *Principled World Politics: The Challenge of Normative International Relations*. Eds. Wapner, Paul and Edwin J. Ruiz. Lanham, MD: Rowman & Littlefield.

 2003. "World Summit on Sustainable Development: Toward a Post-Jo'burg Environmentalism." *Global Environmental Politics* 3.1: 1–10.

 2008. "The Importance of Critical Environmental Studies in the New Environmentalism." *Global Environmental Politics* 8.1: 6–13.

 2014. "Climate Suffering." *Global Environmental Politics* 14.2: 1–6.

Watts, Michael. 2001. "Petro-Violence: Community, Extraction, and Political Ecology of a Mythic Commodity." *Violent Environments*. Eds. Peluso, Nancy Lee and Michael Watts. Ithaca: Cornell University Press.

Webb, Kernaghan. 2012. "Multi-Level Corporate Responsibility and the Mining Sector: Learning from the Canadian Experience in Latin America." *Business and Politics*: 1–42.

Weinthal, Erika, and Yael Parag. 2003. "Two Steps Forward, One Step Backward: Societal Capacity and Israel's Implementation of the Barcelona Convention and the Mediterranean Action Plan." *Global Environmental Politics* 3.1: 51–72.

Weiss, Edith Brown, and Harold K. Jacobson, eds. 1998. *Engaging Countries: Strengthening Compliance with International Environmental Accords*. Cambridge, MA: MIT Press.

Wendt, Alexander. 1992. "Anarchy is What States Make of it: The Social Construction of Power Politics." *International Organization* 46.2: 391–425.

Werksman, Jacob. 1998. "The Clean Development Mechanism: Unwrapping the 'Kyoto Surprise'." *RECIEL* 7.2: 147–58.

Wettestad, Jorgen. 2014. "Rescuing EU Emissions Trading: Mission Impossible?" *Global Environmental Politics* 14.2: 64–81.

Wihtol, Robert. 2014. "Whither Multilateral Development Finance?" ADBI Working Paper Series No. 491. Available at www.adb.org/sites/default/files/publication/156346/adbi-wp491.pdf.

Wilkinson, Rorden. 2012. "Of Butchery and Bicycles: The WTO and the 'Death' of the Doha Development Agenda." *Political Quarterly* 83.2: 395–401.

Williams, Marc. 1996. "International Political Economy and Global Environmental Change." *The Environment and International Relations*. Eds. Vogler, John and Mark F. Imber. London: Routledge.

2005. "The Third World and Global Environmental Negotiations: Interests, Institutions and Ideas." *Global Environmental Politics* 5.3: 48–69.

2012. "Knowledge, Power and Global Environmental Policy." *Handbook of Global Environmental Politics*, 2nd edition. Ed. Dauvergne, Peter. Cheltenham: Edward Elgar.

Winickoff, David, Sheila Jasanoff, Lawrence Busch, Robin Grove-White, and Brian Wynne. 2005. "Adjudicating the GM Food Wars: Science, Risk, and Democracy in World Trade Law." *Yale Journal of International Law* 30: 81–123.

Witter, Rebecca, Kimberly R. Marion Suiseeya, Rebecca L. Gruby, Sarah Hitchner, Edward M. Maclin, Maggie Bourque, and J. Peter Brosius. 2015. "Moments of Influence in Global Environmental Governance." *Environmental Politics* 24.6: 894–912.

WMO/UNEP. 2014. "Assessment for Decision-Makers: Scientific Assessment of Ozone Depletion 2014." World Meteorological Organization Research and Monitoring Project – Report No. 56.

Wood, Robert E. 1986. *From Marshall Plan to Debt Crisis: Foreign Aid and Development Choices in the World Economy*. Berkeley: University of California Press.

World Bank. 2014. *State and Trends of Carbon Pricing, 2014*. Washington DC: World Bank.

World Bank and Ecofys. 2015. *State and Trends of Carbon Pricing*. Washington DC: World Bank.

Wunder, Sven. 2005. "Payments for Environmental Services: Some Nuts and Bolts." CIFOR Occasional Paper 42.

Young, Oran R. 1989. "The Politics of International Regime Formation: Managing Natural Resources and the Environment." *International Organization* 43.3: 349–75.

1991. "Political Leadership and Regime Formation: On the Development of Institutions in International Society." *International Organization* 45.3: 281–308.

1994. *International Governance: Protecting the Environment in a Stateless Society*. Ithaca: Cornell University Press.

1996. "Institutional Linkages in International Society: Polar Perspectives." *Global Governance* 2.1: 1–24.

ed. 1999. *The Effectiveness of International Environmental Regimes: Causal Connections and Behavioral Mechanisms.* Cambridge, MA: MIT Press.

2001. "Inferences and Indices: Evaluating the Effectiveness of International Environmental Regimes." *Global Environmental Politics* 1.1: 99–121.

2002. *The Institutional Dimensions of Environmental Change: Fit, Interplay and Scale.* Cambridge, MA: MIT Press.

2010. *Institutional Dynamics: Emergent Patterns in International Environmental Governance.* Cambridge, MA: MIT Press.

2011. "Effectiveness of International Environmental Regimes: Existing Knowledge, Cutting Edge Themes, and Research Strategies." *Proceedings of the National Academy of Sciences* 108.50: 19853–60.

2014. "Does Fairness Matter in International Environmental Governance? Creating an Equitable and Effective Climate Regime." *Toward a New Climate Agreement: Conflict, Resolution and Governance.* Eds. Cherry, Todd L., Jon Hovi, and David M. McEvoy. London: Routledge.

Young, Oran R., and Marc A. Levy. 1999. "The Effectiveness of International Environmental Regimes." *The Effectiveness of International Environmental Regimes: Causal Connections and Behavioral Mechanisms.* Ed. Young, Oran R. Cambridge, MA: MIT Press.

Yukhanov, Anna. 2014. "World Bank Review Shows Flaws in Social, Environment Safeguards Process." Reuters, July 15.

Zelli, Fariborz, and Harro van Asselt. 2013. "The Institutional Fragmentation of Global Environmental Governance: Causes, Consequences, and Responses." *Global Environmental Politics* 13.3: 1–13.

Zürn, Michael. 1998. "The Rise of International Environmental Politics: A Review of the Current Research." *World Politics* 50.4: 617–49.

Index

Made in the USA
San Bernardino, CA
25 August 2018